THE MAKING OF MALCOLM LOWRY
UNDER THE VOLCANO

THE MAKING OF MALCOLM LOWRY'S
UNDER THE VOLCANO

Frederick Asals

The University of Georgia Press
Athens & London

© 1997 by the University of Georgia Press
Athens, Georgia 30602
www.ugapress.org
Previously unpublished material by Malcolm Lowry
© 1997 by Priscilla Woolfan
Reprinted by permission of Sterling Lord Literistic, Inc.
All rights reserved
Designed by Walton Harris
Set in 10.5/14 Bodoni by Books International

Most University of Georgia Press titles are
available from popular e-book vendors.

Printed digitally

Library of Congress Cataloging in Publication Data
Asals, Frederick.
The making of Malcolm Lowry's Under the volcano /
Frederick Asals.
x, 476 p. ; 24 cm.
Includes bibliographical references (p. [457]–460) and indexes.

1. Lowry, Malcolm, 1909–1957. Under the volcano—Criticism,
Textual.   I. Title.
PR6023.O96 U5327 1997
813'.54—dc20   96–2221

British Library Cataloging in Publication Data available

ISBN-13: 978-0-8203-5709-6

CONTENTS

ACKNOWLEDGMENTS *vii*

A NOTE ON THE TEXT *ix*

INTRODUCTION *1*

PROLOGUE. The Ur-*Volcano* *17*

CHAPTER ONE. The 1940 *Under the Volcano* *29*

CHAPTER TWO. 1941 *71*

CHAPTER THREE. 1942–1943 *92*

CHAPTER FOUR. 1943–1944 *191*

CHAPTER FIVE. 1945–1946 *297*

CHAPTER SIX. The Complete Consort *319*

APPENDIX A. Stages of the 1940 *Under the Volcano* *387*

APPENDIX B. The Manuscript Record *395*

NOTES *407*

WORKS CITED *457*

GENERAL INDEX *461*

INDEX TO *UNDER THE VOLCANO* *465*

ACKNOWLEDGMENTS

Anyone working with the manuscripts of Malcolm Lowry is indebted to those responsible for gathering them into the Special Collections Division of the University of British Columbia library—primarily to Earle Birney, Basil Stuart-Stubbs, and Anne Yandle. I am personally very grateful to Anne Yandle and George Brandak and the staff in Special Collections for their unfailing helpfulness and good humor to one who must over the years have seemed (alternately?) thoroughly tiresome ("Here he comes again") and a part of the semipermanent furniture. If the top of the UBC library came to feel almost a second home, it was because of the people there as well as what they fetched for me; I shall miss it. I am also grateful to the staffs of the Harry Ransom Humanities Research Center of the University of Texas, the Huntington Library, the library of the University of Pennsylvania, the Columbia University library, and to Norman Levi, Betty Atwater, and the late Harold Matson for their helpfulness in making manuscripts relevant to my work available for examination. Herbert Rosengarten and his colleagues in the UBC English department always made me welcome: their warmth and hospitality have been greatly appreciated.

In a somewhat different way, all who labor with the Lowry manuscripts at UBC owe a debt to Victor Doyen, who was instrumental in first ordering and describing the collection there. His 1973 dissertation *Fighting the Albatross of Self: A Genetic Study of the Literary Work of Malcolm Lowry* remains the starting point for scholars studying the manuscripts, and I was very uneasy on the few occasions when I found myself in disagreement with Doyen. His brief published account, based on the thesis, "La genèse d' 'Au-dessous du Volcan,'" is an early forerunner of my work here. The other major predecessors of the current study are Andrew Pottinger, *The Revising of "Under the Volcano": A Study in Literary Creativity*; Douglas Day, *Malcolm Lowry: A Biography* (216-19, 258-74, 286, 293-96, 298-300, 303, 305, 367-68);

and Sue Vice, "Narrator Dethroned: The Making of *Under the Volcano*." Pottinger's study concentrates on Lowry's manuscript marginalia; Day and Vice are quite unreliable in their accounts of the manuscript record (but not necessarily therefore without insight into Lowry's aims and effects). I have learned from them all. I have also benefitted enormously from my conversations with a variety of "Lowryites," from Chris Ackerley, Betty Atwater, Gordon Bowker, Harvey and Dorothy Burt, Kathy Chung, Suzanne Kim, Pat McCarthy, Carol and Bill McConnell, Miguel Mota, Bill New, Norman Newton, Sheryl Salloum, Pierre Schaeffer, Kathleen Scherf, Cynthia Sugars, Paul Tiessen, and Michael Wutz. I owe a special debt to Sherrill Grace, who slogged through the entire manuscript and made many valuable suggestions for its improvement. Neither she nor anyone else bears responsibility for its shortcomings.

Finally, I am very grateful to the Social Sciences and Humanities Research Council of Canada for a grant that enabled me to get this project launched, and to the Office of Research Administration of the University of Toronto for annual grants that enabled me to sustain it.

Portions of Chapter 1 appeared previously in the introduction to *The 1940 Under the Volcano*, edited by Paul Tiessen and Miguel Mota, Waterloo, Ontario: MLR Editions Canada, 1994. Portions of Chapters 3, 4, and 6 appeared in another form as part of my article "Revision and Illusion in *Under the Volcano*," *Swinging the Maelstrom*, edited by Sherrill Grace, Montreal and Kingston: McGill-Queens University Press, 1992.

A NOTE ON THE TEXT

MANUSCRIPT MATERIAL

The largest collection of Lowry's manuscripts and the primary source for my study is the Malcolm Lowry Collection in the University of British Columbia (UBC) Library, Special Collections Division. References to this collection are made, without preceding designation, parenthetically in my text. The first number refers to box, the second to file, the third (when appropriate) to page: thus 12:14, 6 would mean box 12, file 14, page 6. If a file contains both typescript and holograph versions, the abbreviation "ts." or "ms." indicates to which version my text refers. When pages have been refolioed, the new designations will appear in square brackets, (e.g., 20 ["24"]).

Three other collections at UBC were also drawn upon for this study. The following designations identify them, and the same system of referring to location described above is used:

Neilson	The Einar Neilson Collection
Templeton	The William Loftus Templeton Collection
Margerie	The Margerie Lowry Collection

One important manuscript of the *Volcano* is held by the Harry Ransom Humanities Research Center of the University of Texas at Austin. References to this manuscript are designated "Texas," followed by chapter and (where pertinent) page numbers.

OTHER ABBREVIATIONS

All references to *Under the Volcano* are to the 1965 text published by J. B. Lippincott Company. Since this is a reprint of the 1947 Reynal and Hitchcock edition, page numbers correspond—as do those of the Plume paperback issued by the New American Library in 1971. As the version Lowry saw through the press, this is the most authoritative text of the novel. The title is abbreviated *"Volcano"* throughout my study.

Other frequently cited texts will be abbreviated as follows:

DAG	Malcolm Lowry, *Dark As the Grave Wherein My Friend Is Laid*, ed. Douglas Day and Margerie Lowry (Toronto: General Publishing Company, Ltd., 1968)
Letters	Harvey Breit and Margerie Bonner Lowry, eds., *Selected Letters of Malcolm Lowry* (Philadelphia: J. B. Lippincott Company, 1965)
Aiken-Lowry	Cynthia Sugars, ed., *The Letters of Conrad Aiken and Malcolm Lowry, 1929–1954* (Toronto: ECW Press, 1992)
Lowry-Noxon	Paul Tiessen, ed., *The Letters of Malcolm Lowry and Gerald Noxon, 1940–1952* (Vancouver: UBC Press, 1988)
1940	Malcolm Lowry, *The 1940 Under the Volcano*, ed. Paul Tiessen and Miguel Mota (Waterloo: MLR Editions, 1994)

(Unfortunately, *Sursum Corda! The Collected Letters of Malcolm Lowry, Volume 1: 1926–1946*, edited by Sherrill E. Grace [Toronto: University of Toronto Press, 1995], appeared too late for use in my text.)

To minimize confusion, I refer to individual chapters of the *Volcano* as Lowry did, using roman numerals; cross-references to chapters of my own text use arabic numbers: *e.g.*, Chapter IV is a reference to Lowry, chapter 4 a reference to Asals.

INTRODUCTION

The novel's duration is in part the measurable amount of time the novelist needs to apprehend and harness what is before him; time is part of the writing too. The novel finished and standing free of him is not the mirror-reflection of that writing-time, but is its equivalent. A novel's duration is, in some respect, exactly how long it takes the particular author of a particular novel to explore its emotional resources, and to give his full powers to learning their scope and meeting their demands, and finding out their truest procedure.

—EUDORA WELTY, "Some Notes on Time in Fiction," *The Eye of the Story*

Books as well as people have lives, and this study aims to be the partial biography of one such notable life—partial because the material for telling the whole story is lacking. It is a story, a life, that lasted for about ten years and as it proceeded virtually absorbed the life of its creator as well. This was not the case at the beginning: in Mexico, Los Angeles, even at first in Vancouver, Malcolm Lowry certainly had an existence—even a writing existence—apart from *Under the Volcano*. The Lowry of the late 1930s was husband and friend, traveler and drinker, someone who got into and out of difficulties with police and lawyers, landlords and guardians, wife and womenfriends, and who as writer had numerous projects underway—stories and novels, a collection of poetry, perhaps a play—and was actively involved with allies and agents in trying to get them read and published. This is not the Malcolm Lowry of the first half of the 1940s. While he continued to write short poems and probably did some work on *In Ballast to the White Sea*, the Lowry of the 1940s was almost wholly absorbed in the *Volcano*, not simply as a writer, but even as a man. Far from continuing to try to place his work, he did not so much as correspond with his New York agent for a full three years. It is revealing that Douglas Day's biography fills the space of these years with his lengthy analysis of the novel—criticism rather than a more conventional biographical narrative. Yet Day is only papering over an embarrassment, a paucity of material, and doing so by appropriate means, for in these years the *Volcano* virtually *was* Lowry's life, a fact confirmed in Gordon Bowker's more recent account, where the period 1941-44 take up a mere twenty-five pages, by far the shortest such treatment in this voluminous telling. If a writer inevitably inscribes his experience into his work, it should not then be surprising that part of what gets inscribed into the final text of the *Volcano* is the experience of writing it, nor that by the time he had reached the final stages, Lowry himself had become conscious of the self-reflexive dimension and inscribed *that* awareness into his text. To anyone observing the process of the creation of the *Volcano*, something like *Dark As the Grave*, which inverts what might be called the power relations between novel and author, book and world, seems a next step that could almost have been predicted.

So perhaps it should have come as no surprise that study of these manuscripts would involve me in a similar process, that I would find myself for hours on end so fully absorbed both in and into the depicted world of Quauhnahuac that it was with bewildered, blinking surprise that I would emerge into contemporary Vancouver, textual reality only gradually and fuzzily giving way to material landmarks and the dimly recollected actualities of mundane life, a need to stop at the market, say, or a date for dinner. The spell of the manuscripts confirmed the novel's power: it did nothing to answer any of the questions one might have about the significance of those manuscripts, especially how to give an account of them. First, as everyone knows, one needs a "thesis," and I didn't have a thesis: the longer I gazed, the more it seemed to me that Lowry's revisions were aimed at accomplishing a number of ends, pursued often at different stages, and did not proceed in a single discernable direction. If I was not to distort what he had actually done, it seemed I would have to make such multiplicity my thesis, or at least my guiding thread, a solution not likely to please anyone, including its perpetrator. Lowry was especially inconsiderate in not revising in a straight line, that is, by rewriting the entire novel from beginning to end. At least from 1940 onward, the chapter was the unit of revision, so that while between 1940 and 1945 there are many important—indeed, crucial—alterations in his text, there are no new "versions" of the novel as a whole. Even worse, as months and years wore on chapters might get picked up in any sequence out of a "felt need," and since after 1940 all revisions, holograph and typescript, were made on 8½ x 11" foolscap, there were no external signs by which the sequence might be reliably ordered. To complicate matters further, some chapters gave Lowry more difficulty than others and went through many more drafts: there are some six versions of Chapter IX after 1941, for instance, as opposed to only two of Chapter XII. How provide a coherent account of all this?

One initially attractive possibility was tossed out after real acquaintance with the manuscripts, that of organizing the study by "levels" to trace separately the development of individual dimensions of the text. It was, after all, Lowry himself in the famous letter to Jonathan Cape who introduced talk of "levels," although it is a common enough critical concept, and most substantial interpretations of the *Volcano* have seemed unable to do without it. For a study of the creation of the novel, however, it presented evident problems. One was the difficulty of defining "levels" in such a way as to keep material separate. If one spoke of the "religious" level, say, one obviously would include Christian, Buddhist, and Hindu references. What, however, of cabalistic material? Was this "religious" or "occult"? Alchemy? Swedenborgianism? Rosicrucianism? The Tarot? Where did Atlantis fit in? What of the Faust references—was the literary a separate "level" or should it here be treated with the religious? Since dogs are at least partly attached to the Faust story, do we treat of those animals here? And what of the reference to Spengler's view of western man as "Faustian"? Is that a part of the "political," the "religious," or the "literary" level?

I came, in short, to the same conclusion Ronald Binns was coming to around this time: "Critics tend to talk about levels of meaning in *Under the Volcano*, but the metaphor is misleading. The novel's structure is not made up of distinct, discrete elements which can be neatly distinguished like the storeys of a building. There is, rather, an interpenetration and overlapping" (*Malcolm Lowry* 59). Even if evident difficulties could have been moderated by careful definition and cross-referencing, there was another consideration that from my perspective seemed even more compelling. As Binns reminds us, to speak of "levels" is to speak metaphorically; in cold fact, there is only one level the writer can deal with, the level of the text itself, the level of language.

The illusion of other strata beyond the linguistic surface can only be created within it. My study of Lowry's writing and rewriting of his text would have to be literally superficial.

A second possibility was to follow Lowry's own lead and to organize by chapter, tracing, in order, the revisions of each of the novel's twelve units through from beginning to final form. Although this might involve repetitiveness (I would have to mention, for instance, the "Ebro motif" each time it got introduced into chapters IV, VI, VII, and VIII) some repetition seemed unavoidable in any case, and at least these units (unlike "levels") could be kept clear and separate from one another. However, a little reflection reminded me that this was in fact distinctly *not* the way that Lowry had written, that his revising out of sequence affected where individual matters appeared in the text, and that the larger sense of the evolving whole, which Lowry always had in the back of his mind even as he worked on a specific chapter, would be utterly lost in such a static approach.

There seemed nothing for it, then, but to try to follow his own lead, even when it was impossible to be certain what that lead was, and employ a "genetic" approach, to trace insofar as possible the revisions in the order Lowry made them. This is easy enough at the beginning and end of the study, when full "versions" are in question (my chapters 1, 2, and 5); it is most problematic in the center (chapters 3 and 4) where many of the most important textual changes were made. Fortunately, Lowry's final full (or almost full) revision of his text, the subject of chapter 4, apparently did follow sequential order. The material of chapter 3, however, resists that ordering—or, definitively, any other. However, precisely because it is not possible to establish an authoritative sequence here, I felt free to moderate confusion by grouping chapters according to narrative consciousness: thus "Hugh's chapters" are examined as a group, as are those of Yvonne and of the Consul. Some sense of Lowry's method of revision is, I hope, thereby retained while chaos for the reader is averted.

This study tries to be attentive to specifics in Lowry's evolving text. In this, again, my work attempts to follow his, and once more process is reflected in product: Lowry's individual changes had as one major aim giving his novel a more vividly specific texture. He came to see that his early version was hopelessly, inadequately vague and insubstantial in all manner of ways—when was all this happening? what were people wearing? what were they drinking? what did the Mexican scene look like? et cetera—and he labored mightily to make it as concretely apprehensible as possible. In this effort he was guided by a private warning, a handwriting on the wall that he had printed out for himself, like the Consul's garden sign, in black capitals:

> ABJURE THE PLATITUDE OF STATEMENT. FOR IN ART WHAT IS MERELY STATED IS NOT PRESENTED, WHAT IS NOT PRESENTED IS NOT VIVID, WHAT IS NOT VIVID IS NOT REPRESENTED, AND WHAT IS NOT REPRESENTED IS NOT ART.
>
> (Templeton 1:14)

Lowry attributed this "dictum" to Henry James (it is actually R. P. Blackmur's redaction of James), an appropriate guide; as we shall see, Lowry's revisions were Jamesian in at least one other important way.[1]

However, that initial vagueness and lack of specificity may come as something of a surprise to any who, recognizing Lowry's use of autobiographical material, make the not unnatural assumption that such material was "primary," that is, a part of the book's very inception. Is there anyone who now reads the *Volcano* that does not know even before picking it up that Malcolm Lowry went to sea and Cambridge in his youth, lived in Mexico in the mid 1930s, separated from his first wife, drank mightily both then and later, went to Canada, married again and was happy there—and that all this can be found in the novel? Much (not all) of it is both there and not there in 1940, entered in a nominal form, but sketchy, insubstantial, not in James's sense "represented." What the early drafts of the *Volcano* lack is not symbolic extension—this is almost as "symbolic" a work in 1940 as it would be in 1947, although not always in the same ways—but intellectual, emotional, imaginative resonance. Revealingly, it is often bits of Lowry's experience that make a gradual or "belated" appearance in the novel's drafts: "Juan Cerillo," stool pigeons, and the El Popo menu, to choose three quite different kinds of material, were all, we know, a part of Lowry's Mexican sojourn, yet none is included in the earliest versions of the novel. Their later appearance is an index of Lowry's increasing *penetration* of his Mexican experience, not a symbolic working up, but a prolonged contemplation of both the actuality and the significance of an experience he had projected too simply and glibly in its initial forms.

A major absence from the 1940 *Volcano* was the believable representation of the Consul's drunkenness. There is a rather large and obvious irony in the recognition that the making of Geoffrey Firmin as perhaps the most closely observed and convincing representation of an alcoholic in fiction was a function of his creator's sobriety. That is how Lowry described the composition in his Christmas 1944 card to Conrad Aiken: I have, he said, finally finished the novel after more than three years work, eight hours a day, "soberly" (*Aiken-Lowry* 182), and he is, I am convinced, speaking the truth, although by this time Lowry's serious drinking had, at least sporadically, resumed. But in the preceding years, first in Vancouver, then in Dollarton, establishing his new, stable, and relatively serene existence with Margerie Bonner, alcohol had not been an important factor in his life—nor, except imaginatively, in his writing. It was the fire of June 1944 that abruptly ended that period and that acted as a trigger for Lowry the drinker, but by that time the *Volcano* was in what would prove its final stage, and the very intensity of the effort to complete it seems to have helped keep the resurgent drinking within bounds. Yet to encounter the sheer volume of extant drafts for the novel between 1940 and 1944 and, even more, the painstaking care with which sentences, paragraphs, chapters have been written and rewritten, is to view a crafting that could hardly have been accomplished under the influence.

The Consul's letter of Chapter I suggests in several ways the relationship between drinking and writing for Lowry during this period. The very structure of the letter is marked by the alternation between these activities, the mescals twice recorded thereby breaking the written text into three sections, as if one oral function drives out the other, the alcohol reducing the Consul to parenthetically noted periods of silence, the writing forestalling the ordering of further drinks. Yet we are told that the handwriting covering these sheets is "wholly drunken," and Lowry means us to see the connection not only between the fragmentary properties of this prose and alcohol, but also between its visionary, even prophetic qualities and drink. However, when we turn from the connections and disconnections implied in the novel to the acts that created them, from character to author, the manuscripts demonstrate not Lowry's "visionary" composition of the letter (much less drunken handwriting), but his painstaking revisions, the very clearheaded outline of the various stages of the letter on a worksheet (Texas II, verso

12), and repeated drafts of individual passages. We are meant to think of the Consul's script as a single screed written out during the one long night it invokes; Lowry's composings, on the other hand, went through repeated writings, and the letter we read in the published novel bears little resemblance to the one that appeared in the 1940 version.

If invocations of the "biographical Lowry" to account for various aspects of the *Volcano* seem reductive in the face of the manuscripts, so do efforts of the apparent counterschool of criticism, that which construes the work in terms of its patterns and allusions (another face of the biograpical Lowry, after all). This line of criticism takes its cue from the famous 1946 letter to Jonathan Cape, a document from which commentary on the novel has never recovered. Here begins the positing of the novel as a multileveled symbolic construct, totally controlled by the clear if sly intelligence of an eclectically learned creator at every moment conscious of both his immediate purpose and its relationship to the larger system that is the intricately interwelded whole. If this view seems possible to take seriously in a way the biographical, at least at its most naive, does not, we should, I think, recall the occasion and purpose of the daunting letter that appears to authorize it.

The rhetorical intent of that letter, and thus its size and scope, was to bowl over Cape himself and demolish his reader's call for extensive revisions, to so overwhelm the publisher that the manuscript would be accepted without reservation and printed substantially as it stood. Secondary purposes of course crept in as well, as if Lowry couldn't help it—a kind of compulsive history of composition (including, not incidentally, a record of previous revision), justification of his writerly life, suggestions of literary lineage, and so on—but essentially he wanted to overpower Cape, to appear to be able to explain and justify virtually his every word. (Disarmingly, he half admits this, and of course the letter succeeded admirably.) Here Lowry becomes for the first time on record—many more instances would follow—reader and explicator of his own text, but he quite deliberately speaks as if still in the mode of creator. Yet his alternative account of his way of writing the *Volcano*, one that has spawned no critical approach, strikes a very different note: the book was not, he tells another correspondent, "intended to operate on quite so many levels [as I have been expounding]. One serious intention was to create a work of art—after a while it began to make a noise like music; when it made the wrong noise I altered it—when it made the right one finally, I kept it" (*Letters* 200). The point of course is not that one of these is "right," the other "wrong"—Lowry doubtless vibrated between conscious deliberation and intuitive apprehension (indeed, how could it have been otherwise?)—but that the Cape letter gives only a partial account and thus is potentially misleading in its emphases.

Nonetheless, Lowry's declared purpose "to create a work of art" ("turning his greatest weakness—he loathed the phrase—into his greatest strength," as Sigbjørn Wilderness cites Yeats in *DAG* 24; cf. 16, 41, 109–10), while not, even to that correspondent, his only intention, is a usefully loose and open declaration that can suggest his advancing on simultaneous fronts to "improve" his text, to achieve the "art" he aimed at. Thus the textual focus of the current study and its difficulty in pursuing a single thesis. In terms of the traditional camps of Lowry criticism, it situates itself as contiguous to (not to say parasitical on) all, yet fully allied to none. It is not primarily biographical, although it freely avails itself of biographical information wherever that seems useful, and as a "biography of a book", has perhaps a parallel existence to the more traditional form. Nor is it an attempt to identify sources and allusions (although inevitably it has turned up a few): the existence of *A Companion to "Under the Volcano"* happily makes such an enterprise redundant. Nor is it an attempt to give yet one more "interpretation" of the *Volcano*, although it is broadly and inescapably interpretive. Indeed, the study on that level (speaking of "levels"!) argues for indeterminateness, an indeterminateness that is not simply the familiar openness of texts to a variety of possible approaches and "readings," but an indeterminateness written *into* the text, which became both the result and, in its conscious forms, a part of the process of composition. The completed *Volcano* bears a resemblance to the painter's device of anamorphosis, which at first seems to present a single clear image, yet when seen from another angle shows an entirely different one, so that although the viewer can sometimes pick up the shadow of the second image while looking at the first, it is impossible to bring the two into clear focus simultaneously.

As a study intended both for professional scholars and for those unprofessionally fascinated by Lowry's great novel, the present work runs the very real risk of satisfying neither. The Lowry scholar concerned to find a full account of the inception and development of his favorite motif may come away partially or wholly disappointed; in a work already embarrassingly long, the only way to include everything would have been to reproduce the entire manuscript record. On the other hand, the general *Volcano* reader may well hear more talk than he or she wishes about holographs and typescripts, and more detail about the changes undergone in specific passages and drafts than seems profitable or interesting. Descriptions of the manuscript record of concern only to scholars actively researching the novel, however, are confined to notes and appendices.

Nonetheless, this study does hope to prove of value to scholars not by exhausting the subject of the genesis of the novel—I am too conscious not only of other approaches and foci but of how much, even descriptively, has had to be omitted, for such pretension—but by at least making practically and reliably available to the researcher a record of and guide to the known manuscripts involved in the creation of the *Volcano*. In such a way, I would hope, it provides the basis for and opens up avenues to further and more specific explorations of various aspects of the novel and of Lowry's writing generally. Most previous references to various stages of composition have been understandably vague or imprecise or have had to use the catchall "an earlier draft" to designate passages composed in 1940, 1943, and 1945. Now it should prove possible to know what came when and in what general order, and to say whether a feature of the text is early or late, before moving on to draw conclusions from such information.

Both hypothetical readers, the researching-scholarly and the informed-general, might coalesce to object to the lack of a strong single thesis to guide them through the material. The objection is at least partly justified, yet as I have already suggested, there have seemed to me reasons for not attempting to impose too determinant a grid on the process here surveyed. Such a study as this of the making of a major literary work is also at least indirectly a study of the creative imagination. I must leave it to others to judge whether Malcolm Lowry is typical in this respect, but even the abbreviated record of the *Volcano* that we have makes clear that the creation of this work did not move in a single determinable direction. For instance, Lowry's first revision after the 1940 version cut, winnowed, reduced, simplified his book, streamlining it into a triangular romance, yet his subsequent impulse was to expand and enlarge its scope, while at the same time making its historical time and place far more specific—seemingly a reversal of direction. Even when we confine ourselves to those latter developments, there is no single answer to the question, "Expansive in what direction?" If we begin to catalogue the elements added only after 1941, we can easily produce an apparent grab bag. Specifics of the Spanish Civil War, golf, Hindu myth and ritual, the vagaries of human consciousness, disguise, the Cabala, the betrayals of love, drunkenness rendered from both the inside and the outside, the ever-shifting processes of time, Canada-as-paradise, the Mexican Revolution, guilt and remorse, the lure of the sea—all of these (and more) enter the text during the final three years of revision, to be brought together with such extant concerns as tragedy, Atlantis, imperialist exploitation, Christianity, eternal recurrence, sterility. It is this expansive motion that, I will argue, produces the multivalent text published in 1947, a text that both insists on being "interpreted" and simultaneously resists (indeed, makes impossible) a final and definitive ordering. In short, my genetic reading of the *Volcano* is of a process of composition that is in the end designed to open the novel to multiple possibilities, not to bring it to focus on a single one, in order to create the sense of offering as many opportunities as "life" itself.

One of the very last passages Lowry composed for the novel, the description in Chapter XI of the night sky, expresses, I think, what he wanted his book to do by this time: to present a series of interlocking patterns—and of course the huge "wheeling" of the stars overhead is meant to echo and validate the "trochal" structure of his novel—patterns that will raise without definitively answering the great questions, "To what end? What force drives this sublime celestial machinery?" The point is not that answers cannot be derived from the *Volcano*, or that they cannot be derived from scanning the cosmos, but rather the reverse: many and conflicting responses may be derived from either. The *Volcano* is not, of course, the cosmos, but it aspires to being an ordered and patterned miniature, a simulacrum of the complex whole from the point of view of a privileged but far from omniscient viewer. The reader/spectator becomes at first like those generations scanning the heavens of Chapter XI, whose immediate points of entry are quite specific moments, moments both rich and evanescent, demanding response and interpretation yet frustrating both, complicating at one moment what was seemingly offered immediately before. Yet since, unlike the world of space, time, and eternity, the *Volcano* can be apprehended as a whole, it seems to hold out the possibility of being "known," of surrendering its secrets to our understanding, of revealing the order and meaning of its world. But those wheels contain wheels within them, the series of patterns locks and interlocks and does not, finally, tell us how to interpret or relate them, in a cosmos—or a text— in which the only certain law is that of motion.

Thus the thesis of this study, insofar as it can be said to have one, is that the *outcome* of Lowry's revisions was to produce the poetic richness of this multivalent text, which is perhaps to say that this was, necessarily, also the eventual *direction* of his labors. As a result my view of how to "read" the completed novel must be closer to that of Binns than, for instance, that of Day. Day looks for what he calls "a *Gestalt* reading" (321ff.; indeed, his own ambitious and suggestive interpretation is an essay in that direction) and, with reference to the Cape letter, speaks of the book's discrete if interrelated levels. This produces such unambiguous specific interpretations as, for instance, "the Consul *is* damned" (349). For Binns, however, who views the novel as "encyclopedic," "To talk about levels of meaning in *Under the Volcano* is to imply hierarchies of meaning. But encyclopedism is a narrative mode which notoriously resists the privileging of meaning" (63). He thus "adamantly resists the extraction of a single coherent 'reading' which can account for the book as a totality. Ambiguity is rooted in the very grammar of the narrative" (62). The fact that the novel has long been interpreted in the manner adopted by Day suggests that it *allows for* such readings; the problem is that it also became designed to allow for counterreadings as well (e.g., that the Consul is ultimately "saved" rather than "damned"). Yet the determining of "meaning" was itself only one of the fronts on which Lowry advanced through his drafts: indeed, the multiplying of significance may have at first been a by-product rather than a central aim of the revising process.

"How was the *Volcano* written?" At its simplest, the question is directed to the actual activities involved in composition itself. For the pre-1940 period we know as little of Lowry's manner of working as we do of other matters relating to those earliest manuscripts. Malcolm apparently first wrote by hand and then either typed himself (he seems to have had a typewriter in Mexico and Los Angeles) or had a typist make a fair copy of his composings. It is only in 1940, with the arrival on the scene of Margerie Bonner and the move to Canada that we have a clearer picture of how the Lowrys worked.

"The Lowrys": from her entry into Malcolm's life, Margerie became not simply his personal partner but his writing cohort, and even the latter function, deeply involving her in his work, was multiple. She very quickly became muse, sounding board, editor, critic, and codrafter as well as typist, and she more than once described the specifics of how the two worked together on his writing. The following account, given to Andrew Pottinger in late 1974, does not differ materially from others:

> He wrote everything in longhand. Then I typed it. Then I would read it over carefully and type out my suggestions—whether there should be cuts or this should be developed or this wouldn't gibe with something else.... After I'd read it and made my suggestions, then he would read it in typescript and make his suggestions ... and then we'd get together and discuss it.... Then he'd write another longhand version. We'd go through the whole thing all over again until we got it to suit.... He'd have about six or eight piles of manuscript [on his desk] [sic], and sometimes he had piles all over the bed, and he'd go from one to the other.... And sometimes he'd work back and forth in the book; sometimes he'd be doing something on Chapter VII and suddenly he'd think "Wait a minute, that doesn't gibe with something in Chapter IV," and he'd go back to rewrite Chapter IV to make it gibe with Chapter VII.

Pottinger comments, "this account helps to explain the apparent lack of complete versions of the novel between 1941 and 1944."[2] But the matter may be put more forcibly: the method here described is *itself* a powerful deterrent to producing a "complete version." A novel composed in this manner might forever remain "unfinished," the revisions of Chapter VII never quite "gibing" with those of IV (and what about II? or IX? and doesn't X need to be revised in light of VI? and so on and on), the text as a whole never "got to suit."

Margerie does not mention that (at least post-1940) Malcolm's "longhand" was invariably pencil, and her memory long after the fact seems in minor ways erroneous—no typed comments from her are in evidence, and the suggestion that, hummingbird-like, Lowry whirred from chapter to chapter doing minor revisions, making quick changes, seems contradicted by the sustained nature of the surviving holograph drafts:

probably she is thinking of notes of reminder jotted on the opening page of chapter drafts—but the routine of working by chapter and out of novelistic order was established as early as revisions of the 1940 version. And while it is usually easy to distinguish holograph drafts prepared for Margerie's typewriter from those that are not, and thus to see that sometimes sentences, paragraphs, sections, and indeed entire chapters would be revised—often more than once—before being deemed ready for typing, this only serves to underline the implication of Margerie's account: that typing marked the end of a phase, a moment of temporary stasis. The chapter had, for now, been "got to suit."

These accounts refer primarily to their manner of working in the shack in Dollarton, but the first full version of the *Volcano* that we have dates from Vancouver and was composed under rather different circumstances. At least at times, according to Margerie, Malcolm himself made use of their rented typewriter in the freezing attic room on West 19th Avenue that the Lowrys so luridly described to the Aikens in their letters of 1939–40 (*Aiken-Lowry* 56–132), yet she more specifically presents Malcolm as "writing with flying pen" on the *Volcano* in these cold quarters (*Aiken-Lowry* 253–64). Feeling beseiged, desperate, and alone, with the possibility that Malcolm might at any moment face military conscription, driven together both by their sense of isolation and by the earliest, "honeymoon" phase of their relationship, Malcolm and Margerie plunged into work, and it was apparent virtually from the first that she was almost as much involved in the novel as he. Within weeks of the arrival of the *Volcano* manuscripts from Los Angeles, Margerie was telling Mary Aiken, "We are now up to our ears in the Volcano and working like mad to get it done. We wake up in the morning talking about it and go to sleep still sitting up in bed writing" (*Aiken-Lowry* 263). The pronoun is revealing, the description suggestive: the intimacy of composition indeed. They worked rapidly and with a serene sense of accomplishment, and while neither holograph drafts nor any further description of how they functioned survive, it is clear from Malcolm's letters to Aiken that Margerie's involvement from the first was intense—and necessary. As early as January 27 he declares that she is "essential" to his writing: "In drawing together, work has become a communal thing between us. . . . We work together on [the novel] day and night" (*Aiken-Lowry* 100). By April 24 he puts it even more powerfully: "Margie, apart from anything else, is now so absolutely inextricable from my work, that I can't get along without her from this point of view alone" (*Aiken-Lowry* 132). By this time, too, Margerie had clearly taken on one permanent role: "if I did not have her I'd have to pay a typist," Malcolm confided to Aiken (*Aiken-Lowry* 112).

So involved was Margerie from 1940 on in every aspect of the *Volcano* that it is now impossible—indeed, it always was—to keep separate just what "Malcolm" contributed to the novel, what "Margerie." Crucial decisions clearly never reached paper, perishing in the air of their many discussions in Vancouver, Dollarton, Ontario—and who can tell now with which partner individual points originated? Although most of the actual writing is unquestionably Malcolm's, there remain traces of "Margie versions" in extant manuscripts—but the last word was always his. He quickly assessed her specific value to him as a writer of fiction: "I realize my fault is, roughly speaking, too much loquacity and not enough action, and hams in the window, and there she helps me immeasureably by her censorship and suggestions." An unsympathetic witness might argue that these tendencies can easily move in the direction of superficiality and popular formulas, but with regard to the *Volcano* any such debate must remain theoretical: almost nothing pre-Margerie survives, nowhere near enough on which to base a comparison of texts before and after her arrival. Not unaware of the arguments that might be mounted against such quasi-collaboration, Malcolm, at least, was convinced of the rightness of their connection: "Objectively speaking I think that such a dependence might not be a good thing in many cases but in *our* case it definitely works" (*Aiken-Lowry* 112).

I think Lowry was essentially correct about Margerie's particular value to him here, that beyond her importance for his general stability, beyond the psychological and emotional necessity of a partner actively involved with him in his work, Margerie Bonner's awareness of the need of a reader of fiction to be engaged by a dramatic and interesting immediate action did indeed keep Malcolm from maundering into introspective prosings or from meandering too far down Aiken's fictional road where "nothing happens." She may also, by precisely the same token, be instrumental in the failure of the 1940 *Volcano* and even more responsible, as I speculate in chapter 2, for the oddly uncharacteristic 1941 revisions that follow. For these are of course the versions produced while their relationship was at its freshest and most intensely romantic, while they made two against a hostile world, almost without funds, alone in a city and country they did not know, threatened with being parted by a savage war. What now seems strangest about the 1940 *Volcano* is not its failure but its frequent ineptness—Lowry was, we must remind ourselves, already a published novelist and author of a half-dozen short fictions—coupled with his obliviousness, the repeated expressions of his certainty of solid accomplishment. Would he have been so obtusely insistent on the worth of a work in which his beloved had not been decisively involved? The question is unanswerable and further speculation, I think, profitless: whatever the nature and effect of her contributions, Margerie *was* involved and would remain so, and her hand appears repeatedly among the *Volcano* manuscripts. My speculations in chapter 2 aside, there is no reason to believe that Margerie's contributions were made without Malcolm's full knowledge and approval (indeed, when he does not like them, we can see him arguing with or simply reversing them), and I will generally not attempt to make any separation between the two. In the writing of the *Volcano*, and thus in the pages that follow, "Lowry" comes to designate an often indeterminate composite figure.

Minor uncertainties of attribution, however, pale before the larger, genuine mystery with which these revisions confront us: how was the uneven, unsatisfying *Volcano* of 1940, a mediocre fiction at best, turned into the resplendent, powerful novel published in 1947? The achievement, as Lowry himself knew, was improbable, a transmutation as unlikely as the alchemists' aim to convert lead into gold. This question too is unanswerable: even after the process is laid open and examined, what is produced is not an "explanation" but a renewal of wonder. The Consul may or may not have been a magician; his creator, at least this once, most certainly was.[3]

Yet Lowry paid, it seems to me, a devastating price for this literary conjuring act. The young writer who had with confidence sent out manuscripts for placement throughout the 1930s, who even in the spring of 1940 was writing to friends of plans for publishing both fiction and poetry (*Letters* 27–31; *Aiken-Lowry* 115, 139, 143)—this creature disappeared as rejections of the 1940 text rolled in, never to be seen again. It was with the greatest reluctance—and only after the terrifying fire of 1944 that consumed another novel-length manuscript—that the *Volcano* was five years later released once more to the mercies of publishing houses. Despite its success with publishers, reviewers, even book buyers, Lowry never again submitted a book-length manuscript for publication, indeed never finished another novel. If the revising process was an act of justification both to himself and to the hostile world, the *Volcano* had so swallowed him up that it stripped him of everything but his fears and the writing itself. Like alcohol, writing for Lowry was his way of both meeting the world and simultaneously keeping it at bay, but in his final decade the balance in that paradox shifted, the fears gained the upper hand, and not even writing could restore the equilibrium. There was much interesting and significant work done in those years, but it was done by a man whose early courtship of failure had at last met with success.

PROLOGUE

The Ur-*Volcano*

It seems particularly appropriate to a writer who fictionalized his life—and came to believe that perhaps he was living his fiction—that the beginnings of Malcolm Lowry's greatest work should lie shrouded in mythic mists. Lowry's accounts of the inception of the *Volcano* varied very little. Here is the fullest, delivered not by the author in propria persona, but by his character Sigbjørn Wilderness in *Dark As the Grave Wherein My Friend Is Laid*:

> "One day about nine years ago, it was the end of 1936 . . . I took a bus to go to Chapultepec. Not the big Chapultepec, the little one near here. . . . There were several people with me, a person extremely dear to me, whom we will call X, Señora X my first wife . . . and two Americans, one of whom was dressed up in cowboy costume—which was the costume of a character I had named Hugh: he'd come down here in a cattle truck on a bet from Texas, and they'd impounded his clothes at the border. We were going to a bullthrowing, this side of Chapultepec. . . . About halfway there we stopped beside an Indian who seemed to be dying by the roadside. We all wanted to help but were prevented from doing so . . . because we were told it was against the law. All that happened is that in the end we left him where he was, and, meanwhile, a drunk on the bus had stolen his money out of his hat, which was lying beside him, on the road. He paid his fare with it, the stolen money, and we went on to the bullthrowing."
>
> "Go on."
>
> "That's all. The whole story grew out of that incident. I began it as a short story." (150–51)

The account in the famous letter to Jonathan Cape is slightly, possibly significantly, different. Of Chapter VIII of the novel, Lowry says: "It was the first chapter written in the book; the incident by the roadside, based on a personal experience, was the germ of the book. I feel that some wag not too unlike your reader might tell me at this point that I would do better to reduce the book back to this original germ so that we could all have it printed in O'Brien's *Best Short Stories of 1946*" (*Letters* 79). While playing with the notion of taking the *Volcano* down to story length, Lowry does not claim that what he first wrote was such a story, but speaks of a "chapter," implying perhaps a longer work already underway.

Certainly Margerie Lowry not only believed in the existence of an "original" story, but thought she had found it among Malcolm's papers after his death: the "Under the Volcano" published first in *Prairie Schooner*, then in *Psalms and Songs*, and repeatedly so identified by influential commentators since.[1] But Margerie was not around in the 1930s for the creation of such a story; if she believed enough in it to think she had discovered it, that was only the result of her, like everyone else, hearing Malcolm assert its existence. Jan Gabrial, who *was* around at the time, had nothing to say after thirty-eight years of the supposed incident on which the story was based and further claimed that the *Volcano* was never conceived as a story: "it was always going to be a novel" (Bowker, *Lowry Remembered* 120; this is not, of course, quite the same as denying the existence of an inceptive story).

What Margerie had found among Malcolm's papers was not a story written in the 1930s in Mexico, but one culled from a later version of the already-developed novel in 1941 and sent to Lowry's agent, Harold Matson, as harbinger of the novel he hoped would soon follow.[2] If this later story fooled Margerie, one might wonder: did it "fool" Malcolm himself? Several years later, as the creation of the *Volcano* was itself undergoing fictionalization in his mind and under his pencil, did he too recall this story version of 1941 and mythify it, creating an ur-*Volcano* as short story—especially if a roadside incident did lie behind the inception of the novel? Alternatively, was the creation of the 1941 story version an attempt on Lowry's part to get back to the "roots" of his book, to rewrite the incident that had served as a germ for the first story, at a time when his faith in his novel was being battered by publisher's rejections? ¿*Quien sabe?* This much, however, is certain: if there ever was a short story of the 1930s called "Under the Volcano," it has long since vanished.

Nonetheless, there is no doubt that Lowry did begin writing on the material that would develop into the *Volcano* while in Mexico, and if it began as a short story, it did not stay one for long.[3] Malcolm and his friends of the time all attest to the existence of manuscript, although just what and when varies somewhat. Lowry himself recalled that he "conceived" the novel in November 1936 (2:3, draft of Cape letter, 6), whereas Jan Gabrial seemed vague on when he had started writing or what exactly he had achieved before her departure near the end of 1937—he was "working on notes . . . using bits and pieces of places and people" (Bowker, *Lowry Remembered* 117). Conrad Aiken thirty years later recalled reading a "first draft" of a novel on his visit in the spring of 1937 (Killorin 324), whereas Arthur Calder-Marshall, who came to Mexico several months later, remembered after forty-seven years a "long short story" (110), a description that tallies with Lowry's account of Calder-Marshall's reading "a 40,000 word version" during his visit (2:3, draft of Cape letter, 6). However, the only contemporary document attesting to this stage of composition is a letter from the New York office of the literary agent Ann Watkins dated January 31, 1938, addressed to Lowry in Oaxaca and beginning, "Arthur Calder-Marshall has just walked out leaving me with some very clear sailing directions as to what I should do about you! He tells me that UNDER THE VOLCANO is, from what you have told him, probably one of the most exciting books that has come down the line in a long time and although you have virtually completed the first 40,000 word version he is afraid it is going to be a long time before you have finished it to your own satisfaction" (1:71). The final words are all too prophetic and some of the phrasing is curious ("from what you have told him"—hadn't he read it for himself? The answer seems to be that Calder-Marshall privately found this version "*terrible*" [112]), but this contemporary description is at least consistent with (the source of?) Lowry's later account to Cape as well as Calder-Marshall's recall.

It is not only the earliest beginnings of the novel that are lost in memory and myth. Lowry remained in Mexico until July 1938, when he traveled to Los Angeles, where he stayed almost exactly a year before being shipped off to Vancouver by the lawyer hired by his father, Benjamin Parks. During this time, too, the *Volcano* seems to have occupied him, although how much he worked on it in Los Angeles would now appear undiscoverable. There is, however, a witness to the state the *Volcano* had reached before Lowry left for Canada: Carol Phillips (as she was known to Lowry) was hired by him as a typist in the early spring of 1939, first for "The Last Address" (*Lunar Caustic*), then in May for the *Volcano*.[4] What she recalls receiving of the latter was some hundred pages, mostly "yellow canary second sheets" covered in single-spaced, tiny type, with some handwritten pages, all annotated. In the midst of the typing, Phillips was taken ill, and when she next heard from Lowry (apparently in late June or July), he told her he was leaving Los Angeles and asked to see her again. At this final meeting, he requested that she continue typing clean copy even after his departure (done partly on yellow sheets, Lowry clearly did not consider this a publishable version), which she did sporadically over the summer and into the fall. From Vancouver, Lowry wrote first (August?) querying the stage of her typing, then, more urgently (September?), in expectation of being called up for the war, asking her to send the whole bundle of manuscripts to him, perhaps via Parks. What precisely happened next is unclear, but Phillips recalls having retyped approximately three-fourths of the manuscript before Parks collected it to send on to Lowry. Although she was paid for her typing of "The Last Address," Phillips never received reimbursement for the *Volcano*. It was January 1940 by the time the manuscript reached Lowry in Vancouver.

What Carol Phillips recalls of the contents of that manuscript is, after more than fifty years, understandably a bit uncertain. Nonetheless, she remembers the work *opening* with the episode of the bus trip and the dying Indian, which occupied a large portion (approximately twenty-five pages) of the original manuscript. The Day of the Dead was richly described; drinking, on the other hand, played a relatively small part. It was her impression that Lowry was sure of himself in handling the Consul, rather shakier with the figures of Hugh and Yvonne; Laruelle she does not recall appearing at all. In this version, Phillips recollects, the Consul did not die. The tragedy of his life lay in his desiring much and remaining unfulfilled, but this draft left a hope for a future resolution to his difficulties.

At the time—May 17, 1939, to be exact—this was Carol Phillips's description of the *Volcano*:

Such plots, and counter-plots and subterranean intricacies. The theme of this novel "Under the Volcano" is first—life against death.... Then man's inhumanity against man—that is the running thread. Then the actual story which all takes place in one day—that of a father and his daughter and her sweetheart—then the historical significance of revolution in Mexico—the general world unrest, the precipitation of war and rumors of war and general brutality, which is tremendous—the psychological by-play on the part of the father whose own love having been thwarted finds in his daughter's sweetheart a very menacing rival, the Oedipus complex, and the tragedy of Emperor Maximilian and Carlotta. How you like dose![5]

Thematic in its emphases, Phillips's account nonetheless makes clear that the limitation of the action to a single day (not, presumably, two "single days") was in place by 1939 and that the psychological and political concerns, so strongly to be underlined in the 1940 version, were already in some form prominent.

If after half a century and more we attend to unreliable recollections of Lowry, his friends and acquaintances for these earliest stages of composition, it is the result of there being so absurdly little of the actual manuscript of the *Volcano* itself available. Several thousand sheets survive from the 1940–46 period; what remains from Mexico-Los Angeles is two notebooks containing fragmentary material pertaining to the novel and a few loose notebook sheets. More is left unanswered than the matter of whether the novel began as a short story. How much writing was actually done in Mexico? in Los Angeles? what format had the work at inception? and what, of course, was its nature? what were its action, characters, themes, techniques? The glimpses we obtain from the scrappy remnants are mere tantalizations.

Apparently the earliest of these is a notebook containing a group of witty remarks, several of which will persist through to the published novel, that both Lowry and Conrad Aiken identified as deriving from Aiken's visit to Lowry in Cuernavaca in the spring of 1937: "'I expect to see Rousseau riding out of there on a tiger,' 'He thinks I'm a tree with a bird in it,' 'The landscape like New Hampshire,' A sound of whistling: 'The ambassador practicing diplomacy.'"[6] Mentioned briefly in note form are an expression to "Enid" (the Consul's estranged wife in the working draft of 1940) of a sense of triumph "at the bottom of the abyss"; the Trogon *ambiguus ambiguus*; a white and crimson turkey; a bird with a long tail which glides to land "like an arrow"; "gin fish"; the wandering remains of a famous singer; and Puebla and Cholula, with the latter's 366 churches and two barber shops, the Toilet and the Harem. The citations from Aiken alone suggest that whatever new work Lowry gave his former mentor to read during his visit, it predated the contents of this notebook—and that nothing, therefore, of the very earliest phases of the *Volcano* remains.

More extensively developed than these notes are two scenes between young lovers known here as Ed and Joey, each occupying almost three full pages. Joey is the daughter of "the Consul," and the first of the passages is labelled "the Consul overhears." He does so with considerable incredulity, we are told: they are discussing marriage, for which Joey seems eager, Ed less so:

"Do we want to make that overture to the state?"
"It isn't so much an overture. It's the last hope."
"But why marriage?"
"It's a security."
"Against what."
"Against ourselves. It's a security against what Dad calls the burning [luring?] phantasm of the unconscious."

They go on to wonder whether they might "help each other to help some thing," such as Spain, but all they seem sure of is their mutual love. To the "astounded" Consul who hears all this, it appears that ordinary life has "become so unreal that it was necessary to build it upon an even greater fantasy," and the war in Spain seems to him at first as much a delusion as "the other war to make the world safe for democracy." And yet, we are told, "he knew with his best intuitions {to which he never lived up} [sic] that there *was* a difference, in the strictest sense, all the difference in the world." In the second scene, the lovers recall their earlier happy time in Paris (and the abbreviation of this in the form of "Do you remember the bicycles, etc." may suggest that this is a revision of a still earlier draft) and observe target practice in the distance, but since this episode repeats several elements of the first it is probably an alternate version of that scene.

Several pages further on in the notebook, a scrawled two pages present a diatribe by the Consul to an unidentified audience on the "sentimentality" occasioned by the war in Spain. He openly declares his sympathy with the Loyalists, but privately reflects that they are the ones who are "destroying culture—whatever that was," and who would "stop him going further into the jungle with Indians" like William Blackstone. "'Now the Indians are in here—' he tapped his chest . . . 'Genius will look after itself.'"

Quite separate in this same notebook, beginning at the back and written upside down, is a single coherent narrative headed "Escruch is an old man," which occupies 8½ consecutive pages. The protagonist is a Mr. Carruthers, whose house lies "between two huge ambassadorial mansions" in a lush garden that "ran riot": "And he too ran riot, but in the taverns of the town, not in his home, as though something hurt him about the beauty that might have existed there." He is, it develops, "a remittance man, a blot on some aristocratic family in England, paid to stay away." He gives various accounts of himself, we are told, including one that he is or was "the Norwegian Consul in Acapulco." But he is none of these things: now forty and looking sixty, he is a binge drinker who runs up his credit in all the bars of Q. As he drinks in an obscure bar run by a woman, the proprietress, who knows no English, produces a child's exercise book (similar to the one in which Malcolm Lowry is composing this little story?). In it, Carruthers discovers that Dickens's lonely old miser has become a model for basic Spanish-English translation, and with sample dialogue the narrative ends.

There is nothing in Lowry's exercise book to link this tale of an aging drunk to the scenes between the young lovers or the Consul's political tirade, but readers of the *Volcano* will recognize the little book the Consul comes across in Chapter VII. Also resonant is the name "Carruthers," which will get attached to "an old professor" of the Consul (and, later, of Hugh) who also was a heavy tippler and who is associated with classic literary texts, if not those of Dickens. Not surprisingly, at one stage his parallels to the Consul will be rather heavily underlined.

Several loose sheets seem to date from more or less this same period. Two consecutive notebook sheets are headed "Going to Puebla," and comparison of these descriptive notes with the earliest surviving version of Chapter I ("B") reveals that almost everything in these notes was used, and used on two pages (9–10) near the start of Laruelle's walk. The presentation there of the sun, the trees, the cactus, the earth, the changeable landscape (reminiscent of so many others), the boys on the backs of lorries, the ancient Ford propped "against involuntary departure," and the memory of "motoring" to Puebla along "the Mexican lake bed" all derive from the passages on these sheets, often with hardly an alteration.[7] Two other sheets (28:21 and 1:76) sketch out "an ugly child with earrings, a bald patch," swinging in a creaking hammock and transcribe an exchange of "Sank you's."

Finally, a bound set of notebook pages seems to represent a later stage of composition than any of the materials mentioned above.[8] First, we here are given a glimpse of a larger fictional structure, at least in part already extant, to which the notebook passages pertain. While most of the nine recto pages written on contain an extended love scene between Ed and Joey, that scene is headed by a Roman "III" and immediately preceded, on the first extant page, by

II
The letter to the mother.

A later listing (verso of the ninth page) expands:

I
II letter
III—love scene
IV: scene between deQuincey
V scene on porch etc.

Furthermore, near the end of the love scene occurs this self-reminder:

{Here, the horseman out of the last chapter: the blind force:
Here: also in xi: they go to Maximilian's palace; the swimming pool, etc.
And from 2 (chap iii)—much cut—p.2 to 8: all; but much cut: and to some extent, re-cast.}

There is no way of determining just what and how much had been written by this point, but the repeated references to ordering and revision indicate a phase beyond that represented by the exercise book discussed above.

So, indeed, does the conduct of the love scene here. Its very extent—seven consecutive pages—suggests its more mature development. Also, a number of what had been in the earlier notebook merely isolated images—the Trogon, the turkey, the gliding bird—are now integrated into the narrative, while new features of the scene begin to emerge: the Calle Nicaragua itself, "a road of tossing stones, going on for ever into eternity like a life of agony"; coffee beans on the lawn; a sunflower "peering in" a window; the prison watchtower; the ruins of "King Maximilian's Palace"; the covered entrance to an iron mine; a "noise of subterranean collapse" from the barranca; a white goat and dirty brown dog ("'Tragedy and lust are with us,'" quips Ed) that accompany the lovers on their stroll from garden to barranca and back, which is the extent of the physical action here. Ed and Joey have seemingly remet coincidentally at "the dance" the previous evening, and they once more reminisce about Paris and wonder at their luck in finding each other again. But while they exchange declarations of love, there is, as before, a not-quite-identified sense of malaise between them, here vaguely touched on as a question of sexual fidelity: Joey repeats enigmatically "'I'm no use'" while Ed mutters "'I have been faithful to you all.'" They have no trouble agreeing on Joey's father, however, whom they determine to avoid because "'he's still pretty plastered'" and is "'charging about the garden somewhere.'"

Designated here to precede the love scene is a "letter to the mother," at least part of which is given in a page-and-a-half version. The mother in question, it emerges, is the Consul's, while he identifies himself in the letter as "ex-Consul." Here is the letter's opening: "——Mother, mother: how can I say what I want to say to you, without singing Solveig's song, and I on the sole Arabian tree? Midnight denies poursuivant of the dawn and dawn denies finality of twelve! How shall we balance unbalanced childhood, with some fixed decency, with an even tune, to its certainty, to its hollied Decembers?" The letter goes on for some twenty lines more before breaking off, through the white whale and black snow, Ahab and the Fool in *Lear*, "the dark's spinets" and days "upright as tulips." Structurally, it is obviously the forerunner of the letter to Yvonne of Chapter I, but at this stage it is Lowry at his most "poetic" (and indeed there survives a blank verse effort from this period that uses most of these same lines: cf. Scherf no. 102). The addressee is especially astonishing, for this is the outpouring of a character old enough to have a grown daughter of his own.

Although I have presented these notes and drafts in what seems their order of composition, there is nothing in the early survivals to allow us to date the significant entries with any exactitude. Those in the earliest notebook that derive from Aiken's conversation clearly cannot be earlier than spring 1937, but even a dating of all the events that occasioned Lowry's notes would not determine precisely when the passages were incorporated into the *Volcano*, and there seems no way to discover when larger scenes and structures, clearly a part of the developing fiction, got created. Since all of this material seems to belong to relatively early stages of composition, we may guess that these notebook passages well precede the annotated typescript Lowry had compiled by spring 1939, but in the absence of any corroborating evidence, even that remains conjectural.

Barring the unlikely appearance of new manuscript from this period, the contents of any early version or versions—we are not certain even which form to use—can only be glimpsed in the fragmentary mirrors of these notes (none of which, incidentally, makes mention of the episode of the dying Indian). Other relics of the Mexican period will later become part of Lowry's text—as different as "found" objects (menu, train schedule, travel poster, telegram, etc.) and poems written during this time that will be cannibalized for the omnivorous novel—but there is no evidence that these were part of the *Volcano* at this stage of its creation (and sometimes there is clear evidence that they were not).

What, then, can be said with assurance of the Ur-*Volcano* of 1936(?)–1939? That, as it grew, it came to be conceived of as consisting of eleven sections; that central among its characters were a drunken (? see Carol Phillips's recollections above) ex-consul, his young daughter, and her lover; that this division along lines of age was also a division in political allegiance; that the war in Spain was the primary political issue bruited; that virtually all the surviving passages given any real development are from the early sections; and that while much of the language will be altogether superseded, there are some images and even phrasings that persist through innumerable revisions into the published novel—our first instance of a characteristic Lowry compositional procedure, the creation of linguistic nodes, poetic shapes that remain untouchable while all else around them may be radically altered.

Much of this can also be said of the 1940 *Volcano;* let us venture a bit further, recognizing that we are moving now into the conjectural. Since the 1940 version also began with eleven chapters before expanding, it seems unlikely that the structural numerology Lowry will so insist on later, rejecting out of hand proposed modifications to his twelve-part work, had any place in his early conception. Furthermore, although a Chapter 1 is listed in the red notebook, its contents are left unspecified, but there is nothing to suggest the narrative dislocation that appears in all draftings composed after the outbreak of World War II. Chapter I may have focused on the rites and celebrations connected with that day, perhaps including the ball at which "Joey" and "Ed" were reunited; by 1939, according to Carol Phillips's later recollection, it was an account of the bus journey. At any rate, whatever the subject, it almost certainly occupied the same temporal plane as the rest of the action.

The Consul's letter to his mother seems to reinforce the sense elsewhere that the principal narrative dynamic in the earliest *Volcano* was intergenerational and suggests that (however grotesquely rendered) an oedipal theme was even then part of Lowry's conception. Although there is one brief shaft directed at "Enid," she is otherwise unmentioned, and the tensions between Joey and Ed on the one hand and Joey's father, the Consul, on the other seem reechoed in his letter's resentments of a blighted childhood. Lowry's fascination with time was not absent—the Consul's letter is centrally occupied with it, ending "where broken heart meets broken tryst in time"—and the final ("red") notebook contains familiar historical references (the Mexican Revolution, the Conquest, Maximilian's Palace); but temporal concern seems to have been extended through the characters in a series of generational disputes, an eternal return of the failures of age giving way to the renewals and hope of youth. Thus the love theme, which in 1940 will be developed in both generations, here may have been confined almost entirely to the younger couple, who seem to have their own difficulties (is abortion one of Joey's sexual secrets, as it will be Yvonne's?), while no indication of the Consul's marital status (separated? divorced? widowed?) appears.

The main political focus of these drafts, written during the years of the Spanish Civil War, is not hard to guess (although exactly what forms the dispute between elder and younger would have taken is of course undeterminable), but it seems unlikely these matters were more complex than the relatively simple conflicts of the 1940 version. Finally—and here we may move beyond conjecture—some familiar Lowryan counters present themselves in these notes and sketches: Bix Beiderbecke and Eddie Lang, Kafka and Doré, *Paradise Lost* and Adam, Los Manos de Orlac [*sic*] all appear. They often seem dropped like plums into pudding, yet that crudity is simply a sign of the earliness of these draftings. If we make the reasonable assumption that the 1940 *Volcano* was the most sophisticated and polished version to date—it is certainly the only one Lowry released with a view to publication—Arthur Calder-Marshall's blunt private response ("terrible") in 1937 begins to sound less harsh. Fascinating as it would be to be able to scan that Ur-*Volcano*, Lowry's gods were perhaps this time kind to him in permitting most of it to disappear.

CHAPTER ONE

The 1940 *Under the Volcano*

In July 1939 Lowry left Los Angeles for Vancouver, but, as we have seen, the *Volcano* did not go with him. He doubtless anticipated coming back himself to collect the freshly typed manuscript from Carol Phillips, and before summer was out he did attempt one such return, but in fact Canada was destined to be Lowry's home for the next fifteen years. Instead, late summer of 1939 brought two other developments that would have a decisive effect on the *Volcano:* Margerie Bonner joined Malcolm in Vancouver, and war broke out in Europe.

In terms of world history the two events are almost comically incommensurate; in terms of the history of the *Volcano*, it is difficult to know which was the more significant. In any case, Lowry had leisure to absorb the impact of both, for as weeks stretched into months, he remained without the manuscript of the *Volcano*. Repeated pleas to Los Angeles produced nothing until sometime in January 1940. A letter of January 27 provides the first evidence that it has arrived: he writes to Conrad Aiken excitedly that "Margie is now as much interested in Under the Volcano as I am. We work together on it day and night." (*Aiken-Lowry* 100)

Because of the Lowrys' methods of working on this version of the novel, it is uniquely possible to be precise about how and even when portions of the new draft were created (see Appendix A). For some of the same reasons, however, what remains indeterminate is what relation this Vancouver version bears to whatever came up to Lowry from Los Angeles. Nothing of the latter survives; neither do any of the superseded or rejected manuscript or typescript leaves from the Vancouver version remain. So thorough are these absences that the almost inescapable conclusion is that—with an abandon he would never again demonstrate—Lowry deliberately discarded these now "unnecessary" drafts and pages. Thus, as with the pre-1940 *Volcano*—and partly as a result of our ignorance of earlier drafts—there are enormous gaps in our knowledge of how this version came about, the largest being that concerning the construction of the action itself, the sequence of events that led to the remarkably assured Chapter XII. Furthermore, we often do not know when or with what implications portions of action or character entered the novel's development. We know, for instance, that Lowry claimed he did not encounter Juan Fernando Márquez, the original of Dr. Vigil, until late 1937 or early 1938, which would mean that this character could not have been in the version(s) read by Aiken or Calder-Marshall—but this does not tell us when or how he *did* enter the manuscript. We know that Lowry wrote to Aiken on January 27, 1940 that he and Margerie have "got started on an absolutely new and important character in it which is her idea" (*Aiken-Lowry* 100), a reference, one must assume, to Jacques Laruelle; yet although the director comes into existence only with this Vancouver version, we cannot gauge the implications of this figure for the novel as previously constituted.

There are thus great gaps in our knowledge not only of how Lowry got to the 1940 version, but also about the stages *of* that version.[1] But for all we do not know about the origins of the 1940 *Volcano*, still, its finished form is available for description and analysis.[2] And it is worth recalling that we *are* dealing here with a finished text, one intended—albeit vainly—for publication. As such, it doubtless should be read, as it once was, without presupposition or hindsight. Yet the inescapable fact is that virtually no one picking it up now comes to it unfreighted with the knowledge of its published successor: there are probably no "innocent" readings of this quite innocent text. Indeed, it acquires its only interest now in the reflected light of the achieved work, the glory cast back from the 1947 masterpiece. As such, it seems to demand being read with a bifurcated gaze, one that focuses on the text before it yet also cannot help framing that look within a vision of the work to come. We cannot avoid recalling, in short, that there are two quite different works bearing the title *Under the Volcano*.

Whatever we may make of connections and disconnections between these two *Volcanoes*, it is important to recognize at the outset that they are the only two complete versions of the novel that exist (or, doubtless, that ever existed). We have many post-1940 drafts of individual chapters, but no other complete texts of the whole novel until in June 1945

Lowry sent off the typescript that, edited and with a rash of last minute alterations, was published in 1947.

At dusk on the Day of the Dead, 1939, two men sit drinking and talking on the porch of the Casino de la Selva just outside Quahnahuac, Mexico. Their talk concerns their former friend, whom they refer to only as "the Consul," for this day is an anniversary of his death. As they part, they agree to meet later, about ten, in "the place where you know," and we follow one of the men, Jacques Laruelle, as he begins his slow circuitous route back to town. He responds to the variegated nature of the Mexican landscape as he goes and, still thinking of the Consul, pauses at the bridge over the barranca, the deep ravine that runs through the town. Next, Maximilian's ruined palace seems "part of a nightmare," and Laruelle hurries away, soon entering the town itself. As he approaches the cinema a sudden violent storm bursts, causing an electrical failure in the theatre—a common occurrence, the manager remarks. Excusing himself briefly, the manager returns with a book Laruelle recognizes as an anthology of plays that had actually belonged to the Consul, and as he examines it, a sheaf of paper falls out. It is a letter from the Consul to his former wife, the wife who had also been Laruelle's lover. "Dear Priscilla," the letter begins.

Any reader of the *Volcano* will immediately recognize my summary of the novel's opening (reinforced by the quoting of some familiar phrases) but may be bothered by small dissonances before reaching the large one of the name of the Consul's ex-wife, which of course we know as "Yvonne." The account of Jacques's walk, for instance, as well as having stops at barranca and palace in the "wrong" order, may sound oddly truncated, with no mention of his pause at the station, imagined voices in the ruins, the drunken horseman, or the long reminiscence of his and the Consul's adolescent friendship. And why has the reading of passages from the anthology not been noted? Those who know the novel very well will have recognized that the name of the town that is the book's setting has been misspelled, that Laruelle and his companion, Dr. Vigil, agree to meet at half past eight, not at ten, and that it is peculiar to call this day "an" anniversary of the Consul's death rather than "the" anniversary, since it is the first one.

The simple explanation for these omissions and "errors," of course, is that the summary is of the opening of the *Volcano* of 1940, not 1947.

and the point to be made is basic to what follows: the standard ways of talking about fiction will not get us very far when facing the extensive and often radical revising Lowry did on the *Volcano*. From my little summary it might reasonably be concluded that while Lowry changed a few things and added more than a few, the published novel was otherwise rather similar to its earliest surviving version. What no summary can convey is what is in Lowry's case crucial: the texture of the novel itself, the actual encounter with the language that is constituitive of the world there dramatized. To read the 1940 *Volcano* is to find oneself in a universe other than the one created by the book we know, a place that is oddly but somehow always "wrongly" familiar, as when one comes across a faded photograph of a beloved friend taken years earlier, and thinks even at the moment of identifying the blurred features, "But that can't be her! She's much more beautiful than that!"

If, as Wallace Stevens claimed, "A change of style is a change of subject," then the *Volcano* became over the years after 1940 a very different work indeed. Let us look more closely at the beginning of the novel, not this time a summarized version, but the actual opening paragraph of 1940 and of 1947:

It was the Day of the Dead. (*1940* 5)

Two mountain chains traverse the republic roughly from north to south, forming between them a number of valleys and plateaus. Overlooking one of these valleys, which is dominated by two volcanoes, lies, six thousand feet above sea level, the town of Quauhnahuac. It is situated well south of the Tropic of Cancer, to be exact on the nineteenth parallel, in about the same latitude as the Revillagigedo Islands to the west in the Pacific, or very much further west, the southernmost tip of Hawaii—and as the port of Tzucox to the east on the Atlantic seaboard of Yucatan near the border of British Honduras, or very much further east, the town of Juggernaut, in India, on the Bay of Bengal. (*Volcano* 3)

The abrupt, apparently "factual" opening in 1940—somewhat deceptive as to its factuality: compare "It was November 2"—presents unobtrusively an imaginative designation that will be exploited immediately as the text turns from temporality to setting, describing the processions of mourners observed by "the two men." But there is nothing deceptive in the abruptness of the flat rhythm of that sentence, which appears to seek to convince by its very absence of rhetorical flourish. The later opening has quite different intentions, insisting in its panoramic sweep on spatial references that seem global in their reach (only later will we see why Hawaii and India are the specific western and eastern poles of this vista). The paragraph invites us to take the long view in more than a geographic sense: it does not thrust us into the immediacy of the moment and the scene as does the 1940 opening but deliberately withholds a more precise focus (the novel will continue to take its time as the narrator gradually pans downward, using three paragraphs to reach those "two men"). But the geographical vista also implies a suspended temporality. The impression of the long view is reinforced by the use of present tense, for this is clearly the eternal present, a representation of the way things "always" are, no more the designation of a specific moment than the paragraph designates a specific place (it is not even clear at once which "republic" is in question). Furthermore, diction, syntax, sound and movement are all brought into play: the discreet Latinisms, unobtrusive alliteration ("*T*wo moun*t*ain chains *t*raverse the *r*epublic *r*oughly *fr*om north to south, *f*orming...."), and elevated and suspended rhythms (compare "traverse the republic" with, say, "cross the country"; note the withholdings of the second sentence which bring all its force down on "the town of Quauhnahuac"; observe the dying fall of "the town of Juggernaut, in India, on the Bay of Bengal"; and the parallelisms—since geographical parallels are also in question—of "to the west," "to the east," "very much further west," "very much further east"). Through the use of these rhetorical resources, the 1947 opening establishes at once its tone of high seriousness, its implication of consequentiality, which function with the paragraph's other features to lay claim not to historicity (this is the way it was) but to resonant significance (this is important, perhaps on a global scale).

The radical difference in the nature of those two openings epitomizes the intense reweaving of its texture that the *Volcano* underwent between 1940 and 1947. However, I have focused on Lowry's initial chapter for yet another reason: in 1940, its very existence was an innovation that transformed the nature of the existing text. Although nothing remains of the bundle that came up from Los Angeles, it is evident enough that Lowry faced a dilemma as he looked over his manuscripts that January. Whatever their precise nature, a novel in which the chief moral and political touchstone was the Spanish Civil War must have looked hopelessly dated given the developing international scene. Spain was a dead issue. With the fury of the Nazi rush across northern Europe, who could now be concerned with such matters as whether to fight for the Republic, the local implications of a Franco victory, or possible reservations about Marxist ideology? Lowry's working instinct, however, was always to revise and revamp, to rescue rather than abandon, and almost at once he must have seen that his manuscript could be "updated," made contemporary once again, by a kind of prefatory chapter which (in a scarcely original connection) linked the two wars, viewing the Spanish action as a warm-up for the wider confict now underway. It is worth recalling that when Lowry sat down to work again early in 1940, the November 1939 setting of his new opening was only a few weeks in the past. By the time the *Volcano* was published in 1947, of course, both of the novel's temporal settings had become "historical," but the Lowry who wrote rapidly in 1940 with hopes of early publication was writing a thoroughly contemporary fiction, and it was precisely this opening chapter that now made it so.[3]

Although even in 1940 Lowry had begun exploring some implications of setting his opening chapter later than the rest of the novel, what seems most striking now is how "local" it is, how much a product of a particular historical moment, as indeed the text as a whole reflects the preoccupations of the decade during which it had taken shape. The presiding figure of Chapter I, Jacques Laruelle, as we have seen, apparently came into being only with this draft, an inspiration of Margerie's— Malcolm may have loved films, but it was Margerie who had been the professional—yet in 1940 it is at least as important that he is French as that he is a director. When Lowry began reworking the *Volcano*, the German invasion of France was clearly imminent, and by the time he sent his manuscript off to New York, the country had fallen and Pétain had signed an armistice with the Nazis. But in the November 1939 opening, Laruelle can believably articulate his dilemma of whether or not to return and fight for France—a dilemma that echoes not only his creator's but, more to the point for the novel, Hugh's with regard to Spain—and Lowry indulges him at length. As the events of 1939–40 faded from the apparently critical to merely initiatory stages of a long, harrowing conflict, Jacques's political passions faded with them until by 1947 he has become the almost apolitical opening consciousness of a postwar novel who serves as reminder that whatever is happening in the external world, some struggles are perennial: "One side or the other would win. And in either case life would be hard. Though if the allies lost it would be harder. And in either case one's own battle would go on" (*Volcano* 9). There is nothing this politically aloof in 1940.

In its responses to the European situation, Chapter I can only have been created for this draft, but some of the other features of the 1940 text reflect in a more personal, Lowryesque way on nationalism at this historical moment of writing, before the fall of France, before the Battle of Britain, before the entry of the United States into the conflict. Lowry was not only of two minds about his anticipated participation in the war: he was an Englishman who during this period often identified himself as "really" at least as American as British and who was working closely on this novel with a newly beloved native of that America. Both Lowry's wives were, of course, Americans, and his attraction and resistance to this divided identity are projected into the Consul's letter to his ex-wife, where after touching on drink, sacrifice, remorse, and love he adds bathetically *"[p]art of the trouble is perhaps, simply my nationality. Perhaps if I had given in and become a naturalized American, it might have been our salvation. Yet I would never have been able to forget that I am an Englishman."*[4] That Lowry has something more in mind than a rather absurd personal statement (just how was a British career diplomat to become an American citizen?) appears several lines later: *"That they* [Americans] *are the hope of the world I am sure, but that I have a need of any such hope whatsoever in my life is questionable. And just as the sea has divided me in nationality, just as my life has been broken in half, so the Atlantic of my soul, crashing on widely separated coasts of thought, storms in me day and night. Yes, storms in me between the severed halves of what I am and what I would be, and I no longer know which is which. Which is ego, which is super ego,"* and so on (1940 25). The very crudeness of this formulation of a kind of modernist Ahab makes plain the intention to have the issue of nationality reverberate on several frequencies.

With an American mother and English father, the 1940 Yvonne seems to live out the Consul's ambivalence by making easy pragmatic use of it, identifying herself sometimes as one, sometimes as the other, particularly in political argument with the two men. Thus in Chapter IV, disputing with Hugh about Spain, she declares herself "'very proud to think I am really English,'" since she sees nonintervention as the only sensible policy; while in Chapter VI she's "'damned proud to be an American'" as she quarrels with her father about what she now presents as England's irresponsibility toward Spain. In 1940, however, "America" is most insistently identified with the young, naive, idealistic figure of Hugh, Yvonne's twenty-four-year-old suitor, late of Stanford University. Although in a moment of angry frustration he can turn against his country—when the diplomats' cars will not stop to aid the dying Indian—the way in which he does so is itself, we are reminded, typically American: "'My countrymen,' said Hugh . . . *'In God We Trust,* but only on the nickel. No trust! . . . Is that democracy? That's what Melville said too in *The Confidence Man.* No trust. Is that America?'" (1940 254). But Hugh's underlying faith in his country, and his joining of England to it in continuity, is made by way of another literary reference. In Chapter VI he reflects that "it was her [England's] spirit indeed which would never die and it was in him too, as an American, just as Nathaniel Hawthorne had said in 'The Grey Champion'" (1940 167). When at the end of Chapter XI he "hears" that Grey Champion warn once again of peril—"For I am the type of New England's hereditary spirit; and my shadowy march, on the eve of danger, must ever be the pledge that New England's sons will vindicate their ancestry"—the ancestry so invoked runs in unbroken continuity back through colonial America to England's nurturing traditions.

What is division in the Consul and vacillation in Yvonne is reconciled in Hugh, but only because at the end of Chapter X he has identified Yvonne and all that he idealizes with "America." It is an affirmation that in his final moments even the Consul will seem confusedly to make, although distinctly from the European side: "'America, perhaps, France, forgive me,'" he rambles, thus voicing a kind of allegiance to the country of hope, but also giving final prominence to that last stronghold of antifascism on the continent, either about to fall or just having fallen as Lowry writes (and "France" is a pencilled insert, literally a last thought on the working manuscript [26:5, 29A]). Like Jacques's musings about homelands at the other end of the novel, the reference to France will disappear, and while "America" remains to the end, it does so in a context that has grown considerably more equivocal about such nationalistic identifications.

Yet if Chapter I is in one respect quite specific in its reflection of the time of writing, in another it is curiously vague. While Vigil and Laruelle are obsessed on this Day of the Dead by the Consul, they are quite unable to recall just when he died: "'How many years ago today is it?' . . . 'Two, three years ago,'" comes the hazy response, followed by the lame, "'Time isn't our strong point in *Méjico*'" (*1940* 6). This odd indeterminacy is only explained as the novel revolves into the past and the war in question becomes the Spanish one. Although that conflict was presumably the one the developing text had been concerned with now for several years, the 1940 *Volcano* treats it mainly as a political, moral, even metaphysical conundrum rather than a particular set of events, and the rare specific allusion reveals why. In Chapter IX, as the band at the bullthrowing strikes up "Guadalajara," Hugh asks, "'Guadalajara, do you hear that? . . . Jesus, which Guadalajara?'" (*1940* 277) For him, the song evokes not the Mexican town but the March 1937 offensive at the Spanish city, a timing that would place the action of Lowry's novel in November 1937 or 1938. In Chapter VII, however, the Consul hears shouted newspaper headlines concerning "Sangriente Combate en la Garcel Modelo" (25:23, 22; cf. *1940* 208), by which Lowry means Madrid's Model Prison (Cárcel Modelo), where "bloody" executions occurred in the summer and autumn of 1936. That dating, however, would place the novel's action in the year *previous* to the Guadalajara offensive. In short, Lowry was uncertain about the actual events of the Spanish war and knew it, and the entire text in 1940 is left temporally unfixed to cover his vagueness. An ocean away from that struggle during its entire course, Lowry like others of his generation was moved by its issues and implications, but it touched him less directly than the war now menacing England, one in which his own participation threatened not to be a matter of choice. The European conflict is a palpable presence in the 1940 *Volcano*; the particularities of the Spanish war he would have to work up later.

If the concern with the Spanish Civil War testifies to the novel's origins in the 1930s, so does its linking of political and economic issues, a linking more overt and "committed" in 1940 than it will be in 1947. Only two pages into this version we find Laruelle treating Vigil to his analysis of the background of the European situation by way of a Central American analogy that blames the conflict on the cynical betrayal by the "metal industry," which set about secretly rearming the enemy in order to stimulate the domestic economy even though "they knew [this action] would only lead to war" (*1940* 7).[5] Not surprisingly, the figure that most explicitly bears this theme of economic betrayal in 1940 is the Consul, here named "William Ames." Young Hugh's father, it turns out, has been a business acquaintance of the Consul's ("and a very profitable one," the latter recalls), and Hugh himself is vaguely aware that he is dealing with "a wealthy man," but William Ames is more interested in and precise about economic matters than Geoffrey Firmin will be. For instance, the phone call of Chapter III is less enigmatic in 1940 than in 1947. Here, after the "silver rumor . . . denied by Washington" (cf. *Volcano* 76), the conversation turns on government expropriation of foreigners' land. "'I'm glad I had the sense to roll some of your investments away into a sensible obscure corner,'" he tells Yvonne. "'How's the market?'" she responds, and the answer she gets here links the Consul's capitalism to an unrestrained self-indulgence: "'Money,' he said. 'We lose our lands, our wife, our soul, our wits, we no longer need a Consul in Quahnahuac, yet we still do make money enough, God knows how, in the midst of disaster still preserve our taste for *tequila añejo* and *pulpos in su tinta*'" (*1940* 85). In 1940 it is the Consul, not Hugh, who delivers in Chapter X the speech on universal exploitation, an exploitation that in 1940 is insistently economic: "the exploitation of everybody by everybody else" is a matter of "'Loot. Loot. Loot. And it's the same everywhere in the world. Loot. Nothing else but loot. The desire for loot is at the bottom of all things even when there isn't any. Then you get communism'" (*1940* 297; cf. *Volcano* 299–300). The sharp economic note, so characteristic of literature of the thirties, is sounded more persistently here than it will be later.

Focused in William Ames is the association of alcohol, fascism, and death with foreign economic exploitation, a confluence that is repeated and projected in the curious *doppelgänger* figure of a drunken German silver miner the Consul acquires in Chapter XII. Yet even before his appearance in the Farolito makes these associations overt, the final chapter, detailing the Consul's end, presses hard on the theme of economic retribution. Lost in the jungle as the chapter opens, William Ames senses that a "torrent" is about to "sweep down on him, the landed proprietor, who had amassed half a million *pesos* out of Mexican oil, out of Mexican silver, the *gringo*, who, for his own ends had tapped Mexico's very veins . . . there was going to be a reckoning or two." Since all such "exploitations," especially on the Day of the Dead, are ultimately one, the Consul, like O'Neill's Emperor Jones, imagines menacing figures in the jungle, "those Tlahuicans who had died for the valley . . . huddling all around him as they had huddled this morning on the murals" (*1940* 341-42). Yet when he turns on his tormentors in the Farolito, his accusations erase any distinction between victim and victimizer to include them all in a universal process of thievery: "'No different in the world— ha ha, inner markets and munitions! Been going on for years—worse than loot—believe me! I know how I make my profits, don't I? . . . One day the People'll rise up and wipe you out—won't do any good either, they're all thieves too. Whole bloody lot of you are thieves, everybody! Laruelle! Humanity! Me too. Thieves!'" (*1940* 372-73) This is the Consul at his most Timonesque, his cynicism sweeping beyond meaningful economic or political criticism into a full-blown misanthropy. In 1940 he will literally die of it.

Like the counterpoint in Chapter XII between the silver miner's tale of being led to his mother by his little dead sister and Priscilla's yearning letters, the novel as a whole has a larger counteraction to the Consul's movement toward death in the movement of Yvonne and Hugh toward love, an action not without its political and economic ramifications. In Chapter II, as Yvonne reflects on her many failed affairs and recognizes that she has never given herself "*generously*," she makes an immediate association the strictest Marxist might approve: "Had the element in which she lived anything to do with this, the monetary element—was it this that had been so responsibly all-poisoning? A fish takes the water for granted, she thought. And if you suggested to him it would be better to live in the fresh air? What then?" (*1940* 53) A "jingle" starts in her mind that will be revived and completed in Chapter IX, "a song about money" in the composition of which she enlists Hugh and the Consul's aid. A kind of politicized revision of Rupert Brooke's "Heaven," the song is meant to voice Yvonne's sense of "breakthrough" in her feeling for Hugh, but the effort goes on for pages (*1940* 271-74, 283-84) and seems allegorically muddled even to its creators before this tedious whimsy comes to an end. Nonetheless, as an expression of her love, it is meant to be taken as a sign of her redemption from sterile selfishness, one of whose aspects is economic. As for Hugh, his growing commitment to Yvonne is clearly intended to bring him a sense of purpose so that by Chapter XI, when she comes to represent "America" to him, the personal, Lowry would have us believe, is directly translatable into the moral and political.

I have underlined the prominence in 1940 of economic and political themes both because they help locate the matrix out of which this *Volcano* emerges and because to readers familiar with the 1947 novel the degree of explicitness and emphasis they receive is a primary distinction between the two texts. Elsewhere readers may find to their surprise less difference—or, more precisely, another kind of difference—than they might have anticipated. On the correct assumption that the 1940 version is the more primitive of the two, for instance, they might have expected a simpler, more direct, rendering of experience, a less allusive, less symbolic text than the published one. In fact, however, the 1940 *Volcano* quite bristles with allusions and overt symbols (not, of course, always the same ones as those of 1947, nor used in the same ways), and it is the "rendering of experience," however defined, that is the less developed, more primitive aspect of the text. For this curious state of affairs, the novel, if not its author, had a kind of explanation:

> Life was a forest of symbols, was it, Baudelaire had said? But, it occurred to him, even before the forest, if there were such a thing as 'before,' were not there still the symbols? Yes, before! Before you knew anything about life, you had the symbols. It was with symbols that you started. From them you progressed to something else. Life was indeed what you made of the symbols and, the less you made of life the more symbols you got. And the more you tried to comprehend them, confusing what life was, with the necessity for this comprehension, the more they multiplied. And the more they multiplied, that is, disintegrated into still more and more symbols which in the first place never had the slightest intention of meaning anything, let alone of being understood, just like human beings in short, the more they liked it, until, in the end, life itself, like the beautiful insect flying in the cat's mouth, which the cat itself did not know it should eat, fluttered away abruptly, leaving an abstraction behind. (1940 346–47)

This may be a cry of post-Romantic disillusionment, but it is also an ironically trenchant criticism of the book which contains it. The concern with the symbol and its "meaning," here purchased at the expense of "life," points unerringly at the cerebral nature of the 1940 *Volcano*, where the principals are presented as endlessly "thinking" and debating with themselves and one another but have no convincingly presented inner reality, no emotional being out of which their concerns might be rendered with credible urgency. It is a text of gestures, one that points verbally at characters and actions to tell us not who or how they are but what they mean, where the "abstraction" is asked to do the work of animating the novel, where characters all attempt to "understand" each other and themselves. In the cited passage, it is the symbol, not "life," which is primary, originary, at least as alive and determinate as "human beings," who feature here almost as an afterthought. "Life," alas, has disappeared, leaving behind only empty proliferating symbols.

In other words, we are faced not only with the differences between earlier and later versions of the *Volcano*, but with a 1940 text that is at times so unsatisfactory, so amateurish, that it is difficult to recall that Lowry at this time was not a novice but a young professional with a modest career already behind him. How are we to understand the crudities and failures of the 1940 *Volcano*?

We may speculate on any number of personal causes for what we find here, from haste of composition to the unassimilated influence of Margerie to Malcolm's reluctance to confront the deeper implications of his material; lacking earlier manuscripts out of which this version evolved, however, such guesses must remain speculative. The text itself, however, silent as to causality, presents an aesthetic and technical anomaly in Lowry's career that helps illuminate its inhering problems. For that tersely "objective" opening, "It was the Day of the Dead," characteristic of the 1940 *Volcano* and doubtless the result of such thirties' critical shibboleths as "simplicity" and "directness," is closely related to the narrative stance adopted throughout. That stance is peculiar in both senses, in the uniqueness and in the oddity of his employment of it. The point of view Lowry uses here is one of roving omniscience, a perspective whereby the narrator, while he may remain as exterior recording witness to the action, also enters the consciousnesses of the major characters at will, typically moving from one figure to another to present the responses of each to the various unfolding episodes, filtering action through successive minds in turn. What is odd here is not of course the technique itself—it has been used countless times from Dickens to Hardy, Fielding to Lawrence and beyond—but Lowry's employment of it, unsuited as it would seem to his particular gifts. The distinctive vividness and intensity of his best work is generated out of prolonged confrontation by a single consciousness of its circumstances, inner and outer, from which flows, witty and lyrical, obsessive and allusive, that supple, varied movement of language that characterizes Lowry's recognizable narrative presence, his "style," if you will. But as he employs it in 1940, roving omniscience is more suited to dramatizing the exterior world, with brief responses from the characters—that is, to a rapidly fluid movement and action that rests final fictional authority with a colorless narrator who retains responsibility for novelistic coherence as well as decisions of where to shift the view from moment to moment. For Lowry, this stance robs the account of intensity and urgency, flattens it emotionally, so that the inwardness of his characters never acquires depth nor does the exterior action achieve clarity and resonance. He never adopted this narrative stance again—its alteration is one of the first and arguably the most significant of his post-1940 revisions, the one with the furthest-reaching implications—and the emotional superficiality, the reliance on dialogue, the frequently reportorial presentation of exterior action one finds here would all seem closely connected to the particular "design governing posture" employed. The end product is a general distancing and what I have called a fiction of gesture, in which a kind of novelistic semaphoring is substituted for genuine rendering, one which often reads more like the notes toward a book to be written or commentary on one already extant than the realized work itself.

Repeatedly, for instance, Lowry burdens his dialogue with statements of barely disguised intentionality. Yvonne first encounters Hugh in a church "gazing at the votive pictures on the wall," and he turns to her with, "'Hullo Yvonne, hey, how do you like this? . . . I'm just looking at this picture of a man falling off a balcony'" (*1940* 57). The second sentence is inept because of its implausible announcement of the obvious, that is, what would be obvious to Yvonne. In his eagerness to implant an early image of the Consul's end, Lowry has forgotten who the true audience for Hugh's comment is, and the intrusive verbal gesture alienates the reader from the world of the novel. Hugh and Yvonne are particularly given to this announcing of emotions and attitudes whether of themselves or others. I should be fighting in Spain to "prove" my convictions, says Hugh, for "'I do wish to be sincere'" (*1940* 110). Let's avoid Father, says Yvonne, "we'll only find him in an agony'" (*1940* 101). This "gesturing" is not limited to the young: Laruelle in Chapter I pronounces, "'I think the Consul is haunting me.'" Nor is the tic confined to characters and dialogue: the narrator is quite capable of it. In Chapter VIII, as the the bus passengers stand uncertainly around the fallen Indian, the Consul is "so profoundly wishing that he could get as far away from this scene as possible, if necessary even by means of the *peón's* horse, that he was actually beginning to pretend to himself that nothing had happened; but making the decision, just the same, to absorb everything, not to miss a single touch in this glorious little drama of man's contemptibility" (*1940* 240). This is not a rendering of the Consul's response, but a report on it, a reading of it (confirmed by its transformation into Hugh's interpretation of the Consul's "look" [*Volcano* 243]). It is a comment on feeling rather than an attempt to convey it.

One consequence of Lowry's adoption of this distantly roving narrator is that what we are told sometimes seems oddly unrelated to the manner of its telling. For instance, in Chapter IX, as Yvonne sits at the bullthrowing, the account of her consciousness moves across her recollections of her meetings with Hugh to her association of feelings about him with her feelings about cherished writers to her recognition of love and its transfiguration of the world. The latter section goes this way:

> She wondered now as she had wondered then if such an emotion, separated from its element of hysterical identification, could become, truly, the thing itself. And as she was trying whimsically to fancy how she might have behaved had Keats or Shelley been alive, her question was answered, and, simultaneously, she knew that, even now, she was falling in love with Hugh. Looking at him by her side, clear-eyed and proud, she felt herself turning to him as the creative self turns on self for food, but turning, above all, in her heart, to the tenderness in him, which God knows she had never previously awakened in anyone.
>
> The world was now totally different from the world of a moment or two before. Everything was charged with a different significance. The fact that this was Mexico and that Hugh and she had met for the first time in Spain became more important too. (*1940* 269)

This is Yvonne's great epiphany in the 1940 *Volcano*, although one would hardly know it from the prose, the neutrality of tone as unflappable after her realization as before it. The later Lowry might participate with her in the moment, in the "totally different" sense of "the world," which would seem to evoke a stylistic reflection of the emotional discovery; or he might maintain an ironic distance from her failure of self-recognition, her unawareness of the parasitical nature of what she believes is "love" but what the feeding imagery reveals as something more sinister. In either event, tone, rhythm, diction, syntax would establish a response, however complex, however mixed, toward this moment. In the actual case nothing of the kind occurs. The prose continues in its flat reportorial indistinguishability; the narrator displays no awareness either of the character's sense of transfiguration or of the implications of his own imagery.

If such passages seem undeniable failures, abjectly unable to convey or "place" the emotions that are their ostensible subject, the 1940 *Volcano* is not without its successes. Lowry often had a surer, more immediate literary response to inanimate surroundings than to human speech or behavior. When he could find an objective correlative in landscape for the feeling within his character—when, in short, the lyric poet in him could bring together inner and outer worlds—we are likely to discover the prose quickly approaching or even achieving final form. Some of the landscape passages of 1940 are directly traceable to surviving notebook entries, and they tend to persist, even if modified, as depictions of character or renderings of dialogue do not. In addition to establishing a concrete external world, they serve as symbolic expression, of moral, political, and mythic dimensions as well as individual emotional ones, although their significance might shift as the context around them changes. Here, for instance, is a section of Laruelle's walk in Chapter I as it appears in 1940:

> he found himself not only unable to take his mind off the Consul, but to focus upon any point of rest in his recollections of him: these too were as confused, contradictory and as violent as the landscape, and he fell into a strange mood like a vicarious despair. Laruelle crossed another field where a faded blue Ford, a total wreck, had been pushed under a hedge on the slope. Two bricks had been set against its front wheels against involuntary departure.

What are you waiting for, he asked it, feeling a sort of empathy, in his present state, for those tatters of ancient hood flapping, and later, as he approached the bridge, put the same question to himself, wondering whether he would find his "invitation" to return to France at home. (*1940* 16)

That faded blue Ford, we recall (see Prologue, p. 24), first appears on a loose sheet from a Mexican notebook and, wheels propped, will remain a precarious fixture of Chapter I on into the published novel. But as its surroundings alter, so will the kind of resonance it has. Here in 1940 it is the centrepiece of a passage as insistent about the use of landscape as objective correlative as Lowry would ever get. With the opening sentence drawing the explicit parallel between inner and outer, Jacques's "empathy" is made overt by his "put[ting] the same question" ("What are you waiting for?") twice. Its application to himself is given determinate meaning: his reluctance to return to his house, itself a reflection of his conflicted reluctance to return to France, with its undertones of remorseful self-destruction. By the time of publication, where he still questions the car to which he feels "a sort of kinship, an empathy," there is no longer an overt reference to Jacques's return to France, which in this version is an already determined decision. The "involuntary departure" may, therefore, still suggest that leavetaking, with or without the self-destructive undertones, but it no longer insists on this reading, for now Jacques immediately makes a different association altogether: "*Darling, why did I leave? Why did you let me?* (*Volcano* 13). Yvonne's recalled questions on her postcard to the Consul suggest the "involuntary" nature of both her departures, the exit from Quauhnahuac and marriage to which she is referring, and her death, which Laruelle's discovery of the card that very night inevitably brings to mind. As a result, it thereby serves to recall the "involuntary departure" of the Consul as well—like the precariously moored car, into an abyss. So while the basic scene and the technique of correspondence remain— the old Ford, the propped wheels, Jacques's "empathy," his question— the shifts in context inescapably produce shifts in meaning, and it is characteristic of the direction of Lowry's revisions that what is clear and closed in 1940 has become multivalent and open in 1947.

Perhaps nowhere does the 1940 *Volcano* declare its distance from its eventual successor than in the flat, terse, understated "neutrality" of its writing. The sense of movement, the kinetic quality of the prose of the published *Volcano*, dramatizes—indeed, creates—an entire vision of existence as well as the particular emotion of a moment.[6] Although it may seem that the very appearance of an opening chapter set one year after the body of the ensuing fiction would demand a recognition of time as motion, the few indications of this in the 1940 manuscript are thematic, not stylistic. The illusion that the *Volcano* creates of not only being *about* a universe where journeys never end but of embodying it in the very sentence exfoliating before our eyes, pivoting on its own diction and syntax until it finds adequate form, here, now, to convey the inner motion of this moment (which may, of course, be undermined by the next one), yet whatever its complications or interruptions (I am of course parodying such a sentence here) arrives finally after however long a journey at a point of stasis, often an image, which brings it to a close like the brief dropping of a curtain before the next scene—this stylistic transformation would be the achievement of the following years of recasting and, in both senses, of re-vision.

Even when physical motion is the focus, the dynamic quality of the prose is, at best, muted in 1940, deliberately so. Here is the latter portion of the Consul's ride on the "Maquina Infernal" of Chapter VII as it first appears:

> Then the cages began to go in reverse so that the sensation of falling was now behind him. The Consul was uneasily thinking how this recessive unwinding was a thousand times worse than looping in a plane, where the movement is quickly over and the only strange feeling one of increased weight when he realized, confusedly, that articles were falling out of his pockets, a new one at each circuit, his notecase, pipe, keys, his small change he did not have time to imagine being pounced upon by the children after all, his empty flask, and lastly his passport with his bond papers and birth certificate. (*1940* 217)

And here is the same action in its final form:

> All at once, terribly, the confession boxes had begun to go in reverse: Oh, the Consul said, oh; for the sensation of falling was now as if terribly behind him, unlike anything, beyond experience; certainly this recessive unwinding was not like looping-the-loop in a

plane, where the movement was quickly over, the only strange feeling one of increased weight; as a sailor he disapproved of that feeling too, but this—ah, my God! Everything was falling out of his pockets, was being wrested from him, torn away, a fresh article at each whirling, sickening, plunging, retreating, unspeakable circuit, his notecase, pipe, keys, his dark glasses he had taken off, his small change he did not have time to imagine being pounced on by the children after all, he was being emptied out, returned empty, his stick, his passport—had that been his passport? (*Volcano* 222)

The later passage is imagined from within, and the exclamations of horror and adverbs of dismay ("Oh . . . oh . . . ah, my God . . . terribly . . . terribly") acquire force from the swirl of participles that conveys the rapid wrenching movement of the machine. As the catalogue of verbals yields to that of the Consul's possessions, they are turned into half-glimpsed objects by the clausal interruptor ("he was being emptied out, returned empty") and the final question, which underscore the spasmodic and failing efforts of the mind to retain its equilibrium or at least its perceptual power. The ride is dramatized as felt and apprehended by its victim, both the dizzying circuits and the fear and disorientation (and exhilaration!) suggested by the expressive diction and rhythm of the two sentences.

In 1940 the passage also consists of two sentences, but the effect is altogether different. Again, the Consul's response is indicated adverbially ("uneasily," "confusedly"), but these are terms used *about* him by the narrator, not words he himself might employ. No attempt is made here to render his "confusion": the prose keeps all its feet on the ground, observing the ride from a clear distance, reporting rather than dramatizing action and reaction. In 1940 there is nowhere any break in syntax, whereas in the later passage there are two sharp shifts, mimetic of the mind's inability to control its own processes under these conditions. In both cases we are told the Consul has no "time to imagine" his change "being pounced upon by the children after all" (the narrator, however, has "time" to report the unimaginable), but in 1940 the single packet of "his passport with his bond papers and birth certificate" takes its place clearly and "lastly" at the end of an orderly listing, recorded by an eye innocent of the "confusion" of this wild ride. Indeed, nothing is more telling for the 1940 version than the signs in the working ("B") manuscript of the deliberate seeking of narrative detachment. In the first of these sentences the Consul's responses of "colossally" and "in a dreadful fashion" are cancelled, leaving his reaction, coolly noted, to the second sentence.

Descriptive passages, including metaphorical descriptions (the Consul as a stricken town, for example, in Chapter V), are among the most effective in 1940; like the old Ford of Chapter I, they tend to endure, instances where Lowry found his novel making "a noise like music." However, this text presents a much more "extroverted" novel than the one that will evolve out of it—again, a feature that seems closely related to the distant, roving point of view—far more reliant on dialogue than it will be in 1947. Yet with some important exceptions, Lowry seems to have had little in the way of a natural ear for dialogue. Those memorable exceptions are versions of the demotic (see the sailors in *Ultramarine*), such witty oddities as the fractured English of Dr. Vigil and Señora Gregorio, the *double entendres* of Cervantes and his menu. When he must produce dialogue of a more conventional sort, exchanges among members of his own class such as Hugh and Yvonne, the effort was likely to eventuate in such a passage as this from Chapter IV:

"It's so damned good to see you again. We really had no chance to talk this morning—what with earthquakes, airplanes and what have you—"
"Well, let's start now," said Yvonne.
"Now I can't think of anything to say—save that it's wonderful meeting you here. And that I've never seen such a gorgeous garden as this."
"I don't think Dad ever sees it, if he's always as plastered as this."
"Lucky fellow. Not lucky not to see the garden, lucky to be plastered. Well, lucky in a way."
"Lucky! If—but you don't know him as I do. Or did."
"I only know we're together again and it's good."
"Come on," said Yvonne.... "Let's go down the road. Father may be champing about the garden somewhere by now." (*1940* 103–4)

Dialogue must do all the narrative work here, without physical gesture or responding consciousness. Yet these exchanges are banal, awkward, without nuance, and, worse, strangely unconvincing. We are asked to accept this Hugh and Yvonne as two young people who, having met for the fifth coincidental time and falling more and more in love, are carrying on this exchange the moment they are first really alone. Hugh has hardly grasped the "wonder" of seeing her again when he begins commenting on the horticulture, at which point a Yvonne who has never seen her father in this setting counters with what he probably "[n]ever" does here. Then these lovers go on to speak not of themselves or each other or even the garden around them, but of this absent figure. It is not the (plain enough) narrative intentions behind such dialogue one questions, but the plausibility of the rendering itself. "Get this so you can hear it" and "more natural" were the kinds of admonitions Lowry jotted beside passages of dialogue as he revised in the attempt to make both content and cadence carry greater conviction, in every sense to *sound* believable. Yet it is also far from surprising that the novel as it evolved relied less and less on dialogue than did the 1940 version.

This *Volcano* gives the impression of being full of "talk," not simply from the relative prominence of dialogue but from the rendering of consciousness as if it too is mainly constituted of spoken language, as if even internally the characters converse with themselves, elaborate the positions or carry on the debates we have heard them make aloud—as if the inner life comes to little more than silent chatter. Here is part of Hugh's response to a quarrel between Yvonne and her father that he overhears in Chapter VI:

> Hugh now discovered, from hearing part of his own argument against England presented so unsympathetically, that he was considering the possibility he had been wrong. Even if England were blind *now* to what was going on in Spain, did not that merely bring them nearer to the time when they themselves would be in the same position as she? And once in that position of awful danger, which was nothing new to her, mightn't she find that, at last, even against her own will, she *was* fighting the battle for democracy itself? And what was democracy? Ah, if communists and Christians would only stop being bigots and call themselves men! Whatever you thought about religion, what sounder basis upon which to reconcile contradictions could there possibly be than the simple principles of Christianity? One day, if they only realised that and acted upon it, the good people of the England of Shakespeare and

Lovelace and Robert Browning would be waking up with a roar! (*1940* 166–67)

And so on: comparable passages could be produced for all the major characters and from all sections of the text. As a result, the 1940 *Volcano* often reads like a novel of ideas for which the characters merely serve as mouthpieces. Here as later, the Consul finds "people with ideas" antipathetic, but his creator indulges them at length. Opinions flourish, credos are articulated, discussed, modified, revised, defended; and everyone, including the Consul, is full of "ideas," whether about Spain, England's foreign policy, social justice, the nature of America, the best jazz records, economic conditions, the nature of "the people," the condition of Mexico, good writers, or just "life." Lowry clearly *means* such views to be expressive of a deeper, inner self: the Consul is made to say "with confidence" (and Hugh will echo him), "'all these arguments about left and right, about politics that don't concern us . . . are . . . only an expression of a conflict within ourselves between what we are, and what we want to be'" (*1940* 146–47). But in the event they become substitutes for rather than expressions of the character's inner life, so that we seem to be told about these matters rather than having them rendered. The result, again, is "gesturing," the novel insistently pointing toward its concerns (as in the Consul's comment just quoted) rather than portraying them.

One of the effects of this gesturing is that it keeps involving Lowry in problems that he is unable (or unwilling) to resolve. The first statement we encounter of the desire to use the inner as reflection of the outer, the private of the public, the microcosm of the macrocosm, is Laruelle's pronouncement early in Chapter I:

"My God!" said Laruelle, "If I only had the time to put a character like the Consul into a film! Yes, supposing, Doctor, that all the suffering and chaos and conflict of the present were suddenly to take human form. And to become conscious of itself! This is the impression I would want to give of my man: a man to whom, like Jesus, the great betrayal of the human spirit would appear in the guise of a private anguishing betrayal. . . . If I could only convey the effect of a man who was the very shape and motion of the world's doom," he went on, "But at the same time the living prophecy of its hope!" (*1940* 8–9)

It is difficult now not to hear the echo of Jacques's creator, who also feared he might not "have the time" to fashion his grand representative figure before being himself drawn into "the chaos and conflict of the present." But more important is what seems promised for the rest of the novel, where the Consul will somehow contain two kinds of doubleness: he will embody both "the very shape and motion of the world's doom" and yet be also "the living prophecy of its hope"; and while a distinctively public figure "like Jesus," his underlying "betrayal" will be "private." Leaving aside the question of whether any fictional character is likely to survive an overt comparison with Jesus, neither of these aims is realized in the ensuing novel (which is for both Jacques and Lowry, we should remember, not "ensuing" but retrospective: Jacques looks back in time, Lowry from a stage of final revision). For the only "prophecy of hope" in this version rests quite clearly with Yvonne and Hugh, and as for a "private anguishing betrayal," we remain uncertain just what it is. Laruelle, to be sure, immediately suggests a doubleheaded one, but withdraws the possibility before it is fully articulated: "His marriage might be shown as the real basis of his tragedy as a man. . . . Although I doubt that it was. And perhaps the fact that his wife would give him no more children—" (*1940* 9). With the second of these, the desire for children—which the text will, as in 1947, bear out— we find ourselves in a situation that overburdens credulity. William Ames's age is never stated, but he is referred to by others—and refers to himself—as an "old" man. His daughter Yvonne is twenty-four, his hair is grey, he has retired (not resigned) from the British consular service. When he expresses his desire for more children, and when Priscilla's letters in Chapter XII, like Yvonne's in later versions, respond with her eagerness to bear those children, the effect is, at best, grotesque. The nature of this failure is characteristic of the 1940 *Volcano*, where "ideas" (in this case the author's) take precedence over fully imagined human contingency. As a theme, childbearing appears in all drafts of the novel in a quite traditional way, as a sign of the commitment to love, to unselfishness, to the future, and in 1940 it is one of the means by which Lowry plays the younger generation off against the older. Early in the text Yvonne's many abortions are placed parallel to her mother's refusals, but what seems to be her impregnation at the end of Chapter XI—the lovemaking metaphors there bring a ship to "rest" in her "wharf's womb" (*1940* 339)—is set against the unrealizable desire expressed in her mother's letters in the next chapter for just such an impregnation. Lowry's thematic desires have run athwart plausible actualities to bathetic effect, for he has clearly not recognized the incongruity of the middle-aged Priscilla's parental pinings. It is a failure of imagination in the area of the novel that would continue to give him most trouble, that of his female character(s).

But Jacques's comment both proposed and doubted that the Consul's marriage itself was "the real basis of his tragedy as a man," and the failure of the novel to deal with this suggestion is of another order than the question of children. We are made aware immediately that Laruelle has been Priscilla's lover—which casts doubt on his doubt—but we have no means to appraise these matters, not only because they belong irrevocably to the past, but because Priscilla is not a character in the novel. She is repeatedly a reference point and a subject of discussion for the Consul, Yvonne, Laruelle, and even Hugh, but there is no getting around her absence and our resulting inability to gauge the real significance of her "betrayal" or assess Jacques's doubt of its determinative power. However, we look in vain through the 1940 *Volcano* for some other "private betrayal" that might be the source of "the great betrayal of the human spirit" in its protagonist.

Technically, this declaration belongs to Laruelle, but coming as it does early in the text it serves transparently as a statement of Lowry's aspiration, one that remains embarrassingly unfulfilled. Hugh's ersatz "description" of the Consul as looking like "King Lear in full face, Hamlet in profile" (*1940* 69), or his later meaningless superlative that "he was, perhaps, the greatest drunkard the world had ever known" (*1940* 99) are other uses on the authorial level of the "ideas" the characters are prone to, attempts at shortcuts, assertions asked to do the work of representation. We need not go beyond Chapter I to find an instance of the kind of difficulty this intellectualizing could get Lowry into. The Consul's letter here breaks off with an unfinished hope that "somehow, in some way, the future might change the—." Laruelle wonders, "Might change the what? the past? . . . Surely the Consul would have more sense of humour than to quote, from his obscure and different dimension, Ouspensky or Dunne?" (*1940* 26). Apparently not. As Laruelle falls into a dream whereby he "becomes" the Consul, he realizes that he wishes to deliver a "message" to Yvonne and Hugh, and when he hears Hugh say, "'Who's that guy who says somewhere "the future can change the past?"'" he is "satisfied that this [the delivery of the message] was, after all, done." However, in the dream, Yvonne's immediate response to Hugh's question is, "'But I don't want to change *our* past a bit, not *anything*,'" and Hugh answers, "'of course I didn't mean *that*'" (*1940* 43). What then did he mean? How does he imagine altering some of the past without affecting all of it, eliminating the "undesirable" while leaving the rest untouched? The point is not how these questions might be resolved in the pages of "Ouspensky or Dunne" (in Lowry's awkwardly self-conscious reference), but how they function in context, and in context the thinking seems rather on the level of the popular film *Back to the Future*. Lowry is too honest to suppress the objections, but he appears to have no way of coping with them.

If the repeated arguments and "discussions," explicit references to the nature of time, debates over the significance of Spain, and varied authorial signallings of intent and meaning all suggest the intellectualized texture of the 1940 *Volcano*, so too does the attempt to schematize the characters and the developing action. Yvonne usefully remarks in Chapter XI, "'it's always a pity there has to be a story'" (*1940* 322) and here, even more than later, Lowry provides as little of one as he can manage. In this respect, the *Volcano* might be called a book with an evolving situation rather than a traditional plot, and in 1940 that situation evolves in very clear outline. Here Hugh was to emerge overtly as antagonist to the Consul, as youth to age, future to past, but also as lover to drinker ("All the world loves a lover. . . . Why not all the world loves a drunkard?'" asks the Consul twice), leftist to rightist, communist sympathizer to capitalist exploiter, and most sweepingly, endorser of "life" versus exponent of death, a contrast typically made explicit (*1940* 161). The developing opposition between the two reaches its climax at the dinner of Chapter X when, after the confused political-economic argument (here reported in full in order, presumably, to dramatize the "disintegration of values"), the enraged Consul turns on the younger couple and delivers a ranting revelation of Yvonne's abortions. When the two men are left together for a final confrontation, we are invited to view the Consul as a figure wholly given over to the forces of death and destruction. Rejoined by Yvonne in the chapter's final paragraph, Hugh moves with her toward the lovemaking that ends Chapter XI in apparently stark contrast to the Consul's movement toward death in Chapter XII.

If the contrast is in context not quite so stark as my summary, that is a result of Lowry's emphasis on development and of some qualifications in the prose itself. Despite all his political talk, Hugh enters the novel a young man essentially uncommitted, adrift. Having quit his studies at Stanford, he is apparently in Mexico only on a pointless bet about rounding the Horn, but we are invited to see him as making momentous strides on this memorable day, progressively falling in love with Yvonne and coming to believe in those principles that have hitherto been only "indoor Marxmanship." That double commitment is realized in his final act of integration, the coming together with Yvonne at the end of Chapter XI, where she is enabled to "perceive all things hitherto disparate in their knowledge of each other were being joined together" (*1940* 338).

Mildly complicated by this development in the younger man, the sharpness of opposition between Hugh and the Consul is also ameliorated by Hugh's sympathy and a curious sense of connectedness. He is frequently made sensitive to the older man's sadness and pain, and he feels that they are both subject to the same forces: "the very presences, which abandoned the Consul to his doom, were now obscurely, but potently, at the disposal of his own integration" (*1940* 161). Sporadically, too, Hugh's youthfulness and naivete are subjected to a somewhat uncertain narrative irony. For instance, his first impressions of the Consul, which see him as capable of understanding, compassion, cruelty, and destruction, are termed "a flight of fancy," yet there is nothing in the text which follows that seriously challenges this "fanciful" view (*1940* 69). The irony is more secure later (but also more labored) when Hugh reflects on the Consul's apparent love of his own despair and the narrator comments, "The key to it all, of course, was self, and this common knowledge struck him . . . like a revelation" (*1940* 100). Yet while from time to time the narrator exposes Hugh's inexperience, even simplicity, he is placed firmly on the side of "life," and his essential rightness and generosity is endorsed by his growth. His riding of the bull, for instance, becomes now as later not only a movement to action (rather than mere thought or talk) which is both release and mastery, but also an act of maturation, so that Yvonne recognizes in the Salón Ofélia that "Hugh's personality was undergoing a change. He was much more sure of himself. . . . And he no longer gave the impression of being naively impeded by his thoughts" (*1940* 293–94). Thus he holds his own in the ensuing argument, faces down the Consul at his most destructive, and makes his commitment to Yvonne and "life" at the climax of Chapter XI.

Perhaps the greatest strain caused by the schematizing of the two principal men is the mixed burden that as a result is forced on Yvonne. On the one hand, she reflects both her parents. As her father's daughter, her many abortions figure as her version of the denial of life, the act of love turned to destruction, as her father's idealism has been wrenched to misanthropy. In both, "finer" impulses remain, and in the younger Yvonne, they will, with the aid of Hugh, prevail. In the refusal of childbearing, she is also reminiscent of her mother, but the novel thrusts on her a more problematic relation to that mother: to her father (and the narrator), she is less the reflection of than the stand-in for that mother, her representative on the current scene, as the Consul tells her repeatedly ("'You are like Priscilla,'" "'You've got as vile a temper as your mother,'" etc.). On the other hand, she is a young woman on this day falling more and more in love with Hugh. The awkward consequence of this set of roles in the text is a Yvonne who with Hugh is by turns happy, enthusiastic, tender, gay, and spiritedly combative alternating with another Yvonne who in the vicinity of her father becomes an aggressive nag, an antialcoholic shrew whose browbeating quickly becomes repetitive and irritating. "'How could anybody accept you as you are? . . . didn't you divorce Mother because you were drunk all the time and didn't know what you were doing? . . . You were drunk all the time and she couldn't stand you. . . . You're awful when you drink, you get rude and incoherent. . . . Why don't you stop drinking?'" (1940 87, 91). Lowry appears dimly aware of the problem—for instance, Yvonne, who herself has a hangover, is intermittently conscious of the strain of hypocrisy in her behavior—but she continues it nonetheless. And Hugh, who in Chapter VI overhears a particularly nasty quarrel between father and daughter, is made to reflect that despite the shrill "vindictiveness" he detects in her, "there was a mysterious communication between them which prevented this impression from really touching his heart" (1940 169; the reader, alas, has no such protection). Lowry may have been aiming at a quality of feistiness in her, but if so he has miscalculated the effect. Hardly a naturally gifted portrayer of female characters, he is here unable to integrate this mixture of roles, and Yvonne is one of the more conspicuous failures of the 1940 text.

However unsuccessful a creation, Yvonne, like Hugh, is clearly meant to be seen as developing during the course of the action. The late-written meditative passage for her in Chapter II, as she sits alone in her hotel room, is designed as a parallel to Hugh's already created one in Chapter VI: in both, internal conflict is played off against an outer counterpoint (Hugh with different kinds of music, Yvonne with a variety of overheard dialogues) which externalizes that conflict. In Yvonne, dismal memories of her empty and sexually promiscuous past alternate with a longing for some "finer scene." With her American mother and English father, Yvonne's ultimate role as the site of reconciliation and resolution in Chapter XI is anticipated in the overheard American (Weber) in the next room who keeps using the British "Righto," and in the passing group of English sailors who repeat the Yankee "O.K." When she and Hugh improbably meet in the next pages during the portentous earthquake, the internalizing of the event—Yvonne's heart is "pounding so violently it seemed to be shaking her"—begins her reorientation.

Despite her developing feelings for Hugh through the horseback ride of IV, the bus journey and the bullthrowing of VIII and IX, her secret sexual past, with its unadmitted abortions, silently "poisons" the relationship until the Consul's diatribe in Chapter X. That attack, drunkenly conflating Yvonne with her mother, Hugh with Laruelle (the content of which Lowry would thus need to alter very little in subsequent revision), viciously means to undermine their relationship, but ironically has the reverse effect: it clears the air between them so that in Chapter XI they can in their fulfillment move beyond the personal. Chapter XI is the weakest in the 1940 *Volcano*, but its intent is clear: the particularities of the novel's time and space are to be self-consciously included within a cosmic dimension. Briefly Yvonne looks at the stars and feels their own small part in the larger galactic motion; more extensively (and tediously) the lovers recall that it is the Day of the Dead and play at length a game of "Who shall we allow into heaven with us?" If it is difficult to take this seriously, Hugh's sense that the dead are all around them, speaking (in a line borrowed from Hermann Broch), "'To us. Now. . . . "Do yourselves no harm," they say, "for we are all here—"'" (*1940* 336), is clearly meant to bring a social and political dimension into their personal commitment; and the lovemaking that ends the chapter—and this strand of the novel's action—is so densely metaphorical that the two individuals virtually disappear, dissolved into a symbolic act of wholeness and unification, a coming together that is the joining of all disparates, a rebirth that initiates the future.

The love/death contrast of Chapters XI and XII is reinforced by there being no narrative link between them. Hugh and Yvonne consider, then reject, the idea of pursuing the Consul, a decision that seems intended to indicate not indifference or callousness (although it might strike a reader as just that), but a freeing of themselves from the figure of destruction, committing them to each other and to "life." The opposition between the final chapters is thus sharper in 1940 than it will become, and in that schematizing it at last becomes clear why Lowry has kept the figure of Priscilla so insistently and awkwardly both in our minds and off the scene, leaving Yvonne as her sometime stand-in. He means us to see, especially here at the end, not merely that the Consul is alone (in contrast to the lovers), but that his aloneness, rather than indicating independence or self-sufficiency, is simply the rejection of love, a failure on the personal level that is meant to reverberate on others as well. Although Priscilla is a shadowy figure, she too involves Lowry in unsolved difficulties. She is apparently "practical," "intelligent," and decidedly "social." This presumably superficial creature can perhaps be matched with one side of William Ames, the property-owner-capitalist-investor side, but she is harder to recognize as the writer of the eloquent letters the Consul reads in Chapter XII (which include but go beyond the passages familiar from the published *Volcano*). It is perhaps credible that the Priscilla sketched by her former husband would subsequently claim that she had written the letters only as a ploy to get him to stop drinking, but that aim is difficult to reconcile with a rhetorical and poetic power far in excess of such a limited goal. It is not difficult to see why Lowry wanted such moving and even literary letters—we must feel the value and attractiveness of what the Consul has rejected—although they fit with nothing we have been told of Priscilla in the preceding eleven chapters.

Clearly, one result of the schematizing of 1940 was the thinness or implausibility of the characters in both behavior and motivation. For example, how and why has this group of *gringos* come together in Mexico? The flimsiness of Hugh's motivation has been pointed out, and indeed is underscored in the text by Yvonne ("'Going round the Horn seems silly to me, since you've done all that before'" [*1940* 112]). Yet her own reason for being in Mexico seems almost as arbitrary: "'I'm going to Quahnahuac to find out what's what with my Dad'" (*1940* 58). In the postcard the Consul receives from his estranged wife Priscilla says she "*may buy a small car and come back down if you decide to stay and we can return together*" (*1940* 194). The immediate question is not, why didn't she? but, what are we to infer about an absent character from this message? What is the nature of Jacques Laruelle and the Consul's friendship? Why does it continue after the Frenchman's "betrayal"? Why does he insist that this party of three, two of whom are total strangers to him, visit his house in Chapter VII? The so-called level of the *Volcano* most crucially missing or, at best, only sporadically present, is not the symbolic or the magical, but that portion of what Dale Edmonds called the "immediate level" that gives plausibility, density, and thus resonance to individual motivation.

Perhaps all of these characteristic features of the 1940 *Volcano*—the foregrounding of the economic and the political, the "extroversion" of the text, its concern with "ideas," the schematizing of patterns and relationships, the resultant scanting of motivation—best come into focus in the figure of the Consul. Surely one of the major achievements of the published novel, the single point of agreement among differing readers with varied approaches, has been the success of its central character. Indeed, some of the general features of the 1940 text as they are reflected in William Ames have already been noted, such as his concern with economic matters. Another is the verbal gesturing, which results in transparent statements of intention against which one can gauge all too easily what has been achieved. From Chapter I on, where Laruelle projects his former friend as a fictive "character," the paradigm insistently offered is that of the tragic figure (Hamlet, Lear, Faust) very much in the classical mold. The immediate difficulty here is one Lowry seems at this stage unaware of: the drunkard already is a standard figure in both literary and popular traditions, and even if, as Hugh thinks, this one may be "the greatest drunkard" ever, he comes inescapably bearing the credentials and expectations of comedy.

Yet although William Ames himself possesses an ironic wit, he is not viewed from a comic perspective either by the narrator or by other characters. For that matter, after the prologue of Chapter I, he is rarely perceived as fulfilling a tragic role, either. Yvonne is apparently meant to feel some filial affection, but what most convincingly registers is exasperation. Laruelle too, once his "sound" reasonableness produces little impression in Chapter VII, turns simply impatient, while Hugh, who bears much of the burden in 1940 for articulating the Consul's stature, moves between awed sympathy and angry revulsion. The latter, certainly, is easily justified, for William Ames, unlike Geoffrey Firmin, can be not only vicious, but nasty—a lighter but meaner manifestation of the capacity for cruelty. As Hugh hesitates over aiding the dying Indian, the Consul gratuitously whispers, "Go ahead... after all, Spain invaded Mexico first" (*1940* 239); and to and about his daughter and her friend he turns sometimes petty and malicious. A squabble over bathroom rights, for instance ends with, "'Why didn't you say you had finished in the bathroom? I got out of it once already for you!' he yelled. 'And as for you people, you bloody people with ideas!... And that damned little Cithernhead... if he knew what I know about you he wouldn't touch you with the end of a ten foot barge pole!'" (*1940* 168). In its banality this kind of exchange is less likely to conjure up *King Lear* than an ugly episode of, say, *As the World Turns*.

Paradoxically, this "extroverted" novel is frequently vague about the outside world, and events in Spain are not the only casualty of a lack of specification: talk about "ideas" can, it seems, vaporize the external as well as attenuate the internal realm. Nowhere is this more observable— nor, perhaps, more surprising—than in the treatment of the Consul's alcoholism, for in this area of the novel no one has ever doubted that Lowry was drawing on his own experience. But in 1940 the Consul's drinking is often handled hazily and unconvincingly, and any naive assumption that the alcoholic side of the book was a kind of given, a first stage to which Lowry simply added symbolic and allusive complications, will not survive an encounter with this manuscript.

It is typical of the 1940 *Volcano* that while on the one hand a wide-eyed Hugh is speculating that the Consul is "the greatest drunkard the world has ever known," on the other we are rarely told exactly what he is drinking. Had this text been published there would have been no "Drinking Man's *Under the Volcano*"(as Dale Edmonds has called it): although some sort of alcohol gets consumed with regularity, "drinks" is the typical vague designation, creating the impression that neither author nor character is paying very close attention. Nor does William Ames reliably exhibit the obsessive cunning of the truly possessed-alcoholic. For instance, he owns a pocket flask from which he drinks in the obscurity of his garden in Chapter V, but in setting off for the afternoon-long trip to the bullthrowing, he unaccountably neglects to fill this or to secure some other supply, a lapse that undermines his claim to being a truly serious drunkard. Only in Chapter IX does he discover, with belated dismay, his alcoholless state, and so distant is Lowry from his protagonist's anguish that in Chapter X before the oasis of the Salón Ofélia we get the simple announcement, "'I'm going inside,'" followed immediately by the bald, "A little later the Consul, second drink in hand, stood with Señor Cervantes at the door" (*1940* 287). Vagueness about the exterior world ("drink" substituting for a more precise term) seems intimately related to the failure fully to imagine an interior one, to account for an unswerving alcoholic who "forgets" to fill his flask or to dramatize the desperation of that drinkless alcoholic when, already the victim of "jitters" and hallucinations, he approaches the anticipated relief of a bar. It may seem surprising that Lowry in 1940 was blind to comic possibilities in his protagonist's drinking; it is downright startling to discover that he could not handle the alcoholic stratum of his text with any sustained conviction at all.

If backgrounds and motivations of other figures seem dim, the past of the central character is here almost as sketchy. A student of languages "at Liverpool," we hear, he later served as lecturer at Helsingfors, and later still at "Tortu." During the war he had been a lieutenant on the Q-ship *Samaritan* (becoming "Captain Ames" by the time he retired from the British navy), and he recalls in passing the incident of the immolation of the German officers. At some unspecified point he entered consular service (Yvonne has been born in New York before World War I, but her parents' presence there is not explained); however, all we know of his diplomatic career is its most recent phase, which he rehearses to Yvonne in Chapter III (how it could be news to her is quite mysterious). He and Priscilla had come to Mexico three years before and "'fell in love, as they say, with this place and with this house too.'" Suddenly, however, he was transferred to Spain (Algeciras), from which he was apparently transferred back to Quauhnahuac at the outbreak of hostilities. He and Priscilla separated and divorced, and at some recent period he has retired from the consular service.[7] Aside from playing the silver market and drinking, he may not be working on his "book on secret knowledge—alchemy and Atlantis and God knows what" (25:17,

5), which has been a hobby for "'about twenty years'" (as a canceled passage has it).

My paragraph may sound like a bare summary of a richer text, but in 1940 the Consul's background is virtually exhausted in these few details, and gaps and inconsistencies may suggest how little concerned Lowry was here to provide his protagonist with a genuinely imaginable past. Only the Consul's reference to the odd Mexico-Spain-Mexico movement receives any amplification, apparently in answer to Yvonne's frank question of why her parents divorced. Although his "explanation" does not explain, Lowry seems to intend the strangely interrupted Mexican posting to serve as a metaphor for the rupture of the elder Ameses, as if the "falling in love with Mexico" was to signify a renewal of their own love, a hope shattered by the ominous posting to Spain, itself about to be shattered by conflict. However, in any version of the *Volcano*, the Consul's past is more than a matter of curiosity, of adequate or faulty exposition; the novel's action, this final day, is after all for him a culmination, the result of everything that preceded it, the "last stage of his headlong flight downhill" which thereby reveals "the pattern of his own inevitable destruction" (*1940* 362). If the pattern is blurred or left incomplete, the last stage too will not bear its full weight. But there is a subtler aspect of the Consul's past at stake here also, that is not a matter of events and motivations directly, yet is crucial to his investment with the tragic stature that the 1940 text insists on.

Commentary from others not only speaks of his (at least potential) greatness but also presents him in dualistic terms, from Jacques's encomium of Chapter I to Hugh's later assessment of the "idealist" transformed into "a walking, stalking chaos" (*1940* 109). If Laruelle's terms do not seem to fit the novel we are actually about to read, Hugh's, by incorporating the temporal element, more plausibly approximate what we find in 1940. Fitfully, Lowry remembers to keep us aware of a disillusionment in the Consul that can suddenly, if momentarily, give way to a sense of compassion and the larger possibilities of life that has grown almost entirely retrospective. The start of the letter to Priscilla, for instance, after enumerating her failures and shortcomings, opens into a brief celebration of his love and of *"the unity we once knew"*(*1940* 23). The pelado of Chapter VIII produces "a loathing of the whole world" until the Consul is suddenly touched by his sight of the man's absurd attire (*1940* 230). And in the final chapter the "tapestry" he has seen earlier at Laruelle's he turns to personal allegory: those "soaring upwards to the light" and the others "hurtling down into the darkness" (*1940* 361) become respectively figures for himself as he had been and as he now was. But this duality in the Consul never becomes more than sporadically convincing in the present of the novel. He may once have been an "idealist," may once have been a partner in a loving marriage, may once have believed in "the kinship of man for man," but the abstractness of all this aside, there is little force in these as genuine possibilities now. Imaginatively, Lowry has invested all his real hope here in the figures of youth, Yvonne and Hugh, and although he seems to recognize that for purposes of dramatic tension as well as sympathy he *should* give the Consul something with which and for which to struggle, he can hardly imagine what it might be. When in Chapter VI, at the midpoint of his book, Lowry has Hugh reflect that he is committed to "real life" and the Consul to "death," such a stark, monolithic contrast leaves little room for any genuine aspiration or constructive values to be attributed to the latter.

Yet Lowry did intend that the Consul's disillusionment at least provide him with a certain clearsightedness that the other characters, still locked in their thirties' idealism, cannot achieve. "'What depresses me sometimes'" says Laruelle in the opening chapter, "'is that the Consul should not have been so absolutely wrong in his prognostications about Spain, about the rest of the world, for that matter'" (*1940* 8). If his predictions of Franco's victory seem hardly remarkable now, we need to recall the impassioned faith among intellectuals and the young (that is, the other characters of the 1940 *Volcano*) that the Republicans *must* win, in order to see in historical context such a remark as, "'It will be better for everybody if Franco gets that war finished as soon as possible'" (*1940* 261). If this be cynicism, the text implies, make the most of it: it is not thereby false, and the times perhaps demand a measure of cynicism. When the Consul draws Hugh's attention to the bloody coins the pelado has taken from the dying Indian and the younger man responds, "'Perhaps he hasn't stolen it.... Perhaps he knows him and is just looking after it for him,'" this gets greeted with the mocking laughter it deserves (*1940* 249). But when in Chapter X the Consul turns on Hugh to demand, "'what about your own responsibilities.... Your own country,'" it is to begin an attack on American hypocrisy for which his scathing remedy is "'sell them the war fever!'" (*1940* 313–14). The Consul's "disillusionment" thus can run from a clear-eyed view of things as they are to what Hugh feels, in this last instance, as "the sheerest evil."

Yet at this end of the spectrum the Consul's "evil" is not much more convincing than his hypothetical idealism—perhaps inevitably, as they are mirror images of one another. The mock advice to Hugh to run around spreading "war fever" sounds more mischievous than satanic, the naughty prank of an overimaginative child. In the letter to Priscilla he dramatizes the destructiveness he feels without her by writing, "*Everything is smash-smash-smash! I would like to break all the glass in the house!*" (*1940* 24; Lowry's own later marginal comment is, correctly, "This is immature"). In these passages the responses seem attributed from the outside rather than generated from within, part, again, of the gestural manner of the 1940 text. But if the possibilities for evil in the Consul are trivial or unconvincing, then his entire stature is reduced, the potentialities for greatness that Jacques attributed to him likewise rendered suspect. Indeed, in this version it is often difficult to see on what his putative stature is based. It seems revealing that in Chapter XI Hugh and Yvonne can be made so easily to walk away from him. At the other end of the day's action one might inquire—fruitlessly—just why Yvonne has come all the way to Mexico to visit him. Here, other characters do not seem to gravitate in his orbit, not testify, however reluctantly or tacitly, to his preeminence, nor acknowledge a sense of his power in their vary manner of response to him, as they will in 1947. His grandeur here comes largely in verbal attribution, only through the words of others, and it is not enough.

Closely connected with this scanting of one side of the Consul's character is the treatment of his attitude toward drinking. William Ames is from the start an absolutely unswerving drunk. This may or may not make him a less credible alcoholic than Geoffrey Firmin; it certainly makes him a less dramatic one. Geoffrey's letter to Yvonne will cry out in desperation, "come back, come back, I will stop drinking, anything." William Ames's letter discourses in quite different tones: "*I know that I myself would submit to no exhortation to bring us together which implied the sacrifices you would demand. It would not only mean a denial of drink but a denial of the romantic passion of my own remorse in which I am often absorbed to the exclusion of all else. Just as others must die bravely in war, so I must suffer*" (*1940* 25). Aside from the narcissistic posturing in such rhetoric—this is the Consul gesturing toward his Byronically Christlike self—the denial of even the possibility of struggle vitiates the drama in advance, and as the novel proceeds that denial is never so much as questioned.

The Consul's drinking is an action affecting both his own behavior and the responses of other characters, but it is also meant to be a passion, both in the intensity with which he feels it and in the sense of being undergone, suffered, lived inwardly as well as outwardly. However, as I have already suggested, the richness and intensity of consciousness that the Consul will acquire is in 1940 not yet achieved or, at best, is suggested only intermittently. As a characteristic expression of that consciousness, we might glance once more at the letter to the former wife (Priscilla, later Yvonne) which in all versions is our introduction to the characteristic voice and vision of Lowry's protagonist. Between 1940 and 1947, that letter will grow enormously, almost doubling in length (approximately 2170 vs. 1250 words), yet its central thrust remains: it mourns the loss of the wife, declares the need of her love, appeals to the "us" that must still exist somewhere, acknowledges a self-destructive urge that only she can rescue him from, hopes that somehow she may return. But this summary of the core of the letters masks the enormous difference in the kinds of reference they use, and here the openings of the earliest and the final versions are instructive. In 1940 the Consul writes in a way that is at once personal and abstract and opens what can only be called a direct attack: *"since September I have been struggling against my love for you,"* he begins; *"I have fortified myself... by trying to concentrate on what I disliked about you"* and goes on to catalogue those qualities (*"your hardness," "your infidelity,"* and so on). The later version, however, has nothing to say about Yvonne herself; it begins with the evocation of the half-heard, half-hallucinated Mexican night and experiences of the trip to Oaxaca (the sick child on the train, the vulture in the wash basin), a merging of consciousness and world, inner and outer, that gives weight to the projected self as an explorer of "some extraordinary land from which he can never return to give his knowledge to the world: but the name of this land is hell" (*Volcano* 36). Here what might have been simply grandiose in the Dantean identification is underpinned by the specifics of the evoked experience, and metaphors ("daemonic orchestras," "the unbandaging of great giants," etc.) both extend and internalize it, anticipating the explicit identification of this landscape as emotional and symbolic ("It is not Mexico of course but in the heart").

In a general way, both letters move on to set their "negative" openings—Priscilla's shortcomings, the "horrors" in Mexico—against a desired "positive"—the qualities he cherishes in Priscilla (*"your songs, your merriment... your simplicity and comradeship,"* etc.) and the vision of the northern paradise respectively—before moving on, as both do, to appeal to a transcendent "us" created by their love. The close focus on Priscilla's characteristics leaves the letter inherently personal: the Consul emerges as the victim of a broken marriage who understandably has mixed feelings about his ex-wife. Laruelle has led us to expect a representative "greatness," an embodiment of the world's "doom" and "hope," but what we seem to see is simply a man lonely and paralyzed in the wake of his divorce. In 1947, the representativeness of this figure is implied (without being announced, gestured at) by his visions of "hell" and "paradise," visions that dramatize the metaphor-apprehending consciousness without insisting on the merely personal.

Perhaps, then, it is not surprising that in 1940 William Ames will appear at the other end of the novel essentially unchanged from the letter writer of Chapter I, carrying with him into the Farolito a cynicism his long day's experience has only deepened. In consonance with the economic bias of this version are his repeated accusations of a universal desire for "loot," which as already noted reach a crescendo as he faces down his accusers in Chapter XII. Here he is given an improbably lengthy and detailed speech that "reconstructs" the afternoon's crime before sweeping on to include "'everybody.... Humanity! Me too!'" in its vision of universal thievery. That his cynicism seems to rest largely on this materialistic foundation does raise some curious questions in the context of this version. If all are equally guilty, what accounts for the tone of outrage? On what logical basis does the Consul stand to accuse anyone at all? One is compelled to posit a Timon-like sense of disillusionment and betrayal as more appropriate to Ames than Hugh's suggestions of Hamlet and Lear, and indeed Lowry has the Consul identify himself with Timon in the letter of Chapter I. Nonetheless, the 1940 text is almost silent on what illusions may have been lost, and the single identified betrayal is Priscilla's infidelity.

The furious misanthropy thus seems insufficiently motivated, and its overbalancing is perhaps suggested by the fact that while later the

Consul's brief speech of accusation in Chapter XII will be almost exactly countered by his half-coherent lines of hope and possibility, in 1940 those few lines are set against two full pages of diatribe. Nor is the contemptuous accusation "pelado," which in all versions the Consul internalizes, countered here by the compassionate "compañero," which does not appear in the 1940 text. It is revealing that the moment of hope here emerges wholly from outside the Consul, and indeed from outside the human order altogether. A "mask of compassion" materializes "out of gloom," but here that Presence offers "a drink from his bowl. 'But he who drinks of the water I shall give thee,' he murmured, 'Shall have everlasting life.' Now He had vanished" (*1940* 375). Like other forms of externality and abstraction in 1940, this moment impinges from above rather than arising out of the political and social context the novel has presumably been rendering; thus the Consul's self-identification as "the pelado, the thief," adds here "St. Dismas." St. Dismas, as he has explained to Yvonne in Chapter III, was "'one of the two thieves crucified on either side of Jesus'" (*1940* 90), neglecting to add, as he will to the pariah dog in Chapter VII, that this is the thief to whom Christ promised "This day shalt thou be with me in Paradise" (*1940* 223; cf. Luke 23:43). In 1940 the Consul cites the entire line with its benign destination clearly named, and the curious result is that his salvation seems at once almost certain (the text seems to insist on it) and arbitrary: where has this come from, what context been established to explain or justify it? At any rate, in this moment of recognition, the Consul is made capable of judging the extent of his own "thievery" (oddly, it is no longer economic at all but, as in the final version, intellectual: the pilfering "of meaningless muddled ideas out of which his rejection of life had grown") and so of moving from cynicism to salvation, from "pelado" to St. Dismas.

The degree to which this moment is at all credible depends on Lowry's not allowing William Ames to become wholly absorbed into his disillusionment, wholly bereft of fellow feeling and belief in human possibility. Spasmodic and ineffectual as that sense may be, the flash of understanding pity for the pelado, delight in the Mexican horticulturists who visit his garden, evocation of love for Priscilla, and at last, only half-coherent, verbless and thus not quite asserted, the tentative ("perhaps") mumbled litany that, as in the published version, half-articulates the rudiments of a bearable or even lovable world: "'Only the poor, only through God, perhaps, only the people you wipe your feet on ... '" (*1940* 373)—these moments forestall emotional rigidity in the Consul and thus keep at least some measure of readerly sympathy. Since this seems the furthest reach of William Ames's wisdom, however, there is little here or elsewhere to justify his claim that "strange truths are discovered by those who hide themselves in bottles." It is revealing of both versions that while that claim will seem more credible in 1947, it will not be made then.

Indeed, what is most impressive about the Consul in 1940—and about the novel that contains him—is his poetic response to an apprehended scene, real or imagined, the ability to conjure up a particular time and place with all the loveliness or horror it may evoke in the beholder. The "beauty of the cantina early in the morning" (Chapter III here), the cantina when it first opens (III), the Farolito (IX), the extended conceit of the soul as a stricken town and the insect vision in the bathroom (both V) are all familiar to readers of the novel, typically in more elaborate and richer but nonetheless recognizable forms. This power is not limited to the Consul here, although, as later, it appears most often in him: Laruelle's view of the Mexican landscape in Chapter I has already been noted, and a particularly evocative response to the sea by Yvonne in II was only partly salvaged when the Acapulco setting was discarded. It is in these passages that we are closest to the final *Volcano*, for they contain, as much else does not, the texture and feeling (and indeed often the language) that will persist through all revision. It is Lowry the lyric poet in prose we find here, not Lowry the "novelist," and since many of these passages are attributed to the Consul, it is not surprising that William Ames seems not only most familiar to us at these moments, but also most vitally alive.

But there runs throughout the 1940 *Volcano* a motif that troubles the surface again and again until it envelops all the characters and, finally, the fictional structure they inhabit. It is the expression of radical doubt, doubt that takes form as a question of evasion or "escapism." It appears first in Chapter I where Laruelle wonders at length whether or not to return to Europe to fight. The characteristic method of the 1940 text here declares itself—discussion, debate, dialogue—but in Laruelle's unresolved doubt appears also the troubled shadow that dogs this motif throughout. It will surface again in Yvonne's night reflections in Acapulco on her "evasions" of life, in Hugh's recognition of the gap between his beliefs about Spain and his want of action, in the failure to respond of everyone connected with the episode of the dying Indian. Most obviously, of course, it appears in the Consul's drinking: again, early in Chapter I, Jacques puts it succinctly: "'it's too easy to say... the Consul found his escape in drink. The question arises: for instance, was it an escape?'" (*1940* 9). The motif will carry on into the final version, although less insistently, but in 1940 it has also an ironic self-reflexive dimension, a resonance that troubles not the characters but their creator, who is understandably anxious about his fictional world and his "confrontation" with it. For surely in 1940 Lowry *had* evaded really dealing with his material, and on some level he was aware of this. When Margerie wrote to Harold Matson in 1945, "Only a person... who has dominated and disciplined the volcano within him, at what a cost of suffering even I do not understand, could have written such a book" (*Letters* 422), she was speaking of the final manuscript, a manuscript that justified her description. But that version was several years and many drafts away: in 1940 most of those costs were still to be paid. If the theme of evasion was left unresolved to trouble that manuscript with its doubt, there was good reason for this.

For of course far from being through with the *Volcano* as he assumed in June of 1940, Lowry had in one sense hardly begun. What he had achieved in this text was not, as he first thought, a finished novel, but an essential structure, a skeleton of characters and events that would largely hold firm while almost everything else might change. From 1940 onward there will be four major figures, and the basic action of most of the twelve chapters (in its earlier stages the novel had only eleven) will remain the same: Chapter IV will always bring Yvonne and Hugh together in the Consul's garden, followed by a horseback ride that ends at the ruined palace; Chapter VIII will always present the bus trip and the dying Indian by the side of the road; Chapter IX the bullthrowing, and so on (the exceptions are II and XI, in which action becomes extensively different from that of 1940). Relationships among characters will be altered both obviously and subtly, and for one brief moment, even the twelve chapter structure, of which Lowry will speak to Jonathan Cape as being etched in stone, will giddily be toyed with, expanding to thirteen. Nonetheless, Lowry had found his basic fable, and his task in the following years would become successively interpreting it.

In speaking of a "fable" and its "interpretation," I am borrowing Frank Kermode's heuristic terms for addressing the Gospels: positing an earlier narrative, he presents the evangelists as undertaking a "pre-exegetical interpretive act; instead of interpreting by commentary, one does so by a process of augmenting the narrative" (81). Lowry himself, not surprisingly, thought of the revisionary process in another way, as action to realize the work that in 1940 was already incohately "there": although in that manuscript, as he wrote Matson, "the pattern does not emerge properly," nonetheless "within its matrix there *is* a novel" (*Letters* 39, 38). Yet inevitably, as he wrote and rewrote, those original aims became modified and even transformed, and it seems more fruitful to see him as brooding and brooding over the significance of his now-established fable than, by quasi-Platonic analogy, uncovering the "real" *Volcano*. The process would be longer and more laborious than he ever dreamed in 1940, for the manuscript that he sent off to Whit Burnett with exhilaration and relief gave him not a completed work, but simply the essential terms of his fable, with the first of their interpretations.

Lowry liked to see himself as the descendent of his beloved Herman Melville, perhaps indeed as yet another version of the unappreciated American genius, so it may not be altogether fanciful (or at least not wholly *my* fancy) to compare Lowry's task in the years of revision with Melville's approach to his masterpiece. After his failure with the all-too-symbolic *Mardi*, a romance unanchored in lived experience, the American writer turned to the particularities of the realistic *Redburn* and *White-Jacket* before being able successfully to fuse these modes in *Moby-Dick*. What Melville did over the course of several novels is akin to what Lowry did in the writing and rewriting of one. It was not *Ultramarine* or his stories of the thirties that prepared Lowry for *Under the Volcano* (any more than *Typee* and *Omoo* led Melville directly to *Moby-Dick*), but the repeated rewriting of this one novel: Lowry's apprenticeship for *Under the Volcano* is *Under the Volcano*. However we may distinguish it from Melville's great book, the *Volcano*, like *Moby-Dick*, has never been found symbolically undernourished, but, like the allegorical *Mardi*, the 1940 text had a surer sense of the symbol than of a felt life that would make it meaningful. That would only be acquired slowly, painstakingly, over the years in the gradual, unlikely feat of literary transformation that finally, radically differentiates Lowry's experience from that of his predecessor.

For as I have already suggested, the mystery lurking within the 1940 *Volcano*, and one which any study can perhaps only deepen, is how this unsatisfying text became the brilliant book eventually published. There are, I believe, no simple solutions to that conundrum, no sudden revelations, no single addition or revision that accomplished this truly amazing transmutation, but a repeated coming back and back, burrowing further and further inward, fleshing the parts of the skeleton over and over until the bones themselves became something other than dry sticks to support the flesh, rather a necessary, integral part of the body itself. Drafts and drafts of individual chapters—further interpretations of his fable—would pile up in the shack in Dollarton as Lowry returned again and again to chapter after chapter, until, as he came to see, he too had been caught up in the wheel of the novel: he informed Cape that his book "can even be regarded as a sort of machine: it works too, believe me, as I have found out" (*Letters* 66). It is, doubtless, little wonder given his temperament that the later Lowry repeatedly dramatized himself as a man trapped by the novel he himself has created; what such a posture cannot tell us is by what magic that novel had been transfigured in the process.

CHAPTER TWO

1941

In the dense correspondence between Lowry and Conrad Aiken during the winter and spring of 1940, Lowry sent off to his old mentor excited bulletins of progress on the *Volcano*. On February 7, he tells Aiken he is "sure at last [I] have got something"; on April 9, he thinks "it makes an odd but splendid din"; on May 15, "I have not much doubt but that it is a good book." By June 10, the end in sight, he is looking to practical results, expecting "some money" to have accrued from the *Volcano* before funds will reach him from wartime Britain (*Aiken-Lowry* 104, 128, 135, 138).

But with the heady throes of composition over and the typescript off, Lowry became less sure. Through the summer and early fall of 1940, he waited impatiently for word from Whit Burnett and Story Press. Back in the mid-thirties, Burnett had published two of Lowry's stories, and for several years now Lowry had promised Burnett a first look at the novel.[1] Furthermore, he reported to Aiken on May 15 that he had had "an enthusiastic letter" from Burnett restating his interest. During the summer, Lowry's worries about conscription and finances eased; much of the anxiety that remained was that of the doting literary parent. Belatedly informing Harold Matson both of the existence of the novel and of his having submitted it himself to Story, he told Matson in one breath "that I really feel [the *Volcano*] might be important," and in the next "perhaps ... I have overestimated it." It "threaten[s]" to "be a *really* good book," but it has its flaws, including "a few abstractions and meaninglessnesses" (*Letters* 32). Important as it seems to have been to Lowry to have Burnett accept it, he is in the same letter to Matson suggesting other options. This was on July 27; on August 9, he writes again, wondering why he has not heard from Burnett ("He has had it since June 27"), again suggesting Robert Linscott of Houghton Mifflin as second choice, and yet again hesitating between extolling the book and fearing that it is "unsaleable." On October 4, he wrote Matson yet again, and this time he did get a decision, the one he dreaded (1:79).

Matson's letter of October 7 must have been doubly discouraging to Lowry, for in addition to the rejection by Story came the unexpected news that Harcourt, Brace too had seen the manuscript and turned it down. But it was the decision at Story that hurt most: Martha Foley had written, "It is a very unusual book but one that we feel does not quite emerge from under the burden of the author's preoccupation with what might be described as the Dunn [sic] theory of time. We have been so interested in what Malcolm has been trying to do that we hate to give this as our decision" (1:45). Lowry's response of October 12 did not try to conceal how crushed he was

Dear Hal:
Thanks for your letter, after which I believe in my book, rather more, if anything, because I do not think these individuals can have read it carefully: I am somewhat hurt about Whit, who has said not a word to me all this while. As for the Dunn theory of time I just vaguely know what it is but have never read Dunn so cannot be preoccupied with it: perhaps they meant Ouspensky: anyhow the book has nothing to do with such a thing: Martha's remarks prove that she has seen fit to know as little about my poor book as I about Dunn, that's all; which is unfortunate, but not I hope, fatal. Perhaps it was they who were experimenting with the Dunn theory of time by keeping it for so many months without a word when I had told them that I was working against, no theory, but time itself. (1:79)

The limp joke at the end hardly conceals the tone of personal injury, and behind Lowry's anxiety to deny knowledge of Dunne—there is in fact an open allusion to him in Chapter I—seems to lurk his deep fear of being charged with plagiarism, a fear that could only exacerbate the pain of rejection. He wrote briefly to Matson a few days later when submitting a story, and then apparently not again until the following March.

That spring resumption of correspondence announces that perhaps Martha Foley was right after all, and that in any case he is rewriting the book, cutting extensively. To show Matson what he is doing, Lowry goes on, "I am sending you part of it as a short story," which he hopes Matson can place (the story misidentified as the "original" version from which the novel grew: see Prologue, p. 18 above).[2] The activity that lies behind this is, and seems likely to remain, somewhat mysterious. Margerie Lowry's later recollection of this period was that around the end of 1940, having heard from Matson that the *Volcano* had been rejected by four publishers, Lowry "was literally prostrated with disappointment," unable to write, speak, or even eat or drink, immobilized in bed, his face to the wall, a condition from which he recovered only when Margerie herself began to work on one of her mystery novels and called on him for help. It was from this depression, Margerie recollected, that she wrote the January 6, 1941, letter to Harold Matson (*Letters* 37–38) in which determination to proceed with work on the *Volcano* is announced along with the release of Matson himself from any further obligation to either of the Lowrys (Day 286; Bowker, *Pursued by Furies* 307–8).

There are two immediate problems with Margerie's account here. First, there seems to be no letter from Matson announcing four rejections of the *Volcano:* perhaps Margerie is thinking of Matson's letter of March 6, 1941, in which he mentions five rejections thus far, but this comes only after (and in response to) Lowry's letter telling Matson of his resumption of work on the novel. Second, and more important, Margerie has thrice mistaken the date of the joint letter to Matson, first in typing it, next in editing the *Letters*, and finally in recalling the episode for Douglas Day. The letter was actually written a year later, in 1942 (probably misdated as a result of the common inability to recall in January the change in year). It was in fact written in response to the now-famous letter from Matson listing the twelve publishers who had rejected the novel and asking for further direction, a letter dated September 5, 1941, more than four months before the Lowrys' reply (*Letters* 419).

Nonetheless, even allowing for melodramatic heightening in Margerie's account, it seems plausible to accept the substance of her portrayal of Lowry as depressed over his book's rejection while recognizing that her memory of this episode might have become hazy after several decades. Indeed, I would suggest that Lowry's depression is more likely to have occurred after that first rejection in October 1940 than later. He had a good deal of emotional investment not only in the novel's quick acceptance, but in the endorsement such an acceptance would convey, that ratification of merit he had had from Burnett in the past and felt he had every reason to expect for this far more important work. No other single letter from Matson is likely to have affected him so deeply, for his agent conscientiously sent on individual rejections as they came in.[3] Thus, neither the letter of March 6, 1941, listing five rejections nor the well-known one of September 5 cataloguing the round dozen could have come as a shock to Lowry, however discouraging such a view of the full lineup might have been. But the earlier rejection by Story Press confirmed his own privately expressed fears about the book's merit. Story's rejection seemed ratified by the like decision from Harcourt, Brace, and the double blow may well have produced a temporarily debilitating depression.

But if Margerie was mistaken on just when this episode occurred, might she not also have been in error as to the precise means that lifted Lowry out of his funk? She recollects starting to work on her own mystery novel (*The Shapes That Creep*) and, by enlisting her husband's help, gradually bringing him back to life and writing. Given what we find in the surviving manuscripts, however, it seems equally plausible that it was to revision of the *Volcano* that Margerie turned, a work on which she had already served as collaborator and editor as well as muse and typist, and that it was her proposing a line of revision on that manuscript—and beginning to execute it—that brought the discouraged Lowry back to life and hope and work.

In the nature of the situation, any modification of Margerie's account must remain speculative. As revision of Lowry's biography, these details hardly merit such fussy attention. Their value for our understanding of the making of the *Volcano*, however, resides in their power to account for a curious phenomenon: while it is easy to discover unmistakable evidence of Margerie's hand in the first post-1940 reworkings of the novel, there is almost nothing there that can with the same assurance be attributed to Lowry himself. Such routine matters as the pencilled instructions to "see insert," usually found both earlier and later in Lowry's characteristic hand, are here entirely in Margerie's. And there is nothing to go on *but* the typescripts for this stage of revision: no holograph sheets survive, a lack that may be taken as evidence that the Lowrys were still in their early prodigal mode of discarding superseded sheets—*or* that this indicates Margerie's primary role. For while Lowry always composed by hand, Margerie apparently "wrote" directly on the typewriter.[4]

By itself, the mere prevalence of Margerie's hand at any stage does not imply composition undertaken without Malcolm's assent. Nowhere else, however, is Lowry's own hand almost entirely absent. It is nonetheless clear that before pencil touched paper (or fingers keys) at this stage, two crucial decisions had been made, and it is difficult to imagine Margerie taking these entirely unto herself. First, there was to be extensive trimming of the existing version; anything that might be defined as "extraneous" was to be ruthlessly eliminated. Second, the relationship of the three central characters was to be altered from father, daughter, boyfriend to (ex-)husband, (ex-)wife, and brother/lover. Furthermore, the Consul was here renamed "Jeffrey" Ames, a spelling that endures only through this phase of revision. On the carbons that remained the base for these changes, it is always Margerie's hand that makes necessary alteration in names, designations, and forms of address—from, say, "father" to "Jeffrey," or "Hugh Fernhead" to "Hugh Ames," or "sir" to "Jeff." But she is also clearly responsible for eliminating other kinds of inappropriateness: expository questions the Consul in 1940 asked of young Hugh Fernhead, for instance, are no longer appropriate when put to his own brother, and the Yvonne who returns to Mexico after a year's absence cannot have all the same reactions as the Yvonne who, in 1940, is on her initial visit. The mark of Margerie's suggestion of a cut, here and later, is the parenthesis (round bracket); Lowry himself uses the square bracket, the marginal designation "cut," or the direct pencil cancellation of a passage, which seem to indicate three phases rising in definitiveness of rejection. Not only do we find virtually none of the latter that can with certainty be assigned to this stage on the carbons; we find, at least in Chapter I, Lowry's approval of Margerie's independent work: "good cut," reads his hand on p. 13 [refolioed 9] against her parentheses, and "a good, though agonizing, cut" on p. 16 [11] (26:18). It may well be that a depressed Lowry gave Margerie carte blanche to make such editorial changes.[5]

Certainly most of what appears on the new interleaved yellow sheets involves relatively little new writing: it is of the cut-and-paste variety in which typically the trimming of a section combines with the changes in relationships to demand a more extensive rewriting than can be accommodated on the original carbons. What is new in such spots comes to little more than transitional passages, and so while Margerie might have hesitated to compose extensive new prose for her husband's book, she may well have felt equipped to undertake this glorified editorial task. After all, nothing was being actually discarded, and Malcolm could easily reject any changes that he disliked. It is easier to envisage Margerie evoking a response from the despondent Lowry about his own, familiar book than about a new one of hers through the questions that, according to Day, she used to rouse him: "how might one best express this or that? how ought such-and-such a character to behave?" Is this first post-1940 revision largely what Malcolm called a "Margie version"?

Whatever the nature and degree of Lowry's involvement and whenever he became part of the rewriting, much of what distinguishes this stage of revision has certainly been executed by Margerie. In one sense this is perhaps not surprising, for what is most immediately characteristic of the 1941 *Volcano* is also what is most un-Lowryan: its insistence on economy, compression, rejection, resulting in a radical reduction of the text. At some point before March 1941, however, Malcolm clearly did become involved in the revising and recasting process, and in what follows I will refer to "Lowry" without presuming to distinguish between the contributions of husband and wife. In that, of course, this stage of revision is unique only in the possibly unprecedented role of Margerie, for she was a large if indeterminate factor in all her husband's writing from 1939 onward.[6]

Lowry's 1941 letters that mention the *Volcano* keep coming back to the theme of reduction: "I am cutting mercilessly" (1:80); "I have cut and cut and cut" (*Letters* 39). Although there are many gaps in surviving manuscripts, enough remains to determine that the text was trimmed by more than one-quarter: the 402 pages of the 1940 version were cut to approximately 290 before Lowry moved beyond these carbons altogether.[7] There were some wholesale discardings: Chapters II and XI from 1940 were replaced almost entire. More typical, however, is the shaving of the internal musings of his characters, attempting to eliminate altogether what Lowry himself called "Malcolm stooginess"— the obvious use of a character's thoughts as vehicle for authorial exposition—and to reduce, sometimes quite radically, the more indulgent ramblings of his figures. I have called the 1940 *Volcano* a novel that (for Lowry) is rather "extroverted," but in 1941 it was on its way to becoming even more so as thought processes, however superficial or unconvincing they might have appeared, were sharply curbed, and characters seemed correspondingly more responsive to the outside world.

The best way to see the kind of thing Lowry was about is to look at two passages, here from the opening of Chapter VIII:

> At the market they stopped for Indian women with baskets of poultry. They had strong faces, the color of dark earthenware. The weight of the earth was in their movements as they settled themselves. Two or three had cigarette stubs behind their ears, another chewed an old pipe. Their good-humored faces were wrinkled with the sun but they did not smile. The Consul, in a superb humor, felt as he had read in some bogus theosophical work that he ought to feel when confronted by the Sphinx, that he was perhaps less seen than seen through, that something there far beyond death, of which he was not even the temporary symbol, was apprehended by that fixed, unforgiving look. His sunflower at least looked at *him*. But here he could not be sure that what compelled this stare was real at all or belonged to the categories of the world. Pretentious thoughts! For now that the *camión* was welding the old women into a community, he saw faces cracking into smiles. Someone laughed. Two managed to hold an anxious conversation in spite of the noise. Probably that look visible even in laughter did not pierce the future further than the price of fish in holiday week. Why should it? Prices were rising. They were simple busy working women going home from market with their joys and troubles the same as anyone else. (*1940* 226–27)

> At the market they stopped for Indian women with baskets of poultry. They had strong faces, the color of dark earthenware. There was a massiveness in their movements as they settled themselves. Two or three had cigarette stubs behind their ears, another chewed an old pipe. Their good humoured faces of old idols were wrinkled with sun but they did not smile.
>
> Then someone laughed, the faces of the others slowly cracked into mirth, the camion was welding the old women into a community. Two even managed to hold an anxious conversation in spite of the racket.

The Consul, nodding to them politely, wished he too were going home, and he wondered again what perverse force had instigated this ghastly trip. The effort of staying sober was far greater than he had expected. Perhaps it was not the effort of merely being sober that told so much as that of coping with Yvonne's unexpected return, Hugh's ill-timed visit and the legacy of impending doom his recent, even for him, unprecedented bouts had left him. (1941: 30:9, 1–2)

The central feature here of reduction, and reduction specifically of consciousness, requires little commentary: the Indian women occupy half as much prose in the second passage precisely because the Consul's ruminations on their significance and their relation to him have been altogether excised. Some of the subtler alterations, however, are also telling. In 1940 it is not clear whether the Mexican women in the opening sentences appear as the narrator or as the Consul sees them; in either case, the Lawrentian mysticism of their movements having "the weight of the earth" is consistent with the "theosophical" musings which follow. Here the women are quickly absorbed into the character's inner world both in his first impressions and in the correction that follows, as their smiles and laughter seem to serve primarily as the occasion for his recognition of "pretentious thoughts." In short, while the passage explicitly separates inner and outer worlds, speaking of a divorce between the actuality of the women and this outsider's imaginings about them, its *method* in fact blurs the line between the two.

In the revision, Lowry is concerned to mark a sharp separation between the women and the Consul's consciousness in both technique and content. The changes in paragraphing and the elimination of the impressionistic (and repetitious) "weight of the earth" help sharpen the division, but that is mainly accomplished by the definitive splitting of the passage into outer (the women) and inner (the Consul's thoughts) rather than interweaving them, and by having the Consul's musings touch upon the women only in order to define his distinction from them: they are going home, he is not. What accounts for most of the reduction here is that his thoughts are kept almost briskly to his immediate situation—sobriety, Yvonne and Hugh, sense of foreboding—rather than permitted to associate across the theosophical work, the Sphinx, the sunflower, mysteries beyond death, prices, inflation, the "joys and troubles" of mankind. Brief as it is, the passage is characteristic of this stage in demonstrating not only the kind of revision Lowry was undertaking, but the simplifying effects of these revisions.

When he told Matson he intended to cut and "re-create," he spoke generally, saying only that he was "hewing above all to the pattern, the form, the meaning—while at the same time trying to make them [the *Volcano* and *In Ballast*] exciting as stories qua stories" (1:80).[8] Behind that last phrase lurks the change in character relationships that produces the triangle (or, if one includes Laruelle, the "square," as the Consul sardonically calls it here) that will persist from this point forward. The alteration is sometimes made with deceptive ease, a few strokes identifying "Yvonne" where 1940 had read "Priscilla" (that shadowy figure who, of course, now disappears altogether). The immediate benefits are considerable, as Lowry must have seen in making the alteration, for the awkward double role of Yvonne as daughter and as wife-substitute, which helped to undermine the character in 1940, is at once eliminated, while there is an almost automatic increase in the tension of the triangular relationship. The Consul's envy of and malice toward the growing closeness of his daughter and her lover had in 1940 clear Freudian overtones, exacerbated by his drunken conflation of wife and daughter. With the change in relationships, there is obvious narrative cause for the Consul's suspicion of Hugh and Yvonne and a quite conventional suspense over which of the men Yvonne will choose. For in 1941 Yvonne has returned to her former husband, as Priscilla had only threatened to do, but now the unexpected presence of Hugh on the scene raises for her a genuine alternative. As the long day unfolds and Jeffrey continues to drink, Yvonne finds herself gravitating increasingly toward Hugh until, witnessing his danger from the vigilantes of Chapter VIII, she confronts her emotions: "Those few dragging seconds of suspended terror when the policeman was fumbling with his holster had shown her more clearly than years of wondering, of self-examination, just how deeply she felt about her husband's brother" (30:9, 20). While she still feels obligations to her ex-husband, she recognizes that on one level he does not want her back. On the other hand, she remains uncertain of Hugh's reaction to her "desertion of his brother."

Specific passages concerning the romantic dilemma were of course mainly new in 1941, but extensive new writing was obviously not envisaged for this revision. By confining himself to a single set of carbons, supplemented by the familiar yellow sheets, Lowry seems to have imagined that one brisk march through his chapters would suffice to put the novel "right," to meet publishers' objections to the 1940 text's obfuscations and overwriting. Odd as it may sound, even in the change in relationships, simplification was a central aim. Lowry's admonitions to "compress" and "condense" as well as "cut" reappear throughout, and the turning of Yvonne from daughter to wife and Hugh from lover to lover-brother manages both to eliminate the redundant Priscilla and to weave the major characters into a tighter and closer mesh. But in the course of making these alterations, Lowry seems to have stumbled on the other major change of this stage, a change at least as significant as the altered character relationships and one that would ultimately reverse the tendency toward simplification and reduction. It will not be fully accomplished until the next set of revisions, but the radical alteration in the novel's point of view begins during this phase of rewriting: the roving omniscience of 1940 gives way to a focusing of each chapter through the mind of one central figure, no two sequential chapters employing the same character's consciousness. One inescapable consequence of the partial realization of this new scheme was that the text now *had* to be revised yet again in order to carry out fully and consistently this new "design-governing posture." From this time forward Lowry found himself inexorably launched on a round of revision without clear end, one that seemed to acquire a momentum of its own, a *máquina infernal* from which its creator would find it difficult to alight.

Unlike this entirely new approach to the novel's material, which seems to have been discovered only in this course of revisions, the simpler change in character relationships was decided upon before rewriting began, for it is fully accomplished everywhere. Its consequences are apparent immediately—that is, in the new Chapter II which emerges out of the earlier section of 1940's Chapter III. Now, Yvonne as ex-wife has returned to the Consul only to discover almost at once (the new II is very brief indeed) that the other two legs of the "quadrangle," Jacques and Hugh, are unexpectedly also present. Although Laruelle is no longer a romantic interest for her, Hugh is another matter, and the developing feeling between the two required surprisingly little alteration in the middle chapters from the treatment of their younger counterparts of 1940. This time, the Consul's jealousy of the pair through

Chapters IX and X is quite justified and produces arguably the nastiest version of the explosion at Yvonne found in the manuscripts. Railing at her as a "'stinking trollop'" and a "'slut'" (31:4, 21), he crudely advises the two to "'go off somewhere and go to bed together, you've been doing it all day in your minds about as subtly as a dog and his bitch'" (31:4, 22). Eventually, that is exactly what they do, but not until the end of a revealingly revised Chapter XI.

Here Yvonne insists on pursuing Jeffrey, even over Hugh's angry protests that "'He's old enough to take care of himself'" (Templeton 1:5, 2). This decision provides Lowry with a more compelling narrative base than the vapid (and now excised) dialogue about the "good" dead that filled out the 1940 version, and it also makes of Yvonne a more sympathetic figure than the indifferent daughter who dismissed her drunken father without another thought. Here the divided path (which had previously served simply as an emblem of alternatives—love or death—offered by the final two chapters) gains a narrative function: it allows for the wrong choice on the reasonable ground that it will take them by two other cantinas before depositing them at the Farolito, where this Yvonne, familiar with the Consul's habits, suspects he has gone. He will not, of course, be found at either El Petadi (*sic*) or El Popo, and at the latter this search comes to an end. With the storm menacing outside, Hugh successfully persuades Yvonne to pause, and here they declare their love for one another, then engage a room for the night. Yet while this XI, like its predecessor, ends with their mating, here Lowry makes it explicit that their love is too hopelessly compromised to survive. Having arrived only this morning to effect a reconciliation with her former husband, Yvonne is consumed with guilt at the rapidity of her about-face: she judges herself "shabby" and anticipates that although Hugh loves her he will "never quite forgive her" for abandoning his brother, moved by "the peculiar loyalty between males that women could not share or understand" (Templeton 1:5, 15). In her final vision, "the anguished face of Jeffrey, thrust itself between them; her heart felt the weight of the cold core of knowledge that they were already separated" (Templeton 1:5, 18). On this note the chapter, and this strand of the novel, ends. Since the action of Chapter XII was never essentially to alter, at this stage the *Volcano* had suddenly become a very dark tale indeed, a guilty and doomed romance the only proffered alternative to the Consul's commitment to death.

Unfortunately, because of the lacunae in the remains of Chapters IV and VI, our knowledge of Hugh at this stage is sparse. Here there is no question that he and Yvonne have had an affair in Paris (as there might be in the published novel, and as the Hugh and Yvonne of 1940 explicitly have not), that the Consul is aware of it, and that, although he considers himself responsible, he remains resentful of Hugh. As later, Hugh has now flown down from the States, arriving from a Texas cattle ranch wearing a "fantastic outfit" and entertaining, as the Consul believes, the "'naive idea . . . that we could all be just "good friends again."'" But although we can determine from subsequent chapters that Hugh is meant to be a more athletically active and decisive figure than his younger counterpart of 1940, he also may be less politically aware: nothing survives to suggest that at this stage he has any journalistic background (why was he in Texas?) or that he plans to go to Spain. Nonetheless, he appears intended as a somewhat older and more definite man of action than his callower 1940 predecessor—a rather stereotypically dashing romantic hero.

The attractions of Hugh for Yvonne are inseparable from the weaknesses of the other leg of the triangle, her relationship with Jeffrey, which are apparent from the start. Chapter II now opens with Yvonne in the Bella Vista bar, and her motivation for coming, stronger than that of the 1940 Yvonne, is bluntly delivered to (and by) a shaking Consul:

> "Oh *Jeffrey*," she said. "I—I ran into Tom Taylor in Del Monte, and he said you were still here, and that you—"
> The Consul nodded, "It's ghastly, isn't it? I'm sure you've already regretted the kindly impulse—you never could resist trying to help people—no matter, you can catch another train out this afternoon." (29:1, 1)

Yvonne has hardly arrived before Jeffrey is proposing she take the first train back, while she in immediate response to his obvious drunkenness feels "all the old emotions . . . despite her defenses, her good resolutions, her preparedness for this very thing" (29:1, 2). Since she has no real alternative to suggest to him beyond a vague "'let's just go away together,'" her return seems particularly "quixotic," as it is indeed called here. In trying to make his heroine more appealing than either Yvonne or Priscilla had been in 1940, Lowry eliminated both her disavowal of her letters and the Consul's inventory of her faults in his letter. Further, he attempted, with only partial success, to tone down the shrewish note that prevailed in 1940. Yvonne-wife, like Yvonne-daughter, can begin a discussion of their possible future with a briskly officious, "'Look here, Jeffrey,'" carry on with a dismissive, "'How could anybody accept you as you are?'" and follow through with a diminished but still perceptible nagging about drink (29:7, 9–12), all within a few pages in Chapter III. As for the Consul, when Yvonne complains that the public scribe in the square might have been used to answer some of her letters, his cold response of "'There was nothing to say'" (29:1, 4) is so patently at odds with the unsent letter we have seen in Chapter I that it seems a deliberate slamming of the door. It is thus understandable that by midafternoon she should conclude "that he did not want to be 'saved,' that he even resented her coming back to upset his fine romantic picture of a wronged husband, drinking himself to death with a perfectly valid excuse to do so in anyone's eyes" (30:12, 13; cf. 30:9, 20). However, this Yvonne also apparently offers nothing new in attitude or response on her return, and she is off riding with her former lover before the morning is done. Since only a few hours later she will have decided that it is Hugh she loves, not Jeffrey, clearly the latter's suspicions have some justification. This Yvonne, while less unsympathetic than the haranguing daughter, is emotionally too light to embody a plausible counterforce to the Consul's knowing self-destruction.[9]

Indeed, in 1941—here most unlike 1940—romantic love seems hardly a possibility. While Jeffrey will translate the handwriting on Laruelle's wall as "'we can't live without love'" (29:1, 5–6) (not "without loving"), even Yvonne, just after deciding that she loves Hugh, will watch his riding of the bull with "a furious panicky resentment of this unpredictable stranger." This Yvonne is repeatedly given a crypto-feminist awareness of a clannishness among males that automatically and decisively excludes her. If Jeffrey and Yvonne never seem a genuinely possible couple here, the conjoining of Hugh and Yvonne is sharply circumscribed even before guilt over the excluded Consul sinks it altogether. Erotic love may continue to be "doomed" in all future versions of the *Volcano* too, but Yvonne's death in later drafts will somewhat mute this failure: we will not be asked to contemplate a continuing couple who not only will not be "redemptive," as the Hugh and Yvonne of 1940 hope to be, but who are fated to live unhappily ever after, if we can imagine their relationship surviving at all.

In 1941, not only are most of the new passages connected with the romantic triangle, but the triangle has moved sharply to the emotional center of the novel. As a result, such concerns of crucial importance in 1940 as the political, whether focused on the Spanish or the later European war, carry less weight and significance here. A lengthy discussion of sympathies toward Spain is excised from Chapter V, a four-page diatribe from Hugh in IX vanishes entirely, and the dinner table argument of X is radically trimmed, with the highly politicized confrontation of Hugh and the Consul at the end of that chapter excised altogether. Sometimes, too, the wholesale weeding takes with it references and motifs that seem simply victims of the general drive for economy: certainly the 1941 text is much less openly allusive than its predecessor. Whole fistfuls of high-culture names disappear: Hermann Broch's *Die Schlafwandler*, Chubchakum and Atlas, Shakespeare's Caesar, Hamlet, and Lear, Caligula and his horse-consul, *Crime and Punishment*, Poe's *Alfred Gordon Pym* [sic], Rip Van Winkle, Diana of the Ephesians, Hawthorne's Grey Champion, H. G. Wells, St. Dismas, and Mr. Facing Both Ways. The 1941 Lowry is quite severe, and anything suspected of escaping a strict functionalism goes: an apocalyptic parrot joke of V, the anecdote about the unemployed actor from III, the guitarist's oxen song of X, the German miner's story of XII, the description of Laruelle's film of "Alastor" from VII, and of course all of II and most of XI. Rarely is new material introduced, although the carefully wrought new VIII (and its short-story version) makes room for the Consul's likening of Hugh's efforts to those of Don Quixote and for the view of Popocatapetl as a seductive Moby-Dick "beckoning them on, as it swung from one side of the horizon to the other, to some disaster, unique and immedicable" (30:9, 2).

The experienced reader of the *Volcano* will recognize that some of these cuts (and additions) were not final, that the song about oxen and the story of the actor who wanted to "get" somewhere, for instance, will reappear, like Caligula and *Crime and Punishment*, and Lowry will eventually find ways to use a surprising amount of the material of II without returning directly to Acapulco. But those restorations came later; the cutting of such passages evidences again the zeal with which the editorial pencil was wielded at this stage. The *effect* of the cuts, however, is sometimes problematic. To what extent, one might ask, is

Lowry genuinely eliminating material and to what extent simply dropping overt references, subtilizing his text—or covering his tracks? Hugh will henceforth not have read Broch's *The Sleepwalkers*, for instance, but Broch's closing "we are all here" remains inescapably appropriate to Lowry's Day of the Dead, and metaphors of sleepwalking continue to appear in his text (see Saalmann, and Ackerley, "Lowry and Hermann Broch"). On the other hand, Lowry did not need Broch for such imagery: *The Cabinet of Dr. Caligari* and *Macbeth*, for instance, were both a part of his text in 1940, and Djuna Barnes's *Nightwood* (which Lowry recommended to Carol Phillips in 1939)[10] was an equally available contemporary source for the somnambulism that runs through the *Volcano*.

With the sheer amount of trimming going on, shifts in emphasis were inevitable, but some were clearly deliberate decisions. For instance, in 1940 the Consul had viewed his garden as a "jungle," although one embodying a "fantastic beauty," whereas Yvonne and Hugh had found it "breathtaking," "too divine," "a Paradise." By 1941 this paradise is lost once and for all: Yvonne's first glance reveals to her an untended "mess," and the Consul repeats his sense of his "jungle" without the redemptive sense of loveliness (27:9, 1; 26:22, insert 5). Whether we interpret the widely differing responses of 1940 as part of the contrast between generations stressed in this version or as an inconsistency or "blurring" in the presentation of the setting, it is clear that in 1941 Lowry had decided that the sharp, firm symbol of a ruined Eden was to take precedence, a significance to which all the characters agree. Presumably, this is part of what he meant in telling Matson he was "hewing . . . to the pattern, the form, the meaning" in revision, a blowing away of what he later abjectly called "the almost total fog in the *Volcano* as was" (*Letters* 41).

But these individual changes pale beside the momentous decision to focus each chapter through a single consciousness. One suspects that Lowry may have happened upon this expedient almost inadvertantly as he contemplated his new set of character relationships where they first manifest themselves, in Chapter II. With the appearance of the figure of Yvonne, it must have been borne in on him that the Yvonne who arrives here cannot be the Yvonne of 1940. In that version, an original Chapter II had expanded to divide and produce Chapters II and III; in

1941 the new Chapters II and III were formed out of the action of the old 1940 Chapter III. It was a division that suggested a natural alternation between two centers of focus.

Creating a new Chapter II meant creating a new situation for Yvonne—which meant creating a new Yvonne. In 1941, when she finds the Consul in the Bella Vista bar, she is no longer a daughter who has casually dropped in for a visit (nor has she arrived by plane, incidentally: her train trip here plays muted counterpoint to the Consul's maunderings about the corpse and the express). One of her internal reflections—her sense of the "glare" in the Consul's eyes and her fear that it might "swing outward" on her—is simply taken over from the Hugh of 1940, but most of her responses are, as they must be, new. The divorced wife nervously, tentatively returning to her former spouse only to find him drunker than ever and both her ex-lovers on the scene—establishing these new circumstances, however sketchily, meant establishing Yvonne herself. Thus, perhaps almost without design, much of the very brief new Chapter II is concerned with Yvonne's consciousness, her hopes, fears, dismay, anxiety as she responds first to Jeffrey himself, then to his news that both Laruelle and Hugh are in town. Since the seven surviving typescript pages of this short chapter are entirely unmarked, one may only surmise that Yvonne-as-central-consciousness, which is not quite achieved here (Jeffrey's mind is still entered briefly), was a stance emerging out of the necessity of establishing character rather than as a deliberate decision about "technique," and that only later would Lowry see that it might be of considerable (if, as yet, unexplored) use to his book as a whole. But if Yvonne's return was used primarily to establish her and reveal her responses, the natural next move was to explore how the Consul in turn is affected by this sudden and unanticipated event. The surprise return of an estranged wife is, after all, a far more emotionally loaded event than the casual visit of a daughter; a Chapter III focused on the Consul and his reactions would seem necessarily to follow.

One of the few chapters to survive in its entirety at this stage, III suggests that Lowry initially made use of this focusing of point of view chiefly as another means of sharpening and compressing his material. This chapter, like most of the rest, is considerably reduced from the parallel section of the 1940 Chapter III (23 to 17 pages), even with the introduction of the attempt at lovemaking, the only new "incident" in

1941. What is remarkable through the opening pages of the revision is how little alteration Lowry's changes in relationship and point of view actually *demand* in the text. The introduction to the new maid ("Josephina" at this stage), her appearance with whisky and soda, the suppressed anger of both Yvonnes, the Consul's appraisal of the appearance of his daughter/wife—the new version moves through the same events here, making only minor cuts and alterations, until the subject of Hugh arises (*1940* 80, and 29:7, 4), and we begin to see what limiting point of view meant to Lowry at this stage.[11] In 1941 this moment becomes an opportunity for exposition: the Consul is made to recall how the affair between wife and brother developed, assess his own responsibility in it, and reflect on the current situation this creates before the narrative returns to the present. This replaces a much longer (three pages to one) and more diffuse and repetitious passage of 1940, in which the Consul had rambled from daughter to wife to Hugh, ending on a note of paranoia. Although intended to give us a view of the Consul's interiority, its prose is indistinguishable from the more impersonal idiom of the narrator. Here is William Ames, reflecting on Hugh's bet and his accidental meeting with Yvonne in Acapulco, working himself into an angry sense of alienation and persecution:

> That meeting had not, after all, had anything to do with the wager. And as for bringing Yvonne back to Quahnahuac, had that been part of it? The Consul thought not. And would it be really necessary either for both of them to make him feel, as they would, inevitably, make him feel—and had this anything mysteriously to do with the bet?—that they were in league with forces cut off from him long ago at the root, and yet which would reappear to heckle him. Would it be absolutely essential to the fulfillment of the terms of the wager that their conversation should be adapted, as it undoubtedly would find itself being adapted, to a special reality, an insulated category of its own, into which it would always subside when he approached, or, when it did not so subside, would adapt itself patronizingly to what it obviously felt were merely his own circumspections on a far lower plane? (*1940* 81–82)

The upshot of these reflections a few lines later is, we are told, "a paroxysm of nerves." However, violent emotional upheaval is hardly conveyed by a passage where diction, tone, and rhythm remain not only controlled but distant, a report on the Consul's consciousness, not a rendering of it. The formalized, heavily latinate diction alone ("wager," "adapted," "inevitably," "fulfillment," "subside," "patronizingly," "circumspections") goes far to create distance here, making no attempt to identify the particular sources of his developing paranoia (what "forces" does he mean? what "conversations" does he envisage? what "insulated category" is in question? and what in heaven's name is meant by "his own circumspections on a far lower plane"?) He imagines feelings in the future; the passage makes clear their existence in the present, but provides no real sense of their source and no individual voice to convey them.

The much briefer reflection on Hugh and Yvonne that replaces this in 1941 is quite specific about what gives rise to the Consul's musings—the focus is on the past, not the imagined future—but still does little to provide them with a personal voice. Thinking of the situation in Paris:

> The guilt, if any, was all his, he thought again, unconsciously bowing his head, he'd hardly seen his wife for weeks, when he did it was only to have a ferocious row, like the time he had passed out and then made the row at the American Ambassador's reception, which he seized upon as an excuse to rush out to the nearest pub. He'd been vastly relieved when Hugh arrived from New Guinea—or was it Fiji?—broke, in a jam over his passport, which he had lost, and generally at a loose end. He had pulled himself together sufficiently to straighten out the passport difficulties, and then, quite literally, had tossed Yvonne into Hugh's lap and told him to show her Paris. (29:7, 4)

This is sufficiently precise about events, but scarcely more emotionally alive than the earlier passage (and sometimes ineptly written: the repeated "row," the solecism of the "quite literal" tossing of Yvonne at Hugh). Despite the gesture of the bowed head, the brisk rhythms of that first sentence hardly convey any genuine sense of "guilt" in either past or present, and the oddly detached curiosity in the second ("or was it Fiji?") masks the unexplored depths beneath the "relief" the Consul felt on Hugh's arrival. Indeed, one would hardly guess from the passage that these are the recollections of a man who has just suddenly and unexpectedly found himself once more in the situation to which this is the immediate emotional background. Lowry's later marginal comment is succinct: "This seems too much like a synopsis." But the particular *kind* of inadequacy here reveals his priorities in 1941, where the ability of the central consciousness to provide some necessary exposition seems economically to accomplish two aims at once (instead, it merely kills both birds).

Other alterations in the consular chapters III, V, and VII that result from the newly restricted point of view confirm that Lowry at this stage used it primarily as one more means of cutting, reducing, clarifying. Only rarely does he allow the new circumstances created by his alterations to tempt him down the path of expansion, to a reimagining that demands enlargement. Perhaps the most interesting occurs in Chapter VII, at the encounter with Laruelle, a convergence that has suddenly acquired explosive overtones. In 1940 the meeting in the street and the invitation to Jacques's "madhouse" occupied some fifteen lines; in 1941 it has grown to a page and a half as Lowry begins to explore the new possibilities.

At his entrance in 1940, Laruelle exists merely as a name in a brief paragraph that brings the four figures together and moves them up the hill. In 1941, however, the *frisson* of the moment is to be savored, and Laruelle acquires "bold blue eyes" so that they may register a momentary "incredulous dismay" at his first sight of the unexpected Yvonne, and a mouth "under its small, blond mustache" to express his subsequent "full appreciation of the satirical humor of this meeting" in its "engaging smile." Jeffrey's consciousness is our point of reference here, and while he can see Laruelle's expression he has a view only of Yvonne's back. Nonetheless, he is aware of *her* awareness both of him behind her *and* of Hugh at her side, and he feels "a grim and ghastly glee" at the "comedy of manners" aspect of this impossible situation. "Laruelle himself, he knew, would miss not the subtlest nuance, but Laruelle did not know that the situation was not merely a triangle, but a square. And as for Hugh, he too would of a necessity miss the final irony: only he and Yvonne could share the bitter draught this walk through the hot Mexican noon distilled" (30:5, 4–5). The passage is worth preserving if only to rescue from oblivion that final sentence, but it marks too the stirrings of the impulse in Lowry not to cut and condense, but to enter into and explore the larger dimensions of a moment as it registers on a specific consciousness.

However, the use of central consciousness in 1941 seems primarily opportunistic rather than sustained and deliberate: whole chapters, such as VIII, IX, and XI, continue to "rove," others, like II and X, are not fully consistent in their employment of the new technique. In short, Lowry had not reached, as in 1940, a stopping point when he had worked through these revisions using carbons as a base. If only because of the necessity of achieving a consistent "design governing posture" throughout, he had reached, at best, a place to pause rather than a completed and coherent "version" of his novel. It may have seemed that all that was needed was more tinkering, a smoothing over of inconsistencies and rough patches. That appears indeed to be the way Lowry looked on this first post-1940 revision, working from an established text, doing as little truly new writing as possible, trimming, smoothing, polishing, streamlining. What actually happened next, however, was quite different, although its germ emerges in the brief section of the 1941 Chapter VII discussed above. Chapter by chapter, entering into the consciousnesses of each of his characters in turn, Lowry began to reimagine his material. Revision became not a matter of smoothing and polishing, but of a full reapprehension of his work, delving into dimensions that he had avoided thus far, confronting emotional and imaginative depths of response—and the task of articulating them—that would end by transforming his text from the thin mediocre work offered in 1940 to the resonant (and demanding) novel eventually published.

In 1941, by launching into the rewriting of a text still being considered by New York publishers, Lowry set in motion a process that would not stop until 1945, if then. From the moment he first picked up his pencil again, there are no clear divisions, no complete "versions" of the *Volcano,* but rather a constant round of revision, chapters taken up in an order that seemed most needful, some rewritten again and again, others (although rarely) altered hardly at all. And once these carbons are left behind, even a base on paper that can be discriminated by color, watermark, pagination, and so on disappears: we are plunged into a morass of yellow sheets, used for both holograph and typescript drafts, no longer to be discriminated by external markings. But if the term "version" does not truly apply to what is merely a stage on a continuing way, the date "1941" is probably also a heuristic fiction: it is offered here with none of the assurance with which "1940" can be affixed to its predecessor. Only the letters cited near the beginning of this chapter provide any authority for employing this date for the resumption of work on the novel; nothing at all sanctions dating the end of this phase in that year.[12]

These observations have a number of ramifications. One, clearly, is that we can speak of a "1940 version" of the *Volcano* and of a "1945 version," but of no genuine "versions" in between.[13] Perhaps less obvious is the narrowing of Lowry's focus as reflected in his way of working. In 1940, Lowry wrote, in order, the first draft of that version and then revised, out of order, every chapter in it. In "1941," Lowry revised, at least partly out of order, each of the chapters of the "D" carbon. After "1941" Lowry revised, out of order, the individual chapters of his novel, some several times, some only once or twice. While he certainly had his sense of the whole novel "in the back of his mind" (often manifested in scrawled notes and reminders on the top page of the latest draft of a chapter concerning issues raised during revision of another chapter) this development marks a progression away from the novel as a whole as the unit of composition, and indeed from the view of narrative as linear. It also, of course, works against any sense of completion or closure, which helps explain why Lowry found it difficult to consider not only the *Volcano* but any of his writings "finished" or even releasable: more and more, finality began to smack of death for both work and author. Life was motion, a thought vaguely expressed in the 1940 *Volcano* but embodied only by means of the long revising process, a process that, I would wager, gave Lowry precisely his deepest experience of that motion as a coherency—motion in Lowry is never random— that traveled not only "around" in circles or ellipses but also "up" and "down" through the various dimensions encountered at any point on the arc of the larger motion: not only wheels, in short, but wheels within wheels. Eventually, for Lowry everything resonates, and resonates plurally, and the individual consciousness not only mediates and registers the reverberations but may contribute its own force to the universal dynamic. But in 1941, if the larger, outward form of his novel suggested endless motion, he was just beginning to explore the reaches—and the limitation—of consciousness.

CHAPTER THREE

1942-1943

I

In a note to himself written sometime in 1944, Lowry reviewed the history of the *Volcano* this way: "Begun 1936. First version finished 1937. Abandoned 1938. Lost 1939. Found in Long Beach, Calif. 1940. Rewritten in 6 months 1940. Rejected by every publisher in New York 1940. Totally abandoned 1940. Rewritten and abandoned as short novel 1941. Rewritten during recovery from near mortal illness [illegible], 1941-1944. Finally published 1944-1945. Touchwood" (Templeton 1:13). Full of obscure drama, adversity, and abandonment, this account gives us the *Volcano* already becoming part of the Lowry myth (the same worksheet has notes toward a preface for the still-to-be-completed, much less accepted, novel, a preface that would eventually be published with the French translation, (see Woodcock, 9-15) but it makes along the way the same point that a Christmas card to Conrad Aiken will make later that same year: "Just finished to-day after 3 years & 3 months revision 8 hours a day approx, soberly Under the Volcano" (*Aiken-Lowry* 182). Although the longer account shows that Lowry had not forgotten all his earlier work, in retrospect the "real" revisions seemed to be those accomplished after the universal rejection from New York, a version of the rewriting that is accurate at least in its suggestion that until late 1944 there is no break in the process, no emergence of anything he was willing to consider a discrete and independent manuscript. Indeed, even the famous Christmas completion and presentation of the working manuscript to Gerald and Betty Noxon is something of a fiction: Lowry was not finished with his novel. He would not be ready to release fair copies to publishers for another six months—the same amount of time, his little history reminds us, given to the entire 1940 version.

Indeed, it may even be, as these later notes claim, that Lowry briefly considered abandoning the *Volcano* altogether after the radical reductions of 1941. In fact, it would be surprising if he had not more than once entertained the possibility of throwing it over during these years, and from one point of view his deep reluctance to release it again to publishers—so different from the speed and eagerness with which he had sent it out in 1940—can be seen as an alternative to abandonment. This was a kind of having one's psychological cake ("Of course I'm working, never harder") and eating it too ("Oh no, my book is in no shape to be seen by others yet") not unrelated to his own Consul's plans for *his* work in progress: "it is perhaps a good idea under the circumstances to pretend at least to be proceeding with one's great work on 'Secret Knowledge,' then one can always say when it never comes out that the title explains this deficiency.... I've got a publisher interested too; in Chicago—interested but not concerned, if you understand me, for it's really a mistake to imagine such a book could become popular" (*Volcano* 39, 86). The crucial difference, of course, was that Lowry actually was "proceeding with [his] great work," even if his potential publishers were no more sanguine about sales than the Consul's.[1]

The novel to which Lowry returned was a much leaner work than the one sent off some two years earlier. In 1941, characters and relationships had been changed from the outside; now he was ready to begin the much more demanding task of recreating them from the inside. The alterations of 1941 were thus in one sense only preliminary, but they were a necessary preliminary. What they were preliminary to, however, was altogether different from the cut-and-paste process of 1941: Lowry now embarked on full scale rewritings of his chapters.

Again, some revisions had clearly been determined before Lowry picked up his pencil. One necessity was to make systematic and thorough those changes in point of view he had begun in 1941. Lightly sketched on the yellow page nine of the preceding Chapter VII is the distribution of chapters to individual figures just as it will occur from this point forward (Templeton 1:9), and marginal reminders of who must serve as privileged filter appear on many of those 1941 chapters—"Well, Hugh feels this" (30:9, 7); "But all this through Yvonne's mind" (27:2, "26"). Simple consistency is Lowry's immediate priority, and it can create problems for him. For instance, the telephone call the

Consul takes in Chapter III, previously observed through Yvonne's eyes, now bears a question mark and the following marginal note: "must not, then, according to our plan, switch to Yvonne's consciousness." Necessary alterations are duly made, but now the Consul is responding to a conversation he apparently does not hear, so Lowry awkwardly adds that he is speaking "automatically in reply to what he was not concentrating on" (26:20, "7"). Yet how can the Consul make specific rejoinders to a conversation that hardly seems to exist for him? The final passage—the Consul "not knowing what he was saying, hearing Tom's muted voice quite plainly but turning his questions into his own answers, apprehensive lest at any moment boiling oil pour into his eardrums or his mouth" (*Volcano* 76)—may not be Lowry's most plausible inspiration, but it takes advantage of his protagonist's almost frantic state to suggest a "conversation" that does not penetrate his jangling, overburdened consciousness.

With various chapters now assigned to individual figures, the units of the novel had become quasi-independent, a status reinforced by Lowry's practice of revision by chapter. Thus he now began to play with chapter divisions—clearly the scheme of twelve was not so sacred at this stage that he refused to think of altering it—considering ending Chapter VIII, for instance, as the bus drives away from the dying Indian (27:1, 264), determining to begin Chapter VII with the approach to Jacques's house (Templeton 1:9, 9). And although so little remains from this phase of Chapter I that we are hard pressed to know what Lowry intended for it, he will very soon divide it into a "Chapter I" that ends with Laruelle and Vigil parting and a "Chapter II" that moves from Laruelle's solitary walk to the burning of the Consul's letter (28:23). Some proposed changes were apparently never implemented, but whether acted on or not they seem to stem either from Lowry's sense of "dramatic" (as distinguished from narrative) structure or from a desire, reversing Joycean priorities, to open his chapters with a moment of epiphany, a passage striking the revelatory keynote of the action that follows. In showing Lowry beginning to treat his chapters as semi-independent structures, these changes mark an important stage in the creation of the novel.

In a modest sense, this had begun in the 1941 revisions. Since it is only in Chapter II that his narrative proper was to start, Lowry could open it with the line that will in tone and image suggest its characterizing note. "'A corpse will be transported by express'" was not new to this draft; what was new was its placement, providing as it does our first direct contact with the living Consul's characteristic voice. In 1940, the comparable chapter ("III" at that stage) had begun with Hugh and Yvonne entering town, observing the square, making conversation, going into the Bella Vista, discovering the Consul unexpectedly in the bar. Only then did we hear his line about this curious Mexican railroad policy (*1940* 67–68). Ordered by strict chronology, the sequence is typical of the linearity of the 1940 *Volcano* and, for that matter, of 1941 as well. In 1941, however, Yvonne can be placed in the bar to hear the Consul's comment without ruffling the sequence of events, which continues to move forward quite conventionally. But the remark itself, no longer buried amid other action and dialogue, acquires a new and ominous weight, casting its sinister shadow over the ensuing action. When Lowry returned to his manuscript, he seems to have seized on the principle of that dramatic opening as a touchstone for other chapters, and to have made use of the new focus through a single consciousness to achieve it.

His strategy for the opening of Chapter III is similar, but in this case between the 1941 version and the next draft occurs one of the rare, breathtaking leaps forward one sometimes encounters in these manuscripts, not the addition of a sentence, rearrangement of a passage, or rewording of a paragraph, but an entire reimagining that appears suddenly in a wholly new burst of prose. In 1941 and in the current draft, Chapter III begins with a descriptive paragraph preceding dialogue that remains virtually unchanged: "'Is Maria still with you?' Yvonne asked. She held his arm tightly but her voice was almost normal, the Consul thought. 'And Pedro—does he still nurse my/the crimson ramblers along?'" (29:7, 1 and 29:8, 2). But the opening paragraphs that precede Yvonne's domestic questions, while ostensibly ushering us into the same garden, actually introduce us into different worlds:

> They were walking down a winding drive with tall, flaming plants growing in lush, tangled profusion. (29:7, 1)

> The tragedy, proclaimed, as they made their way up the winding drive, no less by the gaping potholes in it than by the tall exotic plants perishing on every hand of unnecessary thirst, staggering, it almost appeared, against one another, yet struggling like dying

voluptuaries in a vision to maintain to the end some attitude of potency, or of a collective, desolate, fecundity, the Consul thought, seemed to be directed and interpreted by a person other than himself walking by his side, suffering, and saying: 'Regard, see how strange, how sad, familiar things may be. To think that which you have known in the blood should ever seem so strange. It is as if your best friend should return after long absence only to strike you viciously across the face. Suffer now the tragedy of all places where man has lived and lost his chance. I am the part of your lives you have left here, who came out to meet you not in sorrow, not rebuking, only bidding you now suffer it, for you will never have to suffer anything worse, not even in hell. Touch this tree you have known; look up at that niche in the wall where Christ is still suffering too, compassionate, who would help you if you asked Him. You cannot ask Him. Look at the rose trees on the lawn, Concepta's coffee beans (you used to say they were Maria's) drying in the sun. Do you know their sweet aroma any more? See, the plantains with their green familiar blooms, once emblematic of life, now of an evil phallic death. They are all the same. They are not the same. They are not the same because you do not know how to love them any longer. You only love the cantinas now; the feeble survival of a love of your fellow man, frustrated and turned to poison, which now is only not wholly poison—and poison has become your daily cure, your food—when in the taverns you draw a little closer to what it once was through those who despise or pity you, but for whom, nevertheless, though you will say precisely the opposite, you have always secretly longed, like Christ, even like your own brother, to die.['] (29:8, 1)

Even longer than the paragraph that will eventually open Chapter III, nothing forecasts this enormous shift but two scattered pencil notes on the 1941 top page ("Tragedy, thought the Consul. . . . Coffee beans drying in the sun") and a single surviving worksheet (29:11) that, in outlining the opening and the later lovemaking passage, presents the alcoholic usurpation of love common to both. But neither of these sketchy notes even begins to forecast the sudden richness of scene, the *symboliste* use of images and vaguely frenchified ("Regard") style of address, the dramatized "speaker" itself expressive of self-alienation, and the enormous range of reference across matters religious (Christ), moral (one's fellow man), natural, and erotic (potency, fecundity, phallic), reaching from the exotic (the plants, the voluptuaries in a vision) to the everyday (the aroma of coffee beans). It is even syntactically enormous, being a single sentence, a fact masked by the more varied rhetoric of the "voice" contained within it (hardly worth comparing with the terse introduction of 1941). Voice and vision arise simultaneously; this garden does not exist in the novel until it gets "spoken," for the particulars here—the tree, the plantains, the rose bushes, the coffee beans, the crucifix—quite literally come into fictional being as they are articulated. Finally, the pretense of a detached notation of scene, plausible in the rather neutral tone and rhythm of the 1941 opening, is cast aside for good: the new opening is only made possible by the foregrounding of Geoffrey's consciousness, which, with his excessive drinking already established in Chapter II, renders unnecessary explanation or justification for the convoluted syntax, fevered images, or semihallucinatory "voice" that suddenly appear here. In fact, Lowry can be said to have it both ways at the opening of Chapter III, at once internalizing the action—we are certainly looking through the Consul's eyes—and, in the creation of a "voice," a persona, for Geoffrey's alienation, dramatizing it as well.

Parallel parts of the novel did not, however, all change at the same stage, as if Lowry were working from a master blueprint; while most chapters would acquire significantly different openings, they did not all do so now. For instance, it is in this immediate post-1941 phase of revision that mescal becomes posited throughout the manuscript as the "fatal" drink—"'I might as well . . . start on the whisky: not on the tequila, of course, that would be the beginning of the end, or mescal, which would be the end,'" the Consul tells Yvonne here (29:8, 5)—and so pencil notes are made on the opening pages of the 1941 X and XII, reminders to dramatize the progress of the Consul's downfall with orders of mescal at the Salón Ofélia and the Farolito (27:3, 27:5). The new beginnings of these chapters will indeed feature such orders, but neither underwent revision until considerably later.

As just these altered openings make clear, it is only after 1941 that the Consul's drinking begins to acquire specificity and direction; as an apparent counteraction, Hugh's strychnine cure makes its initial appearance in notations to the 1941 Chapter III.[2] As with the garden opening of that chapter, these changes are part of one of the major thrusts in Lowry's post-1941 revisions, his determination to give to the world of his novel greater physical solidity and particularity. Laruelle, for instance, has taken on a new importance as the lover of Yvonne, not merely of the off-stage Priscilla, and so Lowry sketches out a fuller physical profile (30:5, 1). Incidental additions frequently function to enrich the specificity of the text: the mention of a bottle of *habanero* in Chapter I draws the direction, "description of the bottle," the Consul's socklessness is called for in the margins of III.

In just the changes mentioned thus far, the post-1941 tendency to expansion is unmistakable. New material affecting the entire novel similarly brought greater specificity to the experience, past and present, of the three central figures. For the first time, the brothers, now given the name "Firmin" from that ambiguous figure in the unpublished "June 30, 1934" (and "Jeffrey" becomes the more typically British "Geoffrey"), acquire a childhood in India. Hugh becomes a journalist, although exactly what professional interest has brought him to Mexico will only gradually emerge, and Yvonne acquires a first husband and a deceased child. Although an inevitable source of tension among the characters in all drafts after 1940, the illicit affair between Hugh and Yvonne is not now to determine the outcome of the present plot; rather, it helps fill the expanded role of consciousness, as do Yvonne's plan to get the Consul "away" and Hugh's political concerns, restored after the attenuations of the previous draft. As for the Consul, what he most immediately gains is the hierarchy of drinks, from booze *ordinaire* (beer, "whisky") through the dangerous tequila to the "fatal" mescal, which marks his *progresión a ratos* through the novel's long day. But these outer stigmata are now matched, as in the opening of III, by the beginnings of a rendering of alcoholic consciousness. In all of these appears a recognition of the novel's need for particulars, signs of an outer world, especially as the role of the characters' inner world is being expanded and deepened. Perhaps there is also a recognition that a novel partly about the burdens of the past ought at least to provide its main characters with one.

Yet at the same time he was expanding, deepening, rendering more precise the landscape and the human situation of his novel, Lowry was in the process of becoming increasingly self-conscious about his prose. Dialogue was always difficult for him, and he could be devastating about his own earlier attempts: "phoney," "stooginess," "false" are among the politer marginalia, and the sweeping "balls" captures a more exasperated response. But the directive "get this so you can hear it" applies for Lowry to more than spoken dialogue: as with that opening garden passage of Chapter III, from this point on he is concerned to obtain an oral effect in his prose, to develop "voice" as the expression of consciousness and to capture in the rhythm of its movement an articulation of the inward sense of experience. "Rhythm" became one of his watchwords, and while it meant other things to Lowry as well, it applied first to the attempt to capture in language the very motion of responding to a ride on the loop-the-loop, suffering a dream transformed into a hammering, obsessive nightmare, or resensing the sounds and sights of a journey in its aftermath. Indeed, creating an oral effect in unspoken passages, sometimes by creating internal voices, came more easily to Lowry than more conventional forms of novelistic dialogue.

Lowry's return to the full-scale rewriting of his chapters almost certainly began in 1942, but for those of us trying to follow him, the precise trail becomes indistinct, for while the general direction remains clear, a number of signposts have disappeared. We are far now from the ability to date stages with fair precision, as with the 1940 text, or even to use the (partly fictive) designation "1941" and point to a coherent, single process of rewriting. Until Lowry again begins to put together a manuscript of his twelve chapters—in this case, the combined holograph-typescript that he presented to the Noxons at Christmas 1944—both chronology and the exact order of rewriting disappear into the boskage of yellow sheets, which are used universally now, and sometimes on both sides, for holograph drafts, pencil revision of individual passages, and typescript "final" versions of each chapter at each stage. Once again, the surviving record is frequently incomplete, although even so one can determine the stages of composition of any given chapter, even to positing wholly missing drafts. What is much more difficult is to arrive at any assurance about the order in which Lowry worked on individual chapters.

There thus seems little to be gained from the pretense that we are following Lowry's order of composition in this phase, and perhaps a good deal to be lost in the resulting incoherence of an account that would seem simply to skip about in a fashion that might remain perplexing even if we could recover Lowry's rationale for taking up chapters in whatever sequence he did. On the other hand, it is clear not only that Lowry did not revise in novelistic order, but that not all chapters were revised equally often; and there are some signs to suggest the relative earliness or lateness of particular drafts.[3] To deal with the material coherently, and yet retain some suggestion of the actual writing process, I propose to take up the chapters by group: "the Consul's chapters," "Hugh's chapters," "Yvonne's chapters," beginning with the one that stands alone, Chapter I, not only because it gives every sign of having been revised early, but because we will not soon meet it again in our account.

II

The survivals of Chapter I after 1941 are the most fragmentary group among these manuscripts. It is clear, for instance, from a notebook (28:22) containing "inserts" for not one but two versions of Chapter I at this stage that both (holograph?) drafts have disappeared: all that remains is the typescript of the later of the two. This is the typescript in which the opening of the novel is divided into "Chapter I" (from the beginnings to Laruelle and Vigil's parting) and "Chapter II" (from Laruelle's walk to the end).

The first of the inserts in the surviving notebook is a long one (twelve pages), moving from Laruelle's entrance into the cervecería to the end of the chapter, omitting (but indicating inclusion of) the calendar and the Consul's letter. Much of the material here remains close to what we found in 1940–41. The major expansion is an extended conversation about the Consul between Laruelle and Bustamente (as the cinema manager is named in this set of inserts, but not, oddly, in the subsequent one or the typescript made from it). Here we see Lowry in an enlarging, specifying moment: whereas the cinema manager earlier was barely characterized, we now have a lengthy description of his appearance, ancestry, haberdashery, toilet, temperament—typically, a fuller account than will eventually be published. When he returns with the book of Elizabethan plays and turns the conversation to the Consul, he takes a much more metaphysical view of him than he will later, but one very much in line with Dr. Vigil's "'Sickness is not only in body, but in that part used to be call: soul.'" The Consul, he claims, was indeed a "'pobrecito . . . for so long as a man is in evils he is also in the love of them. . . . And as man cannot shun the evils in his own strength he must be looking to God. But as your friend had no strength to be looking to God he look to hell instead'" (28:22, 11). It was, says the manager, like being trapped in a cellar, and when Laruelle insists that he had enjoyed the cellar, the other demurs: "'I think he suffered. Suffered more because he was nearly a good man'" (13). There is more in this vein—"Swedenborg stuff," Lowry called it subsequently (28:23, 12)— uncomfortably close at times to Laruelle's explicit analyses in the 1940 Chapter I. But Bustamente describes the other inhabitants of that demonic cellar as "alacranes and espiders," and the latter term, bouncing off the accusation already snarled at the Consul by the "chiefs" of Chapter XII, points to a mystery strongly but opaquely hinted in this stage of Chapter I.

In the typescript, as Laruelle and Vigil discuss circumstances surrounding the Consul's death, Vigil remarks that "'even in the Farolito, do you remember, they knew nothing at all,'" and Laruelle oddly responds, "'How should they know even if they knew,'" thinking silently, "I wonder how much he knows" (28:23, I, 3). Later, when the conversation with Bustamente turns to the Consul, Laruelle feels that the cinema manager's eyes convey, "'I know. I know,' . . . but at the same time 'please understand that I know nothing about it, that it is none of my business, that so far as I am concerned we may assume nothing of the kind has happened'" (28:23, II, 11). Lowry's pencilled corrections do not illuminate what they "know," but they suggest something shameful: "'[I know] what happened, what your friend did, but please don't worry, I'm not going to hurt you by speaking of it.'"

If we read back into this draft the later suggestion that Geoffrey was a spy—and in the want of other plausible hypotheses, this seems the obvious likelihood here—we detect Lowry in a characteristic maneuver, introducing a significant matter unambiguously (both Laruelle and Bustamente—if not Vigil—"know" whatever it was the Consul did) that later will become highly problematic. If this is the case, then Bustamente's at this stage taking the "high" line—speaking of the Consul in broad moral and theological terms, of his love of an "evil" and "death"—is part of his tact, his refusal to embarrass or pain Laruelle by talking concretely of an "evil" deed or deeds that his friend has performed. Nor, as his later stance shows, is there any incompatability between his belief in the Consul's shady actions and his sympathy for the man himself. Indeed, the spelling out of Bustamente's identification of the Consul as a spy may have been the result of Lowry's recognition that he had dealt here with the suggestion impenetrably. Uncertainty will then shift from *what* is being conveyed to the unascertainable basis for the belief—now Bustamente's alone—in actuality.

When the manager says, "'He liked the death and pulque. He liked the death and tequila better. But best of all he liked the death and mescal. When he haved death and mescal then he is flying'"(15), we recognize by the alcoholic hierarchy that we are in the post-1941 phase. In other ways, however, even the final "Chapter I-Chapter II" typescript reveals how close Lowry still was to early conceptions. Vigil and Laruelle's dialogue, shorn of tendentiousness but in some respects little altered from 1940, conjures up a version of the past that will shortly be superseded. "'Doesn't it seem only yesterday when we were going all round the cantinas and all the infamous pulquerias in Mexico looking for him? My God, I felt sorry for his wife. It must have been hell being the woman of such a maker of tragedies.... I thought she would have a decomposition of the mind'" (28; 23, 3). Lowry has not yet sent Vigil on holiday to Guanajuato, and since "we" here seems to include a distraught Yvonne as one of the search party, she is still imagined as a survivor. Plot concerns alone would demand revision here; in any case, the notion of dividing the opening into two chapters cannot have lasted long, for nowhere in the manuscripts is there an alteration in the numbering of other chapters that this change would have necessitated.

This opening chapter has become doubly vague on the precise historical time of the novel's action. We are still given no sense of how long ago these momentous events occurred. "'I think'" Vigil says coyly, "'you are thinking of the Consul and another Jour des Morts'" (28:23, I, 3). The Spanish war is "finito" but amazingly, recalling its centrality in 1940, the European war is not directly mentioned at all. Jacques does not consider returning to France; his plans for the following day are to "go and scratch the land a little" at "amateur excavations . . . at Xocxitepec" (28:23, I,8). Closest to a reference to the war is Laruelle's association of the calendar picture of Cortez and Moctezuma with Hitler and Chamberlain—"or," in pencil, "Franco and Sir Samuel Hoare"(9)— but we are given no notion of the chronological relation of the Munich meeting to any of the novel's events. All of this suggests that in the

"Chapter I–Chapter II" draft we are still early in the post-1941 revisions where, the cinema manager's additions aside, the principal watchword continues to be "concision." Hints of new departures are discernable: Vigil, for instance, acquires physicality, a yawn, an "impossibly handsome" face, delicate wrists with a sprinkling of "coarse black hair"; the Consul's original identification of the pyramid at Cholula with the Tower of Babel is now reflectively interiorized in Jacques's "How admirably he had concealed . . . the greater Babel of his thoughts"; and Laruelle associates his borrowing of the book of Elizabethan plays with a remorseful memory of Yvonne (28:23, "I", 3; "II," 3, 10). The major expansive phase is yet to come, but as these additions suggest, unlike the 1940 text, it will be an expansion into specificity and particularity that will also bring with it a return of the political and the historical not as ideology but as precise events with names, dates, consequences.

Like this opening chapter, the latter two "Yvonne chapters"—IX and XI—bear signs of being among the early revisions. In Chapter IX (30:13), for instance, Lowry still has difficulty holding to her point of view, a technical problem no other chapter suffers by this time. Despite marginal reminders, the typescript presents several unlikely passages in which Yvonne seems to have the ability to read the minds of her male companions. Furthermore, Lowry was still at this point operating in the cutting and condensing mode of 1941: whereas Chapter IX had been slightly trimmed in that phase, it is now slashed from some 30 pages to 17½—as XI will, more modestly, be trimmed from 18 to 17 pages.

Throughout the years of revision following the adoption of central consciousnesses, Yvonne's chapters would continue to cause Lowry the most difficulty. Perhaps his uncertainty helps account for the fact that even as this IX is cut by almost half—excisions of weak dialogue and the falling-in-love-with-Hugh passages—much of what Yvonne "thinks" is actually what Hugh and Geoffrey are thinking. On the opening page of the chapter, she bursts into tears, as she had previously, but instead of making us privy to the responses that produced the weeping, Lowry tells us, "She could sense as though she had seen it the exchanged glance of dismay between the two men behind her," and goes on to distinguish what that glance would mean for each man (30:13, 1–2). Indeed, much of the chapter simply rearranges material remaining from the previous draft to bring it into at least nominal accord with

Yvonne's vision. The tedious song about the fish, for instance, is here given to Hugh, in part, presumably, because if it were retained for Yvonne Lowry would have to give some sense of what she is thinking as she creates these silly lines. Yvonne's proposal that they get away to a farm and her momentary sense, twice felt, of stirrings of the "unity" she and Geoffrey had once shared (30:13, 3, 14) are the only moments genuinely new to this draft.

One might expect the other chapter that makes use of the farm proposal, Chapter XI, to be appreciably different from its predecessor, for it is in this draft that the plot of the *Volcano* takes its definitive turn away from any romantic resolution, ending for the first time with Yvonne's death. Yet the two drafts are almost exactly the same length, and early sections diverge mainly in small but sometimes significant ways (the later draft even incorporates two pages refolioed from the earlier one). For instance, Lowry has Hugh and Yvonne pause over the momentous choice of paths, for from now on the wrong and sinister ("path to the left") choice will determine two fatalities. More extensive were alterations in the relationship between the two former lovers. Now they confront various "impossible" options: Yvonne might catch the train out with Hugh; she might catch the train and Hugh remain to "straighten [Geoffrey] out"; she might remain while Hugh goes. By the time they reach El Popo, her revulsion against "shabbiness" produces not a scathing self-judgment but a desire to escape to her farm alone; and what had appeared in 1941 as a sense of a separate "world of men" that excluded her is now transformed into *her* rejection of "all of them." Here the two versions clearly part company, the later one only glancing toward the possibility of Hugh and Yvonne spending the night together at El Popo before sending them back out into the approaching storm, where Yvonne, climbing over the fallen tree, loses her footing as the rushing horse, "7" brand clearly visible, plunges toward her. That entire final sequence is sketched briefly, the action from Yvonne's arrival at the tree occupying a single terse page. From the perspective of her weariness of "all of them," the desire to get away and be on "her farm" alone, her death is almost a prayer answered. It is also, of course, Lowry's way out of the impossible love triangle.

It is tempting—and plausible—to think that the third "Yvonne chapter," Chapter II, was also rewritten at this time.[4] Yet if this Chapter II comes out of the same period as IX and XI, it is an enormous step beyond them precisely in being an enormous step beyond its predecessor. Yvonne herself is of a piece with her parallel incarnations in those drafts, for instance in her resentment of masculine exclusiveness, a characteristic only of this phase: told by her ex-husband that he and her ex-lover Laruelle "'have terrific times together,'" she thinks, "My God these men, God this locked world of men a woman can never get her nose inside of, God's Jesus these men" (29:2, 14). However, at more than twice the length of the 1941 version, this draft presents the first sustained effort to render the novel's world as apprehended through Yvonne's consciousness, and the change is dramatic. As in the new opening of Chapter III, both world and consciousness suddenly spring into life as if they exist only in terms of each other, the external coming into being only in the act of apprehension. Action and much of the dialogue remain almost what they had been; the change is all in the texture of the prose, in the density of rendered world and self.

Perhaps the magnitude of the alteration can be suggested once more by glancing at openings, from the Consul's pronouncement with which each draft begins to the moment that, catching sight of Yvonne, he exclaims, "My God." In 1941, this is the passage:

> "A corpse will be transported by express," the Consul observed to no one in particular, for the barman was at a little distance and did not have the air of listening. He resumed his study, from various angles, of a blue and red National Timetable. "A corpse, whether adult or child," he added, peering round as if seeing little.
> "My God," . . . (29:1, 1)

It is only at this point that we discover that Yvonne is *in* the scene, much less the privileged observer of it. There is no such confusion in the next draft: the Consul's remark is given its own paragraph (with, now, the line of lead); then we have:

> The precise English voice, coming from the little bar beside the Bella Vista Hotel, was achingly familiar as the hotel itself, but unreal, as though it had come from the stage, she thought, where some intolerable play is being performed one has escaped from into the cold decor and debris and blind walls of the world for a cigarette. (29:2, 1)

If the opening comment has seemed unmediated, this paragraph clearly establishes "she" as the locus of perception, aware at once of what her senses record (the voice, the hotel) and what emotion, memory, and imagination do with these ("achingly familiar . . . unreal . . . as though . . . one has escaped," and so on), suggesting at once the dilemma Yvonne faces of an "intolerable" unreality of life with Geoffrey, and the "cold," "blind" emptiness of life without him. The syntax of the sentence is slightly wobbly, but that too seems the result of the attempt to make a single linguistic structure dramatize the relationships among these matters—the inner and outer scenes, the familiar and the strange, the options offered.

Lowry is partly establishing the landscape of his book, and so for the first time he places Yvonne outside the bar, has her observe the square, the amusements, the ambulance, the banner, the volcanoes. But he filters the scene through her highly emotional perception of it: it is Yvonne's consciousness rather than the square of Quauhnahuac that is the true site of this opening. Furthermore, observation of the present is partly overlaid by past and future: her continuing awareness of the morning's flight from Acapulco (here Lowry begins to make use of material from the discarded Chapter II of 1940), "the horn of Venus," the plane "like a minute red demon," and her anticipation of the later fiesta, all become part of the account. She has once more arrived on the *Pennsylvania,* landing now at "Hornos, Acapulco," which the Consul will pretend to confuse with a trip around Cape Horn (to such has Hugh Fernhead's proposed journey been reduced). As with the new opening of Chapter III, the prose no longer aspires to neutrality, but begins acquiring supple rhythms that can convey the charged and multiple perceptions of consciousness. Compare the following sentence with the opening of the previous draft cited just above:

> She could almost have sworn the taxi-driver winked at her as she looked round the square, the controlled thunder of the plane still in her ears, *their* square, brilliant in the early morning sunlight, silent yet poised, expectant, looking forward to the fiesta later—the festival of the Day of the Dead having started the night before—the booths shut up but with one eye open already, the merry-go-rounds only half asleep, the giant Ferris wheel dreaming. (29:2, 2)

Aware of the square but still "hearing" an aftersense of the plane engine, looking around at the scene but both catching and doubting a glimpse of the single human in view, emotionally appropriating this landscape ("*their* square") and thus animating it, transforming a recollection from the past into anticipation of the future—this is Lowry launched on the characteristic flexibility and motion of a prose that will incorporate multiple awarenesses into a single sustained reflection, transforming an ambitious but immature and unrealized manuscript into a major novel.

By starting outside the Bella Vista, Lowry is also able to make dramatic use of the shift of scene as Yvonne moves from the bright exterior where she can still sniff "the cool sweetness of the dawn" into the "dusk" of the bar where, like the vista, "she felt her heart suddenly contract." He will make more of this contrast later, but here, while Yvonne's heart is contracting, Lowry himself is expanding the scene inside the bar. Under her gaze, the barman, who previously had only nominal existence, acquires solidity, action, purpose: he becomes "a lad of not more than eighteen with sleek dark hair . . . at a little distance drying glasses," who at first seems not to have "the air of listening." But Yvonne's initial impression is "mistaken," she discovers, as the boy goes into a pantomime with the cigarette, advertisement (here, in her first appearance, "a naked woman") and "'Absolutamente necessario,'" familiar from the published novel. The boy's speech and action, giving particularity to the scene, establish the bar for the first time as genuinely imagined and imaginable space. But Lowry is after more than an impressionistic realism, the "absolutamente necessario" playing counterpoint to the corpse that imperatively "will be transported," sex ambiguously juxtaposed with death (even with the woman on the advertisement less overtly associated with Yvonne than the later scarlet brassiere will make her), the "rituals" of the past set against the failing ones of the present. Only now, at the top of the fifth page, does the Consul peer toward Yvonne "a little blurred because the sunlight was behind her" and utter his "My God."

Lowry seemed able to expand the material of II before that of IX and XI because he could more easily enter into the emotional state of Yvonne at this point and so reimagine the chapter from the vantage of her mixture of hope and fear, nostalgia and apprehension, love and revulsion and, everywhere, anxiety. Those feelings were all connected to the specific place and situation to which she was returning, which thereby demanded rendering both in their own right and as objective correlatives of her condition as the action unfolded. The resultant emotional difference can be seen in the difference between the bald demand of 1941—"'Jeffrey,' Yvonne said suddenly, 'what do you get out of it?'"—and the agonized unspoken plea of this draft:

> "God knows I've seen you like this before," her thoughts were saying, her love was saying through the gloom of the bar, "too many times for it to be a surprise anyhow, yet there is this subtle difference this time. I am defeated, I am baffled—how can I hope to help you now when I have not been able to help you before? And do I want to? Would it not be kinder after all to let you have your darkness. Oh Geoffrey, why do you do it?" (29:2, 7)

It is not only a matter of Yvonne's unspoken speech making her more sympathetic: here she is emotionally *involved* in the situation, whereas the Yvonne of 1941 had seemed to stand outside it. At the same time, because the bar has been imaginatively established, its "gloom" becomes the outer and visible embodiment of the metaphorical "darkness" that is her image of his condition, and which now, for the first time, becomes the pivot of the unspoken reply she imagines to her unspoken question: "But it is not altogether darkness.... You misunderstand me if you think it is altogether darkness I seek.... But if you look at that sunlight there, ah then perhaps you'll get the answer, see, look at the way it falls through the window."

Here also Yvonne begins to acquire a past earlier than her marriages, a background that will disappear from Chapter II to be revived elsewhere. There had been, she reflects "a slight element of falsehood" in her marriage to Geoffrey, "the marriage partly into the past, into her English-Scottish ancestry, into the imagined empty ghost-whistling castles in Sutherland, into an emanation of gaunt lowland uncles chumbling shortbread at five o'clock in the morning— ... a husband that was not a husband, but alternately a drivelling impotent old man and a helpless pitiable child" (11). Just as the dead child of her first marriage is suggested in those final words, so Yvonne's actual father is contained in the other end of the analogy, and he too makes a brief, oblique appearance. On hearing that Hugh is in town, Yvonne associates her response with a childhood sense "after a quarrel with her father . . . : that nature, the whole world were disclocated. . . . The sound of Hugh's name, like her father's angry words still hammering in her ears, made her afraid" (22).

While Geoffrey proceeds to outline Hugh's "salvage operations"—the strychnine treatment and Theodore Watts-Dunton here enter the text—Yvonne silently registers her disgust at his alcoholic state, a revulsion that Lowry seems to think explains her immediate emotional gravitation toward Hugh. As the above passage suggests, his unexpected presence evokes a powerful reaction, and she reminds herself, "it was going to be necessary . . . to keep one's reasons for being here, however futile they might have become, very firmly in mind" (22–23). The intensity of response seems to belong to a previous phase of the novel, a phase when she had not yet responded to La Despedida with the imaginative identification that longs for some "geologic thaumaturgy" to restore its unity, not yet invoked the "us" of the love she and Geoffrey had shared. A Yvonne who veers from emotional commitment to Geoffrey to "love" for Hugh within a few pages (and, in novelistic time, a few minutes) can hardly be taken seriously, and passages suggesting her continuing infatuation will vanish quickly.

It is within the revised "Hugh chapters" (that is, Chapters IV and VI, for VIII will not get taken up again until later) that we become aware that Lowry has at last fixed the dates of his Days of the Dead. "Chapter I-Chapter II" is still indeterminate in its reference to the Munich agreement, but the parallel version of IV is quite clear. "'When were you in California?'" Yvonne asks Hugh, who replies, "'A month ago. I landed in Frisco just in time for Munich'" (29:12, 10). This IV is not as specific as it will become: the later Hugh is almost compulsively exact: "'they got the Internationals out five weeks ago, on the twenty-eighth of September to be precise, two days before Chamberlain went to Godesburg'" (29:13, ms. 7).[5] Nonetheless, the date of November 1938 is now set, a fixed point from which both the specifics of the characters' lives and details about public events can flow.

Indeed, one of the first results is apparently Lowry's attempt to devise a precise historicity for his characters: three holograph sheets in Margerie's hand (Templeton 1:14) bear witness to an explicit working out of times, dates, and relationships, all of which are reflected in the various drafts of this stage, but not later ones, where some details change. The first of these is headed "Yvonne" and provides not only the "English-

Scottish ancestry," the dead child, and the unfaithful husband already noted, but several details apparently never made use of—a mother "from Virginia or Maryland," a debut at eighteen, a "finishing school." Altogether, this sketches more of a "society" background than any version of Yvonne definitely acquires and is consistent with what had been intimated about Priscilla in 1940. The second sheet, headed "Geoffrey and Hugh," dates their births in 1895 and 1905 respectively (thus Hugh's 33 years in the VI at this stage—but only there), mentions their father's disappearance "into Tibet" in 1908, their mother's subsequent death, the boys in England at "separate schools," their attendances at Cambridge, Geoffrey's enlistment in the war, his two years at Tortu, and, more vaguely, his diplomatic career until a 1932–33 posting to Algeciras. One reason for the later alteration of Hugh's age to 29 also becomes apparent: what has he been doing all his adult years? Margerie lists him as being at sea from 1926 to 1928, then traveling "aimlessly but adventurously" from 1928 to 1932, rather a long time to be simply on the road. Apparently he was to turn journalist only in 1932–33, receiving "roving commission from paper." The third sheet, headed "Time Table," covers the period from "Spring 1935," when Yvonne and Geoffrey "meet in Algeciras . . . marry and are very happy," to "November 1938," when "Yvonne returns and story begins," dating seasonally the moves (Paris, Mexico), Geoffrey's drinking bouts, the affairs with Hugh and Laruelle, and Yvonne's final departure. With only minor modifications, the information contained on this sheet will carry through into the finished novel.[6]

The fixing of the time of the principal action, coming so amazingly late in the novel's gestation, is one of the key events in its composition, as if only now did Lowry realize that a work as concerned in form and matter with the very processes of time as the *Volcano* could not evade its own historicity. One of the first beneficiaries is Hugh, who at the opening of this next draft of Chapter VI gains for the first time a specific age, the clouds overhead announcing to him the thirty-three years assigned him on Margerie's worksheet. Hugh's anxieties and calculations here about vanished youth, irresponsibility, and so on are very close to those of the published novel—with the notable exception of the age itself. Indeed, in pencil in the margin of this typescript (30:1) appears a doodled drawing bearing the legend "Hugh is 29 in 1938," the "29" heavily circled. Here we glimpse Lowry implicitly acknowledging the measure of self-projection in Hugh that first automatically assigned the character his current age of thirty-three (thus almost certainly dating this draft of Chapter VI to 1942) before adjusting for the historicity of the action—thereby acknowledging, on another level, the continued authorial identification (Lowry too, of course, was twenty-nine in 1938).

The Hugh of these drafts of Chapters IV and VI is not only an older, but a guiltier Hugh than we have seen up to this point. When in 1941 he had become the Consul's younger brother, Lowry had been obliged to abandon some of the neatly stark contrasts he had devised for the earlier version of the two male figures, but he did so reluctantly. Their "shared" love of Yvonne was now a matter for bitterness and irony, no longer conceivable without tension, guilt, animosity, but in 1941 Lowry seems to have solved this potential difficulty by reserving for Yvonne and the Consul the burden of anxiety and guilt, leaving Hugh free to remain the strong, uncomplicated, but principled man of action who steps in decisively only in Chapter XI after Jeffrey's vicious verbal assault. Indeed, as late as the post-1941 "Chapter I–Chapter II" version of the letter to Yvonne, Lowry is trying to maintain simple contrast by having the Consul speak of his brother's "organic and total dissimilarity from myself" (28:23, 20). That characterization, however, left a bad aftertaste of Hugh's unacknowledged hypocrisy in its wake, and as Lowry began again to flesh out his novel, this figure inevitably became more complex, less simply a contrast to the Consul, taking on the kind of partial mirroring that would eventually be expressed in the relationship of half-brother.

Thus the Hugh who now enters a more richly imagined garden at the start of Chapter IV only to be stopped by "something between floribundia and rose woven out of the filaments of the past that looked like Yvonne," is a more guilt-ridden Hugh than we have heretofore seen. The telegram and Hugh's explanation of it arrive, apparently for the first time, almost exactly as in the published novel, and his forays into Texas, California, and China are all here and accounted for by the newly acquired career.[7] He has not, however, been to Spain in this draft, and the sound of target practice evokes all Hugh's guilt for *not* being there (29:12, 14A). But he goes on to recall, as in the novel, his activist friends, a line of thought leading into a virulent attack on fellow-traveling bystanders. Since these are largely journalists, Hugh confesses to Yvonne that much of his revulsion is really self-disgust, but although in Chapter VI he fantasizes about miraculously appearing on the battlefield, he has no genuine plans in these drafts for going to Spain.

If the young Hugh of 1940 had been uneasy about the gap between his leftist sympathies and his absence from Spain, this Hugh is far less young and proportionately more riddled by the guilt of his own inconsistency. Although his meditation at the opening of VI does not yet have the very surroundings seeming to accuse him, Hugh is even here torn between the facts of his age and experience and a familiar and flattering self-conception that he cannot quite surrender. But Spain is of course only part of Hugh's problem; the betrayal of "brotherhood" has a closer and more literal application. He is stunned to find Yvonne on the scene, although the greeting Lowry first gives him sounds simply crudely insulting rather than startled and guiltily apprehensive: "'How terrible. I mean how what. How absolutely something or other,' he was saying. 'I thought you were Louise Bogan's Medusa for a moment. When did you get here?'" (29:12, 3).[8] Her handshake produces a "pain in his heart," and it is his sense of that organ being "exposed" that causes him to button his shirt. More sentimental than he will be later, he has made Yvonne "an arbour in his consciousness he resorted to mostly before sleeping, that was formed out of everything he was able to lay the tentacles of his memory on he could persuade himself was honest or triumphant or kind or good" (8). Suddenly he "remember[s]" that this is his brother's wife and his guilt seems "running around them like a kitten biting at their ankles." The metaphorical kitten soon becomes the actual charging goat, which in turn gives way to the horses and dog of their pastoral ride, from which arises Hugh's sense, persisting from 1940, of their carrying with them "a little world of love."[9] But in a typical Lowryan dialectic, that sense now first seems mere illusion, denied by his guilt—"it is all a bloody lie"—until the harsh dismissal is itself qualified by the recognition that, lie or not, "Are we not happy, indisputably happy, just to be together?" (19).

Nonetheless, it is Hugh's pained consciousness of his false position that leads him to initiate the personal dialogue that accounts for much of the expansion in this part of the chapter. He begins by bluntly declaring his brother a hopeless alcoholic case, but in deference to Yvonne's dismay, backtracks into proposing a geographical cure, which here means escape to a new life in Geoffrey's "genteel Siberia," rather sketchily described by Hugh as "tough sledding" beside wilderness and sea, and avoiding hypocrites and beerparlours "in the town." However, Lowry is not content to let the love triangle remain tacit, at least not this early in the action, and an avoided embrace in the ruins of Maximilian's Palace eventually gives way to a brief reprise of the 1941 romance: "Now she was clinging to him; she was crying, and now they did kiss, half passionlessly, almost with a kind of terror, he thought. 'Hugh, oh Hugh, I don't want you to go away to—I love you, but—' 'You love him too. More.' 'Yes'" (29:12, A–D).

In Chapter VI, this somewhat sentimentalized Hugh turns over in his mind the possibilities of the "genteel Siberia" actually proving workable (to the marginal distress of his creator, who judges him probably too "taken in" for the worldly journalist he is now supposed to be). But while this VI (30:1) is superficially consistent with the current IV, it shows little of the development of the earlier Hugh chapter. For the first time, the action carries on beyond the departure from the house to the meetings with Laruelle and the little *cartero* and the walk towards Jacques's place, ending with the focus on Yvonne's belated postcard. Yet the "new" chapter is at least as terse as the 1941 version had been, the apparent twenty-one pages of the earlier draft not quite matched by the eighteen pages that cover the comparable action of this revision.

In that previous draft, Hugh's opening introspection on the daybed had shrunk by more than half. Now, tentatively and briefly, Lowry begins reconstructing the opening soliloquy, retaining the radio news reports of various disasters—these may have been the germ of Hugh's career as journalist in the first place—but preceding them with a new passage, Hugh's pained reflections on aging. Wavering, ambivalent, still uncommitted, perhaps unsurprisingly the reconstructed introspection here is brief; the Consul's cry for help with shaving comes on p. 4.

Although in this draft Lowry at last cuts the quarrel between the Consul and Yvonne that Hugh had overheard since 1940, her old role as nag and scold is still insinuated by Geoffrey's whispers and pantomimed cover-up, "one hand over his lips enjoining silence, the other hand ... pointing to the radio," and by his first words: "I don't want Yvonne to know, but ..." (4). Now Anglo-Indian, Geoffrey suffers from "rajah" shakes, a background underlined by his "Tit for tat" recollection, Hugh's aid to the nauseated Consul being a reversal of the Consul's ministrations to seasick little Hugh "'On the P and O boat coming back from India'" (6). In this way, Lowry begins to exploit their common brotherly background, as well as the more ambiguous roles of father and son ("Well, suppose I shave you, Papa?" [5]). Both have now been at Cambridge and so share affectionate recollections of "old Carruthers" (here adding the story of Geoffrey riding a "ferocious" horse into college). In this draft Carruthers has become a rather pointed analogue for the Consul, who professes to be "shocked" at Hugh's story of his passing out during a supervision, defensively claims that being a connoisseur of wines "refined" the old man "into the very opposite type from drunkards," but is saddened by Hugh's report of his recent death from cirrhosis.

Much of this scene—talk of the barbering, readings from *El Universal*—dates back to 1940. What the earlier Hugh had read silently, however, is, now that he is a journalist, made the stuff of gleeful banter between the two men. The first altogether new passage is occasioned by the newspaper's report that "certain 'police chiefs' . . . [are] Performing their 'private functions' in public." With the events of VIII and XII in mind, Lowry has the Consul attempt to address the situation:

> I don't think those birds referred to here are even police, let alone chiefs, but belong to a clandestine political organization affiliated to the *military* police, which is different . . . the Inspector General of the State, who *is* the military police, is a member. Also the Chef de Jardineros [sic]. Anyway, their headquarters used to be the Policia de Seguridad. Though maybe it isn't any longer, but in Parian somewhere, I heard. Or elsewhere. They are a sort of survival of Maximilian's iron guard . . . who like to keep order at such times as now, when half the real police are on strike. (30:1, 10)

"It sounds like another fascist set-up," Hugh responds, a side glance at his telegram which also moves rather specifically into the Mexican situation of the time—specifically enough that before his next draft, Lowry would do some research into these matters.[10]

As the travelers leave the house, Laruelle appears, looking "somewhat Jewish" and moving toward them "as though impelled by clockwork." This material, previously part of Chapter VII, had then been reflected through the Consul's eyes; now, while Hugh takes an immediate dislike to this figure, feeling "something . . . wrong," he does not of course know what it is. The Consul's view of the meeting of the four had been bitterly sardonic, but the encounter reverberates only obliquely for Hugh, and although it is in parts ponderously done, the necessity for indirection propels Lowry into expressive physical description, which from this draft forward hints at the bases for Hugh's instant antagonism:

> it was as if the whole of this man, by a curious legal fiction, reached up to the crown of his perpendicularly raised hat, for the gap below seemed to Hugh still occupied by something, a sort of halo or spiritual property of his body, or the essence of some guilty secret perhaps that he kept under the hat but which was now momentarily exposed, fluttering and embarrassed. He was confronting them, though smiling at Yvonne alone . . . [he] wore his coat open, and trousers very high over a stomach they had probably been designed to conceal but which they merely succeeded in changing in character, making it appear instead like an independent tumescence of the lower part of his body. . . . (30:1, 21–22)

Hugh cannot understand why Yvonne seems "reluctant" to present him, and when the Consul does finally make the introduction, it is only to say, "'you ought to get to know one another, you have more than you think in common'" (22). The remainder of the action through the appearance of the postman (who now announces to the Consul "a message . . . for your horse," receiving in reply, "What, nothing for senor Caligula?") and the discovery of the card remains very close to its predecessor, except that Lowry has Yvonne write, "'Darling . . . Why did I make this ridiculous trip? Why did you make me? . . . Hope to find a wire there waiting telling me to come back but oh, tell me where?'" (25). That message quite clearly posits Geoffrey as the agent of the final marital breakdown. "'Cheery little matter,'" he comments to close the chapter, echoing Yvonne's comment on the death of the cats; but he does not, for the first time, throw the card away.

If this Chapter VI is often still close to its 1941 forerunner, one apparently small alteration points to a major development. Into Hugh's monologue at the chapter's start comes, for the first time, a form of animation in which the narrator no longer simply conveys the substance of Hugh's reflections; Hugh himself develops an internal speaker, or rather two internal speakers, who debate the questions of his youth and responsibility ("I am not a prodigy any longer. I have no excuse any longer to behave in this irresponsible fashion.... On the other hand, I *am* a prodigy. I *am* young"). In the next version of VI, they will even briefly be called "the first voice" and "the second voice" (5:96). Yet it is not Hugh, of course, who becomes the principal beneficiary of Lowry's dramatization of "voice," but the Consul.

Indeed, at this stage Geoffrey's chapters begin to exploit the possibilities of this device. Chapter III seems to present the Consul as little more than a locus of voices, which can even take over his actual speech. The "familiar" who begins, as in the published novel, in response to Yvonne's refusal of a drink, "She might have said yes for once" (29:8, 5; cf. *Volcano* 68), is on the one hand recognized by his host, but on the other carefully distinguished: "it wasn't the stranger in the garden for instance, he thought, but that faction of himself perhaps who thrived on deceiving him (though he remained undeceived) ... one whom he often thought of as an actual person." A moment later this voice appears to usurp Geoffrey's spoken address to Yvonne, and a dozen pages further, as he plausibly describes a program for phasing out his drinking altogether, we are left in no doubt: "his familiar was speaking aloud for him" (19).

A richer orchestration of utterances, however, occurs as husband and wife sit silently on the porch. We have looked at part of the previous version of this passage (see p. 88 above) and had occasion then to comment on the impersonality of the rendering, a divorce between the emotional burden of the content and the flatness of the prose. There, the narrator observed a distinction between placid exterior and pained and guilty interior, but tone, rhythm, diction seemed unaffected by the shift from one to the other. Here is the comparable passage in the present draft of Chapter III:

> He relit his pipe: the gulf, he thought, she has brought the damn thing with her, the bloody abyss, the ubiquitous barranca, it is here now, on this porch, yawning between us, only we can't tell yet how much larger, deeper, wider, more malodorous it has grown. He was leaning forward peering intently, as if he were really concerned to see whether Popocatapetl were emerging from the black horizontal columns of cloud like smoke from a forest fire obscuring it, or drawn across the face of the mountain by several trains running parallel....

(*Die glöcke glöcke tönt nicht mehr*).... Nevertheless, it wasn't that I blamed you in yourselves, once the vicarious probe, the surgical shock of the thing had lost its first scorching impact. For we had been perilously close to a break even before she met you. And you ought to understand this, Hugh, when you feel too guilty, when remorse incarnadines you sweating in the night, that at the time of your arrival in Paris I had hardly seen her for weeks and when I did it was only to have as a rule a scene, just such a scene as I fear is now inevitably approaching. I shall pass over the painful exhibitions I was making of myself at ambassadorial receptions, the disappearances into the green wormwood depths of pernod bottles or into the well named Café Chagrin in the Boulevard Raspail. For what I want you to bear in mind too is that I was relieved when you arrived from Aden.... (29:8, 8-9)

At least four kinds of utterance can be immediately distinguished here: the impartial narrative voice that renders the exterior world either in its simple physical presence (relighting the pipe, leaning, peering) or in heightened analogies (forest fire, trains) for the clouds around the volcano; in sharp contrast, the internal voice whose short-breathed fear responds to the encroaching "pit" in a rhythm of rising panic as style itself seems to hyperventilate ("here now... larger, deeper, wider, more malodorous"); the German of Goethe, distinct from the first two not only in its linguistic form, but in its private-public nature, evoked by the Consul as part of his dread but also, in its intertextuality, placing that dread in a larger historical-literary context; and the direct address to Hugh, no less spoken idiom for being silent, and in its longer syntactical structures and heightened rhetoric altogether different from the frightened private voice with its short-winded terror. Unlike the 1941 version, this address is particular ("green wormwood... pernod bottles... Café Chagrin... Boulevard Raspail") rather than general ("the row... the nearest pub"). If Geoffrey was "relieved" by Hugh's appearance in Paris, so the long passage which this recollection begins is another "relief," a second evasion of Yvonne in its postponement of the "inevitably approaching" confrontation.

Even passages that, unlike this direct address, are not literally presented as real or imagined speech are swept into a new sense of the tone and rhythms of the urgently projected. For example, the Consul's conjuration of a cantina early in the morning changes hardly at all in its imagery, but suddenly at this point acquires an intensity it had never possessed previously. Here is the passage in 1940 and 1941:

> Now, again, he wanted to go, seeing in his mind's eye ... the peace changing into the strange fevered preoccupation of a *cantina* at this time.... all sorts of people somehow not a part at any other time of the community of *cantinas* at all.... The newsvendors of *La Prensa* or *El Universal*, standing in the corner with the shoeblacks, their shoestools in their hands, or balanced on the rail—no one but he knew how beautiful all this was! (*1940* 92; 26:20, 94 ["13"])

Here is the comparable section of the present draft:

> But now, now, he wanted to go, passionately he wanted to go, aware that the peace of the cantina was changing into its first strange fevered preoccupation of the morning.... Now, now he wanted to go, aware that the place was filling with all sorts of people somehow not a part at any other time of the community of the cantinas at all ... the newsvendors of El [*sic*] Prensa and El Universal would be coming in, standing in the corner at this moment with the shoeblacks who carried their shoestools in their hands or had left them balanced on the footrail, and now, now, he wanted to go. Ah, none but he knew how beautiful it all was.... (29:8, 23)

Only rhythm and tone differ here, possessed of that urgency that makes "passionately" the keyword and dramatizing for the first time in the hypnotically repeated "now, now" and the yearning sigh of "Ah," the irresistible attraction, rendered from within, that leaves Yvonne sobbing alone on the bed, her beauty no match for the cantina, *eros* invested elsewhere. It was not context that brought about this change—the attempted lovemaking and the vision of the cantina as its rival were there already in 1941—but the reimagining of the episode from the inside, producing the altered prose rhythms that capture its "fevered" feeling.

Chapter III grows from sixteen typescript pages to twenty-six holograph leaves at this stage, and not all of its enlargement can be laid to new interior "voices." Lowry's particularizing is in full swing in this draft, creating domestic dialogue for the newly reunited couple, weaving in the motifs of the infernal machine (the lawn mower) and Oaxaca (the serape on Yvonne's bed), and unable to pass up such an invitation to exposition, expanding the address to Hugh to almost three pages. In an entirely new passage, Geoffrey recalls his and Yvonne's last night in Mexico City, and finding himself suddenly on the verge of tears, he is carried as much by "masochistic sentimentality" (22) as by desire into attempted lovemaking. Throughout the chapter Yvonne's tone holds some of the anger and edge of earlier incarnations; so now she lashes out, "'You maudlin, drunken, useless—'" while the Consul retires to the porch to contemplate with apparent impartiality glasses both of strychnine and of Johnny Walker ("Nacio 1820 y siguente tam campante" [sic]).

But this draft marks the beginning of Lowry's concern to dramatize the alcoholic consciousness from within, and Geoffrey's impartiality, he makes clear, is merely apparent. Thus at the end of the chapter he begins to sketch in the rationalization on the porch, which will become the brilliantly comic set piece of the Consul almost successfully persuading himself that he is still in control not only of his drinking but of his life. When he does take a drink of whisky, it is "almost absentmindedly, as if thus (he knew) to conceal the significance of the action from himself," a complex game of undeceived self-deception. The sound of Yvonne's weeping reminds him of her missing letters, and he persuades himself that it is for those she weeps, a maneuver that masks the recent sexual and emotional failure, but is ultimately just as productive of guilt, for which he knows but one remedy: "he took another sip of whisky." Immediately, his hallucination appears, this time taking the specific shape of "a dead man lying by his swimming pool, with a hat over its face." The apparition necessitates, of course, another drink, but since it is "only a double this time, 'I am tapering off,' he said, 'my hand is much steadier already. . . . I am not only much better, I am actually well,' he said, draining his glass." To prove it, he puts away bottle and glass, pours (but does not drink) strychnine, and arranges the container in a manner "better calculated to catch Hugh's attention." Having successfully convinced himself that "I am cutting the stuff out," he decides that unlike "that last time" he will not rush out to the Bella Vista but will remain and have "a hell of a good time" (25–26), a good time he inaugurates, in the chapter's final words, by falling asleep "with a crash."

Lowry will elaborate this final movement into a comic dance up and down the steps of alcoholic rationalization, but even in the first and simplest form here it is far more successful than the clashes over drinking between Yvonne and Geoffrey earlier in the chapter, querulous wranglings that manage only to trivialize both figures without illuminating either their relationship or the dynamics of the Consul's dipsomania. More moving and convincing than their "scenes" are oblique manifestations of Geoffrey's drinking, such strangely beautiful indices of alienation from the human and natural worlds as the opening of the chapter or the paragraph, new to this draft, where Yvonne and the Consul, their hands barely touching, look out together toward the volcanoes as if inhabitants of separate dreams, far away from an actual Mexico and each other.

Although, unlike III, Chapter V is not greatly expanded at this stage, Lowry's intention of rendering the various phases of alcoholic consciousness is as evident here as in the earlier chapter. Once again, the Consul's voices make their appearance in the chapter's opening paragraph, in a form very close to its final one, as he discovers himself on the move in his garden. Here the difference in tone and effect created from the alteration in point of view—and, indeed, stage of drink—can perhaps be best seen after a glance at the preceding version:[11]

> The Consul, still in his dress trousers, sauntered down the garden with his hands in his pockets, giving furtive glances, every now and then, over his shoulder. Just like this, he thought, William Blackstone must have left the Puritans in South Boston, to live among the Indians; just like this too, had not he himself, as a child in England, and with the same delicious feeling of escape, run away from his quarreling parents into the depths of the Rutlandshire woods? And then, of course, he recalled . . . there was always his poor, but magnificent, ornithologist friend who had once strolled off, and in his dress trousers too, into the wilds of New Guinea, never to return. (26:22, 133 ["1"])

The "sauntered" of this earlier version sets the leisurely tone for what follows. The Consul's thoughts here, the syntactically parallel structures tell us, are as controlled as his movements, the repeated "just like this," the rhetorical question, the casual "every now and then" or "And then, of course, he recalled," all seem to testify to a charmed sophistication (a "delicious feeling"), a pleased indulgence in recollection, even a boredom (the clichéd "poor, but magnificent" eccentric friend) that may be partly assumed but that provides as convincing a veneer to the prose as the Consul imagines he does to his invisible audience.

The new version, however, begins this way:

> The Consul, an inconceivable anguish of horripilating hangover thunderclapping about his skull, and accompanied by a protective screen of demons gnattering in his ears, was aware at last that in the now horrid event of being observed by his neighbours it could no longer be surmised he was merely sauntering, with some innocent horticultural object in view, down his garden. Nor even that he was sauntering. The Consul was almost running. He was also lurching. He tried to stop, without success, plunging his palpitant hands deeper into the sweat-soaked pockets of the dress trousers he had not yet changed. And now, rheumatisms discarded, he really was running. Might he not be suspected then of a more dramatic purpose, of having assumed the impatient buskin, of, for instance, a William Blackstone leaving the Puritans to dwell among the Indians, or the decisive mood of his friend Wilson at the moment of his abandoning the University expedition to plunge alone, also in a pair of dress trousers, into the jungles of New Guinea, never to return? No. (29:16, 1)

In "it could no longer be surmised he was merely sauntering," we catch the text in dialogue with its own earlier self: just when, after all, *might* one have "surmised" that Geoffrey's gait was a "saunter"? However, the replacement of the controlled stroll by the frantic lunge is in more than one sense only the exterior, although like everything else it points toward the heightened intensity and radical alteration of tone, that desperation simultaneously ghastly and comic that is at a far remove from the blasé sophistication of the earlier draft. Lowry's initial "inconceivable anguish of horripilating hangover thunderclapping about his skull" not only takes us immediately inside the Consul at a level beyond deliberate thought but furnishes that interior in a baroque decor, the very excesses of latinate alliteration and onomatopoeia implying the irony that becomes overt as the paragraph proceeds. Somewhere between the thundering hangover within and the exterior world of garden and neighbors buzzes that "protective screen of demons" who will have to "gnatter" at him the point of all this activity, for the Consul *in propria persona* does not know it. But then the Consul is not precisely *in propria persona*, the language of the passage now making explicit the self-dramatization, the trying on of roles, implied in the earlier version (as well as preparing for the *Macbeth* allusions later in the chapter). The comedy of the passage lies not in Geoffrey's pain and desperation, but in the pretensions of the adopted masks of Blackstone and "Wilson," for the Consul not only cannot fill such relatively dignified parts but must be informed by one of his "voices" just why he is out lurching through the underbrush at all. And the superficial sophistication of the dress trousers is now rather severely qualified by the "sweat-soaked pockets" into which he plunges "palpitant hands" in an unsuccessful attempt to arrest his convulsive progress. He is indeed, as one of his voices informs him, in a "deplorable . . . condition," a state to be alleviated only by the thoughtfully hidden tequila, toward which he "crashe[s] . . . through the metamorphoses of dying and reborn hallucinations, like a man who has been shot from behind."

Here at the chapter's start is its significant new "event," for there was no hidden bottle in previous drafts: the cool "saunter" was genuine, the glances over the shoulder merely a mild form of paranoia. Lowry's concern, however, was to render not just the Consul's drinking, but its effects. Thus, while Geoffrey seems outwardly to hurtle toward the tequila bottle, his voices enact a more complex dialectic of desire, justification, resolution, refusal, rationalization, and guilt—at which time, not surprisingly, the snake of previous drafts reappears. However, the tequila also has an immediate effect on his perception: "Gazing back up it after the tequila he did not think his garden seemed so ruined after all, such a chaos as it had appeared from the porch" (2). Indeed, in expounding a few moments later his proliferating theories of the Fall for Mr. Quincey's benefit, the Consul is aware of the source of his eloquence: "it was the tequila, this was tequila talk, he knew—nonsensical, subtly different from mescal talk, which tended to be only too much to the point" (5). When Quincey inquires after Laruelle, Geoffrey's disorientation produces the recognition that "the tequila was wearing off a little" (8). Later revisions will elaborate this alcoholic motif still further, until the tequila bottle will become the central point of reference in the opening section of the chapter.

As the Consul becomes here more visibly drunk and reprehensible, so Quincey is abruptly altered from the amiable (if xenophobic) neighbor of previous drafts into the curmudgeon familiar from the novel. Now Geoffrey's association of him with a censorious God leads smoothly into a streamlined presentation of his Eden theories, while Quincey gets supplied with a "cold" gaze and sardonic remarks about drunken hallucinations as well as direct exhortations ("cut it out") and advice ("see a doctor"). The last serves as cue for Vigil's entrance, which allows Lowry to reactivate the Consul's voices (*"You will not lie to us, we know what you did last night"*), but since an antialcoholic Quincey remains on the scene, Geoffrey for the first time "covers" for the doctor, as in the novel. Out of such dialogue emerges this passage:

> Suddenly it seemed to the Consul that the doctor, who had been regarding him with a real pity, had said, nodding at his dark glasses, something that sounded like 'macropsy y strabismus convergens' . . . simultaneously making a gesture as of snatching an insect out of the air before his eyes; yet so disconnected from the remark did this gesture appear, so unreal, it struck him that this encounter, this conversation might be occurring entirely in his imagination, that it was all part of a dream being dreamt by him on the porch which while now he heard himself repeating the word *'convergens'* became abruptly a nightmare: for it was as though the word convergens were expanding in his consciousness in such an abominable fashion as to [draw together] . . . the trees themselves, the volcanoes, even the maguey growing beyond the barranca like a battalion moving up a slope under machine gun fire. (29:16, [10–12]–13)

I have trimmed the original, and Lowry in the next draft will largely cut it, retaining only the paranoid lines in which nature becomes an attacking army (thereby updating the *Macbeth* allusions). Yet the importance of the passage is that it contains the germ of the next, more radical stage in Lowry's interiorizing of his novel, a stage beyond the "voices" developed in this draft, one that will sometimes even cut the cable that ties interior vision and exterior event. The "routine hallucination"—the dead man in the garden of III, for instance—had been a feature of the text since 1940, but that was identified at once *as* hallucination and thus clearly placed in the epistemological scheme. Now, Lowry begins more boldly to experiment with his subjective points of view, for here, momentarily, the entire scene loses its ontological base, what we have accepted as "real" becoming a dream dreamt by a dreamer situated elsewhere, which, possessing a dynamism of its own, takes on the power to menace the figure undergoing the experience, before the Consul makes "a tremendous effort to pull himself together." Chapter V itself will soon make a double use of the hints contained in this passage, opening with "a dream being dreamt by him on the porch" which turns into "a nightmare," and then, immediately after the moment described here, creating for the Consul a blackout that so disclocates the action as to leave its status hopelessly uncertain.

With the Consul's return to his own property, Lowry faced the portion of Chapter V that had always been the weakest, and expansion here—the episode that had previously accounted for one-third of the chapter now fills fully half—perhaps attests to his attempt to invest it with intensity and significance. But although there are noteworthy additions—Guanajuato for the first time appears a genuinely possible destination, the pool becomes the ambiguously Shakespearean "grave where buried love doth live," the "electric system" becomes also an "eclectic systemë" and a "mesh," the Consul recalls Vigil's remark about "insanes" and wonders if it applies to him—the insipidity of previous drafts remains. If Lowry was uncomfortable with this section, he had not found a way to minimize the trivia that may have seemed necessary to such a "social" encounter.

Chapter VII for the first time opens with the focus on Laruelle's house, where Lowry manages to work the term "latter-day churrigueresque" into his initial sentences. Meanwhile, the initial action on the staircase now acquires a dialogue it had not possessed heretofore:

"How far up to a drink, Jacques?" he asked without turning.
"Don't you think you've had about enough?"
"No."
"Don't you ever think about anything else?"
"Yes: that's why I want one," the Consul answered. (30:6, 1)

This apparently simple passage will continue to plague Lowry, for as the initial exchange between the two here it sets the tone for their confrontation later. The first try will not survive even this holograph (it was rewritten immediately), the Consul seeming too desperate-aggressive for this stage of events, Jacques too hectoring-omniscient; but it forecasts not only the tension between the men, but the difficulty Lowry has finding expression for it.[12]

A parallel difficulty afflicts a new scene between the Consul and Yvonne. Hugh dispatched with binoculars to the roof above, Yvonne and Geoffrey have their first moment alone since the debacle of the lovemaking in Chapter III. It is an important moment in establishing the appeal to that side of Geoffrey's conflict represented by Yvonne, and here Lowry does manage to make her a more sympathetic figure. She is given a convincing emotion and concern for the Consul, proposing that they "get away" from Laruelle's, asking for his "tenderness or love," establishing a clear motivation for her subsequent proposal for departure for the fair. The problem is in the handling of Geoffrey here. His initial shame and awkwardness over the morning's erotic failure is well enough, but this Consul retains a streak of snarling nastiness (as distinguished from outright fury or revulsion, or from sly, sardonic digs) that now surfaces with Yvonne ("Try and be tactful so long as you need me for something practical and immediate. Be polite!") as it had with Laruelle slightly earlier ("I'd be obliged if you'd get me a drink and shut up."). A moment later, as they embrace, the Consul mentions his heart, and to Yvonne's solicitous inquiry, responds, "Nothing. It broke just then, though, I think. . . . Clickety click like a lift stopping. Give it time, sweetheart, and it'll repair itself, I do believe" (30:6, 4), a bit of bathetic self-indulgence that, hard on the heels of the gratuitous sneer at her, makes Geoffrey simply repellent.

Emotionally, this scene on the porch is also played off against the ensuing, extant episode where the Consul, alone in Laruelle's room, wonders, "Was it here that he had been betrayed?" and bitter imagination now adds, "Was this the room that had been filled with her cries of love?" In counterpoint, Lowry inserts the rhapsody on the beauty of the Farolito that had first appeared in IX but had had to be housed elsewhere when that became Yvonne's chapter. The passage is almost unchanged from its 1940 form, but it is followed by an entirely new paragraph:

> Then his thoughts came abruptly back to Yvonne. Had he really forgotten her? Could he have been so callous as to forget her even

for a moment on this day of all days in his life which with some decent sane part of his mind he must have been longing for for months, praying for as his only hope? No, Yvonne was connected with it somehow, that was the queer part: somehow his love for her was connected with the Farolito. He looked round the room again. In just such rooms, just such studio couches, had they found their own love, not at first, not without difficulty, frustration, pain, weeping. But they had found themselves and it had been a triumph. And then all at once it had become too good, too much of a triumph, too good to lose, unimaginable to share, impossible finally to stand, a grief, and a pain, a mystery, a foreshadowing of the pain when he had lost her, deliberately she had betrayed him, and somehow all this too was connected with the Farolito. (30:6, 6)

Forerunner to the paragraph that will put the conundrum, "Could one be faithful to Yvonne and the Farolito both?" this curious passage attempts to answer, "Yes." Here, just before returning to the social scene (Laruelle is about to reappear with refreshments), Lowry seems to want to still the Consul's emotional pendulum—the present, loving Yvonne, the reminder of Yvonne's betrayal; the anguish of the suffering drinker, the calm beyond in the desired, beautiful cantina—by reconciling his two loves "somehow." It is a strained passage, but the central thread seems to go: out of pain had come love, yet that love was so surpassing as to bring the knowledge that it could not be sustained, which first produced pain once more in the anticipation of loss, and then created the loss itself, with its inevitable attendant pain. But uncertainties remain, questions bristle. "Unimaginable to share" with others, a love that so bonded as to deny them the larger world? Or (worse) "unimaginable to share" even with each other finally? "Impossible . . . to stand" because such ecstasy is unendurable for long? (And, if so, is this merely guilty rationalization?) Or "impossible . . . to stand" because of the recognition of the inevitability of its loss? "Mystery" in what sense? Are "he had lost her" and "she had betrayed him" two perspectives on a single event, or references to two separate actions?

One thing seems clear: "deliberately she had betrayed him" makes Yvonne the primary agent of their failure. We seem back in the Garden with a vengeance, "Eve-onne" the underminer of her blameless husband, responsible for the loss of bliss. It seems well from several points of view that Lowry rewrote the passage: even on the clean holograph draft of this stage, the "foreboding that it could not last" had turned Geoffrey's "steps into places like the Farolito," thereby acknowledging his share in their loss. "And now, could one begin over again, as though the Farolito had never been, or without it? Could one be faithful to the Farolito and to Yvonne both?" (30:7, 11). One of the benefits of rescuing the earlier, more complex version of the passage is to forestall too glib a "No" in answer to this last question.

Laruelle arrives with refreshments, sounding now ("Ei, ei, ei, ei, ei, ei") "not unlike the little postman" and (by process of association?) Geoffrey does the "strange thing" of slipping Yvonne's postcard under Jacques's pillow (30:6, 6). Here Lowry sharply abbreviated the social portion of what follows, but the quite different actions in the two surviving holographs of this stage reveal his uncertainty about how to handle the episode. First, the Consul drinks desperately, grabbing the bottle from the cocktail tray as Laruelle passes, and then participates with the others in general conversation. The result was stilted banality, however brief, and in the ensuing holograph references to Shelley and Tolstoy are restored from an earlier version, the foursome breaks down into two pairs (Geoffrey and Hugh, Yvonne and Jacques), while Geoffrey seems to do no more than hold his glass calmly as he and Hugh reminisce. It is not only action and dialogue that varies widely here; tone does too, depending on the Consul's state. First he is both desperate for a drink and snidely insinuating about the sexual "square" that the four constitute; then, apparently under both alcoholic and emotional control, relaxed, nostalgic, even avuncular.

With the departure of Hugh and Yvonne, we virtually reach the end of the 1941 survivals and must proceed in ignorance of what came immediately before.[13] However, despite the absence of earlier draftings, we can see that Lowry characteristically retained his essential structure from 1940 while gradually altering texture, adding density and detail. For instance, only in the "clean" holograph does Vigil telephone to repropose the trip to Guanajuato, and the Consul in turn wonders "suspiciously" how the doctor knew he was at Laruelle's at all, "'secret police'" automatically occurring to him (30:7, ms. 15). The horseman in the square is fully particularized—his almost speaking to them, added here, becomes part of the novel's growing pattern of missed communications—and, now that the date of his action has been fixed, Lowry becomes anxious about Spanish war headlines. The "Sangriente Combate" is first (once more) in "la Garcel Modelo" [sic], then in Barcelona; "Los Aviones" belong first to "el Gobierno" and bomb Salamanca, next are given to "los Rebeldes" and attack San Sebastian: a stickler for such accuracy, clearly he would need to look into this. Then, after all the other sights and sounds of the square, and in association with the singing horseman, comes the Consul's reaction to the panel of lovers on the merry-go-round, and he goes through a gamut of response that by the end of this stage will be almost the finished version of the novel itself. Here again is one of those the sudden appearances, almost full-blown, of a passage for which there is no anticipation whatever. What had begun as mere outward notation, the observation of crude illustrations on the carousel, becomes entirely internalized, an emotional ride that takes the Consul from loss to recovery to joy, from desire to hope to skepticism, from doubt to guilt to determination to impotence, until the outer scene again intrudes to become now a grindingly tumultuous and chaotic equivalent of a hopelessness that knows only one alleviation: "The Consul needed a drink"(30:7, ms. 20). This marvelous passage Lowry seems to have carried through as if in a single motion, an uninterrupted arc of prose. The ensuing episode, the scene with Jacques in the cafe, was another matter altogether.

In a very general way, it was always clear what this encounter was to be about: as the lover of Priscilla/Yvonne, Laruelle obviously stands as the Consul's rival and antagonist. But he is also representative of the "despised sober people, on which the balance of any human situation depends," whose set of challenges to the Consul thus operates on other levels as well. However, this broad purpose of confrontation and articulation of opposed viewpoints was little help in actually writing the scene: dialogue, as usual, proved difficult for Lowry. In the present drafts, the episode begins as before with Laruelle's questions of "why?" to Geoffrey, but adds the alcoholic heirarchy of the later text. When the Consul orders tequila, Jacques comments, "'When I start to drink that stuff you'll know I'm done for.'" Geoffrey, however, claims the tequila as part of his sobering-up program; it is only in drinking mescal again "'that you'll know *I'm* done for'" (30:6, 14; 30:7, ms. 21). But as the scene continues with Jacques warning that Yvonne will once again walk out on her drunken husband, an alternative line begins to get sketched.

First, the Consul asserts, "'Yvonne didn't leave me. I sent her away'" and goes on, "'What if I didn't want her? What if there was something I wanted more?'" The dialogue then develops this way:

> "Not just drink. Not tequila either. Mescal perhaps. But again, not mescal alone."
> "But you just said a minute ago if you ever started on mescal again I'd know you were done for."
> "Did I? Perhaps I didn't mean quite that. Perhaps I only meant that I'd know I was done for and that that was what I liked, not being done for, of course, but the feeling I was done for. However, I think I am misleading you." (30:7, ms. 23)

The exchange is one index of the difficulties Lowry had with this encounter: not only Jacques might be misled by claims at once explicit and evasive. Yet the passage serves as a useful reminder that both here and later Geoffrey's declarations of "finality" are not necessarily final.

But Geoffrey is not through. Rejecting Laruelle's sober world, he produces a grandiose image of his desire: "'the Anglo-Saxon longing for Valhalla, the prospect of an unlimited binge in blazes, without interference from people like you, that's a different thing again!'" Although Jacques repeats the possibility of a certain "clarity" in the Consul's vision—giving Marlowe ("your Faust man") as an alternative source to Jonson and locating the battle on "'his big toenail'"—his voice comes round once more to the "unnecessary" nature of Geoffrey's suffering and to his affair with Yvonne as a mere excuse for "'drowning your sorrows'" (now adding, "I can see the writing on the wall"). The arguments begin to sound familiar to the Consul: "'But haven't I just told you all that myself? Hullo.' The Consul sat up with a start. Laruelle wasn't there at all. He must have gone some time ago and he'd been talking to himself" (30:7, ms. 26).

"Some time ago" is sufficiently elastic to invite us to see an indeterminate part of this dialogue as internal, with "Laruelle" serving as *doppelgänger*, the articulator of arguments Geoffrey has put to himself more than once. Yet this is also the first time a "hole" has appeared explicitly in Lowry's text, an emptiness in the exterior world brought about by a character's consciousness shutting it out. The opposite motion, the "overfilling" of the outer world, we have seen as early as

Geoffrey's hallucination of the dead man in his garden. Here, Laruelle is "subtracted" from his apparent presence at the table, a piece of trompe l'oeil we discover only as the Consul does. In both motions, of course, it is an inner deracination that "distorts" the exterior, and thus it is almost inevitable that the first examples are found in the alcoholic consciousness of the Consul. They will not, however, be limited to him, nor even to Lowry's characters: we readers have no more exact notion of when Laruelle disappeared from the cafe than Geoffrey does. The aporia remains.

The remainder of this stage of Chapter VII contains a number of individual additions and alterations, but no major departures. The closed British consulate gets passed, the Consul's attitude toward the begging children is altered from Scrooge-like to cautiously ineffectual, Lowry worries over whether or not to supply him with a passport, mescal in El Bosque is pointedly refused in favor of tequila, and the parting from Señora Gregorio, fraught with emotion, is given an explicit source in his momentary sense that "he was looking at his mother" (30:6, 23). In the final paragraph Señor Bustamente is added to the passing Dr. Vigil and Mr. Quincey as the Consul prepares to exit the cantina, a powerful reinforcement to his paranoiac sense that they are concerned about "what could be done with him" (30:7, ts. 39). Here, precisely at the midpoint of the Consul's day, Bustamente forms a link between the opening chapter—where by now he is a significant presence in the cervecería—and that final chapter in another cantina where natives will also seek "opinions" about the Consul and where his fears will become thoroughly justified.

Chapter XII was certainly revised at this time (probably 1942), for it bears the tell-tale signs of this stage of composition.[14] There seems nothing remarkable in this, until we realize that this was the final full-scale rewriting this climactic chapter would get. As with Chapter VII, Lowry was not easily satisfied—there are a "dirty" and a "clean" holograph as well as a typescript—but measured against what the rest of the text still was to pass through, the last is first, XII once again shows itself the bellwether chapter, embodying a standard, a richness of vision and brilliance of rendering, toward which the rest of the novel had to aspire.

In one respect, this Chapter XII bears typical marks of other revisions done in this phase: it alters the previous opening to skip over linking material (which, if reused at all, enters later as description or recollection) and begin dramatically. To echo the proposed start of Chapter X, XII too was to begin with the order of mescal, necessarily placing the Consul within the Farolito, a position he had previously achieved only some half-dozen pages into the action. Part of the effect is to recall our first view of the Consul in another bar with another bartender (Chapter II); the comparison is instructive. Next, the Consul was to observe the square that had previously been described as he made his unsteady way across it; now, he simply views it from the doorway of the cantina. Then was to come the return of A Few Fleas and the Consul's renewed attention to matters within the Farolito, followed by a return to the doorway and the square, followed by the entrance of Diosdado and action within the cantina, and so on. Lowry, in short, is setting up a deliberate rhythm of withdrawal and return that becomes more complex and less mechanical as revisions proceed. Initial alternations will be significantly complicated by movements that carry the Consul further into the labyrinthine Farolito, but they will nonetheless hold and take on a particular significance once the sinister "chiefs" arrive: Geoffrey will more than once recognize that doorway as the portal of release, but he will only be able to use it as a release into death.

As the chapter now opens in the empty Farolito, the sounds the Consul had heard while plunging through the jungle in 1940 are made part of his consciousness in Parián, and the incremental associative process by which Lowry often worked becomes especially clear, gradually creating a rich auditory fugue. First come "the voices in argument" from the Salón Ofélia; then, "a wailing of distress: Borracho, Borrachero, Borrracho." (31:12, 1). Then, the clean holograph adds the sound of a voice "like Yvonne's, pleading," and the pervasive "ticking" first heard in another cantina, El Bosque, now sets the tone ("the ticking of his watch, his heart, his conscience, a clock somewhere"), followed by the sinister sound "of subterranean collapse." Lowry having by this time created in the deserted barroom a dissonant prelude to the rich cacophony to come, all of "the voices" are stilled by the drinking of "two large mescals."

One aim of this set of revisions was the simple one of clarification. A marginal note on the opening description of the interior of the Farolito reads, "Get very clear in my and the reader's mind," and as Lowry moves on now to the description of the town square, directives like "to the left" and "to the right" designate precise placements. But clarity involves more than description. The matter of the Consul's payment for these first drinks, which in all versions of XII is one of the accusations later made against him, is a case in point. In 1940 the Consul had several unspecified monetary transactions with A Few Fleas, with the prostitute, with Diosdado, and vague as all these transactions were, they made the charges of the "chiefs" seem entirely trumped up. Now, however, matters become more complicated—and more precise. The clean manuscript, like the novel, presents the double action of the Consul at first recovering no change (as in 1940), then a moment later seeing all his money on the counter and pocketing it, thereby reversing the economic situation—and laying plausible ground for the later accusations. At the same time, he now feels he must stay here "for Yvonne's sake," although he does not know exactly why (27:17, 4-5). Clarity in one area gives way to mystery in another, but mystery is not vagueness.

At the same time, Lowry is at work in other ways to tie in more closely these early sections of the chapter with those that come later. The Consul's nightmare vision of "unearthly animals" had in 1940 no correlative in the exterior world. Now, when he opens his eyes, in the dirty holograph an afterthought inserts "someone leading a horse," and by the typescript that "someone" "looked like a policeman" (31:12, 4; 27:17, 6). In a more extensive addition, where previously the Consul had immediately taken Yvonne's recovered letters into an inner room, from the clean copy onward he pauses to cite Racine and then trace in "spilled liquor" a nostalgic map of Spain, where he and Yvonne had first met. "[H]is Spanish failing him," he tries to relate this romantic connection to the Mexican bartender in English. But we are already within the Tower of Babel, and to Diosdado, "Granada" signifies political rather than sentimental concerns, the violent divisions of the present, not the loving embraces of the past. It is Geoffrey's single public affirmation of Yvonne and her importance to him—and the cost is his life. That is the price of his indifference to politics: he seems entirely oblivious to the implications of Diosdado's "different, harder pronunciation" of the simple place name "Granada." It is the stroke whereby Lowry creates for the Consul that connection to the "wrong" (Republican) side in Spain that, seemingly confirmed by Hugh's anarchist card, gives point to the charge of "'Bolsheviko'" that had been hurled at him since 1940, and helps seal his fate.

Originally, Lowry had followed the Consul's reading of his wife's letters with the solicitation of the whore, María, the ensuing sexual encounter being nasty, brutish, and short, occupying a paragraph of less than half a page. This juxtaposition (involving his discarding of the letters) acted as an immediately effective rejection of the wife's appeal, but the current drafts pick up on the subtler matter of the expressed desire for children and, in the alternating rhythms now established, return the Consul to the cantina doorway, where indeed he observes a tableau of the possibilities of ordinary domestic life: "How happy, how far too happy they [the Mexican family] were. This was Mexico too, out there, not in the Farolito. He hated to look at it, at their happiness" (27:17, 13). Much of this will be cut (Lowry acknowledging the patness of the scene at just this point by calling the family "unlikely"), but it does establish the continued presence of the anti-Farolito pole in Geoffrey. As a result, "Miserably he wanted her [Yvonne] and did not want her," out of which divided state, now, comes the voice of the young prostitute.

Previously, the encounter with María had only symbolic value. In 1940 Priscilla was of course long gone, and in 1941, with his diatribe at the Salón Ofélia, the Consul had effectively turned Yvonne over to Hugh. Now, while in one sense the Consul realizes that the act is "the final unprophylactic stupid rejection" of Yvonne, in another it seems to allow him a reconciliation of that divided self that both does and does not want her. Whereas the first notations had sketched the girl as a grotesque, second thoughts produced her (wishful?) uncanny resemblance to Yvonne: "lightning silhouetted Yvonne's face curiously like Yvonne's [sic]. Her body was curiously like Yvonne's too, he thought, the feel of her, her heart, the passionate breaking heart of her" (31:13, ms. "Thunder blew the door open").

María's room too becomes for Geoffrey an elaborate mnemonic. At first it seems to recall, again, Yvonne and their love: "It was like one of the many curious rooms in which Yvonne and he had once slept happily and slept better for their curiousness." What Lowry shows us, however, is something altogether more sinister. Whereas previously it had been simply a somewhat grimy room "at the back" of the cantina, now it is more portentously approached: María leads the Consul through the labyrinthine public rooms "which got smaller and smaller and darker and darker, until by the mingitorio" a "lightless annex" threateningly contains two faceless figures "drinking or plotting," a framing of lust by filth and retribution, disgust and fear, which recall Yvonne only by contrast. The patio they must cross resembles "the El Popo where he had thought of going [and where Yvonne and Hugh are at this moment looking for him], only more sinister, the obverse of it." Then, María's room takes on another, similarly skewed appropriateness: it seems to Geoffrey to resemble "a student's room," is even "like his own room at college," and on top of a bookcase lies "a Spanish History of British India at the time of Warren Hastings. He thought he caught the word Kashmir and started."[15] In the corner stands "a gigantic sabre" (which, briefly, he will identify with "Excalibur"). "This is a nightmare at once flashed through his mind, then, I am dead," but he realizes he is "in that world which obeys different stranger laws to those men know," a hint of the occult that will not survive even to the fair copy. As the copulation begins, "Yvonne's face was going" (Texas XII, 13), and Geoffrey, as before, focuses his attention on the calendar turned to the coming month of December.

Now, however, as Lowry expands the incident, the calendar acquires an illustration, "a picture of some place in Canada ... the moon rising over the rocks, a coracle pointing at the moon, the risen madness, the stag in moonlight, British Columbia, he thought" (31:13, ms. "Thunder blew the door open"). It is a note the Consul will return to, but first Lowry takes him into the mingitorio, previously unoccupied. Now it is full of voices: those of the Consul, which "hissed and shrieked, yammered at him from the walls," and that of another occupant, seated, who speaks also, from both orifices, the pimp-stool pigeon. It is the Consul's recollection of the pimp's "'Half past sick by the cock'" on the return yet again to the doorway of the Farolito that merges with the calendar picture to produce the new memory of the incident "in Canada, on cold Pineaus Lake" of the search, with rooster, for a drowned Lithuanian. The entire passage, leading up to Geoffrey's own positing (and rejecting) the possibility of new life in Canada is through these drafts worked to almost its final form, the folk belief of the cock crow and the drowned body recalling texts from the New Testament to *Hamlet, Huckleberry Finn* to *The Waste Land*.[16] Even ignoring the phallic pun, the Consul's recollection is neither the first nor last appearance of a cock in the text, a fowl rendered no less ambiguous by this addition.

With his postcoital "gruesome gaiety" (and despite another voice that denies the genuineness of his supposed "feelings" of lively despair), Geoffrey carries this "mischievousness" into his recognition of the horse tethered to the nearby tree. The untying of the bridle, the policeman's abrupt interruption, the Consul's "explanation of this afternoon's events" are all familiar from previous drafts. What is new is a rendering of that "explanation," but careful phrasing makes clear that the narrator neither endorses nor denies the reconstruction now offered, for the Consul's conviction arises "out of some correspondence between the subnormal world and the abnormally suspicious delirious one within him" rather than from hard evidence. Further, in a passage later excised, his very certainty is "already receding, growing vague, confused, disappearing into the Farolito or the forest" in his mescal-driven mind (27:17, 17 ["22"]; cf. Pottinger, "Consul's 'Murder'").

The entrance here of the first of the "chiefs" reminds Lowry again of the need for clarification. Previously the three "chaotic villains" (31:12, 9) had been dressed in similar, "replendent" uniforms and had interchangeable sinister-jocular speech and mannerisms. Now the careful distinction of the Jefe de Jardineros from his two underlings marks the difference with grim clarity: the blustering henchmen resemble grotesque twins, the "silent" and "sombre" man in tweeds, Lowry reminds himself, "just stands there, he is the *deus ex machina*" (31:12, 20). That sombreness, too, helps change the tone of the proceedings, which at first seemed to Lowry "Too cheery" (31:12, 10), and he is at pains to darken it, to show the laughter as mocking, aggressive, contemptuous rather than playful or pleasant, and to remove such whimsy as the Consul's self-identification as a Jew ("He had lost his identity: why should he not be a Jew?") as too light, too frivolous, for the context he was now creating.

Lowry's darkening has the example of Kafka behind it as he now delays identification of these sinister figures ("who were these people, really?") and provides the third "chief" the grimly distinctive feature of missing the "trigger finger" and thumb of his right hand. The repeated "catechism" of the Consul's national identity (ironic for a former diplomat) is made insistent, badgering, until it reaches through the fractured

English of the "chiefs" (a malign echo of Vigil's in Chapter I) to an existential level, a questioning of his right to be, or of the purposes of mankind: "'Why ah are you? ... What ah are you for?'" In contrast, at this moment the accusers identify *themselves* for the first time, and then, mockingly, the Consul as well:

> "That man is Chef [*sic*] de Jardineros ... I am chief too, I am Chief of Rostrums...."
> "And I—" began the Consul.
> "Am *perfectamente* borracho," finished the first policeman, and everyone roared. (27:17, 22 ["27"])

The final line is good enough that it will be given, in a different spirit, directly to Vigil in Chapters I and V; here it is imposed contemptuously on a figure who seems to have surrendered all other identity, to have become nothing but "borracho," a sense apparently confirmed when the Consul can only repeat helplessly, "'Y yo—,'" a self-avowal that hangs incomplete, undefined. The judgment appears underlined when the Consul recognizes in the "black" look of the Chief of Gardens (who in this draft acquires the name "Sanabria," a "health" presumably opposed to drunkenness) "the image of himself when ... he had assumed the Vice Consulship in Granada," as if a younger incarnation from a Granada already in the hands of the enemy has arrived to condemn him.

The open doorway that Geoffrey has so frequently visited in this revision now acquires narrative point. In the ensuing activity, suddenly, for the first time, he realizes that he might leave the Farolito freely, "yet he made no move." Apparent choices are being kept open—this is not the last time he will be aware of the possibility of escape—which work against any simple sense of the Consul as victim. Lowry himself seems in his vacillations on these manuscripts to mirror his protagonist's hesitations. If Geoffrey's contemplation of the wings on his "Alas" package momentarily permits an upsurge of hope in the dirty holograph—"Was it really too late? What was he thinking of? Wasn't he still alive, a man? Hadn't Yvonne come back? He could end all this—he would go find Yvonne now—he would change his life" (31:12, 12)—by the clean copy Lowry gives him only a gaze around the cantina before a "black dog" seems to weigh him down.

The "Babel" that ensues is hardly altered from its first appearance in 1940: surrounding descriptions and circumstances may be altered, but the dialogue persists almost exactly throughout the drafts. At times Lowry will *cut* a phrase or even a sentence; rarely does he *change* the expression of these voices. Major characters, being "his own," may speak very different things and indeed in quite different manners as he writes and rewrites, but the dialogue of minor figures, often based on actual conversations Lowry claimed to have overheard (Bowker, *Pursued by Furies* 212), are treated with an almost superstitious regard, as "givens" from the world beyond imagination, more closely allied in his mind to posters, menus, telegrams, and newspapers than to the speech of other characters. For instance, the figure most readily recognized from his refrain—"'Mozart was the man what writ the Bible'"—began as "a sailor . . . [who] had deserted his ship at Bellize, British Honduras [*sic*]," to which Lowry adds in pencil after 1940, "a Canadian" (27:5, 389). By the fair holograph of the present stage, he has become "of uncertain nationality" but has "walked here through Yucatan" after deserting ship (27:17, 28 ["33"]). Meanwhile, what he *says* changes almost not at all. The most notable alteration is the excision of a comment that perhaps seemed almost too "sensible" for this man of "awful mind." He claims, "'I would dispute my comprehensible stuff,'" which, in a sense, his author has done for him by deleting an almost-intelligible sentence. Otherwise, however, the only change here is that "comprehensible" flips to "incomprehensible" in the fair holograph, and then to the "imcomprehensible" of the final script, which, if a typo, was allowed to stand, form reflecting meaning: the character is identified as "illiterate," after all.

There are small, if significant, new strains in the voices at this stage—the radio's questions receive their negative response; *"Mar Cantabrico"* appears as if out of the air—but after 1941, the largest such addition was Yvonne's voice. With the expungement of the German silver miner, most of the passages from her recovered letters now participate in the larger, more complex counterpoint of the final "Babel" as the Consul begins once more to read from them. *These* Lowry was not slow to alter, adding, cutting, rephrasing. For instance, by the clean holograph, the letters will make clear that Yvonne literally does not know where Geoffrey is, a far stronger argument for her absence than the vague and unexplained "I cannot come to you yet" of the dirty manuscript; and the crude "If you let anything happen to yourself you will be a murderer for you will have murdered me" becomes "If you let anything happen to yourself you will be harming my flesh and mind" (cf. 31:12, 16 and 27:17, 32–33 ["37"-"38"]). Reordering and refining, Lowry made Yvonne's voice a poignant cry amid the babel, and her final word in the novel, in echo of A Few Fleas (who is articulating the plea of a comicbook character) and of the Consul himself, now becomes the broken appeal of "'Save–'" (31:12, 16).

Although Yvonne's "voice" ceases, her role (like Hugh's) in this final episode is far from done. A search of the Consul now reveals Hugh's telegram and (in a late reminder on the dirty manuscript) his Spanish anarchist card as well as Yvonne's letters, so that from this stage onward it is not the Consul's own passport but Hugh and Yvonne's "paper" testimony that reveals Geoffrey as not Blackstone (as he claims in all versions), but "Firmin"—whether "Hugo" or "Geoffrey" seems not to matter—and thus a suspicious liar. The "evidence" of the telegram, which neither Geoffrey nor the chiefs can truly read but which does contain the word "jews," lends plausibility to their charge of "Juden," an identification that in earlier versions was simply unmotivated anti-Semitism. At last stung into motion, the Consul pauses only when the noise of the rabbit suggests "Yvonne and Hugh, perhaps, at last"–a false hope, of course, ironic counterpart to their unwitting paper betrayal, but a hope nonetheless, an indication again of that side of the Consul which refuses to reject "amar," which continues to reach out to human attachment.

In the ensuing chaotic action, once again Lowry is largely concerned with clarification and streamlining. The bird that seems to flap before his face had once been the parrot of the now-expunged apocalyptic joke; it gradually gives place to the more resonant cock, which has played such a large part in the preceding chapter. The Consul's accusing speech is much reduced in length and detail—"This should be better + much shorter + controlled," Lowry had noted ("D," 399)—and overt economic and political implications of the incident are excised altogether. (Nonetheless, as before, the Consul's plausible series of associations, which replaces "France" with "Don Quixote," reaches a pointed and specific climax: "You stole that horse.") The horse's gain in specificity is altogether a triumph of vividness (WHAT IS NOT VIVID IS

NOT REPRESENTED). Using numbers 1 to 5, Lowry rearranged a random listing of details to carry the Consul's eye from front ("the corded mouth") to rear ("the rump"), coming to rest on "the stud behind the buckle" that now is "glittering like a jewel in the light from the cantina" (31:13, ms. E). Finally, whereas in 1940 one shot had been enough to finish the Consul, now three are fired, the second two "spaced, deliberate": we are to be left in no doubt that this is an execution.

Lowry had in the meantime reassessed the religiosity of the 1940 ending. Although the Consul adds a pious/blasphemous "Christ" to his final speech, the explicit Christian references of the earlier version (water of life, St. Dismas) disappear (31:12, 22). The overall result is a more naturalistically rendered climax, where the suggestion of merciful water is carried through an added "It was raining softly," which permits a religious reading without insisting on one. And for the first time, the "'Compañero'" of the old fiddler, which can resonate on several levels, makes its appearance. As a consequence, to the Consul's reflections on his identity with the pelado, which persists with only minor changes through the drafts, now are added his responses to the opposing address of brotherhood, which makes him "happy." Astonishingly, the presentation of sounds that follows persists with hardly the change of a word from 1940 onward, even when "what sounded like the cries of love" are no longer Yvonne's ecstasy, but her death. (The notation "how alike are the groans of love to those of the dying" for Geoffrey's own deathlike act of "love" here in XII will be added later and presumably as a result of these "cries," which do double duty for both).

Nor does Lowry make many alterations in the long visionary passage of Geoffrey's mountainous ascent and fall. Kashmir, at the start of this stunning paragraph, draws together the beginning and end of Geoffrey's life, uniting him with his father, superimposing Himavat on Popocatepetl, "Atlantis" reborn in this final vision, the two halves of the world for a moment reunited. The Consul is relieved of "the original manuscript of *War and Peace*," the ambulance ride to the top modified, the rhythm and phrasing of the apocalyptic "falling" of the last several lines reworked. And with the removal of the garden notice from the mountain top and the firm fixture of the sign itself—not merely its words, but a pictograph of the signboard and its support as well, so that we the readers were to witness it *as* a sign, a warning, just as Geoffrey had—Chapter XII, and the novel, ended.

There were still some revisions and additions to come on this chapter, but what is most amazing is not how much rewriting Lowry did on it, but how little. Chapter XII is far and away the chapter that from 1940 on is closest to its final form—Chapter X is a distant second—and the single set of revisions, described here in some detail, comes close to exhausting the changes made. Yet the chapter is from 1940 a sustained performance, a brilliant close to the sequence of chapters, which, "behind" it, as it were, would undergo repeated alteration, sometimes drastically so: few would, I think, dispute Lowry's boast to Jonathan Cape that it is "definitely the best of the lot" (*Letters* 84). One might argue that the repeated alterations and revisions of the rest of the book were in fact a determined effort on Lowry's part to produce a novel worthy of its climactic chapter, an attempt to discover through its creation just what character, what action, what fictional world could have produced the appalling and beautiful vision of its final pages.

III

The new version of Chapter VIII (30:10) might be said to mark the end of a phase: it is the last of the drafts in which "Chapultepec" rather than "Tomalín" is the destination of the afternoon excursion.[17] On the other hand, it also marks a beginning: it contains the first appearance of the "Ebro motif" so closely associated with Hugh, perhaps the most evident historical fruit of the new specificity in the drafts. Lowry had done his homework on the Spanish Civil War: as surviving notes show (Templeton 1:11) he relied on Henry Buckley's 1940 *Life and Death of the Spanish Republic* for virtually all his information. As in the published novel, Hugh first thinks of the impending loss of the battle in the prescient prediction (for one who has only "smell[ed] the headlines of the unbought papers") that "it would now be a matter of days before Modesto withdrew altogether" (30:10, ms. 1). He goes on to imagine his friend "Jack" as a participant "if he'd not been already evacuated or killed, [at] the railway bridge at Mora de Ebro ... or was it in the news to-day they'd already lost it?"[18] If this reference is almost anachronistically up-to-date, Hugh's recalling of "old Colonel Kopic" is, even to himself, perplexingly old hat. "Why Colonel Kopic? Hugh thought: he'd been withdrawn from the XVth Brigade in June, before the Ebro show began.... This was November, not June. This was indeed perhaps, only too specifically, one's last November" (ms. 3). The ominous final sentence reveals that Lowry has already determined on Hugh's dangerous sailing on the *Noemijolea* which appears in the new draft of IV, but that sheds no light on "old Colonel Kopic."[19] Perhaps Lowry intended through him to develop an analogue to his own characters; if so, he must have found the parallel too convoluted even for his practice: the reference disappears.

The first "new" material encountered is in fact not new to the manuscripts at all. Rescued out of the discarded device of Laruelle's dream in the 1940 Chapter I (*1940* 39), the bus driver and his "two beautiful tame white pigeons" now open this aviary of a chapter. Here, however, they become a part of Lowry's counterpoint, "little secret ambassadors of peace, of love" doubtfully established against the sinister xopilotes of the chapter's end and, more ambiguously, the submissive poultry within the bus (also politicized here, recalling Munich and Chamberlain) as well as the literal diplomats who later pass by the fallen Indian on the other side. In this context, the birds' coats shining "as if with fresh white paint" seem to echo the note of deception struck at the start of the previous chapter (Laruelle's house appearing "camouflaged"), and they now anticipate yet another bird, the parrot outside the undertaker's, reminiscent of the Consul's apocalyptic comic story cut from V but nonetheless persisting here in Hugh's mental summary.

Like the "painted" pigeons, this draft quickly establishes a prevailing tone of superficial pleasantness and amiability: even the Consul seems "in a good mood," now producing his "quod semper, quod ubique, quod ab omnibus" pun (ms. 5). Just beneath those surfaces, however, lurks the potential for disorder, violence, and death. Unstrung by his guilty passion for Yvonne, and now also by his guilty awareness of the combat in Spain (thus the "idiotic false premise" that equates the loss of Yvonne with the loss of the Ebro, emotionally sound if logically absurd), Hugh vacillates between benign possibilities he cannot quite believe in and sinister implications he will not fully face. As a result, "Probably it would be a sound idea . . . to get roaring drunk oneself" (ms. 8).

At El Amor de los Amores (translated here by Hugh as "the Love of Love") the Spanish motif is extended by the Consul's whispered, "'Viva Franco . . . in there'" (ms. 6). Reflections on the pelado, now given to Hugh, become inescapably political in nature. Recognizing, as he believes, the "Spanish" features and hands of the *conquistador,* Hugh evolves the "neat idea" that this stranger represents "[the] confusion [that] eventually tends to overtake *conquistadores.*" Along with such ideological theorizing comes its opposite, a more concrete presentation of the man's apparel: "blue suit . . . of quite expensive cut—the open coat shaped at the waist, the broad-cuffed trousers draped well over pointed brown expensive American shoes" (ms. 7). If he is to serve as a political symbol, even a dubious one, he must be given convincing, concrete physical existence.

Landscape too is fleshed out, sometimes indeed created, in its double role as setting and objective correlative. The railway station, previously unmentioned, appears "closed like a book," and Hugh thinks of the actual book, London's *Valley of the Moon,* that he might have brought with him. To the Indian women the Ebro too had been "a closed book": a variety of unopened books seems ironically appropriate to Hugh. Suddenly he wonders if perhaps he might *not* depart that night, as he had originally intended, a possibility suggested by his "glimpse of the country over which he and Yvonne had ridden that morning. It looked, from the bus, dead, dead as the land between Murcia and Almeria in Spain," and a moment later, "Away to the left, sinister emblem of sacrificial hearts," a pyramid comes into view. As they go on, he realizes, "The country wasn't really dead, he had only wanted it to be" (ms. 8), an acknowledgment of landscape as projection that here exposes his guilty desires; for as he has recognized, only "something calamitous" could prevent his departure this night, and if so, the "sacrificial heart" will not be his own.

Yet it is not long before the bus (now a 1918 Chevrolet) does indeed pass through a countryside that gives unmistakable testimony "quite as Prescott informed him . . . to Popocatapetl's presence and antiquity" and leads Hugh into a meditation on the causes of volcanic eruptions. This too, of course, is landscape as objective correlative, but now (as the naming of Prescott suggests) not as personal projection—Hugh's account smacks of the encyclopedia—but as expressive of explosive forces deep within the individual and collective self that everywhere and in every period proclaim their power but that remain beyond explanation, as "mysterious" as the action of the literal volcano. The counterpart of Yvonne's reflections on volcanic action in Chapter II's "La Despedida," Hugh's reflections here also lead to a sense of inevitability: "All one could say for certain was that there always had been and always would be volcanic eruptions" (ms. 10). The symbolic victims of such violence appear in the "passive" poultry, bound and apparently acquiescing in their fate, that Hugh imagines as aware of the warning over the windscreen: "*Su salvara estara a salvo no escapiendo en el interior de esta vehiculo* [*sic*] [For your safety, no spitting inside this vehicle].... Obviously those pullets knew it" (ms. 10A).

His mood seems to shift like the double aspect of the Day of the Dead. First the speeding camión creates a sense of "gaiety" and "fiesta": "[a] quite different atmosphere now pervaded the little bus," and under its influence "Hugh forgot the women in mourning and the pelado as they rolled and banged along." But this changes as the boys drop off, the landscape alters, and the burned church comes into view with "an air of being damned."[20] Quite unanticipated is the fantasy this church now gives rise to:

> Hugh ... saw the church burning and himself, figuratively, rescuing Christ from the interior. The time has come for you to join your comrades, to aid the workers, he told Christ, who agreed. It had been his idea all the time only those hypocrites had kept him shut up inside where he couldn't breathe. Hugh made a speech. Stalin gave him a medal and listened sympathetically while he explained what was on his mind. 'True, I wasn't in time to save the Ebro, but I did strike my blow—' He went off, the star of Lenin on his lapel: in his pocket, a certificate: Hero of the Soviet Republic—pride and love in his heart. God, what a shatterpated self-dramatising bastard you are: Hugh came to his senses. But the queer thing was that love was real.—Christ, why can't we be simple, he wondered, not knowing quite how his thoughts had got into this order, Christ Jesus why may we not be good, why may we not all be brothers, what is eating the heart out of this corrupt stinking hypocritical world? (ms. 13)[21]

Hugh may not know "how his thoughts had got into this order," but in fact that order is a typical one for him (and often for his creator): the quasi-dialectical structure of initial statement of desire, ironic reaction against one's own "simplicity," and modified restatement of a core of "truth" in the original desire. The fantasy may be "shatterpated," the longing for brotherhood is nonetheless genuine. As to the question of "why not?" Hugh might begin an answer with his own "self-dramatising" and its confession of hypocrisy.

As the narrative reaches the fallen Indian, Lowry's most evident concern (managed with only partial success) is to effect a separation between the argument among the passengers at large and the echoing one held by Geoffrey and Hugh. However, when "the discussion began to take a political turn," Cárdenas's agrarian reforms enter the manuscripts for the first time: "It had been suggested the man was a messenger for a Credit Bank that financed village enterprise under a progressive agrarian law and that he had been waylaid by enemies of the Cardenás [sic] government. But the man didn't look to him like a bank messenger any more than the horse now—one supposed—looked like a bank messenger's horse" (ms. 23) In ensuing dialogue, the significant clue of the saddlebags is established, and the political focus is held by the approach of "three smiling vigilantes," identified by Geoffrey as "'not the real police, only the people I told you about,'" referring to their conversation in VI.

The two new strains here, both of them specific and political—the particularities of the war in Spain and the struggle in Mexico over agrarian reforms—develop out of the encoded telegram that opens Chapter IV, a telegram drawing connections between the European and Mexican political situations that the reader, much like Yvonne in that chapter, would not grasp without further exposition. Lowry himself would have to work up enough information to be able at least to hint darkly at sinister connections, but the Ebro and the Ejido give to the novel a political particularity in time and place respectively which will be extended and elaborated in ensuing drafts. Indeed, "Ejido" itself will be one of the extensions, for although it is pencilled in the margin of the preceding draft (30:9, 4), the word gets used nowhere in this one.

Out of the confusion on the road comes now the only word the dying rider will speak, a "muttered or groaned" "'Compañero'" that extends the political connection between Spain and Mexico (it was the term of salute of Spanish Loyalists) while, of course, in the context of Lowry's Samaritan parable not limited to that significance. On any level, it is both plea and recognition, demanding response; it gets none as, with the onset of the "policemen," the incident is rapidly closed. Hugh struggles until shoved onto the bus, and Yvonne grotesquely reappears to seal this semicomic fiasco with a petulant, "'For heaven's sake, you men, will you stop all this and come back,'" a demand she underlines by "stamp[ing] her foot." Hugh's shame and subsequent reflections on the other passengers and the fate of "tragedy" in Mexico are taken over from Yvonne in previous drafts, but he now adds more personal reasons for self-condemnation: "While as for him, the hero of the Soviet Republic, what of him, old camarado, old companero—companero, he thought, and hid that thought—who was losing the Battle of the Ebro, was he the villain? Not a bit of it. He'd been right in there fighting," but the "fighting" had been ineffectual.

As his attention returns to the exterior world, the gap between Hugh's private guilt and frustration and his surroundings is forced wide. Lowry reprises the "holiday" air of festivity on the bus, adding fare takers who cavort "clownishly" and perform energetic antics while the wasteland dust ("a soft invasion of dissolution") continues to "fill" the scene. In this bizarre theatrical context Lowry sets the discovery of the pelado's own performance ("grinning round at the preoccupied passengers as if he expected some comment would be made upon his cleverness"): his theft of the dying man's money. The parallel with Orlac and Cortez is underlined ("smeared conquistador's hands"), Hugh and Geoffrey comment rather limply, and the chapter is rapidly brought to a close as the pelado enters the Todos Contentos in the company of the driver and his friend, a threesome ominously paralleling the expatriate trio left watching them "in the dust."

Given these developments in VIII, it seems at first odd that Lowry's treatment of Chapter VI at this stage (30:2) should initially result in further reduction. Now, however, he acted on his self-direction to begin with the shaving episode, ignoring altogether Hugh's interior soliloquy with which the chapter had opened since 1940. Initial pages of the previous draft (30:1) are full of marginal doubt and dissatisfaction about the brief meditation there; perhaps Lowry toyed with the possibility of relieving his man-of-action of some of the burden of consciousness. He may also have weighed whether the reduction or elimination of the soliloquy would make Chapter VI counterpoint more powerfully the highly interiorized consular Chapters V and VII that surround it. At any rate, the new draft opens precisely with the words that follow the pencilled line and direction "Begin here" in 30:1: Hugh's jocular-sinister "'Sure. I'll give you the works'" delivered to a shaking Geoffrey ineffectually trying to lather his shaving brush. Once more a chapter was to open on a dramatic and tonally appropriate note, sacrificing linear connection, but this time no later exposition was to fill the gap: Lowry apparently felt that the Consul's obvious difficulties in the bathroom at the end of V were sufficient explanation for Hugh's barbering. Ten tightly written holograph pages here apparently suffice to contain the entire draft; only a single notation reveals that these are not the whole of Chapter VI at this stage.

Almost exactly half way through this manuscript, after the contemplation of the picture of the *Samaritan*, the line "Hugh left the Consul and went out on the porch to wait for Yvonne" is cancelled, and just under the words "(Bracket here)" the parenthetical "(radio passage)" can be made out (30:2, 5). Thus Hugh alone on the daybed was to come at the center, not the start, of the chapter; clearly it was not Lowry's priority at this stage, and the term "radio passage" may suggest that at first, at least, he hardly contemplated an extended meditation, especially since it was to end with Yvonne's entrance shortly thereafter. What later emerged was something quite different, but manuscript survivals clearly indicate that Hugh's soliloquizing passage was written separately from—and after—drafts for the more dramatic sections of the chapter.

In this first manuscript, most of Lowry's revisions are of the sharpening and clarifying type. Perhaps the most troublesome involved the new political material: what had previously been the vague "clandestine military organization" is now named as the "Union Militar." Hugh knows the Union Militar as a "prewar fascist set up in Spain," but Geoffrey explains it as an organization "right here in this state . . . affiliated to the military police . . . those sinarquistas, or whatever they [are] called" (30:2, 3), Lowry's apparently fictional Mexican organization echoing the actual Spanish group, another link between the countries. "'But it's amazing how all this kind of thing can go on under your nose without affecting you in the slightest,'" the Consul is made to add with a dramatic irony that points straight to Chapter XII: "'it doesn't concern me in the slightest.'" In quite a different direction, as they leave the house, Geoffrey produces for the first time "mysteriously, for no apparent reason" his "Plingen plangen" quatrain (which seems to have begun as "Klingen klangen," k's then converted to p's). "'Did you just make that up?'" Hugh asks. "'Yes,'" the Consul responds. "Hugh noticed he didn't say 'You might make it a song.' Everyone had forgotten." From this reference to Hugh's past as guitar player and song writer an entirely new soliloquy will be generated.

Survivals from Chapter VI are anything but complete (parts of it were lost in the Lowrys' fire) but one page of a later holograph (30: 4) and a typescript page (Templeton 1:8) do testify that opening the chapter with the shaving episode was more than a passing whim. Apparently Lowry did not turn to the soliloquy portion at once, but when he did so, almost inevitably it began to grow. The evidence here is somewhat confusing and very incomplete but nonetheless clear in its testimony both to this ordering of material and to the expansion that comes later.[22] For instance, a sheet from a slightly later stage (30:4, ms. 10) reveals that Hugh was to be brought out of his meditation by Yvonne's emergence onto the porch dressed for their outing and asking him the time, echoing his memory of Einstein's similar question to him. What that incident reveals is Lowry's new intention to give the "soliloquy" much of the status of a flashback: for the first time, one of the major characters was to undertake a meditation on his past. As a result, of course, Chapter VI rapidly mushroomed to unprecedented size.

The earliest version of Hugh's new "soliloquy" apparently sketched in his sea journey but spent considerably more time with his guitar and his discovery through music of a social conscience: he passes out in a Chelsea pub after playing his pop love tunes one evening and awakens to hear his friends singing revolutionary songs, "better songs" than he has heard before. Parts of this are more navel gazing and static than anything in later drafts: a twenty-line discussion of what is meant by "song" in music (30:4, 7), a dozen lines of self-analysis of his incompleteness without a guitar (8).[23] Yet the most significant distinctions from the emergent account, which seems to have evolved quickly, are not only the much briefer narrative of the sea voyage but the viciousness of Hugh's planned vengeance on "the Jews."

In his first account, Lowry had Hugh return from the sea to discover that music publisher David Bolowski has, in literal fulfillment of their contract, printed but not distributed his songs. He opens his revenge by seducing Bolowski's wife, then plots "something worse, something almost Mephisophelean" (Texas, I, 5 [verso of 17]): he persuades the publisher to print as his own compositions "barefaced plagiarisms of two American songs" he knows Bolowski is unfamiliar with. The plot fails, Hugh's sins are revealed, and in guilt and remorse he has become a kind of champion of the Jews. A subsequent version put it this way:

> And then from that gradual[ly] develop into a sort of self-styled protector of the Jews, all the while telling yourself that you felt an identity for them culturally, and because were you not yourself a wanderer? Ah yes, you would have led the Jews out of Israel, all right, so long as they didn't give away their benefactor. It is true that you deplored their suffering, though perhaps not half so much as you deplored your own in advance were you found out ... (5:96, B [verso of "The schoolboy's complaint"])

Most interesting here is not one more example of Lowry playing variations on his plagiarism obsession, but the novel's generating of its own interconnectedness, the creation for Hugh of personal springs for his sensitivity to "the Jewish question" that has already appeared in the telegram of Chapter IV (and that will echo ironically in Chapter XII). For the sources of Hugh's guitar and interest in jazz we need to go to Lowry's biography; for the sources of his concern with Jews (and the Bloomish error of leading the Jews "out of Israel"!) we need look no further than other drafts of the novel.[24]

Of the immediate development of this material we gain only fragmentary glimpses,[25] but given typescript numbering on survivals, the chapter must have balloonned to about fifty pages at this stage, Hugh's "soliloquy" fully developed even if placement and details were still to be altered. Despite many missing sheets, it seems clear that this was a relatively easy section of the novel for Lowry; even very early drafts are often surprisingly close to their final order and, sometimes, phrasing. The "journalistic style" of such a "straight" passage (the terms are Lowry's) was clearly less demanding for him than more convoluted introspection or (especially) dialogue. Indeed, it may have been the opportunity to braid some of Hugh's interior passage into the shaving action—rather than presenting it as a single lump in the center of the chapter—that helped determine Lowry to return the soliloquy to its original placement.

Where the early drafts of Hugh's meditation are furthest from final form, it is for typically Lowryan reasons: they are at once too general and too self-involved and, as a consequence, are also likely to fail of a sustained comic tone, that amused irony that is vital to what Lowry called the "ozone" of these passages. Here, for instance, is the earliest treatment of Hugh's life aboard the *Philoctetes:*

> On board the ship Hugh was popular with his guitar. Or he was unpopular with his guitar. But it was never Hugh the individual who was popular or unpopular [. . .]. Anyway Hugh measured these things by what the bosun thought of him. And if Hugh had taken what the bosun thought of him down to the bottom of his soul he would never later have persuaded himself he had made his trip in order to identify himself with the virile solidarity of the proletariat. However, by certain factions Hugh was loathed and despised to a shocking degree. His first experience at sea in brief was hideous, but in a way one could neither confess nor describe. (30:4, 3)

This will get expanded enormously, filling out the particulars of the "hideous" experience on the *Philoctetes* but doing so in a tone captured in the above passage only in the ironic detachment of Hugh's inflated "persuasion" that he has sailed "in order to identify himself with the virile solidarity of the proletariat." The deflation of such posturing will be carried out thoroughly and specifically by a narrative voice that focuses the recollection through the more knowing eyes of an older Hugh but which is not caught up in his guilt and shame, freer than the character to treat this romantic youth with light satire. And, indeed, both the expansion and the tone are achieved in virtually final form by typed versions of this draft (30:3, 7–9, 11–12; Texas, VI, 13, 17, 23, 25).

Nonetheless, guilt, shame, and self-justification became the opening notes of Hugh's flashback, and Lowry must have recognized that there was no plausible or tonally appropriate way to move directly from the wit and cameraderie of the shaving scene into pained introspection. And so, once more and finally, the order of the episodes was reversed, and Hugh's retrospection opened Chapter VI.

We are in the phase of composition in which Lowry is most intent to fix those markers of time and place (November 1938, November 1939, Mexico, Spain, China) that will give the *Volcano* its specific historicity. The same early holograph of VI in which Hugh intended to lead the Jews "out of Israel" also carries the "Ebro refrain" and another of

Hugh's intentions: sailing to Spain "on a shipload of dynamite for the hardpressed loyalist armies" (5:96). These matters get most fully developed in the new draft of Chapter IV (29:13), where they are perhaps the most obvious addition since its previous version. Now Hugh has already been in Spain and "like a heel" has left at the instruction of his paper, and Lowry is able to confer an apparently casual authority on his experience with such a line as, "'I didn't go to China until after Brihuega'" (29:13, ms. 7).

The other obvious addition to this stage of IV is Yvonne's farm proposal, which arrives as a sort of annex to the "genteel Siberia" notion raised by Hugh in the preceding draft (see note 3). Although she claims she "'always dreamed of having a farm'" (29:13, ms. 18), her introduction of it—"'Oh Hugh, I have a wonderful idea,' Yvonne suddenly broke out"—seems so desperately spur-of-the-moment that Lowry will slightly mute this note with minor forethought and tentativeness ("'Hugh . . . I had an idea coming down on the boat . . . [sic] I don't know whether—'"). Nonetheless, unlike the suggestion of Canada in the earlier draft, this proposal comes from Yvonne herself and has some basis in her and Geoffrey's life "'in the old days'"; and in this draft too it is Yvonne, not Hugh, who first mentions Geoffrey's "genteel Siberia" (just as "suddenly" as she proposes the farm, however) as a possible destination.

Since Canada is no longer Hugh's idea, he is now allowed his playful alternatives ("'British Honduras . . . Tristan da Cunha . . . Gough Island . . . Sokotra . . . my favorite island in the Gulf of Bab-el-Mandeb'") and his comic verse on Saskatchewan ("Oh take me back to Poor Fish River. . . ."). The light satire is Lowry's solution to his reservations about Hugh's previous credulity: "Does this make out Hugh too taken in, for a journalist; also could he possibly take this genteel Siberia idea seriously in his innermost mind? Or if he takes it seriously, does it need more subtle qualification?" (30:1, 4). This Hugh is certainly more skeptical than his earlier or later avatars, but he swallows his doubts and launches into a brief for life in British Columbia (derived from a "Canuck" pal in Spain), carrying on in a lyric vein about specific beauties of the landscape that in the novel will become (more plausibly, since he has never been there) unspoken imaginings. Having talked himself beyond his own skepticism, he concludes by pronouncing a blessing that remains nonetheless skeptical: "'You *can* make a new life. And none of this churlish whining about catastrophe such as I indulge in! Well, that's the limit of this little communist's free advice. Live while you can, my children!'" (21A).[26]

In sheer length, the discussion of Yvonne and Geoffrey's future has more than doubled in this draft, but Lowry was also concerned about Hugh's changes in mood, which had seemed too simple, too euphoric in the previous version. Hugh dearly wants to believe in human possibility; on the other hand, as a journalist he has seen too much, both in himself and in the world, to be able to sustain naive faith. In the future of Yvonne and Geoffrey is the chance to encourage hope in others and thereby also overcome guilt in himself, to redeem the Judas within; but that desire is complicated not only by the remorseful consciousness of this Judas, but by his desire to sin again. As a result, Hugh's responses in the current draft have become considerably more modulated, ranging from the noncommittal to the self-justifying, from the dismissive to the hopeful, from the lightly mocking to a qualified enthusiasm which for the moment (aided by his recent beer, Lowry notes) moves him beyond the doubts he continues to feel: "'Of course it sounds phoney. But there's no need for it to be. It's up to you to prove it isn't'"(ms. 21A).

While there is the usual expanding and extending of material, as in this episode, there is also considerable trimming and excising: one of the most frequent directives found throughout these manuscripts is the simple "cut." Here, for instance, recollections of Paris, shortened, now "remain unspoken" in Hugh's mind; and the entire final section in the ruins of Maximilian's Palace is compressed and truncated. Dialogue is severely pruned, and the continued sublimation of romantic possibilities also has the effect of compressing the episode: nothing now persists of the erotic impulse but the brief "half passionless" embrace, which by the next draft will become his protective arm around her shoulders, which then will disappear too, Lowry apparently recognizing that a Hugh who cannot control the Judas within for more than a few minutes can hardly be more than a figure of satire. Instead, landscape and action more subtly convey the difficulties these two face, the momentary sense of release experienced in racing across the plains countered as they are brought up sharply in the ruins of those other doomed lovers, Maximilian and Carlotta. It is from within those ruins that they again gaze out on the open plains, so like the sea, brought up against the volcanoes behind which, in this draft, storm clouds now gather. In every version, after all, Chapter IV is to end neither in euphoria nor in cynicism, but in "immeasurable longing."

With the exception of the Juan Cerillo material, the three "Hugh chapters" (IV, VI, VIII) were substantially in place by the end of this phase. Not so the "Yvonne chapters" (II, IX, XI), which, as a group, would continue to elude satisfactory final form, passing through more rewritings than any others. In the previous round of revisions, Chapter II had been considerably more developed than either IX or XI, but the reasonable assumption that therefore it might receive less work in future proves unfounded.

In its next version, Chapter II went through a suggestive set of stages, from manuscript to typescript, then from that first typescript to a partial second one based on it.[27] The suggestive stage is the last one, for Lowry seemed to move from one (annotated and revised) typescript directly to another only when he felt he had reached finality, as in 1940 and 1945, when preparing copy for publishers. He may have thought, however briefly, that Chapter II had at this stage come close to a satisfactory state. But the movement from typescript to typescript in this instance also admits of a somewhat different interpretation: this may be the stage at which Gerald Noxon "sat on" this chapter, insisting on (and aiding in) revision until it also seemed to him satisfactory (*Lowry-Noxon* 126).

In any case, the changes here are, by now, characteristic. The chapter as a whole is (of course) somewhat longer than it was, and the kinds of additions are themselves typical: incremental, unspectacular, apparently small shifts that gradually transform its fabric. Take, for instance, the opening. Lowry has between drafts recognized an implausibility: why would a returning Yvonne have directed her taxi to the hotel rather than the house? His solution is to metamorphose the vehicle into the Bella Vista station wagon, which, unlike a taxi, has its own priorities. The hotel itself, previously featureless, acquires dimension and particularity, becoming "spacious flowerboxed balconied." The Consul's initial remark is now not merely repeated but varied into questions—Geoffrey interrogating his fate—that demand response, and suddenly voices seem to proliferate, one activating another: Fernando's "'Absolutamente necessario'" followed by "'Ha ha ha!'" then apparently a third, "'Just a bunch of Alladamnbama farmers!'" With the last, Weber has been simultaneously loosed from that other bar in Chapter XII and reborn out of the wreckage of the old Chapter II, brought forward with little alteration of what the young Yvonne there heard from her adjoining hotel room in Acapulco, to be overheard once more in another hotel by a different Yvonne with other concerns.

In the Bella Vista portion of the chapter, the most extended alterations are connected with that speaker on the other side of the partition (which, along with a second bar to contain Weber, the hotel now acquires). Lowry has by this time enough experience with counterpoint to insert Weber's entries in appropriate juxtaposition with the Consul and Yvonne's (as he pointed out later to Clemens ten Holder [Hilton 46-48]) and, not incidentally, to use them to excise some of the more banal exchanges common to reunions. More generally, Yvonne's expectations about the situation in Quauhnahuac must be both established and undermined, hence the gradually extended opening outside the hotel followed by such drops as the one added here, that on entering the bar she feels "her soul, that could have flown to meet his, as if already sticking to the leather" (29:3, 3). Yet this section was in generally satisfactory shape, both here and later causing Lowry less difficulty than the ensuing walk to the house.

The major problem in this later section was one of tone. As Yvonne learns that both her former lovers are currently in Quauhnahuac and that Geoffrey is on close terms with each, Lowry must present her responding to all this defensively, angrily, desperately without seeming either simply emotionally frivolous or shrewish. In trying to convey mounting tension between the couple while avoiding the kind of snarling bickering that had marred earlier drafts, he reached Geoffrey's irony and obliquity, his sardonic distance, quickly: Yvonne's reaction, however, remained harder. Certainly one tack of the previous draft was wrong; no stirring of her girlish heart by the news that Hugh is present can be found here. What could not be excised, however, Lowry shows himself very conscious of trying to "handle." He now avoids an accusatory confrontation over the missing car, for instance, by treating it elliptically[28] and in the final typescript is able to eliminate altogether one of Yvonne's disgusted and silently self-justifying reproaches for the Consul's drinking. Instead, he presents an Yvonne literally off-balance, having her act out her feelings by blaming the Consul for her stumble on sight of Laruelle's house ("'Do look where you're going, Geoffrey!'").

This comic bit of business is now underlined by his having become "suddenly correct, abrupt, army and navy, consular" (29:4, ms. A) on leaving the Bella Vista.

Lowry still has difficulty making the transition to the figure here called (this draft is *quite* explicit) "'my little wandering doppelgänger. Brother Hugh'" (ms. F). Yvonne's consternation is palpable, but as Geoffrey goes on once more to describe the strychnine "salvage operations," her response to the alcoholic scene has been, again, radically altered. Ironically agreeing that the Consul is "'absolutely stone cold sober,'" "Yvonne smiled; and looking at her hands she was surprised they weren't shaking worse than his before the last 'necessary' drink had reprompted him in that other role of one who's never touched liquor in his life, or rarely, or only for a sound reason—at all events he was playing it tremorless and steady as a house, not for her though, mark you, but for Hugh." This she finds "foolishly bitter and somehow beautiful," but there is none of the revulsion of earlier drafts. With her "suddenly lightheaded" change of mood, the chapter comes to a rapid close not far from the novel's text, including for the first time, the lines from the Turner poem that "the Consul hummed."

Predictably, virtually all the revisions to this first typescript—which resulted in the second set of typescript leaves—came in the chapter's second half. The walk back through town receives double clarification. First, the couple's precise movements through the streets of the city, the landmarks passed, the shops observed are particularized in fuller and additional description. At the same time, the "events" within Yvonne's mind were reordered from a psychological jumble to a specific movement that carries her from past to present. Lowry was always concerned with landscape as objective correlative and as symbol, but he seems in these revisions equally interested in its humbler capacity to suggest a concrete physical world in which a credible action might take place. Like Laruelle in Chapter I, Yvonne on her return is particularly responsive to the features of the landscape she has left, a sensitive register through which Lowry can establish his setting even when it has uses of which Yvonne will never know, like "the country lane to the right," now appearing for the first time, that will be the Consul's destination in Chapter III as he heads out in search of "necessary drinks." These were all gains; still, such passages as one in which Yvonne, startled, pretends to develop a limp, or another in which she finds herself in "a towering temper," clearly continued to make Lowry uneasy and almost guaranteed that he was by no means finished with this chapter.

Unlike Chapter II, Chapter IX, when last encountered, was still in a rather primitive state, quite brief, reduced for the second time, proclaiming Lowry's difficulties in creating a consciousness for Yvonne in these circumstances: it is the chapter he took longest to find his way into. The next stage demonstrates—if it demonstrates little else—his conscientiousness, for there again survive three complete drafts, here the more usual "dirty" (30:14) and "clean" (31:1 plus 2:19, verso of 14) holographs and final typescript (Templeton 1:3).

Like most other chapters during this stage, IX comes equipped with a new opening, in this case one that will stick. Lowry's immediate purpose is to strike a particular tone, and to do so he begins *in medias res* with a passage originally found some five pages into the chapter's action. "What a wonderful time everybody was having, how happy they were, how happy everyone was, how merrily Mexico laughed away its tragic history, the underlying death!" as Yvonne delights in the "smiling, bearded giant" of a peanut vendor with his benign little machine. A stop at Las Novedades, news of the decomposed telephone, and her tears—the events that had previously opened the chapter—are now only recollected as she gazes into her compact mirror, her crying judged as "stupid" as her earlier having turned back "not at the sight of, but at the mere suspicion of blood" (30:14, 2). In illustration, Lowry extends the dog motif, having Yvonne recall a bloody dying animal she had years earlier found herself powerless to aid.[29] She goes on to reflect on the afternoon's events this way:

> it had been stupid to cry because the truth was they all [had] been spiritually remote from what they had witnessed that afternoon. Yes, even Hugh whom she admired for trying to help at his own risk, had been remote, was really only helping because of the dictates of his stupid "social" conscience. The poor Indian staring up at the sky, or into his hat, had been associated with them all[,] she persuaded herself, only in the vaguest way. It was not common sense to force too much significance on the nasty little incident.... Obviously it had nothing to do with them whatever. How could they pretend to care in any essential sense about it. (30:14, 2)

There is more in the same vein, all of it insisting on Yvonne's indifference, a remarkably unpersuasive rendering that epitomizes Lowry's difficulties in creating a credible female figure. Indeed, such a passage may have a quite unintended effect: the narrator's fastidious detachment ("she persuaded herself") and the inadequate language given to Yvonne ("It was not common sense to . . . ," "it had nothing to do with them whatever") might well distance the reader not from the character, but from her creator.

Nor is the next try, on the clean holograph, any better. Now, Yvonne wishes they'd "never started to do *anything*" so as not to have made themselves uncomfortable. After all, "the poor Indian himself . . . would certainly have been the first to agree that too many cooks spoiled the broth—hence that sensible law [that anyone who interferes in a crime or accident may be charged as an accessory]" (31:1, 4A). The clichés could hardly be more inept had the author been preparing a brief against Yvonne—which in a sense he is. Having created an Yvonne determined at this stage of the day to be "merry" at all costs, Lowry finds himself furiously disenchanted with his own creature. The marginal comment on the typescript at this passage is thus doubly ironic: "The conclusion is inescapable: the train of thought of the average woman save in bed simply is not worth reporting" (Templeton 1:3, 4). Not, at any rate, by Malcolm Lowry (the side-glance at Joyce's Molly Bloom is instructive), who is at least becoming sufficiently cognizant of his limitations that he will henceforth look for ways around this direct, and damning, portrayal of Yvonne as irresponsible moralist.

Meanwhile, he was trying to build up a sense of action focused through Yvonne in other ways as well. The new opening, with its flashback, was one such way, as was her play with the compact, which is gradually extended over all the initial reflections. By the clean holograph her mirror also literally reflects the exterior scene—Yvonne, however, discovers she can see only Popo ("however she moved the mirror she couldn't get poor Ixta in")—and later, when her eyes seem "playing Geoffreyish tricks," the ominous image of fatality in "the old woman with the dominoes" (31:1, 4–4A). These grimnesses counterpoint Yvonne's mood, her "warm happy sense" that she has never been away, that the experience itself is fresh (she and Geoffrey have, at this stage, been to a past bullthrowing), that there is "hope, above all . . . hope"—a hope Lowry bluntly undermines by terming it "puerile yet eternal" (31:1, 2). Her euphoria is extended to the bull, "a merry bull too," until in the clean holograph he is doubly named, "Ferdinand" to Yvonne, "Nandi" to the Consul. Geoffrey's mood, however, is pedantic rather than playful:

> "I christen him Nandi, vehicle of Siva, from whose hair the River Ganges flows, and who, sitting endlessly in meditation on the snowy peaks of the Himalayas, smeared with ashes and wearing a necklace of skulls, is worshipped under the symbol of the lignam, or phallus and who I might add," he turned round at the weather, "has also been identified with the Vedic Storm God Vindra, correlatively known to the ancient Mexicans as Huracan." (31:1, 4B)

"'Christos,'" comes Hugh's response.

Pedantic this may well sound, taken, even to most of the phrasing, from Lowry's reading of commentary on the religions of India (Templeton 1:10; Asals, "Indian Sources"). Given the use he will make of this material, it is significant that at the top of his first page of notes appears an account of the belief that Christ survived the cross, traveled to Kashmir, was buried in Srinagar, and was associated with the legend of Yus Asaf. This information will most obviously be used in Chapter X, but Geoffrey's "christen" makes the association here, as, more obviously, does Hugh's unlikely response (so uncolloquial that Lowry will try the sailor's demotic literalism of "Blimey" before settling on the plausible *and* symbolic "For Jesus' sake").

Here, then, we encounter Lowry beginning to thread another strand into his "eclectic system." The novel had from the first included Christian material; later came an Indian background for the Firmin brothers. Now Lowry discovered matter that associated eastern and western religious beliefs and practices, that mentioned places (Kashmir, Srinagar) already named in his manuscript, that employed images (the mountain, the bull, the horse, the wheel, the sacred drink) already central to his own text. The legend of Atlantis, important to the *Volcano* from the beginning, posited a connection between the Old World and the New, Europe and the Americas; now, Lowry was finding links that would add the oldest world of all, the Asian. The Atlantaen legend had been recalled by Laruelle in the earliest draft of the opening chapter: "[The Consul] had spoken of the spirit of the abyss, the God of storm, of 'huracan,' that word which testified so suggestively to intercourse between the opposite shores of the Atlantic" (25:17, 11). Now, Nandi, or "Vindra," "'known to the ancient Mexicans as Huracan,'" completes the circle, testifying suggestively, in the Consul's connection, to intercourse between the opposite shores of the Pacific.[30] And Nandi is only the start.

However, "Nandi" is more than a start at this stage of Chapter IX. Lowry here expands his descriptions of the bulls, and one result is that the name, picked up by Yvonne, gets irritatingly applied to both animals that appear, to wit, Nandi I and Nandi II. Worse, during Hugh's later riding, more detailed in this phase than earlier or later, Lowry indulges the animal at some length in its imitation of a cat. Unable to throw his rider by main force, the bull resorts to "every conceivable bovine trick to unseat Hugh," including stalking on his belly, "the game of the darting paw, the twirley-whirley-trill, the galloping frog" (31:1, 12). Meanwhile, in the stands, the Yvonne-Geoffrey connection is mildly extended. As Hugh subdues the bull, Yvonne proposes leaving Mexico, naming the farm (as before). Strangely enough, the Consul then responds: "'I know just the place too. In British—in Ontario. Rich farming country there, flat land—but everything grows'" (31:1, 14A). Has he been boning up on *The Farmer's Almanac* between drinks? In any case, Geoffrey now is "sweating . . . trembling" and wearily leans "his damp head" against her in acquiescence, so that "It ran in her mind that suddenly they were talking—agreeing hastily—like prisoners who do not have much time to talk."

For the first time, this moment of communion between lovers, which intensifies as one moves through the manuscripts, is broken by a scream from across the arena, the real import of which is not in what it conveys about activity in the arena, but in what it does in the stands: "Yvonne pulled herself away from the Consul, clapping her hand to her mouth," and when she attempts to reestablish contact with him, it is too late. Nothing, after all, is to alter the larger arc of the action here. On descent into Tomalín, their shadows in the dust become involved in the "elliptical shade" of the bicycle wheel which, rescued out of telescoped early action, "enormous, insolent, swept away." The wheel is a reminder of the structural circularity in earlier versions of Chapter IX, more subtly conveyed in the image of the two old Indians (with which the chapter closes in every version) who recall Mexico's "tragic history," a history at once evoked and denied by the new opening sentence, reaffirmed through the pathos and power of this final symbol in the abiding "dust."

By the end of this stage, action was no longer so diffuse, and the chapter has been more successfully, if still very unevenly, angled through Yvonne's consciousness. These were real, if modest, advances; but too much of the activity in the arena still seemed unfocused, and the flimsiness of the presentation of Yvonne was becoming more worrisome as the rest of the novel developed. Her chapters, and IX in particular, were beginning to look rather weak next to the weightier and more dramatic chapters given to the men. Almost as though a conscious effort to counteract this problem, the new version of Chapter XI here acquires fictional heft, growing from a seventeen-page typescript to one that must have run to more than thirty.[31] This is Lowry's breakthrough for this chapter, the draft in which he elaborates his material to a richness unprepared for in earlier incarnations.

Beyond individual alterations, Chapter XI here takes on a gravity, a seriousness of tone and treatment not possessed heretofore. In large measure this is a technical or stylistic change rather than a modification in characterization or action: Lowry significantly reduces passages of dialogue and enlarges those of description and introspection, centering the chapter in an increasingly portentous landscape—the approaching storm—and, to a lesser degree, in Yvonne's somber reflections. He told Jonathan Cape that his "object here was to pull out all the stops of Nature" (*Letters* 83), and while the expanded role of landscape does not wholly account for the sense of growth, it certainly carries a considerable portion of the new intensity.

Again, an altered opening suggests the changed tone and treatment. The first dialogue we now hear is Yvonne's, "'Leave with you?'" which telescopes an implied speech or speeches of Hugh's (in the previous draft they were indeed "speeches") that led to the implied proposal. Hugh's only word on the subject is a similarly compressed explanatory one: "'Of course I didn't mean "with you"—not in that sense. Oh, God damn him to hell....'" Until the final section of the chapter, the reduction of dialogue accompanies an increasingly reflective, "internalized" Yvonne—which perhaps also suggested to Lowry a route out of his difficulties in Chapter IX.

The more thoughtful Yvonne is the obverse of the more fully and richly imagined scene of the chapter. Even apparently small descriptive changes seem to carry disproportionate effect. Here is the paragraph in which the surroundings of the Salón Ofélia are initially presented, first in the previous draft, then in the current one:

> The evening air was very still. The smoke from the charcoal fires hung in the air. The mountains in the distance, the ranges of massed clouds, the rush built huts and jacals [sic], the corn in the fields, the organ cactus and maguey, the whole world, appeared stunned. Women wearing rebozos, with glowing faces and eyes lit by the sunset, might have been walking in their sleep as they slipped past them. Yet their carriage was erect and proud. Footprints departed into the dusk. (Templeton 1:6, 1)

> The smoke from charcoal fires hung in the still, palpitant air. The world appeared stunned: the near hills, white with blossoms, the candelabra cactus, the rush-built huts. Like somnambulists, two women wearing rebozos glided by into the sunset. One woman, with the grace of a Rebecca, balanced a light bottle on her head. Footprints pattered into the dusk, going the wrong way. Hugh and she were going the wrong way too—they'd left by the back door as if afraid of meeting too soon in front the decision that must be reached. (31:9, 1)

The staccato sentences of the earlier version, each beginning with its subject, suggests mock-Hemingway, an effect supported by the simple descriptive diction ("still," "ranges," "massed," and so on) and by the impersonal naming of landscape features ("the air," "the smoke," "the mountains," "the corn," "the huts," etc.), but denied by violent metaphors of unconsciousness ("stunned," "walking in their sleep"). Abandoning the pose of impersonality, the later passage substitutes more flexible syntax and rhythms and a polysyllabic diction ("palpitant," "candelabra," "somnambulists") that fosters such alterations. Fewer features of the scene are evoked, but those that appear are more vivid than their neutrally named predecessors: "the near hills white with blossoms," for instance, rather than "The mountains in the distance"; a "still, palpitant air" rather than an evening that is "still" and an air that is featureless; footsteps that "pattered" rather than "departed." Substantively, almost nothing is new in the second passage, but the single clear innovation serves to underline the darker suggestions of the scene, the repeated "wrong way" in a context of the stunned and the somnambulistic appearing more ominous than a mere mistake.[32] Like the pictograph of the hand that makes its first appearance in this draft, the repetition points forward, in this case to Hugh and Yvonne's wrong choice of paths later in the chapter. (Indeed, the sinister underlining goes too far: there is no literal meaning here to going the "wrong" way.)

In the preceding draft landscape had been almost nonexistent until Hugh and Yvonne had approached the jungle. As they do so again, Lowry augments earlier descriptions. Hugh declares that his heart is being torn "'to pieces,'" but Yvonne, always associated with sky and stars, takes a longer perspective: "Above them the evening looked heartbroken too, but not about them, she thought. The sky, wild, but still light behind the red clouds and clear between them, was in distress about something older" (31:9, 3). This is a particularly overt example of Lowry's distinctive form of pathetic fallacy, landscape functioning as an objective correlative that at once reflects and, here, denies the emotional condition of the humans involved in it. Another is suggested in Yvonne's response to the lushness around her where "[f]or a moment" she feels "her spirit bathe almost contentedly in the thought of the stream pushing its torrential way through the verdant foliage that sprang up everywhere around them . . . but the verdancy was the work of the volcanoes, she thought, the soil must be alluvial—volcanic ash" (4). The comfortable identification of woman and water gives way to the sudden realization that the fecundity around her is the offspring of devastation, creation coming out of destruction. When this technique makes the nonhuman world a little too cozy, Lowry can strike a false note. As an image of a mortally ungraspable beauty, beyond humanity, Yvonne's glimpse of the sky can hardly be bettered: "The clouds, no longer red, had become a peculiar luminous blue-white, drifts and depths of them looking more illumined by moon than sunlight, between which roared still the deep fathomless cobalt of the afternoon." But when she turns to the moon itself, only to find there a reflection of her own state, the effect is bathetic: "tired by a long day, it stood down the southwest, preparing to set" (5).

The stop at El Petadi [sic], which occupied two sentences in the previous draft, becomes an opportunity for a reflective passage as Yvonne waits for Hugh outside. The cantina's inner (not outer) walls are covered in the advertisements named in the novel, but here there is an additional one (which has appeared elsewhere in these drafts), "a vegetable compound for female ills: La Sra. Jekyll y La Sra. Hyde":

> She laughed, feeling a queer emotional detachment—did one ever see much more, essentially, of anyone, however intimate?—and leaning against a low thick tree, actually two trees embracing one another; she knew their names this time, an amate and a sabino. Senora Jekyll and Senora Hyde indeed! As if life could be reduced to such cyclic simplicity. The breeze reawoke nervously, blowing spray in her face. The intertwined roots of the two tree lovers flowed over the ground toward the stream, ecstatically seeking it—but they didn't really need it. The roots might as well have stayed where they were, for all around nature was outdoing itself in extravagant fructification. If before you could have heard things growing, now, looking closely in the gloaming, you felt you might even see a bud open, a branch thrust forth a shoot. Yet high above her, the taller trees disdained all this generosity. There was a cracking, a rebellious tearing among them, and a rattling as of cordage, a sense of conspiracy too, as among ships moored together in harbour. They knew all about the approaching storm. And who is preparing a voyage this time, they seemed to be whispering excitedly, and why? For their dream perhaps was to be the masts planted in great sailing ships, of remote arboreal rumour, battling round Cape Horn. (31:9, 6)

Like the later placement of the "little rebellious hilltop" with its light-filled cemetery into the raw violence of the darkly oncoming storm, most of the elements here are not new but, discrete passages appearing earlier in manuscript, they had not previously been asssembled to this concentrated effect. Starting with the advertisement, Lowry brilliantly inserts the embracing trees (two separate creatures coming together) within this commercial use of Stevenson's parable (a single being splitting apart), and then enlarges the scene of burgeoning life as if in endorsement of Yvonne's sense of the inadequacy of "cyclic simplicity" to such "extravagant" and multiple creation. But the "taller trees" know of something else altogether, darker, more mysterious, more dangerous and "rebellious" that seems to "disdain" such earthly forms for the risk of "voyage": their animation derives from the storm, not from the abundance of natural processes.

The passage is not entirely successful: the insistent nautical images of the latter part might have been credible in any character *except* Yvonne, and Lowry finally will omit the dismissive reference to Jekyll and Hyde, perhaps conscious that his own use of *doppelgängers* is not unrelated to Stevenson's tale. Nevertheless, it illustrates the new richness Lowry brings to the chapter, capturing in symbolic form and in a meditation largely appropriate to the character the two orders of being to which Geoffrey and Yvonne, at their deepest, belong. Here, as they approach their ends, those strains divide as surely as the two paths in the chapter, or as the novel which contains all of these and which treats the simultaneous final actions consecutively. Surely Lowry was right in the next draft to move the freeing of the bird from early in the chapter to this later point and to make it Yvonne's action alone rather than one shared with Hugh, for symbolically and emotionally meditation and act belong to this single moment, and while both Geoffrey and Yvonne are contained in that release, Hugh stands outside.

The "Hotel y Restaurant El Popo," as it is now called, expands more than its title: the episode runs to more than twice its earlier length. First, the scene acquires solidity of specification. Out of the jungle, Yvonne feels "a hard road" beneath her and recalls that nearby "the ravine marked the state line, the border." American cars are parked outside, "wildly hot music" seems to emanate from within, a garage bearing a *Euzkadi* sign appears (a reminder of Spain snatched from the 1940 Chapter II especially for Hugh). Someone, presumably Yvonne, thinks ironically, "How good to be back again among one's fellow cannibals leaping around the campfire!" "'Mephistopheles and his hot four,'" is Hugh's unlikely comment. All of this demonic insistence is, however, undermined by the narrator, who comments that the place contains neither campfire, cannibals, Mephistopheles, nor, for that matter, the Consul. At the restaurant, a new figure appears, "a rather tall, stooped Japanese" who is manager and (perhaps) cook. This character seems only vaguely hostile and "dour" at first; as they leave, however, "it seemed to Yvonne that the Japanese ... clearly and with the utmost venom had said an extraordinary thing. 'I *hatee* you'" (10, 17). This Japanese manager seems intended to strike the political note, a reminder of the Pacific theatre of World War II and, together with the references in Chapters IV and VI, of the Sino-Japanese War of the 1930s that preceded it, just as the Spanish Civil War had preceded and led into the European action of the larger conflict. Like the development of the Indian background of the European Firmin brothers and the incorporation of Asiatic religious references, we see Lowry here quite consciously trying to impart to his novel a global range. This may also be an important reason for subsequently deriving the American Yvonne from Hawaii, those Pacific islands where (as any reader in the 1940s would recall at once) Japanese attack had precipitated America's entrance into the war.

The "Pacific side" of the *Volcano* would never be politically developed nearly so fully as the European, and the remark of the current draft got dropped, presumably because it seemed too extraordinary, too gratuitous, too "inorganic." The Japanese figure shrank to a mere nominal presence (in reduction, as in original purpose, parallel to the German miner Bunge of the 1940 Chapter XII). Meanwhile, the roadhouse itself is moving in the opposite direction, acquiring an expanded rendering of premises and patrons—and motion: lightning that "fired the windows," "crepitant" leaves, thrashing trees, the scream of a cockatoo, the "crackling" of Yvonne's fingers in her hair. As they try to decide what to do next, she "half ironically" proposes "'a drink,'" "'Mescal,'" precisely because "'I've always wanted to find out what Geoff sees in it.'" Hugh agrees. Despite the invocation of Geoffrey, the proposal is here presented as part of a symbolic betrayal, a moment that approaches a ritualized reenactment of the adultery: "they were regarding one another with serious attention and there was something, suddenly, almost of Paris between them, out of place" (10A). But, alone, Yvonne suddenly wearies of the entire situation and instead dreams of her farm. She knows this is an "escapist bag of tricks," but fueled by the mescal imagines adopting "squalls of children, rafts of them—she could see them, dancing over the hill, hand in hand, singing" (12), an extravagantly silly fantasy.

Hugh returns with guitar and flashlight, which here seems "a phallic contraption," underlining his role as lover (in the final version, as "a boy scout contraption," it will reinforce his role as youthful idealist), and with that as keynote, this draft stresses underlying sexual tension. Yvonne picks up and plays with the flashlight, observing that in this setting his "absurd" cowboy outfit seems appropriate, that once more he appears to her gallant and splendid and desirable. She watched him: they were watching each other, though their eyes did not meet.

And she thought: "I can see it, we both can see it, through the meshes of the same deep-laid trap, the same bait gleaming beautifully in the same coarse open sack: only this time there would be no escape—." (31:9, 13)

However, instead of acting upon their desire—and despite suitable encouraging effects from thunder and lightning—Hugh picks up a menu, where he reads "solemnly" (in another retrieval from the 1940 Chapter II) that El Popo "se observa la mas estricta moralidad" and returns their conversation to the Consul, rambling into an attempted explanation of his drinking that touches on the peculiar burden of Englishmen, the loneliness of the soul, guilt over the "rape" of Kashmir, the burdens of history, and so on. What has all this to do with Geoffrey? Yvonne wonders aloud. Hugh produces a murky theory involving a combination of personal and "'official, representative guilt,'" but even he recognizes his incoherence, and in an insert Lowry has him try again:

"I realise all this hasn't altogether explained Geoff's loneliness," he continued. "And I'm afraid I've lost the thread. But what I'm really getting at I think is that drinking has become essential to him because it fulfills such a variety of functions. It solves so much so easily. We'll pass over the fact that Geoff drinking alone is different from Geoff drinking in a bar. The suffering of drink is his martyrdom. The bar is his confessional. Just as it's the conning tower for his *Weltansicht*. And again when he drinks in dives," he added, "perhaps he forgets the burden of guilt he carries, not only personal guilt," etc. (31:9, insert 14)

These passages may, I suppose, be read as casting light on the Consul as drinker, but they seem to me more revealing as absence than as presence (they will not survive this draft), a sign of Lowry's recognition of the inadequacy of *any* overt attempts to "explain" alcohol in the life of Geoffrey Firmin. Still, Yvonne here is sufficiently impressed to respond "with sudden insight," that drinking is for Geoffrey "'Just like you and your guitar.'"

Lowry, however, is not through with the Asian side of things, and Hugh moves from the conquest of Kashmir to an anecdote from his brother's undergraduate days. Apparently a loutish Scot had deliberately insulted some Hindu acquaintances of Geoffrey's by scribbling the insulting "wog" before every item on the dining hall menu and passing it to the polite and uncomprehending Indians. According to Hugh, Geoff had apologized for the entire British Raj and then walked out. "'And incidentally walked out of England too—I believe he's only returned there once with you for a brief visit'" (15). The anecdote goes the way of most of the rest of Hugh's mescal-tinged analysis of the Consul, but the image of an annotated menu reminded Lowry he had in his possession just such a document: the El Popo menu appears at precisely this spot in the next draft.

Leaving the restaurant into the impending storm, Yvonne suddenly recalls herself "on a freezing winter night in New York, in Times Square" a year earlier, surrounded by human suffering and alienation, a "darkness" and "desolation" that she experiences again now. (Inspiration for an important strand of retrospection in IX, only faint traces of this retrieval from the 1940 Chapter II will remain here in XI.) As the two strike off on the path to Parián, "the crossbar to the cross" that Yvonne earlier associated with the divided path, they hold a dialogue (punctuated by Hugh's hiccups) all too reminiscent of the 1940 *Volcano*, full of opinions and abstractions—hate and love and saving the world and revenge and simplicity and compassion. Perhaps it seemed to Lowry justified by the tipsiness of the participants, but it was a serious lapse from the new richness and sombreness of the chapter, as he soon saw: the dialogue went.

Technically, it was also a departure from the paucity of talk earlier in the chapter: here, Hugh and Yvonne positively chatter as they stumble along. This first attempt in extending the latter section of the chapter is thus for the most part not a happy one. When not falling back on discarded earlier devices, Lowry is repeating (through Yvonne) the story of Geoffrey's unsuccessful search for her their last night in Mexico City, or having the searchers discuss the possible identity of an animal glimpsed in the underbrush, or (in an attempt to parallel the action of Chapter XII) giving Yvonne such unlikely speeches (in a dark jungle with a violent storm almost upon them) as this: "'Oh, I do love him, I do,' Yvonne cried passionately. 'I tried to tell him how much in my letters, but he never answered them. I couldn't reach him somehow. I don't know to this day even if he ever read them. Oh, it all seems to be such a ghastly mistake. Oh, I feel so lost'" (31:9, 19). And Hugh is made to sing this altogether too-pertinent ditty: "*'Bottle's empty, father's tight–. . . And dashing down the street there comes a maddened horse'*" (18).

Now, for the first time, three distant shots ring out, and, as they reach the hand that points for reader as well as characters, it begins to rain, sending up "a sweet cleanly smell" from the forest floor. Hugh hiccups and loses the path; Yvonne climbs the fallen tree, loses her footing. The presentation of this final series of actions is more detailed than previously, but the passage still does not move beyond the literal. A notable change is that the horse, when it comes into view, is now clearly "plunging sideways, not at her," which plausibly enables her to see "every detail," so that we too can identify the animal unmistakably, but its gait and position also underline the accidental nature of the incident. Yvonne's fear gives way to detachment—"her mind had become calm now, an onlooker"—but the last image she registers is of a Gothic creature, a true night-mare: "The horse reared, poised over her, nostrils dilated: its lips, dripping froth, curled back from vicious yellow teeth." This ferocity seems to exude a purposeful malice quite at odds with the animal's previous sidelong movement, unrelated to Yvonne. There is an obvious inconsistency here that will lead Lowry before the next draft to rethink the entire close of the chapter.

However, in this draft the apparent intentionality of the horse underlines a thematic thrust that in other versions of Chapter XI never appears with such insistence. It harks back to Hugh's anecdote about the maliciously racist Scot at Cambridge, to the Japanese manager's "I *hatee* you," and to the ensuing comments Yvonne then directs at Hugh as they make their way beyond El Popo. "'Oh Hugh, I'm so afraid,' Yvonne said, 'I'm so afraid of all this hate. . . . And I'm afraid you're full of hate too. And revenge. And passion for killing people'" (17–18). Hugh denies her accusation and claims that in fact it is "love" that he believes in (neither seems to notice that this does not quite answer her charge), but Yvonne's fear of the destructive power of unleashed hate is clearly congruent with the ferocity attributed to the horse in that final image. Taken together with the ending of Chapter XII, this would seem not only to leave the powers of evil triumphant, but indeed almost to identify power itself *as* evil. Recalling the parallel love/death closes of the final chapters in 1940, we can see how far away from that balance Lowry has moved—further, finally, than he wished to go.

Far from systematic in his revisions, Lowry picked up (or ignored) individual chapters out of perceived need, a feeling that a particular unit demanded "work," presumably in accord with his sense of the whole at any given moment, a sense shifting as individual chapters altered, wheels revolving within wheels. Of the Consul's chapters, for instance, XII was fully revised only once after 1941; it would not get taken up again until late in 1944. Chapter VII, although it went through a more extensive overhauling than XII, likewise would not elicit another draft until later. Of the remaining consular chapters, only X had heretofore escaped rewriting since the condensations of 1941. It was overdue.

Notes on that earlier draft call repeatedly for reductions ("cut," "condense"), but it will cause no surprise that the new version (31:5) turns out to be somewhat longer than the previous one. A major source of this growth, a helpful stage direction, appears in a note on the mescal that now opens the chapter: "The mescal slowed up his thought: things began to look strange" (31:4, "insert 2 continued"). The progress of the Consul's drinking was to be a primary concern here, the specificity of mescal as the "final" drink justified by a rendering of its effects from the inside. Thus even in ordering his mescal Geoffrey is curiously able to "persuade[] himself" it is not "serious" while simultaneously suggesting that it is serious indeed: "'Si, senor Cervantes,' he whispered, 'Mescal. Grande'" (31:5, ms. 1). Imbibed, the drink immediately produces an "oozing [of] alcohol from every pore," a sense matched by his vision of the nearby waterfall as "grotesquely suggestive of some agonized ultimate sweat," and suspicious reflections on the sinister "mystery" surrounding Tomalín and, more especially, Parián, from which he can recall "few . . . ever coming back." The world seems to bear in relentlessly upon none other than Geoffrey Firmin: on return to the barroom, "Dark coils of shadows . . . sprang at him" and, in an afterthought, gradually "materialise[]" the features of Cervantes's "'Muy fuerte. Muy terrible'" fighting cock (31:5, ms. insert 3).

In this early section of the chapter, "slowing up thought" is too simple a description of the varied reactions mescal produces. As Geoffrey stares into "his second glass of the colorless awful liquid," he feels that he has "forgotten eternity," but "eternity" dissolves into a series of analogies, from the Melvillean figure of the world's "voyage" to a weary sense of the futility of metaphor, a solipsistic arbitrariness that reaches a point where "[the world] was like whatever it would be shortly, after the next mescal, anything at all, even a man going to the Farolito." Indeed, a perceived "world" has become only dimly and sporadically available. Geoffrey hears "confused" voices, including Hugh's and Yvonne's, which now seem "dear, intolerable, shortly to be lost"; scarlet flowers resembling "flaming swords" suggest another, archetypal loss. "Even almost bad poetry is better than life, the muddle of voices seemed to be saying," when they are not a "roaring" that includes "native women in Kashmir, pleading: Borraaaacho! they wailed" (31:5, ms. 3).

Beckoned into Cervantes's private room, the Consul now produces a series of abortive prayers almost as in the novel (except the one for recovering "'knowledge of the Mysteries,'" of which the manuscripts make as yet no mention). Failures though they may be for Geoffrey, these supplications succeed brilliantly and movingly in conveying the anguish of a man whose self-awareness brings only consciousness of "this dreadful tyranny of self." Once again, Lowry's ability in revision to penetrate into the consciousness of his characters cannot be separated from his giving them voice. The previous brief and unconvincing summary—"[The Consul] . . . prayed, wishing for death" (27:3, 310 [4]; do people really pray "for death"? if so, how do they do it, what do they say?)—gives way to Geoffrey's silent articulations, counterpointed in turn by his own self-judgments from an objectifying distance, a dialogue between "I" and "he": "'Nothing is altered and in spite of God's mercy I am still alone. Though my suffering seems senseless I am still in agony. There is no explanation of my life.' Indeed there was not: nor was this what he'd meant to convey. . . . 'Let me sink lower still, that I may know the truth. Teach me to love again, to love life.' That wouldn't do either" (31:5, ms. 4). The current throughout runs between the tormented ego from which prayers tumble in a rage of mingled desire and loathing and the ironically appraising consciousness, a superego who brusquely dismisses each attempt, a tension so fierce one cannot be sure whether it is a matter for hope or despair that "perhaps [the Virgin] hadn't heard" the final annihilating cry, "'Destroy the world!'".

In the restaurant, Geoffrey silently adds "The supper at Emmaeus," but finds himself unable to meet Yvonne's eyes, "For in the end mescal was the drink of solitude, the ghoulish music of one's ultimately spiralling down the drain," and in his guilt he feels that "Everything accused him" (31:5, ms. 7). Now his launching into hostile dialogue about the afternoon's events is charged to the mescal. Nonetheless, he introduces the possibility that the victim "'was a messenger for the Credit Bank, the Ejidal,'" going on to explain clearly the mechanics of the collective, and waxing expansive on the political passions involved. In a curious (and unconvincing) reversal, it is now Hugh who protests that all this is "'dreadfully vague'" and that despite Weber and "'all you've said . . .–in spite of my own dispatches,'" he doubts a serious fascist presence in Mexico.

The argument by this point has met up once more with its earlier version, and familiar elements—the exploitations of Mexico, citing of *War and Peace,* ordering of criollos and a plate of live shellfish, the Russian film with its dead shark, the guitar player—reappear, although often in sharply abbreviated form. A new departure, however, arrives via Cervantes's lighting of their cigarettes, prompting Hugh's "'Feurstick [Fyrstikk] . . . the Norwegians have a better name for match'" (ms. 15).[33] This, in turn, sets the Consul off—"Delicious vistas of interminable monologue opened up before him"—and he holds forth for several pages on, of all things, Hindu beliefs and practices, joined to Hugh's comment by a frail thread of association: "'it's curious how much architecture in Kashmir is almost Norwegian.'"

Here we begin to see Lowry's larger exploitation of the religious implications of the Firmin brothers' Indian background.[34] At this point, the material can scarcely be called assimilated: great lumps of his sources appear with hardly an alteration. For instance, the association of Kashmiri and Norwegian architecture quoted above is simply lifted from Younghusband (Ackerley and Clipper 379). Nonetheless, the connecting of north and south, Europe and Asia, church and mosque are characteristically syncretic, and Lowry has the Consul move on to ground such connections in the Mexican locale, here, the Borda Gardens, "'Maximilian's garden, used to be, and the pool—it's amazingly like the terrace of the Nishat Bagh'" (ms. 16).

Alcoholic that he is, Geoffrey has not forgotten "the sacred fire" and (most important!) his association with it of the mescal he is now drinking:

"Firestick—ah, and soma! The first drink I ever had, Father gave me on the q.t. Bhang, they probably called it, but our old man never called it anything but soma. The curious thing about it is, it's exactly the same as this mescal here, I could swear. The sacred fire, Yvonne, was Agni, called down from heaven to the family hearth, kindled, with his firesticks, by the priest. . . . Soma was the moon too . . . whose cup—Cervantes!—is ever filling and emptying as he waxes and wanes." (31:5, ms. 16)

There is more, but Lowry's "adaptation" of Rawlinson at this point does little more than make slight adjustments to suggest speech rhythms—and to turn the Consul's mescal ("'Cervantes!'") into the equivalent Indian drink.[35]

Fueled by a mescal that can cause him literally to lose sight of the phenomenal world, Geoffrey's monologue rambles on at length, associating Hindu with Greek, connecting both (if only by contrast) with Mexican beliefs, moving from theology to ritual, from ritual to sacrifice, fetching up (under present circumstances) in a sinister discourse on "the immolation of wives":

"In Taxila, at the time I'm thinking about, *that* practice had been generally discontinued, though the widow of a man who died childless might contract a levirate marriage with his [sic] brother-in-law, by the way: Taxila and Tlaxcala—" the Consul hurried on, "not a tequila's worth of difference, when you come to think of it, is there? Taxila used to be at the mouth of the Khyber Pass and when Alexander arrived he'd already been in communication with its king, one Ambhi, who, just like the Tlaxcalans with Cortes, saw in an alliance with a foreign conqueror an excellent chance of ditching a rival."

Alexander, he speculates, probably felt "'just like stout Cortes, that he was on the threshold of a new world. But alas the trouble with all these new worlds is that they are so dreadfully old, Hugh, I feel, so disastrously and calamitously old.'" Finally allowed an entry into this monologue, Hugh can only disagree: "'Oh, on the contrary . . . I think the only excuse for the world is that it's so young, so disastrously and calamitously young'" (31:5, ms. 17).

Lowry is still following sources closely here, but the most important departure is the connection of Taxila and Tlaxcala. This began (Templeton 1:10, 5) as a verbal association, a kind of geographical pun, but by the time it makes its way into the chapter it has begun to gather up historical Tlaxcalan material long familiar to him from Prescott. When Geoffrey gestures toward a tourist poster on the restaurant wall, he brings Tlaxcala into the novel's present and paves the way for its expansion throughout the next draft (Rawlinson 31–32, 57–58; and Templeton 1:10, 3 and 5). However, even the apparently personal exchange at the end of the cited passage, which so transparently reflects Geoffrey's and Hugh's sense of their own ages under the guise of speaking about "the world," was drawn from Lowry's reading. The Consul goes on this way:

> "Ah, the great mountain chain of humanity. . . . No, most mountains are far, far too old for me too I'm afraid—think of the complicated errors they give rise to, the attraction of the great mass of the Himalayas, for instance, a poor look out for theodolites and the drinking classes, since they pull all liquids toward them, just as the moon attracts the ocean. Drunkards, erect, wandering on the timberline for no reason and theodolite plates tilting upwards! At Darjeeling they get as much as 51" out of true level, while at Mussouri—no, not Missouri, Yvonne, about 37", I believe, [cancelled: once in direct contact by land with Madagascar] though talking about Missouri, don't forget that Kashmir did once hold intercourse with America by sea, as with South Africa by land; poor far far too old Kashmir." (31:5, ms. 18)

The addition of bibulous humanity to those sober theodolites (surveying instruments) is Lowry's main original contribution here.[36] The passage underlines again (cf. Nandi of Chapter IX) that one of his primary uses for this Indian material was the extension of the Atlantis myth to the Far East, thereby making it a universal and unifying hypothesis. Younghusband here authorizes going beyond parallels and analogies to literal geographical communication and connectedness. Indeed, in the final use of Indian sources in X, Lowry has Hugh drive the point home with another kind of connection: "'All I remember about Kashmir,' Hugh said, 'is being told Christ, after being taken down from the cross, and under the name of Yus Asaf, went there in search of the lost tribes of Israel, and died there, in Srinagar.'"[37] Lowry's reduction of this "discourse" on India will be more a matter of compression than cutting, but even when condensed, Chapter X will remain the primary locus in the novel for Eastern material.

So thoroughly has the focus shifted away from the concerns of the previous draft that there is a perceptible strain as Lowry attempts to reintroduce the subject of Tolstoy and the question of free will: "'Tolstoy—something distinctly Himalayan about him too!'" (31:5, ms. 19) the Consul tries, and although Lowry now produces a shortened form of the argument that vanished in the 1941 purge, it is little wonder Hugh asks, "'How the devil did we get on to this?'" Confusion continues to reign until the Consul, shifting ground, moves into his diatribe, augmenting the catalogue of "poor little defenceless" countries by adding, immediately after (and perhaps parallel to) Spain, "'Poor little defenseless China!'"—appropriate to a draft suddenly concerned with the East—and, for the "future," Finland, which Lowry seems belatedly to have discovered as menaced by Russia; and finally "even Russia" itself, under German assault by 1941-42. In a similar vein of consular pseudo-prescience, he includes a historical connection, "'your Shelley's [day], when it was poor little defenseless Greece.... As it will be again, of course,'" that is, after the German invasion of 1941. If these last remarks were meant to raise Geoffrey's stature, they are less persuasive than his new and eloquent discourse on the meaninglessness of history and "the survival of the human spirit":

> "Read history. Go back a thousand years. What is the use of interfering with its worthless, stupid course? Like a barranca—a ravine, choked up with refuse that winds through the ages, and peters out in a desert, no use to anyone. Dull, dry for the most part—even the blood turns to a feeble trickle of water in the end everyone has forgotten about: what in God's name has all the heroic resistance put up by poor little defenseless peoples all rendered defenseless in the first place for some well-calculated and criminal reason to do with the survival of the human spirit? Nothing whatsoever. Less than nothing. Countries, civilizations, empires, great hordes, perish for no reason at all, and their soul and meaning with them, that one old man perhaps you never heard of, and who never heard of them, sitting boiling in Timbuctoo, proving the existence

of the mathematical correlative of *ignoratio elenchi* with obsolete instruments, may survive." (31:5, ms. 19–20)

Here for the first time the Consul is allowed to build on views of historical inevitability found in Tolstoy and Spengler (and perhaps Yeats) and to affirm "the human spirit" in however remote and eccentric a form it may appear. The cost of its survival here is enormous, it may be more than most are willing to pay, Geoffrey may in fact be quite deluded in suggesting a causal relationship between vast cycles of destruction and this single obscure figure of affirmation, but an affirmation it is, and it marks a significant moment in Lowry's slow development of the Consul into a figure who himself embodies that spirit.

While he still touches briefly on his old theme, the lust for "loot" (31:5, ms. 11), the Consul is in this draft far more concerned with "'The dishonest mass rationalization of *motive*,'" the first time Lowry has allowed him an insight into the springs of human action beyond economic cynicism. Self-interest is still the issue, but in a subtler, more complex, more corrosive form, for it masquerades as altruism. According to Geoffrey, political "interference" results from the hypocritical rationalizations of those who have no genuine interest in changing matters, "'nothing constructive at bottom, only acceptance of the state of affairs that permits [them] to feel excited or noble or useful.'" Far from being radicals, they are secret accomplices of the status quo, of the "fatality" of historical process, and in their meddling in the affairs of others, what they covertly desire is a "calamity" that ensures they may continue to evade personal responsibility. Hugh musters no protests here, and given what we know of his motives for returning to Spain at this time and in the way he proposes, Geoffrey's charge is not easy to dismiss.

As the diatribe reaches the attack on his companions, Hugh is again accused, of hypocrisy, but the charge of Yvonne's selfishness is considerably more devious. Gone are simple affirmations of Geoffrey's desire for children and the crude name-calling of "slut," yet more is involved than altered rhetoric: "'Where are the children I might have wanted? You may suppose I might have wanted them. Drowned. To the accompaniment of the rattling of a thousand douche bags. Mind you, *you* don't pretend to love humanity. Oh, not a bit of it! You don't even need an illusion to help you deny the only natural and good function you have. Though on second thoughts it might be better if women had no functions at all'" (31:5, ms. 23). The oblique charge of infanticide ("Drowned") and the grim wit of the musical death-rattle of the douche bags are arguably more devastating in their implications than the previous blunt crudeness. Yvonne is exempted from the charge of hypocrisy only because she indifferently perverts the act of life, turns it to death; for although sex is necessary for procreation, since she uses it only for recreation—and not just with her husband—she casts a blight on all women, who might better have been created without sexual "functions." The term "slut" is never used, but the concept permeates this sweepingly misogynistic vision.

On the matter of children, Lowry means to make a subtler point. The 1940 *Volcano* had posited the Consul's desire for "more children," but the issue had seemed to disappear with the revision in character relationships, except here at the end of Chapter X, where Geoffrey's sudden assertion of a burning desire for offspring came, Lowry must have seen, as rather a surprise (Yvonne's letters in XII lament their "postpone[ment]" of children). As a result, the text is now invaded by conditionals, not the flat "I wanted" or the specified "son" of the previous text, but a desire hedged about with "may" and "might" that places, not the children, but his "want" at a double distance. Here we witness Lowry creating for Geoffrey a more complex consciousness, giving him even in the midst of this assault on Yvonne—surely one of the most painful scenes between lovers in modern fiction—a self-awareness that he cannot or will not suppress: he "might" have wanted children (then again, he might not), and although he does not claim to have expressed even this equivocal desire to her, she, for the sake of argument (his), at this moment "may" assume as much. The Consul, in short, is not simply attacking Yvonne, but both creating and doubting the very grounds on which the attack is made, and doing so, in ironic anticlimax, *after* the substance of the attack.

Those conditionals throw doubt on the Consul's attack from any of several possible angles—is Lowry undermining his protagonist's stance? is Geoffrey himself? is the attack partly trumped-up as an excuse to break with the others?—but they do not slow it down. Indeed, the revolted vision of universal copulation that follows is expanded with passages from *Othello* and *The Winter's Tale* that both enlarge the Consul's diatribe and, once again, undermine it: Desdemona and Hermione were, after all, falsely accused. Now too Geoffrey suddenly realizes that "'poor little defenceless me'" has joined nations threatened by destruction (thus Lowry links the personal to the political). He accepts the terms ("'I've got my own piddling little fight for freedom on my hands'") but rejects the proffered "'peace'" of "'a sober and bovine Paradise'" in terms that begin the complex movement toward an antiparadise. "'Mummy, let me go back to the beautiful brothel! Back to where the triskeles are strumming, the infinite trismus'" seems a regression that not only mocks Hugh and Yvonne but, in the triple-pronged "triskele" and the "infinite" teeth-grinding of the trismus, anticipates the "Hell" that he "choose[s]" in the next few lines.

Or does he? Geoffrey may say that he opts for "'Hell'" but this conclusion is "absurd," and while he insists on his eagerness to "'get back there,'" even he is aware that "he wasn't quite serious" (ms. 24). As with the opening of the chapter ("'Mescal. Grande'... it mustn't be a serious mescal") and the accusations against Yvonne, Lowry manages the peculiar equivocation of flat statement ("'I choose ... Hell'") and almost simultaneous ironic disclaimer ("he finished absurdly," "he wasn't quite serious").

Previously, the Consul had disappeared by the final lines of the chapter, but now Lowry's technical decision alone demands that the narrative remain with him. Landscape here has grown more sinister, as if in response to his affirmations of the demonic, but his own reflections produce another unsettlingly ambiguous passage: "He stopped after a while.... None had come after him. Was that good? Yes, it was good, he thought, his heart pounding. And since it was so good he would take the path to Parian: to the Farolito" (ms. 24). Wasn't the Farolito his destination when he said of "hell" "'I can't wait to get back there. In fact I'm running, I'm almost back there already'"? If so, why does it seem to occur to him only now? Is this merely making conscious what he has subliminally known all along? If so, what did he think he meant by "hell" earlier? Or, since he "wasn't quite serious," did he mean anything specific at all? As the close of the chapter that has raised most explicitly the issue of free will and necessity, and that has apparently presented the protagonist in the overt and articulated act of final choice—Geoffrey, at least, claims to have "'just enough [of a melodramatic little mind] to make up'"—this is the last equivocation, the final doubt cast on a matter superficially "settled." Drunk or not, does one truly "choose" at all, and if so, when and how? These doubts, this equivocation, persist into the published novel. What we glimpse in this draft of Chapter X is the shining of a more doubtful ironic light on the Consul, one that, in the very act of seeming to clarify, throws shadows and crosslights, fostering an irony not incompatible with tragedy, but which might just as easily be comic. Is the figure who chooses "hell . . . absurdly" a Faustus, or a clown?

Here at the end of Chapter X, as at its start, Lowry brilliantly renders the effect of the dread mescal in "slowing up thought." In the long center of the dinner-table conversation, however, he seems to lose sight of that aim. Geoffrey's behavior there may bear witness to this new alcoholic stage, but it is not reflected in his consciousness, through which the entire episode is presumably refracted, for the text unrolls as before, clear, full, undistorted. Furthermore, despite all the instructions to himself to "cut" and "compress" (many of which he obeyed) this section was not reduced—the addition of the new Indian material alone would have seen to that—nor, once past the witty set-piece of the punning menu, was it rendered notably less tedious than before. It seems almost perversely calculated to display Lowry's greatest weaknesses as a novelist, his deep difficulty in producing sustained dialogue for middle-class characters that is at once plausible, interesting, and fictionally purposeful. If this episode is not as inane as the similar sequence on the Consul's porch in Chapter V—more is at stake here, both intellectually and emotionally—it nonetheless remains rambling and ponderous, burdened by allusions and confused and repetitive argument. Perhaps it was his sudden discovery of the way around his difficulties in Chapter V that also showed Lowry how to solve the parallel problems in Chapter X.

Lowry was sufficiently dissatisfied with Chapter III at this stage to take it up again, but the new draft (29:9) causes some wonder at its very existence, so little does an entire rewriting seem warranted. "Lowry at his most compulsive," seems the inescapable judgment as one reads through whole paragraphs with the recognition of tinkering—the substituted phrase, the reworked sentence—but with apparently little more fundamental at stake. There are some simple local alterations, often the result of changes elsewhere in the text. The hotel in Mexico City where they stayed on Yvonne's departure, for instance, becomes the "Canada";

the ship on which the Firmin boys had come from India is now the *"Co-canada"* (although Geoffrey still marginally wonders "'or was it the Nawanipur?'"). Both changes, of course, are part of the threading of the Canadian motif through the novel. Similarly, additions of straw Quixotes to Geoffrey's house, and the affixing of the Molyneux watercolours of Kashmir to the walls of Yvonne's bedroom are means of introducing those two significant motifs into the chapter.

The direction of most changes remains that of one major thrust of Lowry's post-1941 revisions: toward the more fully imagined and vividly rendered. The pariah dog, for instance, no longer vaguely "ran away" when addressed by the Consul, but "cringed away, then slunk off down the drive again" (29:9, 1). Geoffrey's inner world, too, is becoming more precise; into the self-serving analogy of himself with a "beseiged town" a note of doubt intrudes—"'there's something about my analogy I don't like, but never mind'" (5)—a dawning, presumably, of the implied admission of enthrallment. After his impotence with Yvonne, he reads the label on the Johnny Walker bottle ("Nacio 1820 siguente tan campante" [*sic*]) and now adds, "Born 1898 and still going flat. I love you, he murmured, gripping the bottle with both hands as he replaced it on the tray" (16). In a new passage, Lowry comically elaborates the Consul's rationalization of his sexual failure:

> "In a sense what has happened was a sign of my fidelity, my loyalty—any other man would have spent this last year in a very different manner. At least I have no disease!" he cried in his heart, the cry seeming to end on a somewhat doubtful note, however. "And perhaps it's fortunate I have had some whisky, since alcohol is an aphrodisiac too. One must never forget, either, that alcohol is a food. How can a man be expected to perform his marital duties without food? Marital?" (17)

"Small" each of these moments may be (although of increasing lengths) yet of such individual tiles is the mosaic constructed.

Furthermore, there is a sustained effort to give to the setting greater solidity and specificity, to fill the chapter's spatial dimension, the Consul's house and garden and the landscape beyond, with precise and suggestive images. As Geoffrey and Yvonne near the house, Lowry tones down the Consul's insistent symbolizing and allows the narrator a more detached view. "The drive widened to a small arena, then debouched into a path that cut obliquely across a narrow sloping lawn, islanded by rose beds, to the 'front' door, actually at the back of the low white house, which was roofed with flowerpot-coloured pipe-shaped tiles overlapping in the manner of shingles. Glimpsed through the trees, with its chimney on the far left, from which rose a thread of dark smoke, the bungalow appeared for a moment not unlike a pretty little ship lying at anchor" (1). Still implicated in the Consul's consciousness, as the ship metaphor shows, the passage nonetheless establishes, in the midst of his exposition of domestic affairs, the domicile itself as an imaginable structure that might be entered. Similarly, Lowry uses the advance of Concepta (as the Consul's maid is renamed after 1941) along the porch to furnish both its features and their general decay: "she glanced neither to right nor left, neither at the drooping plants, dusty and gone to seed, on the low parapet, nor at the stained hammock nor the bad melodrama of the broken rocking chair or the disembowelled day bed or the uncomfortable stuffed Quixotes tilting their straw mounts on the house wall, shuffling slowly nearer them through the dust and dead leaves she hadn't yet swept from the ruddy tiled floor" (3A).

Perhaps the major new matter to appear in this draft is Yvonne's astronomy magazine and the dialogue about the stars and the Mayas it provokes (Clipper, and Ackerley and Clipper 125–28). Lowry wanted an emotionally "safe" subject for ex-husband-and-wife before launching them into the more volatile personal issues raised by her return, and this passage replaces a feebler exchange on reading that had persisted since 1940. The choice of topic may have been suggested by some unlikely remarks in the previous draft: Geoffrey had responded to Yvonne's plea that they "go away" by moving to the door and remarking, "'Do you know . . . I can almost imagine with these glasses on that it's night and I can see your stars up there—the Pleiades—yes, there's Merope and Sterope, or is it the lost Pleiad, I think it's the lost one—and wasn't it Alnitak, the bottom one of Orion, and over to the right there, above Rigel, Eridanus, yes, that's the constellation I like, the River Styx.[38] I even like that one better than Scorpio'" (29:8, 21) (the passage is repeated in this draft with the admission that "he'd imagined nothing of the kind" [13A]).

Typically, the description of the magazine and the ensuing conversation about the stars is approximately twice what will finally appear.

Here the journal is called *Ecliptic* (*Telescope,* the title of an actual publication of the time, is cancelled), the imperial "Roman helmets" of the observatory pictured on the cover are sexualized—"huge circumcised domes"—and a portentous weather appears to extend its menace into the scene itself: "a brilliant tickertape of lightning . . . seemed to emanate from behind a jagged coastline of dark clouds which echoed the 'dome' motif. It was as if he heard the sound of thunder rumbling in the room" (9). Yvonne first speaks of "'reading about Jupiter's Red Spot,'" which unpredictably has enlarged, a sinister cosmic development that might be extended into several ramifications in the novel.[39] This obliquely brings up the Mayas, who despite their sophisticated observations "'didn't suspect . . . [a] Copernican system.'" Before playfulness sets in, however, Yvonne passes on information that, pedantically expressed, Lowry means to reflect on herself: "'The Dresden codex gives Venus tables by the Mayas describing the synodic circle, I think, as 236 days as a morning star, ninety days in disappearance, I forget—.'" The Consul extols the "vague years" and "pseudo years," double ways of measuring time that dramatize its relative value, to say nothing of their distinction from our calendar, which implicitly reinforces the point, a pre-Copernican vision of space and time that, Lowry hints, may also be suggestive in a post-Einsteinean world. And if perhaps time is not an immutable dimension, then playing with its designations (as they now proceed to do with Mayan month names) may be an appropriate response.[40]

However, aside from the rewriting of extant material and the introduction of new, there is another kind of activity at work in this draft, something observable in other chapters—we have noted it in the revision of XII—and, at times, between chapters (e.g., the girl and armadillo): the shifting of material from one spot to another, a process that typically occurs in conjunction with other additions and alterations (cf. Costa, chapter 4). The most obvious move in this draft is that of the Consul's address to Hugh, which had created the impression of a long, long silence between Geoffrey and Yvonne on the porch while the Consul implausibly "spoke" at great length to his absent brother. Now Lowry found a spot where this lengthy monologue might come—while Yvonne bathes, which heretofore had simply been an unfilled gap of novelistic time—and has even created a more or less plausible occasion for its appearance: tempted to sneak a drink, the Consul guiltily senses

"Hugh standing at his elbow." Although "the illusion vanished instantly," it makes a satisfactory transition into the ensuing passage. Furthermore, placed now between the two scenes with Yvonne—on the porch, in the bedroom—rather than awkwardly in the midst of the first, it becomes a function of Lowry's sense of novelistic "rhythm," a monologue between two dialogues that, arising out of the tensions in the first, also casts its tonal shadow over the second.

Whatever we may think of the revisions in this draft of Chapter III, the fact that it survives only in holograph form seems symbolically just. A clean manuscript prepared for typing, nonetheless no typescript remains, an inadvertant testimony to its relatively primitive development: of the Consul's chapters, III at this stage is still farthest from its final form. The next version of Chapter V (29:17), on the other hand, takes that chapter far down the road to completion. This is the breakthrough draft of V; no one could think that here Lowry was just tinkering.[41]

The opening dream passage makes its initial appearance full-blown, almost exactly as it will go into the novel, enacting a movement of disintegration: the measured, stately lines from the *Mahabharata* give way to increasingly agitated rhythms, the communal "they" becoming the isolated "he," the active and purposeful pilgrimage fragmenting into a series of postures suddenly glimpsed or passively assumed, a lofty seriousness of tone replaced by the half-waking self's comic interruptions that question the dreamer's obsessive images ("—how could he be drinking . . . ?"), which have become the wholly immaterial "promise of lightness" and "certainty of brightness." The suggestions of seasonal decline—blossoms and lapping lake superseded by mosquitoes and dust—and the fading of "the mighty mountain Himavat" from a goal to a mere reflection are counterpointed by the swelling demands of frustrated thirst as the paragraph descends from "souls well disciplined" to the frantic compulsiveness of "light, light, light, and again, of light, light, light, light, light!"[42]

This passage heralds a bold new departure not only in the chapter but in the novel as a whole: the freeing of consciousness from its ordinary daylight functions of "perceiving" or "thinking," opening it to the darker, more ambiguous possibilities of dream, obsession, fantasy, hallucination, blackout, vision. Although speaking of the completed novel and not the process of its creation, Lowry appropriately chose Chapter

V as the occasion to say in his letter to Cape, "The book is now fast sinking into the action of the mind, and away from normal action" (*Letters* 73). He had had a model for such a departure before him since 1940 in the Consul's dying illusion that he is at last climbing Popocatapetl, a passage that becomes explicitly linked to the dream of Chapter V by the later addition, "He was in Kashmir. . . ." Yet only now, at this advanced stage of revision, does Lowry really start to exploit the device, to begin investigating both the more expressive range of consciousness and the effect this has on "normal action," that is, on the novelistic world that now must be rendered through it. The disjunction of consciousness created by the Consul's drinking (Lowry, like Dostoyevsky, may have discovered the effect first in Poe) gives a sheen of plausibility to the sudden gaps and impositions in his chapters, but if his is the most extreme example of an inescapable solipsism, it is not the only one.

The new opening of V seems to set off a number of related effects as this draft proceeds, the most important of which is the blackout at its other end. But by itself the dream sequence creates ambiguities, uncertainties, false assumptions that draw reader as well as character within its net. Least troublesome is the precise relation of this passage—I have been calling it a "dream," although the text never calls it that—to the paragraph that follows, a modified version of the previous opening in which the Consul discovers himself, hungover, on the move in the garden in search of the tequila bottle. In Lowry's draft the gap is dramatized thus:

> . . . of light, light, light, light, light!————————————
> . . . . . . The Consul, an inconceivable anguish of horripilating hangover . . . (29:17, ms. 1)

Line and dots (in the published novel, italicized print will stand in for the line) emphasize the disjunction, the somewhat uncertain relationship between the paragraphs, before the narrator himself seemingly fills in a few lines later: "The Consul (who had woken up a moment or two ago on the porch and remembered everything immediately). . . ."

Not all difficulties, however, are resolved with such apparent ease. For instance, within the chapter's second paragraph there appears, for the first time, an actual dog, echo of the "visionary" one of the opening lines. Or does there?

On the path before him a little snake he had thought a twig was rustling off into the bushes and he watched it a moment through his dark glasses, fascinated. It was a real snake, all right. Not that he was much bothered by anything so simple as snakes, he reflected with a degree of pride, finding that he was gazing straight into the eyes of a dog. (It was a pariah dog and disturbingly familiar.) "Perro," he repeated as it still stood there—but had not this incident occurred, was it not now as it were occurring an hour or two ago, he thought in a flash. Strange, yet a brute fact. (ms. 3)

The momentary doubt of the snake, a survival from earlier drafts, probably suggested to Lowry the far more uncertain dog, for although the snake is "verified" (Mr. Quincey seems skeptical later, however), the perceptions of a character needing the self-reassurance, "It was a real snake, all right," are clearly suspect. After all, he has just been described moving through a series of "dying and reborn hallucinations"; and as he is quite sure the snake is real, he will later in this draft recognize a "routine hallucination" of a figure in mourning standing in the garden. The dog, however, remains even in the Consul's mind unplaced, its ontological ambiguity reinforced by the verbal uncertainty of "repeated" ("said it twice now," or "said it now as he had earlier," in Chapter III?) and the mischievous punning of "a brute fact" (what precisely is the "fact"?). At issue here is not just the status of the dog, but also the temporal dislocation he effects, the possible overlapping in time created, and the consequent suggestion of the flexibility of that dimension (recall the Mayan calendar). The possibility of a folding-over of time is raised briefly here: it will be taken further by the blackout at the other end of the chapter.

Before that, however, Lowry will have built on the devices of the previous draft and introduced new ones. Now, for instance, the text makes it quite clear that nothing is more a consular "illusion" than the belief in the "'normal,'" whether that consist of Yvonne quietly asleep in the house (we know she is not there) or of the "exuberance" and "charm" of the garden, now termed a "dishonest vision of order" (ms. 6). The encounter with the accusatory garden notice is of course not new, but the Consul's doubt of his translation is—"Perhaps the sign didn't mean quite that—for alcohol sometimes affected his Spanish adversely"— while the sinister fork nearby now seems "nakedly impaling the mind."

Capping this series of "illusions" comes the extension of Geoffrey's complex game of role-playing in which "honesty" and dishonesty are inextricably mixed, a moral cocktail induced precisely by the latest round of drinking:

> [his] opportunity to be brilliant was, in turn, more like something else, an opportunity to be admired; even—and he could at least thank the tequila for such honesty, however brief its duration—to be loved. Loved for precisely what was another question: since he'd put it to himself he might answer: loved for my reckless and irresponsible appearance, or rather for the fact that, beneath that appearance, so obviously burns the fire of genius, which, not so obviously—indeed it is devoutly to be hoped not obviously at all—is not my genius, but that of my old and good friend, Abraham Taskerson, the great poet. . . . (ms. 7)

Although almost certainly first written into a lost draft of Chapter I, thus do the Taskersons make their initial appearance in surviving manuscripts.

As a result, the scene between the Consul and Quincey acquires another dimension altogether, for Geoffrey's "burlesque" is maintained until, tequila waning, it drops "abruptly," replaced by waves of guilt that suddenly send him into the "vertigo" of paranoia. With the disappearance of Quincey and his replacement by the momentarily unidentifiable figure approaching across the lawn, the alcoholic effect inverts itself, and instead of proliferating visions of world and self, everything narrows to a point, comes to focus on none other than Geoffrey Firmin. Vigil's arrival "meant one thing: his visit had been timed to coincide with his own probable visit to the tequila bottle—though he had fooled them neatly there—with the object, naturally, of spying upon him, of obtaining some information about him, some clue to the nature of which might all too conceivably be found within the pages of that accusing newspaper" (ms. 14). Reassured by Vigil's attitude and a glimpse of the headlines which, concerned with the Pope's illness, "certainly could not apply to him" (ms. 16), Geoffrey apparently feels the need of a booster from the tequila bottle. He does "seem" to drink from it again, that action itself producing a mild narrative dislocation and in the Consul an "amber glow" so that "the day before him stretched out like an illimitable rolling wonderful desert in which one was going, though in a delightful way, to be lost ... he was drawn on beautifully by the dissolving mirages past the skeletons like frozen wire and the wandering dreaming lions toward ineluctable personal disaster, always in a delightful way of course" (ms. 17). This brief re-heightening of sensory awareness, productive of further visions, suddenly crashes into the blackout that reaches almost to the end of Chapter V.

Aside from the fact that Geoffrey's drinking in this chapter makes the blackout plausible simply as alcoholic symptom, the narrative disruption enables Lowry to solve the exasperating problem that weighed down all previous versions of Chapter V, that full recounting of dialogue and action on Geoffrey's porch that by the previous draft had occupied more than half the chapter (some eighteen holograph leaves). The most immediate and startling effect of the new technique is to reduce this section to five tightly written pencilled sheets, approximately one-quarter of the chapter, a contraction made possible by the alcoholic holes in the Consul's memory through which has sifted much of the trivia of earlier versions.

Lowry's problem here was one not of length, but of intensity. Conventional technique seemed to demand full reportage, but this social episode was of a low fictional temperature that Lowry was unable to invest with heightened imaginative or emotional power. Now, however, the sequence has been removed from the novel's present; as recovered through Geoffrey's problematic memory, polite small talk drops away and obligatory transitional passages are dispensed with. Geoffrey's consciousness is now truly the center of focus, but it is a consciousness apt to suffer sudden skips and gaps, to cast up shadows and fragments, rendered in a prose in which long, fluent (or fluid) sentences sit next to sudden dashes or dots, the jagged punctuation of ellipsis. Previously, narrative syntax had held, even as the Consul's consciousness gained fuller prominence: while his observations became looser, they never lost coherence, and dialogue always returned the focus to the scene unfolding before him. Now, however, the following passage, the material of which occupied three holograph pages in the previous draft, is typical:

> he knew not only that they had been talking about him but obscurely, from that bright fragment of conversation, its round meaning, just as, he reflected, producing at last the freezing bottle of Cartablanca, had he at that moment glimpsed the old moon with

the new moon in its arms, he might have been simultaneously impressed by the shape of its complete face, though the rest were shadowy, illumined only by earthlight.—Then,—"We saw an armadillo," Yvonne was saying;—"What no Tarsius spectres!" and Hugh was opening his bottle of beer for him, prising off the foisting cap on the edge of the parapet, and decanting the foam into the glass, the contiguity of which to his "strychnine" bottle had now lost some of its significance.—"Nonsense." And he had told him with impressive consular authority that he couldn't leave immediately anyway; at least not for Mexico City: that there was only one bus today, the one he'd come on, which had now gone back, and one train that didn't leave until 11:45 P.M.—"But wasn't it," Yvonne was asking—"wasn't it Bougainville, doctor, who discovered the bougainvillea?" (ts. 21)

I have abbreviated Lowry's long first sentence (which swallowed up three sentences of the previous draft), but its loose inclusiveness remains evident, as do the sudden shifts, the abrupt halts and starts, the lacunae—what has Hugh said to produce "Nonsense"? when did Dr. Vigil arrive?—that render the mind not as recording current experience, but as striving after pieces of the past that come sometimes in a gradual associative flow and sometimes in sharp elliptical bits.

In this first version of the blackout, Lowry is satisfied to provide paragraphs that frame the recalled past from the perspective of the present in the bathroom, with only an occasional hint at the dubious status of what now emerges ("When he returned to the porch with his new bottle of Cartablanca . . .—or had that been before they went in the water?" "It seemed that Dr. Vigil had said this several times. . . ."). Nonetheless, even in brief form, the opening frame raises many of the radical questions created by this shift in technique. Like the ending of Chapter V's first paragraph, the dream sequence, this shift too is attended by a long line of solid type:

————Why then, should he be sitting in the bathroom? Was he asleep? dead? passed out? Was he in the bathroom now or half an hour ago? Was it night? (ms. 18)

To wonder about one's state of consciousness is of course to connect this experience directly to the one with which the chapter begins (and perhaps to invite us to ask again just what the provenance of that opening paragraph is), while to question whether an experience apparently present is occurring "now or half an hour ago" is to raise the same issue as that raised by the dog in the paragraph that followed the opening, and thus to make this sequence in every sense climactic for the chapter.

I have called what happens on these pages "recall," but this initial passage casts even that assurance in doubt. The Consul's first hesitant query here elicits not an answer, but a proliferation of further questions, all of them unsettling. Apparently a state of awareness, a condition in which one might pose questions and perceive oneself as sitting in a bathroom, is not incompatible with being simultaneously "asleep," "dead," "passed out." (Is that series climactic, anticlimactic, or in any order at all?) Given this remarkable state, how much of what follows is, perhaps, dream, vision, hallucination—not, in short, "recall" in the usual sense at all? What, indeed, under these conditions, would "recall" mean? These ponderables are given a further turn by the devastating temporal question that, like the one applied to the dog, undermines altogether any assumptions about the status of the novel's world of time and space: what seems "present" may be hallucinatory, visionary, a warp of linear time that, even as we read the words, has already occurred "half an hour ago" and is thus over. But if we are reading it "now," as the Consul is experiencing it apparently for the first time "now," then in some sense (which, precisely?) it cannot really be "over." If you can see yourself, by apparent daylight, sitting in a bathroom, how is it meaningful to ask "Was it night?" unless you conceive yourself as at least potentially detached from your own experience? And if that is the case, then that experience may have an independent existence, inhabit a realm outside time altogether, which like a film might be run or rerun before your eyes at any moment. The Consul's questions, in short, breed yet further questions, enabling us to view the episode that follows either as the partially clarifying answer to Geoffrey's confusion or as rendered hopelessly uncertain by the very questions with which it is introduced.

I have lingered over some of the disturbing questions raised by these episodes because, if this is the first place where Lowry has begun to exploit those techniques that render the text problematic, it is hardly the last. From this stage onward, action and dialogue that have up to now appeared in the drafts as fictionally determinate (whatever we may make of the textual information, we do not doubt that in the world of the novel the words were said, the events occurred) will sometimes be rendered as quite uncertain—indeed, unascertainable—while as the novel continues to "sink into the action of the mind," gaps in the phenomenal world it presents will suddenly open before our questioning eyes. However, while this is surely the most significant set of changes in this draft of the chapter, it is not the only one. Moving in a quite different direction are the alterations designed to increase the comedy.

In a sense, this bent is also implicit in the new chapter opening, which begins by aligning the Consul with the loftiest spiritual aspirations and then enacts a descent that is also a comic deflation. That paragraph retains a perspective that reminds us what is at stake here, and perhaps because of it Lowry felt free to indulge in the comedy of the drunk, often a low comedy indeed. For this is the draft that introduces the Consul's uncontrollable hiccups ("The agony in the garden, struggling with the hiccups" [ms. 4]); this is the draft of the gaping trouser fly. As these suggest, much of the heightened comedy comes in the Quincey episode. Geoffrey's hiccups begin as an implied comment on the "sentiment" of his imagined return to Liverpool and England, but their comic potential only gets exploited with the sudden appearance of Quincey. The open fly, however, discovered as the Consul holds forth on Genesis, is both comic and ironic: reminiscent of the ancient notion that it was sexuality that lost us Paradise, it is more immediately a reminder of the sexual failure of Chapter III (which makes the Consul's use of the odd "J'adoube," here explained as "the term customary in chess when touching a piece without meaning to make a move" [ms. 11], seem wildly unnecessary).

Poor old Quincey himself completes his metamorphosis from the amiable figure of earlier drafts to the snarling *senex* of the novel, even the Consul's conventional "'good morning'" subjected to a grumping "'What's good about it?'" With Geoffrey more tequila-expansive than before, Quincey now gives nothing: even such charmless questions as the previous "'Did you survive the ball last night?'" and "'Goodness man . . . why don't you cut it [drinking] out'" (29:16, 5) disappear, replaced by an interrogative that is actually a fastidious request: "'Might I ask you if the next time you inspect your jungle you'd mind being sick on your own side of the fence?'" (ms. 9). Needless to say, the sharpening of the contrast between them augments the absurdity as the increasingly fanciful Geoffrey crashes again and again on Quincey's "realpolitik" unresponsiveness, only to bounce back with alcoholic resilience for one more doomed try.

Similarly, the comic exchanges between Consul and Doctor, hungover survivors of the previous night, are enhanced by the need for secrecy in this draft. Previously, Quincey had been a miffed presence at Vigil's friendly reunion with the Consul; now, however, as morning-after conditions are compared, possible remedies broached, an invitation issued—all with a wary eye to the whereabouts of the walnut-grower—Lowry extends and even "raises" the comic tone (replacing the tasteless pun of Vigil's "'Who is the booful layee?'" [29:16, 13] with the much better "Katabasis to cat abysses" [ms. insert 14]).

Much of the Rabelaisian humor in the novel was added relatively late in composition: the parallel bathroom (*excusado*) scene in X, for instance, does not appear until the next (and almost final) version, and it is only in this draft of V that the barranca takes on its identity not only as "general Tartarus," but also as "gigantic jakes." Unsurprisingly, the Prometheus imagined as inhabiting it is now "cloacal" and comically approachable: "one might even climb down, if one wished, by easy stages of course, and taking the occasional swig of tequila on the way" to visit him (ms. 7-8). That reflection follows the drunken lurch that almost precipitates Geoffrey into the ravine ("One was . . . always stumbling upon the damned thing"), a small alcoholic almost-pratfall pitfall that is no less comic for its anticipation of his eventual fate. Much of the humor in the early portion of the chapter—the Consul's self-conscious rush down the garden, desperately hoping no one is noticing, the wonderfully smooth self-deceptions of the dialogue with his voices—had been part of the previous draft, which served to set the tone for revisions that heighten the comedy of later passages. But even in this early section Lowry is alert to small extensions of comic possibilities. Here, for instance, is the Consul harrumphing on the domestic advantages of having booze hidden about: "it was fortunate he'd remembered about the tequila bottle: now he had a chance to straighten up a little, which he never could have done on the porch, before greeting [Yvonne] again. There was altogether too much difficulty involved, under the circumstances, in drinking on the porch: it was a good thing a man knew where to have a quiet drink when he wanted it, without being disturbed etc. etc." (3A).

The heightening of comic elements does not cancel the frightening or portentous—the accusing garden sign, the Consul's paranoia, the insect vision, the closing chorus of haunting voices (balancing, and partly echoing, the familiars near the start, these now seem to emerge from a "rolling of drums heard by some great dying monarch"). Stylistically too, the chapter is becoming more various, not only in the uneven rhythms of the blackout section, which break up earlier conventional narrative sequences into the alternately abrupt and discontinuous and the fluidly associative, but in such newly added passages as that in which Geoffrey anticipates donning the persona of Abraham Taskerson. Here (see p. 184 above) syntax and rhythm closely follow the devious turnings of the Consul's mind as it moves step by step from the spied chance to be brilliant, on to the desire to be admired, then to the desire to be loved, and yet (pausing, wondering) loved for what exactly? Why (he answers himself), for certain appearances, or rather (correcting) for what is beneath those appearances, which is actually a borrowed power, the borrowing (as he now hopes is *not* discernible) being from his old friend Taskerson. A series of appositives seeming to exfoliate out of one another, the sentences pause, interrupt to consider ("in turn"), to qualify ("indeed it is devoutly to be hoped . . . ," "or rather . . ."), to comment upon ("and he could at least thank the tequila for such honesty . . ."), and as the narrator's light irony gives way to Geoffrey's own language, create the impression of burrowing inward, presenting the mind step by step not only discovering what its own desires are but all the while remarking on its discoveries. The new passage does not end here, but carries on to sweep into this movement of desire the longing for drink, and, beyond that, for the Farolito ("Parián! . . . It was a name suggestive of old marble and the gale swept Cyclades" [ms. 7]), but catching up in its single sentence Geoffrey's movements in the garden, his hallucination of a mourning figure and his response to it, and his view of a friendly sky—a seamless web of the mind's motions in all its multitudinous complexity of perceiving, reflecting, yearning, responding, correcting, associating, interpreting, wondering. As the novel "sink[s] into the action of the mind," such passages, whether altogether new or revisions of earlier, simpler, material, become more and more frequent.

CHAPTER FOUR

1943–1944

In a letter to Gerald Noxon dated June 15, 1943, Lowry wrote, "The *Volcano* smoulders to a finish in reverse, first chapter last" (*Lowry-Noxon* 55). This announcement of an ending was not unique and might be dismissed along with similar bulletins to Noxon or Aiken, but this time, at least, manuscripts suggest that Lowry was trying to bring his novel into some kind of final form. He had already demonstrated his ability to postpone closure almost indefinitely in proliferating revisions (a tendency that after the *Volcano* will run unchecked), yet what we now seem to find is not, of course, the "finished" novel announced here, but rather the *beginnings* of a final phase of revision. The approach to finality is suggested by Lowry's moving through his text in narrative order, beginning—not ending—with this new version of Chapter I and proceeding through II, III, etc., until, by June of the following year, probably having reached Chapter VI, he was interrupted by the fire that destroyed the Dollarton shack and took with it almost all of *In Ballast to the White Sea*.

It is that fire, I would hazard, that so terrified Lowry that he moved beyond toying with completion to genuinely working toward publication. The announcement to Noxon of a "finish" was, after all, a year later still far from fulfilled, but the cosmic forces that haunted Lowry's existence had just given him a warning, a sideswipe (that was also a devastating act of criticism) in the destruction of another manuscript, and he feared a similar fate for the *Volcano*. Had not the completed typescript of *Ultramarine* been stolen years before (and, according to Lowry, an earlier version of the *Volcano* temporarily lost in California or Mexico)?[1] As someone remarks to Lowry's alterego Sigbjørn Wilderness, "you spoke to me of the sense of security you had when you were writing it [the fictional counterpart of the *Volcano*], and which was destroyed by the fire" (*DAG* 156). Later Margerie would recall that as they traveled east after the fire to take up residence with the Noxons in Ontario, Malcolm would not permit her to put down the suitcase containing the manuscript (Day 301). Sometime, probably soon, after their arrival in Oakville, she set about making a clean copy of the chapters completed thus far—the first five, when she began.[2] This was not, of course, a typescript to be sent to agents or publishers—fire or no, by this time Lowry's reluctance to let go of his book ran deep—for it was still on the yellow second-sheets the Lowrys used for everything *except* final copy. Nonetheless, it was a move in that direction and at the very least provided a kind of protection, a second typescript in case of further disaster. Writing to Aiken after the Lowrys' return to Dollarton in 1945, Noxon perceptively observed, "The danger is that Malc will want to keep on working at it although it is finished. In a sense he dare not let it go away from him. But I have lectured him about the necessity for getting it off to a publisher pronto and I'm hoping that Margie will be able to accomplish it." If he succeeded, it may have been in part because, as he recalled years later, he did *not* insist on finality: "I think I did persuade Malcolm that it was time to—not perhaps to produce a definitive version of the Volcano but one which he was willing to send to his agent or the publisher and say that he would abide by this if it were accepted."[3]

Whether truly committed to a course of completion or not, Lowry had in June 1943 embarked on a round of revisions that a year and a half later would replace a group of individual chapters with a single coherent manuscript, much of it consecutively numbered, which was not of course finished—to Lowry the *Volcano* would never be "finished" (*Letters* 393)—but which in its very consecutiveness and coherence raised the possibility that its author might abandon it to a publisher. To reach that single manuscript ("E"), his chapters received quite uneven kinds of attention, ranging from several full drafts for the deeply dissatisfying (Chapter IX) to alterations in only selected passages for the essentially completed (Chapter XII). Thus, this round of rewriting, however many drafts it involved, and whenever precisely they were executed, reached a point of logical pause only when Margerie had typed out the fair copy of a state-of-the-novel manuscript sometime in December 1944.

All of this, however, takes the long, clear view of hindsight. In June of 1943, Lowry's perspective was neither sweeping nor prophetic when he wrote his old friend: he simply contemplated with a kind of complacent self-mocking the perverse compositional habits that brought him to "first chapter last." There is of course an ironic appropriateness in his revisionary circling here, as he himself surely recognized ("when you get to the end," he would tell Jonathan Cape, "if you have read carefully, you should want to turn back to the beginning again"), for chronologically speaking, Chapter I does come "last." Almost uniquely in the post-1941 revisions, we find ourselves on solid temporal ground, for the June 15 letter not only announces work on Chapter I but, as if to confirm it, contains a description of the sight seen "the other evening" from the beach. Readers of another letter, the Consul's fictional one, would recognize the passage at once as part of his description of an imagined landscape "somewhere far north." That the description was new, not borrowed by Lowry from an extant fictional text to grace a personal one, is doubly confirmed by the survival of a holograph draft of the final page of the Noxon letter marked "keep" (Templeton 1: 2, n.p.) and a draft of the Consul's letter where the time of his vision is specified as an "evening in June" (Texas I, verso 35). We cannot determine just when work on this stage of Chapter I began or ended, but we can say with unprecedented certainty that Lowry was involved with it in June 1943.

It is a relief to return to this crucial opening unit, for in truth Chapter I is an embarrassment to any discussion of the composition of the *Volcano*, so fragmentary in its survivals that it becomes almost impossible to say anything substantial about it between the relatively early "Chapter I–Chapter II" draft discussed in chapter 3 above, and the much later manuscripts involved with the Texas version. Enough remains to make it clear that there *were* intermediate drafts, but beyond that it is difficult to go. A typescript page headed "3"—the only sheet to testify to the existence of this entire stage—may suggest why, its burn holes apparently witness to its presence at the June 1944 fire, which may have consumed other intervening drafts. For, uniquely, not enough survives to reveal how many drafts there were.[4]

But if it is no longer possible to speak authoritatively of the stages passed through between the "Chapter I–Chapter II" (28:23) typescript and the Chapter I of the Texas manuscript, we can catch glimpses of some of the significant transformations—as well as some abortive experiments, like that of splitting the chapter, a notion quickly reversed. Other departures did get tried out before disappearing or turning up elsewhere, transformed. For instance, a marginal suggestion as Jacques sets out on his walk to town, "Goes to station bar—presented with C.'s bill" (28:23, II, 1), became, "Perhaps drops in at the station bar for a drink" only to be presented with a bill of the Consul's, which was to "establish[] that Consul likes to drink in lonely places" (Texas V, verso 51). The scene got sketched out (Texas VI, verso 57), complete with bartender and cat "who sleeps all day and works all night," and may have been part of a draft of Chapter I before being divided between El Popo in Chapter XI and the unreached cantina of Chapter III. Less likely was the directive, "Have Laruelle go to Senora Gregorio—find her dead" (28:23, II, 15). Nothing remains to suggest the demise of the widow, but a holograph draft of Laruelle's entrance into town by way of a rather pointless stop at El Bosque does survive (Texas VI, verso 41).

More often, it seems, alterations proved happier as well as more predictable. Not surprisingly, for instance, the desultory opening Laruelle-Vigil exchange, with its obvious expository burden, was severely trimmed, opening on what had been the fifth page of the earlier draft (a dash, however, indicates that we have entered *in medias res* [*Volcano* 4]). Here, as elsewhere, we see Lowry reducing dialogue, interiorizing his opening, intensifying the slow, "brooding" quality it comes to have. In line with that effect, Jacques's walk around and into town, and with it his character, have been considerably expanded. If the suggestion that he stop at the station bar did not last, the passing of the station itself did (and by the Texas typescript, the graphic of its sign, QUAUHNAHUAC complete with borders, is penciled in). Furthermore, Jacques is given a substantial reflection on his Mexican sojourn. His time in Mexico, he considers, has not been "constructive": there has been the odd lecture—he recalls "*La exposicion Sobrealist en Paris*"— but no films, and his original purpose of a brief stay for "readjustment and renewal" had given way when "he had found the Consul here and stayed on and like him played the silver market" (Texas I, 9–10). Of his Mexican experience, only the quarrelling mistress and the Mayan idols persist into the novel, but the passage gives rise to a revealing example of Lowry's indirections in technique.

An earlier draft of the walk (Texas VI, verso 49) presents Jacques thinking, "He had fallen in love with the wife of the British Consul," a strangely belated, blunt, and formal way of putting it, the kind of flat statement that Lowry called "bad, undramatized, hence unwritten" (Texas I, 7). A second try makes an explicit symbolic equation as Jacques recalls a storm "out of season": "There was a calm, but the calm was within the storm. So that one might have said that the storm was like anything else, that the love was like anything else" (Texas I, verso 6). By the time the passage emerges in the Texas typescript—almost exactly as in the novel—it has become more oblique, elliptical: Jacques's recollections of his Mexican mistress and his Mayan idols, associating his female and his archeological acquisitions, bring Yvonne to mind (confirming the Consul's suspicion that Yvonne "in the aftermath of her passion" was "confronted" by these idols), but now the painful memory is not permitted to surface: Jacques's thought breaks off, "and he had—." Instead, he looks out at the landscape, which obliges by producing storm clouds "out of season," and he reflects abstractly on a love that is also out of season, that "came too late" (Texas I, 11. Lowry is here cannibalizing his earlier poem; cf. Scherf no. 51). A few pages later, the encroaching storm cloud by itself produces the associated thought of Yvonne. Lowry called this projection of the suppressed his "old idea about how to do the Yvonne passage, namely by the change it caused, so to speak, in the Mexican landscape" (Texas VI, verso 18). Elsewhere, he refers more simply (as I have) to the use of landscape as objective correlative.

The same draft that contained "He had fallen in love with the wife of the British Consul" also contained marginal notes on the stop at Maximilian's Palace, an indication that the order of incidents has been modified so that the pause at the bridge follows rather than precedes the stop at the ruin. This allows for the association of Geoffrey and Laruelle "looking into an abyss" to lead back easily into the recollections of boyhood friendship. But although this "flashback" section is entirely unanticipated in earlier drafts, virtually nothing survives of discarded or superseded tries, which may suggest, as with Hugh's parallel passages in VI, that Lowry found these relatively light sections much easier to write than the present action of the novel.

In any case, although we can say virtually nothing of the coming into being of the retrospective material, we can note some of the purposes it fulfilled in this phase of composition. Like the recollections given to Hugh and Yvonne (only Geoffrey has no such sustained passage) it is one manifestation of the novel's movement into the past, the weight of history here established on the personal level. To whatever extent it helps "account for" the characters, it certainly allows for connections between past and present, whether on the level of image and symbol—this recollection emerges from the explicit connection noted above, one that can be extended to all actual or metaphorical "abysses" in the novel—or on the level of behavior. For instance, the Taskerson insistence on a "manly erect carriage" even (especially!) when drunk, appears several times in Geoffrey, never more so than in the incident in Chapter III of the encounter with the fellow Englishman (apparently not yet written, it may have been suggested to Lowry after and by the Taskerson material of Chapter I). We may easily find a psychological link between the adolescent incident of the "Hell Bunker"—sexual failure, shame, drink—and patterns observable in Geoffrey's present existence. However, we are to note distinctions as well: the "Hell Bunker," say, is an altogether less sinister abyss than the barranca into which Jacques gazes. This is part of what Lowry called his "musical" sense in the novel—here, the appearance of themes or motifs in different keys, as it were. Later, for example, in looking at the passage in which Jacques connects his quarreling with the Consul in Mexico and the estrangement "years before at Leasowe," Lowry will wonder whether "perhaps the situation is not analogous—save for my obscure musical purposes—... at all" (Texas VI, verso 22). Finally, these "flashback" passages are as a whole "musical" in the sense of a deliberate lightening of tone and prose: largely comic, they are much less densely written than the "present" sections of the *Volcano* that surround them, which seems to assure us that, only memories, they are thereby distanced from the more ominous foreground action. At this late stage of composition, Lowry himself seemed to feel the novel's need for such a lightening, "ozone," he called it. And indeed at this same late stage, they are a part of the deliberate dropping into the text of comic passages, whether past or present: the Consul's gaping fly and hiccups of Chapter V, that encounter with the Englishman in Chapter III, the placing of Dekker's *Shoemaker's Holiday* among the *sortes Shakespeareanae* here in Chapter I. More than a DeQuinceyan "comic relief," such passages raise the question of the most appropriate perspective from which to view character and action.

Elsewhere (Texas VI, verso 41), Laruelle in approaching the town is made to reflect that most consuls, he has heard, are spies. This appears an early development from the mysterious and never-articulated "knowledge" shared by Jacques and the cinema manager in that preceding draft (see pp. 101–2 above), but when we next see these two confront one another, Bustamente has explicit, expressed suspicions of the Consul, while Laruelle denies the very possibility of espionage (Texas VI, versos 40, 39). Bustamente is armed with his father's experience; in refutation, Jacques cites, for the first time, the Consul's role in the capture of the German submarine.[5]

The *Samaritan* incident had existed since 1940, where a single sentence records the Consul's memory of the German officers placed in the ship's furnaces, but its inclusion in Chapter I and much of the development beyond brief reference are lost. Apparently it was first designed to testify to both the Consul's courage and his guilt. A note directs "Give the Consul a D.S.O. [Distinguished Service Order]" (Texas VI, verso 42), and he was to have been sensitive about this honor because of the deaths of the officers: "But the fact remained that the Consul did not approve of his decoration. If you spoke of it, he bridled. And in his own eyes he had apparently been responsible" (Texas I, verso 38). Jacques produced literary models to justify Geoffrey's idealism, first Rider Haggard's Allen Quartermain, then Conrad's Lord Jim. In both cases, however, Lowry became skittish about seeming to offer a simple peg on which to hang his protagonist: of each figure we are warned that it does "not explain the Consul." The ultimate solution is entirely characteristic of his practice in late revision, giving with one hand what it takes with the other, a teasing assertion that refuses to assert: "it was easy to think of the Consul as a kind of more lachrymose pseudo 'Lord Jim.' . . . Yet this was far from the case" (28:24, 10) This later Geoffrey is no sensitive plant, riddled with unworthiness, taking all responsibility onto himself, heavy with guilt, etc.—or is he? For at times he proclaims that he is indeed responsible. But the Consul is by now himself a master fictionizer and ironist: the Conradian reference reappears only to be, in the same breath, seemingly dismissed: "Unlike Lord Jim. . . . "

Yet while its content was undergoing significant change, the dialogue form of the Laruelle-Bustamente episode remained until Lowry came to see that the comic and resonant Spanglish he had used for Dr. Vigil only worked sparingly: overused, as by the cinema manager here, it began to sound labored and, worse, false. Thus as the episode grew, with Bustamente elaborating his theory of spies and counterspies and Laruelle imagining a more detailed version of the incident of the submarine and its repercussions (Texas VI, verso 44 provides an early glimpse), the entire later section of the exchange was cast into *oratorio oblique*. In a typically late-Lowryan decision this move was managed by means of a time shift that turns the section from the simple narrative past ("he said") into the pluperfect ("he had said") (28:24, 5-10). It is now not only whether the Consul was a spy that has become problematic, but what either of these figures of the novel's present has had to say on the matter, turning readers from witnesses of the action to viewers of it only retrospectively, privy not to what was actually said, but to how it later seemed to one of the participants.

If we get only glimpses of the alterations of much of Chapter I, we do have more extensive survivals from two of its most significant passages, one early, the other late. The very opening of the chapter (and thus of the novel) like so many of Lowry's openings undergoes a series of transformations, reaching by the time of the Texas typescript final form. From 1940 onward, the *Volcano* was to have opened with the simple declarative, "It was the Day of the Dead," the only modification being that—in accordance with the directive "Not so many paragraphs" (26:18)—it became the lead sentence in a paragraph that moved on to the mourners and the fiesta rather than set off by itself. The first sign of dissatisfaction with that beginning and the sense that Lowry might want to lead more gradually into his foreground action comes on a single holograph sheet (28:23) that shows him toying with two possible openings. One is the original "It was the day of the Dead—" [*sic*], the other an entirely new passage taking a more distant view, locating the action spatially rather than temporally:

I

The streets and lanes of Quahnahuac were tortuous and [the foregoing all cancelled]

> The walls of Quahnahuac were high, the streets and lanes tortuous and broken, and the roads winding. The thoroughfares are dirty, and there are open shops on both sides of the road with appropriate signs. In coming and going the people keep on the left side of the road while the cars go to the right. The houses are surrounded by low walls and form the suburbs. The earth being soft and muddy the walls of the town are mostly built of tiles.

Adapted from his major source on Eastern religion, this is seventh-century India as seen by a Chinese pilgrim, with only the minor adjustments of transforming "stalls" into "shops" and introducing autos needed to turn it into twentieth century Mexico.[6] In the end, of course, most of this would disappear and the rewritten paragraph would become the novel's second one, but in the first sentence medieval India will continue to impinge silently on this New World setting.

The next phase, while remaining spatial, takes a longer view still, rising far above the town to view the country that contains it:

> Two mountain chains traverse the republic from north to south, forming between them a number of valleys and plateaus. The plateau of Anahuac, on which the capital is situated, is the largest and most important. The eastern edge of the plateau is formed by the Sierra Madre Oriental. On the western edge of the plateau the Sierra Madre Occidental shows a steep front and narrow ridges broken by canyons; in both Sierras the highest peaks are about 10,000 feet. South of the Tropic of Cancer, south of the capital and situated in a valley between the Sierra Madre Oriental and the Sierra Madre Occidental lies the town of Quanahuac [sic]. (Texas VI, verso 52)

Lowry's first draft of this was longer still, carrying on into a second paragraph dealing with the Mexican form of government, which reinforces the school primer-like tone.[7] After this abbreviated version, again comes the description of the town, now appearing as the second paragraph, and at the bottom of the sheet the lightly written sentence, "A fine American style highway leads in from the north, but is lost in its narrow streets and comes out a goat track." Yet Lowry was dissatisfied too with the new opening, which sounds cribbed from an atlas, and the next holograph, dropping the emphasis on mountains and plateaus, establishes the volcanoes and reaches out west and east along the nineteenth parallel, to Pacific (Revillagigedo Islands) and Atlantic (Tzucox) Oceans. More playful is the enumerating of the eighteen (first, "thirty seven") churches and fifty-seven ("one hundred and . . ." cancelled) cantinas, as well as "two barber shops, the Toilet and the Harem," and the many swimming pools and "splendid hotels" of new final sentences. That last reference, in turn, leads into a rough sketch of the Casino de la Selva before we strike once more "It was the Day of the Dead. . . ."

The original opening is now four paragraphs into the novel, and Lowry's slow, evocative start was approaching finished form. Having moved beyond what even an airborne eye might perceive by including Pacific and Atlantic poles to his perspective, he takes the final step of making his reach at once global and precise by naming Hawaii and, portentously, "the town of Juggernaut, in India, on the Bay of Bengal" (Texas VI, verso 32), lands of origin of his three central figures. The "haunted" Casino gets filled out, and the fourth paragraph now begins, "Towards evening on the day of the Dead—or All Souls Day—in November 1929 [sic]—two men in white flannels. . . ."

The importance of the change here should not, I think, be underestimated. Lowry has moved from a flat assertion of the novel's central metaphor, left understated, to the much more gradual descent to a precise focus (no longer, incidentally, the mourners, but the two men), a descent that makes clear the novel's ambitions both in its spatial sweep and in its somber evocations of the tragic and the supernatural. It replaces the mid-range establishing shot, of mourners on a hillside, with the long pan of a tracking shot, a favorite device of the openings of so many Hollywood movies of the 1930s and 1940s. However skeptical one may feel about applying cinematic language to a novel becoming rapidly more interiorized, these terms for the opening are underwritten by Lowry himself: we find him worrying to Margerie about "problems of technique" in the novel's fourth paragraph, specifically about "the 'camera eye' who is the narrator so far" (does it "know Christian names"? he comically wonders) (Texas VI, verso 20; cf. Binns, *Malcolm Lowry* 44). Lowry calls this narrator "objective," yet he approaches neutrality only in his tone and (literal) distance, for his account is both selective and evocative in establishing what Lowry called (to Jonathan Cape) "the slow melancholy tragic rhythm" of what is to follow (*Letters* 58). But the initial paragraphs evoke also the scope that the novel aims at, the range of its aspiration, the length of its metaphorical reach: "This is not," the opening now informs us, "a modern novel of understatement, but fiction in the grand manner."

The later item of Chapter I that we can obtain more than a glimpse of is the Consul's letter. In its early form(s), the letter is throughout entirely personal in its references, and while in almost the only lines that persist throughout it affirms the centrality of love and the sacramental value of drink, it closes on the words "my own despair—." The strongest directive in the marginalia is to reverse this emphasis: "Note here should be. For God's sake come back, come back, I'll do anything if you'll only come back..." (28:23, 15). That note will indeed be struck, but the personal appeal gradually becomes set within a very different structure and texture. At a later stage, Lowry paused to outline it this way:

1. The night, the horrors of the night, and how he cannot stand it, and so gets up in the night to go to some bar, preferably desolate, that is open all night and where he may drink in peace. I write this at night, not at the Bellavista, which is only open on holidays, but in El Bosque—the Farolito in Parian [*sic*]. When I heard about the divorce I [took?] a taxi right out there in the middle of the night. {There was another Farolito at Oaxaca I might tell you about it} [*sic*]
2. I have just heard about the divorce; the immediate result has been I dream about a new life: the smoke of the train, the lightning in the white clouds.
3. very much abbreviated, how he cannot read her letters, etc. etc. Why did you send them—first one—to Wells Fargo? Can it be you didn't know I was still here. That is very peculiar. It would be so easy to find out too.
4. Memories of their life
5. But we can't leave things like this. For Christ's sake come back, etc. (Texas II, verso 12)

Then, at the bottom of this sheet, the plaintive bracket: "{In five paragraphs: cut to two pages in toto}." He of course would never be able to do so.

Indeed, revision and expansion are more obvious than cutting. In the ensuing draft the letter begins not in assertions of emotion, but with an almost Ignatian composition of place, the dreadful night that has been the Consul's true habitation ever since Yvonne's departure. Out of its evocation comes the journey to Oaxaca, that "hell" from which he reports, "it is not peace with me. It is war. It is time for the nightly struggle/battle with death" (Texas II, verso 10), an awkward handling of the crucial matter of Geoffrey Firmin's personal war in the midst of the violent military struggles that form the backdrop of the novel, but useful for its very baldness. However, Lowry is in this draft unsure himself how seriously he wants to take his Consul. No sooner has Geoffrey declared himself a "great explorer" of hell than he is made to fall into posturing. "People like Rimbaud and Dante are mere renegades beside me," he boasts, and carries on, "But right through hell there is a path, as Blake knew, a path that could perhaps only be taken and survived by an Englishman. . . . Yes, I repeat, by an Englishman. For an American could never tolerate for long its lack of modern conveniences. A Frenchman would divide hell against itself for his own profit, while a Russian. . . ." And so on (there is more). Little wonder that "Laruelle could not help laughing" (Texas II, verso 10). Here, again, is an example of Lowry's late adoption of a comic stance, although in this instance he came to feel its inappropriateness.

Eventually, this Geoffrey returns to his original point: "But what is it, you ask, I see beyond this path? I sometimes have visions that are not of hell, but of a life, Yvonne, that you and I might lead." Thus the first evocation of the counterplace, a paradisal *topos* of visionary reconciliation rendered in the lyrical prose and imagery of "a light blue evening in June," "sunlight and spring and clear water," distant mountains, clouds like "alabaster lamp[s]," and redemptive, eastward-rolling trains that they view "like Swedenborg's angels." "Ah—could I but make this into poetry? had I only the strength," he sighs—and here is the first hint in the letter of any writerly ambition, however faint—before he returns to "the human plane" and his struggle "against my love for you" (Texas II, versos 10–9).

Thus the point at which earlier versions of the letter began, Geoffrey's direct, personal address to Yvonne, has this long foreground. Blame of her behavior is now muted, and her unanswered letters—merely mentioned in previous drafts—become more central. Then, unexpectedly,

"Do you think of me as working on my book? What book? There never was a book and never will be." But an insert tempers this: "Or at least not much of one. Ben Jonson's Alchemist without the humor, gone bad and without the genius." With that, he veers back to the familiar territory of the happiness they knew together, which itself now becomes tailored more to pattern than to feeling, to "shadows of our fate." At this point, after three crowded holograph pages, the draft, if not the letter, breaks off, although apparently little more than the appeal for Yvonne's return has been lost.

Lowry's indecision about the Consul's supposed book is suggested in the brief dance noted here (it never existed; well, maybe it did, slightly) an uncertainty that will characteristically crystallize into a teasing ambiguity. However, behind the matter of the book is the deeper question of the essential nature of the Consul's mind, here manifested in his two quite separate references to potential writing. In the next surviving draft, Lowry brings them together, all the while sustaining uncertainty about the existence of writing:

> Meantime, do you still see me as working on a book? What book? There never was a book, not what you could call a book, and never will be. Were there one, I suppose it would be something in each word of which would grin some dreadful prophecy. But to express myself, I think I could have woven once such material as that about the alabaster cloud, into great poetry. Yet I can only see clearly when drunk. No use working when drunk—you lose things. And you can't go back, can't use what you see when sober—it hurts too much. Just the same. . . . (Texas I, verso 7)

Maundering on, the Consul proceeds to illustrate his point by "losing" the thread in a rambling eulogy of universal drunkenness. Scattered notes continue to proliferate questions, refusing answers, referring finally to a "quest" that by the fair holograph of this stage (28:24, 16) takes the form, "Do you find me . . . between Chesed and Binah? . . . As if I ever were at Chesed." Thus do cabalistic references make their first appearance in the manuscripts, and a characteristic appearance it is, too, for while it evidences the Consul's familiarity with such terms, it leaves indeterminate his commitment to them.

Survivals allow for only glimpses of the elaboration of the letter, both permanent—noises of slaughtering in the hotel kitchen and the vulture in the washbasin of Oaxaca, for instance—and transient—"the ghost of D. H. Lawrence" intoning, "'My son, endure, pull through, you are English'" (Texas I, verso 36; Lowry still trying the comic note). The simultaneous news of the Firmins' divorce and the breach in British-Mexican relations is introduced to become a structural pivot on which symbolic landscapes turn, the recollection of hell (Oaxaca) giving way to the vista of heaven (Canada) as divorce seems to make possible the envisioning of a "new life." A continuing problem was the attack on Yvonne; Lowry suppressed it in one spot only to have it spring up in another. Personal blame ("what I disliked about you") might be written out, but it was replaced by an assault on her letters, which, to make matters worse, Geoffrey admits to not having read. "I do not have to read them to know their burden," he claims. That "burden" is the possibility of a new life that he too envisions but that in her he calls false. "I feel they are hypocritical, letters written to your conscience" (28:24, 14A). The charge of hypocrisy here seems a persistence from the Priscilla of 1940, whose letters *were* "hypocritical," confessedly written only to persuade her former husband to stop drinking. Here, as elsewhere, Lowry gives up reluctantly and gradually the Consul's outright attacks on Yvonne, leaving only the muted "too long digested" and the ironically unjust "too late" as epistolary criticisms. The final sense becomes one of the pain rather than the anger the letters cause him, but the charge of hypocrisy disappears only with the ultimate holograph draft (28:24, 15).

Finally, each of the major movements in Lowry's outline for the letter becomes at this late stage marked by rhetorical collapse and the resumption of drinking: the image of the ship "like a great wheel . . . whirling across the bay" dissolves the paradisal vision, the sinisterly powerful "desire to destroy myself by my own imagination" stutters into the incoherence of "—not at least to be the prey of—ghosts—," and the final cry simply breaks off without concluding. One oral function drives out another, apparently, a conclusion perhaps confirmed by the Consul's role as "frustrated poet," unable to write either prose or verse. The "nightly grapple with death" is thus partly enacted in the letter as a struggle between those instruments of the grappling hand, pencil and glass. Yet this too may oversimplify, for, as that earlier passage had it, one can only see clearly when drunk, at which time it is impossible to work; and while Malcolm Lowry was in the act of disproving this through the creation of the *Volcano* itself, it remained a hypothesis he never fully surrendered (and would all too convincingly live out in his last decade).

Dealing with incomplete survivals provides fascinating glimpses into various sections of Chapter I while denying us a view of the development of the whole. They can only partially prepare us for the full version, which we do not reach until the Texas Chapter I, a version very close to finality. As we might have guessed, it is now a chapter far more particularly evocative of the dimensions of time and space than it had been previously. Political and historical awareness, stripped away in earlier revision, has been restored to it, but inevitably not as in 1940. Now rather than being merely the subject of debate, it pervades setting and consciousness: the Jacques who is to return to France on the morrow is fully aware of the conflict there, and such new touches as the headlines of the newspaper *Quauhnahuac Nuevo* or the poster for the German actress Maria Landrock testify in their different ways to the European war. Meanwhile, the overt politicizing in Señor Bustamente's view of the Consul not only conjures up a local question applicable to ensuing chapters, but directly evokes two specific—and almost contemporary—historical situations, the First World War (the *Samaritan* incident) and the Díaz regime, both of which cast long shadows over the novel's present. Jacques's recollection of Hugh introduces the immediate political past of his projected trip to Spain, and Jacques himself (hardly politically involved) acquires both a recent (Mexico, Hollywood) and distant (Ufa films, student days) history more specific than any suggested before. The Taskerson recollection, of course, takes us back to a yet earlier past for both Geoffrey and Jacques.

At the same time, what was spasmodically apparent on the fragmentary drafts discussed above is now clear. Jacques's walk, for instance, has developed greatly in richness and precision. He no longer seems to wander directly from a "field" into the bustle of the town. Perhaps Lowry followed his own marginal directive to "See Digest Map"; at any rate, when Laruelle describes his course as an "eccentric orbit," it is now quite literally imaginable. The approaching storm, the ruined Palace, the drunken horseman appear with a fullness of detail heretofore only suggested, and specific memorable images make their initial appearances as fixtures in the text—the pitchfork-brandishing devil on the bottle of anís, the bordered station sign, the darkness that has "fallen like the house of Usher," and, tested in the margins of earlier drafts, the sad, Dantesque bell, and the backwardly revolving "luminous wheel." Specific, and significant, verbal additions are the inclusion of Dekker's lines in the midst of *sortes Shakespereanae*, Bustamente's use of the resonant "Compañero," and, as we have seen, most of the Consul's letter. Finally, the view of the sinisterly shadowed cinema, its audience awaiting the "suspended function," is elaborated to suggest its double role as an image of the world of 1939 and as site of the "film" that in Chapters II–XII is about to unreel before us.

With the revision of Chapter II we have come to late summer 1943.[8] It is a chapter Lowry seemed to think of as needing only tidying up. Marginal comments on the previous typescript (29:3 and 29:4) call largely for clarification and extension, enlargement, deepening; the fact that several earlier typescript pages were simply refoliated as part of the new version suggests the partial nature of the revision here.[9] And yet an unusually large amount of specific rewriting also gets called for on the previous typescript, and some matters that seem to begin as simple clarification lead into significant features emerging only at this stage. Lowry for instance appears to realize belatedly that the narrative's movement into the past needs to be quickly marked if his reader, coming from the 1939 of Chapter I, is not to be baffled. "Get year clearly," he directs, tries an insert in the opening paragraph (the Quauhnahuac airport "had been built this year, in 1938"), but realizes that dating comes more naturally further along where "as though it were November 1936 and not, as it was, November 1938" is added. Similarly, and still on the opening page, "'–Just a bunch of Alladamnbama farmers!–'" is underlined and followed by an explanatory "The last was another voice." It is precisely at this juncture that Lowry recognizes that Yvonne as well as the reader might be misled by this "other" voice, for, still out in the square, she now makes an assumption that Lowry will go on to exploit.

Expectant and apprehensive, Yvonne's energized self-consciousness, playing upon what she hears, reaches a plausibly anxious conclusion: "So the bar, open all night for the occasion, was probably full, even at this strange hour." By the new draft, the irrelevant final phrase has been snipped and her hesitant anxiety made overt in her double "reluctance" both to face this "crowd" herself and cravenly to send the taxi-driver in for her. But it is her anxiety that has made a "full" bar out of three voices, and this is the start of Lowry's enlarging, thickening of Yvonne's consciousness, the creating moment by moment of that mix of assumptions, impressions, perceptions, memories, fears, and desires that is her apprehended world. The first fruit of that enhancement, indicated only by the marginal direction "½ a page of journey, sea—etc.," is the astonishing sentence that by the final holograph of this draft has achieved almost finished form. Lowry begins with her emotions about the immediate scene ("Ashamed, numb with nostagia and anxiety . . .''), superimposes the still-present afterimages of her journey ("she still seemed to be travelling, still, sailing into Acapulco harbour . . .") in which the recalled "commotion" of the greeting butterflies recreates her initial impression of sudden "fountains of multicolored stationery," so that while she recognizes that the square now before her is "really tranquil" it remains overlaid by the reiterated image of the butterflies. The result is that the dual perception of stillness and motion gives a new kinetic thrust to the extant ending of the sentence, the square "silent yet somehow poised, expectant, with one eye half open already, the merry-go-rounds, the Ferris wheel lightly dreaming," as the slower and longer rhythms bring the suspended syntactical structures back to earth with Yvonne's consciousness, which now unites the recent past ("she'd been confidentially informed") with the immediate future ("a taxi strike that afternoon") to end the sentence with her gaze attached to the present scene.[10]

The ironic upshot of all this activity of consciousness, where several time frames overlap, is "The *zocalo* was just the same," an assumption anticipated in the previous draft by the "eternal" pointing of an unidentified statue, the repeated "stills" of flowing fountain and drooping trees leading to, "God, how familiar it all was!" (29:4, 1). The statue, however, is the "eternal" form of the historical moment, a moment now identified by making it a statue of "the turbulent Huerta" (overriding the marginal suggestion of the more benign "Juarez" and perhaps suggested by Lowry's reading in Gunther, the equestrian Huerta is named with an eye to his later use in XI).[11] The sinister note evoked by Huerta is underscored by the reminder that the "horn[ed]" planet Venus is also Lucifer, the morning star, and the red plane that has brought Yvonne now becomes his "winged emissary."

But Lowry is not finished with the overlapping of Yvonne's journey onto her present awareness, "the sea that morning going in with her" as she enters the bar. Her recollection of that sea—the tide's "ellipses," pelicans "moving with the precision of planets," boys blowing on "their mournful conch shells"—has, like the butterflies greeting the *Pennsylvania*, been rescued out of the discarded 1940 Chapter II. Those pages were a well Lowry returned to repeatedly: Weber's dialogue had been retrieved during the preceding revision. The quite distinct appearances of superseded materials show that Lowry fetched them only as he had precise uses for them, and the passages themselves resound rather differently in their new contexts. Here, the lyrical rhythms and the fresh imagery and romantic metaphors drawn from the morning seascape both jar against "the swift leathery perfumed alcoholic dusk" of the bar and contribute to Yvonne's "myopic" vision of the darkened interior. It is only now that Lowry, fully entering into the moment, realizes that the sudden shift from bright sun to evening-like dusk on Yvonne already half-seeing those early-morning sea-sights, might produce a misapprehension of the scene before her. In the previous draft, she had merely noted in passing the "surprisingly deserted bar." Now, when she enters, Lowry tries first "Surprisingly, the bar was empty of all save one figure," then, more daringly, "The bar was perfectly empty" (29:3, ts. 2) before, in a paragraph by itself, "The bar was empty, however," followed by the correction, "Or rather it contained one figure" (29:5, 3). The distinction between the two drafts is one of those apparently small differences that is in fact crucial to the Lowryan world of the *Volcano:* the radical difference between reporting the *product* of perception and dramatizating the *process* itself.

This far more elaborate and sustained dramatization of the complexities of consciousness, and especially its kinetic nature, the moment-to-moment alterations, corrections, shiftings, may owe its inception, in this chapter at least, to Yvonne's responses to the interplay between the Consul and the barman that follows in the text, but which had been developed by the preceding draft. Both passages give us an Yvonne subject to illusions, yet these are followed by an instance of the reverse, which we might call "exclusions." To Lowry's sense of the multiple possibilities and limited powers of human consciousness, every awareness implies a corresponding unawareness, a focusing of the mind here creating a blurring there, an overpowering emotion momentarily blocking a less compelling perception. Chapter II's eeriest example of the excluded arose in the previous draft with the unexpected materialization in the bar of the old woman from Tarasco. She has been a part of the chapter from 1940 onward, always striking Yvonne as ominous, but there is no mystery about her very presence until the 29:3 draft, when the Consul's gaze draws Yvonne's attention to this strange figure in the corner: "It was true, it was almost uncanny, there *was* someone else in the room she hadn't noticed until the Consul, without a word, had glanced behind them" (29:3, ts. 7 [9]). Doubtless Yvonne, emotionally focused on her reunion with Geoffrey, has simply "excluded" the old woman from awareness, unless, that is, we are willing to take seriously the insinuated possibility that the Consul has magically conjured her up (her stick handle here appears like "some animal claw or a goat's pollex perhaps"). However we explain it, the old woman's sudden presence makes Yvonne—and us—aware of her previous absence from Yvonne's consciousness.

More mundane is the exclusion, the "disappearance," of Laruelle's house from Yvonne's memory, for she has simply "forgotten" this unforgettable site of her adultery—that is, guiltily repressed it in her idealized mental reconstructions of the town.[12] Again, this lacuna first appears in the previous draft, but only in the present version does Lowry add the elaborate sentence that extends Yvonne's imagined Quauhnahuac and makes clear its guilty base: "It had vanished some time before, leaving not a trace, it was as if the house had never existed, just as in the mind of a murderer, she had read somewhere, it may happen that some prominent building in the vicinity of his crime, a landmark of both, may be obliterated so that upon returning to that neighbourhood, even though familiar with it all his life, he scarcely knows where to turn" (29:5, second 5).

The earlier form of a sentence describing Yvonne's response to the square as she and Geoffrey leave the Bella Vista perhaps provides a kind of rationale for her various illusions and exclusions: "The whole scene before her, striking Yvonne as so strangely familiar once more, and yet so sharply strange after the year's absence, the severance of thought and body, mode of being, began to appear, as if some mysterious lymph separation secreted had affected her vision, oddly confused and out of focus" (29:3, ts. 8). The bizarre physicality of the metaphor here points forward to Yvonne's ensuing meditation on La Despedida, her desperately emotional effort to "heal" the "severed halves." The language carries its built-in irony, the physicality of this emotional-mental effort, but in his new draft, Lowry creates another "exclusion" that drives the irony in that meditation home. While Yvonne so identifies herself and Geoffrey with the sundered halves of the rock that she imagines "the other half" speaking to her in the Consul's voice, the actual Geoffrey by her side has said something that Yvonne (and we) will never hear: "'—in Tortu' the Consul was saying, though she was not following." She does, however, notice that he is "beginning to shake again":

"Geoffrey I'm so thirsty why don't we stop and have a drink?
"Geoffrey let's just be reckless this once and get tight together before breakfast?"
Yvonne said neither of these things. (29:5, 2)

These are, certainly, "illusions" for the reader: however briefly, fictional conventions—typography, punctuation, syntax—have asserted these as spoken by Yvonne, and their retrospective cancellation by the final sentence cannot undo them, make them as if they never were. *She* may not have "said" them, but the *Volcano* ineradicably has. Their status for her, however, remains problematic: if she did not say them, did she at least think them? However queried, the text remains mute.

These gaps in consciousness—part of Lowry's complex play with the appearance/reality split—are among the most resonant ways in which this chapter and indeed the novel explores the motif of severance or "divorce." One of the most compelling passages in Chapter II to dramatize this gap appears only in this draft, when the seemingly reunited couple pauses before the print shop window. Here the very image seems to affirm the bridging of gaps, healing of splits, the closing of "the frightful cleft, the eternal horror of opposites" (male/female, past/present, old world/new world, time/eternity, etc.). Both the previous draft and the current one have "They stood as once, as forever, looking in" (29:4, 9 and 29:5, second 1; cf. Wallace Stevens's "the intricate evasions of 'as'") before this draft cancels "as forever." Indeed, the phrase is meaningless; to a description that had until now been concerned only with the contents of the shop window is added a reflection of and by Yvonne that mocks the appearance of oneness, the illusion of timelessness. A marginal note on the previous draft—"A creature of sun here"—suggests the connection between this passage and the earlier ship, air, and sea additions made at this time, but the connection with sun and sea, while associating her again with Venus, manifests only her fragmentation. Mirrors are instruments of dissociation and partialness, as Yvonne will rediscover in Chapter IX: while they seem simply to duplicate, they invert the images they present, and even in appearing to restore us to ourselves, they sever the outer image from the inward sense, placing at a distance our imaged and imagined selves:

> From the mirror within the window an ocean creature so drenched and coppered by sun and winnowed by sea-wind and spray looked back at her she seemed, even while making ["mimicking" cancelled] the fugitive motions of Yvonne's vanity, somewhere beyond human grief charioting the surf. But the sun turned grief to poison and a glowing body only mocked the sick heart, Yvonne knew, if that sun-darkened creature of waves and sea margins and windrows did not!

Thus they "stood, as once," not "as forever"; "forever" belongs to "that sun-darkened creature" who is beyond humanity in her ability to be simultaneously in the window ("looked back at her") and elsewhere, dominating the elements ("charioting the surf"). Yvonne can no longer identify this demigoddess with her "poison[ed]" mortal self; the image "mock[s] the sick heart" even as the couple before the window, by summoning up the past ("as once"), mocks their present state, even as "the wedding invitations" mock the reality of severance pictured in La Despedida, even as that photograph, precisely in being an image rather than the thing itself, mocks the actual violence of the split it proclaims.[13]

The irreparable nature of this series of gaps is further driven home by their lack of congruence, the gaps between *them*, as it were. Just as the past is not the present, the outer not the inner, the image not the thing itself, metaphor not actuality, so is a human marriage not an unsevered rock, as the mixture of poignance and absurdity in Yvonne's meditation on La Despedida shows. Yet the fruitlessness of her effort lies not only in the inherent hopelessness of restoring a broken rock nor, finally, even in the failure of analogy revealed by the comedy but, as already noted, in the juxtaposition of the imagined speech of Geoffrey-the-rock and the remnants of the consequently unheard one of the actual Geoffrey beside her. The gap has not only not been healed, it has been widened by Yvonne's very passion to close it.

As we have seen, Lowry was also concerned in this chapter with a more mundane "gap," the growing tension between Yvonne and the Consul, especially during the walk to the house, when the presence of Jacques and Hugh is made known to her. Direct dramatization of Yvonne's responses made her appear shrewish; attempts to convey her indignation and dismay through action produced a preposterous repertoire of stumbles and limps. Two devices to extend (and minimize) these more traditional techniques get introduced in this draft: the boxing advertisements, used to comment on the couple's verbal sparring; and the silent "reaction," indicated by the quoted dash, thus: "–." The latter is surely a specific borrowing from film, the visual reaction shot that cannot be conveyed by words, but (Lowry here demonstrates) is not altogether beyond the resources of print. Both devices, in their different ways, enhance the outer world of a novel that is, like this chapter, becoming progressively interiorized.

Little is excised as a result of these devices—typically, they supplement rather than replace (although Yvonne will stumble only once from now on!)—but Lowry does refine this section of the chapter. For instance, rather than the Consul blithely quoting the "'No se puede vivir sin amar'" [sic] on Jacques's house, we are reminded of the words more obliquely by a peon's "gazing curiously" up at the house as it comes into view, a momentary ambiguity now created when Geoffrey says, "'And he's still there too. He hasn't budged an inch.'" Already off balance, Yvonne falters (rather than asking "sharply" as previously), "'Who—who hasn't—'" and looks back to see the peon "going into an alleyway" (29:5, second 6). According to Bustamente, spies are to be found at "every alley entrance," a locale that may link this figure with the sinister types lurking outside the Bella Vista, equipped now by Lowry with dark glasses to match the cinema manager's description and the Consul's own affectation so that Yvonne can almost grasp the wrong arm (10A). But Geoffrey here hurries on to specify some particulars of his and Jacques's "terrific times" ("'everything from Bishop Berkeley to the four o'clock *mirabilis jalapa*'"), dubs Quauhnahuac "'Cuckoldshaven,'" and (Lowry keeping one eye on Hugh's recollections in Chapter VI) informs Yvonne that his brother has "'become quite famous lately. For the second time, in case you weren't aware of the first'" (second 6, second 7, 9). Meanwhile, we are quietly being apprised of the wearing-off of Geoffrey's drinks: the sharply "correct,"

Taskerson-like bearing with which he had briskly left the Bella Vista gradually deserts him. After the disclosure of Hugh's presence, "they moved on, this time more slowly"; as Yvonne tries to question him about Hugh, he walks "more and more slowly," now also losing his mental place: "'What did I say' he asked at length." Pain and encroaching sobriety bring Geoffrey almost to a full stop: "the Consul's voice had grown hoarse, and he seemed also at this moment to have great difficulty in placing one foot in front of another" (9). Geoffrey's condition as a result of his drinks (or lack of them) continued to occupy Lowry on into the typescript (Texas II), for in this Yvonne-chapter it must be conveyed indirectly by small touches. The margins of the pages of the walk home contain tiny circled numbers against tell-tale signs (speed of movement, hoarseness, trembling or steadiness, mental alertness), for while Yvonne may not always be aware of what each of these signals means, Lowry was seeing to it that his drunk exhibited appropriate symptoms at each alcoholic stage. Nor was his concern confined to this chapter: on the Chapter III typescript, Geoffrey is made to grow hoarse "again" (Texas III, 28), and when he speaks in a "deep voice," Lowry quickly inserts "false" (10).

The exterior world gets extended in other ways, some of them relatively straightforward—shop names and advertisements surrounding the city square first appear here, like the boxing posters doubtless out of Mexican material then still in Lowry's possession—others more suggestive, like the lounging men outside the Bella Vista with whom the Consul has an "enigmatic" exchange and the man "resembling a carpenter" who says something like "'Mescalito'" to Geoffrey and whom he salutes in "dubious greeting" (29:5, 10A, B). The most substantial addition of this sort is a wholly new episode on the walk arising directly out of the Consul's alcoholic need. As they pass the opening shops on the Calle Tierra del Fuego, the Consul suddenly disappears into one with a hasty "'momentito,'" and Yvonne is abruptly deserted in the street to wait and wonder. Once more, Lowry dramatizes the moment-by-moment process of response: she walks on past, retraces her steps in order to join him, "repents" that decision, experiences a "mood of martyrdom" at being "abandoned," forgets all about Geoffrey in renewed wonder at being again in Quauhnahuac, and so on. Within the abarrotes, it is clear, the Consul is having some kind of drink(s) and a more enigmatic conversation, snippets of the interlocutor's side of which emerge in the *double entendres* of Lowry's Spanglish suggesting alcohol (do the numbers "two . . . tree . . . quatros" refer to the drinks being consumed?), sex ("*layee*," "*Eggs*," taken from an earlier version of Vigil in Chapter V), the demonic ("*diablos*"; we are, after all, on the Street of the Land of Fire), and, oddly, gangsters ("you—ah—Al Ca*pone*!").[14] As if to deny any rupture, the Consul, without missing a beat, emerges to resume his discourse exactly where he left off: "'In Tortu,' he was saying . . ." (second 4).

In the final holograph of this draft, the child's funeral, also salvaged from the 1940 Chapter II, follows Geoffrey's reemergence onto the street, punctuating his celebration of "'the business of—*look out!*—drinking,'" moving past "swiftly" in a chapter where a "little corpse" is prophesied to be "'transported by express.'" But if its most obvious application is to Geoffrey himself, the different placement of an earlier worksheet gave the incident another thrust. Lowry first sketched the end of his new episode this way: "She hears strange dialogue about you diablo—you tree diablos—haw haw haw, you Al Capone—and eggs—suddenly the child's funeral passes then Geoffrey comes out" (Texas II, verso 25). The earlier placement of the child's funeral, present here only to Yvonne and juxtaposed with "eggs," suggests that it was first intended as a comment on her childlessness rather than as a portent of the Consul's death. However, Lowry came quickly to see that, via her dead child also named Geoffrey, already a part of Chapter III, the child's funeral could play more than one role; after all, it was not only the Consul whose death might be thereby foreshadowed.

Another "gap" new to this draft is entirely Yvonne's willed creation. As Geoffrey recounts Hugh's efforts to "straighten me up" and asserts facetiously that of course he's "'absolutely stone cold sober now, as you can readily see,'" she responds with apparent good-natured aplomb, "'Oh absolutely' Yvonne smiled, walking on slowly beside him." Her unspoken reaction, however, is another matter. In previous drafts, her thought had been congruent with the outer situation, reflections occasioned by Geoffrey's drinking, followed by an apparently unconnected passage of responses to the familiarity of their street, her last glimpse of it, and so on. Lowry began to see how these two could be more closely integrated—an integration that would finally eliminate her tedious mental rehearsal of the various stages of his drinking. Beside the paragraph of responses to Calle Nicaragua, Lowry wrote, "make clear that she's thinking about this deliberately in order to avoid thinking that her two ex-lovers are here. She was prepared for tirade and humiliation: chaotic and despairing frame of mind. While in the back of her mind: Box!" (29:4, ts. 17). He does better than this, for Yvonne's response is not just to Hugh's and Jacques's presence but to Geoffrey's condition as well, for which she has *not* been fully "prepared":

> full of thoughts that gathered her up like a whirlwind and had already swept her a thousand miles off. For with her whole soul she seemed frantically running away from all this. On the other hand she was not running away, she was not being gathered up, she was all this while walking on slowly, inevitably, toward their house. But deliberately as a man on a high unguarded place looks up at the pine trees above on the precipice and comforts himself by saying: "Never mind about the drop below me, how very much higher those pines are" she forced herself out of the moment: she stopped thinking: or she thought about the street again, remembering her last poignant glimpse of it—and how much more desperate things had seemed then! (29:5, 11)

Lowry will smooth the passage and eliminate repetitiveness, but that very repetitiveness here underlines the gap (and Yvonne's deliberate cultivation of it) between exterior and interior, the divorce of body and voice from mind and feeling, and then of conscious thought from underlying emotion, so that the Yvonne who continues to walk, automaton-like, toward the house, fills her head with perceptions of the landscape, suppressing her panicky responses and, for a time, even the presence of the man next to her. Little wonder that a moment later she feels "lightheaded"!

No chapter of the *Volcano* is more concerned with "divorce" than this one, and a final significant addition at this stage extends an association that deepens its resonance. Picking up the revised opening of the letter of Chapter I, the Consul now tells Yvonne directly that he's been away from Quauhnahuac only once, to Oaxaca, and Lowry's repetitions create an echolalia of sadness: "'Oaxaca.—Remember Oaxaca?' '—Oaxaca?—' '—Oaxaca—'—The word was like a breaking heart . . .'" (29:5, 7). The new passage this introduces is almost exactly that of the published novel: what it does (aside from becoming a link in the Oaxaca-motif that runs literally from first to last chapters) is precisely to dramatize "divorce." It is no accident that in a passage that begins by insisting on the reverberations of a name ("Oaxaca"), Yvonne ponders the word *divorce* itself: "She had looked it up on the ship: to sunder, to sever. And divorced meant: sundered, severed." The two words are then equated: "Oaxaca meant divorce." But if the name now conjures up "divorce" for her, it is only because it once evoked the reverse, the unity both Geoffrey and Yvonne refer to as "us": "In Oaxaca they had found each other once." "Divorce" lies in the gap between what she recalls—the roses, the great tree, the buses, the notice '*damas accompañadas de un caballero gratis!*' which promised drinking shared and harmless, and especially "their cries of love, rising into the ancient fragrant Mayan air"—and what she now sees, the Consul "straightening out the leaflets on the bar ... changing mentally from the part played for Fernando to the part he would play for her." " 'Surely this cannot be us' she cried in her heart suddenly 'this cannot be us—say that it is not somebody, this cannot be us here!' " It is this draft that first notes what these former lovers do *not* do on reunion: "They did not kiss." Hearts that can be broken, hearts that can utter passionate cries, give way to the "heart" that is, like the kiss, an absence, for Oaxaca becomes now "where the Consul had gone when she left, as if into the heart of the sundering, of the severance." Between the "fragrant" metaphorical language of the remembered past and the cold and divisive abstractions that designate their present lies the gap now designated by the sound "Oaxaca," repeated once more to end the passage with the "weary ... sigh" of accepted death.

If the previous version of Chapter III seemed hardly to justify the rewriting (see chapter 3, pp. 177ff.), now, perhaps feeling himself on the last lap, Lowry compensated. Most obvious is the entirely new action that takes the Consul out in search of a cantina, only to bring about his collapse in the street and the encounter with his "frightfully English" countryman. Surrounding and, in part, including this episode is the recasting of Geoffrey's dealings with Yvonne, which, in turn, involved the still-closer focus on his alcoholic condition. Chapter III is the first direct presentation of the mind of the novel's protagonist, a truth that would have been borne in upon Lowry by his taking up the chapter in sequence; and with the blackout of Chapter V behind him, he had already discovered that the most efficient way to alter the outer world of his novel was to unfix Geoffrey's inner one. Suddenly and belatedly, Chapter III, like the other consular chapters (if more mildly), becomes epistemologically problematic.[15]

In the new III Geoffrey's alcoholic state is clearly more advanced than in any previous version. In his heightened desperation, Yvonne's bath becomes an opportunity that drives him out toward a cantina, and his uncertainty of the line between inner and outer reality places him for the first time under the illusion that on falling in the street he is actually addressing a returning Hugh. The dash from the house is an early manifestation of the lure of the cantinas rather than just of alcohol—there is, after all, a prominent bottle of Johnny Walker available—and, *mutatis mutandis*, a dash away from Yvonne. For this purpose, Lowry created a lane stretching off "to the left" up the Calvary-like hill of the Calle Nicaragua, and a small cantina with bartender and sleepy cat transplanted from the discarded station bar of Chapter I (see p. 194 above).

The Consul's belief that he is actually addressing Hugh, which now anticipates the outright hallucination of the dead man by the pool, involved Lowry in some recasting of this already lengthy monologue. The oral touches, the "are-you-listening-Hugh?"s and rhetorical questions, become intensified, more numerous: only punctuation (the use of a dash rather than quotation marks) gives the reader a clue that the address may not be uttered aloud. The expository burden of the passage, ostensibly unaltered, is utterly transformed by a strand of the previous version that now governs, more subtly and complexly, the very structure of the speech: the partly genuine, partly hypocritical and always tricky theme of mutual concern, of brotherly love.

The address now opens on this note, invoking a Hugh perceived as literally in the act of "lending a hand," a move immediately chalked on a scoreboard of brotherly assistance ("it is perhaps indeed your turn these days to lend a hand. Not that I haven't always been delighted to help *you!*"). Geoffrey was most recently so "delighted" when Hugh had turned up suddenly in Paris, but this reminder of brotherly betrayal (I was helping you out, remember: look how you repaid me!) is ostensibly yet another form of assistance: "Why do I say this?—Is it in part [what is the other "part"?] that you should see that I also recognise how close Yvonne and I had already been brought to disaster before your meeting! Are you listening, Hugh—do I make myself clear? Clear that I forgive you, as somehow I have never wholly been able to forgive Yvonne, and that I can still love you as a brother and respect you as a man" (29:10, 10). There has been "all too little opportunity" to act as a brother toward you, the Consul goes on, although I have in the past "acted as a father" [to your brotherly guilt, Hugh, add the Oedipal burden]. Of course, "I never dreamed for a moment such a thing as did happen [the adultery] would or could happen . . . that I trusted you goes without saying." Now, I know you tried to "justify yourself," and that what you did "you did impulsively and have tried to forget in the cruel abstraction of youth." But I fear that, precisely because you are really "a good and simple person," later remorse will bring you "a suffering on account of it more abominable than any you have caused me [you may not be in pain now, but you will be, especially after I get through telling you how much pain you've brought *me*]. How may I help you? How ward it off? How shall the murdered man convince his assassin he will not haunt him?" [I promise not to haunt you, Hugh, even though you *have* destroyed me] After all, "*I* realise to what degree I brought all this upon myself," in fact my "cast[ing] Yvonne upon you in that fashion was a feckless action—almost, I was going to say, a clownish one, inviting" and deserving of comic retribution. Does all this "help?" "I sincerely hope so" (11–12).

The speech is a brilliant mixture of blame and self-blame, accusation and forgiveness, exculpation and renewed indictment, resentment and affection as the Consul casts himself and Hugh in a rapid series of mutually shifting, sometimes contradictory, roles: the fallen sinner and the good Samaritan, the dutiful elder and the irresponsible child, the generous Christ and the ungrateful Judas, the good father and the incestuous son, the trusting husband and the disloyal friend, the wounded cuckold and the self-righteous seducer, the condescending sage and the noble simpleton, the victim and his assassin, the irresponsible drunkard and *his* victim, the clown and his punisher. Structurally, tonally, psychologically, it is a considerable advance on the previous version, where the Consul had managed to be convincingly unconvincing in "excusing" his brother's adultery. That earlier Geoffrey was nobler but less interesting or credible than the later one; furthermore, his "nobility" was hardly consistent with his more mistrustful and antagonistic responses to Hugh elsewhere.

Hugh may not be on the spot to give aid, but someone else is. The wonderfully comic encounter with the traveling Englishman that now follows seems to have been achieved with relative ease; an unnecessary daughter (?) in the passenger seat and the excessive prop of a long cigarette holder disappear from early attempts, but except for the Venezuelan card the Consul discovers in his pocket, everything is in final place by the fair holograph. One reason for the epsiode's success appears in the marginalia of an early worksheet—"Act out with Margie"— the same draft that discloses the cinematic model(s) for the Englishman—"Nigel Bruce Arthur Treacher playing Nigel Bruce" (Texas III, verso 15; perhaps not surprisingly, this is the one scene the film version got tonally *almost* right). In the insistently "British" voice of his compatriot, we hear the Consul's alienation in Mexico: he is truly a man without a country. And without a function, as the Englishman's reference to "'this oil business'" and Geoffrey's interrupted—and powerless— offer of consular help reminds us. Brief as it is, the incident conjures up not only Geoffrey's Cambridge past (developed in ensuing chapters) but, in the small contretemps of the Trinity tie, the entire British class system. The nameless Englishman may be comically stereotypical, but he is not unaware of the situation he is dealing with in his kindly way, as the draft makes clearer than the novel: even in offering the Consul his "Burke's Irish" with "'Have a nip?'" he is having second thoughts: "'But perhaps you'd better not'" (29:10, 13). By then, of course, it is too late: Geoffrey is "taking a long draught," ironic mnemonic of *"Might a soul bathe there and be clean or slake its drought?"*

However, perhaps the central point to be made about this parodic Samaritan incident (which, again, has its ironic echo in the "dead man" by the pool later) is precisely its humor, another instance of Lowry's late addition of comic versions of figures, actions, motifs elsewhere treated with full seriousness, the deliberate inclusion of ironic or absurd perspectives that complicate our responses. While he added individual humorous touches throughout, comedy most easily made its way through new material. Thus, in the sentence that closes this incident— "Erect as Jim Taskerson, he thought, married now too, poor devil— restored, the Consul glided down the Calle Nicaragua"—the source of comic effect is not simply Geoffrey's effortless "glide" on the wings of the whiskey (recall his "toiling" drinkless up this "road . . . of agony"), nor his avuncular assertion of fellowship with all other bedeviled sods of husbands (*husband,* Señor Firmin?), but our awareness from that other comic addition that the "erect manly carriage" of the Taskersons was a sure index of their inebriation. However, the comedy here reaches forward as well as backward, spilling over into the ensuing action both in the compulsively "English" accent the Consul discovers he has adopted with Yvonne and in Lowry's employment of extravagantly sinister simile when Geoffrey enters her bedroom "innocently as a man who has committed murder while dummy at bridge" (29:10, 14).

As comedy seems to infect the ensuing scene in the bedroom, Lowry discovers how, with a boost from the Consul's latest drink, to rid that episode of its remaining traces of mean-spirited quarrelling. Having displayed earlier the unreliability of Geoffrey's consciousness, Lowry simply finesses Yvonne's dialogue here. When she makes her proposal that they leave Mexico (with whatever arguments or commentary she might surround it), we do not witness it because "The Consul scarcely heard what she was saying." Thus in a single bold stroke Lowry eliminated the wrangling over the marriage and drinking that had marred previous drafts. There is a sleight of hand here: the interior response that so preoccupies Geoffrey that Yvonne's words are swallowed up in it should logically be his reaction to those words, not the replacement for them. However, the moment works because Lowry has already carefully established the Consul's uncertain hold on the distinction between external and internal reality, and the growing primacy of the latter.

Once again, this shift is part of the novel's tendency to "sink into the action of the mind," dialogue giving way to consciousness. Heavy with tension and blame in earlier versions, the scene is now invested with ironic comedy as emphasis shifts from a dramatization of both figures to the contemplation of Geoffrey's reactions. The elaborate horror in his initial response, for instance, stems from his "flash" of understanding that he might be robbed of "the occasion for desperate celebration" in favor of "—Good God!—his salvation." To counter this menacing possibility, he produces ("with passion, with anguish") the anecdote of the out-of-work actor, from which he draws "with perfect seriousness" a wildly inappropriate, highflown "moral." Part of the comedy, however, lies in the absurd reflexiveness of the story, for Geoffrey himself is here doubly an "out of work actor," replacing his "English accent" with that of "a Becker street dereliction [*sic:* in the Texas typescript he becomes "a Beeker Street mummer"!]" and "shaking violently with the emotion of the poor actor," whom, in fact, he has never encountered: the entire story is second-hand.

But it is Yvonne's quiet suggestion that they "'cope with'" the possibility of leaving "'in a day or two, when you're sober'" that affords Lowry his most extended comic opportunity here. Both the suggestion and Geoffrey's indignant silent reaction are new, the latter a brilliantly elaborate fugue of self-justification that stutters through initial outrage at "the enormity of the insult" ("As if, as if, as if, he were not sober now!"), withdraws slightly ("he was not sober . . . not at this very moment he wasn't!") only to surge forward righteously again ("what had that to do with . . . ? . . . what right had Yvonne to assume . . . ? . . . What right had she . . . ?"), rolls mental eyes at the blindness, the ignorance, the insensitivity of the uncomprehending ("Ah, a woman could not know . . . ! From what conceivable standpoint of rectitude did she imagine . . . ? And she knew nothing whatever of . . . ! What a world."), discovers self-justifying wheels within wheels ("And the trouble was she had now spoiled the moment. . . . Because the Consul now felt that he might have been able. . . . But who could agree with someone who . . . ?"), and with pained aplomb, irrelevantly, self-pityingly, approves the correctness of his unappreciated decorum ("no one could tell when he was drunk. . . . He was not the person to be seen reeling about in the street. True, he might lie down in the street, if need be, like a gentleman. . . . Ah, what a world it was. . . . !") (29:10, 17–18).

This silent diatribe has all the shifts in tone, the rhetoric, the rhythms of speech; it does not differ appreciably from the ensuing passage, apparently, delivered aloud ("he said almost tragically"). Not surprisingly, perhaps, the next two "speeches"—that is, passages within quotation marks—are irreducibly ambiguous; "He either thought or said" and "thinking or saying" constitute the respective introductions. Some of the material for Geoffrey here is altogether new, and some is particularly suggestive, like that stemming from an "interested but not concerned publisher in Chicago": "'it's amazing when you come to think of it how the human spirit seems to blossom in the shadow of the abbatoir! How, not far enough below the stockyards to escape altogether the reek of the porterhouse of to-morrow people can be living in cellars the life of the old alchemists of Prague! . . . What am I talking about? Copula Maritalis? Or from alcohol to alkahest. Can you tell me?'" (29:10, 19–20) This constitutes a significant portion of the occult references introduced in this draft, where Geoffrey asserts his adeptness "in the rigging of the Cabbala" (15), refers to "the paths and spheres of the Holy Cabbala" (18), and in the attempted lovemaking (where it is the only substantial change) thinks of the cabalistic "neophyte, Yesod-bound" (22). Yet these allusions are also, as in the passage quoted above ("'What am I talking about? . . . Can you tell me?'"), tipped into a draft in which Lowry is intent on unsettling the status of the Consul's utterances, unmooring his text, taking with one hand what he has seemed to give with the other.[16]

As Geoffrey moves uneasily between bed and door, between Yvonne and the reassuring sight of the whisky bottle, new "images of grief and tragedy"—the lost butterfly, the duck and the hen, Oscar Wilde at Clapham Junction—flicker. These, again, are part of the unsettling of the phenomenal world, the interiorizing achieved by exploitation of symptomatic features of his alcoholic condition, an "alcoholic realism" that has been established much earlier in the chapter. Alone on the porch with Yvonne, awkward and self-conscious, Geoffrey becomes aware that his earlier feeling of "pleasant . . . tightness" is fading (29:10, 3), and with the play of scotch versus strychnine, the insistent proffering of a drink to Yvonne (less embattled here than on previous drafts), and the awakening of the voices of familiars, Lowry for the first time makes the effect of alcohol on the Consul's consciousness crucial to the ensuing text. Self-absorbed, listening only to his internal voices, the Consul belatedly becomes aware that Yvonne has been speaking to him—it will be the first spot in the novel at which *we* become aware that Geoffrey's internal world, like Yvonne's in Chapter II, can eclipse the external one—and that the resentment his familiar expresses toward Yvonne is in fact unwarranted, for she, "laughing," has authorized "'a decent drink.'" A moment later, uncertainty will be compounded: for the first time we are literally unsure of what is happening: "They were embracing, or so it all but seemed, passionately" (5–5A).

As time seems to slow ("The swimming pool ticked like a clock") and the Consul discovers Vigil's card, the novel establishes his susceptibility to blackout: "What had he done?" he wonders, the previous night. Out of this radical uncertainty about his own experience comes a questioning that asks for reassurance: "'—Have you really come back? Or have you just come to see me?' 'Here I am, aren't I?'" Yvonne's response of course refuses Geoffrey the assurance he requests, but he here adds: "'Yes, here you are. Or are you?'" This final question was quickly cut, perhaps because it seemed redundant or simply silly, but the Geoffrey who hears voices (and knows he is "hearing voices"), whose mental loss of the previous night has turned it into a threatening *"ursa horribilis,"* wants sensory clarification perhaps even more than emotional reassurance. What he means is, "Tell me that you are here in the flesh, that you are not an hallucination, a vision, a projection of my desire, a manifestation from the world of spirits." "Spirits," by this draft, may point toward alcohol or toward the occult; the double reference is potentially more than a verbal quibble, as the vision of the dead man by the pool will soon suggest.[17]

As they go on to exchange compliments, the text insists on its own uncertainty. "She seemed to have said," "Had he said that?" "Yvonne had apparently replied"—the pluperfects force the action into the past while at the same time leaving irresolvable the status of the dialogue, experience receding uncertainly from the present moment. The couple is trying, apparently, to find safe small talk, but time hangs heavy. "The swimming pool ticked on," but it brings along with it a potential counter to indeterminacy, the line from Marvell that raises the question of another order of time and being altogether: *"Might a soul bathe there and be clean or slake its drought?"* Ostensibly associating the liquidity of the pool with Geoffrey's desire for a drink, it actually points in a different direction, for Marvell's Damon has recently encountered Pan (Christ), a "late change" that presents to the shepherd alternate refreshment for the soul. The icon of Christ has been hovering over the opening of Chapter III for several drafts, and the line from "Clorinda and Damon," ironically repeated in the episode of the Englishman, now becomes a part of the ambiguous threading through the chapter of a countermotif to the infernal (as in the two voices of Geoffrey's apparently opposed familiars). It is a brilliant late addition here, telescoping such matters as the alcoholic cycle of drink and remorse, of desire for relief and the question of where to find it, of a yearning for Yvonne and deep mistrust of her, of the varied possibilities of the locus of "there." The kind of literary uncertainty created by this allusion is familiar, traditional, although not all writers employ it this richly; but taken together with Lowry's quite untraditional unsettling of the epistimological status of action and dialogue and his growing introduction of elements of the comic, the ironic, the parodic, Chapter III has become by this stage a clear example of his deliberate creation of a multidimensional text.

When he turned to Chapter IV, Lowry came to a unit of his novel that seemed less in need of alteration than any of the chapters preceding it. Easily the most important addition here is Hugh's evocation of his Mexican friend Juan Cerillo.[18] Hugh's pained but rather grandiose sense of guilt as he and Yvonne rode through the countryside in the previous draft had concluded, "No peace man will ever find but that must pay full toll to hell" (29:13, ts. 16), a line surrounded by pencilled qualifications and extensions, some having to do with Mexico ("But it was a lie so far as Mexico was concerned"), some urging Hugh to imitate Mexico ("Can you not be a man as brave as Mexico, follow her example."), one universalizing the experience of Mexico ("In a sense, Mexico was man—"), and one epitomizing it ("What made the Mexicans nicer than any other people? He had known one in Spain, the Credito Ejidal").[19] What Lowry's surviving notes show is his attempt to compress these various senses into one, to present the experience of Mexico as a universal one, but bodied forth in an individual who will simultaneously act as exemplar for Hugh—on a smaller scale, a revival of the ambition Laruelle had expressed for the figure of the Consul in the opening chapter of the 1940 *Volcano*. Lowry did not then have the resources to fulfill such an aim, and his success here with Juan Cerillo is a measure of the enormous artistic distance he has traveled since that clumsy start.

Although two worksheets show Lowry making notes for the qualities of Juan Cerillo and the process he is meant to exemplify, the new passage seems to have reached final form fairly quickly; in any case, surviving drafts are remarkable for their fullness and sophistication. Hugh's sense of "poisoned peace" provided the cue: now, an upbraiding voice—once more, the centrality of the spoken voice in these revisions!—in counterpoint to Hugh's gloom breaks in, a "good angel" not unlike the Consul's familiars, but, appropriate to the simpler Hugh, the voice of an actual acquaintance speaking in affectionate paradox ("'Firmin, you are a poor sort of good man'"). From a voice, Juan Cerillo becomes a ghostly presence, "an invisible member of their caravan," then a symbol of Mexico's generosity to the Spanish Republic.

His dangerous work with the Ejido is an outward and visible action in "a human cause" far less uncertain than Hugh's dubious attempts to "save" either his brother or Spanish democracy, and in it he manifests his triumph over both the outward forces of brutality and oppression—the horrors of the Díaz regime of his childhood—and the inner ones of guilt and remorse—for to give the most dreaded thrust to his Oedipal theme, Lowry has made Juan Cerillo not only a murderer, but a parricide (as one "who had fought with Huerta, but turned traitor," the father extends the betrayal theme). And so the lesson that unites all these dimensions—the individual, the moral exemplar, the epitome of his land, the symbol of mankind—is drawn, once more as if in the voice of the man himself: "For man, every man, Juan seemed to say, even as Mexico, must ceaselessly struggle upward. What was life but a warfare and a stranger's sojourn? Revolution rages too in the tierra caliente of each human soul. No peace but that must pay full toll to hell—" (29:14, 11).[20]

As he revised to make way for Juan Cerillo, Lowry saw an opportunity to create a plausible preparation for the new figure through Hugh's horse-like whistle. At first Hugh claims, as before, that he acquired this device in Texas, but Lowry, in afterthought, has him catch himself up: "Why had he said Texas? He had learned the trick in Spain from Juan Cerillo" (10). The Mexican having been brought to Hugh's mind, his reappearance a few moments later, aided by an inserted "now" ("Hugh imagined Juan Cerillo distinctly now") becomes simply the result of an associative process. The central Juan Cerillo passage is also responsible for such other touches as Hugh's association of Díaz with Maximilian—"[Juarez] should have had old thingmetight, Diaz, shot at the same time and made a job of it" (23)—as recent embodiments of the twin nightmares of Mexican history, exploitation from without and betrayal from within. Closely connected to this material from another direction is an addendum to Hugh's guilty association with Judas slightly later in the chapter, a poisonous remorse for which Hugh upbraids himself in terms similar to those of the imagined Juan. Now, his sense of the "necess[ity] to go out and hang oneself" is followed by these new sentences: "Ouch! Here indeed it was again, the temptation, the cowardly, the future-corruptive serpent, remorse, in itself a worse than Judas: trample on it, stupid fool. Be Mexico. Have you not passed through the river? In the name of God be dead. And Hugh actually did ride over a dead garter snake, embossed on the path like a belt to a pair of bathing trunks. Or perhaps it was a Gila monster." Here as later, horsemanship becomes metaphorical: as he rides on "by himself for a while," horse "reined in" (in a sentence later excised), "After all, he had not given in; now, he held his thoughts in check" (29:14, 14).[21] If Hugh is to fulfill his role as a figure of hope, however compromised—for Yvonne and Geoffrey in this chapter, for the world at large throughout the novel— he must not be left simply immersed in his own guilt.

Nothing else in this draft of IV is nearly as important, in itself and in its radiating effects, as the introduction of Juan Cerillo. The numerous small touches that make Hugh's urging of Yvonne and Geoffrey's new life in Canada seem, while still somewhat skeptically amused, more genuinely hopeful than earlier surely come from this source, producing in addition to the previous "Judas had forgotten," the triumphant "nay, Judas had been, somehow, redeemed" (29:14, 22). As if to dramatize this redemption, for the first time the two do not touch at chapter's close, the hurried embrace disappearing in the holograph, and even a brush of hands and arms excised in the typescript. Nonetheless, Lowry was well aware that Yvonne's unexpected presence served to complicate and, in part, undermine Hugh's intentions. Since their playful talk of climbing Popocatapetl had been a feature of Chapter X since 1940, when the pair were young lovers, to have Hugh here reflect that "he'd entertained a quite serious notion of finding time to climb Popo, perhaps even with Juan Cerillo—" (23) was to merge early the action and the figure associated with aspiration, "the desire to be, to do, good," since these were to separate in the later flirtatious exchange with Yvonne. Perhaps Hugh never mentions Juan Cerillo to Yvonne because the Zapotecan epitomizes those values that, for him, oppose her influence: public good vs. private satisfaction, service vs. betrayal, action vs. passion, male vs. female, agape vs. eros. And perhaps the combination of these conflicting appeals is what makes his affirmations (as he knows, so "passionate, yet so nearly always hypocritical") often grandiosely self-indulgent. Here, he considers that he has tried to persuade not simply England but "the world" not to cut its own throat (29:14, 7), and fantasizes for himself a central role behind the wheel of the *Noemijolea* (8). Yet these seem mere variations on his posturing, of which we are now in little doubt: he is made "secretly enormously proud" of his cowboy costume (2), and as he hooks his thumbs under his belt in "western" pose, announces, "'I'm completely through with newspaper work, it isn't a pose'" (7).

There are numerous miscellaneous adjustments and alterations in this new Chapter IV, but the base of this version, the previous typescript (29:13), does seem revised with a view to completion. As his major method of cancellation, Lowry there employs a series of small oblique lines (rather than his usual single vertical line or the marginal direction "Cut"), an oddly formal, neat practice which, with the relative paucity of new passages and the general sense of verbal tidying, confirms the impression that this version was to be "final." In a last brisk run-through, the draft supplies Hugh with a counterweight to Yvonne and his own guilt and thus gives his character a stronger sense of hope and new possibility, but other than weaving in those touches that will bring the text into consistent line with developments planned elsewhere and refining the responses of its central consciousness, Lowry appears to pronounce the chapter essentially finished.

Chapter IV was not extensively changed, but it was, literally, completely rewritten. With Chapter V we see a simple but telling compositional sign that Lowry just might accede to finishing his novel: not all of it is revised. The first part of the chapter, up through the encounter with Mr. Quincey, is left substantially unaltered.[22] What most concerned Lowry now, what received sustained attention, was the blackout section, which *as* a blackout had emerged only in the previous draft. Along with some briefer changes to the pages surrounding Vigil's arrival in the neighboring garden, this meant that about one-half of the chapter was rewritten at this stage. The remainder was simply taken over from the preceding version and, when necessary, refolioed.[23]

Geoffrey's first encounter with Vigil is a sudden reminder of his loss of the previous night. "You cannot lie to us," his voices now say, "We know what you did last night" (Texas V, insert 15–16). But Geoffrey himself does not know, and Lowry's revisions to the blackout section of Chapter V associate these two events. On an early worksheet the explicit connection also supplied motivation for the major thrust of the revision: "And then what had happened? Oh Oh the Consul said aloud. Perhaps nothing very bad after all, but his day already had another night in it, and he felt a pressing need to reconstruct" (Texas V, verso 29). The "Oh Oh" ("All this should be permeated with guilt" Lowry reminded himself [29:17, ts. 22]) demands the "need to reconstruct" manifested in the major textual alteration in this draft, the intercutting of anguished present—the Consul in the bathroom, glass of flat beer in hand—with bits of recovered past. What becomes dramatized is thus not, as in the previous version, what is "reconstructed" from that past, but the act of reconstructing itself—again, process rather than product. This is Lowry's more radical and problematic use of Conrad's framed narration, but where the latter's Marlow repeatedly turned from his tale to a human audience, the Consul reawakens to the pain of isolation, and what he regains from the past is not, as in Conrad, a coherent narrative, but a discontinuous set of fragments, full of uncertainty and ellipses.

On one level, very little seems to change between these versions: recollected dialogue and action on the porch remain almost exactly what they were. But the context in which that material appears has been crucially altered; the most important set of additions here are those that return us again and again to the Consul in the bathroom, thereby reminding us of the mental nature of the action. Thus we no longer have "He was steadily crossing the porch" but "in his mind too he was steadily crossing the porch," and in a new introductory passage: "But what had happened then? 'Oh' the Consul said aloud again. 'Oh.' The faces of the last hour hovered before him, the figures of Hugh and Yvonne and Dr. Vigil moving quickly and jerkily now like those of an old silent film, their words mute explosions in the brain" (29:17, ts. 20; 29:18, 1). "In his mind, "in the brain"—once again, the sinking of the novel into consciousness, more radically than in Chapter III, for here the status of the Consul's experience is complicated by the temporal factor. In this revision, the pluperfect becomes insistent: we, like the Consul, witness not what happened but what (perhaps) *had* happened ("But what had happened then?").

Within the interstices of this new technique, Lowry exploits his altered situation inventively. For instance, Vigil's "magnificently giving the whole show away" by blurting out before Hugh and Yvonne how "'perfectamente borracho'" the Consul had been appears in the new version almost exactly as it had earlier. What is significantly different is that rather than moving on at once to the doctor's proposed trip to Guanajuato, the narrative now pauses ("A strange fellow") to bring us back to Geoffrey reflectively sipping his flat beer, a bibulous savoring that allows *us* to savor the humorous situation created by Vigil's tactlessness. The comedy is furthered by the Consul's sighing, self-righteous "Why couldn't people hold their liquor?" which unexpectedly gives way to genuine alcoholic pathos: "In the final analysis there was no one you could drink to the bottom of the bowl with. A lonely thought" (29:18, 2). Only then, the moment enriched, does Lowry return to his previous text.

The single sustained addition to this section of the chapter that is not simply a function of the recovery of lost time is the two paragraph "parody of . . . meditation" that follows the Consul's conceit of his soul as a town "ravaged and stricken in the black path of his excess" ("'why couldn't it have been a white path?'" queries a marginal note [29:17, ts. 24]). Here, however, the Consul feels divorced from time altogether, ominously so, for while he can still "see" his earlier self crossing the porch "it was as if something he could not put his finger on had mysteriously supervened to separate drastically that returning figure from himself sitting in the bathroom,—the figure on the porch, for all its damnation, seemed younger, to have more freedom of movement, choice." Yet not only the past seems lost, but the entire stream of time: to the almost-drinkless Geoffrey, that envisaged self also appears "to have, if only because it held a full glass of beer once more, a better chance of a future" (29:18, 4). When Lowry plays, as here, with the sense of temporality, the occult is probably not far away.

Attaching itself to Vigil's remark about "insanes," the passage quickly moves into a condition beyond medical powers: "how interested would the doctor have been in one who felt himself being shattered by the very forces of the universe?" The personal thus becomes the cosmic, Vigil's "practised eye" becomes the Consul's, who reads a handwriting on the wall for world destruction and, going further still, raises the possibility that he is not only victim but agent of this armageddon, whether in his own person or as an "innocent" child, a kind of antilogos of ran-dom de-creation. The passage pointedly incorporates an ironic citation of Yeats's "uncontrollable mystery on the bestial floor" ("bestial" will on second thought revert to "bathroom," but even here the line refers to the wet footprints of the adulterous swimmers), Lowry's parodic evocation of the salvific Child, Creator and Redeemer of historical process.

That Lowry had occult matters in mind during these revisions is confirmed not only by Geoffrey's dark musings here (or by the Cape letter's mention of "the infant Horus" [*Letters* 74]), but by marginalia (including the "white path") on the previous typescript: "Mem: write down the Cambridge cabbalists and Platonists. Henry Moore etc. Old Carruthers—the old Crow—knows about Henry Moore etc."; "For Saturn lives at fifty-two/Bahomet lives at fifty-one" [cancelled]; "Somewhere in last chapter: the Consul pretends to be: 'No, my real name of course is Theophrastus Bombastus von Hohenheim' (Paracelsus)"; "the thousand tongued murmur of the world of shells" (29:17, 21, 24). Even marginally some of these are marked for other chapters (and perhaps, in one case, meant for a poem), and none gets used anywhere in V, but they certainly suggest one of Lowry's preoccupations while rewriting here and may well contribute to the single significant addition to the bewildered queries Geoffrey poses on first waking in the bathroom. "Where were the others?" the previous draft had wondered simply (29:17, ts. 20). Now questioning runs this way: "Where were the others? But now he heard some of the others' voices on the porch. Some of the others? It was just Hugh and Yvonne, of course, for the doctor had gone. Yet for a moment he could have sworn the house had been full of people" (29:18, 1). Nothing that follows will support this sense of "other people" (yet on what basis would we judge?), but "people" may not be the precise term. That Geoffrey hears voices we already know: that he may sense other "presences" will be suggested a few pages later even without use of cabbalistic marginalia. Having established the Consul's voices, hallucinations, experiential doubts, and now blackout—in short, having rendered radically uncertain the ontological status of the world as filtered through Geoffrey's mind, Lowry becomes bolder in opening the possibilities of the occult apprehensions of that mind. As in Poe's tales, however, the "reasonable" explanation of derangement, here with a mighty alcoholic assist, is always available.

Lowry was not quite through, however. Although Atlantis lore is not truly "occult" and had been a part of the novel at least since 1940, Lowry's delvings into other spiritualist and cabbalist material seems to have reopened that earlier vein of interest. Now in his corrections he went out of his way to add, via Jules Verne, "Down, down to the frightful 'poulps.' Meropis of Theopompus. . . . And the ignivome mountains" (27:10, ms. "E").[24] This indeed is a descent to a spot "under the volcano," one Dr. Vigil confidently attributes to alcoholic illusion, to tequila, to mescal. But the Consul, of course, has been talking not simply of himself, but of the world. As if to underline the importance of this comment, Lowry on the typescript alters his form of address from "'Arturo'" to "'compañero,'" Geoffrey's only use in the novel of this loaded term (Texas V, 29). He and Dr. Vigil may indeed be "major adepts," but their shared ranking "in the Great Brotherhood of Alcohol" appears confined to consumption, for it is only the Consul who believes in the validity of his bibulous visions. In the end, it seems, there truly is no one he can drink with to the bottom of the bowl.

Lowry was, he told Jonathan Cape, at work on Chapter VI when his fire occurred, taking with it some of his revisions (*Letters* 77), and the pencilled directive on the typescript opening confirms the situation: "Page 43 missing—burned—in last analysis use p. 34 of copy and cut accordingly" (Texas VI, 1). There is no telling just how much was lost in the fire, but burn holes in some of the surviving leaves (30:4), the radical incompleteness of the records for this chapter, and the holograph page 43 called for in Lowry's note all testify to its effect. It is perhaps the last of the chapters worked on in Dollarton, and presumably brings us to spring 1944.

As we have seen (chapter 3, pp. 147–49), losses from this chapter make it sometimes impossible to speak authoritatively of exactly what was introduced when. Like Chapter V, it did not now seem to Lowry to demand a wholly new draft: indeed, in addition to those typescript pages that, revised, become part of the base for the new fair copy, some of the leaves from the previous version, after being added to this "mixed" draft, moved on yet again to get incorporated directly into the finished typescript. In any case, there certainly was at some point in Dollarton a complete manuscript-typescript from which Margerie made the Chapter VI now a part of the Texas *Volcano*, and almost all of that document does survive.[25] Thus if it may not prove possible to trace all changes as they emerged, we can nonetheless discuss the chapter as it stood somewhere around the middle of 1944.

Lowry's general aim seems to be the double one of both individuating Hugh and suggesting his underlying reflective relation to his brother. The restlessly guilty note on which Chapter VI opens on the one hand leads into his very particular past while on the other resonates as a lower-keyed version of Geoffrey's. Thus the meditation now begins with Hugh brooding on the opening of Dante's *Commedia* (cited, presumably from memory—Lowry's, that is—inaccurately). Since Lowry is working to dramatize consciousness rather than just report it, he creates expressive interactions between inner and outer states. For instance, an earlier worksheet at this point reads simply, "With one hand Hugh turned the dial of the radio back and forth" (30:4, A). Now, "—*Ahhh!* Hugh, as if to rid himself of these repulsive thoughts, turned the dial back and forth," the frustrated sigh and "erasing" motion acting out the connection between his self-accusation and the restless gesture. The Mexican voices on the radio seem to take up the theme, like the Consul's familiars, persuading Hugh that even his superficially selfless actions, like the desire "to lead the whole Jewish race out of Babylon" (Lowry having at last found an appropriate land of exile), is rooted in dishonesty.

Lowry has by now mastered the fine line that he walks with Hugh throughout his self-examination, the establishing of which is one of the prime purposes of these early passages, that line between the naive, even painfully sincere, desire to see oneself honestly and to "do the right thing," and the helpless absurdity of the moral posturing this leads him into, an absurdity not dispelled by those flashes of self-awareness that serve only to start the round again. No sooner has he recalled a London church with its accusing "Is it nothing to you all ye who pass by?" than, thinking of his impending journey to Spain, he finds himself falling into the role of the sacrificial Christ, silently addressing heedless passers-by—then guiltily catches himself in the self-serving act (Neilson 1:2, 2–3). The entire paragraph in which Hugh considers his belated gesture toward Spain is shot through with that mix of moral earnestness and self-consciousness that impels and taints his actions, making them both daring and desperate, the combination captured in the oxymoronic "stupid beauty" of the proposed journey.

"Straight" passage though Hugh's recollections are, Lowry makes use of them to develop themes at work elsewhere. For instance, the significant motif of the destructive as perversion of the creative enters the flashback in the juxtaposition of Joe Venuti's melody with radio news of disaster. Venuti's violin had been heard since 1940, but only now does it seem to counter the chaos of the destructive world not by separating itself from it, but by participating in and ordering anarchic passions: it soars "in some remote summer of its own above all this abyssal fury, yet furious too, with the wild controlled abandon of that music" (Neilson

1:2, 4; a reflexive metaphor for the *Volcano?*). The theme reappears, more darkly and personally, in the startling comparison of the young Hugh hawking his songs at London music publishers to "another frustrated artist, Adolf Hitler" (Neilson 1:2, 6; formerly "Insert 17-18-19"). Hugh may have disliked the anti-Semitism he found at school, but his vengefulness toward Bolowski aligns him with the century's most vicious persecutor of Jews, and this, too, in a sentence that points again Hugh's symbolic parallel to the Consul: he recalls carrying song sheets about London in "another old Gladstone bag of Geoff's." Similarly, the well-publicized gesture of "running away to sea" (all too clearly the wrong expression) is now presented not as a shrewd or rebellious individual act, but as representative of a larger malaise: "Hugh was convinced he'd been amazingly clever, and the extraordinary letters of 'congratulation' he received from shipless buccaneers everywhere, who found their lives under a sad curse of futility because they had not sailed with their elder brothers the seas of the last war, whose curious thoughts were merrily brewing the next one, and of whom Hugh himself was perhaps the archetype, served only to strengthen this opinion." (30:3, 8).

The long account of Hugh's youthful sailing experience is now firmly woven into the comic fabric of the text. Much of the comedy here results from filtering the adolescent romance of the sea through the older Hugh's (and the narrator's) wider awareness of both literature and life. The technique is essentially that of parodic deflation, the confronting of the bloated image with its ironic counterpart, both usually suggested by a literary prototype. The episode is shot through with such models, both those the young Hugh has encountered—Sir Walter Raleigh, Jack London, Eugene O'Neill (marginally suggested)—those he has not—Melville, Conrad—and those implied in the name of his ships—*Philoctetes, Oedipus Tyrannus*—of whom he has never heard.[26] Yet Lowry's interest in that last-named ship appears far in excess of its obvious narrative uses in delineating Hugh's experience, and the vessel itself is presented in a way that seems to emphasize its strangeness. It is introduced, in a curious phrase (30:3, 15), as a ship "of a different century" (not, say, "of the last century") in the same sentence in which its Sophoclean link to the *Philoctetes* ("another Greek in trouble") is stressed and in the same paragraph where the two ships are almost literally "linked" by colliding—the passage that Lowry called the heart of his book. The language hints at a ship of mystery, one which has been sailing the equivalent of "an eternity" (the neutral "old" will be changed to the more evocative "ancient"), like that Wandering Jew of the sea lanes, the Flying Dutchman. Watching it swing "rebelliously close," Hugh feels bound to it "as to the tether of his mind," but oddly cannot quite keep it in single focus, the ship "appearing now on one quarter, now on another, one instant near the breakwater, the next running out to sea." Despite her battered appearance, "there was something youthful and beautiful about her, like an illusion that will never die, but always remains hull-down on the horizon." Seeming possessed of magical powers, the ship stirs Hugh's imagination, and as he tries to decide whether to volunteer for service on her, suddenly thinks, "Ah, Geoff, too, knew these seas, these pastures of experience, what would he have done?"

Perhaps this is the clue to Lowry's emphasis on the *Oedipus Tyrannus*, a clue lurking in its name all along, once again an echoing link of the brothers. It is Geoffrey who is most insistently associated with Oedipus: the dark glasses, the limp, the desire for a "daughter" to "lead him by the hand . . . homeward." In a post-Freudian time, however, the role is hardly exclusive; in Hugh's movement from younger to older ship we may see an enactment of transference, the adoption by the young man of the elder's role, with its responsibilities and tragic burdens. An early draft, using a phrasing that will occur to Hugh later, draws the connection: "his guitar a prop—just as Philoctetes' bow had been and Oedipus' daughter" (30:4, 7). "Papa" is Hugh's repeated term for the Consul, and it is to this figure of "experience" he figuratively turns now. When he does transfer to the other ship, it becomes Hugh's first gesture of brotherhood, a giving of the self "so that another sea-weary man, homesick longer than he, might take his place." Thus he becomes a "comrade" of those on the *Oedipus Tyrannus* and achieves a measure of understanding of and peace with his shipmates on the *Philoctetes*.

But in the present of the novel there is a brotherhood still more intimate. If Geoffrey is sometimes identified with Oedipus, sometimes cast as Laius to Hugh's rebellious, incestuous son (capable, as in the "address" of Chapter III, of exploiting the role himself), it is the latter relationship that the second half of Chapter VI explores. The anthropological transference (old king, young king) is enacted in the shaving episode a few pages later, where Geoffrey's cry of "'Help'" echoes that of the *Oedipus Tyrannus*. The shaving episode of course has persisted since 1940: later, Hugh's change of ships restates that action in a sociopolitical context. Only now, however, with his reordering of the material, is Lowry enabled to structure the connection between them by interweaving the final passages of Hugh's recollections with the present action of shaving. Hugh's failures, enacted as sexual betrayals (Bolowski's wife, Yvonne), follow his awakening at sea, yet it is with that awakening that Lowry establishes in Hugh a genuine sense of brotherhood *to be* betrayed. Presumably it was at least partly to some such sense of the episode's importance that he responded in resisting (for reasons he professed not fully to understand himself) Albert Erskine's plea that Hugh's recollections be cut.[27]

The major innovation in the second half of the chapter is the structural one of intercutting late stages of Hugh's flashback with the extant shaving scene, a counterpointing not unlike the more intimate tensions between past and present in the Consul's blackout of Chapter V. The point of *frisson* comes with Hugh's memory that after the Bolowski affair he had "calmly gone up to—" and at that moment is interrupted by Geoffrey's "'Help.'" Both mind and dialogue in the ensuing scene run on the suppressed word, "Cambridge," but Geoffrey's "'Help'" supplies a different kind of completion. One implication is, of course, the brothers as doubles, even syntactically—Geoffrey completes Hugh's unfinished mental sentence—but another is the imperative to "help," the imperative of brotherhood laid on Hugh by the generosity of the wronged Bolowski, claimed first by the literal brother, for whom Hugh's first service (aid when sick) is already a return, "'Tit for tat . . . I did that for you once'" (30:3, 25).

Into the present action that follows Lowry now ambiguously begins to introduce cabalistic and "magical" material. An early draft of this stage presents, for instance, both the possibility that Hugh in going to the porch cupboard for the whisky bottle is "as if absentmindedly obeying the other's wordless instructions," and the possibility that Geoffrey knows nothing at all about it (Texas VI, verso 46). In similar vein, it is in this version of VI (Texas VI, verso 46) that the Consul acquires a library which Hugh observes on his return from the porch. Some books listed here will disappear, others will be added, but the mystical note is struck by "cabbalistic and alchemical books"—as is the comic by *Peter Rabbit*, along with the Consul's summary comment, "Everything is to be found in *Peter Rabbit*" (and the news that "in fact he had stolen the book when tight aboard the Aquitania").[28]

If these occult references raise the possibility of moving beyond ordinary dimensions of time and space, so in another sense do Hugh's reflections on Cambridge. Indeed, the questioning of time brackets his entire meditation. Lowry makes this focus seem to arise out of the intercutting itself, beginning with Hugh's picking up of Geoffrey's phrase "'in my time'" and wondering, "But what exactly does that mean?" and closing on the encounter with Einstein, who has "upset the whole world's notions of time and space," but who asks Hugh the time of day. Is he, Hugh now begins by asking, "really" in Quauhnahuac or in Cambridge, more truly alive in mind or body? (A question compounded for the reader, to whom the 1938 of Chapter VI is "past" from the 1939 perspective of the opening, and who is reading the entire *Volcano* in a "present" that casts both its historical moments into the "past." But then, since the novel is "present" to him at the moment he reads it. . . .)

The question "In my time?" here forestalls the commonsense answer of simply citing the historical moment as Lowry shifts ground by asking: "What, if anything, did one do finally at Cambridge, that would show the soul worthy of Siegebert of East Anglia.—Or, say, John Cornford!" (27). John Cornford would of course have been a contemporary of Hugh's, Siegebert a predecessor by many centuries, and if it becomes a matter of the worthiness of the *soul*, to what degree is one confined to the historical moment? What if the university's "enduring beauty . . . seemed part, not . . . of one's stupid life there, though maintained perhaps by the countless deceitful memories of such lives, but the strange dream of some old monk, eight hundred years dead"? Is this one such "deceitful memory"? If so, why does it contain not only the sense of "enduring beauty" but also the recollection of "one's stupid life"? Am I "there" now as I recall it, and more or less so than when I walked there? Why did it seem even then more truly a "strange dream . . . eight hundred years dead"? Lowry moves deftly between presents and pasts, the experienced and the recalled, the material and the spiritual. Cambridge may have been "a dream," and not even a contemporary one, but it had, like Mexico, its actual garden signs: "a dream jealously guarded: Keep off the grass." In a parallel imperative, however, it evoked responses far different: "And yet whose unearthly beauty compelled one to say: God forgive me." From what recesses of being did such pious sentiments spring? After all, "oneself lived in a disgusting smell of marmalade and old boots." What, in short, is "my time," and in what manner can I be said to be "in" it?

These musings may seem beyond the sophistication of Hugh, but time can also seem fluid in more mundane ways. At matriculation, for instance, he felt himself "aged . . . beyond undergraduate years," and reencountering the class system in full flower gave him the sensation of "running once more full tilt into the past" (28). Against such disillusionments and confusions, Hugh brandished his instrument, which one undergraduate artist saw as his bid to remove himself from time altogether: he is pictured "as an immense guitar, inside which an oddly familiar infant was hiding, curled up, as in a womb," a vision balanced almost at once by Hugh's recurrent dream of his death in a desert, "strumming to the end," two exits from the temporal.

As Hugh's recollections close, the focus subtly shifts to the Consul, the way prepared by the preceding counterpoint, the attention to his physical preparation, and underwritten by the quiet development of the *doppelgänger* motif. Hugh's reflection on the "otherness" of his brother, on how little he really knows of him, allows Lowry a suitably mysterious introduction of further occult materials. Late in the chapter Hugh takes a second look at Geoffrey's books. This time he sees a clutch of mystical works. Reading the final title, which claims the existence on earth of "rational creatures besides men," he asks, "Are there?" and receives from his brother a catalogue of demons along with the claim of their visitation (37). As they leave the house, the Consul contends that Hitler's annihilation of the Jews is motivated by a desire "to obtain just such arcana as could be found there in those bookshelves" (a story he terms "'right down [Hugh's] alley,'" which is indeed more than professionally true, although "alley" by now also hints ambiguously at espionage). Shortly thereafter, the Consul turns to another facet of the subject:

"It's true that at Cambridge, Hugh," the Consul said, . . . "You may have learned about Guelphs and so on. . . . But did you know that no angel with three wings is ever transformed?"

"I seem to have heard that no bird ever flew with one wing," Hugh laughed.

"Probably you remember that statue of Milton in Christs. With a chamber pot on his head.; but did you know that Thomas Burnet, author of the Telluris Theoria Sacra, entered Christs in 1654, when Ralph Cudworth was master. Henry More must have been about my age then. Who were all these old blokes anyway, you may ask? Who was that Eirenaeus Philalethes you were looking at, for example? Certainly I can tell you this, Hugh," the Consul staggered almost imperceptibly. "He was not Eugenius Philalethes, who was Thomas Vaughan—"

Hugh said as if this were a shaft of wit: "No relation to the man who saw eternity the other night, I take it—"

"And who said: 'Whoever shall know the quality which is the secret of darkness shall know why the evil demons are more hurtful in the night than in the day?'" (30:3, 41)[29]

Surviving notes suggest that, as with Spanish, Mexican, and Indian material deliberately researched for the novel, Lowry also distributed his occult references from a common source. That "source" was almost certainly not as compact as the individual volumes used in other cases; doubtless it was his magician-friend Charles Stansfeld-Jones's collection. Two sheets survive (Templeton 1:11), headed in Lowry's hand "Chapter VI—with notes," which includes the titles of those mystical works that show up in both passages inventorying the Consul's books. Unsurprisingly, occult references in the novel were as deliberately "worked up" as other historical, geographical, political, or religious materials. At first here, the Consul was so to bombard Hugh with names and questions about such creatures that a marginal note indicated the latter's vertigo: "'Good God,' said Hugh, doubting, for a moment, his existence" (Templeton 1:11, n.p.). He will not, finally, be allowed such an explicit response, but a questioning of the dimensions of reality is very much on Lowry's mind late in this chapter.[30]

He continued, of course, to fuss with individual passages, but the only other substantial addition is Hugh's long reflective paragraph about Yvonne and, beyond her, "American women," the brilliant fluidity of which ranges from what she is wearing to the "situation" in which they are now caught, from what he knows of her emotions to what an observor might surmise, from the tact and freshness of her conversation to her aloneness, from the roles of such women as both "angel" and "succubus" to their pampered political indifference (38). Underscoring the duality of Yvonne as seen by the men in her life, it is appropriately, for Hugh, balanced by the new paragraph in which his unanswered hope for a message from Juan Cerillo draws him into the novel's pattern of frustrated and missed communications. That disappointment is underlined by the bad guitar-playing he now hears, as Lowry brings in a final "musical" reference to the instrument of Hugh's that has dominated the earlier part of the chapter, as, indeed, it apparently dominated the early part of his life.

The important Chapter VII (pivot of the Consul's day, if not quite of the novel that contains him, to which it is slightly eccentric) had been lying fallow for some time, so it is not surprising that the previous typescript (30:7) fairly bristled with suggestions. Many of those were for additions, individual touches that provide both density and internal structure—the use of golfing allusions, for instance, or the listing of Jacques's books—and even though not all were acted upon, those that were made relatively easy insertions. However, a more general observation on the opening page of the old draft had larger consequences: "This chapter exhibits a strange change of style: cut and cut and cut." The "change" Lowry refers to is doubtless that from the previous consular chapters, III and V (rather than from the immediately preceding Chapter VI or from earlier versions of this one): Geoffrey's earlier chapters had become progressively more convoluted and internalized, sporting time-shifts, hallucinations, a blackout, and everywhere a feverish intensity of perception that seemed, as one encounters this chapter sequentially, inexplicably to have relaxed. Indeed, stylistically it resembles more the "journalistic" directness Lowry has devised for Hugh's chapters than the growing complexity and rapidly associative consciousness dramatized in the Consul. Lowry's steps to rectify this problem took essentially two forms. On the one hand (as his note directs), there was a cutting and local rewriting to intensify passages that now seemed too slack, too controlled, too "normal" to represent Geoffrey's condition on "the drunken madly revolving world" (a new insert) at midday. On the other, Lowry entirely recast key episodes—Geoffrey at Laruelle's after Hugh and Yvonne leave, on the telephone, with Jacques in the cafe, on the Máquina Infernal—to capture the feeling, the "rhythm," the *inwardness* of these episodes as apprehended by his protagonist.[31]

Thus the very opening of the chapter, the lengthy, cool description of Laruelle's house, now is placed and "justified," attributed to a "mood of detachment" in the Consul. That mood only slowly dissipates, the Consul's latent hostility expressed in silent contempt and in the incohate "threat" of his movement after the departing Laruelle. At the same time, the reduced exchange between the men now has a double function, for it reestablishes the uncertainty of Geoffrey's point of view. Whereas in previous drafts dialogue carried conventional narrative authority, now: "'Don't you ever think of anything else [but drinks],' it *seemed* Jacques had said" (Texas VII, 3: italics added).

It was the preceding draft of this chapter that first introduced the effects of the solipsistic consciousness when Laruelle melted away at the Café Paris and the Consul discovered that he had been holding a dialogue with himself (see chapter 3, p. 129). Now, Lowry prepares for that later vanishing act by following up this early consular indeterminacy. Previously, Yvonne had repeated Jacques's question to Geoffrey when they spoke together on the "porch," but neither author nor characters gave any sign that "'Don't you think of anything except how many drinks you're going to have?'" (30:7, ts. 4) *was* repetition. Lowry's marginalia directed him to exonerate Yvonne altogether: "make it clear she hasn't said it." Yet in the end he refuses this clarity too, leaving Geoffrey (and us) to wonder "(but wasn't it Jacques who'd just asked him this?)" (Texas VII, 4). Once more, the entire fictional situation has changed, and we can no more resolve Geoffrey's query than he can, no longer discover whether Jacques, Yvonne, both, or neither has put that question. As the novel's texture becomes at once richer and more compressed, its tauter dimensions pressed into double and triple service, that richness turns out to be quite compatible with indeterminacy.

Indeed, indeterminacy pervades Geoffrey's and Yvonne's moments alone on what is now "the flying balcony." Does the Consul, as before, move tenderly toward her? "Apparently." Does he again speak about what her "astronomical mind" might suggest? He would at first appear to, "but no, he had not said it. . . . He had said nothing." Does Yvonne speak, as before, lovingly and tenderly of their reunion? "Apparently." When his seeming assertion of love is left incomplete, qualified, there is no telling what this may signify: "'I do love you. Only—' 'I can never forgive you deeply enough': was that what it was in his mind to add?" (Texas VII, 4–5) That question now gives rise not to an answer but to the remarkable paragraph that manages at once to convey Geoffrey's pain, anchor in the past his inability to escape it, and present the resulting self-division that forestalls action in the very passage that dramatizes its current manifestation. Thinking of the "desolation" of his suffering without Yvonne, he can recall a comparable bereavement only "when his mother died. But this present emotion he had never experienced with his mother: this urgent desire to hurt . . . had commenced with his step-mother": "Even now, of all times. Even though here was God's moment, the chance to agree, to produce the card, to change everything: or there was but a moment left. . . . Too late. The Consul had controlled his tongue. But he felt his mind divide and rise, like the two halves of a counterpoised drawbridge, ticking, to permit passage of these noisome thoughts" (5). The rapid series of phrases embodies the mounting sense of urgency, the Consul's desperate desire to desire, to feel a single emotion sufficiently that he might act on it; but the most he can do is "control[] his tongue," not shout out his anger, his "hate," and the rhythms of the paragraph subside, come to rest in the conceit of the drawbridge, the ironic image of a device whose opening is designed to "permit passage," allow fluid ingress and egress, here expressive of the self-division that leaves moment after moment stillborn, recessive, disappearing into the introspective, irrecoverable past—"Too late." Anticipating the later moment in the square when Geoffrey again feels the unique opportunity at hand, the opportunity that will never recur "until it was too late," these are perhaps the most intense glimpses the Consul has—precisely at the midpoint of his narrative—of the irrecoverable moment, the moment when the day might be seized, destiny altered. The silent metaphor of the drawbridge, replacing the spoken heart-as-a-broken-lift, deftly enables Lowry to suggest the Consul's self-division without having a maudlin Geoffrey himself ask for unearned sentiment. This paragraph, at least, could not be accused of "a strange change of style."

Jacques's reentry with cocktails brings the four together for the chapter's sharply contracted social encounter. The previous chitchat that had surrounded Laruelle's film of *Alastor* now shrinks to little more than the Consul's witty summary, and the breaking of the foursome into two couples (Yvonne-Jacques, Hugh-Geoffrey) gets reduced to the brief exchange about Shelley's drowning before Yvonne proposes departure. Despite the fraught relations among these characters, the social interval here, as in earlier versions of the porch episode of Chapter V, had dissipated the novel's tension: Lowry had little talent for (or interest in) these staple scenes of traditional fiction. Now, he partly replaces excised dialogue by two interiorized passages (Texas VII, 8–10) in which Geoffrey, taking the binoculars from Hugh, views the entire landscape as a cosmic golf course involving both Prometheus and Golgotha. But if this carries his imagination outward to mythic greens and deeps, it also carries it backward to his own past where the projected fairway leads "over the hills and far away, like youth, like life itself." All journeys, however, seem to lead to a single destination, the nineteenth hole, the Farolito, where indeed "The Case Is Altered." (Thus does the Consul's narrative at its midpoint repeatedly glance backward to Chapter I and forward to Chapter XII, Lowry revising Eliot: in my middle is both my beginning and my end.) Well might Geoffrey wonder "what on earth" he is looking for "out there," for this is the first of several passages in which he will express a sense of lost identity, here, that "figment of himself" that had enjoyed the "simple healthy stupid good" game of golf. The passage itself is full of a punning that is anything but "simple," the natural "Ozone" giving way to the astrological "Zodiac Zone," "blind holes" and "new silver king" evoking Geoffrey's own Oedipal role, and the entire paragraph moving from evocations of the outdoorsiness of the game to the celestial parody "played" through Donne's "Hymn to God the Father." These paragraphs may long for a lost "ozone" (for Lowry, "fresh air") but they hardly supply it to the novel—nor does Lowry wish it here. For while they are going forward, Lowry is building on the undischarged tension of the Consul's alcoholism.

Now when Jacques appears with cocktails, Geoffrey accepts one but does not drink from it, an "absence" that becomes a tense presence as the narrator keeps us apprised of this reluctance: "oddly he had not touched this drink" (8); "and still he had not touched his drink" (10). In part his recent evocation of the Farolito, lingering, has calmed him, assuaged his need; then too, he has the scorn of the serious drinker for that concoction, "the cocktail" ("despicable repast"); furthermore, he wants to show everyone (not least himself) that when it comes to liquor, he can take it or leave it; finally of course the very presence of the drinks, promising him relief any time he chooses, releases him from the pressing fear their absence creates.

Thus alcohol here become as potentially explosive as Chekhov's dramatic gun, and Lowry, applying the screws, makes us wonder when it will "go off." As Jacques sees Hugh and Yvonne downstairs, a new paragraph appears, carefully surveying the alcoholic situation on the balcony, wholly concerned with the drama of the Consul's to drink or not to drink, a decision that may indeed have Hamletesque consequences, but clearly has its comic side as well: Geoffrey feeling his bicep to check for moral "strength," deciding to eat to keep up that strength ("So the Consul ate half a canapé"), imagining his momentarily quiescent demons as "taking their siesta perhaps." Aware of the complex weave of lies that his existence has become, he wonders again where he might discover that sense of self on which a new start might be based, but by the time Jacques has returned, "the Consul was still gazing drinklessly—where was he gazing? He didn't know himself." Almost precisely what appears in the published novel (*Volcano* 204–5)—only the response to entering a sanatorium will be altered, indeed, reversed, from "what was worse" to "though for a second the thought was not too bad"—the paragraph is typical not only of the interiorizing trend of the revision, but of the dramatic rendering of consciousness, the tracing of processes of mind. Here it can take the form of dialectic, even dialogue—the Consul's "familiars" may be at siesta, but he doesn't seem to suffer the lack—as he is represented both "speaking" and responding to that speech ("'Yet I shall face it.' How? When he not only lied to himself. . . . 'Horror,' he said. 'Yet I will not give in.' But who was I. . . . 'The will of man is unconquerable.' Eat? I should eat. So the Consul ate"). This flexible technique—one can distinguish direct speech, *oratorio obliqua*, and surrounding narrative discourse—is capable of moving rapidly across a range of tones and degrees of emotional and rhetorical involvement from the anguished to the ironic, the poetic to the self-mocking, the tentative to the stalwart, the interrogative to the descriptively declarative.

By this time Lowry, always more sharply attendant to his own inner voices than to the ordinary speech of those around him, was a master of the plasticity of "speaking" discourse in these internalized passages, as even brief examples show. On Jacques' return he cries at the Consul, as before, his incomprehension that even with Yvonne back the other "'continue[s] only to care where the next drink's coming from.'" But the external situation has changed—Geoffrey now has not had a drink at Laruelle's—and, in a new paragraph, he basks for a moment in his own self-righteousness: "For this unanswerable and staggering injustice the Consul had no word: he reached for his cocktail; he held it, smelt it: but somewhere, where it would do little good, a hawser did not give way: he did not drink; he almost smiled pleasantly at M. Laruelle. You might as well start now as later, refusing the drinks. You might as well start now; as later. Later" (Texas VII, 12).

The opening line here is serious indeed, but it is the seriousness of deadpan, the overblown terms measuring the distance between Geoffrey's sense of outrageous persecution and the implied-narrator's ironic smile. The Consul savors a disdainful superiority to his ignorant tormentor in the controlled theatricality of his ensuing actions, as the point of view appears to shift briefly to the exterior. That shift may be only apparent, for the final lines certainly present an internal voice, a voice that, as in a comically malicious echo chamber, is progressively edited until it conveys a message directly opposed to the one it began with. By this time our consciousness of a narrator has faded: that last voice belongs to Geoffrey. But to whom should we assign the parenthetical irony in the middle, the "where it would do little good" qualifier of the Consul's self-approval? Surely to the narrator? Yet Geoffrey is, after all, capable of both self-awareness and self-mockery. Lowry's free indirect discourse, with its rapid shifts, does not always permit sure distinctions.

The Consul's apparent calm and poise are of course precarious, and while he remains virtuously dry—he reenters the house "leaving, yes, all the drinks untouched"—there lies ahead of him the shock of Laruelle's nakedness and the graphic physicality of his imagining of the adulterous act. Now, however, Lowry applies further pressure with Vigil's phone call. First, he elaborates the Consul's paranoia: the suspicious "'How did he know I was here?'" previously answered by the seemingly sensible "'I told him'" in this draft gets another screw-like turn: "'But what could have made you tell Vigil I was here, if you didn't know he knew me?'" Next, he further builds on the undermining effect of the Chapter V blackout, momentarily rendering the doctor hallucinatory: "who was Vigil?—the good fellow seemed by now unreal to him as some figure one would forbear to greet for fear he was not your acquaintance of the morning, so much as the living double of the actor seen on the screen that afternoon" (Texas VII, 13). Furthermore, should these seem insufficiently "disturbing," Lowry now reintroduces—whether actuality or hallucination there is no way of determining—the observation plane of Chapter VI, which seems to come "out of nowhere . . . straight at the balcony, at the Consul, looking for him, perhaps, zooming" (15A).[32]

Geoffrey's horrified vision of Laruelle's genitals produces this time a more sweeping revulsion than heretofore—"How loathsome, how incredibly loathsome was reality" (15)—and for refuge he turns to the director's books. Before naming what he finds, however, Geoffrey for the second time in this draft records that he "still didn't see his Elizabethan plays," a notation Lowry seemed to want to carry an obscure burden of significance: "how mean was man, it had only occurred to him now, that their friendship seemed to be at an end (not because of Yvonne but because of his plays)" (6). "Books, too many books" are what he *does* see, although he names only a few of these, beginning (cruelly) with "Les joyeuses bourgeoises de Windsor" (*The Merry Wives of Windsor*), ending with a title that Lowry found among those given for Guizot's translation of Shakespeare, but used by the Consul as a dismissive comment on the whole, "Beaucoup de bruit pour rien" (*Much Ado about Nothing*). For they seem to him irrelevant ("Banal whimpering," an earlier worksheet calls them), an inadequate counterweight to the horrors of actuality, an insufficient guide to its common beauties ("how to look at an ox-eye daisy"). Seeking desperately a more direct assuagement, he plunges a moment later incohately toward the telephone.

Before he does so, however, we might pause over the first occcurance of a significant phenomenon in Lowry's later work. A holograph sheet survives (Templeton 1:9, A) listing a number of French authors and titles, followed by a draft of the passage just discussed. Against the former is the marginal comment "Too many books," the same editorial remark that had appeared against an early listing of the Consul's books in Chapter VI. The comment does not appear in that draft of the novel passage, an attempt otherwise quite close to the finished version; yet, here it is, in the holograph fair copy. Clearly, between the early worksheet and this manuscript, the comment has moved from margin to text. As Lowry goes on to revise, especially when he comes to Chapter XI (see note 47 below), his notes to Margerie will make clear that he has become aware of the ambiguous relation between margin and text;

by the time of "Through the Panama" several years later, the complexities of that border relation will have become a central principle of composition. Although he was remarkably sensitive to borders of all kinds, here, to my knowledge, is the first of *this* kind of crossing in Lowry's work.

The Consul's rush to the telephone, ostensibly to call Dr. Guzman, is altogether new, but it follows the rising tension Lowry has been establishing, Geoffrey's drinklessness since leaving his house, a drinklessness of which he is every moment conscious, subject to increasing pressure both personal (Yvonne, Laruelle) and impersonal (target practice, the observation plane), now reaching a crescendo whose form is suggested by the naming of that other doctor, Vigil, and bursting into the jerky rhythms ("his nerves gibbered") and frantic repetitions ("He'd already forgotten the number, forgotten the number . . . he'd already taken the receiver off the hook, the receiver off the hook, off the hook") that make the Consul cry out deperately for a more potent doctor than Guzman: "'Que quieres? Who do you want . . . God!' he shouted, hanging up" (17). As with Yvonne, whom he both does and does not want, the action denies the words, and for such unresolved states, Geoffrey Firmin knows but one remedy: "He would need a drink to do this." In his frenzy on the staircase, uncertain where the drinks are, driven first up, then down, then up once more, he enacts in miniature the duality that moves him throughout the novel, the topographical pull of ascent and descent seen here in their most naked, most compressed form, until the gun "goes off," the desperation that lay behind his superficial sobriety bursts through, and the unbearable strain is (temporarily) eased: "He came on the mirador and drank down all the drinks in sight." The effect is instantaneous; as soon as he does so, the very rhythms of Lowry's sentences change: "The Consul finished the contents of the cocktail shaker and came downstairs quietly, picked up a paperbacked book lying on the table, sat down and opened it with a long sigh." The sentence is itself a "long sigh," its measured movement and paratactic construction imitating the calm connectedness of a man at peace, a quiet scholar perhaps.

As a kind of preface to the dialogue between the two men, Lowry now inserts the paragraph that accompanies them into the street, juxtaposing them first in physical size, then in other kinds of stature. The passage turns on a series of reversals (Jacques the taller now, Geoffrey when they were young; Jacques physically larger, Geoffrey spiritually "larger"). The "English influence" the Consul here detects in his boyhood friend reinforces the suggestions in Chapter I that Jacques might be viewed as a lesser version of Geoffrey. Now, he thinks he detects "almost an ex-consular sort of litheness about [Laruelle's] movements," and reflects on "how all-permeating" on Jacques's life and character their early friendship has proved. This is perhaps the most explicit establishment of Jacques as a "double" of the Consul and an important preparation for the moment in the cafe where dialogue shifts and the Consul discovers he has been engaged not in conversation, but in inner dialectic. But the current paragraph goes still further, and in considering Jacques's more recent coming to Quauhnahuac, plays with Geoffrey's possible occult powers. The sentences in question convey the Consul's silent thoughts, but they are cagily handled, both interrogatives, both employing "it-was-almost-as-if" structures, asserting nothing unequivocally: "Was it not much as though he, the Consul, from afar, had willed it, for obscure purposes of his own? . . . Was it not almost as though the Consul had tricked him into dishonour and misery, willed, even, his betrayal of him?" (19). "Suggestive" as these reflections may be, Lowry is giving nothing away.

Now Jacques acquires a scarab ring, companion to the bottle of El Nilo that he drinks in the cafe. A "man also in dark glasses who seemed familiar" appears and street cries are interpolated, although the status of both is doubtful, for "the Consul's mind [was] constantly filling with harmless deliriums." However, little in the long central section of the chapter was altered until Lowry reached the dialogue in the cafe, long a problem spot. That entire episode is reduced by one-third, simplified, given a clear, unrepetitive structure. Opening dramatically, the Consul's "'Tequila'" announces at once the focus of the dialogue. For the first time Laruelle is not complacently in command in this episode: his nervousness, his "shaking," is apparent immediately, and the tequila he sips leads as if naturally into the two men's declarations of which drinks would signal "the end." In a late insert (Texas VII, 24), "'Name of a name of God,'" Jacques shudders, like a pious cabalist avoiding the Tetragrammaton. His discomfort makes him to Geoffrey a kind of temporal double ("all the desolation of the months following Yvonne's departure were now mirrored in the other's eyes"), which, by a bizarre logic, recalls to him Hugh's role in their complex affairs (as

Jacques was to Geoffrey, so is Hugh now to Jacques) with the crucial difference that Jacques remains unaware of the full situation.

Geoffrey's command of such knowledge is part of what now gives him the dominant role. Following up on the passage in which the Consul assessed his power in Jacques's life, Lowry makes him the controlling figure in the dialogue. His assertion that "'I have never once told you the truth about my life'" establishes his superior position, and when Laruelle ventures that "'once or twice . . . you have told the truth,'" he is brusquely dismissed: "'I have never told you the truth. I know it, it is worse than terrible. But as Shelley says, the cold world shall not know'" (25). Jacques is reduced to, "'I'm afraid of you, . . . old bean.'" One result of the Consul's disdain (and, now, a second tequila) is that Lowry is able to compress the bulk of Jacques's tiresome exhortations to snippets of "well-meaning phrases" and to move quickly (it had taken three pages previously) to the center of their opposition. Echoing the start of the letter to Yvonne, Geoffrey now makes the large claim—and there is no precedent for this in earlier drafts—of being engaged in a "'great battle. . . . Against death. . . . My battle for the survival of the human consciousness.'"

This is worth pausing over, for its central declaration seems a reversal of the Consul's previous position. Granted, the confrontation between the two had been more diffuse and meandering heretofore; nonetheless, Geoffrey had allowed Jacques's description of his project, a psycho-religious reading of alcohol out of late Freud and William James that connected being "in love with death" and desire for the "release[] [of] the mystical," to stand essentially unchallenged (30:7, ts. 25).[33] Geoffrey's redefinition in the current draft, on the other hand, casts him in the heroic mold (a role reinforced, ironically, by Laruelle's new allusion to Aeneas) as the battler for man's consciousness "against death." We may of course, like Jacques, find this absurdly grandiose—and Lowry's having the Consul "s[i]nk back easily in his chair" as he makes his claim to heroic action can be read as sly commentary—but the central point is what Geoffrey himself asserts as his role, and that has sharply changed from any earlier version. When Laruelle carries on (in streamlined versions of extant passages) to distinguish Geoffrey and his like ("'Ben Jonson . . . or perhaps it was Christopher Marlowe'") from "'us despised sober people,'" Lowry sets up an opposition comparable to *Moby-Dick*'s distinction between Ahab and Ishmael, between the vision that defines itself as heroic and that of the ordinary mass of men. Jacques, like Melville's narrator, can grant at least some of the claims of the self-proclaimed heroic figure, but neither can fully share the other's vision and, prudently aware of the risks of such dangerous single-mindedness, both foresee the destructive potential in hewing to an undeviating course. Even in the short run, Laruelle notes as he had earlier, "'what you have excluded ... returns,'" but this time he gets a full response (as in *Volcano* 218–19) that gives these "returns" a meaning other than the one he seems to intend. From "returns" to "remorse," the Consul implies ("Consider the word remorse"), is but a syllable, the pain an accepted part of his role, just as the Qliphoth, perhaps, is its risk. Why, after all, is there "all that biting ... in the etymology?" As with the additions to Hugh's chapters at this stage, the enormous power of "remorse" moves (if more obliquely) to the motivating center.

That the arguments expressed by Jacques are familiar to the Consul is the central point of his belated discovery that Laruelle has disappeared, that the dialogue is with himself, the latter part of which gets shrewdly altered now simply by repunctuating, so that the final paragraph spoken by "Jacques" seems progressively to fragment before our eyes ("Break up into incoherence" directs a note): "'But Yvonne knows. And so do I. And so do you. That Yvonne wouldn't have been aware. If you hadn't been so drunk. . . .'" Similarly, the claims of the ordinary and the ethical are the burden of the extant paragraph in which the Consul observes the roundabout that seems to suggest all his missed opportunities "until it was too late." In this draft, he inquires, "What opportunities precisely did he mean?" and the radio's "Samaritana mia" returns us to human compassion, to the German officers and the man by the roadside, who, like Melville's captain of the *Rachel*, find no succor from the individualist bent on his own quest.

By now, the *Volcano*'s movement toward self-consciousness is well under way, and as the Consul lurches away from the Paris (recalling the start of "The Wibbly-Wobbly Song"), a new paragraph appears, beginning "Dies Faustus" and reflecting on the drunkard's tendency to suffer the collapse of time, morning becoming night "in a trice." This day, however—and the novel that contains it—has seemed to reverse the process: "It was already the longest day in his entire experience, a lifetime." Indeed, as the Day of the Dead, it is potentially without temporal limit, moving back beyond Chapter I to the beginnings in the Garden and onward beyond Chapter XII, with its intimations of apocalypse, to the final day (Dies Irae). Here, at the midpoint of this day, "Dies Faustus"—Day of Fortune, day on which Faustus dies (see Ackerley and Clipper 301)—the phrase gestures toward either end of the novel that contains it, and out beyond.

With a single important exception, the rest of Lowry's alterations in this chapter comprise individual small insertions and local stylistic changes. Yet the major revision is neither a new passage nor, in the usual sense, an alteration in "content." Against the previous version of the loop-the-loop ride appears the marginal direction: "NB. See original where the *motion* is got [far?] better" (30:7, ts. 32). Lowry here went back yet again to his working copy of the 1940 *Volcano*, that is, the "D" carbon plus its 1941 yellow-sheet revisions (which for this passage are, alas, lost).[34] If his return to this earlier version was primarily to rescue its kinetic properties, it enabled him also to recover some specific features that had dropped off along the way—the child's exercise book, the Chinese hunchback, the Consul's actual boarding of the ride—and add, among other things, the information that when the Consul is at the top, the opposing cage, "which, significantly, was empty" is at the bottom, that Geoffrey upside-down sees "999," and that he resembles "that poor fool who was bringing light to the world." Whatever else these additions do, they prolong the suspended moment (as does the added, reflexive, "interminable") in which he hangs inverted. Lowry does little to alter the depiction of the forward motion of the ride, but when it reverses itself, he does a good deal, as we have already seen (chapter 1, pp. 46–48).

This return to a considerably earlier version of a passage is another reminder that Lowry's direction in his revisions is not always straight-ahead. However, while his infernal machine here receives its definitive treatment, he is not quite finished. A late, pencilled insert (27:12, 275), an addendum to Geoffrey's sense of the ride, casts some doubt on his mythic and cabalistic erudition, for it is, he feels dimly, symbolic, "of what he could not conceive, but it was undoubtedly symbolic." Even when the ride is over, however, the motion, and the attempt to render that motion, does not end with it. Earlier drafts had briefly and belatedly, some dozen lines later, asserted that a Consular dizziness succeeded the actual whirling. Now the aftereffects ensue at once, and with much of the rapidity of the original motion. As the landscape spins round, a bare list of nouns again suggests the "madly" whirling sensation from within, and the gradually diminishing disorientation as the children restore his goods leads the paragraph to a new sentence that, in its ordered rhythms and syntax as much as in the deliberately exteriorized actions conveyed, presents the Consul in a comic performance of complete self-possession. "He replaced his dark glasses, set his pipe in his mouth, crossed his legs, and, as the world gradually slowed down, assumed the bored expression of an English tourist sitting in the Luxembourg Gardens" (31).

In Geoffrey's belated regret that he has given nothing to the children, a regret underscored by thoughts of his and Yvonne's childlessness, Lowry now finds the appropriate spot for the reintroduction of the exercise book and its archetypal English miser, lonely, loveless Scrooge. The exercises here are exactly those it displayed in El Bosque in 1940, although only in the typescript does Margerie's hand add the three concluding words of the Pegaso notebook that now first enter the *Volcano*: "Alone. World. On." (27:12, 277) The notebook appears at precisely the spot where Lowry called for "the scribe somewhere" (30:7, 33), that scribe Geoffrey and Yvonne had passed in Chapter II, who is echoed by the soldier in Chapter XII "inscribing" a document in the square at Parián, for which the exercise book becomes the symbolic substitute. This is a final, small indication of the pivotal nature of the chapter. Chapter VI may be, as Lowry told Jonathan Cape, "the heart of the book," but VII is literally the center of the Consul's day (Dies Faustus) and thus the chapter that most insistently points to beginnings and ends, repeatedly declaring its role as the hub around which the infernal machine of his life whirls, telling us that we are, with Geoffrey, precisely halfway up—or down—the slippery pole. Many of the features manifesting that role were already in evidence, but this revision alters, sharpens, adds, focuses. Lowry will make very few further changes before final copy.

When he came to Chapter VIII, Lowry seemed to feel he knew just what was needed. "Cut and cut and cut where possible" is underlined at the top of the latest typescript (30:10), but he also sounds a contradictory cautionary note: "Not so much cutting perhaps." Cuts there are, although almost always in the nature of trimmings and tightenings, condensations and reworkings, rather than wholesale eliminations. If the directives are much like those found elsewhere, it will not by now come as a surprise that the new version nonetheless turned out to be almost exactly the length of the old one.[35]

An important part of the rewriting here involved Lowry's sharpened sense of the character who is the chapter's central consciousness and the stylistic difference this should make. Appropriately, "Henry James" is invoked in the margins to preside over these revisions; more mundanely, a note directs simply, "Eye on Hugh." Lowry is especially alive here to the need to distinguish the Firmin brothers in the most basic way, that is, in the language associated with each. Thus for the simpler Hugh, he prescribes "short sentences" and "Shorter paragraphs," the latter order repeated halfway through the chapter: "More paragraphs to get the dramatic effect" (30:10, ts. 12). That comment comes as the bus reaches the fallen Indian, and we see Lowry's matching here of consciousness and action, the focus on the "drama" in the exterior world through the eyes of the figure by temperament and profession best suited to apprehend it in all its immediacy and urgency.

From the start, however, Lowry is sensitive to the kinds of alterations needed to bring Hugh (and thus the chapter) into sharper relief. Recollections are now denied until after the incident on the road; references to Paris, to his friend Jack, are eliminated. Now stress falls on his almost willed simplicity—his focus on present and future, his hopes for Yvonne and Geoffrey's life together. We are meant to see—as we could not, wholly, in previous versions—Hugh's essential decency, even if that decency is purchased at the cost of some intelligence. As a result, his ominous sense of possible "calamity," associated with Aztec human sacrifice and the memory of "dead" land in Spain (30:10, ts. 6–7) gets replaced by a paragraph describing his euphoria, a "strange exaltation" that is also somewhat fatuous: "Like a child Hugh wanted everyone to be happy on a trip." Unsurprisingly, "a pint of bitter" now contributes to his "blurred" apprehension of "the naked realities of the situation" (Texas VIII, 6).

Consciously, at least, Hugh's benevolence radiates outward to embrace Yvonne and Geoffrey: "May she be happy. May everything come, somehow, right. May we all be happy. God bless us." Ignoring the devastating "somehow," Hugh thinks of the "very small pinch bottle of habanero" in his pocket, wonders whether to offer his brother a drink, an association that of course undermines his silent prayers, perhaps with a certain unconscious malice. Despite the fact that we now learn that he and Yvonne had talked only of the Consul while in the plaza and that it had been "a joyful relief" to her when Geoffrey had met them at the bus terminal, one part of Hugh does *not* hope for their happiness, the part that within a half-dozen lines will produce, as before, the "idiotic syllogism" equating Yvonne and the lost Ebro (8). Not incidentally, in what had heretofore been the only dry chapter of this very wet novel, alcohol now enters in the form of the ironically named bitter and the *habanero* that will be tapped before the chapter ends.

"Rewrite the beginning. End mostly good," Lowry told himself, and indeed the first half of the chapter reveals a preponderance of changes. Counter to Hugh's euphoria, the ominous opening word of the chapter becomes "Downhill." Despite the obvious association with Geoffrey, however, what that word most immediately and literally applies to is the route of the bus; it thus not only suggests a downward plunge toward disaster, the abyss, but also (especially in a vehicle described marginally here as "coasting") the easy descent, the undemanding glide that seems to require almost no effort, where energy and alertness may relax, be virtually suspended, thrown into neutral—not a bad description of Hugh's mood as Lowry has recast it. However, the new opening required some rearrangement of existing material, and it apparently sent him back once more to the 1940 manuscript.

As a result, this version, like that much older one, begins as the bus gets underway rather than with the driver's display of pigeons, which is postponed; and the opening movement of the chapter becomes an alternating rhythm that rocks from interior to exterior as the bus moves through town, passing landmarks new to the chapter ("Baños de la Libertad, the Casa Brandes [La Primera en el Ramo de Electricidad]") as well as a revival from 1940: "The clock over the market arch, like the one in Rupert Brooke, said ten to three." When Yvonne had noted that time in 1940 (*1940* 227), it was apparently correct, but Hugh here observes that his watch registers twenty to three. Typically, Lowry manages now to have it both ways, evoking in Mexico (as Brooke from Germany) the yearning sense of timeless English pastoral (which Yvonne had sentimentally followed up with nostalgic recollections of Cambridge), then undermining it by suggesting that the time is all too out of joint.

As they pass the "Inhumaciones," the undertakers' parrot is observed, but all traces of the joke associated with it have disappeared, so that the bird, now connected only with the sign above it (Quo Vadis?), seems still played off against various other birds of the chapter (pigeons, poultry, vultures), but to less obvious purpose. It remains, I think, because Lowry has recognized immanent in his material the important motif of disguise, of performance, a motif hardly limited to VIII (it runs throughout the novel), but appearing here in particularly concentrated and politicized form. The parrot, traditionally the performing bird, the ape of speech, brightly plumed, is not a bird usually associated with death. That unexpected juxtaposition may be precisely the point, for on its present perch, it is inescapably the undertakers' bird, and the resonant question (Quo Vadis?) points most directly to the chapter's end where its hovering, carrion-seeking associates, unmasked, await the travelers.

The new opening demanded by the initial "Downhill" emphasizes the performance given by the bus driver, who speaks a stage "Irish-American" for his tourist audience—"'Let in the clutch, step on the gas. ... Sure, Mike. ... Look! O.K. ... My—ah—my aerial pigeons'" (1). This is not new, but only in this draft does the bus itself become masked, "hooded," as they move through the town, and the associations return us to the change of mood in Hugh here. For the new Hugh and the (old) bus do at last dovetail in a way that illuminates Lowry's alterations.

The bus is in every sense a vehicle, in the action of the novel a ramshackle means of transport, for the author potential metaphor. In 1940 the Consul, observing its interior details (which endure almost unchanged), had reflected "from less than these could a universe be constructed" (*1940* 233). Within three pages, the bus had become the microcosm of a "world ... going to sleep," "whirling them on to their doom, like some planet whose gods are dead." The insistent cosmic allegory vanished with the change in point of view, but Lowry retained and later extended other passages that gave it a more quietly metaphorical life. The ability of the camión to create a sense of "community" among the marketing women, the speed and color that briefly spark "a sense of gaiety" among the passengers, a sense whose renewal after the fruitless stop for the wounded man seems ever more inappropriate, its "holiday" air wildly incongruous—in abbreviated form, these passages, well within the range of Hugh's social-political observations and concerns, were there as early as 1940. A new one, however, aligns it not only with the human figures of the novel, but, more obliquely, with the world itself as presented at the opening of Chapter VII, thereby subtly reviving the cosmic metaphor: leaving the Indian in the road to the mercy of the vigilantes, "The bus thundered on, reeling, cannonading, drunk."

In the new draft, Lowry's concern is to position Hugh clearly within the prevailing mood of "fiesta," of stupor, euphoria, mindless—and dangerous—abdication of control. One way to do so was to move his reflection on volcanic eruptions—hardly, on the face of it, a "fiesta" theme—and add two new sentences that give a quite different thrust to the passage:

> In movies of eruptions people were always seen standing in the midst of the encroaching flood, delighted by it. Walls fell over, whole families moved away their possessions in a panic, but there were always these people, jumping about between the streams of molten lava, smoking cigarettes. . . .
> Christ! He hadn't realized how fast they were going, in spite of the road. (Texas VIII, 10–11)

The juxtaposition now invites us to see the similarity in the celebration-in-the-midst-of-danger themes: the sense of release, of holiday, the invitation to irresponsibility offered by the belief that a condition lies beyond individual control—one of the novel's important motifs that in this draft begins to situate Hugh clearly within it. In this context, the new description of his Panglossian mood ("This trip now seemed to him the best of all possible ideas") takes on another coloration: fortified by his drink, "The noonday languor had passed him by: yet the naked realities of the situation, like the spokes of a wheel, were blurred in motion" (6). The wheel is the novel's most resonant metaphor, but it is embodied in this chapter as the wheels of the bus, whose "hooded" character is here echoed in the "blurred" effect of its speeding course.

Hugh's euphoria feeds easily into grandiose daydreams, fantasies that are literally "unreal high events," whereas the bus is in fact traveling toward an incident both real and common, "high" only in its symbolic reach. Yet Lowry's alterations in Hugh's state were partly intended to associate him with the figure of the pelado, who remains almost unchanged throughout the drafts. From 1940 on, the Consul had been more obviously connected with this other drunken figure who posesses considerably more awareness and control than his outer semblance may suggest. Hugh's similarities are subtler, even perhaps somewhat strained, but in his self-regard, his irresponsibility, his daydreaming, his hypocrisies, he seems intended to display less blatant versions of qualities evident in the repellent pelado.

That creature is of course in all drafts the most obvious embodiment of "performance" in the chapter. With his two hats (a Homburg on a sombrero, they suggest the German presence in Mexico) he looks like a refugee from a down-at-heels vaudeville troupe, and he elaborately acts out the roles of "stupor" and "death" (soon to be presented in undisguised form by the man in the road) while remaining altogether "on guard." Cruelly, Lowry has him hypocritically make a "gesture of hopelessness, which was also like a gesture of sympathy" toward the wounded Indian, a performance not unlike Hugh's own, as the latter is all too aware. In a particularly naked enactment of the age-old ritual of all exploitation, the pelado openly pays his way with his stolen money, an action that is, again, clearly a public performance.

Building on this material, Lowry now elaborates the pelado's final performance—in this version *called* a "performance"—in the longest single new passage, a page and a half in which Hugh gives silent voice to the gesture language of the thief for which he and his companions seem the chosen audience ("this performance was undoubtedly rather for their own benefit, as witnesses and foreigners"; Texas VIII, 23). In fact, Hugh gradually understands that the pelado is not making an effort to conceal the money but, on the contary, is displaying it as part of a brazen rhetorical strategy of rationalization, of "furthers" and "thens," of "buts" and "therefores." This strategy reaches its climax not in feats of "juggling" and legerdemain by which bloodstained coins slip into various pockets—sleight-of-mind, not of hand, is what is in question—but in the cynicism of his final rhetorical reach, which finds justification in its own bold rapaciousness: "it was open and above board, for all the world to know about. It was a recognized thing, like Abyssinia." Although Lowry doubtless could not resist the extension, and the political analogy is certainly appropriate to Hugh, this new passage ends by blurring his guilty identification with the pelado (and likewise calls into question the Consul's identification at the end of the novel): the bold shamelessness of the thief, after all, is antithetical to Hugh's remorseful self-castigations.

If the pelado ends by paradoxically revealing his true nature in a final elaborate performance, he enters this draft for the first time under the metaphor of disguise. "'He's not an aerial pigeon,'" the Consul here tells Hugh, itself an assertion so oblique, so "hooded," that Lowry amends it by having Hugh respond "'A what? ... Oh'" (27:13, 288A), thereby calling attention to the underlying, unspoken "stool pigeon," an identification that ties the pelado into the political version of disguise—spying—that runs through the novel. Nonetheless, the consideration of the social and political identity of this man Geoffrey also calls simply "a Spaniard" continues to cause Lowry difficulty. Now given to Hugh (originally it had been the Consul's), the passage is distanced by heavy irony ("it was perhaps Hugh's too neat idea," "Hugh consulted his ignorance further"), and when we discover that his understanding depends on a nameless "informant," it seems almost certain that the screen of disclaimers reflects Lowry's own insecurity in this territory. What Hugh's source has told him about "pelados" is precisely what will appear in the novel, but here it seems so flimsily based that Lowry feels obliged to end with the limp, "Without knowing quite why Hugh put the man down as a pelado" (4-5). Uncertain about his terms, Lowry is sure from this time forward that he wants a flexible and ambiguous definition of his comic-sinister "Spaniard," one that keeps disguise and performance at its center.

Hugh's euphoria in the early part of the chapter, his wanting "everyone to be happy," culminates in a pastoral sense of home, of hedges "so reminiscent of England one expected at any point to see a sign: Public Footpath to Lostwithiel." That is not, of course, the sign Hugh sees: the following word in the text is *"¡Desviacion!"* and with this "deviation" (detour) the entire edifice of Hugh's benevolence collapses.

This central episode had long since taken essential form. Nonetheless, there are a number of individual adjustments in this draft that create notable differences in the impact of character and action. Long paragraphs are broken into several shorter ones without the change of a word in order to achieve, through Hugh, a more "dramatic effect." The Indian's impossible posture—"lying on his back with his arms stretched out behind him towards [the] wayside cross"—is questioned, "behind him" dropped; a larger space is drawn around the small human drama by single images that twice draw the eye and ear upward, to a bird in flight and to a distant plane; Hugh and Geoffrey's dialogue over the wounded man is trimmed, given immediate point. Hugh is no longer certain from his first glimpse that the wounded man is dying—which makes the issue of aid even more urgent—and Lowry is so concerned not to make the Consul here entirely unsympathetic that he violates the chapter's point of view to assert that "it was a fact he was about to take some action, when the pelado anticipated him" (15).

When at last dust "obliterated the scene" on the road, what is obliterated with it is Hugh's too-easy sense of well-being, his superficial benevolence. If his euphoria early in the chapter had spared him backward looks, he now seems at the mercy of the most grisly memories, full of such guilt-ridden reflections that he first fails to see, then to comprehend, the pelado's elaborate display. In an entirely new paragraph, Yvonne's fear of "the sight of blood" has thrown up to the seasoned journalist yet another paradoxically "real" performance, the gruesome sights that are "among the stupid props of war's senseless Titus Andronicus," a gory catalogue of fragmentary images rhetorically echoing the severed body parts that make up their content, rapid flashes that constitute a brief antinarrative (they "could not even make a good story" [18A]). These horrors only feed Hugh's guilt that he "could have done something," and he is now obliquely reminded of the "stiflingly hot" sun on the road, of the *habanero* in his pocket ("Keep the patient absolutely quiet in a darkened room. Brandy may sometimes be given to the dying"). His bitter estimation of his own conduct culminates in the final devastating reflection that possibly "nothing would have done any good . . . non-feasance was impossible. Which only made it worse than ever" (20).

And so the bus hurries on as before, boys playing, bright tickets "wink[ing]," "holiday" sense superficially restored as, in echo of the opening, the vehicle (like the chapter) "circled," "downhill," into Tomalín. Yet the tone has subtly but decisively shifted, even the performance of the men on the exterior of the bus "grinning . . . clownishly" or "joining hands over the radiator cap" carries a slightly sinister air, and a marginal gloss Lowry did not explicitly follow up suggests why: "As if they had sprung from the pages of Franz Kafka."[36] Colored by the pervasive "dissolution" of the dust and the malicious fatuousness of the pelado, the final movement downward, emergency brake "screaming," is in a new sentence revealed in all its menace, "sheer unguarded drop" gaping on the outside of the now overtly "dangerous" road. This time, when Hugh observes the waiting xopilotes who hover "beautifully," he includes them silently in the Consul's "'Everybody happy, including me,'" and the vocal abstention seems to measure the depth of his emotional drop in this darker version of the journey.

In the summer of 1944, not long after arriving in Oakville, Lowry turned his attention to Chapter IX. He did not like what he found. Writing to Margerie in New York, he told her, "I've suddenly become completely fed up with the bull chapter, which merely seems to me to be well named!" (2:1, n.d.).[37] No other surviving chapter draft carries on it such a severe articulation of its author's radical dissatisfaction: Lowry's disapproval is expressed on his current typescript (Templeton 1:3) with a rhetorical formality (and even an orthographic clarity) unique in these papers. The self-consciousness here is, surely, an awareness of audience, of Gerald Noxon (certainly, of another man) as reader of a piece that Lowry was genuinely dissatisfied with, but which he now views, as it were, through the eyes of an outsider. His strictures become olympian: the comment on "the train of thought of the average woman" (noted in chapter 3, p. 156 above) is one such. The opening page carries another, more general: "brilliantly reported, this nonetheless strikes me as dishonest writing. Yvonne appears an impossibly superficial person with quite different, though womanly—she is a woman—problems; & the objective correlative is all to pieces." In the event, Lowry apparently decided that the objective correlative of the scene was not so "all to pieces" that it demanded total recasting, and that the weaknesses in the portrayal of Yvonne might be papered over if not altogether eliminated by new passages of introspection. Nonetheless, his dissatisfaction was real, even if he was not quite sure where the problems lay.

Despite an air of puzzlement—"Christ knows what's wrong but it sure *is* wrong: the tone, dialogue, everything. . . . Why?" (Templeton 1:3)—marginal directives abound, and many are the familiar calls for cuts and clarification. One, however, demands "make point Yvonne's drink has gone to her head," indicating that the important motif of alcoholic alteration of perception in characters other than the Consul—begun with Hugh and Yvonne's mescals in the preceding draft of Chapter XI, repeated in Hugh's pint of bitter in VIII—was to get another extension. A new image is called for: "Right in the centre of her brain was a figure of a woman, like a puppet, having hysterics. It was perhaps herself but detached from herself too, conquered [conjured?], this convulsive figure on wires" (Templeton 1:3, 1). And more than once Yvonne was to feel in the action in the arena "the boredom of it."

That "boredom" would allow her mind to wander away from the scene, and through it Lowry would find a way out of the thinness and repetitiveness of her "superficial" reflections. While Yvonne's imagining of a future and remembrances of the past both make appearances in this draft, indications are that the former was the first hit upon: it is certainly the more fully developed. Anticipation of "the future" is indeed one of the first notes struck now, just those two words added to the extant sentence about "sorrow that would be overcome, of hope, above all, of hope" (31:2, 1). Immediately, however, Lowry introduced the contrapuntal chord by appending a parenthesis to the peanut vendor of the next sentence: "A smiling bearded giant (who for some reason vaguely reminded her of her father)." But the look of this opening on the page has also been radically altered: even before we distinguish its words, typography is to make its impression.

As Lowry would make clear to Albert Erskine, he was acutely conscious of the visual impact of typographical layout. In his drafts, this concern most frequently gets articulated in marginal notes that dialogue should be either "horizontal" or "vertical," that is, either run together within a single paragraph or set out in dramatic form, paragraphs changing with speaker. The former method creates a slight "blurring" in what characters say: it lacks the stark clarity and weight of speeches arranged individually and distinctly down the page and conveys an almost subliminal sense of diminished importance to its exchanges. Here in Chapter IX, other matters of layout and typography seemed to Lowry inappropriate, just as they had in his revision of Chapter VIII, and the parallels are instructive. "Shorter paragraphs, more paragraphs" were called for in the preceding chapter; now, "Too few paragraphs" is the terse comment on the previous opening of IX. As a result, just as those units got altered in VIII, what had been two long paragraphs running from Chapter IX's start to the moment when Yvonne began to powder her nose has, with very little change of content, become in the new draft (as in the novel) no fewer than *twelve* much shorter ones!

Again, Lowry is conscious of implied meaning in the appearance of the page: two long, sustained paragraphs carry a misleading suggestion of meditative rather than dramatic focus. Thus, the very format had appeared to invest Yvonne with weight and importance, yet on rereading her author had found her "impossibly superficial." Now, neither author nor character need be seen as "superficial": that burden can be shifted to the alcohol (parallel to the effect of Hugh's bitter on the early portion of Chapter VIII). Hence, paragraphing now subtly undermines the view presented in the opening, the rapid shifts in themselves suggesting a flitting mind, the slightly boozy inability to focus long in any one spot, to view closely the scene at hand. In much the same spirit, the few changes here are almost entirely small trimmings that clip sentence rhythms and reduce any impression of reflectiveness, so that Yvonne might maintain her drink-induced sense that what she sees is just "fun."

All this could be achieved with minimal change. More challenging was the question of what to do with Yvonne when her gaze shifted from outer to inner worlds, from the arena to the events of the afternoon—those reflections Lowry had dismissed as "not worth reporting"—the inward turn signaled and symbolized by her opening the compact mirror. The solution turned out to be remarkably simple: the Yvonne who is determined to align herself with the hope and happiness she believes surround her, to project that hope into the future, is thereby also determined not to focus on the "unpleasantness" of the earlier incident. Thus Lowry creates two plausible ellipses that obviate her restless rationalizations, replacing her memory of the injured dog and her view of the events on the road with the dash of the broken-off reflection ("so that once—but what was the good of thinking of that?"; "she couldn't understand why—She gave her hat a final pat"). This is in one sense a confession of failure, of Lowry's inability to portray "feminine" moral reflection in such a way as not to undermine either himself or the character. That failure, however, would not be grossly apparent to readers of the finished novel: he must also have recognized that by retaining the portentous image of the old woman with the dominoes that had flashed into Yvonne's mind in the previous draft, he had a subtler and more effective rendition of the return of the repressed than any rationalizations or memories he might produce for his heroine.

Now, when Yvonne returns to the exterior world "with a smile," she is "met with no answering smile" but with a general "gloom," a recognition that the boredom she now feels had existed "all the time" and that the gaiety she had detected had simply been her own projection: "All that had happened was that Yvonne had had a drink in the bus that had taken effect and was now wearing off" (31:2, 3). As she tries to focus once more on the arena, the marginal direction—"all this more serious after the drink wears off, she has a heavy feeling" (Templeton 1:3, 6)—becomes embodied in associations the bull calls up of the uncomprehending entanglements of her unsuccessful father, "a Major in the American army with a craze for invention." This first appearance of Yvonne's more distant past is brief and crude, a summarizing of her father's failures and her own movie career, marriage, and divorce. The recollections are interrupted only once by action in the arena, yet even aside from its unassimilated structure, the passage reads more like a précis than a reminiscence, however stylized.

As her attention returns to the arena to witness the "death" and "resurrection" of the bull, Hugh's habanero is produced and Yvonne, drinking, spies a couple she guesses to be "lovers . . . or on their honeymoon." Contemplating their "pure and untrammelled future," her heart "soaring into the future on the brief wings of the habanero" moves in immediate association to the shack that in her mind she has transformed into a "home." Lowry will cut the alcoholic basis for Yvonne's imagining; it is repetitive of her condition earlier, and now has the wrong effect, rendering her desired future as insubstantial as the pipe dreams of one of Eugene O'Neill's characters. Although her aspirations will not be realized, Lowry does not want them dismissed as mere fantasies; whatever they mean for Yvonne's existence, they are an expression of fundamental human yearning, of the hope of a home or of the need to believe in the possibility of paradise—something more, in short, than a simple "mistake" like the earlier projection of her mood onto the crowd. So powerful is her vision of this new life that action in the exterior world now seems hardly to interrupt it; in the infectious silence that falls on the arena, her mind turns to a filling-out of the particulars of her vision, a lyrical imagining of health and beauty and creativity that flirts at times with mawkishness (Geoffrey, for instance, is imagined as "a sort of father-confessor" to local fishermen, and projected fame and success will somehow leave untouched their "isolation, and simplicity and love").

This new material allowed Lowry to reduce considerably the sheer bulk of the action in the bull ring, which had become repetitious. He was here facing the old problem of imitative form, particularly acute for an insistently symbolic writer: how to dramatize meaningless action without falling into meaninglessness oneself? The parallel of the encounter with the first bull to the stages of human life had long been established, and Hugh's ride was to impose order and purpose on the potential power embodied in the animal, but in the long middle action between these, the chapter wandered. Now, however, such is the power of Yvonne's vision that Lowry can plausibly create another focus of attention, an inner world that elaborates itself as against merely glimpsed actions in the bullring. While she seems to be staring down into the arena, what she actually sees is a view as through clear water at the shack, where she gazes not at bulls and ropes and disgruntled spectators but, for instance, at "an archipelago . . . and . . . brocaded stones like pincushions, over which the brocaded crabs scuttled among a few drowned leaves—" (31:2, 14).

Against increasing tumult in bullring and sky, the focus was now to move to Geoffrey and Yvonne, quiet in the midst of growing chaos. Her vision returns to the imagined scene of tranquility, and she "whisper[s] suddenly" to the Consul her proposal that they "'go away, immediately, to-morrow.'" The comparable passage on the preceding draft had been savaged by its creator as "too bloody for words: where the hell is my sense of humor that I don't strike out such gibberish?" But in fact the earlier exchange was not remarkably different from the one that here replaces it. Geoffrey had remained calm, even detached, in the face of Yvonne's proposal, and although his ensuing sweating and trembling had reminded her of the conspiratorial haste of doomed prisoners, the couple remained self-possessed enough to be "smiling at each other" in their newfound harmony.

Perhaps Lowry found the "gibberish" of that rendition at least partly in its emotional dishonesty, the relative ease and lack of conflict in the Consul's acceptance of Yvonne's proposal. In any case, the scene that replaces it (up to a point it is the scene of the novel) resounds far more convincingly with the emotions such a proposal must stir in Geoffrey, "hysterical" and terrified refusals collapsing into a "weary" acquiescence that for a moment seems to become more than surrender, to contain a real surge of hope, of the possibility of "rebirth" that a marginal note reminds Lowry to make explicit. But as Yvonne's mind now runs on silently to elaborate her vision—"a train that wandered slowly through an evening land of fields beside water," etc.—Geoffrey in odd counterpoint begins speaking: "'I went to sleep just now and had a dream about twenty three nuns . . . like king penguins, or people in mourning [in] . . . a broken down motorboat . . . at ten o'clock on Easter Monday'"; while she dreams of the smoke of the train and a shingle mill mingling, he speaks of "'white smoke from chemical factories'" and the boat, now in motion, carrying the sound of the laughter of the nuns over its slow "'phut-phut-phut'" (31:2, 21).

The precise implications of this bizarre vision are by no means clear (is this Lowry's notion of a recovery of his "sense of humor"?) but the Easter Monday evocation of "mourning" then "laughing" nuns in an outmoded boat certainly seems meant to undermine the possibilities of genuine "rebirth." Aside from the implausibility of Geoffrey's instantaneous "dream," however, the passage seems tonally wrong, blatant where subtlety is needed, mocking where such mockery seems mean-spirited (it will, nonetheless, persist as far as galley proofs). Now, however, as the couple's attention returns to the arena, their moment of communion ends, and Lowry's marginal comments make explicit that the Consul's recourse to the habanero bottle constitutes a repudiation of their short-lived "pact," an "[appeal] to the bottle and not to her."

Cutting two-thirds of a page, Lowry sends his characters immediately down into Tomalín. Now Yvonne immediately counters the wasteland mirage of the broken greenhouse with, "But the shack was in her mind now: their home was real," and the remainder of the paragraph, as in the novel, establishes the solidity of the structure, at least as mental construct, viewable from every conceivable angle, at varied times of day and night and in different seasons (31:2, 24). But Lowry brilliantly undercuts her assurance by moving easily from the shack as seen from the sea to the metaphorical "little boat of their conversation . . . moored precariously" and then to the wholly foreign and ominous figure of the helplessly hysterical woman. The skein of association is clear enough: Yvonne's final vision of the shack is from a distance as an anti-Farolito ("a haven and a beacon"). But she herself is thereby placed at "sea," unable to rescue the little boat "banging against the rocks," a helpless victim of destructive motion in turn echoed in the "banging" fists of the hysterically jerking woman.

For the chapter's close, Lowry makes an unnecessarily obvious alteration by having the Consul whisper of the two aged Indians, "'It's his father, Hugh,'" a whisper followed by five repetitions of "'Buenos noches'" and Geoffrey's emendation, "'Unless it's the old man of the sea.'" The same point is simultaneously made more suggestively by the single addition here that will remain: the aged bearer is made "trembling in every limb under this weight of the past" (Templeton 1:4, 23). There is, however, another type of change occurring as well, one that returns us to the chapter's opening in the alteration of the very look of the page. What had been three paragraphs between "'Forward to the Salon Ophelia!'" [sic] and the chapter end has become three times that number with almost no change of material. There will be some consolidation before publication, but essentially this arrangement will remain.

These changes in the one section of Chapter IX that had been left almost untouched since 1940 seem Lowry's way of emphasizing the chapter's return to its point of origin (like echoing stops at Las Novedades in earlier versions). Mexico's "tragic history" has been evoked at the opening only to be dismissed, "laugh[ed] away," the apparent powerlessness of that past embodied in the genial figure of the peanut vendor, who reminds Yvonne of her father. Now not only does the father-figure reappear in all his burdensomeness, underlined in explicit identification, but the very typography seems to mock the alcoholic-euphoric effervescence of the opening, its rapid shifts and insistence on "happiness." For here the series of brief paragraphs does not underline Yvonne's perception; indeed, the shift from the previous "Yvonne noticed what looked like the bottom of a crutch" to "they noticed" shows Lowry subtly objectifying these final actions; the arrangement places in dramatic relief the individual image, allowing the full weight of each to register. In short, the breaking of solid paragraph blocks, underscored by the somber tone, here slows movement as the dark images march before us, throwing their shadow (a key image here) back over the entire chapter, turning to "noches" hopes engendered in the arena under late afternoon sun.

Anxious as he was about this chapter, Lowry recognized quickly that he had only partially solved its problems. Yvonne's projection of a future life with Geoffrey was basically sound: congruent with the Consular vision in the Chapter I letter, and drawing as it does on its author's loving memories—all the more loving from exile in Ontario—the scene is richly and lyrically imagined. But the sketch of a past for Yvonne parallel to those already devised for Geoffrey and Laruelle (Chapter I) and for Hugh (Chapter VI) is rudimentary when compared either with those others or with her envisioned future, and it is flatly written, a brief piece of pedestrian exposition. It demanded either excision or enrichment, and given the thinness and brevity of Chapter IX, its prevailing theme of the weight of the past, and Lowry's native propensities, it is no surprise that he chose the latter course.

Thus while the next versions of Chapter IX receive inevitable adjustments, the new draft(s) are distinguished by the enormous enlargement of Yvonne's retrospection early in the chapter.[38] Typically, Lowry begins by dramatizing his material, setting it into motion. Now Yvonne's past, in the person of her father, enters with the uncomprehending, entangled bull, rather than as an appendage to the proud "giant" of the peanut vendor, but Lowry first introduces Captain Constable (demoted from the earlier draft's "Major") almost as awkwardly as he had previously: "Yvonne thought suddenly, with a pang not felt for years, of her father" (27:14, 5). Only then does he make Yvonne *see* him (as Hugh is made first to *hear* Juan Cerillo in Chapter IV), moving in his characteristic manner, making "his way toward her, through the seats, hovering, responding eagerly as a child," establishing him as a concrete physical presence, before moving to the career that proved so disastrous to him.

Given the novel's concern with the manifold burdens of the past, the parent Yvonne was provided with probably had to be psychologically "significant." Lowry was no doubt right to make the parallels between Geoffrey and Captain Constable—military and diplomatic careers ("Consul to Iquique! . . . or Quauhnahuac!"), alcoholism—a part of Yvonne's own awareness, although at first he seems to think that awareness needs justifying. We are told of attempts to rationalize her feelings for Geoffrey "by saying (which she would perhaps never have done had there not with the advent of the home radio come to be a mass-produced statue of King Oedipus—or would it be Electra?—in every American's back yard) it was merely the 'passionately protective love for her father transferred to him.'" Confused and confusing as that parenthesis was, Lowry jettisoned the entire overstrained structure, persuaded that his heroine's awareness of pop-Freudianism did not need explaining. "Explained" or not, the Oedipal (or Electral) configuration places Yvonne parallel to the Firmin brothers, each of whom, like the Indian at the chapter's close, bears the burden of his own paternal figure.

The expanded treatment of Yvonne's father grew out of the outline in the previous draft. For the similar sketch there of Yvonne's own earlier life, equally flat and journalistic, Lowry had a different solution: make it *really* journalistic, give it the kind of jaunty, dishonest "liveliness" movie magazine columns can possess. And thus the press release, the puff interview was born, which Lowry clearly enjoyed enough to let it carry him further than was strictly necessary. Outside it, too, he used the opportunity to flesh out the pattern of Yvonne's life by having her "caught in a ravine with two hundred stampeding horses" and make the cowboy-togged Hugh evoke her former leading man, Bill Hodson.[39] And in one of the best touches in the entire presentation of Yvonne, far more effective than her previous railings against an exclusive "world" of males, she is now made to recognize her essential aloneness even—perhaps especially—among the men most important to her: Hugh, who knows nothing whatever of her past career, and her father and her husband, bracketed again, who, vaguely embarrassed, do not want to think about this part of her life or its effects on her. "Geoffrey might have nightmares, like her father in this too, be the only person in the world who ever had such nightmares, but that she should have them—ah, never!" (27:14, 9). It is a momentary drop, a swift bitter recognition, yet it does more to impute to Yvonne an inner life than all of the press release.

That very American pastiche, with its hopped-up rhythms, addiction to nicknames (Boomp Girl, Honolulu Hellion, Boss-Boss), its clichés of both word and action, nonetheless gets used for other than expository purposes by Lowry, concerned to extend the patterns of Yvonne's experience and her role in the action. Once again associated with the goddess of love (the interviewer presents her as "a honey-tanned Venus just emerging from the surf"), she is nonetheless known as "Yvonne the Terrible," and her trumpeted "comeback," ironically echoing the action of the novel, which dramatizes another attempted return, is portentously a failure. "Star" for her has at the University of Hawaii acquired astronomical rather than cinematic meaning, an evolution that apparently permits no reversal, for "Yvonne Constable had not become a star for the second time" (13). In the passages following the interview, as Yvonne's life seems to roam aimlessly, Lowry returns once more to the long-superseded 1940 *Volcano* for some of her phantasmagoric wanderings on the streets of Los Angeles and New York. Wholly unanticipated, however, is Laruelle's film about Yvonne Griffaton, a *mise en abyme* for the fictional Yvonne Constable and one of several openings in the novel that allow us to consider Chapters II-XII as yet another film by Jacques Laruelle.

What of course *Le Destin de Yvonne Griffaton* most immediately seems to do is to suggest pattern and meaning in the life of Yvonne Constable, a pattern and meaning ironically unknown to her, if not to the rest of the audience (whose "knowledge" is useless), for they have apparently seen the film from the start, whereas she has come late and cannot stay for the next show's beginning. (Lowry seems to hint at a universal belatedness.) Yvonne is a natural skeptic, but she recognizes the possibility that for her too what "conceivably lent some meaning ... to her own destiny was buried in the distant past, and might for all she knew repeat itself in the future" (17). Echoing the fictional Yvonne Griffaton, however, Yvonne Constable wonders whether repeated pattern, "an endless succession of tragedies," was "just frankly meaningless." Some kind of "faith," however misguided, seems to her necessary to impart value. Lowry manages to have it, as usual, both ways: the "pattern" imputed to the career of Yvonne Griffaton is both reflective of and reflected in that of Yvonne Constable—even the dullest member of the novel's "audience" can hardly miss the huge horse that, "filling the whole screen, seemed leaping out of it at her" as she enters the cinema—yet that pattern need not imply significance, may suggest a pointless grinding, mere repetitive doom. Picking up the language of the ending of the previous draft, Lowry ties both Yvonnes into the novel's central historical question: "What could she do under the weight of such a heritage? How could she rid herself of this old man of the sea? Was she doomed to an endless succesion of tragedies ... ?" The Yvonne Constable who thus reflects on Yvonne Griffaton then reemerges into the novel's 1938 present as Yvonne "Firmin" only to see yet one more pattern, a very old and, again, repetitive one, in the struggling bull in Arena Tomalín brought down into "a sort of death, just as it so often was in life; and now, once more, resurrection" (18). A series of fictions, a series of patterns, a series of metaphors—and the question of meaning left open. At this point, Lowry reengages his previous draft, where we almost at once find Yvonne discovering a kind of "faith," a growing belief in the possibility of love grounded in the landscape, the "home," that her imagination amplifies through the remainder of the chapter. That home, that love, is not an earthly possibility, as Chapter XI will demonstrate: whether this denies Yvonne's "faith," however, is another question, one which (once more) Lowry characteristically leaves open.

Chapter IX was hard slogging for Lowry, although he would insist to Jonathan Cape his satisfaction with the result (*Letters* 80), but Chapter X was more like serious fun: it brought out his creative playfulness. Throughout this round of revision the Consul's chapters had grown progressively bolder, wilder, more hallucinatory, dislocated, with skips and breaks, uncertainties of attribution, dubieties of action, delirium, blackout. In its previous incarnation, however, Chapter X, where the Consul first takes the dread mescal, had been quite conventional in technique. Geoffrey's consciousness had been "slowed" by the drinks, mood and tone becoming more agitated and paranoiac, but his mind— and the narrative—had remained thoroughly coherent. Given the development of the Consul through the preceding chapters, however, there could now be no question of a Geoffrey only mildly transformed by his mounting intake of alcohol, or of an account unaltered by his transformation. With the action that continues to open the chapter, the ordering and drinking of the first mescal, the change is virtually instantaneous.

It was not instantaneous in the writing, however. Surviving manuscripts indicate at least three stages before Lowry arrived at a satisfactory version, and even this solution rapidly proved unstable.[40] The most obvious and important changes are additions: despite condensations elsewhere, the chapter swells from twenty-seven to forty-five pages. Curiously, the largest of these come from quite old and quite new sources—from a Tlaxcala tourist folder (now, alas, lost) that Lowry presumably brought with him out of Mexico in 1938, and from local trips, just prior to the time of writing, to the Oakville railroad station, Inn, and environs. The previous typescript (31:5) contains holograph notations concerning both, but it is worth noting that the Tlaxcalan theme evolves from a poster in that earlier draft, whereas the train-vision not only comes from later in Lowry's experience but has no such hook in the previous text.

These additions in themselves, however, did not require any significant change in technique, and many annotations on the previous typescript suggest modest alterations in the spirit of that more conventional draft. On the opening page, for instance, we find this: "The Consul's point should be that Hugh has absolutely misinterpreted everybody's motives, that only kindness is to be interpreted in the business of the Indian, that people were looking after him really," a modification of the dinner-table argument that clearly conceives of it as still a fully coherent discussion. Here too the matching set pieces of Hugh's citing of Arnold on Marcus Aurelius and Geoffrey's diatribe on the elements are marked for entry, the latter an invocation of the Consul's cosmic opponents in the battle for "human consciousness" (31:5). None of these demands dislocation in design or method, however. It is the opening train passage that, in dramatizing the usurpation of the Consul's mind by mescal-charged vision, signals a new and more radical technique ahead, although the passage itself requires little more than careful insertion into existing material, typically, in echoing passages near beginning and end of the chapter.

The vision is insistently sinister. Trains, like buses and ships, vehicles of transit and transition, always stirred Lowry's imagination; here they induce a semihallucinatory state where the ordinary apprehension of time and space seems suspended and the landscape takes on a menacing life of its own. Into this world without time threatening trains thunder relentlessly, again and again, the frightening sight and sound intensified by the surrounding infernal details—coal, smoke, fire. Those are in turn set within a nature (cornflowers, dandelion, meadowsweet) itself turning violently unnatural (a tree "like a green exploding sea-mine, frozen") just as the inanimate awakes to grotesque life ("Rows of lamps like erect snakes"). Intensifying this sense of time suspended and landscape of menace are the linguistic resources of sound and rhythm, the thundering, hypnotic *clipperty*s, which create the sense of relentless recurrence, a hammering obsessiveness that stamps the entire passage as situated within, an event of the mind, not the world. Nor, whatever source we may posit for an "Oakville" in the

Consul's past, is this experience undergone at the Salón Ofélia merely a matter of "memory": the disorienting, frightening passage seems to straddle the line between dream and waking, partaking of each, and thus unresolvable, held between the precision that could anchor it to daylight familiarity and the pure associativeness that might label it "only" a psychological product.[41] It is a stunning overture to the dislocations which lie ahead.

The darkness and insistent demonic references are set in relief by the elliptical anecdote involving one "Mr. Quattras, the negro . . . from Codrington, in the Barbados," who somehow has provided the Consul with that ordeal to which he has declared his commitment, a "battle against death" that, in this instance, "had been won." The real battle here has been internal, as a cancelled passage makes clear, Geoffrey's victory seen in his ability to act on "one unselfish thought," which is to "save" Quattras from deportation (31:6, 4). Quattras is not only an outcast in danger but a black, and thus in the traditional symbolism of the vision—*"It's a black business but we use you white: Daemon's Coal"*—the Consul's saving embrace of this unfortunate seems doubly potent.[42] It does not, however, prevent the imagery of darkness and death—the shadows, the night, the cemetery, the transportable vault that brings the Consul once more to "A corpse will be transported by express"—from closing out the passage, returning Geoffrey from this vision associated with his past to the ominous portent of his future.

However disturbingly surreal, the vision is almost detachable from the surrounding text: with the addition of wibberlee-wobberlee transitional sentences ("It was as if, more, he were waiting for something, and then again, not waiting") that modulate from the coherent outer world with which the chapter opens, the new passage could simply be dropped in, both here and in the reprise near chapter's end, a reprise that repeats exactly the early section of the vision (although its first version [31:6, 42-43] was three times the length it eventually became). Yet if the vision itself required little textual change, its locating the center of perception within the Consul implied and authorized a far less conventional handling of material to follow. After all, if Geoffrey has a blackout after tequila in Chapter V, what might we expect after mescal?

Whatever we might expect, the first thing we get is another deft installment of the ironic comedy of the drunk. In two stages, Lowry establishes first the Consul's mescal-fueled self-congratulation ("How sensible!"), the preposterous reassurance that he is "now fully awake, fully sober again," followed by the "continual twitching and hopping within his field of vision, as of innumerable sand fleas," which undermines the rationalization and prepares for future strangenesses within that "field of vision" (31:6, 5). They are not long in arriving.

"Mescal was the drink of solitude," Geoffrey had reflected in the preceding draft, a cue that Lowry now accepts by dramatizing it. Whereas previously he had guiltily been unable to meet Yvonne's eyes at the table, here he does so with "a long look of longing"; but ironically the blend of yearning and mescal causes the present Yvonne to fade into nostalgic memories of their meeting in Granada, a brilliant paragraph that merges the continuous upward movement of aspiration—he imagines them traveling constantly "up, up" the long hill to the Alhambra and Generalife Gardens—with a benign transformation of the train-vision (*"chuffery-puppery"*). It is the imagined arrival at this "summit" that causes him guiltily to drop his eyes as the hill metamorphoses into a mountain of bottles, "a babel of glasses" that crumbles and smashes beneath him as, in anticipation of the novel's close, the ascent becomes a descent in the enormous ensuing catalogue where each element seems to divide and branch into the next, a proliferation that syntactically enacts the disintegration at its center: the question of where in all this multiplying chaos is *his* center, "the cohesive factor of his personality" (while the character seems to wonder on his author's behalf, "Or was all this bloody nonsense?") (31:6, 15).

Immersed within Geoffrey's consciousness, the narrative now moves through personal stocktaking, the seriocomic reflections of the rationalizing drunk, before reemerging into an awareness of fragmented snatches of dialogue. As it seems once more to engage the outer world, we gradually discover that during his self-absorbed reflections the Consul has moved from restaurant proper to the nearby toilet, from which we will soon receive, as in Chapter V, an abrupt series of glimpses of elided exterior action. Now, however, it is not possible to pinpoint just when his move has taken place, nor to identify with certainty other features of the ensuing episode in the "stone retreat." Geoffrey himself wonders, "Why was he here? Why was he always more or less, here?" (recalling the bathroom blackout of V, anticipating the mingitorio of XII), a reasonable question since, "fully dressed," it is not even clear he is seated there for the usual purpose, despite Cervantes's grim offer of a hygienic "stone." How has he obtained the mescal beside him, and why, when he seems able to hear Yvonne and Hugh quite clearly, are they unable to hear him? Or is he in fact "hearing" them in the usual sense at all? Since other "voices" appear that we can hardly believe come from outside the Consul—his familiars, the out-of-work actor, Weber, the Englishman in the sportscar, Dr. Vigil, Yvonne, Geoffrey himself earlier in the day, and so on—there seems little basis on which to discriminate "real" from "imagined." Indeed, there are some voices it appears impossible to locate: who says "'Mar Cantabrico'"? "'no pasarán'"? "'Madrid'"? (31:6, 23, 25) Has the Consul indeed ever left the restaurant table, where he will again find himself doing precisely what he was doing when we last saw him there: "And now, once more their eyes met across the table" (31:6, 26)?⁴³ Much more radically than in V, and much more disturbing to the bases of fictional orientation—where is all this? when? who is speaking?—the center of Chapter X resists determinacy.

The revised technique of course permits (as did the blackout of Chapter V) a telescoping and editing of material for which a more traditional approach demands (and in previous drafts received) fuller treatment. "Break up the conversation into nonsense" (31:5, 9), Lowry marginally directs, and the discussion of the afternoon's events is thereby reduced to key words and phrases to telegraph the essence of positions and indicate the drift of argument rather than provide a transcript, sharply reducing the entire, somewhat ponderous dinner-table episode. This turned out to be an opportunity for some other housecleaning, eliminating more than verbiage. The strain that insisted on history as a mere scramble for "loot," part of the chapter since 1940, finally disappears. (Lowry was particularly sensitive about this material, borrowed from Claude Houghton—as he felt obliged to say.)⁴⁴

The ambiguous textual upshot of Geoffrey's condition is sustained in the action that follows his return to the table (however we understand that "return"). Full of suspicion and paranoia, the Consul now insists on traveling to Tlaxcala, reviews "the drink situation," and announces his battle with the elements (followed by Hugh on Matthew Arnold). Expansion here is partly balanced by contraction elsewhere. The Consul's rambling monologue on the rites and religions of India was ripe for reduction, and Lowry shrewdly catches it up in the alcoholic confusion of the chapter, in the fluid borders already established between consciousness and world. What had previously covered more than three pages of quoted speech shrinks here to half that in indirect discourse, a technique that permits considerable condensation while retaining almost all the substantive issues and associations raised in the original, indeed, even slightly amplifying them with a trail of allusions out of Sir Thomas Browne. However, we are assured that the *oratorio oblique* on the page before us is a representation of the Consul "once more, in top form," that he is speaking "soberly, brilliantly, and fluently again," an assurance kept before us in the repeated "He was talking . . .," "The Consul was talking. . . ." Even more deceptive than the "speech" to Hugh from the stones of the Calle Nicaragua in Chapter III, this error cannot be detected before Geoffrey himself realizes, "there was a slight mistake. The Consul was not talking. Apparently not. The Consul had not uttered a single word. It was all an illusion, a species of brainstorm, a whirling cerebral chaos" (27:15, 33-34).

It is not, of course, a "chaos" as we read it, but a richly complex series of associations, in its compressed form the most convincing single passage in the novel to suggest a Geoffrey Firmin capable of writing that syncretic book on universal religion first mentioned in his letter. If this be chaos, the "order" that follows from it—the citation from Tolstoy on free will—is thin and obvious by comparison. The price of articulation seems simplification, a "little" piano piece (as the new metaphor puts it) cast up by memory. In the Consul's now persuading himself that this was what sent him to the "excusado," in likening it to Hugh's citation from Arnold (to which it has become Geoffrey's competitive counterthrust), we see Lowry binding the strands of the chapter more closely.

Geoffrey, however, is soon launched on his diatribe, which differs from its predecessor primarily in the interruptions Lowry contrives, largely to keep drama alive. The line about "determinism in the fate of nations," for instance, draws from Hugh the objection, "'you're quoting Spengler'" (which will shrink to the vaguer, "'Not exactly original'"). As the attack shifts from the political to the personal, the assault on Hugh and Yvonne, the major alteration is Geoffrey's self-consciousness, his helpless moments of awareness of what he is doing coupled with his powerlessness to change it, an intimate, ironic dramatization of the Tolstoyan debate on freedom and necessity, appropriate to an attack on his companions that simultaneously brings it home: "What was he saying? The Consul listened to himself, almost in surprise at this cruelty, this vulgarity. And in a moment it was going to get worse. . . . Must the Consul say this? It seemed he must, that something from outside which was also drawing him like a magnet, was making him say it" (27:15, 40–41).[45] That last sentence, however, muddied waters by appearing to posit another agency, a gambit Lowry hardly wished to pursue, whereas the revised "He was saying, had said it" returns the issue to the personal and becomes a part of the novel's motif of "too late," of opportunities missed altogether or glimpsed only as they receded, became unavailable, part of the past, the pluperfect.

Much of this, however, was essentially adjustment, the refinement of extant passages. In an altogether different category is the Tlaxcalan material. In earlier drafts the Tlaxcalans had been the Consul's example of preconquest exploitation within Mexico, and he had argued plausibly that they were "tickled to death at the rumors . . . that they'd soon be free of Moctezuma, the exploiter" (31:5, ts. 14), allying themselves with the Spaniards in an act of revolt. Now, however, as Lowry most fully explores this material, long available to him from Prescott and the travel folder, that earlier significance is reversed. What Tlaxcala means from now on is "betrayal," not revolt, most insidiously a betrayal from within, a self-undermining. The Consul, in short, now comes to view sixteenth-century Mexico much as Hugh had in earlier drafts, as a land vulnerable to imperialism, a prey to European invasion and exploitation. With "Mexico" the operative entity, the Aztec-Tlaxcalan opposition becomes an internal affair, the Spaniards alone viewed as outsiders, the enemy, and the Tlaxcalans thus as "treacherous." From this perspective, "betrayal" may suddenly find analogues ranging from civil struggle in Spain—thus Tlaxcala "resembles" Granada in more than appearance—a war that betrays all of Europe and the West to German incursion, to Hugh's remorse over his political and sexual betrayals, a remorse that by dividing the will and undermining action, further betrays the integrity of the self. From Judas and Peter's betrayals of Christ to Yvonne's infidelities, the novel had long been full of betrayals, including of course the Consul's betrayal of himself. Here in Chapter X he first takes that drink that he has declared would be "the end"; here too, at last, Lowry brings his theme of betrayal fully to the surface by rooting it in Mexican soil.

The center of the Tlaxcala material is the travel brochure, but Lowry weaves it in elsewhere as he rewrites, sometimes dropping it literally and casually, as if in "natural" connection with Cervantes—his greeting with "Tlaxcaltecan pleasure," training the cock for a fight "in Tlaxcala," possessing a ten-volume "History of Tlaxcala" (formerly "of Oaxaca") (27:15, 7, 10). Other references extend the motif metaphorically, as in the early connection of it with the train vision, which appears as, "And did not the soul too have her savage and traitorous Tlaxcalans, her Cortes and her noches tristes, and sitting within her innermost citadel in chains, drinking chocolate, her pale Moctezuma?" (31:6, 8) Later the Consul will quite inconsistently invoke it with boozy sentimentality—"'Why should any one have interfered with the Tlaxcalans, for example, who were perfectly happy by their stricken-in-years trees, among the webbed footed fowl in the first lagoon'" (31:6, 36).

This last example depends upon our encounter with that Tlaxcaltecan "document," the travel folder, that materializes somehow while the Consul reposes in the toilet (itself "probably a purely Tlaxcaltecan fantasy"). We read it there, in one of Lowry's favorite devices, contrapuntally, the dry, formal, not quite idiomatic English of the brochure played off against the various speaking voices that swirl through the episode. The essential comedy thus created is announced even before the arrival of the folder by the unexpected appearance in the stone "tomb" of Cervantes, who enigmatically utters, "chuckling," the single word "'—Tlaxcala!'" As if a signal, two overlapping dialogues now create between them a series of cloacal puns, a reference to the horse's "'rump'" juxtaposed with "the Consul's plight" on the toilet, which seems to Cervantes best solved by "'a stone.'" "'Branded'" warns the other voice, as if anticipating the upshot of Cervantes's "'Clean yourself on a stone, señor'" (31:6, 16).

The folder itself, entitled SEAT OF THE HISTORY OF THE CONQUEST, punning on the Consul's present posture, is heralded by an outside voice, announcing "'—and then there was this Indian—.'" Under the same heading in Spanish—SEDE DE LA HISTORIA DE LO CONQUISTA [sic]— we hear the echoing "'—Indian sitting with his back against the wall—'"; and "'—What a glorious morning it was!—'" seems to introduce the brochure on CLIMATE ("regular and healthy" is its phlegmatic verdict). As the episode proceeds, counterpointing becomes more complex, voices played against one another as well as against the folder. While the

Consul comments ("although it was strange, nobody seemed to have heard him") on Hugh's need to see the pelado as a Spaniard in order to support his political-historical "illusions," Hugh himself (or Yvonne?) is recalling "'—crossing the river, a windmill—'" the evocation of Don Quixote underlined by the Consul's call for "'Cervantes!'" Soon "overheard" dialogue can no longer all be ascribed to actual voices, speaking now. Yvonne's commentary on events at the roadside is followed by another voice (the Consul's own) from the event itself ("'Move his hat further down though, so he can get some air'"). "Perhaps," Geoffrey has reflected earlier, "there was no time ... in this stone retreat." As voices begin to appear from other parts of the day, from recollections of other days, from who knows where or when, the usual boundaries of time (and space? and consciousness?) do seem to dissolve. Is this, then, "the eternity he'd been making so much fuss about"? (31:6, 16–25) Whatever one's answer to that question, in the reverberations here orchestrated Lowry was working to create more complex effects than the spare literalism of the previous political discussion, or even than the simple counterpoint between past and present, folder and voice(s), with which at this stage he began, for as the episode begins to echo with other voices, other passages, it resonates on several frequencies simultaneously.

Characteristically, the earliest version here is the longest, the typescript marked for numerous cuts, but basic structure and method were now established. From the first, Lowry was as much concerned about "seeing" as hearing the passages from the brochure. Even, apparently, before working them into his own manuscript, he knew he wanted them set off from surrounding text. In notes for the holograph draft, "the typography of the passages from the folder" is made a topic to discuss (Templeton 1:9, B), and on the typescript, he calls for "single spacing, possibly smaller print throughout" and "all these [sub-headings] capitalised ... in centre of page" (31:6, 18). Late in discovering the usefulness of a "found" object he had had all these years, once he did take it up he seemed to see more and more possibilities in it. Not the least was its strange, stilted speech, a formality and awkwardness studded with sober gaffes ("inhibitants," "corpulent ash-trees") distinct from the multilingual punning of Cervantes's menu or the Spanglish of Dr. Vigil and Señora Gregorio. If this was wordplay, it was of the most dignified kind, and thus all the more delighted Lowry in its pompous lurches into absurdity. He would be henceforth reluctant to surrender any of it.

The two major additions, the train passage and the Tlaxcalan material, develop out of quite different sources, and they provide the mescal-imbued Consul with two quite distinct inner visions: the threatening, demonic world of frantic, ceaseless action, dominated by a traditional blackness (coal, trains, smoke, night, Negroes), and "the beautiful cathedral city," entirely white and entirely empty, where instead of being surrounded by sinister and threatening figures, he is accompanied only by an ideally benign Yvonne, where the single clock is "timeless," and the measured, calm sentences reflect an existence quite opposed to the hyperventilations that convey the rushing trains and suddenly telescoped scenes. The hell and heaven of the mescalito, undoubtedly, yet, counterposed as imagery, tone, rhythms seem to make them, there can be little doubt of their equal deathliness. In his manipulations of traditional counters, Lowry shows himself worthy of his forbears, Melville and Conrad, for the white silences of this ideal Tlaxcala are the whitenesses of sterility, barrenness, the tomb, the whiteness of darkness. It is Geoffrey's own Tlaxcalan self-betrayal that he takes this to be his paradisal city, his goal, the eternity toward which he yearns, tricked out in the churches and towers, sanctuary and cathedral, that deceptively seem to endorse and justify his desire: endless bibulous satisfaction at no cost.[46]

Little wonder, then, that the chapter's climax resolves the apparent opposition, bringing together the two visions, the two new strains, to suggest their underlying oneness. With the reappearance of the train vision, the compulsive repetitious element, the rushing *clippertys*, gets replaced by the obsessive stutter of "Tlax" ("*Tlax: tlax: tlax: tlax:*"). No longer indicating a vision of timelessness, they at one point denote the tick of the "orderly little clock" situated (where else?) "behind the bar," and in the now enormously suspended syntax of the Consul's sentence asserting his power of choice, the first thing he "chooses" is "Tlax," with which "Hell" is in eventual, "absurd" apposition. Geoffrey may not quite know what he is saying, but Lowry most certainly does. The ontology of the train vision is questioned belatedly (in both senses: it is a pencil insert on the typescript, as well as coming only at the end of the chapter)—"had he gone?"—and the name of the ideal city reduced to little more than a hiccup, ironic counters brought together in the place that for the Consul dissolves their superficial opposition, "the paradise of his despair," the Farolito (31:6, 42–43).

Chapter XI was the last of the novel's units to receive a full rewriting, and perhaps because the end did now really seem in view, Lowry was anxious to get it right. The final Yvonne-chapter, it had, like her others, presented him with more difficulties than those mediated by the male characters. Despite the leap forward of the preceding draft, much still seemed to demand attention: survivals, again, are incomplete, but several phases of holograph and typescript were passed through before Lowry arrived at a fair copy ("E") that satisfied him.[47]

The great set-piece of this revision is the passage about the stars, echoed in the richly metaphorical ending he now devises for Yvonne. Both combine the intensified focus on nature with an increased internalization of the chapter. From a brief opening exchange between Yvonne and Hugh until conversation in El Popo, for instance, there is now no dialogue at all other than a terse exchange outside El Petate. Lowry can hardly have been unaware that this reduction would at last virtually purge the Yvonne-Hugh relationship of all direct reference to the love-triangle. The sexual tension between the two of course remains as subtext, but it is no accident that the focus in that new initial exchange has become the Consul, Yvonne opening with, "'You know perfectly well I can't just run away, and abandon him'" (31:10, 1).

Meanwhile, literally in place of diminished dialogue, Lowry introduces other (and more stylized) kinds of utterance, mainly in Spanish. As in Chapter X, a long-retained object—here, the menu—is brought belatedly into play, and wherever he obtained them, Lowry provides Hugh with appropriate revolutionary songs on which to exercise his guitar. Once more he makes imaginative use of contrapuntal technique, substituting these other expressive forms for one side of a reduced dialogue. In the case of the menu, while Hugh is delivering a sharply abbreviated version of British distaste for conspicuously virtuous action, his speech is simply set against the card that we read, as it were, over Yvonne's shoulder. With the revolutionary songs, roles are reversed: we hear Hugh's verses against Yvonne's speeches expressing more personal emotion.

The songs are perhaps the simpler of the introductions here. Doubly set off from their surroundings by typography and language, the excerpts reverberate ironically against Yvonne's words and situation. As she speaks of Geoffrey going "'from restaurant to restaurant'" seeking her ("'just as we're looking for him now'"), for instance, Hugh sings of workshops and arsenals and exhorts everyone *(todos)* to war *(a guerra!)*; while she balances precariously on the log, his song advises that "if your existence is a world of pain, choose to die, choose to die" (31:10, J, L). Love played off against war is an ancient configuration; it is not the least of Lowry's ironies that song, introduced so late into the scene, is placed not at the service of its traditional amorous ally but serves to celebrate battle and, finally, death.

The menu, on the other hand, has a double aspect, corresponding to its two sides. Unlike what we find in Chapter X, where the characters in the Salón Ofélia are also said to be scanning a menu, this is distinctly (as it is called) "a document," something to be read, closer to telegram and postcard of Chapters IV and VI. "Reprint in *full*," reads Lowry's directive on the surviving original (Templeton 1:24), but of course he neither "reprints" nor even describes "in full" what is there. The actual menu is covered on both sides with Lowry's handwriting (some clearly from 1944, when he is at work on the novel, much of the rest doubtless dating from Mexico). But the fictional menu is entirely clean on its face: Yvonne must be told to turn it over to discover why Hugh has shown it to her. That "impersonality" is, surely, part of the point: like the other document that needs to be turned over to be fully read, the postcard, its face speaks of the world beyond the self; only its back inscribes the individual.

Nevertheless, the printed face acts on Yvonne as if it were a directed missive, which, since Hugh has "skimmed" the menu onto the table "for her," in a sense it is. Her study of it "with alcoholic deliberation," is Lowry's opportunity to describe it, and the straightforward bill of fare—there are no puns, no jokes here—establishes the "objectivity" of the menu, as do the notices Lowry now copies from the lower part of its face: *"Recuerede Usted que A partir del 1º de Enero de 1938 Sorteos Lunes-Miércoles y Viernes"* and "Loteria Nacional Para La Beneficia Publica." The latter acquires resonance by appearing in "a design like a small wheel," the words "which created another circular frame within where [sic] appeared a sort of symbolic trade or hallmark representing a happy mother caressing her child" (31:10, F). The first notice, being only literal, is quickly cut, and Lowry will drop the "symbolic" insistence on the second, simply allowing the implications of wheels and mother-and-child to operate.[48] The "smiling young woman" on the left side of the menu, who holds in one hand her block of lottery tickets featuring horse and rider while with the other she raises her forefinger, is indeed prominent on the actual menu, but the admonition to observe "la más estricta moralidad"—the hook into the fictional menu from the preceding draft—is not a feature of the actual menu at all.

Despite the apparent impersonality of such a card and Yvonne's phlegmatic spoken response—"'Well'" is all she says to Hugh—her identification of the cowgirl on the lottery tickets as her "own reduplicated and half-forgotten selves waving goodbye to herself" indicates that she has taken (and will continue to take) the face of the menu as composed of encoded messages that would indeed make it a sort of "letter," one very much directed to Yvonne, if not exactly by Hugh. Yet if the printed face of the menu suggests to her an ordered world of total correspondence with directives meant for herself, the other side appears in every sense a "reverse," a blankness "almost covered by the Consul's handwriting at its most chaotic." This side too is encoded, containing what seems a poem, but so encumbered "as to be almost undecipherable." This, however, is the Consul's "code," and both Hugh's endorsement and the familiar handwriting seem to promise potential meaning, so that Yvonne persists until she discovers a "semblance" of coherence.

Despite exaggerating the difficulties of decipherment, Lowry here is fairly faithful to his source. The actual menu's verso does indeed contain a "Recknung" at the top left, and several drawings that are at least open to the readings Yvonne gives them. The novel's major alteration to the cited poem (headed "The Comedian") has been to collapse two drafts into one and to ignore some of the more desultory markings. Now, the line that haunts Yvonne—"Who once fled north"—has a resonance for the novel it could not have had before the Canadian vision was developed; at the same time the poem's motifs of "escape," "thronged terrors," "foundered soul," and (the other line Yvonne repeats), "There would have been a scandal at his death," all reverberate on Geoffrey's frequency. Lowry simply sidestepped more prosaic (or irrelevant) lines—"made no further effort, took no chance/spent no money, to secure him, thought him not worth/Even the price a government pays for a cell," for instance (Scherf, no. 108). Finally, it is the drawing of the "wheel" that imagistically links this "personal" side to the other, printed one, also containing a "small wheel." "My life is firmly and forever joined to yours," her letters had been telling the Consul since 1940 (26:5, 14). Now, impelled through the jungle by reading his poem, Yvonne hurries toward the fate that will join her to Geoffrey in death as in life, an inseparability as close as two sides of a menu.

Lowry's notes indicate that with the urgency lent to Hugh and Yvonne's quest by the menu came the immediate jettisoning of the political discussion of the previous draft: "on having read this [the poem] . . . Yvonne should . . . say we must go, and they should go out quickly, all the business of I hatee you etc., being cut" (15:14, verso 12). Now the menu and Hugh's flashlight produce "illusions" that extend the range of the ensuing action. Plunging back into the forest, Yvonne glimpses "her own wrong shadow . . . or the shadow of a giantess," and moments later seems to make out "beckoning her on at the end of the path, the fixedly smiling woman with the lottery tickets" (31:10, H, J), interchangeable images of her fate that seem also (via the lottery tickets) to associate this looming figure with the goddess Fortuna. The sudden illusion of "a ruined Grecian temple" raises other associations, suggesting, especially in its "perfection," Yvonne's imminent removal beyond earthly flaws, a connection more openly expressed in an earlier draft: "such was one's life too, a walking home through a long night of such illusions, as if one were approaching a temple lit by moonlight, and oneself in a dark forest" (15:14, verso 12).[49] The sense Lowry develops throughout the new draft of Yvonne coming "home," particularly in association here with a Grecian temple, is designed to evoke the myths of the lost Pleiad and of Demeter and Persephone, both of which involve transformation (metamorphosis) and the removal to a different sphere of being.[50]

With these matters, we move into the area of Lowry's elaboration of setting, the insistence on nature. Yet as well as celebrating the natural, its terror as well as its beauty, he wants to raise the Romantic possibility of finding in its sublimity the suggestions of something beyond. Thus the chapter now opens not with the prosaically setting sun but with a sentence plucked from the second page of the previous draft, "Eddies of green and orange birds scattered aloft with ever wider circlings like rings on water" (31:10). Aside from its suggestiveness, that opening image can be echoed in transformation at the chapter's close,

Yvonne feeling herself borne upward "through eddies of stars scattering aloft with ever wider circlings like rings on water, among whom now appeared, like a flock of diamond birds flying softly and steadily . . ." (31:10, second C). The repetition underscores the transcendence, the natural birds becoming the diamond luminescence of their heavenly counterparts, echoing "rings on water" retaining the sense of movement, fluidity in the very image of perfection—as the circle here, in motion, is relieved of its sinister overtones, returned to more traditional senses: "I saw Eternity the other night / Like a great ring of pure and endless light."[51]

It is altogether appropriate that the opening should contain an image of birds, creatures that move between earth and sky, for that motion is now central to Chapter XI. Yvonne is no longer left dying under the hooves of a vicious-seeming horse; feeling herself "gathered upwards" she becomes part of the cosmic motion depicted in the new passage about the stars. But the action is birdlike too—the Pleiades are even on their first appearance here "like a flock of birds"—for with this draft birds become the undisputed creatures of concern, all others dropping away. The caged gazelle, the presumed ocelot of earlier drafts are nowhere to be found. The chapter's most important bird gets transported to El Petate, becoming after some debate an eagle rather than a hawk, but other birds (with an assist from Nuttall's *Ornithology*) have by this time made their entrance.

Birds are the most literary of creatures, as Lowry was aware: a Chaucerian caged bird had served as epigraph to *Ultramarine* (and indeed he repeatedly tried to work the passage into the text of the *Volcano*). The turn to Nuttall now was first as simple compositional aid— "Get some dope about a hawk out of the Niag[ara] library to imagine from" (27:17, verso 16), he told himself—but it was also a means to staking out his own ornitholological territory. "Shall I call the hawk a corsair, thus getting away from Yeats and Westcott and Atlantic Monthly . . . [?] SEE NUTTALL" directs a later draft, clearly after looking into *Ornithology*. Some five pages of notes taken from and suggested by that handbook survive (Templeton 1:22), yet what they reveal is Lowry's use of them not for his hawk (or eagle), but for the introduction of other birds.

The first are the vultures Yvonne observes high above. Having glimpsed them on arrival early in Chapter II, now she invests them with somewhat surprising significance. "Infernal bird of Prometheus," they measure not only the distances from earth to sky, but from hell to heaven, from the depraved to the sublime, "on earth ... defiling themselves with blood and filth ... yet capable of rising above the storm, to heights shared only by the condor, above the summit of the Andes—." A longer draft, headed simply "Vultures," made plain the human analogy: a graphic recounting of vultures feasting violently and "jealously" on a carcass nonetheless queried, "are you not even as man, friend to the sun ... and ... even as he capable of sublime flights ... ?" (Templeton 1:22, n.p.)[52]

Yvonne's reflections here link back to the responses of Hugh and Geoffrey to vultures in earlier chapters. Other kinds of linkings-back are made through quite different birds, however, linkings into Yvonne's past rather than the novel's. The largest of these comes from her hearing a whipoorwill, a song that seems "calling one home." "Calling one home," she repeats; then asks "to where?" only to answer (in marginal afterthought), "To her father's home in Ohio." The passage continues, "And what should a poor whip-poor-will be doing so far from home herself, in a dark Mexican forest? But the whip-poor-will, like love and wisdom, had no home. And perhaps as Hugh said it was better here than routing around Cayenne, where she was supposed to winter" (31:10, 7). The somewhat confused use of pronouns ("it"? "she"?) for the bird makes overt Yvonne's identification, and the fact that only an afterthought responds to her question of where she might be called "home" *to* suggests Lowry's attempt to destabilize the idea of home. For of course the other obvious answer to her question is the "home" she has projected for Geoffrey and herself, "their little home by the sea." That home too will have to be surrendered, for the point is that Yvonne, "like love and wisdom," like all of us, must finally pass beyond such earthly homes.[53]

The most significant bird in the chapter, however, is the one that has been there all along, the caged hawk. Lowry's moving the bird to the cantina now gives Yvonne something to do while she waits outside, and since the freeing becomes her action alone (yet another step in breaking her ties with Hugh), some sense of the meaning it holds for her became obligatory. At its furthest reach, Yvonne is made to see the bird as "a little world of fierce and hopeless memories and dreams, of ancient wretchedness, or of the sea, of Barbary or Greece, or of floating high above Popocatapetl itself, mile on mile, to fall—pure marauder!—through the wilderness, and settle, watching, in the timberline ghosts of ravaged mountain trees" (31:10, 6). The hawk will become an eagle—"that kind for which the Aztecs named Quauhnahuac" (31:10, insert 5–6)—and the presentation of its flight get extended, but the new description also integrates Yvonne's response.

The bird, as before, emerges hesitantly, moves to the nearest roof, tests its wings, then takes flight:

> with a rapid and continuous motion of wings, but not up to the nearest tree, as might have been supposed but ... up, up, avoiding the trees altogether, with a swimming gyration, soaring—and this was the miracle, it knew apparently it was free, she was right, it hadn't betrayed her—up, up, with a sudden powerful cleaving of pinions, into the infinite, the deep dark blue pure sky above, in which at that moment appeared one star.[54] No thought of this being a shabby trick touched Yvonne. She felt only an inexplicable secret triumph and relief: no one would ever know she had done this: and then, an obscure reaction, as if her drinks were beginning to wear off again, which in point of fact they were.

Once more, this new version attests to Lowry's ability to suggest in syntax and rhythm the very motions his text describes, here conveyed through Yvonne's exultant participation in the bird's sustained soaring, the very animal motion of freedom and aspiration in the repeated "up, up," that Lowry will, again, pare back (perhaps too much in this case, fastidiously calling it "bad poetry") in later modifications.

The bird works as metaphor precisely because it is so concretely invested with particularity and feeling through Yvonne's vicarious response. This makes it the more peculiar that Lowry should clearly wish to undercut his character at this point. The climax followed by reaction is emotionally convincing; it makes the ponderous judgment rendered feel gratuitous. Once more, as Lowry's "again" acknowledges, we are invited to find her exultation a mere alcoholic "mistake," like the misreading of the crowd's mood in the bullring of Chapter IX, an invitation rather insisted on by the narrator's "in point of fact" detachment, heavily elbowing us toward condemnation. Lowry will find it easier to lighten the judgment than to expunge the boozy misreading, which will not disappear wholly until the galleys.

The reference to Yvonne's "drinks" reminds us of the attention Lowry gives throughout this stage to matters alcoholic; we are about to read that those drinks, "relatively few though they were," in his wonderfully surreal image, "lay like swine on her soul" (2:19, verso 8). But her most important intake within Chapter XI is, of course, the mescal she has at El Popo. That is not new, although in now helping herself to Hugh's glass, she considerably raises the quantity; thus the repeated "Yvonne now felt cold sober . . . Yvonne was sober" (31:10, I)—too much of protest indeed—seem designed with her new ending in mind, the rendering of a consciousness whose visionary qualities arise out of the plausible bases of fear, pain, shock—and drink. However, the immediate effect of the mescal on Yvonne has by this time opened to Lowry an entire new strain.

In the previous draft, Yvonne on sipping the mescal had felt invaded by a "nauseating fire" (31:9, 11). That of course was written well before the June 1944 blaze that took the Lowrys' shack. In the months following, both Malcolm and Margerie remained tautly strung, inordinately sensitized to "fire" in any of its manifestations (cf. *Aiken-Lowry* 186–93; *Day* 300–302). Now Malcolm turned the disaster to account, most literally in Yvonne's dying vision of the burning of the seaside home. Since this "home" has existed only within Yvonne's mind, it is there that the conflagration must occur, and Lowry begins early to prepare for it. Watching Hugh question the Mexicans in El Petate, she feels "as if something within her were smouldering, had taken fire, as if her whole being were going to explode—" (27:17, verso 16), a reaction repeated—Lowry here returning to the germ of it all—as she sips her first mescal. Now, however, her sense has developed: "But no, it was not herself that was on fire. It was the house of her spirit. It was her dream. It was the farm, it was Orion, the Pleiades, it was the shack, their poor little home that had caught fire. It was the shack. But where was the fire? It was the Consul who had been the first to notice it" (15:14, verso 15). Another mescal "and the fire went out, was overwhelmed by a sudden wave through her whole being of agonized love and tenderness for the Consul."

At the same time, Lowry characteristically roots "fire" in his setting, placing El Petate, now festooned with advertisements like "a complicated postal stamp," as the sole survivor "of the once prosperous village of Anochtitlan, which had been burned" (31:10, 4), a minor note reprised precisely when Yvonne and Hugh reach the point of no return. About to see the graphic hand commanding "A PARIAN," in "a lightning flash brilliant as day they had seen a sad useless arrow pointing back the way they'd come, to the burned Anochtitlan" (31:10, K). "The burned Anochtitlan" no longer exists; Yvonne follows the hand rather than the arrow not to Parián, but to another nonexistent place, burning, a final purifying vision that moves her beyond all earthly destinations.

For the treatment of Yvonne's "burning dream" Lowry suggested (half in note, half in draft form):

> But the shack was on fire, she saw it now from the forest from the steps above, heard the crackling, it was on fire, everything was burning, they stood for a moment {have the Consul and she stand for a moment, wringing their hands as we did, everything all right as it was, save that it is on fire, and there is this noise as of leaves blowing along the roof} and then have the whole thing much that is mentioned in Chapter X [IX], the windows, the tree, the desk, etc., but burning in reverse, the last thing mentioned first, so to speak, though of course you can't use it all ending: the Consul's manuscripts, his poor book, were scattered burning along the beach, the tide was coming in and washing them away, the tide washed under the ruined house, the pleasure boats sailed homeward silently on the dark stream that earlier had ferried song upstream. Their house was dying, only an agony would go there now. {*Or* Only an agony went there} {*Or* The sun set on the smouldering house: only an agony lives there now.} (15:14, versos 5–6)

Partly stating, partly enacting Lowry's aims, the passage even suggests the dreamlike shifts in perspective (they are outside, they are inside; the house is on fire, the house is "all right") and the dazed fluidity of the run-on of the finished draft, breathless and unstoppable in its syntax and rhythm until it is "too late," rushing forward before, in a short separate sentence, pausing on the last of the participles, one that describes equally Yvonne and the house: "dying." The conditional "would go" that Lowry opts for at this stage (31:10, second B) puts an effective period to the seemingly endless process of "burning, burning," but like the Eliotic, purgatorial, third "burning," the superior finality in the simple past "went," devoid of future possibility, struck him only later.

Presumably with Yvonne's climactic vision in mind, Lowry first proposed that nothing be "reported straight" after A PARIAN (15:14, verso 9). In the event, however, he decided for somewhat longer to register the literal, to get clear the final action. Paths (as in Dante, as in Frost, as in Chapter VIII, as in the cabala) can, with no violation of the mundane, suggest more than themselves: thus when Yvonne realizes that the fallen tree is the divider between her path and the one "the Consul must have taken," when Hugh strays "'off your path,'" the wooded trails evoke divided and conjoined destinies (Lowry's deliberation here seems indicated by his cancellation of the casual profanity in Hugh's original "'off your damned path'") (31:10, K–L). It is at this moment, with storm approaching, atmospheric but still literal, that Lowry surprises us, attempts something he does nowhere else in the novel.

His narrator, who has remained either laconically at the elbows of the characters or, more typically, focused through or into their consciousnesses, suddenly pulls back from Yvonne and comments *in propria persona*, generalizing, in a witty conceit, about the bustling actions of "another person," an interior double figure who "sometimes in thunder" seems less a part of the individual than an agent of Cosmic Powers, who on the one hand sees to it that an appalling chaos in the universe remains hidden from ordinary mortals, but on the other is careful to leave an opening for "the unprecedented." The passage may originate in Lowry's notion that material after A PARIAN not be presented "straight," but as it developed it also became distinct from the rendering of Yvonne's dazed visionary consciousness. It is as if for "the unprecedented"—for this is lightning that does *not* hit the next street—an unprecedented narrative stance became necessary, a technique comparable to the sudden taking-over of "another person." And so "another person" unexpectedly speaks, a voice not bound to conveying the characters and their narrative—there is no suggestion that these are Yvonne's thoughts—one capable of generalizing on matters pertaining to this world and the next in a rhetoric that can contain both porch furniture and insanity in heaven, the locking of windows and the advent of Jesus, all within the confines of a single sentence (Lowry called for three dots and a change of paragraphs to create "a slow pause for dramatic effect" [31:11, 3]). It is a daring and shrewd performance, its domestic imagery of the threatened house picking up the chapter's "home" theme, its opposed motions of closing and opening, of menace and promise, insanity in heaven and Jesus walking in the door suggesting the ending of Yvonne's life—this disaster *will* strike her here, now—while leaving open the possibilities of how to understand it.

Even now, Lowry postpones the shift out of "report[ing] straight" in order to give a closer, more vivid rendering of the actualities of Yvonne's final minutes—"One foot doubled under her with a sharp pain," for instance, and the horse, depicted with clear specificity, is now simply "the animal"—which serves to counterweight the extended passage of her dying delirium. He knew, however, from an early stage (15:14, versos 8, 7, 5) exactly the structure he wanted in that final passage, a series of "whirlings" dissolving into each other, then into dreamlike mergings of key scenes from her earlier existence, a single grand sentence combining the traditional life-flashing-before-one's-eyes with a vision of the cosmos as a series of wheels within wheels.[55] The circling motions shift back and forth convincingly from the local fiesta to the circuits of the heavenly bodies, then gradually dissolve as the dying Yvonne leaves the courses of mundane life, passing the images that bracket her arrival in Acapulco, on earth (the butterflies) and departure from Mexico, from human existence (the horse), touching along the way the personal, aesthetic, political, apocalyptic, archetypal spheres in the Consul, Yvonne Griffaton, Huerta, the universal stampede, the dark wood that she moves past on her way to her "escape," an escape that deposits her before the burning house. New as it was at this stage, Lowry's vision of this passage seems to have emerged almost complete. Even more complete was the brief final paragraph in which Yvonne feels herself "gathered upwards and borne toward the stars" (15:14, verso 6).

The heavens and earth of her last moments are anticipated and linked in the earlier "Pegasus pounded up the sky unseen" (Texas XI, 18), but this final passage, of course, rests upon the earlier one, also new, in which Yvonne gazes silently and at length at the great wheelings of stars and planets above her. Interestingly, the passage at chapter's end was composed before the prior one that gives it full resonance. Indeed, in the first typing of this draft the passage on the stars was a combination of notes and partial drafts, a preliminary sketch. Cancelling "GIGANTIC is the keynote," the holograph instructed: "A terrific passage, yet somehow not *too* purple, to be made out of Margenius [sic] and the following rough notes." The key to what he would do with these "notes" is found in a second self-directive, near the end: "continue the procession of the constellations . . . but get the thing now as a GIGANTIC WHEEL" (31:10, 8–9). Some early suggestions do not get enacted, but Lowry's most important refinements have much less to do with content than with order and rhythm—motion, in short. He knew he wanted to convey birth and death, creation and destruction on a cosmic scale, all life running on "to eternity," and the individual human response to these vastnesses of time and space. Yet the passage had to arise out of Yvonne, and thus begin and end with this time, this place—and so start with the sinister "giant Scorpion" and conclude with "the beneficent Pleiades," who return "everything good one had ever done . . . everything that was sweet and noble and courageous and proud in the spirit." With those as fixed points, Lowry set to work on a passage whose rhetoric had to be elevated, yet somehow "not *too* purple."

His method of so doing was by ever enlarging units to move toward the single grand sentence whose syntax and rhythm would themselves suggest the processes of time and space and motion—the coordinates of Lowry's universe, visible and invisible—brought at last to bear on the single "hopeless eternal question" of meaning; then, reintroducing Yvonne and the precise configurations before her, to return with gradual diminuendo, to present time, space, character, through which narrative can resume. And so the paragraph builds gradually through a series of enlargements and variations of tone, rhythm, and voice to reach the vision at its center. Grand (and complex) sentences such as this climactic one Lowry sometimes wrote out in lines, breaking them into their syntactical units, thereby revealing their similarity to free verse. Here is a still fairly early version of this longest sentence:

> The earth still turning on its axis,
> the earth revolving around the sun,
> the sun revolving around the luminous wheel of this galaxy
> the countless unmeasured wheels
> of countless unmeasured galaxies
> whirling into infinity, into eternity
> through all of which life, all life
> ran on
> all this too
> men would still read in the night sky

> Winter spring summer autumn winter [all cancelled]
> As the earth turned through the seasons
> they would watch
> rising, culminating, setting
> and rising again
> the constellations: Aries, Taurus
> Gemini, Leo, Virgo, [Libra, Scorpio: cancelled] the Scales and the
>   Scorpion
> [Sagittarius: cancelled] the Archer, the Goat and the Water Bearer
> [Capricornus: cancelled] Pisces, [Aries: cancelled] once more
>   [Aries the Ram: cancelled] Aries (Texas XI, verso 25)

Lowry expands first the spatial then the temporal vision, enlarging outward through the cosmos and down through the seasons, toward "infinity" and "eternity," moving from the sky to the earth and then, climactically, to the sky as seen from the earth—the constellations in zodiacal order, a merging of temporal and spatial. Still somewhat crude, nonetheless, the repetitions, the reliance on participial forms, the suspension of syntax—all are characteristic of the final version, which will intensify the sense of vast structures "turning, turning." Lowry's concern with the rhythms of his prose is perhaps most openly revealed in the handling of the constellations at the end, the decisions on their names based solely on rhythmic effect, the clumsy trochee-dactyl of "Libra, Scorpio," for instance, replaced by the more euphonious double dactyl of "the Scales and the Scorpion."

If the biblical wheels within wheels are in place by this time, the questions of ultimate meaning ("to what end? What force drives this sublime celestial machinery?"), which would develop out of the cavalier subjectivity of "fateful conclusions that were wrong or right, just as one preferred" (31:10, 9), had yet to find its way to this sentence. The central problems were rhetorical, the need to find adequate form for this vision that by its very nature, for Lowry, opened on metaphysics. The last important passage here to get tackled, it is also one of the several that, coming at this surprisingly late stage, create its resonance, make it truly the climax that it is. Chapter XI, Lowry told Cape, was "a double contrast to the lesser horrors of X and the worse ones of XII" (*Letters* 83), but in fact it had been in danger of becoming a contrast of another sort. A weak sister since 1940, the chapter had only in the previous draft begun to take on the density and particularity to make it more than an embarrassment to its neighbors, and only here at the very end does it acquire the imaginative reach to bring it truly up to their level. The major thrust of Lowry's revisions moves along paths already laid down—the radical elimination of dialogue and the extending and deepening of landscape and natural scene—but now he probes deeper, discovering there the theme of home, which can be extended in several directions: into the past (Ohio, Yvonne's childhood home), into the imagined future (the shack by the sea), and into unimaginable Otherness (the stars). The search is not new, but the homeward call is, and together they lead to those passages on the house and the stars that link them and give them a universal dimension (the pun proves unavoidable here). Analogously, the menu, presented in such detail, yet giving portentousness and urgency to the action and resonance to motion ("who once fled north"), and Hugh's songs, providing an equivocal exit on the double note of the music and politics so central to him, operate too as counters in the particular that reach beyond themselves. Improbably, Lowry toward the very end turned one of his least effective chapters around, making it an exciting and worthy counterpart to Geoffrey's surrounding pieces.

And this *was* the end, too—or almost—of this crucial round of revisions. Although every other chapter received extensive rewriting, Chapter XII astonishingly continued (almost) to escape Lowry's restless pencil. Only the opening page and two later patches were found to need sufficient revision as to demand a new typing, and in only one of these is there an extensive addition to the chapter. Most of even these new pages reveal nothing more radical than reordering, adjusting, small inserts, rewordings.[56]

The new opening page is in this respect typical. There are a few rearrangements of words, and a new typography that breaks a single long paragraph into three, but possibly the most significant alteration here is an excision. The earlier version of the chapter had begun this way: "'Mescal,' said the Consul. 'Si, mescal doble, por buen favor, senorito! Si, mescal grande'" (Texas XII). The unqualified echo of the opening of Chapter X, now in the simpler form of "'Mescal,' said the Consul," still marks Geoffrey's advancement, but there may be a subtler, more dramatic reason for this alteration than mere measurement of alcoholic progress.

The almost ferocious addition of "mescal doble . . . mescal grande" seemed to announce total commitment to everything implied by the deadly mescal, nothing remaining but celebration, in fact revelling, in a decision so finally made there can be no turning back. This is a man who has indeed chosen "hell" and is (as we have been told Geoffrey is not, "not quite") entirely serious about it, and the striking of this note at the opening of the final chapter seems to pronounce the struggle over, the Consul now utterly passive in the grip of his fate. Yet as the extant text of Chapter XII showed, the struggle was *not* over: thoughts of Yvonne, responses to her letters, spasmodic impulses to leave the Farolito, and the final furious (if ineffectual) rounding on his tormentors, revealed a Geoffrey who has not fully accepted defeat—who, if he is to attain the stature Lowry means him to have, must never entirely do so even when he seems to rush headlong toward it. And thus the briefer opening that, while marking an advancement in the sinister mescal, does not with the fierce glee of the previous order seem to proclaim the battle over, a proclamation that would rob this superb chapter of its most fundamental source of drama.

The alterations to the opening page are brief and simple to execute. The other two revised passages are at least not brief. The first extends from the entrance of Diosdado up through the Consul's initial reading of Yvonne's recovered letters—some five pages—although even here there is only one major change. This is a new passage of almost 1½ pages in which, as the Consul begins reading the letters with Yvonne's disjunctive question, "'Do you remember tomorrow?'" he feels that "he was losing touch with the situation." The form of his "losing touch" seems a response to her query (as well as Lowry's riposte to *The Lost Weekend:* Geoffrey "was drunk, he was sober, he had a hangover all at once." Could Charles Jackson do as much?). Although it is evening, he feels "back in the early morning again: it was almost as if he were another kind of drunkard, in different circumstances, in another country, to whom something quite different was happening." That "something quite different" is elaborated into a semi-hallucinatory scene and scenario before collapsing back into the Farolito. In part, these dislocated visions serve the Consul's attempted "escape," an evasion of the self that stands accused by these recovered letters; but the forms his imaginings take—an affronted wife departing, pieces of frenetic chaos—declare the escape a failure. The passage itself, however, is not a failure, serving Lowry's rather different purposes as, among other things, a sign of Geoffrey's inability to sink complacently into "the paradise of his despair."[57]

The most extensive and important addition, however, appears in the other revision, Geoffrey's encounter with the whore María, where the long evocation of "El Infierno, that other Farolito" is now dropped into the midst of their copulation, thereby extending that act considerably beyond the brief, efficient transaction of previous drafts. Its placement makes it reverberate ironically against several earlier passages, most obviously the attempted lovemaking with Yvonne in Chapter III, where a comparable evocation of desire for the cantinas rendered the Consul impotent. Here the vision has no such effect: although Geoffrey finds the girl's face (in an added qualifier) "for a moment" reminiscent of Yvonne's, and her "body was Yvonne's too," that body quickly becomes a manifestation of the infernal machine: at the start of the new passage, "a calamity, a fiendish apparatus for calamitous sickening sensation; it was disaster, it was the horror of waking up in the morning in Oaxaca ... after Yvonne had gone" (15). This is in every sense the climactic appearance of the Oaxaca motif, inviting especially our recollection of the passage lately added to Chapter II in which Yvonne and Geoffrey nostalgically remember the joy of their days and nights of lovemaking there, and repeating the images in his Chapter I letter (vulture in the washbasin, sounds of slaughter in the kitchen), extending that account as if in a sequel—or a conclusion.

However, the form of this new passage is as significant as—indeed, finally inseparable from—its content, for this is a single, three-page (15-18) sentence that is precisely equivalent to the act of intercourse it accompanies, sustained just to the moment of the Consul's "crisis" before Lowry puts a period to it and returns to his previous text. The longed-for drink that Geoffrey's consciousness recalls to him is itself a form of lust, and the "penetration" of that anticipated and deferred entrance to the demonic holy of holies, El Infierno, is openly paralleled to the sexual act, which longs for its own consummation. Furthermore, Lowry with some acuteness ("you old rascal") finds, without breaking the surface of the memory, appropriate images in the Consul's past for his present activity—the recollection of "sinking into the soft disaster of the carpet," for instance, or "the dark well of the dining room," "the dark open sewers," the carefully trickling wine, his "subsiding on the couch," "the secret passage"—and, throughout, the old pun on "die," reaching "the violet dawn which should have brought death, and he should have died now too." So, in a sense, he does—this dying fall marks his moment of orgasm—but Geoffrey's intercourse goes beyond word-play: it is quite literally an embrace of negation, his mind filled throughout with a lust that is deeply perverse in finally being not sexual at all. "The escape!" he repeats with mounting excitement as he approaches that consummation devoutly to be wished, "still the escape!" But what El Infierno represents is ultimately the escape from life itself. "How alike are the groans of love to those of the dying" indeed.

It is the grandest of the *Volcano*'s grand sentences (or at least the longest) and a partially surviving early draft shows Lowry typically dividing it syntactically, here because of its great length numbering individual units that are born each time there is a shift in subject and placing summary descriptions next to a few of the early ones (27:17, verso 19). Characteristically, too, the construction of the sentence depends on verbals that impart and sustain motion ("running . . . going . . . sinking . . . waking . . . trying . . . and failing . . . going down . . . sinking . . . sinking . . ." etc.), the motion of consciousness here conceived as reflective of the motion of the body. Yet the sentence presents fewer difficulties than some shorter Lowry constructs, for the syntax remains relatively simple, individual units pivoting either on these verbals of action or on a noun or noun phrase in what remains essentially a paratactic structure. The driving force here is still narrative, for which the "and . . . and . . . or . . . and . . . but . . . then" construction suits sexual intercourse as easily as the events of a characteristic night in Oaxaca.

None of the other alterations approach this new passage in importance, but some are noteworthy. The Consul's world, for instance, continues to open up indeterminately: the dead scorpion that in the previous version had been marked by "a sparkle of phosphorescence and it had gone," now has added, "or had never been there" (19). When he returns to the doorway, the change in the time on the clock appears unpredictable, arbitrary, "as if it had just moved forward with a jerk" (20). Lowry had been trying for some time to work a passage about the monster Typhoeus into his manuscript, and in now at last succeeding, the book's title finally entered its text; "Under the volcano! It was not for nothing the ancients had placed Tartarus under Mt. Aetna, nor within it, jolly old Typhoeus, with his hundred heads and, relatively, fearful eyes and voices" (insert 3). Meanwhile, Lowry clearly feeling he needed to "account for" the style of Yvonne's letters, the crude (and self-revealing) "Was Yvonne plagiarizing, and if so, from whom?" was replaced apparently casually with "substitute something as . . . —had Yvonne been reading the letters of Heloise and Abelard?—" (12; 31:13, 2). Finally, and surprisingly late, only now, "A bell spoke out: *Dolente . . . Dolore!*" (46).

With such individual alterations, this climactic phase of Lowry's revisions sputtered to its end. By Christmas of 1944, he had finished his rewritings and Margerie her typings of fair copy, and they assembled the manuscript to present to the Noxons as a token of thanks for their friends' succor after the fire and particularly for Gerald's help with the novel. Not so incidentally, the gesture of gratitude was also an insurance policy against loss of the fair copy, an act of prudence after Lowry's experience with the manuscripts of *Ultramarine* and *In Ballast to the White Sea*.[58] It might have been mildly excessive to announce, as Lowry did on his Christmas card to Conrad Aiken that year, that the *Volcano* was "finished," but certainly his major work on it was complete by the time he and Margerie left Ontario to reclaim what was left of their little house by the sea in Dollarton.

CHAPTER FIVE

1945–1946

When the Lowrys returned to Dollarton in early February 1945, they faced two important tasks. The more immediate one, which they began dealing with soon after arrival, was the creation of a new dwelling, a job beset by more difficulties than they could have anticipated from Ontario (*Aiken-Lowry* 186–90; *Lowry-Noxon* 104, 106–8; Day 304–5; Bowker, *Pursued* 333–37). Nonetheless, they quickly made time to sit down in their rented accommodation with the working copy of the *Volcano*, and by April 3 Margerie was able to tell the Noxons that "we are typing the *Volcano* and are more than half finished." On May 14, Malcolm reported that Margerie was "just finishing typing the tenth chapter" and, aware of Gerald's fears, assured him they were "finishing the benighted *Volcano*—we still are, really are, this time" (*Lowry-Noxon* 104, 107, 110). Indeed, "this time" he meant it: around the beginning of June, the manuscript was mailed to Harold Matson.[1]

After the major revisions of 1943–44, the rest is, if not silence, at least anticlimax. There were and would be alterations—Lowry could never stop tinkering—but he essentially acquiesced to Noxon's view that the book was, if not complete, at least for the time being "finished." To Lowry's signifying mind, that may have been one meaning of leaving his penultimate manuscript with the Noxons, an act of faith as well as insurance, an earnest of future intent as well as gratitude for past kindnesses personal and literary. In this role, the Noxons were not simply friends, rescuers, advisors, and—Gerald, at least—editor, but a small readership, token of the larger audience to whom his book ultimately must be submitted. It was a full five years since Lowry had last released a manuscript of the *Volcano* to *anyone's* scrutiny, and the apparently private act of the Christmas gift to the Noxons may to him have been a small ritual, symbol of that larger submission so fraught by this time with hopes and fears.

At any rate, posting of the manuscript signaled Lowry's willingness to allow his novel to congeal into the temporary immobility of typeface, binding, covers (perhaps not quite the same, after all, as "finished"). This, therefore, may be the place to lay to rest the myth that he undertook major rewriting either before sending the manuscript out to publishers or at the galley-proof stage. Douglas Day, for instance, leaves the impression of extensive revisions, writing that throughout the spring of 1945 Lowry "had been holding onto [the manuscript] since Niagara-on-the-Lake, making dozens of last minute changes" (305). Most of those changes, however, were both brief and minor. Later, Day reports that whereas most writers "would have taken two weeks to correct their galley proofs: Lowry took four months" (367). Assisted by Margerie, often an enthusiastic collaborator in the creation of the Lowry myth—she wildly told David Markson that "Malc practically rewrote the Volcano in the galleys" (Margerie 1:5, "Friday" [1977?])— Day is probably confusing the correspondence between Lowry and his editor at Reynal and Hitchcock, Albert Erskine, in June and July 1946 with the galley proofs, which Lowry received near the end of October and returned sometime before mid-November of that year. These three quite distinct post-Ontario stages will be discussed below: here it is sufficient to say that at none of them did Lowry undertake major revisions on his novel.

Nevertheless, faced with the necessity for a new typing, he of course went through the manuscript yet one more time, making "final" alterations and corrections. These would, naturally, not always prove final: some pages that Margerie typed would be rejected, to be rewritten and retyped still again. However, most of the changes were forms of housekeeping, adjustments in wording, local clarifications, correctings of inconsistencies. By the time Conrad Aiken, primed by Noxon, wrote to urge his old pupil to "cut the umbilical cord" (September 14, 1946; Killorin 263), the manuscript had been out of Lowry's hands for several months. It was a noteworthy moment: never again would Lowry release a book manuscript for publication.

As he set to work, however, he could, as usual, find plenty that dissatisfied him. Even the epigraphs were not fixed: the three that would remain were at this point accompanied by a fourth, from Francis

Thompson's "The Hound of Heaven"—"My days have crackled and gone up in smoke ... the lute the lutanist" (ll. 121-24; in 27:6, n.p.). The poem was important to Lowry, but the sense of failure and the implicit Christian context in the quoted passage were already conveyed by the citation from Bunyan, and perhaps Lowry felt this overbalanced his careful weighting of hopeful and despairing lines toward the negative pole. Whatever the reason, the epigraph was cancelled.[2]

Most revisions now were of this sort, brief insertions or deletions that did not involve extensive rewriting. For instance, in Chapter I a boastful-sounding (and unsubstantiated) claim in Geoffrey's letter—"I tell you, I have known earthquake, typhoon, fire at sea, war, and the extremeties of physical torture" (42)—became the lower-keyed, "I think I know a good deal about physical suffering." Even simpler were such afterthoughts as Hugh in Chapter IV imagining himself at the wheel of the *Noemijolea* as "Potato Firmin or Columbus in reverse" (27:21, 141) or, in Chapter VI, on the sense of the creeping of time at sea, "(Hugh had not yet read Melville either)" (27:11, 202). Two changes in passages concerned with Yvonne suggest clarifications to plot and motive respectively. In Chapter IX, she is made to recognize that Hugh is quite unaware of her early career as a film horsewoman despite "that day in Robinson," which may imply that their "affair" was a single encounter. In Chapter XI, a new paragraph following the second drink of mescal alters our sense of her lingering in El Popo. Whereas originally the effect of the drinks seemed one of simple inertia—Yvonne "no longer wanted to make any move whatsoever"—a new paragraph dramatizes it as her immersion in an interior vision of their imagined home so powerful and so "real" that it blots out any alternative. In this manner, ironically, she fulfills her wish to discover "'what Geoff sees in it'" (27:16, 14, new 14).

The simpler alterations concerned with the Consul seem designed to intensify uncertainty rather than resolve it, to render the novel's protagonist more rather than less problematic. In Chapter VII, for instance, to Geoffrey's certainty that he has taken his passport with him ("he remembered he had brought it"), Lowry now adds the countercase: "Or hadn't brought it" (28:3, 310) ("The Consul shouldn't be *too* sure ... ," he comments [30:8, 5]). His grasp of the exterior world is put in further doubt when the sense of someone entering and passing through El Bosque gives way to "the next instant the Consul felt this was not the case" (27:12, 282). The material world being uncertain, the immaterial here plays a slightly greater part, at least in his thought: the precarious piles of Laruelle's books wittily seem "[stacked] as by some half-repenting poltergeist" (245). In a different way, individual changes in Chapter XII both sharpen the prose and deepen our sense of Geoffrey's climactic situation without pointing it in any single direction. Early in the chapter, for example, having drawn the attention of A Few Fleas to a dead scorpion on the wall, the Consul overhears the boy mumbling from the magazine he reads, "'Suelte me!'": "Save me, thought the Consul, as the boy suddenly went out for change, suelte me: but the scorpion, not wanting to be saved and in spite of Dr. Johnson, had apparently stung itself to death." Now in revision this becomes, "Save me, thought the Consul vaguely, as the boy suddenly went out for change, suelte me, help: but maybe the scorpion, not wanting to be saved, had stung itself to death" (27:17, 2). The alteration not only condenses, but clarifies and intensifies the ambivalence inhering in the sentence's two halves. In the new version, the echoed plea for help in the first part is depersonalized by "vaguely"; certainly Geoffrey is not focusing on his own situation—or is he? The sharp imperative added at the end, the stark "help," seems to suggest that on some level he *is* asking for aid. The latter part of the sentence, with its simple "maybe," now frees the Consul both from definiteness and from apparent identification with the scorpion (and defiance of Dr. Johnson), committing himself neither to the suicidal creature nor to its rejection of salvation. If Geoffrey cannot be said exactly to be seeking help, neither is it clear that he is seeking death. More than in the first typing, salvation and destruction both seem possibilities: the tension remains operative, even if its ironic effect on the Consul is to paralyze him where he is, pulled in both directions, and thus immobilized. The adverbs—"vaguely," "maybe"—leave options open. With comparable effect, "A black dog settled on his back" becomes "And it was as if a black dog . . ." (32), the "as if" form conveying not only the metaphorical nature of the image, but Geoffrey's consciousness of it *as* metaphor, and thus its potential rejection.

Not all revisions were this simply done, nor were they all focused only on the situations of individual characters. After Margerie had typed Chapter I, for example, Lowry discovered he wanted to make two inserts that required redoing several pages. The ragged, conversing Indians ("grandees," in his shorthand term), who had wandered the manuscripts of the *Volcano* for several years now, had inadvertantly been left out of this final draft altogether, and he decided to insert them early on his Day of the Dead. If they seem to suggest the magical possibilities of that Day, the other insertion—Jacques's recollection of Yvonne's postcard and the circumstances under which he found it— raises a more directed form of "magic"; he wonders whether "the Consul had calculated it all, *knowing* M. Laruelle would discover it under his pillow at the precise moment that Hugh, distraughtly, would call from Parian" (27:6, second set, 14–16A).[3] Appearing as pure message, lacking salutation or signature, the postcard thus becomes the first of the novel's communiqués that are lost, delayed, unsent, misdirected, unread, unheard, misused. Coming early in the opening chapter, Jacques's attribution of "malice" to the Consul balances the use the "chiefs" make of Hugh's telegram at a comparable moment in the final chapter, to which Jacques's memory here alludes. The postcard has been recycled "inappropriately," reaching a recipient to whom it is cruelly ironic, just as Hugh's telegram will be/has been reused "inappropriately," falling into hands for which it was never intended.

A single new action of Chapter III, requiring much the largest emendation there, also involved a marker of missed connections: the Consul discovers in his pocket an unrecognized card from the Venezuelan Embassy requesting "acknowledgement" (27:8, insert 96). The discovery is ironic at least twice over: first, in its immediate context, for the now-added "'wait, here's my card—'" (96) begins an offer of professional services to the fellow Englishman encountered in the road, Geoffrey's attempted reciprocation for Samaritan-like aid. That incident, however, follows hard upon the silent monologue to "Hugh," where Geoffrey had boasted that helping his half-brother out of difficulties demonstrated "that I was still not so divorced from life as to be incapable of discharging such duties with dispatch" (92). Since the Venezuelan government clearly has received no "acknowledgement," the claim of consular competence has lost its force. Indeed, what force could it have? The mistaken card reminds Geoffrey and us that he is now a man without an office.

Several notations and changes give some indication of Lowry's state of mind as he approached the end of his years of labor. In Chapter VII, he rightly notes a weakness in point of view—Hugh "a moment ago had almost drifted into a political argument" with Laruelle—but passes it off with "–through Consul's eyes? Doesn't sound like it: but it might be" (30:8, 2). He needed some such moment to justify Jacques's first impression of Hugh as recounted in Chapter I, but his obvious reluctance to work on this spot suggests how little eager he was to take up major revision now. On the other hand, he did pause to rewrite the little paragraph in Chapter XI about the location of El Popo, a paragraph of suggestiveness disproportionate to its size. The earlier typing had the establishment "so to speak, nowhere" because it appeared to sit upon the state border, which placed it "neither in Parian nor Tomalin nor technically in Anochtitlan" (27:16, 11). The formulation dissatisfied him: "Cut that the restaurant is nowhere: we want to feel that it is damned real" (31:11, 2). Instead of cutting, he rewrites to *insist* on the "border," which is now "not far from here" (insert 10–11). This is, after all, a threshhold chapter, straddling borderlines between past and present, earth and heavens, home and exile, this world and the next, life and death. Terrified of borders himself, Lowry was not about to let one resonant of the Border of Borders escape him. Finally, one insert that appears only on the final typescript (it is not in "E" and will not reach galley proof) is significant in revealing the degree of Lowry's self-consciousness at this stage. When in VI accused of plagiarism, Hugh had wondered whether he has been looking forward to "the publication of someone else's songs, paid for by himself," and the "F" typescript now adds "(or rather, typographical error, his aunt)" (28:2, 238). The self-reflexiveness has no basis in Hugh's experience (*he* is not typing), but the Lowry to whom nothing is more real than his own text is glimpsed in its insertion.

For all the many smaller revisions, there were only two passages of significant length that occupied Lowry at this stage. The first, Hugh's reflections on the man who boards the bus in Chapter VIII, he fussed over again without getting it right. An initial try with local changes (27:13, 289–90) seemed insufficient. Thus new sheets appear in which Hugh, who had been uncertain of the meaning of "pelado," now has a new word at his disposal, "gachupine," which serves to muddy the waters thoroughly. At first, the new term seems synonymous with the old, for when Hugh asks if the man is "'a gachupine,'" Geoffrey responds, "'Si.... A pelado.'" Hugh's understanding of "gachupine" is as "one of those [Spaniards] whose oligarchy once ran Mexico ragged." Can this apply to a newly arrived Spaniard, one landing since the Moroccan war? Hugh has no idea. "But pelado itself might imply, so to speak, 'ragged'" (hardly the same as "to run ragged"). The ambiguity of this latter term is now rehearsed as before, but instead of being attributed to a nameless "informant," its complexities become part of an argument Hugh has had with the Consul (second 289). Lowry will find this portion of the new draft useful, but the play with "gachupine" is odd and confusing, suggesting that even this late Lowry has not grasped that he needs one Spanish word—and one only—to resound antiphonally against "compañero."

By far the most extensively revised unit at this stage was Chapter X: more than half the leaves of the "E" typescript were rejected, many in the name of cutting.[4] (The new version, of course, is almost exactly the same length as the old.) Despite a typical rash of small inserts and alterations, the unusual amount of rewriting reflects the extent of the new material—the train vision, the Tlaxcala folder—that had recently entered the chapter. Here as elsewhere at this stage, the aim was a honing of what already existed, not a launching of new departures, and Lowry's greatest concern was with the Tlaxcalan material. Thus, for instance, he extended the sowing of that motif throughout the chapter. Cervantes gains a motival "'Si, I am Tlaxcalan'" (27:15, 12), and an early sentence establishes "the traitorous Tlaxcalans," those "who had succeeded in making Mexico great even in her betrayal," as (not incidentally) founders of Parián (31:6, 5). But it was the toilet episode that most occupied him, and did so in ways revealing of some of the aims of that section. Indeed, he had Margerie make a typed "Margie-version" (31:7), which, annotated and revised by Malcolm, became the basis for the fair copy of "E" (which, in turn, lightly revised, became the basis for the final typescript "F," which, after all, was the Lowrys' concern at this stage).

The most obvious goal here was excision, not merely to prune the "unnecessary," but also to sharpen the drama, strike contrapuntal sparks by making juxtapositions flash against one another. The first aim Margerie's version usually fulfilled admirably, and Lowry generally approved her trimmed and tightened version of the episode, with the important exception of her cutting of portions of folder excerpts. These he almost unfailingly restored to earlier lengths (while rarely making such restorations in her cuts to dialogue), and he sometimes inserted new bridging passages in his own text. For instance, the folder passage on HYDROGRAPHY is now preceded not only by Cervantes' ironic offer of "'a stone'" (with no water available, this presumably must suffice), but (in an insert) by a voice recalling "'crossing the river.'" Again, Lowry's marginal note insists, "La Sepultura should be in juxtaposition" with CITY OF TLAXCALA, and the parallel to the Consul's current situation is underlined (literally) by the repeated emphasis on *"four clean, seats all over"* (31:7, B–C).

Margerie's efficient cutting sometimes sheared away the flavor of longer folder passages. For instance, from the SAN FRANCISCO CONVENT excerpt she cut almost half, including the early baptisms of the Tlaxcalans, the Spanish conquerors serving as "God-Fathers"; the secret passage; the tower "which is rated as the only one through America"; and the enigmatic final sentence, "The ceiling is the only one in the whole Spanish America." At other times she seemed to miss specific points, excising altogether, for instance, the entry on OCOTELULCO, apparently not recognizing that the preceding and following fragments—"'If I only knew where you could get to!'" and "'It will be like a rebirth'"; "'I'm thinking of becoming a Mexican subject, of going to live among the Indians'"—were played off against the town and its palace, and specifically against the sentence, "In that place, according to tradition, took place the baptism of the first Christian Indian" (31:6, 24). In the end, almost all the fuller versions from the folder received Lowry's "stet."

A "Margie version" of another kind, however, he quite approved. The Tlaxcala folder had been the only *new* piece of material the Consul acquired in the stone toilet, but he had also read there the railroad and bus timetable, reproduced for us, but preceded in the earlier draft by a reproduction of rules for the transportation of corpses. Aside from simple repetition of material from Chapter II, the fact that this is clearly the same timetable he was studying back then might raise awkward (and pointless) questions. Why only now does he think of a journey to Tlaxcala? Why didn't it occur to him back in Chapter V, when the matter of where to go today got raised? So the "rules" section is excised, the timetable like the folder seems a new acquisition, and Lowry declares, "In full agreement with your cuts here" (31:7, "H"). He was even more enthusiastic about her cuts to the ensuing vision of Tlaxcala—a "masterly job," he termed it—which is now tightened, more rigorously focused.

One of the most telling alterations at this stage is placed marginally against Hugh's description of the Ejidal: "Break up as M. Laruelle's is broken up in VII. Effect will be got if dialogue is rewritten as free verse" (31:6, 20). The reference is to the fragmented final speech in the Café Paris, which seems to come from Jacques but actually is part of the Consul's own internal dialogue, and the comparison reveals Lowry's conception of Geoffrey's state here, a state that combines the blurring of interior and exterior (thus our uncertainty about what is actually spoken, what recalled or imagined) with sudden insightful or suggestive juxtapositions. But he was also in earnest about "free verse," or at least a more rhythmic utterance. Against some passages in the "Margie version" (31:7, C), he places a check of approval, then twice complains "but rhythm wrong at the end." One so designated first read, "thinking, Hugh, there is such a bank, in Quauhnahuac, just by Cortez Palace." Lowry's alteration gives; "Why, I think there's a bank like that in Quauhnahuac, Hugh, just by Cortez Palace." The second might, I think, be termed "free verse"; in any case, it is written with a finer ear for rhythm than the first. "Poetry" for Lowry did not stop with his efforts to compose in metrics.

Margerie dutifully typed up the revised pages, some twenty-seven of them, to provide, with the sheets retained from Ontario, an authoritative base for the new fair copy of Chapter X that in turn was duly produced to take its spot in the accumulating manuscript. Lowry thankfully made only a few adjustments after typing, and the longest of these revisions was done. Chapters XI and XII demanded no such extensive rewritings, and at last copies of the typescript were sent off to New York and later to London.[5]

With the *Volcano* off his hands, Lowry had no pressing projects to occupy him, and after the years of work and the trauma of the fire, a holiday seemed in order. Nothing immediate hovered but reports from publishers, so the Lowrys in the fall of 1945 decided to winter in Mexico.[6]

They were in Cuernavaca when on the final day of December a letter arrived from Jonathan Cape that, while recounting mixed responses to the *Volcano* from his readers, was still encouraging (*Letters* 424–25). Lowry had had a much stronger letter from Cape before leaving Dollarton, reporting an "impressed" first reader and his own excited anticipation (*Letters* 87), and the tempered enthusiasm of this second letter, together with the enclosed, more negative reader's report, while deeply disappointing, galvanized Lowry into action. The result was his own monumental, now famous letter of defense, explanation, justification, explication, a tour de force designed to sweep all readers' reports before it, to devastate hesitations, and (especially) to demonstrate the shallowness and folly of any ill-considered demands for revision. Lowry in one stroke became not only the creator of the *Volcano*, but its expositor, a role he retained for the rest of his life, willing, even eager, to expound to all who asked (and even, in *Dark As the Grave*, to those who didn't) on the circumstances, analogues, influences, meanings of his book. The letter went off in mid-January 1946; it was several months before he received further word from either New York or London. Then, on April 6, he heard both from Cape and from Matson, on behalf of Reynal and Hitchcock: the *Volcano* had been—or was about to be—accepted at both firms.

The terms of the acceptances, however, were at first somewhat different. Lowry's letter had convinced Cape (overwhelmed him, more likely), and the *Volcano* was taken unconditionally, although there was talk for a time of a preface. Reynal and Hitchcock, on the other hand, like Cape earlier, would want revisions, extensive enough to require Lowry's presence in New York. Clearly he acceded to this, and he and Margerie had arranged to proceed directly from Mexico when a telegram from Matson cancelled those plans, explaining later that Curtice Hitchcock had decided "that the revisions and changes he wants to recommend ... could be handled through correspondence" (1:45). So, in the event, they were, but Curtice Hitchcock dying suddenly, it was Albert Erskine who became editor of the *Volcano* and who wrote Lowry on June 14 with his first round of queries and suggestions.[7]

The correspondence that developed was remarkable in a number of ways; for our purposes, however, it began Lowry's march through his twelve chapters yet again, this time in June and July 1946 as, once more in Dollarton, he responded to Erskine, raised doubts, questions, suggestions of his own, or made inserts and alterations arising out of his and Margerie's recent venture into Mexico. Erskine's first letter winningly expresses his great admiration for the novel and his willingness "to set up and print the manuscript as it stands" should Lowry so wish it. Nonetheless, he continues, he has brought up, very tentatively, a few points for consideration, which he then sets forth on separate sheets. These range from the trimming of Hugh's sea life in Chapter VI ("a little out of proportion") to the cutting of the border around the station sign for QUAUHNAHUAC, from the insertion of Chapter XI into a Chapter XII broken in two at the end of the María encounter to questions of the rewording of complicated sentences. Several of Erskine's problem areas Lowry acknowledged at once—the obtrusive parenthesis after "'J'adoube'" to explain that chess term, the apparently "impossible" description of the pelado's theft, the syntactical difficulties or outright lapses in some sentences. It is characteristic that Lowry's response to the three pages of Erskine's notes runs to more than twice that length.

But the letter (June 22, 1946: *Letters* 112–14) also expresses a more general anxiety. He had been aware that his Spanish was sometimes shaky—the Consul in Chapter V, for instance, had been made to suspect his translation of the garden sign, although clearly his creator did not have the means to correct him—and the recent trip to Mexico had driven the realization home. "Los Manos," as he says, should everywhere be "Las Manos," "rumpopo" "rumpope," "manzanillo" "manzanilla," and so on, but he hadn't had time to "verify" everything. Was "La Despedida" possible? Did the term "Borracheros" exist? In fact, Lowry's Spanish was worse than he, or even Erskine, at first suspected. Not until August 28, after a copy editor armed with dictionary, then a professional translator, and finally a teacher of Spanish had been over the manuscript, was Erskine able to report not that the language was entirely correct, but that what remained was "routine, and would be done quickly." What had taken so long? "There is quite a lot of it there ... and most of it was wrong."[8]

Even before his recent trip, Lowry had known that the Spanish of the sign was a problem; coincidentally, the final page on which that sign appeared alone had got misplaced in the manuscript at Reynal and Hitchcock, and one of Erskine's questions was about its correct positioning. In commenting on its intended finality, Lowry used a suggestive musical analogy: the close of his book, he said, was "like those old swing tunes" that seem to have ended "and you are about to take the record off, when it ends again, and you then proceed (one hopes as in this case) to put it on again." But he was also eager to correct the sign, first its Spanish—although he insisted he "copied it down" in its incorrect form in Oaxaca in 1938—then its more accurate translation (he still does not get the Spanish quite right). Nonetheless, finding the sign "immeasurably more dramatic as it is, even though wrong," Lowry here thinks his way through to having his cake while eating it: "possibly in VIII, Hugh should see it in its correct form and translate it correctly: in fact that is what I shall have to do if I am to make my point at the very end" (2:5, 5).

On other matters Erskine has raised, Lowry resists suggested cuts and argues against any "disarticulation" of XII in order to insert XI, claiming that he himself "once tried to write it like that" (if so, the attempt has not survived). Problems in grammar and syntax he disarmingly acknowledges but makes only minor suggestions for clarification. The tone throughout both letter and notes is open, friendly, cooperative; he waxes expansive with this new editor-admirer, telling him far more about his book than Erskine has asked. At the same time, he has only just made the acquaintance of "Mr. Erskine" (as he will remain throughout this stage), and Lowry is not easily to be moved on his long-meditated text by any outsider, however well intentioned. The response to Erskine's suggestion of cutting the border around the station sign QUAUHNAHUAC is characteristic. Indeed, agrees Lowry, if "nothing is gained" by the border, by all means cut it. However, he goes on, he had thought the border might universalize this "esoteric" name; furthermore, it probably looks odder in typescript than it would in print; in addition, perhaps the sense of the sign would help realize his intention to evoke "'station' and 'parting.'" And, oh, by the way, he has just discovered from his recent trip (via yet another sign) that this name is actually Aztec for "Near the Wood." Given all the "woods" already in his text, he would like to slip this in somewhere, but where? "Perhaps you could make a suggestion."9

The border around QUAUHNAHUAC stayed.

The actual changes to result from this first exchange of letters were a cutting of the parenthesis after "'J' adoube'" (Chapter V); a correcting of the typo "brug" for "grub" in Chapter VI, an error which Lowry claimed to have let stand for its "expressiveness" (but if "it expresses nothing let us by all means restore it to grub without further brugging around"); and the inserting of two clarifying words into a slightly obscure sentence in the same chapter. The important process of correcting the text's Spanish (and checking other foreign terms) was set in motion, but this is editorial housekeeping (in Lowry's case, more like spring cleaning), a realizing rather than a shifting of intentions. Other possible alterations raised here would be acted upon later—the description of the pelado's theft, the handling of the garden sign—but Lowry had made it clear (in the friendliest, most cooperative way) that while he was willing to listen to suggestions, he was not easily moved to make changes.

That first letter was written without benefit of his copy of the final manuscript, which had been left in Mexico. By June 30, he had it once more and wrote to propose going through it "with a fine tooth comb" and sending on results, not stopping to revise, "time being of the essence."[10] For the next two-and-one-half weeks, that was exactly what he did.[11] Most matters taken up were simple editorial tasks (punctuation, grammar, accents, proper Spanish); what is remarkable about them is that, as surviving correction sheets also demonstrate, Lowry was in fact keenly interested in such minutiae. Erskine saw this quickly, with some dismay: "Your precise notes about inserting or shifting commas have frightened me a little, because we have done a few things on our own with them, and then here you come knowing exactly what you want" (July 8). For Lowry, these were a part of the visual and aural impact of his text: often, punctuation for him was expressive ("for the sound or movement"), whereas Erskine went, as he put it, by "the Rules." Nonetheless, he recognized Lowry's tendency to overpunctuate (the use of commas in addition to parentheses or dashes, for instance), and while trying not "to do violence to the sound or sense of the prose, but indeed to help (if anything) in the sense," he continued judiciously to edit punctuation. On his end, Lowry did too. (We have had studies of Lowry the cabalist, Lowry the symbolist, Lowry the expressionist, and so on; when will we have Lowry the punctuator?)

Most such specifics are of little concern now: what is important is Lowry's intense interest and involvement in every phase and level of the publishing process. What follows will thus focus on substantial alterations made at this point. There seems no reason not to follow Lowry in proceeding sequentially and in note form (for convenience, pagination is that of the published *Volcano*):

Chapter I. From the recent Mexican trip emerged a new passage about the "obscene concourse" of birds (*Volcano*, 13–14), grotesque creatures "something like monstrous insects" that seem to suggest a primal chaos at the very heart of nature. Only three sentences long, their sinister presence appreciably darkens Jacques's walk.

In addition, Lowry inserts "Tlaxcaltecan" before "friend Cervantes" in the Consul's letter (36), commenting, "I feel the chord of Tlaxcala might be faintly struck here."

Chapter II. Lowry finds a place for the correct meaning of "Quauhnahuac," adding Yvonne's response to the "massive shining depths" of the fresno trees to "Or did it really mean, as Louis said, near the wood?" (44) Realizing he had named no shops in the square, Lowry now adds one he assumes Yvonne would remark—"*La China Poblana, hand embroidered dresses*" (53)—and, later, "the Molino para Nixtamal, Morelense" (55).

Chapter III. The outright lie "'I ate'" in response to Yvonne's wondering why Geoffrey isn't breakfasting becomes (with the Burke's Irish in mind) the slyer "'I partook'" (82).

Chapter V. Neither the garden sign nor the Consul's interpretation were altered, but brief inserts were made to help "account for" the incorrect Spanish: "(... perhaps the sign itself, inscribed by some Aztec, was wrong) ... [it] certainly seemed to have more question marks than it should have" (129).

Chapter VI. The Consul's pronouncement on *Peter Rabbit*—no longer a book "stolen ... when tight on board the *Aquitania*"—is made habitual rather than unique by the phrasing "the Consul liked to say" (175). In his description of the *Samaritan*, "a fake" becomes "a ruse," "that's false" becomes "that's a shift" (184). ("Fake and false have too direct a bearing upon Hugh," Lowry comments.) Finally, the designation of "666" is altered from "a cough mixture" to "an insecticide" (188), that is, from a more or less correct identification to a deliberate (?) "error," perhaps to link the apocalyptic designation to the dead scorpion, a creature with which Geoffrey is repeatedly identified. (The number of the Beast of Revelations 13:18, one recalls, is also "the number of a man.")

Chapter VII. An omission Lowry described as "very important" was rectified: the placement of "fight one's way back" into Geoffrey's appeal to Christ for guidance to begin "all over again" (201).

The title of the picture on Laruelle's wall becomes "Los Borrachones" (199) (with the appropriate alteration also made in XII).

"La Mordida!" is inserted among the "rodents in the etymology" (218). Consistent with the Consul's catalogue here, it also provides a hook for the novel Lowry was planning since his recent Mexican trip.

The problem of the garden sign is here handled by reducing it to its first line (219), at the same time eliminating another "666."[12]

Chapter VIII. Lowry here makes his largest alteration of this phase. To accommodate Hugh's correct reading of the sign, he creates early in the bus journey a garden in which the sign can be observed and translated (the Spanish of which is still not quite correct on Lowry's typescript), populating this garden with doves, goat, and "devil," adding "a sound as of clashing machetes" and a couple "by the church." But he carries straight on to rewrite the troubling "pelado" passage, handling it by simply cutting all the "gachupine" material, leaving "pelado" to stand alone in its "pretty ambiguous" meanings (232–35). Further, the paragraph describing Hugh's glimpse of the money on the Indian is rewritten to make possible the pelado's theft (243), and Hugh's later realization of that theft is dramatized by its placement in a paragraph of its own (250).

Chapter X. Lowry's proposals for this chapter consumed four typewritten pages, a result once more of the amount of new writing recently done here. Most of these however, are small verbal adjustments. A more substantial suggestion that did not get acted on was to put Mr. Quattras's words into dialect, as in "'Ah'm a race track man an' Ah was brought up with whites'"(283). (Erskine objected sharply [Oct. 23] that the dialect was "downright bad": "And rather illogical, don't you think, since what the Negro is saying is in itself an explanation [implied if anyone needs one] of why he doesn't talk like a minstrel show.")

The most extensive changes Lowry allows are cuts to the Tlaxcala folder excerpts—although Erskine finally makes none of them—out of which is resolved the issue of typography in this section of the chapter.[13] Lowry had long wanted distinctive type used for the folder passages: "pearl type or even diamond, or both (or occasionally extra-condensed) for some of the folder stuff . . . combined with black letter for the headings by way of contrast," he had suggested in his first letter. Erskine opposed typographical flourishes, terming them "frivolity . . . a crutch which you don't need." Instead he proposes "to set the extracts narrower than the body of the text (indented from both sides) and with less leading" (July 8). Now, Lowry counters with effusive agreement, followed by the suggestion of "slightly smaller type." And thus it is decided: indentation and smaller type will be used.

Two brief additions emphasize Geoffrey's subjectivity. "The Consul had not been away long" becomes "had not been away very long (he thought)" (303), and the notion that his "brilliant" discourse was making Yvonne happy is qualified by "he was sure" (306). Finally, "Dangerous Dan Magoo" achieves its rightful chowdery identity as "Dangerous Clam Magoo" (294).

Chapter XI. In a brief change, "Huerta, the drunken murderer" becomes "Huerta, the drunkard, the murderer" to accommodate ambiguously the next term in this series, "the Consul" (336).

"My hand! My hand!" Lowry exclaims, willing to "sacrifice" almost "anything else you like" for the "sinister emotional effect" of the graphic of a pointing hand. "Very important, very original (straight out of Jude the Obscure, in fact)," he notes, uncertain whether it is on the typescript at Reynal and Hitchcock (333).

Finally (in every sense), the past tense of "only an agony went there [to Yvonne's burned house] now" (336) implies, as he noted, "utter dislocation of time."

Chapter XII. Several changes cluster around the recovery of Yvonne's letters. The "strain" in the Consul's effort to speak is dramatized: "When he spoke he could not recognize his own voice" (342–43). The cynicism of his immediate response to the letters is deepened by the italicizing of "Yvonne had certainly been reading *something*" (346). On the other hand, just afterward, his longing for her is intensified: now he not only "wanted to take her in his arms," but "wanted more than ever before" to express and receive forgiveness (347).

However, perhaps the most startling note is rather in the nature of a musing, the passage in question being the last appearance of "No se puede vivir sin amar" (375). It begins by acknowledging a debt, here to "a book of art criticism" by Somerset Maugham. In Maugham, the line is "thematic," Lowry says: "I do not mean it to be thematic here precisely, it is just a bit of irony." However, he worries, "does it not look as though I *did* mean it to be thematic? In that case . . . please cut it right out here together with the sentence it is in." Not only have readers taken the line to be "thematic," they have frequently (see posters for the film) taken it to be *the* primary theme. Perhaps Lowry foresaw precisely this possibility, the complexities of his novel, and of his sense of human existence, reduced to this simplicity, a simplicity of the basics of life that he himself sometimes subscribed to. At any rate, although a hand, presumably Erskine's, pencils "write" next to this note, there is no record that he did so—and of course the line stayed in.

"Well! we got here!" Lowry exults at the bottom of this last sheet. It was not, however, quite the end; galley proofs were still to come.

On October 23, Erskine wrote that proof was on its way, and in a letter mainly taken up with deadlines and dust jackets, mailings and typography, managed also some last minute proposals for cuts. Near the end of the month (2:9, undated draft) Lowry reported that the galleys had indeed arrived ("complete with an enormous 7 stamped on the envelope") and responded to Erskine's suggestions. He began, characteristically, by agreeing: he was in accord "hands down" with the advice to cut from Chapter I a passage on Laruelle's time in Hollywood and Mexico. What got excised were specifics of Jacques's career: success in Europe, failure in Hollywood, retreat to Mexico for an anticipated brief "period of readjustment and renewal." "Instead he had found the Consul here and stayed on, and like him played the silver market." (With the disappearance of that last sentence, the final clear reference to this activity of Geoffrey's also goes.) Jacques was to feel himself an exiled failure (with an explicit resemblance to Eisenstein), his only work in Mexico being his lectures on "La exposición sobrealista en Paris" (28:9, galley 3).

Having begun with agreement, Lowry went on to resist the other cuts Erskine proposed, but decided on his own to remove the "dream about 23 nuns" from Chapter IX ("it looks as though the author was actually out of touch with his material"), and as a whole declared himself "inarticulate with gratitude and admiration for what you have done." Then, trying to meet the deadline of November 7 for the return of corrected proof, the Lowrys settled down to systematic work.[14]

At first there seemed few alterations beyond inevitable editorial corrections and, sometimes, confirmations (that Lowry wants, for instance, "Vine," not "Vino," "Argal," not "Ergo," "cohabations," not "cohabitations," and so on). He gives no sign of noticing that his prosy transposition of Marlowe—"Then will I run / fly headlong"—had been silently corrected to "Then will I headlong run / fly" (28:9, galley 12), and in Chapter VI curiously accepts the emendation "'Is what right?'" as answer to "'Is that right?'" in his echoing responses (28:14, galley 60). Early in Chapter IV, an indicated violation of Hugh's point of view when Yvonne tugs down the back of the borrowed jacket "knowing it Geoff's" is easily fixed: repunctuation—"(knowing it Geoff's?)"—places the reflection in Hugh's mind (28:12, galley 32). An awkward phrase about Judas after the betrayal—"that very morning of all mornings after the night before"—becomes the terser and smoother "after that madrugada of all madrugadas," but the sense of hangover is thereby sacrificed (37). In VI, "Sanabria," a name slated to appear in the telephone directory of VII, is replaced in the little postman's list by "Sandoval" ("Sandovah" appears in the text).

The second half of the novel elicited more, and more significant, alterations than the first. Perhaps appropriately, Lowry first adjusted the time scheme: the opening designation in Chapter VII of "1:35" gets altered to "1:20 P.M." presumably to add a plausible fifteen minutes to the events that must transpire before 2:30, when the Tomalín bus leaves. The first substantial revision in the chapter comes with Geoffrey's reflection on the relation of Laruelle's house to its occupant. The difference between the two miradors, which had seemed "appropriate to Jacques as denoting the contrast between his life and his ambitions," now appears "obscurely appropriate to Jacques, as indeed was that between the angels and the cannonballs" (28:15, galley 65), an association both more suggestive and more specific, less pathetic, more sinister. Two galleys later, the intensity of the Consul's longing for the Farolito darkens, moving from the language of love to that of struggle and compulsion. His "soul" is now "locked with the essence of the place" rather than "embracing" its spirit, and he is "gripped" rather than "possessed" by the thoughts of the returning mariner. Those are no longer thoughts of greeting a mistress; now it is a wife that awaits an embrace at the end of the voyage (67). The replacement of "mistress" with "wife" here is ominous, for even as it provides the cue for Geoffrey's mind to "return to Yvonne," it suggests that the Farolito has become not just her rival, but her successor. Moving from the opening of the sentence to its close, and now governed by "locked" and "gripped," the embrace no longer has the aspect of a free act: love itself seems forced, compelled.

Not for the first time, Chapter IX evoked considerable attention. Three inserts underscore Yvonne's hopefulness by disclosing the weak bases on which it rests: at the chapter's start, "for had not Geoffrey met her at the Bus Terminal?"; as he identifies the bull with Nandi, Hindu vehicle of divine violence, "(and ah, had he not taken her hand in the bus?)"; as he holds the habanero bottle without, for the moment, drinking, again, "And had he not, too, met her at the bus terminal?" (28:17, inserts galleys 85, 86, 90). But the most extensive, most poignant, and most daring change in the chapter is the new passage that replaces Geoffrey's unlikely dream of nuns in a motorboat. That dream had played ironic (or at least absurd) counterpoint to Yvonne's hopes, to her proposal for a new life "like a rebirth." Now, amazingly—it is the only such moment in the novel—Geoffrey reaches out to her:

"Yvonne?"
"Yes, darling?"
"I've fallen down, you know. . . . Somewhat."
"Never mind, darling."
". . . Yvonne?"
"Yes?"
"I love you . . . Yvonne?"
"Oh, I love you too!"
"My dear one . . . My sweetheart."
"Oh Geoffrey. We *could* be happy, we *could*—"
"Yes. . . . We could." (93)

It is astonishing that only now, at the very last minute, does Lowry create Geoffrey's single unsolicited declaration of love for Yvonne, the moment strengthened by the removal of "He said wearily" from his earlier response, given urgency by her eager proposal to leave "'now, tomorrow, today'" (93). The larger pattern of the action has long been established, the conquered bull Hugh is riding continues to carry obliquely ironic commentary—this is, after all, only a moment—but the glimpse of the genuine possibility of love intensifies the emotional life of the novel and grants stature to both principals. It rescues Yvonne from a merely fatuous hopefulness and deepens the tragic end of the Consul by showing him capable of entertaining a vision of life in a fulfilling human relationship. In another moment, of course, Lowry has undermined this communion by sending the Consul back to the habanero bottle as Yvonne now brokenly appeals to him ("'I don't expect you to—I mean—I know it's going to be—'").[15] However, this only reminds us that the pattern of these alterations reveals Lowry up to old tricks, working simultaneously in two opposed directions, weakening Yvonne's hope by showing the flimsiness of its bases, strengthening Yvonne's hope by giving it the support of Geoffrey's response.

After the extended late revisions and proposals for yet more, Chapter X ended by being left almost as it was. In line with the changes in IX, two brief inserts here reflect on Geoffrey's concern with Yvonne's "happiness." Jealously imagining that her banter with Hugh about climbing Popocatapetl might suggest to them "a lifetime together," the Consul now suddenly wonders "or was Yvonne simply, alas, happy?" (97). If that addition seemed to show that he, at least, gives no lasting value to their moment together at the arena, the other suggests he is still concerned to please her. Holding forth "brilliantly" on Atlantean connections (or so he thinks), he imagines he is making her happy "once more" (103).[16]

Chapter XI received a miscellany of small but significant emendations. Yvonne's first words now announce that she "won't" rather than "can't" abandon Geoffrey, one of the subtle adjustments in the novel's interplay of freedom and necessity (28:19, galley 106). The most extensive alterations come around the end of the stop at El Petate; Lowry at last repents of tying Yvonne's reaction to the freeing of the eagle to her drinks, now allowing "the sense of utter heartbreak and loss" to speak suggestively to the "losses" to come (107). Hugh's rather open-ended comment at El Popo that having decided he is not going to Mexico City tonight, "'there're various things we might do,'" gets qualified by the addition of "'about Geoff'" (109), which both removes the sexual overtones and places Yvonne's response in a sharply ironic light: "'I'd rather like to get tight.'" (Taken together with her ignoring of Hugh's "'Couldn't we phone?'" the developing implication has become that *in this part of the chapter* the failure to pursue the Consul vigorously is primarily Yvonne's doing).

"I hope my cuts in the last chapter were O.K. I can't bear to look, but I sort of feel they are right. I went there rather beyond your advice" (2:9), Lowry worried to Erskine on November 21. The most extensive changes to XII surround the Consul's play with the tethered horse. As he moves toward it, both his explanation of its presence outside the Farolito and his intentions toward it get altered. The first changes from a question to an assertion:

> In any event, why was this horse, instead of in Tomalín, or even Quauhnahuac, here in Parián, near the Comisario de Policia? (28:8, 506)

> It had been those vigilante hombres who'd turned up on the road this afternoon, and here, in Parián, as he'd told Hugh, was their headquarters. (galley 118)

Curiously, the correction here seems to answer the original, or at least the question, "why Parián?" for "the Comisario de Policia" is no longer at issue once the "vigilante hombres" become the putative villains. The alteration neither proves nor disproves Geoffrey's theory of the incident, but it does make that theory self-consistent.

The change in his actions and intentions toward the horse is more measurable in its effect. What Lowry does is cut ten lines of internal musing that had a definite aim, "to lead the horse away to a spot where it couldn't be found." That impulse was "half playful, childish, harmless," we are told, but it was also secretive, and out of the latter side came the partly disingenuous response to the Chief that disclaimed all intention, protesting "'I was merely looking at it, admiring it.'" What he had been doing, however, in the now-excised passage—what the Chief saw—was something else: "he took hold of the bridle preparatory to untying it" (119). In short, while the Consul may have been "innocent" (childish, harmless) in his own mind, what he had actually been doing made him not unreasonably the object of suspicion. With the cutting of this passage, the crucial encounter with the sinister "chiefs" begins with a rendering of Geoffrey's own suspicions, but since he himself now intends no action (surely it would be uncharacteristic), he appears, on this point, unjustly accused, a victim.

Many of the cuts, however, were snippings, as Erskine had suggested, from the speeches of the pimp and the "man who resembled a sailor," and, as the chapter moved toward its climax, of descriptive passages, repetitions, anything that might rob his action of its full intensity. The paragraph most trimmed in this manner is the one where Geoffrey turns on his tormentors and strikes back at them—"Papers. Cabrón. You har no papers" (*Volcano* 372), where at last the phantom parrot disappears—the only bird the Consul "confronts" now is a cock—and the sense of external agency seems, intriguingly, both increased and reduced. As action moves outside the cantina, he is no longer "propell[ed]" by the Chief of Rostrums, but "dragged" by both that individual and "someone else." However, he is not now "pushed" out into the road, but "stumbled backwards," and again later not "pushed back" but "stumbling backwards" until he falls (125). These latter moments can indeed be read as the acting out of Geoffrey's own lack of "equilibrium," but the earlier one may well suggest the self overcome by exterior forces beyond his control. The alterations, in short, clarify Lowry's opposed tensions; they do not resolve them. And finally—whatever we may make of it—at the moment the dying Consul imagines he has reached "the summit" of his mountain, repenting of his thinking "evil of the world when succor was at hand all the time," Lowry inserts: "Ah, Yvonne, sweetheart, forgive me!" (126). It is not, of course, the final line of the novel, but as Lowry's ultimate word, as the last sentence to appear on the galleys, it is somehow fitting. With these corrections and changes, the long composition of the *Volcano* had at last come to an end.[17]

CHAPTER SIX

The Complete Consort

The history of the composition of the *Volcano*, even if we can trace it only between 1940 and 1947, presents anything but a straight line. The manuscript expands, contracts, expands once more; some passages are cut never to be seen again; others disappear from one spot only to be placed elsewhere; still others, snipped from one draft, languish in limbo before third thoughts reinstate them on another. It seems an open text, in constant flux, and indeed in one part of his mind Lowry appears never to have accepted it as completed, done. As late as 1956, when Margerie was reporting buoyantly to David Markson that Malcolm was writing better than at any time "since he finished the *Volcano*," Lowry's own comment was, "Except that he hasn't finished the *Volcano* yet" (*Letters* 393).

Nevertheless, whatever his private view and future plans, publication in 1947 set *Under the Volcano* in cold print once and for all.[1] If his revisions open to us a single truth about the novel, it is surely this double one of a text constantly in motion, yet fixed, completed, yet not completed, a truth central both to the process of composition and to the product, the achieved novel, "process" and "product" being yet another way of expressing the tension between motion and fixity, openness and closure, mutability and finality that runs through the *Volcano*. We have been looking at process, the struggle of composition invisible to a novel's readers, and the question naturally and properly arises: What— or what more than has already been suggested—can this tell us about "product"? What can we discover from this perspective that we could not see, or could not see so clearly, from simply examining the published *Volcano* itself?

The beginnings of an answer lie in the paradoxical doubleness of the novel's conception, a doubleness Lowry was committed to once he had created in the 1940 Chapter I an introductory epilogue. The dimensions of that doubleness, the full implications of what that apparently simple device to save his "dated" text committed him to, would take years to realize, but the dual time scheme created in this fashion and never thereafter questioned gave him an action that was always "finished" before it began—and at the same time never finished. Once Chapter I became both (structurally) the beginning and (temporally) the end, it cast the rest of the novel's action into a curiously double perspective, at once static and dynamic: it is the historical past, and like any past, over, fixed, immutable (the Consul is dead), but it is also the fictional present, unrolling before us now, as we read, like any other narrative (the Consul is not dead). Fixing *all* of the action of the novel on two Days of the Dead, as Lowry had by 1940, was a statement of this doubleness—indeed, the 1940 text has several even more explicit "statements" of this kind, and Hugh's anguish at the opening of Chapter VI (my youth is over, my youth is not over) will enact it in a minor key—but as brilliant a stroke as it was, it was hardly sufficient by itself to sustain the fictional life of the entire work.[2]

Lowry would not or could not see this until publishers' rejections began to roll in. The stripping-down process that followed in 1941, however, revealed that while almost everything else might change (character relations and point of view, for instance, to say nothing of the texture of the prose itself), the 1940 blueprint of action, although it was perhaps not wholly immutable—minor chapels of this churrigueresque cathedral may come and go, inner partitions get moved—still, the central structure outlined there would essentially hold, the supporting walls and towers, pillars and roof, nave and choir hewing closely to the basic plan. Yvonne's death rather than lovemaking at the end of Chapter XI, for example, would gradually send reverberating ripples throughout the text, but it would not disturb the structure even of that chapter ("how alike are the groans of love to those of the dying"), just as the Calle Nicaragua would sprout a lane in Chapter III and send the Consul toward it without in the least affecting the extant action there. Chapter divisions might shift (between VI and VII, for instance) or incidents fully recounted in early drafts appear later only as recollections (the stop at Las Novedades in IX, for instance), and while this certainly modifies the structure of the *novel* (or "discourse"), it has no impact on the structure of the *action* (or "story"), which continues to be made up of the same events, unaffected by the alterations of the text that mediates them.[3] From 1940 on, the *Volcano* had a skeleton that was essentially fixed: it was the processes of the flesh, which both depended from it and made it manifest, that occupied Lowry in the ensuing years.

Given his particular gifts and limitations, the decision to sustain for the length of a chapter a single perspective was almost certain to produce a novel far more interiorized than the rather conventional texts of 1940 and 1941. Dialogue would inevitably shrink, meditative passages increase. Yet his very gravitation toward the inner world of his characters would itself, as if by recoil, evoke the counter impulse, a determined attention to the exterior world. In *Ultramarine*, his only previous novel, Lowry had dealt with this problem by alternating sustained passages of interior monologue and apparently neutral reportage, a method insufficient for the more ambitious and complex *Volcano*. In part, he dealt with the challenge by bringing to bear his essentially poetic gifts, his sensitivity to the concrete image, whether it manifested itself in the presentation of landscape or as the metaphorical expression of consciousness. It is no accident that the actual passages that persist from 1940 onward are almost invariably of these kinds nor, indeed, that Lowry would work intensively throughout the revisions with a technique of "objective correlative," the creation of descriptive passages emotionally expressive of an appropriate phase of the mind.

His gift for dialogue was partial, eccentric—sensitive to odd, "boundary" forms of speech (the multiple possibilities, comic and expressive, when one language meets another, correctness error, or slang propriety), his more conventional conversations are often leaden, pedestrian—but he could through painstaking revision forge convincing and witty monologues, create distinctive "voices" that were essentially masks, and sustain them through the deployment of expressive rhythm, tonal shifts, and commanding rhetoric. Recall simply the interior "voices" gradually developed for Geoffrey in Chapter III: the saddened imperatives and accusations of the "guide" who escorts him down the drive, the febrile and righteous jabberings of one "familiar," the accusatory whine of a second, the half-wheedling, half-blaming, alternately patronizing, affectionate, and angry "address" to Hugh, the outraged righteousness of the response to Yvonne's "insulting" intimation of his nonsobriety, the erotic urgency of his evocation of the opening cantinas, the comically desperate rationalization of his alcoholic condition of the moment. In these we glimpse Lowry's true virtuosity in the form. And this is to ignore the Consul's voiced roles here (the "almost uncontrollably 'English'" idiom borrowed from his compatriot, for instance, or the morose "accent... of a Bleecker Street mummer"). Of all those interior passages, only an evocation of the cantinas existed in 1940, and there it has none of the rhythms and repetitions of urgency and desire that mark the *spoken* word. For of course in these monologues, Lowry marries inner and outer worlds; private to the Consul, they are created with all the dramatic power (and sometimes the punctuation) of the delivered utterance. Indeed, Geoffrey—and the reader too, at first—believe the address to Hugh actually spoken aloud.

As the focus of the novel gradually shifed from event to response, to "[sink] into the action of the mind," Lowry began to recognize that this movement demanded more, not less, specificity, greater, not reduced, attention to the features of his external world. The spatial dimension, landscape, itself would become closely connected to the psychological through objective correlative, but the temporal too needed fixing, rendering. Here was a novel set on quite specific days, evoking specific events of recent history, and while it was clear from the start exactly when Chapter I took place, a curious vagueness pervaded the rest of the novel. Certainly the Spanish war was on, but was this 1936, 1937, or 1938? A work partly about the burdens of history should surely exhibit some; if this was a truism for the novel generally, it also applied to its characters. Thus, soon after Geoffrey and Hugh become related, they acquire a childhood background in India, and a little research into the Spanish Civil War produced not only some specifying references but the more fundamental information that in early November 1938 the Battle of the Ebro was in progress, and thus the date of Chapters II–XII became fixed. Then Lowry recognized that Mexico itself, vivid in flashes though it was from his own sojourn there and from the memorabilia he had brought back, was also in several areas terra incognita. Prescott and Spence, for instance, had been invaluable in tuning him into ancient and mythic Mexico, but how much did he really know of its recent history, including the political situation during his own stay? Further trips to the library were indicated.

In these phases of revision, his Jamesian motto (see Introduction, p. 5) was a particularly appropriate guide, for Lowry's efforts at vividness and representation emerge out of his shift from roving omniscience to alternating centers of consciousness, which produced a gain in intensity, a sharpening of focus as he began to discover their possibilities. The initial concern with mere consistency soon gave way to an exploring of the double thrust created by the technical shift. Exterior and interior worlds of the novel still exist, Lowry saw, but the former now appears only through the latter, a dual focus that both allowed for the sustained exploration of each consciousness (a burden in the case of Yvonne), and almost of necessity brought about a gradual intensifying effect. Still later, Lowry realized that the true locus of his book had inexorably shifted to the interior and that this might produce more radical effects, coloring decisively the very presentation of the exterior world, blotting it out altogether, for instance, or changing it decisively, substituting dream, hallucination, fantasy, false impression, uncertainty for the unquestioned clarity of simple perception. And since "interior" was plural, each of the major characters filtering the world in his or her own ways according to temperament and the conditions of the moment, what emerged was, from this perspective, less an authoritative narrative than an exploration of serial solipsism, a condition from which the reader is not exempted.

The final movement of Chapter V, as we have seen (Chapter 3, pp. 185ff., and Chapter 4, pp. 227ff.), handily epitomizes the kind of change this process of discovery brought about in the text. In all versions, exterior action, summarized at sufficient distance, shows the same elements: the skeleton, established by 1940, holds. Returning from his encounter with Mr. Quincey and Dr. Vigil, the Consul finds Hugh and Yvonne discussing bougainvillea on the porch. The three talk, Vigil arrives, and the conversation turns to where to go in the afternoon. Hugh and Yvonne swim, the closer bullthrowing is preferred to the doctor's more distant Guanajuato, and Vigil takes his leave. In 1940, this section consumes some fourteen pages (approximately 4200 words), of which the following uncut passage is entirely typical:

> "Cheerio! [the Consul said] I'm always glad to see Yvonne's old friends, of course." He leaned against the parapet. "This is better than Algeciras, what?"
> "Well—"
> "Of course, this is a hell of a climate—so was that by the way—but it's a pretty nice place, don't you think?"

"Yes indeed."

"What's all this I hear about a bet?"

Hugh told him the story, stammering like a schoolboy about his clothes, blushing.

"So you quit Stanford," the Consul said, and suddenly laughed loudly. But his eyes did not laugh, holding a fixed stony despair.

"And you see, sir," Hugh added nervously, "I ran into Yvonne here, in Acapulco, and that kind of upset everything. Mexico is awfully interesting, it must be a difficult place to leave."

"Too true," said the Consul. "Unless you get thrown out. But still, after all, what is particularly interesting about it?"

"Oh, I don't know—"

"Of course I don't have to say that the social situation interests you, since that's the fashion. Just as it does Yvonne here, eh Yvonne?"

"I wasn't aware there was one."

"And what about Spain, Hugh? I suppose you're on the side of the Loyalists too, that goes without saying—"

"I think every good American is, surely."

"You must have some interesting conversations with your pro-Franco friend, Yvonne."

"I never said I was pro-Franco, Father!" Yvonne said heatedly. "It's you that are pro-Franco! I only told Hugh that he's a fool to go and fight for the Loyalists, which is what he's thinking of doing, the jackass!"

The Consul laughed again, loudly, with still the same stony expression in his eyes.

"The bougainvillea reminds you of home, doesn't it," he said, after a long silence.

After another silence, the Consul said: "Wasn't it Bougainville who discovered the bougainvillea?"

"Why yes," Hugh nodded. "Now I come to think of it, I believe it was Bougainville."

"Hence the name, bougainvillea," Yvonne said feebly.

"That's right, hence bougainvillea."

The conversation languished. (1940 145–46)

So, needless to say, did the novel.

The method here is entirely characteristic of 1940. Governed by a "neutral" but informative narrator (in a fine example of James's "platitude of statement," he advises us that the Consul's expression does not match his laugh, that his eyes hold "despair"), the text is committed to a conventional reportage. While the narrator will not repeat a story he has let us hear earlier or force us to undergo the actual emptiness of the silences, he otherwise feels bound to re-present precisely what transpired on this banal occasion. This is mimesis with a vengeance: the slackness of the exchange, its awkward silences and *politesse* stretched over the tensions of people who do not know each other well (or, alternatively, know each other only too well), its desultoriness and inanities—the dialogue conveys all too faithfully the pointless wanderings of actual "social" conversation. In 1940, long narrative stretches simply reproduce dialogue, depending on verbal interaction among characters to create resonance, and the results are often as thin as in this passage.

The ensuing 1941 version (26:22) introduced not only the change in point of view, but also the realignment of relationships among characters, which relieved the expository burden so that the porch episode shrank from fourteen to ten pages. The following draft (29:16), however, expanded the episode once more (eighteen manuscript pages), adding both consular reflections and, to the dialogue, consideration of local bus and train schedules. But here Geoffrey was for the first time in rather desperate alcoholic shape, and Lowry apparently began to see how that might allow him a whole new approach to the end of the chapter. However it came to him, the blackout that appears in the next draft (29:17) was an inspiration that solved various problems presented by the porch episode at a single stroke. Given the new emphasis on vividness of representation, it was easily plausible: in addition to the tequila bottle, we have witnessed Geoffrey's intake in Chapters II and III and are about to hear Vigil's indiscreet references to the previous night's gargantuan consumption. A superficial realism is appeased by shifting its locus from the outer world (conversational exchange on the porch) to the inner (the Consul's alcoholic loss of touch with his surroundings) while the social minutiae that had so clogged earlier versions drain away into the holes in Geoffrey's recollections. This draft thus shrinks to about half the length of the preceding one, and most of the disappearances are from those emptily literal exchanges, which, not having registered on the Consul's soaking brain, simply vanish. The shift in focus and compression of material itself generates a rise in intensity, but this receives its final turn in the ensuing draft (29:18) where Lowry fully realizes—and dramatizes—not simply the result of that blackout, imperfect recall of the events of the previous hour, but the *process* of recovery. The novel's present thus becomes not the scene of the foursome on the porch, but Geoffrey alone in the bathroom an hour later, where his anguished groans now repeatedly recall us to this moment and to the current action, the strained attempt to *recover* that scene on the porch.

Inevitably, Lowry would refine and polish this episode until the end, but even in its first and roughest incarnation, the blackout passage achieved stylistic distinctiveness. As we have seen, in the hands of the neutral narrator, the porch episode had been everywhere conventional, and even as the Consul's consciousness gained fuller prominence, narrative syntax had held: Geoffrey's observations became looser, but they never lost coherence, and the centrality of dialogue always returned the focus to the present scene as, moment by moment, it unfolded before him. But with the blackout, the Consul's mind itself becomes the subject, and the text dramatizes its unimpeded flow as suddenly and without warning it begins to undergo mnemonic hiccups, to hurl up questions and fragments, disconnected images and shards of dialogue, uneven and lurching prose mediating non sequiturs, a thread of continuity held out only by a recurrent evocation of the bathroom, where in the strain of dubious recollection the Consul sits with his glass of flat beer, a deferred promise that all coherence has not fled the text. Syntax and rhythm signify, however, not only that the real locus of the novel's action has shifted decisively to the interior, but that this interior, where now at least two temporal levels reside, is the site of an uneven struggle for recovery.

A late addition to the bathroom sequence points up a further ramification of this crucial shift. For a moment, the Consul, his beer finished, feels released from the struggle to recover that hour shrouded in blackout; he simply contemplates with detachment a clear, single vision of his earlier self crossing the porch what seems "a terribly long time ago— it was as if something he could not put his finger on had mysteriously supervened to separate drastically that returning figure from himself sitting in the bathroom—the figure on the porch, for all its damnation, seemed younger, to have more freedom of movement, choice." The struggle to recover the past gives way to a sense of its achievement—here is the past moment crystallized, seen in and for itself—but the price of this clarity is separation not only from "himself" in the present but also from the entire stream of time: that envisaged Geoffrey appears "to have, if only because it held a full glass of beer once more, a better chance of a future" (29:18, 4). This new passage seems to emerge from a full recognition of what the superimposition of time frames in this draft implies, the distance it creates. Whether in such shifts as that from "he was steadily crossing the porch" to "in his mind too he was steadily crossing the porch" or in the switch in tenses so implied ("*said* the doctor," for instance, becomes "the doctor *had said*"), the focus on the recovery of the "lost" hour moves the earlier action firmly into the completed past, a "drive toward the pluperfect," in Matthew Corrigan's useful phrase (422).

As the focus shifted gradually but decisively away from directly represented action, the entire day of Chapters II–XII, and not just such retrospective passages as this in Chapter V, had been moving into the pluperfect, as if all the characters—and readers too—were now inevitably placed in the position of the Consul in Chapter VII, "missing the next opportunity, and the next, missing all the opportunities, finally, until it was too late" (*Volcano* 218). What the blackout of Chapter V writes large is the ineluctable "too late-ness" of all apprehension, the space, whether gaping as here or so small as to seem infinitesimal to the "normal," attentive perception, between action and response, experience and consciousness. Between the reality and the idea (to reverse Eliot) falls the temporal shadow, and while we may not always miss the meaning of experience, that meaning trails, disconsolately, the experience itself. "Life changes," Señora Gregorio wisely advises the Consul; "You can never drink of it," never become one with it, for as soon as you try, life has moved on, what you attempted to "drink" no longer exists except in recollection, mixing memory and desire. In Señora Gregorio's adaptation of Heraclitus, you can never imbibe the same stream twice. There is no way of determining the relationship between what the Consul retrieves from his lost hour and the events that transpired on his porch.

At times, Lowry dramatizes this gap not simply for his characters, but for the reader, writes it in stylistically so that we can recognize only retrospectively the experience presented. Two instances, in the first and last chapters, are the achievement of revision, both, not coincidentally, concerned with the reappearance of objects from the past, *Las Manos de Orlac* in I, the Consul's pipe in XII. In each case, earlier versions had respected conventional narrative sequence. The simpler alteration, the exchange about the pipe in Chapter XII, was also the first made. In 1940, the Consul recognizes it in the possession of Diosdado, and the bartender makes no attempt to deny it:

> The Consul politely explained about the pipe.
> "*Sí, sí*, mistair," replied Diosdado, preoccupied, "*Claro*. You were *borracho* one day."
> "*Un poco–*" (1940 349)

Here, Diosdado's "*Sí, sí*" seems to constitute an admission, a reading confirmed by the narrator when he terms the Consul "compensated" in receiving back Priscilla's letters, but not the pipe, from the barman. The "retrospective shift" comes on the post-1941 holograph. Again, the Consul recognizes his pipe; then:

> "Si, si, mistair," replied Diosdado, preoccupied/listening to the Consul's query about his/that pipe. "Claro. No my ah pipe/Monterey pipe. You were barracho one day. No.
> "Un poco. Possible." (31:12, 4)

And the Consul is no longer "compensated" to receive his wife's letters. Now the presentation of Geoffrey's question follows its apparent answer which, in another shift, is no longer an admission, but simply acknowledgment ("Claro") of the query, for the barman immediately presses on to a denial. "Yes, yes," says Diosdado, "I understand. No, this is my pipe."

By the time we reach that sequence in XII, it constitutes an echo of the comparable passage in Chapter I (see below for Lowry's construction of such echoes). Laruelle, like the Consul a year before (but eleven chapters later), enters a cantina and asks the presiding figure there if he does not recognize an object the other possesses. In both cases the inquirer receives a negative reply followed by the unexpected presentation of another article, one left at that cantina previously (a bundle of letters, a book containing a letter), the recognition of which stuns the recipient. After conventional exchanges of thanks, each proceeds to read from what he has just been handed. Lowry's late alteration of the query about the *Orlac* film may be a deliberate paralleling, even to the form, of the exchange in Chapter XII about the pipe. It is, in any case, even more deceptive.

In 1940, Laruelle had recalled previously seeing the *Orlac* film at the cinema, but he did not question the manager about it until a later draft:

> "Do you mind my asking," Laruelle asked anyway, as they found two seats, "Haven't I seen this Manos de Orlac picture here before? Why have you revived it? Is it popular?"
> "No," laughed the Guatematecan . . . "uno–?"
> Laruelle hesitated. "Tequila," he said. (28:23, "II," 9)

Slightly modified versions of this appeared until it read (Texas I, 27) as in the published novel:

> "Do you mind my–"
> "No, hombre," laughed the other–M. Laruelle had asked Señor Bustamente, who'd now succeeded in attracting the barman's attention, hadn't he seen the Orlac picture here before and if so had he revived it as a hit. "–uno–?"
> M. Laruelle hesitated: "Tequila," . . . (cf. *Volcano* 25–26)

Now, Bustamente's "No" appears his response to Jacques's *politesse*, whatever it may have concerned: "No, I don't mind. . . ." Only later is it possible to determine that it is actually the reply to queries about the film (although since in all versions there are two questions, we can't determine whether it answers the first, second, or both). Furthermore, the "–uno–?" seems initially a hesitation over idiom–perhaps the Mexican does not grasp the English "hit"?–until Laruelle's answering hesitation reveals that Bustamente is asking his guest for his drink order, a focus, again, determinable only after the fact, in retrospect.

One effect of such trompe l'oeil passages is always the same: whenever the reader recognizes that his understanding has been (necessarily) incorrect, the mind is forced back over the episode for a revised interpretation. Not only, it turns out, is the Consul's speech to Hugh from the stones of the Calle Nicaragua in Chapter III unspoken, but

Hugh is not present; the brilliantly learned disquisition on Indian myth and ritual of Chapter X, punctuated by the refrain "the Consul was talking," is revealed as "a whirling cerebral chaos"; the figures who appear at the start of Chapter V are not, as they first seem, Hugh and Yvonne resuming their excursion; Yvonne's invitations to drink as she and the Consul walk toward home in Chapter II are not, after all, spoken aloud; Jacques's final upbraidings of Geoffrey in the Café Paris of Chapter VII do not, in the event, come from Jacques at all. With the exception of the last, none of these passages appears in 1940 in *any* form, and most make their first entry into the text in quite conventional ways: Geoffrey briefly thinks in III of a Hugh he is perfectly aware is not present, he speaks his piece about India's religions in X aloud in extended monologue, Jacques does deliver in VII all the advice Geoffrey attributes to him, and so on. If such passages force the reader into revision, they are the product of revision themselves; our reading becomes a curious mirror image of Lowry's acts of writing, a reversal that in carrying the mind back into the past of the text performs one of the novel's principal strands of meaning.

Yet in the blackout passage of Chapter V, curiously, that is *not* what happens: the Consul's mind is carried desperately back into the past of the previous hour, but since this is not a textual past, the reader's is not. There is something of a paradox here, an odd tension, for as the text has become more complex, overlaying the past with the present struggle to retrieve it, it has also become more fragmentary; only glimpses of the past are recovered. And if that lost hour moves irrevocably into the pluperfect, only partially and unreliably available to us as to the Consul, the novel's focus—not the Consul's—remains firmly on the present, on the attempts "now" to wrest back time's hostages. That action is almost wholly interior—in the very last drafts we are returned to the outer world by the Consul's groans and sips of beer in the bathroom—yet it is far more vivid, more intensely "present" than the banal dialogue and movements that had been the focus in earlier drafts. Of course the very structure of the novel, the relation of the rest of the work to Chapter I, had since 1940 made the most visible statement of a text that moved ahead by moving backwards, yet only in revision did this tension acquire urgency, as the dramatization of the *mind* carried back into the past moved to the evolving center of the novel. That growing intensification is not limited to individual passages: it was the shift in point of view that freed Lowry from the 1940 pose of neutrality, from a distant and objectifying narrator, and made possible the more expressive and flexible stance of later drafts.

Chapter II, for instance, as it comes to focus firmly on and through Yvonne, gradually exploits the double sense, compounded of familiarity and unfamiliarity, memory and perception, past and present, of one coming back to a well-known and loved place after long absence. The Yvonne of 1940, of course, is in Quauhnahuac for the first time, but all her successive incarnations are the returning former wife, and although little is made of this double dimension at first, the 1941 draft does contain one sentence from which her response will sprout: "The scene [outside the Bella Vista], so sharply familiar, yet so strange after a year's absence and the severance in thought, smote Yvonne like a sudden blow" (29:1, 4). But, as Lowry saw, if that "blow" strikes Yvonne on leaving the hotel, must it not have struck her even before entering? Subsequent versions will open with her outside the Bella Vista, hearing the Consul's "achingly familiar" voice, being moved by the "familiar" landscape, recognizing and appropriating once more "*their* square," an affirmation of the oneness of Yvonne and Geoffrey made possible by the apparent collapse of past into present. This initial sense of unity will be ironically undermined as the chapter develops—the presence, as if "out of the past," of both Jacques and Hugh, the recognition from bitter memory of Geoffrey's alcoholic behavior—and will be further complicated in later versions by the overlay of the recent-past-persisting-into-the-present images of her journey until neither "present" nor "past" is a single dimension in Yvonne's consciousness. Nonetheless, the feeling of reconciliation will continue to provide a major key to Yvonne here. The other end of the chapter will more ironically strike that note of temporal and emotional unity: it is almost as if "they were returning from marketing as in days past," an impression that will bluntly be called "false, . . . a lie" (29:5, 12), undermined by the separableness of present from past:

> when she'd half imagined the Consul back in England, she'd tried to keep Quauhnahuac itself, as a sort of safe footway where his phantom could endlessly pace, accompanied only by her own consoling unwanted shadow. . . . Then since the other day Quauhnahuac had appeared though emptied still, different, purged, swept

clean of the past, with Geoffrey here alone, but now in the flesh, redeemable, wanting her help.

And here Geoffrey indeed was, not only not alone, not only not wanting her help, but living in the midst of her blame, a blame by which he seemed to all appearances curiously sustained— (29:5, 11–12; cf. *Volcano* 63)

Not only have "past" and "present" become all too easily separable for Yvonne, but even the present of the chapter's opening (adumbrated in the second vision above, "since the other day") has become, quite distinctly, "the past," literally no longer imaginable.

Although the past manifests itself in consciousness through memory, whether of the previous hour (the Consul in the bathroom) or of months and years before (Yvonne in Chapter II), as it does so it ceases to be wholly past (it is present to the mind, after all) without, on the other hand, becoming entirely present (it is not actually occurring at this moment, after all). This ambiguity, the fluidity of consciousness as it moves among its functions of perceiving, remembering, "thinking," imagining, responding, and so on, allows for Lowry's gradual construction of the complex texture of his chapters, indeed demands (or so he saw it) this construction once consciousness becomes the central locus of action. That construction *was* gradual, however, the fitting of more and more brightly and complexly colored tiles within a pattern already established, flexible without being fluid, able to expand or contract to accommodate new or newly patterned passages. Take the opening of Chapter II. Once Yvonne becomes the returning wife rather than the visiting daughter, the chapter begins with her overhearing the Consul's remark about the transportable corpse from within the Bella Vista bar, and she is assigned no initial reactions to Quauhnahuac. Next, she is placed outside as the chapter opens and responds briefly and nostalgically to the square, associating it "with the cool sweetness of the dawn that morning at the Acapulco airport" where Venus and vultures were in attendance, before entering the "dusk" of the bar (29:2, 2).

The following draft (29:3) adds balconies and flowerboxes to the hotel and fountain, trees, and taxis to the square ("what is not presented is not vivid": indeed, for the novel it does not exist), but it also adds another voice or voices ("'—Ha ha ha!—' . . . 'Just a bunch of Alladamnbama farmers!'") and, in a complementary passage, characterizes Yvonne's inner state ("Ashamed, hesitant, numbly excited") before having her enter the "alcoholic dusk" of the bar, where she is now "myopic" at the sudden change of light. Next (29:5) comes her identification of "another voice" and her drawing the conclusion that the bar is "evidently full." This gives rise to the expanded, epic sentence containing her response ("Ashamed, numb with nostalgia. . . ."), which forges new material with old. The square now resembles "slumbering Harlequin" and acquires a bandstand and the equestrian statue of Huerta, the plane becomes "winged emissary of Lucifer," and on her myopic entrance into alcoholic dusk this time, "the sea that morning" enters with her:

> The bar was empty, however.
> Or rather it contained one figure. (29:5, 3)

The opening of Chapter II is thus enlarged, of course, but this enlargement is actually a thickening, an intensifying, for nothing new "happens" here after the placement of Yvonne outside the hotel except the appearance, in a single line, of another voice. However, the sense of the density of these moments, which become fuller and fuller of sensory and emotional information, expands enormously as Lowry gradually, through three full chapter drafts and who knows how many throwaways, specifies more and more the features of the square and interweaves these both with Yvonne's afterimages of the recent past (the plane, Acapulco, the sea) and with direct and indirect renderings of her expectant emotional state. Inner and outer worlds develop together, from Yvonne's simple expansive identification of "*their* square" and the subsequent emotional "contract[ion]" when entering the bar, on through the introduction of a foreign voice, which evokes a shame and hesitation in her so that she lingers in the expanded square before becoming "myopic" when entering the bar, on to a more fraught hesitation in a consciousness now overlaid with such a vivid sense of voyage that Yvonne literally hardly knows whether she is here or there. Nothing seem to have changed in the ever more fully evoked square, yet her sense of the immediate past of Acapulco and the sea is so potent that it "go[es] in with her" when she enters the bar. These images and the "myopic" semiblindness of the sudden loss of light produce a vision of an "empty" bar.

That impression is erroneous, of course, and takes its place in the pattern of Yvonne's errors, misapprehensions and illusions—the old woman from Tarasco, Laruelle's "forgotten" house, the Consul's unheard statement on Tortu, Yvonne's own unspoken invitations to a drink—already noted (chapter 4, pp. 206ff.). The point here is to suggest the role of the felt past in the creation of such displacements of the "actual" present, and even more broadly, that focusing in and through consciousness that leads to such complexities and uncertainties. Chapter II thus reveals these absences and presences as features of the novel, not simply (as Chapter V, for example, might suggest) as offspring of the Consul's overburdened brain. In a book as steeped in alcohol as the *Volcano*, Lowry establishes early in a stone-cold sober Yvonne that "hallucinations" and false perceptions, misleading assumptions and partial glimpses, are inevitable features of consciousness that color, obscure, even transform our perceptions of and responses to the world around us. In this respect, as in others, Geoffrey is simply an extreme figure on a continuum. For Yvonne early in Chapter II, mixed and varying emotions—anxiety, nostalgia, hope, fear, guilt, longing, revulsion—and impinging stimuli—brilliant sunlight, sudden "dusk," the sound of voices, images from recent and more distant pasts—are enough to produce the illusions and lacunae she undergoes. Even Hugh, whose extroversion results in the chapters least subject to these eruptions and distortions, feels the world stop (IV), hears wind and trees speaking to him (VI), and is literally unable to see the pelado's theft of the dying Indian's money (VIII). His apprehension of the Cervecería Quauhnahuac in Chapter IV (and Lowry's construction of that apprehension) is, in this respect, instructive.

In 1940 "a little brewery" where Yvonne and Hugh are served beer by "a sort of ostler, wearing a huge visor" (25:20, 21) constitutes the full "vividness of representation" for this episode. Next (29:12, 24), the building seems "at first sight a huge French Château." As they come closer, it "now looked different, like a mill, sliced, oblong, which emitted a mill-like clamour and on which flitted and slid mill-wheel-like reflections of sunlight on the water of a neighbouring stream" and "out of a sudden glimpse of its very machinery" comes the visored, ostler-like man bearing beer now described as "dark." In the subsequent version (29:13, ms. 13A), the apparent château acquires "a sort of courtyard" and "a high wall" with a "massive gate" (as well as a much fuller approach through what appears "a somewhat neglected park"). Hugh discovers the name on the wall of the building: "So the château was a brewery, but of a very odd type—one that hadn't quite made up its mind not to be a restaurant with a beer garden." The dark beer brought to the riders now becomes "German." On the next draft (29:14, 15), the "gamekeeper" (no longer "ostler") after serving the riders "vanish[es] through an ostiole back into the machinery; the mill-like clamour was closed out again, as on board ship, by the shutting of a door, is closed out the clamour from down below." Now Hugh pays for the beers, hearing "the renewed clamour of the plant: *dungeons: dungeons: dungeons,* it said" (16).

Thus the simple "brewery" expands to a "huge . . . château," then becomes a "mill" (enabling Lowry to stitch in his motifs of the wheel and, reinforced by the insertion of the child with the armadillo, the infernal machine). When it next suggests a "restaurant with beer garden," the identification of the beer as "German" is almost unnecessary, but its "darkness" too begins to take on metaphorical weight. Finally, the association with a ship, with sounds "down below," and with "dungeons," completes the sinister shading of the presentation. These developing and changing perceptions, adding, correcting, belong, of course, to Hugh, although he shows no sign of recognizing the motif of disguise suggested in his presentation nor its political overtones. Disguise had been implicit in the "huge visor" of the "ostler" of 1940, but that sense was developed and darkened through ensuing drafts until "down below" suggests not only "dungeons" but the below-deck furnaces of the masquerading *Samaritan,* as well, of course, as the infernal regions (a sense underlined, once more, by the burrowing armadillo). This kind of shifting, changing set of perceptions is more typical of Hugh than the outright illusions and blankings both Geoffrey and Yvonne (and even Jacques) are subject to, as is his failure to draw for himself troubling conclusions. Nonetheless, within those shifts and changes, the brewery, which had only nominal existence in 1940, becomes much more richly, if more ambiguously, represented as a solid presence in the novel's landscape.

What the manuscripts show us, of course, are the stages of Lowry's *own* apprehension of the brewery, dramatized in the final text as changes in Hugh's perception. Similarly, in 1940 and 1941 Yvonne discovers the Consul in the Bella Vista "talking, apparently to himself, for the barman was at a little distance and did not have the air of listening" (25:19, 1; 29:1, 1). When the barman next appears (29:2, 3-4), he creates precisely the same first impression, but now follows a correction: "Then she saw she was mistaken about the barman, who was listening after all. Or rather, while he might not understand what the Consul was saying, he was waiting, his towelled hands swivelling the glasses more slowly, for an opening to say or do something" (cf. *Volcano* 45-46). Lowry's second thoughts become Yvonne's (and I would wager that his third thoughts, the "Or rather" sentence, were exactly that, coming third in the text because they occurred "third" to Lowry). We are looking, of course, once more at Lowry's grasp of process, his rendering of the movement of the mind creating a sense of immediacy of apprehension that is a crucial component of the kinetic quality of his prose. Still another component, however, is an adequate representation of the moment beyond "platitude of statement," a bestowing on the bare "barman," as on the equally naked "brewery," of a solidity of specification that gives Yvonne's altered perception substance: "towelled hands swivelling a glass," the picking up of the Consul's cigarette, inhaling, "closing his eyes with an expression of playful ecstasy," and so on.

Lowry no doubt intended the novel to convey his kinetic sense from the start. One of the many "statements" of the 1940 *Volcano* is an only slightly different casting of Jacques's early observation on his walk, "How continually, how startlingly the landscape changed!" (*Volcano* 9; cf. *1940* 15). The key reflection that in its implications would bring this abstraction to life by placing a perceiver at the center, however—"if you cared to think so"—does not appear until later (28:23 "II," 1). Jacques's comment concerns spatial change—Lowry is establishing Mexico as microcosm, evocative of the Cotswolds, Windermere, New Hampshire, the Sahara, and so on—but to a peripatetic observer, those "changes" occur only over time, and once the observer himself becomes central ("if you cared to think so") such "change" no longer depends wholly on the exterior world. In Lowry's day book, as in Joyce's and Woolf's, clocks strike and bells chime to mark the relentless forward march of time, but the minds of the characters, just as relentlessly carried back to retrieve some part of the past, create a countermovement to the forward drive of *chronos*. What distinguishes such passages in Lowry is guilt, the remorse over past acts felt by all his characters, bringing forward the painful past until it "poisons" the present moment (to borrow Hugh's metaphor) and thereby invests it with its troubled kinetic power. Geoffrey groaning in the bathroom over the hour lost to his blackout bears more than a family resemblance to Hugh writhing on the day bed over his various irresponsibilities, and a Laruelle whose mind as his recollections approach the affair with Yvonne snaps into an association of the approaching storm with "love which came too late" is not very different from an Yvonne who stumbles in confusion because her imagination has managed to erase Jacques's unique house from her memory of Quauhnahuac. None of these passages existed in early drafts: the urgent impingement of the guilty past had to await the creation of consciousness to contain it.

But action tends to generate counteraction in Lowry: every movement contains the seeds of its opposite, its reversal. If the unshriven past gradually invades present consciousness, so does the struggle to overcome that past and create a possible future. Only gradually does Lowry discover that this is the real thrust of Yvonne's return, however compromised by her thoughtlessness, her romanticism, her attraction to Hugh; only gradually does he find genuine content for Hugh's idealism, despite his self-aggrandizing, his ineffectuality, his longing for Yvonne; only gradually does he create in Geoffrey a true desire for Yvonne and all she represents, despite his bitterness, his love of the cantinas, his drinking. Only gradually, in short, does Lowry discover that these are the real interlocking dramas of his novel, replacing the static set piece of youth vs. age, love vs. death, Hugh and Yvonne vs. the Consul that had constituted the 1940 *Volcano*. The Consul's is, of course, the most complex case, but the simpler example of Hugh can stand as illustration.

A distant supporter of the Spanish Republic, young Hugh Fernhead had been an almost stereotypically idealistic American, but his life had no real focus, as exemplified by the flimsy bet with his uncle that supposedly lies behind his rather casual trip "round the Horn," and he worries vaguely about his lack of commitment to much of anything other than "doing good." When in 1941 he becomes the Consul's brother and the former lover of Yvonne, now his ex-sister-in-law, the text has been simplified, much of the political talk apparently excised, although Hugh retains his allegiance to the communist movement. What his age is, why he is in Mexico at all, what he has been doing with his life are now far from clear. Nor, despite acquiring a past affair with

Yvonne, is it apparent how deeply he is disturbed about that. What *is* clear is that when he and Yvonne once more declare their love at the end of Chapter XI, that love is doomed not only by the global war now underway, but by the shadow of the abandoned Consul, who, in Yvonne's final vision, already "separates" them.

In the subsequent phase, Hugh is saturated in guilt. Now a journalist, his savage attack on that profession reveals, he admits, his own self-loathing. He has been to China, but not to Spain, yet despite regret over his absence, he has no plans to go there. His guilt on reencountering Yvonne is quite explicit, and their remorseful embrace at the end of Chapter IV (29:12, A–D) is fraught on both sides with longing and reluctance. In the next drafts, Hugh's concern with Spain focuses for the first time on the Battle of the Ebro and his own absence from it, but this guilt is underlined now by his having been in Spain earlier and left at his paper's instruction, an act he judges as feckless. In atonement, he intends to sail with the *Noemijolea* and its load of dynamite for the Republican armies. This is the countermove of the future to guilt from the past, yet this act too Lowry cannot leave uncountered, making clear that part of Hugh's motivation is a deep, even suicidal, need for punishment: he half expects (and contemplates with apparent equanimity) both that the gesture comes too late to aid the Republic and that he will in any case be "blown to smithereens." Meanwhile, as a way of relieving his guilt over Yvonne, he now encourages her plan for getting Geoffrey away from Mexico while trying to quell his own skepticism over its possible success. A brief "half passionless" embrace tones down the end of IV.

Sexual tension between Hugh and Yvonne is a feature of all post-1940 drafts, but Lowry gradually subtilizes his presentation until, in the published novel, a reader may be uncertain just how determinate a factor it is, and in precisely which ways, in motivating actions and responses on this fateful day. Certainly Hugh's reactions mix memory and desire, as he is often aware, but Lowry will, for instance, reduce even the awkward embrace at the end of IV to one arm thrown protectively over her shoulder, then to a stance "side by side," without physical contact. Has "Judas been, somehow, redeemed," as Hugh thinks near the end of IV? The long retrospective passage that next enters Chapter VI wrestles with other guilts until, belatedly, Hugh himself draws the connection between those and his response to Yvonne: "All his resolutions of this morning were to no avail. It seemed useless to struggle further with these thoughts.... At least they would take his mind from Yvonne for a time, if they only led back to her in the end" (27:11, 184). Again, Lowry's sense of the motion and change of life prevents him from showing any "resolution" as final, any battle as definitively and lastingly won. By this time, however, we are aware of Hugh's tendency to "pose," and not just by the cowboy outfit he's decked out in. His private projection of himself on the *Noemijolea* in the next draft of Chapter IV now further complicates that act of dedicated and half-suicidal expiation with a characteristic moment of grandiosity as, fantasizing himself at the wheel, "it was not a ship he was steering now, but the world, out of the Western Ocean of its misery" (29:14, 8). It seems fitting, then, given Hugh's guilt and his always compromised gestures of atonement, that this is the same draft that introduces the balancing figure of Juan Cerillo, with his moralized life: "the banality stood: that the past was irrevocably past. And conscience had been given man to regret it only in so far as that might change the future. For man, every man, Juan seemed to say, even as Mexico, must ceaselessly struggle upward. What was life but a warfare and a stranger's sojourn?" (29:14, 11). This salutary reminder (echoing the novel's epigraph from Goethe) of "the passionate, yet so nearly always hypocritical, affirmation of . . . the desire to be, to do, good, what was right" (29:14, 23) is of course, whatever Juan "seemed to say," a lesson drawn by Hugh himself.

The Hugh that emerges is thus a figure whose idealism, while genuine, is also riddled with guilt and serves as a form of escapism. It rather resembles his relation to the guitar, explored in the late retrospective passage of VI. Hugh is convinced that "it had strung [me] to life," but an undergraduate cartoonist had drawn an "immense" instrument, "inside which an oddly familiar infant was hiding, curled up, as in a womb" (30:3, 31, 28). Connected to "life," retreating from it: both can easily find support in the text. Consider our "last" views of Hugh, characteristically dual. They are indirect, Hugh reflected in articles that are extensions of him or in the eyes of a sympathetic/unsympathetic witness. One occurs in Chapter XII. It is our final sense of Hugh when the novel is read in traditionally linear fashion, Hugh manifested in his anarchist card and telegram, both left in the pocket of the Consul's borrowed jacket to be discovered by the chiefs and become instruments in Geoffrey's end. This Hugh both believes in the vision of a new world order (even if naively skeptical of the fascist presence his own telegram announces) and is typically careless, even irresponsible, in the immediate actualities of life, a carelessness that contributes to his brother's death precisely at the hands of those fascist sympathizers whose existence he doubts. At the other end of the novel—Chapter I—is our final chronological view of Hugh, here as he figures in Laruelle's recollections. Jacques had first found him "an irresponsible bore, a professional indoor Marxman, vain and self-conscious really, but affecting a romantic 'extroverted' air." Yet by the time Hugh had departed, "an eternity had been lived through," and the figure who had gone was the genuine (if, it now seems to Jacques, naive) idealist who "still dreamed, even then, of changing the world . . . through his actions." It is hardly surprising that these passages are late entries to their respective chapters (31:12, 19; and Texas I, 7–8), nor that the one in Chapter XII is the earlier—nor that they strike similar notes, chiming on a frequency that provides a complex, even contradictory glimpse, a summation of the essential Hugh.

At its uncomfortable beginning and end, Hugh's retrospective passage in Chapter VI fits the kinetic, past-impinging-on-the-present pattern I have described above, yet the lengthy central section, proceeding unruffled, narratively undisturbed, like the parallel ones given to Jacques in Chapter I and Yvonne in Chapter IX, was designed as a "long *straight* passage" (*Letters* 74–75). Whatever other functions they may serve, these were intended to introduce "a much needed ozone" (*Letters* 75) into what had by that stage of composition become the *Volcano* at its unrelievedly densest, characterized by a prose wrought to the fiercest intensity of consciousness Lowry could manage. It was, he decided, too much, or too much of a single muchness, an urgency so unbroken, so oppressive, that it risked losing its power, to become at last monotonous, tedious. Thus here we have one manifestation of what Lowry called "rhythm"; indeed, he told Jonathan Cape that the Taskerson episode of Chapter I was justified "musically . . . as relief" (*Letters* 68–69). Reinforced by his extensive trials with poetry during the years of the *Volcano* revisions, Lowry's already developed musical sense seems to have come into play with everything from the movements of individual sentences to the structuring of blocks of material and the designing of whole chapters as contrapuntal pieces in the book he called "a kind of symphony," or "a kind of opera" or "hot music."

Although the metaphor this time is aesthetic, once more we are dealing with a sense of the novel as constantly and everywhere a figure in motion.[4]

On the level of the sentence, rhythm is one vital component of the notion I have been calling "voice" (which encompasses such matters as tone, idiom, and syntax as well)—almost entirely a phenomenon of the revising process. Examples are everywhere: the introduction of the repeated "now, now he wanted to go" into the extant passage on the cantinas in the early morning to invest it with erotic urgency (Chapter III); the revision of the silent "address" to Hugh from the stones of the Calle Nicaragua to give it the interjective quality of the spoken word, and the parallel recasting of the internal disquisition of Chapter X on the religious rituals of India; the deliberate diagrammming of the passage on the stars of XI to create its great "wheeling" rhythms; the abrupt undermining of the sudden paragraph "The bar was empty, however" in Chapter II; the chopping up of syntax and dropping of connectives from "Laruelle's" fully coherent speech of Chapter VII (30:7, 28–29) to create the ellipses of fragmentation at the Café Paris. Indeed, ellipsis in the *Volcano*, creating repeatedly a rhythm of broken or incomplete discourse, is a topic in its own right: is there another novel that can boast a comparable display of dashes and dots? More often than not, these are genuine textual suppressions, the result of Lowry's clipping of a longer passage to create interruption, a lacuna in awareness, a pause or abrupt shift, gaps, in short, of various kinds and various lengths (he tried in vain to convince Albert Erskine of the need for different length dashes). If these omissions can hardly be apparent to a reader of the final text, the created rhythm of ellipsis— interruption, breakdown, incompletion—can be felt everywhere.

Lowry was conscious of rhythm in another sense when building overt or implicit arguments among his figures. Here, "rhythm" was characteristically a form of counterpoint, although sometimes of a complex kind. The bus passengers' debate over what might be done to help the dying Indian, a passage somewhere between *oratorio oblique* and fully dramatized dialogue, was originally termed a "fugue," and Hugh and the Consul's contribution called a dispute "with rather than against one . . . another like two musical instruments" (26:1, 16). Although the designation (but not the passage it characterizes) disappears, the use of "refrain" to describe the antiphonal keynotes "Pobrecito" and

"Chingarn" (26:1, 15) persists. The disputational passages of X and XII are more complex and required fuller orchestration, but the principle of their development is analogous. Indeed, the very use of the Tlaxcalan folder in the late revision of Chapter X owes much to Lowry's musical sense of structure for such episodes. The extended dinnertable argument of earlier drafts, while ideologically muddled, was a coherent passage reported in conventional fullness. The introduction of the travel folder, however, permitted Lowry not only the counterpointing of the stilted and unidiomatic English of the brochure by the voices of the characters, but, with the further reduction of those voices (and others!) to brief broken phrases, created a fugal playing of them against one another, thereby anticipating the barroom episode of XII. Although his intentions in that climactic chapter were evident from the first, the final version of XII presents the *Volcano*'s most elaborate antiphony. In 1940, the episode in the open barroom was preceded by a rather mechanical intercutting of passages from Priscilla's letters with portions of a dream recounted by the German silver miner, a love vs. death duel entirely separate from the later scene. Lowry quickly saw, however, that those letters, since their plea was to be defeated, had to enter more urgently into the larger dispute, to become one of the potent, if finally lost, voices in that auditory microcosm. "Babel" he might openly call it, yet this was not a chaos of incoherence, but an elaborately structured disorder. One need only compare the final section of Joyce's "Oxen of the Sun" episode in *Ulysses* to see the difference: the melange of voices in Burke's pub spews out a jumble of dialects and argots almost impossible to penetrate and, unrelieved by narrative context, usurps the discourse, creating a verbal soup where individual voices can be identified only occasionally. In the *Volcano*, however, while meaning may not always be certain, voices are clear, separate, and almost always recognizable: the Consul, the various "chiefs," the pimp, the "sailor," Yvonne, the radio, Weber, Hugh's telegram all have their distinctive modes of utterance. "The confusion of tongues" it may be, but individual tongues are immediately distinguishable.

A different kind of rhythm is involved in the orchestrating of various motifs or themes through the texture of the work. Some of these are largely in place by 1940 and persist, with modifications, through the drafts. The dog, for example, is in one respect more prominent in 1940 than in 1947, for not only do the foreboding pariah variety and the benign "woolly" creature of Chapter IV appear there, but so does a Scotty belonging to the neighboring ambassador. First called "Angus," later "Ferdy," his role will gradually be reduced until it becomes a mere ride-on in the back seat of one of the diplomatic vehicles of Chapter VIII. On the other hand, and perhaps surprisingly, the particular pariah that provides the ominous final note of Chapter II, recurs at the opening of III, and then is ambiguously echoed near the start of Chapter V will make these related appearances only later, while the metaphorical Faustian "black dog" that seems to settle on the Consul's back in the Farolito enters the drafts only in Texas XII (25). Even a pattern as well established as this one thus undergoes thematic and structural modification as revisions proceed.

Pursued far enough, this dimension of Lowry's sense of rhythm can lead to an unstringing of virtually the entire novel. His manner of weaving such references through his text is most easily seen in his introduction of new material. In its narrowest use, it may be as simple as Hugh's guilty refrain, "They are losing the battle of the Ebro." That line enters the revisions with a number of other references to the Spanish war, most dropped into Hugh's chapters (IV, VI, VIII), but several sown elsewhere, as briefly but pointedly as the mysteriously uttered name of the ill-fated munitions ship intercepted by Franco's blockade, "*Mar Cantábrico.*" This reference crops up first in Chapter XII (Texas XII, 28), then, much later, in Chapter X (31:7, F). In both cases the name seems to materialize out of thin air, attributable to no recognizable speaker; nor is it clear what relation the two utterances might be said to bear to one another. What *is* clear is that, however these appearances are explained, they become a part of a complex web of references not only to the Spanish war generally, but to Hugh's intended journey on the *Noemijolea* specifically and, in the context of X, in counterpoint to Cortez's ships, with which they are juxtaposed. However, as a ship on a disguised mission, the reference also recalls the Consul's *Samaritan* (thus perhaps its juxtaposition with Weber in XII?), which is of course ironically related to the incident of Chapter VIII.... (and so on and on).

Similarly, if we begin with material related to India, we are soon enmeshed in the many-stranded fabric of the novel. Starting with geographical references once the Firmin brothers have been born in Kashmir, moving on to a few Raj idioms ("pukka," "wog," "rajah"), following with religious and historical references, Lowry gradually integrated

Indian matter into evolving drafts. As with the references to the Spanish war, there are usually dense nodes for such matter—geography in Chapter III, for instance, religious ritual in Chapter X—but these are only centers from which allusions radiate throughout (Asals, "Indian Sources"). Again, these may be simple textual additions, like the analogy to "a dream of a dying Hindu" affixed to the boy of Chapter VI, who was already "steering [some cows] by their tails" (30:2, 7), and *the wheel of the law, rolling*" dropped into the description of the Ferris wheel of Chapter VII (Texas VII, 27). Or they may be as extended and important as the "dream" that opens Chapter V. In any case, once begun, the references to India appear literally from beginning ("the town of Juggernaut, in India, on the Bay of Bengal") to end ("He was in Kashmir, he knew, lying in the meadows near running water among violets and trefoil, the Himalayas beyond"), making connections with extant matters of psychology, geography, politics, religion, myth, forming a suite in their own right, but also orchestrated into the larger polyphonic harmonics of the evolving text.

Part of Lowry's notion of this "musical" interweaving of elements of his text is articulated in a letter to his German translator, Clemens ten Holder. Ten Holder had questioned him about the voice "from beyond the glass partition" in Chapter II, the voice of Weber. Lowry first explains using the language of structural dynamics: "Weber . . . belongs to a kind of sub-sub-sub plot of the novel. He is not very important, in one way, and yet he has to be there, bracing something far down within the substructure of the whole" (Hilton 46). He goes on to point out his reappearance in Chapter XII and the bearing of this on "the Consul's fate," as well as the "obscurely . . . suggested . . . reactionary uprising" his presence in Parián might imply, then comments, "I am aware that this may seem insanely complicated as well as needlessly obscure in Chapter II, but the purpose seems to have been musical more than anything in that chapter . . . a contrapuntal device, as it were, that at the same time is a motif of fate. As such . . . he almost seems to answer Yvonne's and the Consul's voice [sic] and make comment on *their* situation." Weber seems to complete Yvonne's sentence, Lowry says, "as if he were another instrument taking up the theme on a different plane." "What I was striving for [in the novel]," he concludes, "was richness of orchestration" (Hilton 47–49).

The retrieval of Weber out of the discarded Acapulco chapter and his local "contrapuntal" function illustrates another level of "musicality" in the text, the arranging of blocks of material within a chapter. Like the creation of the "flashback" episodes of I, VI, and IX, the discarding of the German miner's story and moving of some of Yvonne's letters into the barroom passage in Chapter XII come out of a similar sense of rhythmic fitness. In this respect, Lowry's handling of late revisions of Chapter IX is instructive. Having decided that the keynote of the chapter is to be "hope," he first elaborated Yvonne's vision of the seaside home she and Geoffrey will share, a vision that in its rich natural images and sense of fulfillment counterpoints the present scene of dusty barrenness and irresolution in the bullring before her. Yet taken by itself the vision, coming late in the chapter, seems a confirmation of its opening, Yvonne's sense of the ease of shucking off the burdens of the past, a sense based on little more than her earlier drinks. The vision of a personal future needed, Lowry realized, the counterweight of a personal past: thus the appearance of Yvonne's flashback, a history that, like Mexico's, cannot simply be "laughed away" ("The novel . . . is as it were, teetering between past and future" [*Letters* 81]). Yet intercut as it is with the situation in the arena, not only does the flashback as a whole counterbalance the later imagined future, but it seems both to arise out of present action—the entangled bull, Yvonne's encumbered father—and also to reflect back on it: "Consul to Iquique! . . . Or Quauhnahuac!" Immediate counterpoint is even more intricate. Sketches of Yvonne's father and her early life and career were part of Lowry's earliest effort with the flashback (30:14 and Templeton 1:3); the press release and the film of Yvonne Griffaton came only later (Templeton 1:4). The first, with its fan magazine prose of ersatz excitement and hollow predictions of a "happy" future (Yvonne's comeback), is played off against the nightmare journey through New York, culminating in the symbolically portentous film. Thus both the sinister possibilities hinted at by the film and the falseness of the press release's predicted future subtly undercut Yvonne's own increasingly concrete imaginings of the shack and her happy life to come with Geoffrey.

This is to look only at the arrangement of large blockings of material—closer examination of the prose of Chapter IX, for instance, would reveal how elaborate Lowry's interweaving of motifs and counterpointing of themes can be—yet an even wider lens brings into focus the counterpointing of entire chapters. The commentary to Cape repeatedly stresses their "contrast" to one another; of Chapter IX he says that "musically speaking [it] ought to be a good contrast to VIII and X" (*Letters* 80). The contrasting was rooted in the alternation of central consciousnesses so that no sequential chapters would be mediated by the same figure, but Lowry was not about to rest his contrapuntal sense in mere "character," nor to leave his chapters as simple contrasts to one another. "Each chapter," he insisted to Cape, "is a unity in itself and all are related and interrelated" (*Letters* 65). Since after 1940 he largely took his plot for granted, he was freed to devote himself to concerns of structure and texture that would realize both the individual unity of his chapters and their "interrelat[ionships]."

For instance, he notes to Cape that the emphasis of Chapter III is "the action of the mind," whereas IV presents physical action (which also "supplies a needed *ozone*"). Chapter V, then, "is a contrast in the reverse direction, the opening words having an ironic bearing on the last words of IV," for now the novel is "fast sinking into the action of the mind" (*Letters* 73). Yet if the opening passage of V is ultimately "ironic," it is so because it at first must seem a *continuation* of Chapter IV. As the "dream" disintegrates into the Consul's compulsive desire for a drink, what disintegrates for the reader is the illusion that we are following Hugh and Yvonne and the dog as they resume their journey. The landscape at the close of IV had "resembled a sea," and Hugh had sensed "beyond the volcanoes . . . the wide rolling blue ocean itself"; now, "they reached the briny sea." Chapter IV ends on the note of his "immeasurable longing," the "desire to be, to do, good, what was right"; the travelers of V journey "with heaven aspiring hearts" (29:12, A–D; 29:17, 1).

The dream is, of course, a late addition to Chapter V, appearing in the same draft as the initial version of the blackout toward the other end of the chapter, the reciprocal alterations most profoundly responsible for this chapter's movement "away from normal action." For Chapter V did not always "fast sink[ ] into the action of the mind." When the Consul "sauntered" in the 1940 garden, his calm observations occupied only the opening sixth of the chapter, the remainder being primarily devoted to dialogue with Quincey, Vigil, Hugh, and Yvonne. The "feverish" quality of the whole, the keynote of which is struck as the dream dissolves into the obsessive "light, light, light, and again, of light, light, light, light, light!" (29:17, 1), the desperate plunge for the tequila bottle, the voices, the vision, the "routine hallucination," and so on are all the product of revision, as is the imitation of Taskerson, the hiccups, the open fly, the desperate comedy of the drunkard. The chapter always ended with the insect vision and the hallucinatory sound of warning, pleading voices, but only when he devised the obsessive dream and the tempting "familiars" of the opening did Lowry find a start to match it.

The same draft that introduces the dream also first presents the doubtful pariah dog (see chapter 3, pp. 182–83): "'Perro' he repeated ... but had not this incident occurred, was it not now as it were occurring an hour or two ago" (29:17, 3). Or, alternatively, a chapter or two ago? An echo of the dream dog, the passage more deliberately echoes the revised opening of Chapter III, in which the Consul's same address to a pariah dog sends the animal skittering back down the drive. Chapter V had always begun with the Consul walking in his garden, and with the addition of the "same" dog encountered at the start of Chapter III, where the Consul had been walking up his drive, we are invited to compare these chapter-opening strolls. In V he is now no longer walking (or "sauntering"): he is "almost running," indeed "lurching." Once more, he seems to hear voices, but rather than the mournful interlocutor and commentator ("Regard ... Look ... See") of III, "a protective screen of demons gnattering in his ears" is the accompanying chorus, which ultimately separates, much as in III, into the recognizable tones of the familiars. This deliberate echolalia creates for Lowry a pattern—ultimately all of the *Volcano* is one vast echo chamber—whereby we may recognize both sameness and difference, the repetition that simultaneously denies advance and measures a further stage along the narrative path, the tension between motion and fixity in still another guise. It is one of the subtlest yet surest means by which chapters are "interrelated."

However, the matter is (as Lowry would say) more complicated. We may fairly easily recognize the echoes of III in V (particularly with a nudge from the repetition of the dog incident): after all, as sequential chapters mediated by the Consul, why wouldn't they have some such connection? The intervening Chapter IV, however, is Hugh's first chapter, and Lowry speaks of it to Cape in simple terms of contrast to its surroundings. But at the same stage of revision (post-1941: 29:12), the opening action became another walk down the same drive that the Consul had traversed to start the previous chapter, this time taken at a different pace and with a different focus. Hugh is moving so slowly he "less than sauntered"—Geoffrey at the start of V will "hardly be supposed [to be] just sauntering"—and he stops on the edge of a "deep pothole," one of those same "gaping potholes" noted on the Consul's walk of III. Geoffrey's alienation is proclaimed in words, articulated by an internal voice that both addresses and manifests his distance from a world defined in natural and religious images; Hugh's alienation is expressed in his action—or inaction, for he not only "stops" on the drive but has also stopped, with the telegram he holds, his professional career. The Consul gazes at a world "livid and crepuscular through his dark glasses"; Hugh thinks he must have "eyes in my feet" not to have fallen into the pothole, but when he raises his gaze, "his heart and the world stopped too." Geoffrey had seen a sinisterly eroticized garden, plants "struggling like dying voluptuaries in a vision"; Hugh sees a sublimated erotic glory, an Yvonne apparently "clothed in the sunlight filling the garden." The connection is underlined, a little awkwardly in the earliest version, by the information that Hugh carries "his brother's jacket" toward "his brother's house," and that his bag is "also borrowed from his brother" (29:12, 2–3). Since he is dealing with the same setting, Lowry can even move the image of weaving "between floribundia and rose" from Chapter IV at this stage (29:12, 2) back to a comparable spot in Chapter III at the next (29:9, 1).

I have underlined parallels and connections here, for the differences are obvious enough (sufficiently so that, to my knowledge, no one has noted resemblances). We are of course being introduced to the characteristically individual manner of perception and response of these two figures; more subtly, Lowry is at work setting them up as doubles; perhaps more subtly still, he is creating those "interrelat[ionships]" among his chapters that reach beyond matters of "character." For instance, the opening of IV will be recalled again in another direction in V: I have already noted the echo of "saunter," an echo all the more evident in that as description it is raised in V *only* in order to be denied ("it could hardly be supposed he was just sauntering"). But by this phase of revision, both chapters are also set to open with enigmatic passages, passages that seem to float detached from any context or mooring that would enable us to grasp them on first encounter. Always aware of the visual impact of the printed page, Lowry will later cast both into italics as if to ratify their mysterious textual status. At once (but nonetheless retrospectively: again Lowry places the reader in the pluperfect, forcing the mind backward) we will learn that what we have read in IV is a telegram, yet that information will hardly be enough to decode it ("What is this—the message from Garcia? What in the world does it mean?" [29:12, 5]): our understanding must await Hugh's still-later explanation. Analogously, in V, although we are never told directly that this is a dream, we may infer it from, yet again, the *later* information that the Consul "had woken up a moment or two ago." Meaning here is, of course, never glossed, one difference between telegram and dream, message and myth, politics and poetry. Further, beyond italics, the physical movement of both men, different as the gait may be, is toward the alternative to all that is implied in those opening passages. Hugh's antipolitical walk toward Yvonne will be underlined in the next draft by the introduced refrain, "He was advancing (just as, on the Ebro, it occurred to him, they were retreating)" (29:13, ms. 1), whereas Geoffrey's nonsauntering lurch-becoming-a-run is toward the secreted tequila bottle, hardly a sign of a soul "well-disciplined." Hugh seems to undergo a single vision, a figure "woven from the filaments of the past," which turns into the solid-enough person of Yvonne, whereas Geoffrey "crashe[s] on through the metamorphoses of dying and reborn hallucinations" (29:17, 2) to his vision of the dog, whose ontological status remains impossible to determine.

The "musical" echoes among the openings of just these three chapters help us see what Lowry meant by terming them "related and interrelated." However, he also claimed that "Each chapter is a unity in itself." That, indeed, would seem to be a product of his very method of revision by chapter, focusing on them as quasi-independent entities to be dealt with separately. Since each was provided with its distinctively presiding consciousness (and even as they recur, they do not reappear in the same phase: Yvonne's nervous anxiety of Chapter II, for instance, is not her hopefulness of Chapter IX), Lowry from 1941 had provided himself with a putative intrachapter unity that he then had to realize. One of the ways in which he did so was congruent with his conception of the novel as trochal: if the *Volcano* was to be a wheel, then individual chapters might be wheels within the wheel. Once more, motion and stillness, process and product, the dynamic and the static would be satisfied, for while each chapter moved narratively forward, it would circle back at the end to echo its beginning. Thus Lowry in revision paid a good deal of attention to openings and closings, sometimes moving chapter divisions set up in the 1940 version, more frequently devising new beginnings. Closings, curiously, tended to be arrived at early and to retain their original forms.

Nowhere is this structuring clearer than in Chapter IX—and this had been true since 1940. Indeed, in that version the organization had been too clear, mechanically so, the echoes too blatant, the "mirror" structure too obviously a formalist device. The chapter had opened and (almost) closed at Las Novedades with dialogue about telephones and requests for the time of day, in which Lowry had to strain unconvincingly to work both his puns—"Half past tree by the cock," "Half past sick by the cock"—into an action that appears to occupy about one hour (*1940* 253, 285). After both requests, the clock from the San Francisco church is heard to chime. Then, working in inverse order, at the start of the chapter the conversing "grandees" pass our travelers, just as immediately *preceding* the time request near the chapter's end, they pass again. At the front of the chapter, the trio next observes an apparent lake that they discover to be glass; near the close, just *before* the passing grandees, they note "the glass roof was a lake of silver" (*1940* 284). This rather elaborate paralleling, however, is somewhat undone by the very end, which takes them to the Todos Contentos y Yo Tambien (thereby echoing the close of the previous chapter) and the sight of the two old Indians, much as in the published novel. It is a powerful image, but it has no bearing on the structure—and little, in this version, on the contents—of Chapter IX.

Lowry's initial alterations (30:12 and 13) tone down and cut away the more mechanical parallels, but a new observation of the crowd in the arena points Lowry toward a revised structure: "What a good time everyone was having, Yvonne thought, how *happy* they were, how happy everyone was, how gaily the inhabitants of Mexico laughed away its tragic history, the underlying death" (30:13, 5). With some adjustments, that became the next draft's opening sentence, and with this evocation of mood and theme, the entire previous opening, reduced to the exchange at Las Novedades, becomes Yvonne's recollection, passes into the pluperfect ("Geoffrey had said ... she had cried"), a moment of "history" itself, to which, now, a piece of Yvonne's individual past gets attached, her memory of fainting at the sight of the blood of a dying dog (30:14, 1–3, and 31:1, 1–4). There is little enough "history," still, to deal with, and Yvonne is not yet overtly mistaken about Mexico's "laugh[ter]," but the opening is now echoed ironically by the closing, a reassertion of "history" in whatever sense one chooses to take it.

It is not necessary to rehearse again ensuing stages of Chapter IX— Yvonne's visions of the future, her recollections of the past—to see that in a sense the securing of the structure of opening and closing has suggested the themes to be orchestrated in the body of the chapter.[5] Yvonne's eventual mistake about the mood of the arena and its implications is the result not simply of drinks on the bus, but of her deep desire to overcome her own and Geoffrey's "tragic past," to move on to an envisioned future. Thus Lowry will develop her gradually enlarging visions of life in the shack *before* recognizing that her misreading of the crowd necessitates a confrontation with her own past, a confrontation that ends indecisively, trailing off into vague "hope." So the structure of the chapter comes to depend not on verbal parallels and echoes, as did the 1940 version, but on the more richly explored themes of "history," evolved out of that final episode that had refused to become a part of the earlier structure. The two old Indians of course present to the protagonists an impersonal vision of history, "Mexico's history," if we like, and so it is only proper that the chapter begin by invoking this larger perspective before wheeling round to the soberly ironic refutation of that keynote opening, the reassertion of "this weight of the past."

Like the novel as a whole, whose final chapter in 1940 was far more richly developed than its opening, Lowry seemed to have the knack of finding resonant closings for his chapters before devising openings that satisfied him. As the only ending to get relocated, that of Chapter VI illustrates Lowry's gradual discovery of his structure. In 1940 and 1941, the chapter ended at a seemingly logical narrative point, just as our trio was to leave the Consul's house, closing on a note of Hugh's slightly hysterical laughter at their indecisiveness (*1940* 186–87). Chapter VII then opened with the departure, its events little different from those that endure. In early versions the Consul discards the unexpected postcard after a glance at message and picture; here it has no special importance, seems merely one of a number of incidental events (that the Consul receives in the same mail an appeal from a conservation charity further diminishes it). Only in the next draft when the chapter's action is carried on beyond leavetaking, does the postcard achieve its permanent prominence.

By making the confrontation with the postcard the climactic act of this mid-chapter of his novel, Lowry confirms the significance of the theme of missed communications. Now the Consul does not throw the card away, and the last thing we contemplate in the chapter is the description of its face: "There was a picture of the leonine Signal Peak on El Paso with Carlsbad Cavern Highway leading over a white fenced bridge between desert and desert. The road turned a little corner in the distance and vanished" (30:1, 25–26). The concentration here of the novel's symbolic geography—mountain, abyss, pilgrim's road—extant since 1940, now comes into sharp focus through placement. Yet it will take two more drafts (2:19 verso 2, August 1951 letter to Markson) for Lowry to find the Dantean opening ("Nel mezzo del cammin . . .") to echo this geography at the chapter's other end, and still another to repeat, underline, and translate it ("In the middle of our life, in the middle of the bloody road of our life") (27:11, 183). With that opening, the postcard at the closing takes on another dimension, affording the brothers who contemplate it—and who, after Hugh's contemplation of the road of his life, have shared the space of this chapter—a New World depiction of Dantean geography. It is not accidental that at the end of this chapter we are precisely *nel mezzo del cammin* of the novel.

As Lowry labored on, the evolving novel seems to have become both more complex and progressively clearer to him, like a tapestry in which the weaving of newly colored threads brings the central design into sharper relief. As a result, intrachapter echoing became a device more deliberately and rapidly deployed. Late (1944) additions of the train vision and the Tlaxcala folder to Chapter X afford an example. The very first and last things in Chapter X had been fixed in the previous draft: "'Mescal,'" already identified by the Consul as the drink signalling his end, was to open it, and the hints of personal and cosmic "end"— the choice of "Hell," the approaching storm, the ominous looming of "massive interests"—to close it. Immediately within, however, first fruit, as it were, of the mescal, comes the new train vision with its thundering *"clipperty"* refrain, and later in the draft, the contrapuntal employment of the Tlaxcalan folder. As we approach the other end of the chapter, and the Consul, rounding viciously on Hugh and Yvonne, declares that he has "'made up my melodramatic little mind,'" once again the train vision intervenes. What is of interest here is that this is *exact* repetition, word for word matching that portion of the earlier vision to which it corresponds (Texas X, 1–3, 46–48). The sole modification here is that framing the train vision is the stuttering recall of the travel brochure, the "Tlax -Tlax" becoming an alternative refrain echoing and merging with the "clipperty's" and "lickety's" of the rushing trains, bringing together here at the end these two new major strains in the chapter in a feverish, obsessive climax. The Consul is fast passing into his "whirling cerebral chaos"; Lowry, on the other hand, has never been more controlled. As one manifestation of his "musical sense," structure has become so intimately woven into texture that the two have become finally inseparable.

On the largest scale, this echoing of beginnings and ends is seen most clearly in the opening and closing chapters of the novel. As Lowry said to Cape of Chapter XII, "This chapter is the easterly tower, Chapter I being the westerly, at each end of my churrigueresque Mexican cathedral, and all the gargoyles of the latter are repeated with interest in this. While the doleful bells of one echo the doleful bells of the other, just as the hopeless letters of Yvonne the Consul finally finds here answer the hopeless letter of the Consul M. Laruelle reads precisely a year later in Chapter I" (*Letters* 85) Yet as he also said, the chapter had to serve as culmination—"All the strands of the book, political, esoteric, tragic, comical, religious, and what not are here gathered together" (*Letters* 84)—and the two analogies, drawn from architecture and weaving (?), at once spatial and temporal, embody his recognition that the echoing felt here had to be, as it were, both static and dynamic, causing us to look back particularly hard at the novel's opening chapter (indeed, even to reread it, and thus perhaps begin the whole round again), but striking the notes of the action developing from Chapter II onward as well, making us feel the chapter as climax.

Lowry had some sense of this double function of Chapter XII even in 1940, and as revisions unfolded the final chapter remained his bellwether. It was not, of course, untouchable—nothing was—yet he clearly sensed that the remainder of his novel needed to achieve the level of its climax, the other chapters be brought up to the standard of this one, not only in general richness of conception and execution, but in quite specific ways. What we often find him doing, therefore, is "revising backward," taking for granted an image, a motif, an action already in Chapter XII and inserting its anticipatory echo in earlier chapters, most particularly Chapter I. To be sure, new material appears in Chapter XII—the deadly "Mescal" with which it opens, for example—that needs to be incorporated into the body of the novel, and as we have seen (chapter 3, pp. 131ff.), early action is given more careful structuring (again, "musical," the contrapuntal rhythm of withdrawal and return suggesting the Consul's conflict), but the general paucity of revision after 1940 testifies to Lowry's sure recognition of his accomplishment here.

What of his echolalia had Lowry achieved in the 1940 Chapter XII? Certain matters must culminate here, like the recognizable horse, which has already appeared three times (although not in Chapter XI), immediately identifiable by its branded "7." However, this version also contains the anticipation of the horse and rider of Chapter I, although, in keeping with the simple role here assigned the Consul, in brief and uncomplicated form. True, the horseman carries a machete that the Consul, in echo, will wield in XII, where the "chiefs" punningly deny him the identity of "wrider," but Laruelle's vision in Chapter I is only of "maniacal, uncontrolled, senseless force" (*1940* 42; compare "this maniacal vision of senseless frenzy, but controlled, not quite uncontrolled, somehow almost admirable" [*Volcano* 23]). There are also replays of the banner from the Red Cross Ball (III), "con German friends" (X), Weber's distinctive speech (II), the old Tarascan woman (II), the self-identification with William Blackstone (III), the charge of "pelado" (VIII), "Old men carrying their fathers" (IX). The writing corporal recalls the morning's scribe, the Consul recollects the print-shop window and the photo of the crumbling rock (II) and thinks again of the temperance poster in Jacques's house (VII).

Still, of echoes and repetitions already in place, the most significant are those that take us back directly to Chapter I. The two notices for Dr. Vigil's practice, the more respectable visible to Jacques in town, the other "secretly" available in the mingitorio of the Farolito, complement each other. The important Babel-like confusion of tongues is already largely there (if not quite so richly orchestrated) in 1940, anticipated by the Consul's recollected identification of the pyramid at Cholula as "the original Tower of Babel" (it is one sign of what I have called the extraversion of this text that Jacques here does not speculate on "the babel of his thoughts"). Crucially echoing actions—a man enters a cantina and has returned to him, out of the past (these are, after all, Days of the Dead) writings he has forgotten he left there—these appear in 1940. The returning agents, Diosdado and the unnamed "cinema manager," have little role to play beyond these returns; they have few views of the Consul, do not appear to know him well. The letters, however, already "respond" to each other, echoing the length of the text. Priscilla/Yvonne's letters will be shifted and trimmed but will otherwise remain unaltered; the Consul's letter will be largely recomposed and extended. However, a central portion that addresses his feelings for and appeal to her is retained, and it is here that the letters, as Lowry said, "answer" each other.

"*Do you remember tomorrow?*" Priscilla/Yvonne begins. It is perhaps the earliest sign of the novel's self-consciousness; for if the Consul cannot recall the future (in 1940 he does not react to this extraordinary question: can Lowry himself not have realized its implications?) we readers certainly can, in the future/past that is the temporal mode of Chapter I. When she moves on to appeal to their love, their sense of "*us,*" to "*what we built together,*" she echoes his letter's invocation of love and of "*the unity we once knew.*" Both term themselves "*haunted*": he sees her "*in visions and in every shadow,*" she "*see[s] us in a hundred places with a hundred smiles.*" If she claims for the first time to "*understand the meaning of suicide,*" he speaks of "*a desire to destroy myself myself.*" And so on, through "*madness*" and "*sanity,*" help and helplessness. In perhaps the loneliest repetition started by the letters, the Consul's exhortation not to "*allow what we created to sink down to oblivion in this dingy fashion*" is echoed in the final chapter not by her response, but by his own recognition when, shot, he literally sinks down, alone: "'This is a dingy way to die'" (*1940* 22–26; 351–56; 375). Lowry refined and extended the contrapuntal possibilities in these letters, but his drift was clear in 1940.

Most of the deliberate construction of these echoing motifs, the interweaving of them through the text, was the work of revision, no small portion of which seems to have begun with a hint from Chapter XII. The Consul's final move toward the horse, for instance (in 1940 he does not manage to release it) is of course the germ of Yvonne's subsequent trampling. Less conspicuous is another passage that will persist almost unchanged into the published novel, but will have an altogether different import there: "The chords of a guitar too, half lost, mingled with the distant clamour of the waterfall and with what sounded like the cries of love" (*1940* 375; cf. *Volcano* 374). In 1940, what the Consul heard *were* "cries of love," Hugh and Yvonne's lovemaking at the end of Chapter XI. Guitar sounds, on the other hand, were as imaginary as the other music (Mozart, Gluck, Bach) he seems to "hear" as he lies dying. Yet within those words lies implicit both the irony of "*what sounded like the cries of love*"—Yvonne's dying moans ("how alike are the groans of love to those of the dying")—and Hugh's *actual* guitar playing that will sound out of the jungle of XI. Indeed, in that 1940 sentence lies the germ of the entire account of Hugh's guitar-playing career.

The tracing of Lowry's construction of motifs could send us trundling endlessly back and forth across the novel. Prudence demands limiting ourselves for illustrative purposes to two sets of static relationships extended through the revising process from Chapter XII. The first, and simpler, is that established with Chapter II; the other with the novel's "westerly tower," Chapter I.

The view back to Chapter II is the more "natural," for much of it can be made through the Consul's own consciousness. Even in 1940, his mind travels back via the barranca to the print-shop window, and a later passage (largely retained) rehearses a number of the day's events beginning with Yvonne's early morning arrival. Yet as he revised Lowry did not depend only on his protagonist's recollections. There is no sign, for example, that Geoffrey recognizes in XII the voice of Weber, which he has heard and commented on back in II. Nor does he seem aware of other ironic echoes of that early morning bar scene in this evening one. The neglectful A Few Fleas and his more sinister father Diosdado had been established firmly in XII from the first, but the barman of the Bella Vista had been barely noted in 1940. In revision, Fernando acquired not only a name and activity (drying glasses, smoking, exhaling, pointing, speaking, repeating), but a particular relation to the Consul, one of solemn joking, attentiveness, courteous "ritual," as Yvonne gradually recognizes. The initial impression of indifference—there was nothing to contradict it in 1940—is all the more powerfully revised in Yvonne's process of correction, and Lowry creates Fernando's respectful yet friendly presence to set against those bartenders who manifest neglect (A Few Fleas) and contempt (Diosdado) at the other end of the day. Indeed, the latter's insolence marks "the implied extent of [the

Consul's] downfall," and the longer process by which Geoffrey has reached this point of public scorn is adumbrated by the journey from his first barman to his last.

Once having established Fernando and, more gradually, his characteristic line, "Absolutamente necessario" (cf. 29:2, 4, and 29:3, 1), Lowry then evoked it in a very different tone at the other end of the Consul's day (as well as, later still, inserting it ambiguously into the mid-chapter, VII, of that day [Texas VII, 18]). Fernando pronounces his tag-line three times and is echoed "in a kind of agony" of laughing agreement by the Consul. In the Farolito, however, it is Geoffrey who first uses the emphatic Spanish adverb in denial of the "chiefs'" insuinuation that he is a Communist: "'Absolutamente no.'" The echo that comes back is a mockery, a derisive aping: "'Ab-so-lut-a-men-te hey?' The policeman, with another wink at Diosdado, imitated the Consul's manner" (Texas XII, 19). In the background, a sinister parody of Fernando, Diosdado stands "angrily drying glasses." In Chapter II it is the "woman wearing a scarlet brassiere" who is pronounced "absolutely necessary"; in Chapter XII the Consul is suspected of not paying "for Mehican girl," the "scarlet woman" María, and of being a "red" sympathizer with the Spanish Republic, the double accusation compressed into "You Bolsheviki prick?" which the Consul denies "Absolutamente."

One of the most powerful connections between Chapters II and XII occurs in the passages in each evoking Oaxaca, which Yvonne remembers in II as the place "they had found each other once" and Geoffrey in XII as "where Yvonne and he had once been happy" (*Volcano* 49, 349). But it is also where Geoffrey has gone after their separation, and so the word has come to mean "divorce" to Yvonne, and in the Consul's fevered evocation during the copulation with María, he both remembers and reenacts their "sundering." Neither of these passages, nor anything approaching them, appeared in 1940: indeed, the entire Oaxaca motif is a product of revision. Although Geoffrey, in a late addition, will associate it with Parián because of "that one other terrible cantina" (Texas VII, 7), El Infierno, that he recalls in the still later addition to Chapter XII (a compliment returned in Vigil's reference to the Farolito, "Es un infierno" [25:21, 26]), Oaxaca comes to have more ambiguous overtones than the altogether sinister Parián. Ignoring its various other appearances in the novel (nonetheless *en passant* recalling that Hugh has very different associations with Oaxaca through Juan

Cerillo), we may see how the passage in XII manages to respond to that in II (as well as to the quite distinct initial evocation of Oaxaca in Chapter I).

To Yvonne in Chapter II the name "Oaxaca" itself sounds poignantly "like a breaking heart." Associated with her and Geoffrey's love, it now seems to symbolize its loss, a loss personified as a figure "stumbling and falling" in a wasteland, "dying of thirst in the desert" (29:5, 7). The Geoffrey of Chapter XII recalls himself in Oaxaca indeed dying of thirst, literally unable to drink from a carafe of water, hearing again Señora Gregorio's *"you cannot drink of it,"* desperately in search of the alcohol that appears only obliquely, harmlessly—*"damas accompañadas de un caballero gratis!"* [sic]—in Yvonne's recollection. But Geoffrey's hallucinatory memory is the mental counterpart of his sexual act with María, who in this version both recalls Yvonne and simultaneously is her antithesis. Previously María had been presented as a broken, grotesque figure, the whore ironically named for the Virgin, the opposite in every sense of Eve-onne, Lowry's play with the inversion of these biblical female archetypes. Now, however, given the special significance of Oaxaca for Yvonne in II, the town's reintroduction here casts a more ambiguous light over the prostitute, who becomes in this version attractive, "shapely," "young and pretty," and—or so the Consul persuades himself—physically reminiscent of Yvonne; he can almost imagine for a moment that it is she to whom he is making love. This association and the girl's strange speech, "possibly Zapotecan," help to make the connection with Oaxaca, which is perhaps completed by the sudden sense that he has fallen into the infernal machine in its most treacherous form: "her body was . . . a calamity, a fiendish apparatus for calamitous sickening sensation." Yvonne's desert is replaced by a "desolate" Wagnerian sea where "one huge black sailing ship, hull down, sweeping into the sunset" suggests for this Tristan an ironic *Liebestod,* a love-as-death where Yvonne's memory of "their cries of love rising into the ancient fragrant Mayan air" is replaced by the recognition, soon to prove and reverse itself, "how alike are the groans of love to those of the dying" (Texas XII, 12A–12D). The very prose rhythms distinguish the passages all too clearly, the elegiac and wistful lyricism of Yvonne's replaced by the pounding and compulsive repetitions of Geoffrey's.

Oaxaca thus suggests not only, like Parián, pain, destruction, death, but also love and its loss (and, if we recall Juan Cerillo, possible redemption), although "the lilac shaded dawn that should have brought death" at the end of Geoffrey's Oaxaca so closely echoes "the violet-shaded" dawn of his remembered Farolito that there may for him no longer be a genuine distinction. But Geoffrey's Oaxaca passage is not simply a "response" to Yvonne's, or even, more generally, the culmination of the novel's Oaxaca motif, although it is both; it also specifically echoes, repeats, and fleshes out the opening of his letter of Chapter I. Lowry's "composition of place," apparently originating with this late version, is artfully designed to fill a number of purposes, one of which is to anticipate Yvonne's Oaxaca in the next chapter, to chime so closely with her unspoken response that we feel the attunement of this pair, to make credible their references to that entity both refer to as "us." When she left, he tells her, "I went to Oaxaca. There is no sadder word" ("'Oaxaca.' The word was like a breaking heart") and stayed "in the hotel where we once were happy" ("In Oaxaca they had found each other once," "where Yvonne and he had once been happy"). His journey there (as Yvonne imagines the fate of their love) is literally "through the desert" and indeed "terrible," but not finally so; however thirsty the Consul, "tequila out of my bottle" became balm for "the child whose life its mother and I saved by rubbing its belly" with the alcohol. Nonetheless, the Consul's Oaxaca justifies his terming it "hell," for it anticipates not Yvonne's response to their shared experience in II, but the fuller fleshing of this same trip in XII. There, again, although in less feverish rhythms, is met the sound of slaughtering from the hotel kitchen, the vulture in the washbasin, the noise of the Mexican night.

This mature version of the Consul's letter, coming late in revision, shrewdly makes use of material already established in Chapter XII. Since 1940, Priscilla/Yvonne's letters had drawn an analogy between the Consul's silence and the absence that war imposes (*"the war was not like this, it never had the power to so chill and terrify my heart"* [1940 351–52]); now Geoffrey begins by invoking a private war, "the nightly grapple with death" (28:24, 12A). "For myself," he goes on by way of introducing Oaxaca, "I like to take my sorrow into the shadow of cathedral cities, my guilt into cloisters and under tapestries, and into the misericordes of unimaginable cantinas where sad faced potters and legless beggars drink at dawn, whose cold jonquil beauty one rediscovers in death" (28:24, 12A). This imagery, embodied as experience in XII, has long since existed in Parián, where his letter is, after all, being written, in the same "little room off the bar" where in the final chapter he reads Priscilla / Yvonne's letters; there, the apparent "monastery" of the Military Police barracks and the "legless beggars" have been ensconced since 1940, joined later by the "potter," dispensers and recipients of both the misery and compassion that "misericordes" suggests. Oaxaca, "where we had been happy once," has thus already become a locale in Geoffrey's nightmare world, an extension of the "hell" typified by Parián. Further, the transposition in place occasions no surprise, for the late version of the letter (quite unlike its 1940 predecessor) has unobtrusively moved the Consul through the geographical landscape, actual and symbolic, of the entire novel, touching not only those places that suggested "shadows of our fate" before the action itself begins (Hollywood, Spain, Paris, etc.) but, in addition to Oaxaca and Parián, Quauhnahuac, Tomalín, and a visionary Canada.

Like Oaxaca, Canada has no part in the 1940 *Volcano*, although this motif had been sown through the text before Lowry reached the late version of the letter. At no time, however, is Chapter I's ecstatic vision of shared paradise matched by anything even approaching it in XII: the illustration on the calendar and the recollection of the wilderness there, the ominous search for the drowned Lithuanian, present Canada as "an undiscovered, perhaps an undiscoverable paradise," a future closed to them, Geoffrey feels, by his act with María if nothing else (Texas XII, 15). (Calendars hang in Cerveceria XX and the Farolito from 1940 onward, but the Mexican illustration of the former is not matched by a Canadian scene until later [Texas XII, second 13].) Indeed, the cock of his recollected search for the dead man has its echo in the letter's "cocks that herald dawn all night," especially as those dawns are of a "beauty one rediscovers in death." The only "paradise" of Chapter XII is the Farolito itself, the ironic "paradise of his despair" (31:12, 1), and echoes from the vision of his letter are all inversions; "the white white distant alabaster thunderclouds beyond the mountains" (28:24, 14A), for example, give way to the dark clouds of gathering storm and thunder over Mexico. For this material, the opening is indeed recalled in the closing, but with the effect of ironic loss and repudiation.

Lowry was not doctrinaire about working back from Chapter XII—a reference to Trotsky, for instance, appears in Chapter I before the Consul gets likened to him in the final chapter—but the overwhelming tendency was this inverted construction. One of the clearest instances appears in the "chiefs'" accusation in 1940 that the Consul is an "espider," a charge that in that version has no textual underpinning whatever, no mysterious figures lurking outside the Bella Vista or at Arena Tomalín and, most important, no anticipation in the opening chapter. For in 1940 Señor Bustamente does not exist; although there is a cinema manager, his anonymity befits a minor figure who has little to do beyond delivering the lost book to Laruelle. As Lowry later develops him, however, Bustamente takes spying so for granted in Mexican life that he creates an atmosphere of intrigue that can be drawn on throughout the novel. Specifically, he can be made to drop plausible hints for events already established in XII. The mysterious telephone calls there to higher authorities, the discovery of Hugh's telegram and anarchist card in Geoffrey's pocket that allow the "chiefs" to confuse him with his reporter brother, and Hugh as already a figure of suspicion are all (28:24, 7) suggested through Bustamente's (ostensibly random) example: "he, M. Laruelle, could not cross the border in a cattle truck, say, without 'them' knowing it in Mexico City before he arrived and having already decided what 'they' were going to do about it." But Lowry's development of Bustamente not only buttresses the "espider" motif; it also gives substance to a passing reference to the incident of the burning of the German officers aboard the *Samaritan*, for which Geoffrey is, Lowry notes, "paid back in coin . . . at the end of the book" (*Letters* 70). The passage taking up these matters appears under the plausible aegis of Laruelle's attempt to "explain the Consul" to Bustamente, yet it also enables Lowry to work in two contemporary pieces of wider history, Mexican and European, as enlarging contexts for his action. Thus, this extension of the Jacques-Bustamente encounter has enabled Lowry to reinforce his echoing structures in first and last chapters.

That echoing only begins with simple "spider" identifications made by both the cinema manager and the Chief of Rostrums. Building on the parallel roles of the two presiding figures as returners of lost goods, Lowry picks up Diosdado's assumption that the Consul, like other Anglo-Saxons, is American and in revision has Bustamente repeat the error. The reinforcing of roles works back and forth: as Bustamente develops the suspicion that Geoffrey was a spy, so Diosdado, who in 1940 had no further dealings with the Consul after returning the letters, now responds to his drawing of a map of Spain which features Granada with a darkly "suspicious" look, and as a result takes an active part in events that follow (Lowry is also careful to insert a reference to Granada in the revised letter of I, as well as developing this theme in late drafts of X). Even in their toilet there is a small echo, for if the cinema manager is "inflexibly *muy correcto*," the bartender enters his scene in a "spotless white shirt." Again, the management of tone marks a crucial distinction—Bustamente's genial, sympathetic view of the Consul, spy or no spy, gives way to the insulting and sinister Diosdado's cooperation with the fascist tormentors—but that is a distinction within an established parallel.

Indeed, having elaborated Bustamente's part, Lowry makes use of that expansion for the introduction of several motifs. First, his generous sympathy for the Consul establishes, with Vigil, some "good Mexicans" at the novel's outset to help allay Lowry's concern that his presentation of the Mexican people is too harsh: in the final chapter he will give added prominence to the old Tarascan woman and the aged fiddling potter, both of whom try to aid Geoffrey, as counterweights to the sinister indigenous figures there. Bustamente is also the first in the novel to pronounce, in a casual context, the term "Compañero," the address used as plea and claim by the dying Indian of VIII and then, in XII, in "compassion" to the Consul by the old fiddler. The late insertion of the poster for the actress María Landrock not only suggests the German presence in Mexico, already established in XII, but anticipates the other María of that final chapter. Even minor matters achieve specificity. In early drafts, we have no indication where and how Laruelle and the cinema manager are situated after they enter Cervecería XX. Nor, at a comparable point in Chapter XII, the Consul reentering the Farolito in the company of the "chief" who has accosted him outdoors, is it clear where exactly they end up once inside. However, when the opening chapter places the two men precisely "standing at the end of the short bar where there was room for two" (28:24, 1) we can hear (however subliminally) the echo in the final chapter's "they made for one end of the bar which was empty" (Texas XII, 17), and even, in the "chief's" "Americano, eh?" another repetition of Bustamente's error.

Again, of course, the recollections mark out a distinction, for the manager's cordial invitation to Laruelle to enter and "have a drink" is in marked contrast to the abusive "shove" in XII. Bustamente's brief departure is marked by the courteous "—momentito, señor. Con permiso" (28:24, 2); the "chief" precedes his temporary leave with an unmistakably terse order: "Wait, aqui—comprendo, señor?" [sic] (31:12, 10). In Lowry's words to Cape regarding last and first chapters, "all the gargoyles of the latter are repeated with interest in this" (*Letters* 85).

One such repetition is the line concerning "the correspondence between the subnormal world and the abnormally suspicious," which Laruelle recalls in I as a saying of the Consul's and which we indeed find Geoffrey using in XII outside the Farolito (adding, characteristically, "delirious" as interest). That line also appeared twice in 1940, but not as one of the links between Chapters I and XII, nor as between Geoffrey and Jacques. There it had been Jacques's line alone, "first" thought of in VII (*1940* 205), recalled by him in I (*1940* 28). That line is not, of course, the only evocative link between the two figures in the opening and closing chapters. In 1940, the connection between them was apparently based on their shared love of Priscilla, expressed there in the fused consciousness of Jacques's dream at the end of the opening chapter where the Day of the Dead mysteriously "comes true." Repetitious and implausible, the dream device was quickly abandoned, and Lowry later grounded the men's relation in a credibly shared boyhood friendship, a closeness that had developed into tension and rivalry. Still later additions to Chapter VII, the only chapter really shared by the two, gave to Geoffrey reflections on his influence over Laruelle to provide a basis in plausibility for the echoings of the two in Chapters I and XII (while also allowing for the magical possibility that Jacques's role both before and after Geoffrey's death has been willed by the Consul [Texas VII, 19]).

To begin with the simple, on their different Days of the Dead, Laruelle and Geoffrey both wear tweeds, a fact to which our attention is drawn indirectly, by Bustamente's "fingering" of Jacques's jacket in I and by the echoing references in XII to the Jefe de Jardineros, whom the Consul sees as a version of his younger self, as "the man in tweeds" (a reattiring of that character from the resplendent uniform he had first shared with the two other chiefs). The link that is meant to make this more than a mere coincidence (or an author's trick) is Chapter VII, where we discover that on this day in 1938, both men are wearing tweeds. Jacques admits to himself in Chapter I, "it was only during the last year that he'd been drinking so heavily" (28:24, 5), that is, since we last saw/will see the Consul, drinking heavily, in another cantina in Chapter XII. In VII, where he tries Geoffrey's tequila, Laruelle shudders, "When I start to drink that stuff you'll know I'm done for" (30:6, 14), and in the Cervecería XX Jacques begins by ordering a tequila. He will alter this to an anís, but in his original order followed by Bustamente's request for a gaseosa, we hear an anticipatory/retrospective echo of the precise orders given by Geoffrey and Jacques respectively in the Café Paris of VII. Even such a minor detail as Jacques's sucking on a lemon soon after entering the Cervecería and Geoffrey doing the same soon after entering the Farolito passes through the intermediary stage of Jacques's observing Geoffrey suck a lemon in the Paris. (If one protests that sucking lemons is customary practice when drinking tequila and mescal, as the Consul is in VII and XII, there remains the question of Jacques's "reflective" behavior, with anís before him, in I.) A particularly cruel link between the two is the Consul's action of placing Yvonne's delayed postcard under Laruelle's pillow in VII: recalled by Jacques in I, the postcard both anticipates and echoes Yvonne's other belatedly read missives in Chapter XII.

Other, more miscellaneous, echoes draw the two chapters together, help complete the circle of the novel's structure. The "doleful bells" that Lowry pointed out to Cape seem a repetition so obvious one might think it established from the start, but in fact they do not appear in early drafts (they are first pencilled in on typescripts of 28:23, 20 and 27:17, 46 [41] respectively). When the Chief of Rostrums derisively pronounces the Consul "'perfecta*mente* borracho'" (Texas XII, 21), he merely restates, even to emphasis, Vigil's more compassionate words to Laruelle. Geoffrey had embraced the Farolito as "sanctuary" in XII of 1940, but it was not until much later that Bustamente recalled him running into El Bosque "shouting something like 'Sanctuario'" (28:24, 7) (and later still that the "Santuario" in Tlaxcala will be entered in Chapter X). The image of sunset as cosmic wound, "a mercurochrome agony," was moved from late in XII to near the opening (27:17, 3), where it corresponds to the image early in I of "the gigantic red evening ... whose reflection bled away in innumerable deserted swimming pools" (28:22, 25 ["insert 2"]). A later cosmic image, that of the lightning that bursts with the bullets fired at the Consul, appeared in the 1940 XII this way: "There was a flash of lightning, like an inch-worm going down the sky, and as he fell the Consul saw above him the shape of Popocatapetl, plumed with emerald snow and drenched with light" (26:5, 31). The final phrase will be modified to "drenched with brilliance" to recall the climactic act of I, Laruelle's firing of the letter, which suddenly reveals the entire human frieze of the cantina "in a burst of brilliance" (28:22, 81 ["insert 4-5-6"]). Other echoes of the passage get developed in late pages of I: the burning letter appears to be made up of "tiny red worms" (28:24, 18), and the lightning itself finally reappears cabalistically in Geoffrey's letter as "the all-but unretraceable path of God's lightning back to God" (28:24, 16).

Starting, then, in 1940, with several recollections of his opening in his closing, Lowry, Penelope-like, patiently, obsessively wove and re-wove the text of his novel to create a dense echolalia that often insisted on difference rather than simple likeness, but nonetheless depended on similarity for the perception of distinction. To emphasize likeness is to recognize the static qualities of the novel, the completedness of its 1938 action from the perspective of 1939; to insist on difference is to recognize the novel's focus on process, on incompletion and unfolding. Both concepts, perhaps, are enclosed within the governing trope of the Day of the Dead, a day when nothing is "finished" because all time has become fluid and thus potentially available, yet when, by the same token, everything must be "finished," somehow completed and "there" if it is to be available; or in the pervasive metaphor of the wheel, that circular object which is a traditional symbol of the completed, the enclosed, the finished and static, yet which, set spinnning, is the very image of dynamic change and motion. Neither figure can be reduced to only a single aspect, and Lowry's exploration of their implications throughout the revisions of his text attempted to insure that the same was true of the *Volcano*.

The 1940 *Volcano* had been conceived as tragicomedy, but tragicomedy of a quite particular kind. Structurally, its double ending, bringing death and love, gave us the traditional closes of tragedy, with its focus on the individual (the Consul), and romantic comedy, with its social concern coming to focus on a set of young lovers (Hugh and Yvonne). That text was clear—indeed, insistent—about these intentions, especially the tragic ones, and references not only to Faust but to Shakespearean tragic heroes abound. The developing Yvonne-Hugh relationship, although not saddled with allusions, was likewise clear enough in its thrust: in the climactic Chapter XI, their playful construction of an ideal society, which leads in turn to their lovemaking finale, enacts a recognizable version of traditional comic resolution. In this, as in other ways, the 1940 *Volcano* is generically familiar, even conventional.

Yet the claims made there for the Consul's tragic stature ring hollow; it is to Lowry's discovery of the richer possibilities of internalizing his novel that we owe his construction of a figure with the capacity for vision and suffering that fills out the role claimed for him. In the process of revision Geoffrey Firmin gradually gained the mind and imagination and emotional range imputed to, but never credibly embodied in, William Ames: bit by bit, the Consul acquired the imagery and rhetoric that created a believable figure of perception and anguish whose persecution and death in the final chapter seem to deprive the depicted world of its grandest, most significant humanity. At the same time that Lowry was giving substance to overblown claims to "tragedy," he was also in the process of discovering the texture of genuine comedy, not in an alternative action or set of characters, but in the same tragic figure of the Consul. In the course of development, the consciousness of Geoffrey Firmin comes to express both pain and posturing, brilliance and nonsense, Lowry sometimes fusing the two so closely that we seem invited both to admire and to laugh, as in the late passages of Chapter X: the superb monologue on Indian rites and religions that turns out not to be a monologue at all—silent, it is "a whirling cerebral chaos"—or the Tlaxcalan episode, with its theme of betrayal, its recollection of the tragic road incident, its complex counterpoint—and its intermediary ensconced on the stone toilet.

The 1940 *Volcano* may have had as one strand a recognizable comic structure, but its comic texture was at best limited. Lowry's great witty set pieces, all dependent on the confusion of tongues, were there (Cervantes's menu, the fractured English of Dr. Vigil, Señora Gregorio, *El Universal*) but little more. William Ames is preposterous at times (and, when such, rendered dubious as putative tragic hero), but he is only fitfully witty, and rarely the subject of amusement. In this first casting of his drinker as monolithic tragic figure, Lowry forgot that inebriation is more usually the stuff of comedy, the drunk a stock butt of innumerable jokes. What happens through revision is that he develops the Consul's wit and exploits not only traditional forms of drunken behavior perceived as comic, weaving, staggering, falling down, hiccupping, rambling, leaving one's fly undone, sneaking drinks, getting caught sneaking drinks, passing out, but, more originally (indeed, brilliantly), phases of the alcoholic mind that, dominated by its monomania, views self and world only in relation to drink. The results can be horrific—hallucinations, shakes, guilt, terror, anguish—but they can also be darkly (and not so darkly) funny, whether in the jabberings of an internal voice, excessive umbrage taken at perceived slights, rationalizations of past (or even future) behavior, roles mentally adopted, grandiose resolutions silently sworn. What's more, while the sufferings so dramatized would help realize the merely notional "tragedy" of the Consul, these could at the next moment slide suddenly into comedy, from the vision of the dead man by the pool into bland assurances of one's mounting sobriety, for instance, or from the terrifying ordeal of the Máquina Infernal to the immediate assuming of "the bored expression of an English tourist sitting in the Luxembourg Gardens."

As Lowry's revisions stretched on, his involvement with his text became matched by a detachment from it. In consequence much of the altogether new material brought to the novel struck primarily the comic note, not merely such episodes as the encounter with the fellow Englishman on the Calle Nicaragua, but the retrospective passages given to Laruelle, Hugh, and Yvonne. As these last examples remind us, comedy is not confined to the Consul. While Yvonne may be largely exempt from it—Lowry was never sufficiently at ease with her to exercise the kind of humor he brings to his male figures—the naive young Hugh of 1940, sporadically treated ironically but never there rising to real comedy, becomes enough older to metamorphose into a figure of such anxiety that spasms of guilt and remorse repeatedly hurl him by way of compensation into grandiose poses whose absurdity even he sometimes punctures.

The comedy that finally emerges is thus unlike the structural variety of 1940, with its separable strands of love vs. death, past vs. future, youth vs. age, and so on. Tragic markers are still in place, and they still point primarily toward the Consul, but comic markers now appear also, many of which point toward him too. Instead of being given a separate action, we get another perspective on the same action. Indeed, the conception of comedy is enlarged: Chapter XI, which now ends in death, can be read not as romantic, but as a species of "divine" comedy; Yvonne, like *Faust*'s Marguerite (*Letters* 84) seems to be lifted "up," transported toward the stars. If so, then the Consul's being hurled "down" (as Lowry reminded Cape) becomes an image of damnation. But then what of the dog in Mexican myth that guides its master to the afterlife, and what of the "Wonders are many, and none is more wonderful than man" to which Lowry also directed Cape's trochal attention (*Letters* 88), followed by the salvation offered those "aspiring upward" in Goethe's epigraph?[6] These questions are a reminder that no view in this novel is truly final, that all has become open to irony. As Lowry revised and revised, the growing complexity of his method and the vision it expressed could hardly help creating not only local ironies of tone and action, but a pervading one, a function of the very structure he had built. As individual chapters became mediated by alternating consciousnesses, all views were subject to the re-vision not only of the ensuing action and consciousness, but of the circling author, whose enlarging conception discovered more and other sides to the relatively stable action of his text. The very subjecting of the Consul, for instance, not only to the generic "tragic" sense with which he began, but to a developing comedy, created a gap, and each of Lowry's major characters were laid open to these shifting perspectives.

Why, then, privilege Marlowe's damned Faust over Goethe's spared figure, especially when it is imagery from the latter that gets incorporated into the revised drafts? Indeed, the Marlovian version is most prominent at the start, not the end of the novel ("start" here designating both Chapter I and 1940, as distinguished from Chapter XII and 1947). As he reads them in the opening chapter, Laruelle is particularly responsive to passages from *Dr. Faustus*—he has planned a modern film version—and thus these texts resonate on a frequency he is already attuned to: early and late, he sees the Consul in them as a figure of tragedy. But between the bracketing passages from Marlowe, Lowry inserts another: *"And what wonders I have done all Germany can witness. Enter Wagner, solus.... Ick sal you wat suggen, Hans. Dis skip, dat comen from Candy, is als vol, by God's sacrament, van sugar, almond, cambrick, end alle dingen, towsand, towsand ding"* (28:24, 11; cf. *Volcano* 34). First stunned, then "[s]haken" by his findings in Marlowe, Jacques simply "close[s] the book" on this intermediary text (actually an elision of three passages), which would seem to enact a parodic declension from the grandiose, through the replacement of master by servant (Wagner), to a demotic low comedy that appears to reduce "God's sacrament" to "Candy" and tragic overreaching to clownish greed and gluttony.[7] If Laruelle ignores it, Lowry obviously does not, breaking up the too-neat paradigm of the Faustian analogy, allowing for another, more skeptically comic perspective to emerge. This was a late addition, the deliberate introduction of a discordant note; later still was the overt identification of "Dekker's comedy," underlining the countering of the tragic by the comic, thereby freeing the text from the monolithic tyrrany of Laruelle's view.

Most readers have gone with Laruelle's (and Lowry's early) vision and seen the *Volcano* as presenting the tragedy of the Consul, but in order to do so they must, like Jacques, overlook or downplay such countersigns as the inserted passage. It is no accident that we are looking here at the first dramatization of "reading" in Lowry's text, the scanning of a volume reflexive of what is at that moment being enacted on another level with his own book, for what this episode presents in miniature is the deliberate interplay of crosslights, the complicating of the question of *how* to view the figures and action the work has long been concerned with. It is a dramatization, in short, of the play of multiple perspectives, and perhaps, in Laruelle, the impossibility of bringing them all to bear simultaneously. The multidimensionality of the *Volcano* is not simply a matter of the familiar piety that this text, like others, is open to various interpretations; rather, Lowry has so deliberately constructed it, like this episode, that it will respond at different frequencies, contain within itself conflicting perspectives that forestall resolution, indeed perhaps genuinely be the work Lowry described to Jonathan Cape, at once story, symphony, opera, horse opera, poem, song, tragedy, comedy, farce,"and so forth" (*Letters* 66). The designations sound casual, extemporized, tossed off, yet I suspect that on one level Lowry took them seriously indeed. In any case, the catalogue, diverse, playful, contradictory, suggests the multidimensionality that he has written into his book.

The key step in the realization of this multidimensionality was the interiorizing of the novel, the focusing of action through plural consciousnesses and then "dislocating" these consciousnesses, revealing them as limited, partial, dubious in their constructions of the world beyond the self. Yet, like Jacques's misreading of Marlowe's text—he sees "fly" where the play has "run"—or the Consul's of the garden sign, what is unreliable in one dimension may be meaningful in another. On the opening page of Chapter II, Yvonne overhears the words "Absolutamente necessario" as if in response to the Consul's "'Why shouldn't a corpse be transported by express?'" (death theme) but when she enters the bar and sees the advertisement featuring a woman in a scarlet brassiere and hears Fernando speak the phrase again, "Yvonne realized it was the woman . . . he meant . . . was necessary" (love theme). But the "scarlet"-clad woman is in fact dubious (betrayal theme), connected to Yvonne herself in the ensuing paragraph by the "scarlet bag" she carries. Conflicting as they may be, *all* these associations of necessity, inevitability, are in some sense relevant, even "true" to the action about to unfold.

The multidimensional possibilities in that single phrase—and a few pages later it will be connected to Geoffrey's drinking—were created by Lowry over successive stages. The Consul's announcement of a transportable corpse existed in 1940; two drafts later an advertisement featuring a naked woman appeared, was called "Absolutamente necessario" by Fernando, and Yvonne acquired a scarlet bag (29:2); the next draft (29:3) adds Geoffrey's question and Fernando's apparent response, and the woman is outfitted in a scarlet brassiere. Yvonne's "error," in short, her initial hearing of the phrase as if in response to Geoffrey's questioning of the prediction of death, is thus the last to be written, Lowry's belated discovery of how misperception can itself generate meaning, a simple enough example of how the uncertainties of consciousness can unmoor fixed readings of the novel's events.

Yvonne's "error" and "correction" neither cancel one another out nor exhaust meaning here. Neither, of course, is it adequate simply to grasp the solipsistic nettle, to take the events of individual chapters/minds as sufficient unto themselves, whatever their ontology, to say, for instance, that whether or not a dog actually materializes in the Consul's garden in Chapter V, since he sees a dog there, the dog is for fictional purposes "real." This problem is, I take it, the burden of the Consul's Chapter XII meditation on Laruelle's picture of Los Borrachones, a version of which had existed since 1940. Revisions here sharpen, even crucially identify, the nature of the difficulty. When he had aspired upward, Geoffrey reflects, the world beyond the self had seemed identifiably *other*. More recently, sinking downward, "those features [of life] had tended to dissemble, *to cloy and clutter*, to become finally little better than ghastly caricatures of *his dissimulating inner and outer self*, or of his struggle, if struggle there were still[.] Yes, but had he desired it, willed it, the very material world, *illusory though that was*, might have been a confederate, pointing the wise way" (*Volcano*, 361; italics identify key additions of post-1940 revision). In acknowledging his plight, his difficulty in separating inner self from outer world, the Consul now acknowledges the distinction between them and in the very act of so doing, also acknowledges the "cloy and clutter" that comes into view with that distinction, product of the increasing complexity so introduced. Playing a role for others is one matter; simultaneously adopting a different yet equally dissimulating role for oneself is another, especially when that inner role begins to bifurcate and fragment (think of Geoffrey's "familiars" or his meditation on lost identity in Chapter X). And so even the material world becomes thus blurred and lost—"illusory as that was." "Illusory" because Geoffrey as mystical adept knows its insubstantiality? "Illusory" because Geoffrey even now—and this is symptomatic—cannot acknowledge its reality? Or are these two ways of saying the same thing? However we "account for" Geoffrey's refusal or inability to grant reality to the world of matter, that denial is literally in this final chapter a matter of life and death.

Nor can this question—or any other—be somehow resolved by pointing to the late (1943-44) addition to the text's multidimensionality, the insertion of cabalistic material. The fact that it *does* appear only late in the novel's composition is not, it seems to me, an argument either for its minor importance or for its all-determining power. Whatever significance it may be deemed to have in the *Volcano*, Lowry was able to drop it into a late-maturing text as easily as he did only because he recognized its congruence with the methods and materials already extant there. Neither is the essential question whether Lowry "really believed" in a cabalistic universe or in the existence of occult forces described by the likes of Swedenborgians, Rosicrucians, theosophists, and so on. What is crucial *for the novel* is what of these matters we, the readers, are required to believe, and here the study of revisions can, I think, shed some light. As we have seen (chapter 4) Lowry repeatedly begins with a flat assertion of the occult and then modifies it, tones it down to an ambiguous possibility, never posits its certainty. This is slyboots at work, insinuating into the novel a system to which perhaps no one, including the Consul, has any genuine adherence. The matter is left equivocal, much as Lowry himself left it in the Cape letter. Sketching out the central symbols of the Cabala, he then seems to dismiss it: "all this is not important at all to the understanding of the book." Within a few pages, however, recurring to cabbalistic use of the Garden, the Tree of Life, and the Adam and Eve story, the tone suddenly shifts: "Be these things as they may—and they are certainly at the root of most of our knowledge, the wisdom of our religious thought, and most of our inborn superstitions as to the origin of man...." But a little further along, mentioning "the evidence of ... the magical basis of the world" in the Consul's books, he asks, "You do not believe the world has a magical basis, especially while ... bombs are dropping in Bedford Square? Well, perhaps I don't either" (*Letters* 65, 71, 76). "Perhaps" indeed. For what it's worth, I suspect Lowry himself was of mixed mind, quizzical eyebrow raised one moment at what he passionately believed or feared was the case the previous (and the next) moment. But the central issue, again, is not Lowry's private conviction but the manner of his inscription of the novel, and here he has left us free to make as little or as much of these occult matters as we may wish.

Lapsed magus or not, Geoffrey Firmin is certainly a visionary of some kind, however ironically one might use the term. It may seem a long way from the doubtful appearance of a dog in Chapter V to the Consul's end in Chapter XII, but to a figure who has grown inured to "routine hallucinations," the distinction between inner and outer worlds seems no longer of great moment, perhaps no longer even reliably possible. After all, if his battle is "for the survival of the human consciousness," this is in essence a battle enacted internally (although the object of that consciousness, what it is to exercise itself *on*, remains unspecified). Yet the merging that the Consul so mercilessly condemns in Chapter XII is also the enabling condition of the *Volcano* itself, the certainty of separation between portrayed consciousness and world repeatedly dissolving, sometimes lost altogether. What the Consul thus judges in himself has become the very lifeblood of the evolving novel, with the crucial distinction that we know Lowry knows the object of *his* consciousness, for it is the world of the novel itself. Or rather, more precisely, it too is immaterial, both illusory and actual, for it is the novel's language that is his immediate object.

One of the ways the *Volcano* evinces Lowry's growing self-consciousness is in its proliferation of texts, of "signs" to be decoded, which emerge during composition. Even in 1940, of course, the novel had boasted several of these, but in simple, unproblematic form. True, Jacques had noted the poster for *Las Manos de Orlac* and recalled "with a shock" that it had played on the Consul's last day, but if a billboard for the Day of the Dead, it was not then a "hieroglyphic of the times," both demanding and resisting interpretation. Two key internal "texts," the book of Elizabethan plays and the garden notice, appeared virtually transparent in 1940: Jacques read the passages from *Dr. Faustus* and was suitably traumatized; the Consul gazed at the garden sign, translated it, and applied it to himself. Neither discovered—Lowry himself, surely, had not discovered—that their readings were in fact misreadings, with all that *that* might imply. Other textual "objects" appeared only in the course of revision, the most important of them "difficult," demanding interpretation, each associated with one of the three major characters. The earliest was Hugh's telegram of Chapter IV, a piece of journalistic shorthand designed to deceive the uninitiated. It works well enough on Yvonne, who first asks, "What in the world does it mean?" (29:12, 5), receiving a terse, partial explanation. Suppressed in IV, the anti-Semitism that is its coded burden surfaces in Chapter XII in a misreading that validates the message: although the Chief of Rostrums can no more decode the telegram than can Yvonne, he does not hesitate to construe it: "'It say you are Juden.'" In a novel in which all misreadings are in some sense "true," we are left to ponder just how much this identification tells us about the Consul as cabalist. Or does it suggest his resemblance, however skewed, to that ultimate Jewish scapegoat whose words on Calvary he'd echoed to the dog of Chapter VII? No likeness is apparent to the Chief of Rostrums, who nonetheless raises the issue by inversion: "'You antichrista. . . . And Juden'" (*Volcano* 370).

The difficulties of the telegram are all on the surface; the difficulties of the other two texts, both of which appear very late, rest less in their form, than in *how* they are to be interpreted (see chapter 4, pp. 276–77 and 280–82). The travel brochure of Chapter X and the menu of Chapter XI are impersonal documents brought into contexts inescapably personal, thereby transforming their original utilitarian, informative functions. The travel folder appears at first to be unviolated, its stiff unidiomatic English reproduced without alteration, but closer inspection notes the heading without text and the dots and dash that confess not all entries reprinted in their entirety. Excisions and suppressions are matched by italicized repetitions (*"said to be like Granada," "secret passage,"* etc.), both revealing the presence of the Consul: these are, it seems, not simply what is printed in the brochure, but what, and how, he reads. Furthermore, the task of deciding how to understand the folder entries is complicated by their context, the ambiguous status of the snatches of dialogue that go on contrapuntally around them. Interpretation here faces a more problematic "code" than it does with Hugh's telegram, for the text in question cannot be separated from the surroundings against which it is played, and by which it is invaded.

Problems thrown up by the menu of Chapter XI are different from but analogous to those presented by the folder. As we have seen, the menu of El Popo is very much "a document" (as it is called), apparently "objective" on its face, covered with the Consul's handwriting and drawings on the back. Yet Yvonne, mescal-inspired, identifying the face with her own fate, appropriates its public images, then pores, fascinated, over the verso, which suggests Geoffrey's, the inseparabity of the menu's two sides manifesting the linking of their destinies, just as Yvonne's letters will maintain in Chapter XII.

But there is another connection between the menu and Chapter XII, one that entwines it with the travel folder of Chapter X. In the new, monumental "Oaxaca sentence" composed at the time these "documents" were added (that is, near the very end) the italicized "secret passage" of the folder and the motif of "escape" from the poem on the menu come together, the mounting refrain of "the escape!" eventuating in "the escape through the secret passage" in XII. Even as we see these connections, however, the problem of interpretation persists. Is this, as it seems to be, simply Geoffrey's pipe dream, a reflection of the escapism of his drinking that is given an ironically punning twist at this moment, where the possibly diseased "secret passage" of María with whom he is copulating provides him with the final excuse for his "escape" from the salvation represented by Yvonne? Or, just possibly, is the "secret passage" another form of the Blakean path "right through hell" that his letter of Chapter I refers to? That "path" had led him in the letter to the immediately ensuing vision of the northern paradise; the phrase that sticks in Yvonne's head from the poem of XI (she repeats it five times) is "who once fled north," even as she recognizes that neither she and Hugh nor the Consul are going north, that all are headed toward the Farolito. But it was from the Farolito that the Consul had written that "I seem to see now, between mescals, this path, and beyond it strange vistas like visions of a new life together . . . in some northern country" (*Volcano* 36). Is the Consul on the downward path, hurried on by fantasies of "escape" to the aptly named El Infierno, or is there another sense to his coming to focus on the calendar's "picture of Canada" ("the escape, still the escape!") as his hellish encounter with María ends? Is he now finally Bunyan's lost soul who could not "desire deliverance," or the figure identified in the epigraph from Goethe, "Whosoever unceasingly strives upward . . . him can we save"?

Unlike Hugh's telegram, these two late texts are not involved in misreadings only because no "readings" are given of them: instead, they inspire to action, to the Consul's proposed trip to Tlaxcala and Yvonne's hurried departure for the Farolito. Interpretation is left to us, as is, indeed, the question of why they are in the novel at all. On those levels their paradigm is not the Consul's or Yvonne's letters of the opening and closing chapters, but the postcard that arrives precisely midway through the novel. What meaning, the Consul asks himself in Chapter VII, has its arrival on this day for his and Yvonne's situation? In the drafts, his response evolved through several stages, successively more complex: it ought to have been a good omen (30:6), it might have been a good omen at another time, but one cannot imagine it arriving at another time (30:7), it might have been a good omen, etc., but "how could he know whether it was a good omen or not without another drink?" (Texas VII; cf. *Volcano* 197). Like the menu, the postcard has two sides, one impersonal, one personal, but while both are reported, no interpretation is offered. Yet if neither Hugh nor Geoffrey offers a "reading" of the card, or even, finally, a view of what kind of omen it might be, it also (in revision) inspires the latter to action, an action that draws from the narrator a rare comment: "the Consul did an odd thing; he took the postcard he'd just received from Yvonne and slipped it under Jacques's pillow" (30:7, ms. 11A; cf. *Volcano* 201). The card itself may not get interpreted, but this "odd" act will be: in an addition to the final typescript, Jacques recalls that card in Chapter I—thereby sowing Yvonne's plaintive, unanswered pleas in beginning, middle, and end of the novel—and terms the Consul's action "malicious."

However we may interpret such objects and actions, on the evidence of the readings that *are* offered up by the novel it seems safe to assume that our readings will be misreadings. Indeed, misreadings are everywhere, from Laruelle's of *Faustus* and the Consul's of the garden sign to everyone's interpretations of events. However, it is a premise of the novel that in the universe it projects there is neither simple "wrongness"—everything has some kind of meaning, every meaning some kind of validity—nor a final, fixed significance. The very structure of the book proclaims that this is a universe without finality, a journey that never ends, as, in another way, does the governing metaphor of the Day of the Dead, by reversing the motion of the earth, which spins "forward" in space-time: the backward turning of the luminous wheel is also the earth itself on this day, making potentially available all past times and places. Thus the invocation of various historical periods—the Conquest, Maximilian and Carlotta, World War I and the Mexican revolution—because they are, none of them, simply "past." And thus the introduction of India and (to a lesser extent) Hawaii, both landscaped with mountains or volcanoes and thus reminiscent of Mexico, spatially as well as temporally extending the novel beyond the local setting. These matters of history and geography also testify to "the very material world" beyond individual consciousness, as do, in their different ways, the various myths the novel alludes to and the cultural artifacts that appear in its pages—posters, newspaper headlines, radio broadcasts, calendars, menus and so on—which manifest the persistence of a social presence.

Some of these images, and certainly the principle of the use of mythic allusions and cultural signs, were established by 1940. What changed under revision was the kind of weight they come to bear in the text, the giving-way of the univocal sign to the multivalent possibility: When Jacques does not simply read *Faustus* in Chapter I, but misreads *Faustus*, corrects himself, and then goes on to read and ignore "Dekker's comedy," we have been apprised that each consciousness is not only partial, but even on its own terms a doubtful guide. The upshot even in Chapter I is not that we arrive at a transcendent perspective larger than Laruelle's, definitive in a way his cannot be; rather, we recognize that such a perspective is unavailable, that we are thrown back on ourselves and our own "construction" of meaning, realizing that it must be as partial, as limited, as much a misreading as Jacques's. Later experience will show us that it is, like the novel it reflects on, without true closure, constantly in motion, necessarily subject to modification and revision each time we reconsider or simply open the book again.

For the reader, Jacques's misreading of Marlowe is the first moment when the novel thrusts him into self-consciousness, when its sudden, belated correction of *Faustus* forces on him an awareness of his present role *as* reader. It was certainly for Lowry a moment of self-consciousness, a moment when the novel, as it were, became aware of its action as novel, presenting suddenly two possible texts to be "read" within Lowry's own. He did not discover his mistranscription of Marlowe until late in the revising process—the erroneous reading, with correction, appears only with the 1943-44 text of Chapter I (28:24, 11)—just as he did not develop misgivings about the Consul's translation of the garden sign until well advanced in revision (29:17, 6). Yet in a sense, these are tips of the iceberg, visible results of the revising activity that Lowry permits to stand within the text itself, signs not only of the Consul and his fate but of the very processes whereby these were brought into existence. For as Lowry went back and back over his manuscripts, he became as much reader as writer, scrutinizing again and again not his imagined world but his words on yellow sheets, interpreting and reinterpreting his essential "fable" (in Kermode's terms). As months and drafts slipped by, the novel moved further and further "into the past," its inception, its basic structure of chapters and events subject to second thoughts and second words, the entire process an exercise in "belatedness." All revisions, Lowry's of his novel, Jacques's of his reading of Marlowe, Yvonne's of her impressions on arrival, Geoffrey's of the conduct of his life, are belated, an attempt to alter that which, in suddenly becoming the past, eludes us, acquires a life of its own that may be re-placed (both "placed elsewhere" and "have something else in the space where it was"), but cannot be effaced. This is, after all, one of the implications of the Day of the Dead.

Thus *Under the Volcano* repeatedly forces *us* to revise, to "view again" what had first seemed clear, unequivocal. The result, as Lowry well knew, is not to cancel the first view, but to query in what ways both are relevant, how both "to run" and "to fly" pertain to Geoffrey's final day, and how Dekker just might be as appropriate as any version of Marlowe; how both the Consul's mistranslation of the garden sign and the correct one bear on his situation, and ours; in what senses "absolutamente necessario" can characterize love and death, booze and betrayal (and perhaps even such palliatives as *Cafeaspirina*). Indeed, the revised situation of the novel is itself based on an act of attempted revision: from 1941 onward, Yvonne's return provides the proverbial second chance for her and Geoffrey, an attempt to refute the ghostly voice of Chapter I crying, "Never a chance like that again!" The novel, typically, refuses a single view of the situation for which that is the paradigm. For they are together again, and yet not together; they are the same, and not the same, and so on. For the individual, life marches forward inexorably until, like Geoffrey "missing all the opportunities finally, until it was too late" (*Volcano* 218), no revision is possible. But the premise of the Day of the Dead, and the structure of the novel, rests on the suspension of "finally," posits the "revision" possible in another dimension, including the dimension of art. Thus Lowry's allowing for Chapters II–XII to be seen as a film by Laruelle; and thus the example of the *Volcano* itself, which never changes however often we circle it, yet which ever changes in our renewed interactions with it.

Insofar as revision implies change, its alternative would seem to be stasis, the unmoving, unchanging. But stasis is not even a possibility for Lowry; nothing, in his world, can remain still. Recurrence, repetition, however, which might be called, paradoxically, stasis in motion, certainly is possible, indeed inevitable. At its most benign, repetition seems to answer to some deep human need, from the child's desire to have again its pleasurable piggyback to an audience's demand for the revival of a fascinatingly enigmatic movie, the mysterious slow wheelings of the fixed stars, the myth of the eternal return, or the echoing patterns of art. At its most sinister, repetition threatens an inescapable determinism, a fixity that warns, for instance, that "The same thing will happen again ... it will happen again" (*Volcano* 219). Yet in the *Volcano* as in life, "the same thing" never really occurs twice; even precise verbal repetitions—"*dolente ... dolore,*" "absolutamente necessario," "perfecta*me*nte borracho," "¿Le gusta este jardín?"—are altered by context, and although the very density of Lowry's echolalia in the novel reveals the importance of recurrence to him, just as essential are the changes, the differences we recognize within the sameness. That to Lowry was the essence of revision, a deeply conservative process of slow, sometimes infinitesimal, incremental change, evincing a profound reluctance to let go altogether of anything once given verbal form. The entire 1940 Chapter II (Yvonne in Acapulco) may get discarded, but an astonishing amount of its material will gradually be reinserted in the evolving text over the next years, and Lowry will not until the very end give up looking for some spot to drop in his beloved citation from Chaucer that had provided the epigraph for *Ultramarine*. The latter is a reminder of Lowry's repetition between as well as within works, the sense of his life and writing as inscribing patterns as they evolve, always changing yet always coming back, again and again, to play variations on recurrent themes.

Yet why should this be so? Why might not one's life alter in unanticipated, spontaneous ways, rupturing patterns, striking off in new directions, marking fresh beginnings? Why can't (to put the question in the novel's terms) Yvonne and Geoffrey realize their Canadian dream? Deeper than any belief in the continuity of personality, myths of eternal return, or the persistence of archetypes, the emotional center that for Lowry guaranteed recurrence and made precious both his own experience and the writing that sprang from it was, I believe, the quality of remorse. Remorse spreads like a stain throughout the *Volcano*, not in 1940 (there it is a property only of the Consul, and only sporadically at that) but ever more deeply in the evolving drafts until, at last, Juan Cerillo is created to articulate a way out of the impasse it creates. For all four major characters are dogged by it and its crippling effects. As the word itself suggests—and the Consul considers it together with cognates and relatives in a late addition to Chapter VII—*re-morse* (compare *re-vision*) throws the mind backward, compels it to experience in the present the painful bite of memory, and so forestalls the future, a poison paralyzing the psyche, holding it thrall to the past. Lowry's darkest speculations on its power came not in connection with the Consul, but with Hugh, and they were not permitted to stand.

Once Hugh has been made into the Consul's half-brother and Yvonne's former lover, Lowry developed in consecutive drafts of Chapter IV increasing waves of remorse until, in notations on the typescript of 29:14, Hugh even seemed to see it "glint" in the beer that he drinks at the Cervecería Quauhnahuac (ts. 21), and when a leaf falls "like a sudden footstep," Lowry adds, "It was the footstep of the spectre of indefatigable remorse, disguised this time as guilt. Next time it would be the spectre of atonement" (ts. 22). This intensifying of Hugh's remorse perhaps would have made clearer Lowry's sense of its sinister seductive power: it cripples not simply by arresting the moral faculties before a past transgression, but, by declaring oneself already hopelessly guilty, undermines the moral sense altogether (see chapter 4, note 20). Hugh's most insidious temptation lies not simply in Yvonne's continuing appeal to him, but in the counsel of despair, the whisper that since he has already, Judas-like, betrayed his brother by seducing his wife—since he is already *unforgivably* guilty—there is no reason not to do so again. The diabolical power of remorse would at least have been implied had Lowry not excised on the ensuing typescript, "remorse, in itself a worse than Judas" (Texas IV, 135) with the odd query, "too odd?" Instead, he lightened Hugh's burden by introducing in that draft the counter-balance of Juan Cerillo as (among other things) an exemplar of the ceaseless "struggle upward" whereby the past may be transformed: "conscience had been given man to regret [the past] only in so far as that might change the future" (29:14, 11).

There was for Lowry no route "around" that past, only, as the Consul sensed, a route "right through hell" from which one might glimpse a paradisal vision. Whether or not his characters paid "full toll to hell," the *Volcano* was of course Lowry's own attempt to transform the past, and the late addition of Juan Cerillo may be taken as his articulation of how that might be done, the "toll" paid for *his* Canadian paradise the confrontation there of the remorseful "hell" he carried within him out of Mexico. Re-morse and re-vision were the sides of a blade down whose edge Lowry walked in those years in Dollarton and Ontario, the second designed to re-deem the first, the first threatening to abort and undermine the second. The person closest to Lowry during those years, his cohort and near collaborator, Margerie, put it this way: "only a person whose whole existence *is* his work, who has dominated and disciplined the volcano within him, at what a cost of suffering even I do not understand, could have written such a book" (*Letters* 422). According to Juan Cerillo, picking up one of the novel's controlling tropes, all life is "a warfare"; to the Consul, the "great battle" is "for the survival of the human consciousness." Beyond the playful self-reflexiveness of such references (all appearing in revision, of course) as "eclectic systemë," "churrigueresque," "overloaded and embellished style," or the proliferating images of wheels (and wheels within wheels) lies the grimmer inner struggle of these wartime years, consciousness of battle (as with Hugh) perhaps all the more acute to the uneasy non-participant. As Laruelle is made to reflect, whatever the outcome of the war, "one's own battle would go on." The struggle that would make the *Volcano* a work of great imaginative and emotional power had only begun in 1940: Lowry's private warfare turned out to be almost coterminous with the great world's convulsion.

What remains most difficult to demonstrate, although I must hope that it has been suggested, at perhaps tiresome length, in preceding chapters, is the enormous alteration in the very prose of the novel, the bodying forth of Lowry's world, that texture which in the *Volcano* even more than in most novels conveys the very substance of the writer's vision and which Conrad Aiken praised as "all vascular with life and sensation" (Killorin, 278). We have already compiled enough examples of rewritings to observe the obvious tendency in these specifics, as in the novel as a whole, toward expansion and complication, the enriching and enhancing of the individual linguistic moment that contributes to the same tendency in the day—and the day-book—at large. Perhaps, however, in order to suggest briefly the difference in texture, it would be salutary to enumerate, à la Henry James's famous catalogue of the absences in American life, those passages that make no appearance before the 1941–45 revisions, that have no predecessor, however faint, in 1940. Chapter I may serve as our exemplar (no one could endure a comparable trek through the entire novel).

Thus, in the *Volcano* of 1940 we find: no large macrocosmic opening, no general paragraph describing the town of Quauhnahuac, no evocation of the "ghostly" palatialness of the Casino nor of the growing meaninglessness of tragedy in the "horrors of the present," no physical description of Vigil nor characteristic gesture with his cigarette lighter. No anticipation by Laruelle of departure from Mexico, nor walk by the station, nor framed station sign; no recollection of Hugh and his departure after the Consul's death, no anticipation of Paris nor phlegmatic assessment of the outcome of the war, no evocation of the Earthly Paradise, no recollection of a Mexican mistress nor Mayan idols, no paragraph associating the approaching storm with "love which came too late," no encounter with the courtly ragged Indians, no association of his passion for Priscilla/Yvonne with Chartres Cathedral, no evocation of the surrounding mountains, no recollected postcard from Priscilla/Yvonne, no watchtower and grotesque birds in the twilight, no sense of "ghosts" in Maximilian's Palace, no noting of the ferris wheel and the model farm. No boyhood friendship between Laruelle and the Consul, nor visit to Leasowe, with recollections of the Taskersons, the Hell Bunker, the Case Is Altered. No deliberate evasion by Laruelle of his own house, nor notation of the "eccentric orbit" he was enacting; no recording of newspaper headlines nor shop window placard nor the uniforms of soldiers nor the "Washington Post March" nor the hen apparently seeking service at the box office nor recollections of "the old . . . Ufa days" nor reflections on the symbolism of the *Orlac* films. No description of "the manager" (nor naming of him) nor ordering of drinks nor poster advertising Maria Landrock nor view of the interior of the theatre. No naming of the Consul by the cinema manager nor misidentification of him as American nor discussion of him between the two men: no suspicion of spying, nor review of the Consul's career, nor mention of the *Samaritan* incident and the ensuing court-martial and the Consul's later responses. No correction to the misreading from *Dr. Faustus* nor citation from Dekker. No description of the Consul's handwriting on the letter, no evocation in its contents of the terrors of the night nor of Oaxaca nor of news of the divorce nor of the breaking off of relations between Mexico and Britain nor of the sense of being in hell nor of the vision of a Canadian paradise nor of his book of a kind of universal religion nor of his awareness of the Cabala nor of those places that suggest "shadows of our fate" nor of a vision of Priscilla/Yvonne returning by the Acapulco mail plane. The Consul's letter burns undescribed, no bell "speaks," and no "luminous wheel" revolves, in any direction, over the darkened town.

Crude as such a mere listing is, it provides perhaps a rough dramatization of how different the moment-by-moment experience of Chapter I, and by extension the entire novel, was in 1940. What it cannot do, of course, is tell us anything about the actual encounter with Lowry's language, with the achieved style of the work published in 1947. Despite interesting partial attempts, that style has eluded successsful analysis (nor is this the place to launch another try), largely because, I believe, of its variegated nature.[8] Although Lowry's use of it has been compared with Faulkner's, the highly rhetorical, multibranched, latinate-dictioned, syntactically suspended complex sentence—while it (or something not unlike it) does indeed appear in the *Volcano*—is less determinately characteristic of Lowry than of the American writer.

While he might himself in playful rhyme describe his prose as "flowery" and "glowery," his old mentor Conrad Aiken more fully caught the variegated nature of the novel's language in the encomium he produced for the dust jacket: "Here it is, all renewed and alive again, a changeable shot-silk sun-shot medium of infinite flexibility, which can adapt itself to the subtlest shade of perception or mood, or suffuse with the bloodiest of horrors, or vanish upwards in air like the most mystical of rope tricks." That "infinite flexibility," the varied tones, structures, and "voices" of his novel were precisely the product of Lowry's repeated rewritings. If it is indeed revision that produces his most elaborate structures (the novel's longest sentence, for instance, that which accompanies the copulation with María in Chapter XII, was virtually the last composed; immediately preceeding it was the "purple passage" about the stars of Chapter XI), it is also revision that produces its simplest, such as Chapter II's terse, deflationary paragraph, "The bar was empty, however," followed by, "Or rather it contained one figure." The three retrospective passages of Chapters I, VI, and IX, after all, were late insertions, deliberately designed to be stylistically simple and direct, a form of "relief" from the intensity of the novel's present, and the style in which that "present" is rendered. And at least two of those flashbacks, Hugh's and Yvonne's, involved Lowry in deliberate pastiche, the imitation of journalistic reportage and of the movie magazine interview respectively.

As we glance toward the imitation of "other" modes of utterance, other styles, can we maintain that the *Volcano*'s extensive use of documents drawn from elsewhere is somehow not a part of Lowry's "style"? Yvonne's fan magazine interview, we may be fairly confident, Lowry composed himself: Hugh's telegram and the menu from the El Popo, we can demonstrate, he did not. However, what exactly do we mean by "Lowry" in such instances, and what by "compose"? If it is possible, for example, to show that the El Popo menu items and some of the printing were transcribed directly from an actual document, what do we say of the descriptions of the artwork from that document? Of the descriptions and transcriptions of its annotations, some (all?) of which were made by Lowry at an earlier period? What of the changes Lowry made to the original printed menu in including it in the novel? If the El Popo menu seems not sufficiently troubling, what of that of the Salón Ofélia? Here no document (if there ever was one) survives, nor does the novel pretend to present us with one, dissolving its offerings into the dialogue of the characters. Are the multilingual puns that make up Cervantes's dishes, then, a part of "Lowry's style," and if so, more or less than the straightforward offerings of the El Popo menu, or the traceable accuracy of "Hugh's" telegram? If we cannot be certain whether or not Lowry made up, say, the newspaper headlines he includes, are they "his"? Is the decision to include any "external" reference, whether in fact created by the author or borrowed from actuality, a *stylistic* decision? We are on the borders of a more familiar literary intertextuality here, and of course of Lowry's plagiarism anxiety (we are also, of course, on the borders of his later practice in such works as "Through the Panama").

These questions are not without their tangles, but it seems to me clear that, at least in the case of the *Volcano*, the inclusion of "real" documents (with their "real" language) must necesarily be termed a *stylistic* decision, that whatever their actual sources, Lowry means the reader to experience a wide range of language and "styles," which make the novel a textbook case of what Bakhtinians would call heteroglossia. In this respect, the cacophony of voices that creates the "babel" of Chapter XII is merely a culmination, and it is worth recalling that that uproar of language is attributed not only to voices raised in the bar of the Farolito, but also to such disparate sources as broadcasting (the radio), print (the telegram, Hugh's anarchist card), and the written word (Yvonne's letters). And if, making the traditional assumption that the style is the man, we ask to locate "Lowry" in his greatest work, we might take our cue from the late-composed passage of Chapter X (31:6, 15; *Volcano* 292–93), where in a great catalogue of multitudinous bottles, an alcoholic thesaurus promiscuously consumed in the random locales of his chaotic life, yet another "babel," Geoffrey Firmin wonders skeptically "How . . . could he hope to find himself," discover amongst such anarchic fragmentation "the solitary clue to his identity"? For Lowry, I would argue, the central (if not solitary) clue to identity was discovered in the act of writing itself: when he was not writing, or living in anticipation of writing, chaos was come again, with or (less often) without alcohol. Thus while he was occupied with the various themes that the novel takes up, with love, war, betrayal, belief, poetry, religion, film, the occult, alcohol itself, and so on, it was finally in the orchestration of these that "Lowry" became most himself; it is as conductor rather than as any individual instrument that he is most present in the novel. This is not the Olympian detachment of a Joycean, godlike creator, for the novel itself radiates a kind of poised desperation, the implied awareness that all that separates a Malcolm Lowry from a Geoffrey Firmin is precisely the ability to dominate the demons to the extent of articulating them within an aesthetic structure. Emotional urgency comes out of Lowry's own experience, irony out of his contemplation of that experience, richness and complexity out of his years of writing and rewriting.

Thus, to make the assumption, as so many readers do, that what is central to the *Volcano*, what is most "Lowry" in it, are those inward passages of the Consul, those renderings of his longing, suffering, absurd, insightful, prescient, alcoholically overburdened consciousness, is, unquestionably, to grasp its imaginative core, but it is also to deny (or at least downplay) the structures within and against which this figure has been placed, the renderings of other consciousnesses, the creation of the larger world of the novel. This is the romantic reading of the *Volcano*, but it is also a reading with stylistic implications, a privileging of the more complex and elliptical passages of the novel as somehow most characteristically "Lowry," so that the surrounding context—which here means the surrounding context of language, of other "styles," which sometimes resound through Geoffrey, more often resonate around him—becomes essentially a "placing" of him, the necessary contextualizing demanded by the fictive form, subordinate to the monumental figure at the center (whose importance, as Douglas Day put it [326], derives from the fact that he "is, partially" Malcolm Lowry). Certainly this popular view continues to be available to those who desire it, yet a study of the manuscripts suggests that, whatever the germ of the work, its evolution involved Lowry in far broader concerns than just the rendering of its central character, that it was a conception of the novel as a whole that drove him, a sharpening, clarifying, enriching, enlarging observable throughout the revisions and responsible, finally, for the varied rhythms and differing styles incorporated into the text. Holding firm to the action, the temporal span, the group of characters, the chapter-structure that he had achieved by 1940, Lowry poured his energy into weaving and reweaving the very texture of his book until it was that variegated creation, far more fully than any of the humans contained in it, that became the true mirror of its creator. If the young Lowry is suggested by Hugh, and the Mexican Lowry memorialized in Geoffrey, the figure who emerged out of both of these to create the work containing but hardly limited to their experiences can be glimpsed only in the vision of the *Volcano* as a whole.

APPENDIX A

Stages of the 1940 *Under the Volcano*

Watermarks on the bond typing paper used for the 1940 typed draft, which clearly read "Made in Canada," confirm that we are not dealing with any leaves of previous versions. Further, surviving letters that either speak of work on the novel or whose ribbon or paper correspond to that of the novel typescript enable us to estimate with some accuracy not only dates for the draft as a whole but even those of its various stages. As noted in my text, the Lowrys began work sometime in January 1940. A letter from Lowry to Harold Matson of August 9, 1940 (1:79), claims that Whit Burnett of Story Press has had the *Volcano* "since June 27," and letters to Aiken of June 10 and July 19 confirm late June as the time of Lowry's mailing (*Aiken-Lowry* 137-39, 142). These dates mean that this version of the *Volcano* was entirely assembled in less than six months, and even though we have no way of determining how much actual rewriting was involved, the rapidity and the eagerness it demonstrates are for Lowry altogether unparalleled.

The working typescript (UBC typescript "B") remains almost complete, that is, as the base of the fair copy that was made from it and sent off to Whit Burnett. The typescript can be divided into six separate stages distinguishable by the brand of bond typing paper (or in the final stage, the use of yellow foolscap), the color of the ribbon used, and the style of typeface. In order, these stages are:

1. Superfine paper, black ribbon, pica type.
2. Colonial paper, black ribbon, pica type.
3. Colonial paper, blue ribbon, pica type.
4. Willson paper, blue ribbon, pica type.
5. Willson paper, black ribbon, elite type.
6. Yellow foolscap, elite type.

Extant letters and the Lowrys' move in May 1940, which also brought a change of typewriters, enable us to establish a range for each of these stages:

1. While it is impossible to determine precisely when typing began, letters to the Aikens of January 27 and February 7 correspond to paper, ribbon color, and typeface of this first stage (Aiken Collection, Huntington Library, nos. 2507, 2509).
2. An undated draft of a letter to Arthur Osborne Lowry, to which the elder Lowry replied on April 5, is made up of two pages, the first of which corresponds in paper, ribbon, and typeface to stage two of the *Volcano* draft. However, the second page of the letter draft switches to blue ribbon, thereby dating the transition to stage three in late March (1:38, 1:79).
3. See 2 above.
4. In a letter to Mrs. John Stuart Bonner dated April 16, the ribbon is still blue, the type pica, but the paper has changed to Willson brand (1:79).
5. The Lowrys' move from 19th to 11th Avenues in Vancouver, and the change of typewriters that came with it, occurred between May 7 and May 15: a letter to James Stern on the former date is headed "19th Avenue" (*Letters* 27), and one to the Aikens on the latter date bears the new address (*Aiken-Lowry* 134). The change of typeface is evident on the latter (Aiken Collection, Huntington Library, no. 2513).
6. At some indeterminate time after May 15 (presumably when the Willson paper was used up) the switch to yellow paper was made.

It is clear from the extant manuscript that a full draft of eleven chapters had been created before the Lowrys' move from 19th Avenue in May and that revisions were already underway to make the twelve chapter version, which was achieved by the splitting and rewriting of the original Chapter II. However, it is also clear that although each of the chapters is folioed individually, the typing—and thus, given the Lowrys' later practice, probably also the writing—was carried out in order from I through XI. Revision here, however, also establishes Lowry's characteristic practice: the chapter, not the novel, becomes the operative unit, and rewriting does not necessarily proceed in novelistic order. Thus, for instance, Chapter II was clearly the first to be revised here, but it was also revised more than once. After the extensive enlargement and splitting that made Chapters II and III out of the original II, Lowry returned to each chapter individually for further revision. Furthermore, close inspection shows that although, for instance, both III and IV were revised in the Willson-elite stage, the revisions on IV preceded those on III: in IV "Enid" is still typed as the name of the Consul's former wife, while in III the typewriter has made the change to Priscilla (here too is the first typed change of the film director, originally "Lacretelle," to "Laruelle," thus indicating that both name changes were relatively late decisions).

Thus, a description of the first surviving novel version of the *Volcano* as a function of its typescript is as follows:

CHAPTER NUMBER	NUMBER OF PAGES	PAPER AND TYPE INDICATORS	APPROXIMATE DATING, 1940
I	2	Superfine black pica	Jan.–Feb.
	35	yellow elite	May–June
II	15	Willson blue pica	April–May
	7	Willson black elite	May
III	2	Superfine black pica	Jan.–Feb.
	17	Willson blue pica	April–May
	9	Willson black elite	May
IV	6	Superfine black pica	Jan.–Feb.
	24	Willson black elite	May
V	9	Colonial black pica	Feb.–March
	23	yellow elite	May–June
VI	11	Colonial black pica	Feb.–March
	3	Willson blue pica	April–May
	13	yellow elite	May–June
VII	12	Colonial black pica	Feb.–March
	4	Colonial blue pica	March–April
	21	yellow elite	May–June
VIII	17	Colonial blue pica	March–April
	9	yellow elite	May–June
IX	22	Colonial blue pica	March–April
	11	yellow elite	May–June
X	1	Colonial blue pica	March–April
	32	yellow elite	May–June
XI	20	yellow elite	May–June
XII	24	Willson blue pica	April–May
	11	yellow elite	May–June

As the "elite" indications alone show, all chapters, whether or not they received earlier revision, were again revised in the final stage, that is, the last month, of composition, conveniently indicated here by the change in typewriters. It is worth noting that in a typescript totalling some 360 pages, 215 of those are revisions in this final stage, although, once more, lacking knowledge of what was superseded we can gain no real sense of how extensive the rewriting was.

What this listing cannot reveal is the refoliation that necessarily went on when there were several stages to a chapter's composition, but which is sometimes revealing in unpredictable ways. For instance, in Chapter X the yellow elite sheets are themselves sometimes folioed more than once, indicating not only that Lowry found his first version of the chapter unsatisfactory (only one page of the original remains) but that the final phase was also not without its difficulties. On the other hand, in Chapter XII, which like all the rest went through at least two stages here, the pages, both bond and yellow, are entirely without refoliation, suggesting Lowry's relative assurance and satisfaction with this chapter (reflected also in its content: in both action and language this is the chapter that most nearly anticipates its final version). Chapter XI, however, remains indeterminate: while the fact that no bond pages remain reveals Lowry's radical dissatisfaction with its original form (whatever that might have been), the surviving yellow pages are entirely unrefolioed, suggesting either that he easily arrived at this second version or that the chapter went through an undetermined number of total rewritings. Given Lowry's ususal practice, I would hazard that the first is the more likely possibility, but obviously no certainty is attainable.

Typescript "B" seems to survive complete with the exception of missing p. 13 in Chapter IV. It is prepared for further typing in Lowry's usual way: that is, while there are pencil additions, corrections, and instructions, there are also erasures and the general appearance of an attempt to keep the pencilled markings legible for Margerie. The fair copy made from it is the typescript resoundingly rejected by the New York publishing world, and Lowry eventually instructed Harold Matson to destroy it (*Letters* 38). (Matson, however, eventually returned it.) Lowry kept in his possession two carbons of that ribbon copy (UBC's typescripts "C" and "D"), which when compared with "B" do reveal some minor discrepancies (cf. in Chapter I, pp. 24 and 34-35 of "B" and pp. 29 and 41 respectively of "C"; in Chapter II, pp. 16-17 of "B" and 61-62 of "C"; in Chapter X, pp. 11-12 of "B" and p. 318 of "C"). These changes may have been made orally or on inserts subsequently lost.

Beyond the notebook passages discussed in the Prologue that seem either to have gone immediately into the *Volcano* or to have been originally designed for it, Lowry can be discovered plundering other fictions, which already had a life at least in draft form, for some very specific borrowings at this stage of the novel. For example, not only does the child's exercise book surface in El Bosque in "B," as noted in the Prologue, but a discussion between old Carruthers and his barber about the deprivations of the poor appears almost unchanged in the dialogue of Hugh's flying acquaintance Weber (*1940* 64). Hugh recollects for Yvonne's benefit his sight of corpses in New York City in an only slightly abbreviated passage from the already published story "In Le Havre" (cf. *1940* 113-14, and *Psalms and Songs* 465-66). In Chapter VII the Consul accuses Laruelle by identifying himself with "'The Cyclops.... You ate his mutton, drank his wine, and then you poked his eye out'" (*1940* 211), a charge already made against another womanizer in "Bulls of the Resurrection" (6). From that same story, in one of the few such passages that will survive even in abbreviated form, Lowry lifts "'*Thalavettiparothiam* . . . Or strength obtained by decaptiation'" (cf. *1940* 175, and "Bulls," 10). "The Last Address" (later *Lunar Caustic*) seems to have provided Lowry with the most durable of his prose self-cannibalizings of this period. Here we find "the eternal horror of opposites" (15:1, 2), the film in which a dead shark continues to devour live fish (15:2, IV, 2), and in a connection not strictly verbal, the association of grotesque scenes of surgery with a drunken "horror of the rats." Whereas the protagonist of "The Last Address" believes he can see into hospital operating rooms, the Consul in Chapter V of the 1940 *Volcano* is made to recall several horrifying drawings in Dr. Vigil's office, and in both episodes the vision gives way to a fear of DT's, a "progresión a ratos" (cf. 15:2, V, 3, and *1940* 139–40).

Lowry's self-borrowings were not limited to prose. Poems of this period (that is, those known to have been created before the move to Vancouver) also proved to be fruitful sources, and the fact that poetic borrowings are more likely to persist into the final version than prose may suggest the central role of language in the completion of the novel. For instance, "lightning like an inch-worm going down the sky," which appears here in Chapter XII, occurs also in an early poem (cf. *1940* 374, and Scherf no. 90), and flashing lights that create a "St. Vitus of the City of the Angels" in a poem (Scherf no. 46) simply shifts coasts and genres to become "a St. Vitus dance of electric light" in New York (*1940* 45). The couplet from the Strauss song that first occurs in a dream in the *Volcano* is used in an early poem (cf. *1940* 35, and Scherf no. 61).

But no poetic worksheet was more thoroughly plundered for the novel than a Mexican typescript, with pencil annotations back and front (6:7), of the poem later called "Thirty-five Mescals in Cuautla" (Scherf no. 25). The poem apparently began as an exercise for Conrad Aiken, written in a bar in Cuernavaca during Aiken's visit, and since it reflects on its site of origin Lowry not surprisingly found a home for much of it in his descriptions of El Bosque in Chapter VII. Not all, however: when Chapter I has "khaki water sousing down the gutters" (*1940* 21), it has done no more to the poem's phrasing than make "gutter" plural, and both the poem and Chapter XII contain a "calendar set for/to the future," although the novel's is unillustrated at this stage (*1940* 357), whereas the poem's already has its reindeer and coracle/canoe. Nonetheless, the most extensive uses are those of Chapter VII. The poem has "This ticking is most terrible of all / . . . the death watch beetle at the rotten timber of the world / . . . the hearts [*sic*] silent tick failing against the clock / . . . the tick of real death / not the tick of time. Uno mescalito? / In the cantina throbs the refrigerator / while against the street the gaunt station hums / . . . real death's inside no need to let it loose / the lieutenant carries it though I can't see his face."[1] In the novel the Consul does drink mescal in El Bosque—the drink has no special significance in the 1940 version—and the relevant passages go as follows: "The death watch beetle at the rotten timber of the world. The heart's tick failing against time. The tick of real death not the tick of time. Or was it just the refrigerator? No, that was more like a hum. . . . [the Consul looks at his watch:] This was where the tick was coming from. . . . Somebody else entered and went right through to the back room, glancing around furtively" (*1940* 223). Perhaps the setting helps explain the association when on the verso of the poetic draft one finds pencilled notes for the catalogue of available alcohol that will turn up in El Bosque as well as for the speech of Señora Gregorio, including "So it is. You must take it as it come. It can't be helped," precisely the words that occur in the *Volcano* (*1940* 221).

Lowry seems to have had the originals of virtually all of the "found" materials of the *Volcano*—notices, menus, travel folders, calendars, and so on—in his possession in Vancouver: typescript "B" is full of instructions to "correct by original" in preparing the fair copy, so often so that by the time he has reached Chapter XII he mocks his own practice: next to the Spanish meant to express the old joke about the world going round and waiting for one's own house to come by, he pencils, "Correct by something, God knows what—probably by another note which says correct by this one" (26:5, 17). An exception seems to be the menu of the Salón Ofélia as read out in Chapter X (it may be worth noting that we are never presented with this menu, as we will be that of the El Popo of Chapter XI and for which an original does exist). Notes for the fractured English and the trilingual punning survive in at least two places, suggesting that there was a Mexican "original," whether written or oral. Again, on the verso of the poem typescript discussed immediately above we find, precisely as in "B," such items as "Cawliflowers Poot tootsies Pricked petroot Pep with milk," and "B" will make only one significant alteration: the "special soup," which on the poem typescript is attributed to "Dr. Moises L. Guevara" becomes in "B" the provenance of "Dr. Moise L. von Schmidthaus," presumably to accommodate the "German friends" refrain (26:3, 7). More of Señor Cervantes's remarkable fare turns up in the margin of an early version of the poem later titled "For *Under the Volcano*" (4:84), and here there are alterations between notes and "B". While "divorced eggs" remains unchanged, "octopus in his ink" becomes "sea sleeves in his ink," "the spectral turkey of the house" becomes a chicken, "a somersault to the queen" is elaborated to "Vol-au-vent a la reine. . . . No somersaults for the queen today." This leaves a number of items unaccounted for—"onans in garlic soup," "poxy eggs," "tunny fish," "brambleberry con crappe Grand Duc," to mention only the more delectable—but recalling that the "gin fish" had turned up in the early Pegaso notebook, one may suspect other items recorded on pages now lost. However, since these are meant to be comic transmutations of the "original" Spanish (unlike, say, the menu of El Popo, which is to be taken straight) it is not difficult to imagine Lowry gleefully playing his own punning variations on the bawdy or political themes already suggested by recorded items. In either case, Cervantes's remarkable menu is virtually complete in the "B" typescript.[2]

APPENDIX B

The Manuscript Record

What follows is a listing, for the use of other scholars, of the currently known manuscripts pertaining to *Under the Volcano*. Included here is only material directly relevant to the novel—not quite as banal an assertion as it might appear. There survive materials other than manuscripts—a menu, a telegram—that played significant roles in the compositional process (see the final category of this listing); on the other hand, many other Lowry manuscripts are tangentially rather than directly related to the evolving novel. For instance, in a letter of May 7, 1940, to James Stern, Lowry tells how he came under suspicion for "drawing a map of the Sierra Madre in tequila on the bar counter" in Oaxaca and confides that he learned there the "true" meaning of "stool pigeon" (*Letters* 29). A reader will recognize these anecdotes from the published *Volcano*, but they had not become a part of the manuscript of the novel Lowry was completing at the time he wrote that letter. Often, other documents he had brought back with him from Mexico, the menu, for instance, or the Tlaxcala folder, were available to him for years before being incorporated into the manuscript. All of these materials, manuscript and other, are of interest to anyone studying the creation of the novel, and in my text, I refer to biographical documents whenever it seems helpful or revealing. The following listing, however, confines itself strictly to materials that are a part of the manuscript record of the novel, insofar as it is determinable, in the order in which they entered the working text. Scholars are advised, however, that Lowry was not a neat writer, keeping works clearly separate from one another, genres (poems, letters, novels) in their proper places, and art sharply distinguished from life: thus light on the *Volcano* might suddenly flash from almost anywhere in the manuscript records.

Since, however, for reasons that I argue in the text, there are only two genuine "versions" of the novel (the 1940 circulated fair copy and the 1947 Reynal and Hitchcock publication), and since Lowry revised by chapter, it seemed most sensible and useful to follow his example and, after noting the few known pre-1940 manuscripts and describing the 1940 *Volcano*, to treat the ensuing record on a chapter-by-chapter basis. However, even here, Lowry's methods of composition prevent a neat separation: because he used a carbon ("D") of the 1940 *Volcano* as the basis for his next revisions, the 1940 and 1941 manuscripts have had to be listed together.

Once past these initial shoals, a further discrimination seemed useful. Lowry composed in pencil. When he achieved a chapter draft by which he was satisfied, he gave it to Margerie to type. He tended to keep, held together by paperclips, the full versions, both holograph and typescript, of the various drafts of his chapters even after they had long been superseded by more recent versions. These "final" drafts, both holograph and typescript, might be made up of several stages, but the discards, the false starts, the superseded tries with individual passages were treated cavalierly, often ploughed back into the Lowrys' stock of usable sheets, where clean versos became available for still other drafts. What has tended to survive, then, are those once "complete" drafts (now, alas, not always complete) which are, at every stage, the state-of-the-chapter, whereas there is no way of estimating what percentage of the discards has come down to us (far fewer, certainly, than the proportion of complete drafts). Thus two columns, one headed "drafts," the other "discards," will list, by location, the extant manuscripts from each stage. Drafts will be designated as holograph or typescript, complete or incomplete (unless otherwise indicated, discards are holograph). No attempt at full description of materials or analysis of such complexities as refoliation and reuse of leaves of earlier drafts will be undertaken here: for these, the reader is referred to the appropriate pages and notes in the preceding text. Finally, a brief separate listing will indicate materials directly related to the creation of the novel—maps, notes, sketches, "found" objects—which are not an actual part of any of the manuscripts of the text.

The location of all materials other than the "Texas" manuscript is the Special Collections Division of the Library of the University of British Columbia (see "A Note on the Text" above). Although the McFarlin Library of The University of Tulsa holds the ribbon copy of the manuscript edited at Reynal and Hitchcock, the listing below refers to the photocopy at UBC, there designated the "F" manuscript of the novel.

I shall continue using other designations devised at UBC—the "B" manuscript, the "E" manuscript, and so on—because they are the terms that past and future Lowry scholars, for whom this listing is intended, encounter there. Numbers without preceding designation indicate, as in the text, box, file, and page (where existent) in the Lowry Collection. "T" will designate typescript, "H" holograph draft, "N" notebook, "n.p." no page heading; "C" after a draft will indicate a complete surviving draft of that stage, "I" an incomplete one. Individual leaves will be listed as catalogued at UBC: that is, a superseded draft of the *Volcano* found on the verso of a manuscript catalogued elsewhere will appear as, say, "11:6, verso 18." Finally, "MBL" designates Margerie Bonner Lowry, "AE" Albert Erskine, Lowry's editor at Reynal and Hitchcock.

A. PRE-1940

1. "Libreta Pegaso" notebook 12:14
2. Two loose notebook leaves, possibly from (1) above. 28:21
3. Two loose notebook leaves, not from (1) above. 28:21
4. One loose writing tablet leaf 1:76
5. "Red notebook" (currently missing from UBC)

B. 1940-1941

1. The "B" manuscript. An annotated typescript of 362 pages including pencil inserts, complete except for a missing p. 13 of Chapter IV. 25:17-26:5
Discards: 25:17, verso 9; 25:20, verso 21; 1:38, verso
May 7, 1940 letter from A. O. Lowry; Texas IV, versos 33-34.
2. Fair copy of the "B" manuscript, a typescript of 404 pages, existing as a ribbon copy with two carbons.
   (a) Ribbon copy (circulated to New York publishers, 1940-41), now the possession of Mr. Norman Levi, Victoria, B.C. Missing title page, first epigraph page, final page; corrected, lightly annotated.
   (b) First carbon ("C" manuscript). Complete, corrected, unannotated. 26:6-26:17
   (c) Second carbon ("D" manuscript). Incomplete, corrected, heavily annotated. Base for first post-1940 revisions, bond sheets supplemented by yellow newsprint, latter sometimes catalogued with former, sometimes separately:
      (1) "D" (alone or with yellow leaves): 26:18-27:5
      (2) Supplementary yellow leaves catalogued elsewhere:
         I 5:52, n.p., verso
         II 29:1
         III 29:7
         VII 30:5 (except 25-28/9); Templeton 1:9, 9

The Manuscript Record | 397

VIII	30:9. See also 25:16 ("A" manuscript, the story version written during this period)
IX	30:12; Templeton 1:7
X	31:4
XI	31:11, 12; Templeton 1:5, Templeton 1:6

C. 1942–1946 (BY CHAPTER)

DRAFTS	DISCARDS

Chapter I

1. (a) [H ?]
   (b) 28:23. T, I
2. (a) [H ?]
   (b) 28:25, 3. T, I
3. (a) 28:24. H, I

   (b) Texas I. T, C

4. "E": 27:6. T, C
5. "F": 27:18. T, C

6. (a) Correspondence with
   AE: 1:20; 2:6–9
   (b) "G" (galley proofs): 28:9

(a) 28:21 N, 28:22 N

(b) 28:23, T "21"
(a) 28:23, n.p.;
Templeton 1:8, versos
T 40, 42, 53; 30:4,
n.pp.; versos Texas I, 1
4, 6–9, 13–15A,
22, 27–47; Texas II, 7–14;
Texas VI, 12, 30–33,
36–42, 44–45, 48, 52,
54–57
(b) Templeton 1:8, T 40, 42;
30:4, n.p.; versos Texas VI,
5–6, 14–22; 15:14, versos
2–3

28:25, T 14, 15, 16, 44;
28:25, 7 n.pp.; 27:6,
T 14–16A

(a) 28:25, 2 n.p.p.

Chapter II

1. (a) 29:2. H, C
   (b) 29:5, 5; 29:6, 12, insert 12–13, 13, 19, insert 19. T, I

2. (a) 29:3, Hpp.
   29:4, Hpp. C
   (b) 29:3, Tpp. + 29:5, 14A-15.
       T + H, C
   (c) 29:4, Tpp. + 29:3 Tpp.
       2-3, 5-8. T, C
3. (a) 29:5 + 29:3, T "4," "8,"   (a) 2:2, "1945" [?] letter to
       "9" + 29:6, 10. H, I   Matson, versos. Versos
                                         Texas I, 3, 5, 10-12A,
                                         20-21, 26; Texas II, 1-5,
                                         15-27; Texas VI, 1, 3-4,
                                         7-11, 24-24A, 26-29
   (b) Texas II. T, C
4. "E": 27:7. T, C
5. "F": 27:19. T, C   28:25, n.p.
6. (a) Correspondence with AE: (a) 31:11, verso 1 [?]
       1:20, 2:6-9
   (b) "G" (galley proofs): 28:10

Chapter III

1. (a) 29:8. H, C   (a) 29:11, n.p.
   (b) Templeton 1:19, 22. T, I
2. (a) 29:9. H, C   (a) 29:11, n.p.
   (b) [T ?]
3. (a) 29:10. H, C   (a) 5:42, n.p., verso
   (b) Texas III. T, C   (b) Versos, Texas III, 1-9,
                                         11-25, 27-29, 31, 33-34;
                                         Texas IV, 29-32, 35-36, 39;
                                         Texas VI, 2A; Harvey Burt
                                         Papers 1:2, n.p.
4. "E": 27:8. T, C
5. "F": 27:20. T, C
6. (a) Correspondence with AE: 1:20;
       2:6-9
   (b) "G" (galley proofs): 28:11

Chapter IV

1. (a) 29:12. H, C   (a) 29:12, D verso
   (b) [T ?]

The Manuscript Record | 399

2. (a) 29:13. H, C

(b) 29:13. T, C
3. (a) 29:14. H, C

(b) Texas IV. T, C

4. "E": 27:9. T, C
5. "F": 27:21. T, C

6. (a) Correspondence with AE: 1:20; 2:6-9
(b) "G" (galley proofs): 28:12

(a) 2:2, "Oct. 25" letter to Matson, verso; 5:115, n.p.

(a) 5:75, n.p., verso; 29:15, 14A
(b) Versos, Texas IV, 1-12, 15-28, 37-38; 29:15, inserts

29:15, T 144-145; 29:15, A-C, 144; 30:8, versos 5-6; Texas, versos, letter of 13/4/52, John Davenport to Nancy Cunard, carbon T 144-45

Chapter V

1. (a) 29:16. H, C
(b) 29:16, 8-9. T, I
2. (a) 29:17. H, C

(b) 29:17, 15-17, 19-27
Texas V, 1-14, 18, 28. T, C
(c) 29:18. H, I

(d) Texas V, 15-30 + 29:17, 28. T, I
3. "E": 27:10. T, C
4. "F": 28:1. T, C
5. (a) Correspondence with AE: 1:20; 2:6-9
(b) "G" (galley proofs): 28:13

(a) 29:19, A-B, A-B, 1, 2 n.pp.; Templeton 1:12, 1; Versos: Texas IV, 14, 31; Texas V, 16-17, 23

(c) Versos Texas V, 15, 19-21, 24-30

27:10, E

Chapter VI

1. (a) [H ?]
(b) 30:1. T, C

2. (a) 30:2. H, C (a) 30:8, 7; 28:24, verso 6; 30:4, n.p.

   (b) Templeton 1:8, 8, 43-44 (?); 30:3, T 7-9, 11-12; Texas VI, 13, 17, 23, 25. T, I
   (b) 30:4, 3, 7-8, 10, A, 2-3, A-E, 2 n.pp.; 5:96, verso; 5:44, verso; versos Texas I, 16-19; Texas VI, 2, 46-47; 28:25, verso 3; versos, Texas, letter of Feb. 1944 to Gerald Noxon

3. (a) 30:3 + 2:19, verso 2, August 1951 letter to Markson + Neilson 1:2. T + H, I

   (b) Texas VI. T + H, C
   (b) 30:4, T 34-35; Templeton 1:8, T 53

4. "E": 27:11. T, C
   30:4, 198 alternative, A(2), D, n.p.

5. "F": 28:2. T, C
   30:4, D

6. (a) Correspondence with AE: 1:20; 2:6-9

   (b) "G" (galley proofs): 28:14

Chapter VII

1. (a) 30:6. H, I (a) Templeton 1:13, n.p.
   (b) 30:7 + 2:19, versos 3, 11-12, August 1951 letter to Markson. H, I
   (b) 30:8, D11(2), D12, 13, E14, E15, E16, F18(2), F19, G23, G24, I34, 6 n.pp.

   (c) 30:7 + 30:5, 25-28/29. T, C

2. (a) Texas VII. H, C
   (a) Templeton 1:8, versos T 43-44; Templeton 1:9, 11, F(?); Templeton 1:13, verso sketch; versos Texas VI, 34-35

   (b) "E": 27:12. T, C
   (b) 30:8, 2 n.p., 2-3, 5-6; Templeton 1:20, 2 n.p.

3. "F": 28:3. T, C
   30:8, 272, T 272, 285, 1-6

4. (a) Correspondence with AE: 1:20; 2:6-9

   (b) "G" (galley proofs): 28:15

Chapter VIII

1. (a) 30:10. H, I
   (b) 30:10. T, C
2. (a) Texas VIII. H, C   (a) 22:20, versos 4 n.p.
   (b) "E": 27:13. T, C
3. "F": 28:4. T, C   30:8, 1; 31:7, 2-3
4. (a) Correspondence with AE: (a) 13:14, N; 30:11, T
      1:20; 2:6-9   324, 339, 5 "O.C."
   (b) "G" (galley proofs): 28:16

Chapter IX

1. (a) [H ?]
   (b) 30:13. T, C
2. (a) 30:14. H, C
   (b) 31:1 + 2:19, verso 14, August 1951
      letter to Markson. H, C
   (c) Templeton 1:3. T, C
3. (a) 31:2. H, I
   (b) Templeton 1:4. T, C
4. (a) [H ?]
   (b) "E": 27:14. T, C   (b) 4:40, n.p., verso
5. Texas IX. T, C   31:3, A, D, B, C, 2 n.pp.,
                                          T A; 31:7, versos A, B, E,
                                          F, H, I
6. "F": 28:5. T, C   31:3, 5 n.pp.
7. (a) Correspondence with AE: 1:20;
      2:6-9
   (b) "G" (galley proofs): 28:17

Chapter X

1. (a) 31:5. H, C
   (b) 31:5. T, C
2. (a) Texas X + 31:7. H + T, C   (a) Templeton 1:9, 10, A-D;
                                          Templeton 1:22, 3
   (b) "E": 27:15 + 31:6, 28. T, C   (b) 31:8, n.p.; 31:6, 2 n.pp.,
                                          T + inserts, 4-5, 8,
                                          14-27, 29-31, 36-39,
                                          42-43

3. "F": 28:6. T, C 27:17, 3; 31:8, 1-2, n.p.
4. (a) Correspondence with AE: 1:20;
    2:6-9
   (b) "G" (galley proofs): 28:18

Chapter XI

1. (a) [H ?]
   (b) Templeton 1:6. T, C
2. (a) 31:9. H, C
   (b) 15:14, versos 16-18 + 16:2,
    verso 5. T, I
3. (a) 31:10 + 2:19, versos 4-8, 13,   (a) 15:14, versos 4-15;
    August 1951 letter to Markson.   27:17, versos 1, 7-11, 15-16;
    H, I   versos Texas XI, 1-9,
        11-26; Templeton 1:22, 3
   (b) Texas XI. T, C   (b) 16:1, verso 8; 16:2,
        versos 1-3
4. "E": 27:16. T, C   16:2, verso 4; 31:11, 1-3
5. "F": 28:7. T, C   29:15, 2-3
6. (a) Correspondence with AE: 1:20;   (a) 31:11, 1-3, 2 n.pp.
    2:6-9
   (b) "G" (galley proofs): 28:19

Chapter XII

1. (a) 31:12. H, C
   (b) Texas XII. H, C   (b) 31:13, A-E, D-E, 39A,
        14-14A, 22, 25, 3 n.pp.
   (c) "E": 27:17, 2-6, 10-12, 17-44.   (c) 31:13, T 4 + insert, 9-10,
    T, I   15 + insert, 32(2),
        33 + insert
2. (a) Texas XII, 1, 7A-9A, 12A-13.   (a) 27:17, versos 17-21, final
    H, I   page; 31:13, 2 n.pp.;
        Templeton 1:13, verso, n.p.
   (b) "E": 27:17, 1, 7-11, 15-21. T, I   (b) 31:13, 1-4, 2 n.pp.
3. "F": 28:8. T, C   31:13, T 480(2), 2, 1-2, A,
        n.p.
4. (a) Correspondence with AE: 1:20;   (a) 29:19, T, n.p.
    2:6-9
   (b) "G" (galley proofs): 28:20

The Final Typescripts of *Under the Volcano,* "E" and "F"

Almost all of typescript "E" (the only exception is the major part of Chapter XII) was made in Ontario late in 1944 as the fair copy of the chapters now gathered as the "Texas" manuscript. That grouping, a combination of holograph and typescript drafts, annotated and corrected, was then presented to Gerald and Betty Noxon at Christmas 1944. The "E" typescript was made on the sheets of yellow newsprint the Lowrys favored for all but final drafts, except for portions of Chapters V–VII: for the latter part of V, a thin yellow paper was used, and for the basic draft of VI and the early part of VII, a white paper, watermark "Revenue Bond" (?). Including title and epigraph pages, this was a typescript of some 473 pages ("some," because it is not always possible to be certain whether pencil inserts and typed supersessions were done at this stage or the next ["F"]).

Annotated, partially revised, typescript "E" became the basis for the fair copy typescript "F," made on bond paper in Dollarton in the spring of 1945, a typescript of 543 pages (its greater length largely a result of wider margins). Presumably at least two carbons were made (the ribbon copy to New York, one carbon to Jonathan Cape in London, another carbon retained by Lowry): both are apparently lost.

Other Materials Directly Pertaining to *Under the Volcano*

FROM LOWRY COLLECTION:

2:1, undated letter [July 1944], ML to MBL	Chapter X

FROM TEMPLETON COLLECTION:

1:2, the telegram that is the basis for Hugh's	Chapter IV
1:2, draft letter to G. Noxon [June 15, 1943]	Chapter I
1:9, n.p., directions on exchange of manuscripts with G. Noxon [late 1944]; verso, MBL, "Final notes for Malc"	
1:9, A–B, "Laruelle's books"	Chapter VII
1:10, 1–10, notes from Rawlinson, *India: A Short Cultural History*	Chapters I, V, IX, X, XII
1:11, 3 n.pp., titles for Consul's library, trial dialogue regarding demons, Platonists	Chapter VI
1:11, 1–6, notes from Buckley, *Life and Death of the Spanish Republic*	Chapters IV, VIII, X

1:12, 1–10, notes from Younghusband, *Kashmir*	Chapters III, X, XII
1:13, sketches, the wounded man in the road, paths between Tomalín and Parián	Chapters VIII, XI
1:14, 3 n.pp., notes on chronology of Yvonne, of the Firmin brothers, of events 1935–38, mainly in MBL's hand	
1:15, n.p., headed "General Points to be kept in mind when book is completed"	
1:16, n.p., timing of storm, mainly in MBL's hand	Chapters XI, XII
1:17, n.p., quotation from Dante's *Purgatorio*	
1:18, n.p., sketches for Laruelle's house	
1:19, verso T 22, H map of Quauhnahuac	
1:21, 1–7, notes from Gunther, *Inside Latin America*	
1:22, 5 n.pp., notes from Nuttall, *Ornithology*	Chapter XI
1:23, 2 n.pp., notes from Bates, *Fields of Paradise* [?]	
1:24, the menu on which that of El Popo is based	Chapter XI

NOTES

INTRODUCTION

1. *Letters* 61; see Blackmur xi. I am indebted to Kathy Chung for this identification.
2. Pottinger, "Revising" 30–31. See also Deck.
3. Perhaps this is the place to put to rest any lingering notions that the 1940 version of the *Volcano* was an unappreciated masterpiece rejected by philistine publishers. Such a conception might have been fostered by Conrad Aiken's curious (mischievous?) public statement after Lowry's death about the relationship of an even earlier version to the published novel: "It has always been said that *Under the Volcano* was written *after* the Cuernavaca period. Not so. I read . . . while we were there . . . the whole of *Under the Volcano*. The first draft, but complete, and with a different ending: the horse theme had not then been developed. In short, that book was going to be rewritten for the next nine years. No wonder, given his genius for language, that it is such a miracle of English prose, which, I think, is its chief virtue. . . . But the novel was already substantially *there* in July 1937" (Killorin 124). As a poet and novelist himself, to say nothing of his role as Lowry's literary "father," Aiken's view here seems unaccountable without hypothesizing a posthumous round in the mutual cannibalizing of these two friends/rivals. Indeed, the aim appears so relentlessly undermining that it even discredits Aiken's description of what he actually saw in Cuernavaca thirty years earlier. Compare the account of Arthur Calder-Marshall (Prologue, p. 19 below), who visited Lowry in Mexico several months after Aiken.

PROLOGUE

1. *Prairie Schooner* 37, no. 4 (Winter 1963–64), 284–300; *Psalms and Songs*, 187–201. See Stephen Spender, Introduction to *Under the Volcano*, vii–viii; Day 216–19; Ackerley and Clipper 312.
2. See *Letters* 39. Victor Doyen long ago showed conclusively from both internal and external evidence that the typescript identified in Margerie Lowry's

hand as "First version—a short story" in fact dated from several years later than the putative 1936–37 composition date of such an "original" and thus reflected a later phase of the novel's development. See Doyen, "Fighting the Albatross" 230–32, and O'Kill, "Stylistic Study." This story version, known as "A" at UBC, is found in 25:16.

3. There is a fuller account of composing done in Mexico in the unedited manuscript of *Dark As the Grave,* but since it is Sigbjørn Wilderness's account, never given by Lowry in propria persona, and highly unlikely given other testimony and surviving manuscripts, it seems worth recording in a note. According to Sigbjørn, while still in Mexico and before his wife left him, he had "written the story as a short novel and found myself unable to sell it. . . . It then occurred to me . . . that nobody had written an adequate book upon drinking . . . and so while the first short version of the book was getting turned down by publisher after publisher, I began to elaborate upon that theme of drunkenness . . . out of this kind of thing came the character of the Consul." However, a few pages later, Sigbjørn gives a partially contradictory account, one that posits the creation of a drunken Consul as a very early phase of composition: "After having written the story about the Indian by the side of the road, and first got the inspiration to make the whole thing a larger novel—I wrote the end . . . first. I had him, the Consul, shot by a bunch of policemen in a pub . . . above the barranca." This figure was called, Sigbjørn goes on, "William Erickson," and he had just completed his account of the murder, relying on the conversation of "a bunch of complete borrachos" he had recorded in his notebook, when he read a newspaper account of the shooting and throwing down the barranca of an American, whose name also turned out to be William Erickson (9:5, 330–39). The latter coincidence, of course, fits all too neatly into the concerns of *Dark As the Grave* ("Erickson," Lowry claimed, was the name he had given to the figure representing Nordahl Grieg in *In Ballast to the White Sea* and was also the Lowrys' telephone exchange in Cuernavaca) but even without that correspondence, we can recognize in publishers' universal rejection of the manuscript and the subsequent revision to include examination of an alcoholic phases of the later history of the *Volcano.* In short, Lowry is at least in part fictionalizing for his own purposes in *Dark As the Grave;* and indeed *both* of these accounts simply cannot be true (the Consul was created almost at once, the Consul was not created until after a "short novel" was complete). Lowry *might* have written some version of what became Chapter XII very early (although the Cape letter, for instance, will not imply this), but since the only testimony to this posssibility is *Dark As the Grave,* the ground is extremely shaky.

4. "Phillips" was her married name; she was born Carol Betty Osborne and is now, after another marriage, known as Betty Atwater. I am most grateful to Betty Atwater for the following account, gleaned from a tape she made in 1991

and an interview with me, July 18, 1991. To avoid confusion, however, I will in the text continue to refer to "Carol Phillips," the name by which Lowry knew her.

5. Letter from Carol Phillips [Betty Atwater] to her mother, May 17, 1939. Quoted by permission of Betty Atwater.

6. *Aiken-Lowry* 126; Aiken, *Ushant* 357. This (Mexican?) school composition book measuring 9" × 6½," brand name "Libreta Pegaso" (12:14), contains several poems and material pertaining to *In Ballast to the White Sea* as well as to the *Volcano*.

7. 28:21. The size and quality of the paper makes it possible that these are from the "Pegaso" notebook. Strengthening this suggestion is the content common to notebook and sheets: description of the trip to Puebla, draft passages relevant to *In Ballast,* and the poem that will become "In the Oaxaca Train." Against this, however, is the testimony of one draft of *Dark As the Grave Wherein My Friend Is Laid* (8:10) in which "Martin" on a second trip to Mexico takes from his pocket what is called a "black notebook" and reads "Going to Oaxaca via Puebla on the train, Feb. 1937" (13). This he recalls as a trip taken with his wife, "Ruth," just before "Daniel" (Aiken) had arrived, and "some of it he had used in his Chap I of The Valley of the Shadow of Death" [*Volcano*]. What follows on pp. 13–14 of this manuscript is a precise transcription of the passages appearing on the two leaves under consideration, the first of which is headed simply "Going to Puebla." "The Volcano" also appears at the top of the page, apparently a later pencil addition, and there may be a few other additions on these pages from the *Dark As the Grave* period of the later 1940s. If so, they are very minor.

8. This 9⅞" × 7¾" set of bound pages was removed from its original composition book cover and inserted within a smaller (9³⁄₁₆" × 7") red composition book cover with no identifying marks (in spite of this anomaly I will refer to the present item as "the red notebook"). With the exception of the draft of a poem on the verso of the final sheet here, the nine unpaginated leaves contain only material for the *Volcano*.

This red notebook has been mislaid at UBC. My citations from it are taken from my own transcription of the contents made in 1983.

CHAPTER ONE. **The 1940** *Under the Volcano*

1. Despite all that is missing, we can glimpse part of the process by which the Lowrys' working text ("B") was arrived at. For instance, during composition the second chapter underwent a great expansion, followed by its being split into Chapters II and III. The enlargement, it appears, was in a sense an

expansion "backwards." Only two pages remain from the original Chapter II, but they are the final pages, now the last pages of III, and they present the Consul on his porch reflecting on his condition, having his hallucination, pouring himself a drink, and as the chapter ends, observing hovering vultures. Since this portion of the chapter remains firm throughout, it seems that the greatest expansion here was precisely of the material that now makes up the 1940 Chapter II, which presents Yvonne in Acapulco. Chapter II may once have begun much as it does in the published novel (and as it will in subsequent drafts) with Yvonne looking for and/or finding the Consul in the hotel bar in Quahnahuac [sic] the morning after the ball. Later, however, with a completed draft before him, Lowry may have come to feel that a good deal of exposition was needed to "account for " Yvonne here—more than for the Consul, for instance, of whom we had heard a good bit in Chapter I. As the draft had developed, Yvonne had become a character second in dramatic and thematic importance only to her father—but who was she exactly? what was she doing in Mexico? what were her desires and concerns? In trying to sketch in some answers, Lowry may thus have hit on the expedient of dramatizing her directly—thus the Yvonne-in-Acapulco section that grew to such a size that it split off into a chapter of its own.

If something like this is what occurred, it helps account for a curious vacillation throughout the working typescript ("B") that suggests Lowry's uneasiness about this new chapter. For instance, all of the pages of Chapter IV here are headed with a typed "III," and the chapter's opening page, typed late, in May, has repeated "III's" and "IV's" crossed out before settling, finally, for a pencilled "IV." Two notes elsewhere seem to confirm Lowry's uncertainty. The first is a reminder on the opening page of Chapter VIII, a yellow page (which thus postdates all of II, III, and IV): "I think Yvonne says something like this in 3." But the reference is found in IV. The second is a pencilled note in Chapter XI (all yellow sheets) in Margerie's hand in which Yvonne is made to recall thinking about cages "this morning in Acapulco." The final two words are canceled, yet they appear on the fair version of this page in "C" (cf. 26:4, 4 and 26:16, 345), again suggesting vacillation on the inclusion of Chapter II. In the end, Lowry retained Yvonne-in-Acapulco for the 1940 *Volcano*, but immediately did away with it—while redistributing some of its material—in his next revision.

Yvonne is also the center of some other anomalies that reflect incompletely made transitions from an earlier stage or shifting intentions in the course of the 1940 rewriting. Throughout this version she is on this day visiting her father in Mexico for the first time, yet in Chapter VI she immediately addresses a neighbor's dog by name and refers to what could have been seen "in our garden yesterday" (25:22, 24). When in IV Hugh spots some horses nearby, Yvonne responds, "That's funny, I didn't know there were any" (25:20, 18; *1940* 115), but it is the form of her remark that is "funny": why *would* she know? Similarly, when Hugh offers in V, "'You don't have to think up any trip on my account'"(25:21, 22; *1940* 148), he speaks as if conscious he is the only newcomer on the scene. We should recall here that in the red notebook, Ed and Joey, forerunners of Hugh and Yvonne, had remet each other only the previous evening at "the dance," implying that Joey had been residing there in Mexico with her father while Ed had just arrived. And all this may strengthen the speculation that the original Chapter II had contained a search for the Consul on the part of Hugh and Yvonne, precisely the kind of search that in the current Chapter XI they consider briefly, then reject. It is worth remarking in this connection that in Chapter I Laruelle is made to reflect, "'my God, that was awful, looking for him in those days'" (*1940* 7), as if such searches were habitual.

2. The finished stage of the 1940 *Volcano* is represented by the fair copy of "B," of which there are three manuscripts extant, the ribbon copy and two carbons (for a complete listing, see Appendix B). My text refers to the published version edited by Paul Tiessen and Miguel Mota (see "A Note on the Text").

3. Bowker (*Pursued by Furies* 142) claims that Lowry adopted the notion of placing "last chapter first" from John Sommerfield's *They Die Young*, which he read at Cambridge. Indeed, he may have recalled Sommerfield's novel in 1940 when he came to recast his own, but the device clearly was not a part of his original conception of the book.

4. The theme was not new to Lowry: the divided self can be seen literally projected in "In Le Havre," a 1934 story consisting almost entirely of dialogue between an Englishman and an American who at the end turn out to be "a man and his ghost"—a story of doubles.

5. This reading of the situation is repeated in the story "June the 30th, 1934" (alternative title: "Metal"), which Lowry was working on at the time (see *Letters* 31). Here the protagonist does not "quite understand why in order to promote peace it should be necessary for the French inner market to be stimulated by closer contact with the German steel cartels" (*Psalms and Songs* 36). Set on the "Night of the Long Knives," Hitler's purge of the S.A., or "brownshirts," the story has several links with the 1940 *Volcano*, including the lines—in the story they are questions—"Was there really a sort of determinism about the fate of nations? Could it be true that, in the end, they got what . . . they deserved?" (*Psalms and Songs* 43) and a character called Firmin, a name that will not gravitate to the Consul for some time yet. Although an Englishman, he is the agent for a German company, a prospector in metals, and thus caught up in the theme of economic betrayal prominent both in the story and in the 1940 *Volcano*.

6. Stephen Spender was the first to articulate this important characteristic of Lowry's prose in his Introduction to the 1965 *Volcano*, xix.

7. None of this is very clear and is not helped by apparently conflicting details. According to the Consul, Priscilla had accompanied him to Spain and again back to Mexico, where they planned to begin a "new life," only to separate and divorce instead. However, he also tells Mr. Quincey that Yvonne left Spain with him but rejoined her mother in Los Angeles, implying that he and Priscilla had already separated before leaving Spain. Needless to add, this background is not clarified by the text's fuzziness about the Spanish war and the time of the present action of Chapters II–XII.

CHAPTER TWO. 1941

1. "On Board the West Hardaway," *Story* 3 (October 1933): 12–22; and "Hotel Room in Chartres," *Story* 5 (September 1934): 53–58. The January 31, 1938, letter to Lowry from agent Ann Watkins (see Prologue, p. 19) expressing interest in the *Volcano* notes that Arthur Calder-Marshall has reported that Lowry "had it in mind to send it direct to Whit Burnett," a course she advises against (1:71).

2. The story apparently never was sold, but no surviving correspondence clarifies this minor Lowryan disappointment.

3. See 1:45 for Matson's letters. Mr. Matson kindly gave permission for examination of his own company files, which contain a carbon of a letter of October 16, 1940, not in the UBC collection. This reports the decision of Duell, Sloan and Pearce on the *Volcano*, thus confirming that Matson scrupulously sent along rejections as they came to him.

4. The revisions at this stage employed the second carbon from the 1940 fair copy, the "D" version, as the base for change, and alterations were made either directly in pencil on the bond leaves of that carbon or, if more extensive, on newly typed yellow sheets that served as inserts or replacements for passages superseded. Repagination was done on a chapter-by-chapter basis.

The exception here is Chapter VIII, of which the remaining "D" sheets are very lightly annotated: Lowry may have briefly considered this as a base for revision before deciding that he wanted not only a new chapter, but also a potentially saleable story from the material. Thus two "new" creations come into being here: an entirely recomposed Chapter VIII of twenty-four yellow sheets, which incorporates the altered character-relationships and wholly supersedes the "D" version; and the story announced to Matson in the March 4 letter, which uses the original character relationships with bits of material from elsewhere to provide some exposition and continuity.

The alteration of the relationships in the chapter version here plausibly suggests that the story version was the first of these two written. However, the manuscript evidence is less clear: scholars wishing to pursue this question might especially compare p. 13 of 30:9 (chapter) with pp. 14–15 of 25:16 (story), and p. 19 of the former with p. 20 of the latter—and both typescripts of course with the 1940 version (see 26:1 for "B" and 26:13 for "C").

An examination of the newly added yellow newsprint sheets reveals only two marginal type settings, which suggests that perhaps we can divide the revisions into two groups, those made "earlier" and those "later." In the first group, with a left margin setting of 1"/16", are Chapters I, II, III, V, X; in the latter group, with a marginal setting of 2", Chapters VI, VII, VIII, IX, XI, XII (no yellow sheets for Chapter IV survive). Corresponding to the first setting are two letters to Matson of March 4 and August 4, 1941; using the second setting is the letter to Matson of January 6, "1941" [1942] and the yellow sheets on a draft of "The Last Address," which Lowry informed Matson he had been working on in a letter dated January 30, 1942. Although it is now impossible to be very precise about dating, I shall refer to the revisions based on the "D" carbon as the "1941" revisions (not "version," for reasons to be given in the text).

5. Pencil annotations on the "D" carbon are a problem (those on the yellow sheets from this stage are not problematic, of course: they clearly postdate this phase of revision). Some certainly were made for this stage; others certainly were made for a later stage. For instance, pencil notes on the first sheets of X and XII dramatize the openings as the Consul's ordering of mescal, but mescal has no more special significance in 1941 than it did in 1940: in the text the Consul orders tequila at the Salón Ofélia.

As a result, I have taken a conservative view of revisions here. If a page from "D" is not refolioed or (whether refolioed or not) if it is replaced by an extant yellow sheet, this almost always constitutes clear evidence of supersession ("almost" because XII here may be an exception: the lack of refoliation and the paucity of revision in the final twenty pages suggest that Lowry may have begun reworking this chapter but dropped it before completion). As for the pencil markings, I have taken the editorial ones done by Margerie as certainly of this stage, but have ignored substantive changes of hers and almost all of Malcolm's. My reasoning is this: Margerie, as I have argued in the text, was at this stage clearly given (or took) charge of alterations stemming from the new character relationships and those designed to cut anything extraneous to "the pattern, the form, the meaning." As confirmation there is the clear continuity between her changes on "D" leaves and the content of the new interleaved yellow sheets. But while Lowry's hand appears copiously on the surviving "D" sheets, there is very rarely any evidence to suggest that his changes were for the 1941 revisions, and sometimes clear evidence (see above on Chapters X and XII) that they are for a later stage. As a result of this policy I have doubtless not indicated all the changes made at this stage; however, I have also probably not imposed alterations made at a later phase on this one.

6. With the exception of the March 4 letter to Matson, through the fall and winter of 1940 and on into the spring and summer of 1941, Lowry has nothing to say in surviving letters of work on the *Volcano*. Indeed, the only writing he speaks of doing is poetry, about which he writes frequently to Aiken in this period. Only on May 9, 1941, does he mention to Aiken writing prose ("three long short stories," of which we may assume one is the new "Under the Volcano" sent to Matson in March), and not until August does he say to Aiken that he has been working again on the novel.

7. The following table gives a gross chapter-by-chapter sense of the 1941 changes using the "D" carbon as base. The figures in square brackets show the number of pages in the 1940 fair copy with which Lowry began, "R" indicating refolioed, "U" unrefolioed, and "M" missing leaves of that "D" carbon. Because the survivals are incomplete for more than half the chapters, the question marks indicate estimates:

	"D" LEAVES	YELLOW LEAVES	TOTAL
I [42]	R 12, U 28, M 2	1	21?
II [24]	R 0, U 24	7	10?
III [33]	R 5, U 28	12	17
IV [33]	R 4, U 29	[13]	17?
V [35]	R 25, U 9, M 1	7	31?
VI [31]	R 16, U 15	5	21
VII [41]	R 2, U 10, M 29	10	38?
VIII [29]	R 0, U 21, M 8	24	24
IX [36]	R 18, U 9, M 9	9	30?
X [34]	R 18, U 16	10	22
XI [23]	R 6, U 17	13	19?
XII [41]	R 10, U 29, M 2	2	40?

Scholars who may wish to pursue further this stage of revision will find the documents in the UBC Collection as follows:

I   26:18, 5:52 [verso of holograph "Old Blake was warm"].
II   26:19 [and the first part of 26:20 for the earlier version of the action of this chapter in this and subsequent drafts], 29:1.
III   26:20, 29:7.
IV   26:21.
V   26:22.
VI   26:23.

VII	26:24, 30:5 [N.B. yellow tss here numbered 25, 26, 27, 28-29 belong to later stage of revision], Templeton 1:9 [ts p. 9 only].
VIII	27:1, 30:9 [25:16 contains the "story," UBC's version "A"]
IX	27:2, 30:12, Templeton 1:7.
X	27:3, 31:4.
XI	27:4, 31:11 [yellow ts p. 12 only], Templeton 1:5, 1:6 [yellow ts pp. 9, 13, pencil refolioed 8, 11 only].
XII	27:5.

8. Robert Linscott wrote Lowry directly on November 19, 1940, to decline the *Volcano* on behalf of Houghton Mifflin. In his letter he quoted an adverse reader's report that said, in part, "above all, the pattern of the story fails clearly to emerge, lost as it is in meditation, description, and verbal pyrotechnics" (Templeton 1:1).

9. I am ignoring here the age factor, which looms larger to one coming to the revision after the 1940 version than it could to a reader who has only the newer version at hand. In 1941 Lowry is content to leave the ages of his characters vague. Jeffrey Ames still has gray hair, and the passage in VI in which Hugh reflects that after the barbering and dressing the Consul does not have "the haggard look of a depraved, worn out, old man" is allowed to stand. However, Margerie's hand adds in pencil, "Well, why should he? After all, he was only ten years older than Hugh himself" (26:23, 187). There is, however, no way of determining whether this emendation, accepted in modified form in the subsequent surviving draft of VI, was added at this stage of revision or the next (see n. 5 above). Indeed, just how old is "Hugh himself"? As for Yvonne, although she appears more mature than the twenty-four-year-old of the 1940 version, no age is given for her, nor is there any indication in surviving sheets of how long the Ameses have been married.

10. Interview with the author, July 18, 1991.

11. In 1941, unlike 1940, Lowry dramatizes the introduction of Yvonne and the maid to make here (and subsequently) the indirect point that at the end of their marriage, the Consul and his wife were not sharing a bed. The Consul's "I daresay you want your old room. Anyhow, Hugh's in the guest room" (and variants in later versions of III) clearly assumes that Yvonne will want to continue these "private" arrangements, with a quick oblique glance at one of the causes/results of their estrangement in the location of Hugh's sleeping quarters.

12. Indeed, it seems likely from surviving evidence that this phase carried on into early 1942: the letter to Matson of January 30, 1942, claiming that "the Volcano is almost rewritten again" (1:81) probably refers to this stage (see also n. 4 above). It is important to remember that Lowry was doing other things

than rewriting the *Volcano* during this period; that in 1941, for instance, he and Margerie were finding a new shack to inhabit, moving in, fixing it up, building a pier, and so on; and that even if we confine ourselves to writing, Lowry's letters make clear that he was working on poems, *In Ballast*, and "The Last Address," as well as the *Volcano* during 1941.

This timing raises the minor mystery of the returned ribbon copy of the 1940 *Volcano* and its place in the story of Lowry's composition. For despite the instruction to Matson not to bother returning that typescript (*Letters* 38), his agent did send it, and Lowry subsequently made annotations on some of its pages. By the time he received it back, however, he had long been launched on the revisions discussed here, which use the "D" carbon as their base: the very letter to Matson cited in the previous paragraph as announcing the almost-completed rewriting of the *Volcano* is the same letter that acknowledges receipt of returned manuscripts. Why, then, would Lowry begin annotating yet another version of his 1940 text?

The mystery is hardly dispelled by the recognition that revisions on the ribbon copy are almost never incorporated into the novel's evolving text. Granted, these are relatively sparse—only in Chapter VIII could they be considered anything more than brief and scattered rewordings—but they are also sometimes apparently anachronistic, applied to sections of the novel, such as the original Chapters II and XI, already discarded from the "1941" working manuscript. Furthermore, this typescript contains several self-conscious holograph footnotes that comment on the time of original composition of passages and draw attention to Lowry's political prescience in the light of the development of World War II. "Written in 1937," "Written in 1938," "Written in 1938–39" are not revisions but invitations to an audience (posterity?) to admire the author's foresight, issued over the head of the text, as it were.

Perhaps we may imagine a Lowry early in 1942 well aware of the universal judgment on this version of his novel and in possession of some general remarks from publishers' readers, looking through the typescript newly returned from New York for specific commentary. This he would have found disappointingly sparse and unhelpful—confined to pointing out typos and misspellings, querying foreign words and phrases, and other such editorial particulars—but as he read on, pencil in hand, discovered himself unable to resist "improving" what he saw, however redundant or impractical such changes might be in light of the revisions based on "D." Either then or later, however, he would have recalled that this was, after all, not his working manuscript and, admiring his own prophetic powers, may have salvaged nuggets of insight from the general debacle of the rejected text. This, of course, is to posit a Lowry who was a compulsive rewriter, beyond any utilitarian end, an image nowhere discredited by surviving papers. Thus the post-1940 changes on the ribbon copy of that version, I conclude, stand to one side of the line of revision being traced in this study. (I am most grateful to Mr. Norman Levi of Victoria, B.C., for the opportunity to examine the original typescript of the 1940 *Volcano*, which is in his possession.)

13. I must continue to use the *word* "version," as applied to passages or to entire chapters, but not as appropriate to the work as a whole. My argument runs against the common assumption in Lowry criticism that one can speak of several discrete versions of the novel, a position first and most compellingly taken by Doyen.

CHAPTER THREE. 1942–1943

1. In rejecting the *Volcano* on behalf of Houghton Mifflin, Robert Linscott wrote to Lowry (November 14, 1940) that although he liked the novel, "I do realize it is a very special taste and that it would be a devil of a job to publish it with any chance of commercial success." In this he echoed the adverse reader's report included in his letter: "I must confess to some alarm at the thought of trying to describe this book to a bookseller in such a way as to induce him to order it" (Templeton 1:1). On November 25, Linscott wrote again suggesting that the novel can probably be sold "as is": "it is simply a matter of finding a publisher willing to run the risk—and a pretty good sized risk—of losing money on it" (1:31).

2. The special importance of mescal and the attempted strychnine cure are good examples of Lowry's autobiographical material making only a "belated" appearance in his text. See Hilton and Calder-Marshall.

3. In the absence of bond paper with its possibility of distinguishing weight or watermark, in the presence after May 1940 of the same typewriter and, after 1941, of indistinguishable yellow leaves, only margin-setting and (after a half-century!) the relative darkness of black ribbon remain as shaky external guides to the period in question and to chapter groupings. One attempts to fall back on content, where there are apparently a number of indicators of order: the town where the bullthrowing is held is first "Chapultepec," later "Tomalín"; Hugh is originally the Consul's brother, later his half-brother; he first works for the London *Echo*, later for the London *Globe*; Yvonne at one point wants to spirit Geoffrey away to a farm, at another to his "genteel Siberia"; Hugh is in early stages not aware of the battle of the Ebro, later he is. But while these are usually adequate indicators to distinguish the chapters "vertically"—which version of, for instance, Chapter V came before which other?—they are much less useful in distinguishing them "horizontally": assuming that these drafts of IV and IX, for instance, come from the same general period because they both

speak of Tomalín and the genteel Siberia rather than Chapultepec and a farm, which was written first? The situation is in fact worse than this, for although, say, Hugh does get changed from full to half-brother of Geoffrey, the language of the text, even in the published version, does not always reflect this (e.g., "his brother's house ... his brother's jacket ... his brother's small gladstone bag" [*Volcano* 94]), and while apparently the references to a farm precede those to the island "genteel Siberia" as alternatives to Mexico, Lowry will quite typically go on to make use of *both* rather than choosing one and excising the other. Furthermore, not all chapters contain references to Hugh's relationship to Geoffrey or his employer or the site of the bullthrowing or the destination proposed for the Consul and Yvonne. And of course the appearance of a new motif, such as the Ejido, in one chapter—say, Chapter IV, in connection with Juan Cerillo—does not necessarily designate the timing of its appearance in other chapters, such as VII, where the Banco Crédito y Ejidal is a late insertion (before? at about the same time as? a later afterthought to?) the reference in IV. Acquiescing to the uncertainty principle, one turns again to see what such externals as ribbons and margins can tell us.

A margin of $1\frac{3}{4}$" and a very faded ribbon are common to the earliest surviving typescripts of chapters I, II, V, VI, VII, IX, and XI and, with a slight shift of the margin to $1\frac{5}{8}$", to III as well. This is in itself rather rickety (and not altogether consistent) evidence on which to proceed, and of course it does nothing to sort out which of these chapters preceded which others. But for the reasons given above, definitive answers may not be obtainable, and rickety evidence is still presumably preferable to none whatever. The surviving files involved are the following:

Chapter I. 28:23 contains an incomplete typescript of this chapter, here divided into a "Chapter I" of 7 pages (complete) and a "Chapter II" of 19 pages (incomplete) (see p. 100 above). The missing page "18" from the "Chapter II" phase is to be found in 26:18, where typescript page 22 of the "D" carbon has been refolioed several times, its final refoliation being as "18" of 28:23. The designation "Chapter II" is circled in pencil and struck out in ink; division of the novel's initial chapter did not survive this stage.

The holograph base for 28:23 has not survived, but 28:22 contains a notebook made up of inserts for that base *and* apparently for an earlier version (complete? incomplete? holograph? typescript?) of this chapter, none of which has survived. This notebook has been paginated in pencil by Lowry: "p.81" makes reference to a "Maytime" notebook (now lost) containing other passages designated for inclusion in this draft of I.

Chapter II. 29:5 and 29:6 contain one and five pages respectively of typescript, a very incomplete survival the basis for which is the complete holograph manuscript contained in 29:2.

Chapter III. Templeton 1:19 contains the only typescript from this stage, a single p. 22, the radically incomplete survival of the complete holograph draft of 29:8.

Chapter V. 29:16 contains two pages of typescript ("8" and "9") the basis for which is the complete holograph manuscript contained in the same file.

Chapter VI. 30:1 contains a complete typescript for which no holograph base survives.

Chapter VII. 30:7 contains a complete typescript for which an incomplete holograph base survives in the same file, three of the missing four pages of which are to be found on the versos of pp. 3, 11, 12 of the August 25, 1951, letter to David Markson (2:19). However, in 30:8 can be found 19 holograph pages discarded from the holograph phase of 30:7, and an even earlier holograph phase is to be found in the almost complete (p. 11 lacking) manuscript of 30:6. The holograph versions in 30:6 and 30:7 provide a good contrast between manuscript not prepared for typing and that which is.

Chapter IX. 30:13 contains a complete typescript for which no holograph base survives.

Chapter XI. Templeton 1:6 contains a complete typescript (including pp. 9 and 13 of the "1941" yellow sheet draft, refolioed 8, 11) for which no holograph base survives.

(Although there exists a complete holograph draft of the new version of Chapter IV [29:12], no typescript for this revision survives: thus it has not been included in the foregoing analysis of these revisions, based as that is on typescript evidence. Nonetheless, given the internal references linking it to this stage's V and VI, in my text I treat this draft of IV as from the same period as the other chapters here analyzed.)

There is a network of assumptions and references that involves these chapters with one another without by itself providing answers to questions of order. For instance, we find mention of Yvonne's first marriage to Cliff and their dead child, Geoffrey, in Chapter III (29:8, 6) and again, more obliquely, in XI (Templeton 1:6, 13). In the latter instance, the recollection arises as Yvonne considers adopting a child: momentarily tired of "all of them," she thinks of leaving Mexico alone, buying "her farm" and living there with only children for companions. This thought of the farm is her later revision of the proposal she made to the Consul in IX that they together leave Mexico and "buy a farm, in Ohio, or Canada, or Africa—I don't care where" (30:13, 14). "I see," Geoffrey laughs in response, "But what if he just won't go?" thereby referring to the conversation he has overheard in the garden in V, where Yvonne has worried to Hugh, "'But suppose he just won't go,'" a line the Consul has at that point mockingly quoted back at the two "conspirators" (29:16, 15). These stages of V and IX are further related as the only drafts in which it is noted that Yvonne has been to a bullthrowing previously. However, this V also has clear links to IV and VI of this stage, to the former as the source of the "conspiracy" between Hugh and Yvonne to get Geoffrey away, and to the latter as Hugh reflects on the likelihood of this coming about. Chapter VI is tied even more closely to this version of V in that only here is Hugh presented as taking a drink in V (scotch, neat) and recalling this at the start of the next chapter (30:1, 1). But the possible new life for the Consul and Yvonne that she and Hugh discuss in IV and that he reflects on in VI is envisaged not on a farm, but in Geoffrey's "genteel Siberia."

Here one comes up against the complexity and apparent inconsistency of these manuscript survivals. Perhaps a simple solution was visible in drafts now lost; more likely it exists only in ghostly conversations in the Lowry shack. Subsequent versions reveal his recognition of the inconsistency and his determination to continue using both the farm and the Canadian "genteel Siberia" to designate the goal of the "plot" to get the Consul away. The next stage of IX "explains" the apparent contradiction awkwardly, and thereby suggests a hypothesis to account for the earlier inconsistency: in a "dirty" pencil draft Yvonne proposes to Geoffrey, "Why *don't* we go away really somewhere, I don't care where—and buy a farm and start again. What's to stop us, Geoffrey." In the margin appears this reflection: "She would not mention the 'genteel Siberia' just now in case he had overheard something about it and it might make him antagonistic though there was no reason why they couldn't have a farm on his island on Lake Pineaus" (30:14, 8).

This apparent reduction of the farm to a mere ploy is confirmed in the next version of Chapter IV. Hugh is here more openly skeptical of Yvonne's farm notion than in the published novel, but he does admit, "Though you might use the farm as a sort of lure, a chimaera, a pied piper's flute to spirit him away? I imagine it might work if you got him in the right mood" (29:13, ms. 19). Why, one might well wonder, did Lowry not simply cut the farm proposal from late drafts? Its displacement is easy enough to understand: Lowry knew no more about farming than Yvonne did, and must have quickly realized that he was incapable of developing it further. But perhaps he also recognized that the very ignorance he shared with Yvonne was itself the value of the farm proposal, that it could embody the unreality of her notion of "escape." There is no irony in Yvonne's original reflections in XI as she lyrically imagines the future: "when Arcturus swung over the horizon on cool spring evenings there would be ploughed fields and growing things and little young animals and hard work to do, and when Scorpio crawled low across the Southern sky on hot summer nights there would be the coming harvest to think of—." But the vagueness here is all too revealing, and in pencil Lowry adds, "This was the sentimental phase, she reflected" (Templeton 1:6, 13). Yvonne herself, of course, cannot be this aware, or she would see through her own proposal: something else, clearly, was needed. A "genteel Siberia" in Canada—the farm, as Yvonne suggests, might have been anywhere—was close enough to Lowry's own experience to have possibilities for development and, since Geoffrey is posited as already being the owner of an island, is less blatantly unattainable than the dreamy farm.

4. While precise sequence may be impossible to establish, Chapter II can be shown to predate IV, which is itself closely connected in key motifs, and thus probably in time of composition, to V, VI, and VII. The clue here lies in the presentation of Hugh. In Chapter II, the Consul describes his brother as Hugh is never elsewhere described, as "Mexican correspondent for the London Echo" (29:2, 19A). Apparently he has no intention of resigning from the newspaper. By the time of IV, however, Hugh is employed by the London *Globe*, not the *Echo*, and the cablegram he has just sent is "the last he intended to send the paper from which he had held for the past two years, one week, five days and twenty minutes what was to laymen, and accurately described in his case, as a 'roving commission'" (29:12, 2), which allows for the varied travels he will recount to Yvonne in subsequent pages. The "roving commission" also helps account for his recently being in Texas (as the post of "Mexican correspondent" does not), just as his resignation allows him to offer later in IV to leave the scene precipitously, this very day (Hugh has not yet determined on a trip to Spain).

5. Binns, "Materialism and Magic" 178 and 185, argues that Hugh is erroneous here and that his "defective" knowledge of contemporary events undercuts his supposed political commitment. Lowry, however, appears to be using information he transcribed from Henry Buckley in good faith (Templeton 1:11, 5, and Asals, "Buckley's Spanish Civil War" 21–22).

6. In mutual confirmation, see Walker, which is much fuller than Margerie's holograph worksheet, but differs from it only where the novel itself differs (Granada replaces Algeciras as the place of meeting and marriage) or is more precise (Yvonne's final departure in December 1937, not just "Fall").

7. Indeed, Lowry did not for this draft bother to copy out the telegram itself since he was using the carbon of an original (which survives in Templeton 1:2). The only differences between the actual cable and what appears in *Volcano* 94, is that the actual cable is addressed "DAILY HERALD"; does not misplace a comma in the address, which should precede rather than follow "Esq."; is unsigned; and has in pencil "June 25" in the upper right corner and "140 words" in the upper left. Lowry has omitted the large WESTERN UNION from his cable. One further difference has occasioned some perplexity, but is probably simply a Lowry slip: where the first word after the name of the newspaper is "inteltube" on the telegram, Lowry has transcribed (and the novel prints) "intelube" (see 29:13, 1).

8. Although the reference sounds simply unflattering, Lowry here seems to be paying an oblique debt for some earlier imagery in his text. In Bogan's poem "Medusa," the narrator arrives at a scene not unlike the Consul's house and garden (a "house, in a cave of trees") where "Everything moved,—a bell hung ready to strike, / Sun and reflection wheeled by." With the sudden appearance of the title figure, "This is a dead scene forever now. / Nothing will ever stir," including the bell, the grass "growing for hay," and the motionless "yellow dust." (Bogan 3). Motion and stillness were of considerable interest to Lowry, and just before the reference to Bogan's poem Hugh had been moving up the drive until:

> eyes in my feet I must have, as well as straw, not to have fallen into it, he thought, stopping on the edge of the crater and then, glancing up, his heart and the world stopped too: the horse half over the hurdle, the diver, the guillotine, the hanged man half way down, the murderer's bullet and the cannon's breath, in Spain or China frozen in mid-air, the lover with erect phallus, the wheel, the piston, poised. . . .
> "She, Yvonne . . . was wearing yellow slacks and from a little distance appeared to be clothed in the sunlight filling the garden." (29:12, 2)

The conjunction of sun, reflection, and wheel in Bogan's image may well be the source of the novel's twice-used "millwheel reflections of sunlight." At any rate, his debt to Bogan apparently came to seem to Lowry not direct (or detectable) enough to demand this unlikely textual acknowledgment.

9. Lowry wrote to Aiken (*Aiken-Lowry* 147) on November 22, 1940, "we have been viciously attacked by a goat," which might well be a "symbol": "No more tragedies . . . Yeah." This hardly seems its significance in the *Volcano*, however. Given the cutting that went on in the 1941 drafts, it seems likely the charging goat made its first appearance in the version of IV under discussion.

10. An echo of Blake that gets suppressed after this draft should perhaps be recorded. Viewing Geoffrey as ultimately helpless, Hugh reflects: "What use to the dying tiger were talons and fangs? Quite a lot, doubtless. But perhaps the tiger was not dying. Perhaps it wasn't even a tiger but a lamb" (30:1, 14). Lowry's revisions strengthened the passage considerably, but sacrificed the Blakean matrix out of which it emerged.

11. Among the partly legible pencil notes on the opening page of the "D" typescript (26:22, 133 ["1"]), only those that expand the first sentence might have affected the opening in 1941, but since they are an early try at rendering the Consul's consciousness, they probably postdate those revisions. What I cite in the text is thus typescript that dates back to 1940.

12. We find here for the first time the survival of more than a single holograph or typescript draft from any stage. It was evident that in 1940 all the

original chapter typescripts had been reworked, sometimes more than once, but only final versions remain. In the rewritings of 1941, again only final typescripts survive, so that any earlier phases of composition are hidden from us on lost holograph sheets. After 1941, while the holograph stage is frequently represented in survivals (and the fact that for the versions of VI, IX, and XI discussed above this stage has not survived may well be another argument for their closeness to the 1941 drafts) we have not thus far encountered more than a single pencilled draft of any chapter (although deletions, marginal additions, inserts, and the like on existing sheets make clear that individual passages have frequently gone through more than one version). With Chapter VII, the first post-1941 survival is an almost-complete draft of "dirty" copy—that is, not prepared for Margerie's typewriter—as well as a later "clean" copy, which likewise survives almost entire. Here, however, there is almost an embarrassment of holograph riches, for not only are there the two larger manuscripts, but another nineteen pages of individual discards from the later pencil draft (30:8). Nonetheless, there is no deviation here from Lowry's considering a stage of composition unfinished until a typewritten version appeared, and a complete typescript of the "clean" holograph survives (30:7, ts. + 30:5, 25–28/9).

This "dirty" holograph is also the first draft in which Lowry can be seen adopting another method for labelling his material than that of numbering pages: here he also divides his chapter by marginal lettering (in the current chapter ranging from A to I) according to blocks of material. Thus, "A" designates the description of Laruelle's house, "B" the action until the Consul separates himself from the others and enters the studio, the Consul on his own constituting "C," which ends with the return of Laruelle with refreshments; the following sequence with all four characters makes up "D," and so on. Like building blocks or sub-chapter units, they seemed to help Lowry keep a grasp on the structure he was working with; once more, although the texture might be woven and rewoven, the basic structure was to stand firm. It may be no accident that this technique first appears in a chapter where the structure *has* been altered, for Chapter VII is for the first time without the action since leaving the Consul's house. In any case, as a form of reference—perhaps also convenient for discussions with Margerie—it was retained on the next holograph draft, the "clean copy" prepared for typing.

This practise should probably not be confused with Lowry's sometime-adoption of lettering to order sequential pages. The purpose of this latter use of lettering seems to be to distinguish different drafts of the same material. In this case, the letters normally appear at the top of the page, like numbers; in the use of letters for "blocking," they normally appear to one side rather than at the top, where numerical sequence usually continues. There are, however, times when Lowry uses both methods, e.g., D18, D19, E20, etc.

13. The Consul here (30:6, 9; 30:7, ms. 14) refers to Hugh as "my stepbrother," the first indication after the alteration of character relationships that the two are anything other than full brothers. The designation is probably an error for "halfbrother," for it appears nowhere else, but it is possible Lowry briefly toyed with cutting the blood relationship between the two.

14. See n. 3 above: the site of the bullthrowing is "Chapultepec," the final draft displays a faded ribbon and a margin of 1⅝". This rewriting apparently postdates such other drafts of this period as those of I and VI: "Anis del Mono," which first appears at this stage of I, is a marginal addition to the drinks the Consul observes behind the bar at the Farolito on the opening page of the dirty holograph and then incorporated into the following drafts; and all stages of XII refer repeatedly to the Union Militar, which the Consul has "told Hugh about," but in the dialogue of VI thus alluded to, "Union Militar" is only a pencilled addition to the typescript.

15. Hastings (1732–1818) was the first governor-general of British India. Like Geoffrey, he was born and orphaned there and (again like Geoffrey) went through a period of upbringing and schooling in England. He returned to India and imperial service later in life. His tenure as governor-general was troubled, and on his return to England he was impeached, tried, and acquitted of all charges against him. This part of Hastings's career may have suggested the court-martial and acquittal of Geoffrey in the *Samaritan* affair, complications that at this point have apparently not entered Lowry's manuscripts.

That Lowry was toying with historical parallels to his fictional action is confirmed by the appearance of the name "Suraj-ud Dowlah" above that of Hastings on this holograph. In revolt against the English imperialists, this "Indian with ideas" captured the stronghold at Calcutta, resulting in the infamous incident of the Black Hole. Despite such victories, of course, Indian resistance to British rule was finally no more successful than was that of the Mexicans to the Spanish.

16. One quite deliberate allusion, however, was buried when Lowry deleted the information that the cock had been brought "from the Tarnmoor farm": the proprietor of that farm is Herman Melville. Melville used the pseudonym "Salvator R. Tarnmoor" when he published his series of sketches "The Encantadas." However, Lowry's reference—characteristically oblique—is to Melville's story "Cock-a-Doodle-Doo!" There too a cock crows not only over a dead body, but apparently over death itself: "Oh! death, where is thy sting? / Oh! grave, where is thy victory?" the narrator crows with St. Paul at story's end, and all the other characters agree. However, all the other characters are also by this time dead, as is the cock, and Melville's own view is debatable.

17. See n. 3 above. "Chapultepec" and "Tomalín" both appear on the "dirty" holograph of IX that follows (30:14), but "Tomalín" prevails in the clean holograph and the typescript of this stage (31:1; Templeton 1:3).

No one, incidentally, has explained the significance of this change. Lowry may have decided to eliminate "Chapultepec" so that his town not be confused with the well-known park in Mexico City (as Day does, 216), but why "Tomalín" was chosen remains as mysterious as why the Consul's street bears the name "Nicaragua." A British writer and intellectual named Miles Tomalin served with the International Brigades in Spain (Wintringham, 330, for instance, mentions him), but I am aware of no evidence Lowry knew him, much less that he was the basis for the name change.

In an undated letter to Albert Erskine (c. June 1946), Lowry says darkly, "There is a town spelt Tomellin in Oaxaca, near a town Parian. Tomalin is made up, may be impossible, but its spelling must stand" (2:6).

18. Jack is based on John Sommerfield; some of the material here will be moved to Chapter IV where Hugh has already briefly referred to this friend. The reference to Mora de Ebro will end up with other newspaper headlines in Chapter VII: it was safer to refer generally to "bloody combat" at that spot than to make Hugh's knowledge of a distant battle too precise. Furthermore, this reminds us that the Battle of the Ebro—and the Spanish war—is a matter of public concern, not merely Hugh's obsession, the stuff of newspaper headlines as well as of guilty private refrains.

19. The source of these references is, again, Buckley (Templeton 1:11, 4). As Ackerley and Clipper surmise (158–59), the original of the "Noemijolea" is a British steamer that Buckley has as "Noemiejulea." Lowry transcribed this accurately in his notes (Templeton 1:11, 3), but when he first made it part of the *Volcano* (29:13, ms. 8), the second "e" disappeared, and it was not clear whether the vowel following the "j" was a "u" or an "o": Margerie typed "Noemijolea," and thus it stood thereafter.

20. In a chapter that has already referred to *Moby-Dick*, this association of a church with fire, blackness, and damnation may recall the Negro church stumbled into by Ishmael in chapter 2. Lowry had quoted part of this chapter to Conrad Aiken in a letter of 1931 (*Aiken-Lowry* 32–33).

21. Hugh's fantasy seems a politicized relative of that of Nathanael West's Miss Lonelyhearts in the final chapter of that novel. West's feverish journalist also has an ironically presented dialogue with "God": "God said, 'Will you accept it now?' And he replied, 'I accept, I accept.' He immediately began to plan a new life and his future conduct as Miss Lonelyhearts. He submitted drafts of his column to God and God approved them. God approved his every thought." It seems to him that, when a cripple arrives, "God had sent him so

that Miss Lonelyhearts could perform a miracle and be certain of his conversion. It was a sign." (57) West's hero, in turn, owes something here to Joyce's Leopold Bloom in the Nighttown episode of *Ulysses*, particularly his parodic religious fantasies of the New Bloomusalem.

Lowry seems indebted to West's novel in other ways as well. A passage that persists through the drafts is the Consul's comment on zoos in Chapter VI: "One always heard they had a therapeutic quality. They always had zoos in Mexico apparently—Moctezuma, courteous fellow, even showed stout Cortez around a zoo. The poor chap thought he was in the infernal regions" (*Volcano* 187). Minus the demonic overtones, Miss Lonelyhearts's girlfriend has a similar view: "Betty took him for a walk in the zoo and he was amused by her evident belief in the curative power of animals. She seemed to think that it must steady him to look at a buffalo." Like Yvonne, Betty also believes in the restorative value of farms, but Miss Lonelyhearts is at first as vague as the Consul about her intentions: "He began to realize that there was a definite plan behind her farm talk, but could not guess what it was" (36). Unlike Yvonne, Betty manages to get Miss Lonelyhearts out into the country, but her "cure" does not succeed.

More generally, both writers are ironists alive to a pain that irony cannot cancel; perhaps as a result, they are also highly responsive to the grotesque. West's hero like Lowry's attempts to probe to the metaphysical or religious bases of existence, and both simultaneously attempt to evade those struggles and muffle the pain that drives them. In both novels, the protagonist is usually known by his title rather than his name: indeed, Miss Lonelyhearts has no name of his own. And both books contain a trio at their center: a journalist concerned with universal human suffering, a cynic who mocks the naivete of the "brother" journalist, and a well-meaning but ineffectual woman who attempts, unsuccessfully, to rescue the protagonist from his self-destructive rush toward death. The experience of reading West's terse, economical book is entirely unlike an encounter with Lowry's churrigueresque construct, but it is worth recalling that many of these West-like features stem from earlier stages when the *Volcano* was simpler than it finally became.

In a letter dated October 14, 1951, David Markson praised *Miss Lonelyhearts* highly to Lowry, and noted "a delightful little 'Eden' scene not too much different, in purpose, from Volcano's" (1:43). Lowry responded noncommittally on October 31: "I agree *Miss Lonelyhearts* is an important book" (*Letters* 269), but he confided to Derek Pethick (2:16, n.d. [c. 1950]), "I think Miss Lonelyhearts is a semi-inspired abortion, not good as they say." The last may of course have been a "covering" comment out of Lowry's usual plagiarism neurosis.

22. The relevant documents are found in several places:

1. Holograph pieces of the "flashback" or "solioquy," those reflective sections of Chapter VI that in the published novel make up the opening movement of the chapter and which continue to intrude (between parentheses) even later, while Hugh is outwardly occupied in shaving the Consul. The earliest holograph drafts are numbered and are to be found in 30:4, 3, 7, 8, 10, and on the versos of Texas Chapter VI, pp. 16, 17, 18 (6, 5, 4 respectively). Later pieces are lettered: 30:4, A; 5:96, B (verso of "The Schoolboy's Complaint"). Still later holograph pages are found in 30:4, A–E, 2–3. Most of the holograph pages of this stage are missing.

2. Typescript. Earliest are "light" ribbon typescript pages, left margin 1⅞" found in Templeton 1:8, 8, 30:3, 11, 12, 13, 15, refolioed three times. Following those come "dark" ribbon pages, which replaced some of the "light" typescript: these are refolioed twice in 30:3 and three times in the Texas manuscript, and their typed pagination corresponds to the first holograph refoliations of the "light" typescript. Bearing a slight reduction in margin-width (1¾"), the "dark" typescript pages are found in Templeton 1:8, 43, 44; 30:3, 24; and Texas VI, 22, 25, 31, 33. The refoliations on most of these typescript pages—sometimes as many as four—reveal the moving of the flashback material from late in the chapter to early: for instance, "light" ts. pages originally numbered 11, 12, 13, 15 above, were next refolioed as 19, 20, 21, 23 respectively, then 11, 12, 13, 15 again, before finally becoming 7, 8, 9, 11. (Later, when preparing the chapter for the Texas typescript, considerable rewriting was done yet again, which survives in holograph in 30:3 and elsewhere.)

23. The first passage runs as follows:

> In one way, of course, the only thing that meant anything to him in a jazz piece was the "song." But it depended what one meant by "song." It had occurred to him that whenever, say, any of Joe Venuti's band opened their mouths that record was a failure. That clearly was not what was meant by song. There was an enormous incomparable "song" in Beiderbecke's long break in "Singing the Blues" just as there was in some colossal playing by Venuti at the end of The Blue Room, though the actual singing that had preceded the fury was merely an embarrassment. There was, tremendously, a song,—however bloody people might sneer at "jazz" or equally bloody people compare it to Bach, for the truth was of course that it was something quite different, it was an art analogous in its effect perhaps [to] those of ballet—a statement which was also mistaken—conveyed in the furious form of all those records but that was another kind of song for you. But to Hugh breaks were the units of value by which one

judged the whole. A band was only constellated for him when it allowed its individual performers their breaks like leonids flashing across the night sky. (30:4, 7)

Despite incoherencies, the passage is of interest, even, perhaps, importance; but Lowry was surely right to excise it from the novel.

24. This is not to deny that there may have been some such incidents in Lowry's life, merely to suggest that they are not the immediate source of the novel's concern. The telegram of Chapter IV, after all, was not Lowry's: he told Erskine (2:7), he had "sat in on the concoction thereof," but it was the reporter from the *London Daily Herald* who had sent it.

25. Some seven holograph pages survive (30:4, ms. 2–3, A–E) that are probably (there are minor divergences) the base for the next typescript (30:3 and Templeton 1:8, both light and dark ribbon pages; Texas VI, 22 [refolioed 13], 25 [17], 31 [23], 33 [25]).

26. The advice of this "little communist" seems a comic echo of Strether's well-known exhortation to Little Bilham in James's *The Ambassadors*, "'Live all you can. It's a mistake not to....'"

27. The holograph draft of this phase is divided between 29:3, 1–7A, and 29:4, A–K. Despite different systems of pagination (which suggest the supersession of an earlier portion of manuscript, now lost), these together make up a complete draft which is the basis for the ensuing typescript.

That typescript, with pencil supersessions and inserts, is to be found, almost complete, in 29:3; it is completed by holograph pages 14A and 15, which supersede original typescript for the chapter ending and which are now to be found in 29:5.

From this combined typescript-manuscript, with holograph revisions, comes the ensuing complete typescript. That new typescript partly reuses the leaves of the 29:3 typescript (for pages 2, 3, 5–8), but mainly is a fresh draft based on the (revised) sheets of 29:3, creating new pages 1, 4, 9–19. These new sheets are to be found in 29:4.

28. Lowry continued to have difficulty with the mechanics of transport. The cabs are not yet on strike, and the Consul in this draft offers Yvonne a taxi for the trip to the house. Later, all the "ranged rugged taxis" in the square will have miraculously "disappeared" when the two emerge from the Bella Vista—a conjuring act by the author rather than a transportation crisis in Mexico. In the present draft, since the man picking up her bags at the chapter's opening is called "the taxi-driver," we might wonder why a few pages later Yvonne would unquestioningly entrust her luggage to a seemingly different and unknown man who enters the bar silently. Lowry will in future finesse this problem by

identifying the latter figure only as "a dark god," who may or may not be the same as the taxi-driver of the opening.

29. In the clean holograph here, Lowry extends the passage still further: "so that once—it was during the last year of her first marriage after little Geoff had died, when she'd been having so much trouble with her periods—on being startled in a boat by a rising seal, . . . she'd almost fainted again, thinking for one horrible ludicrous moment it was the dog itself, dripping and groaning sibilant reproach, returning for her perhaps, begging her to share its tumescent fate in the abyss" (31:1, 4). This feminized the return of the repressed with a vengeance ("trouble with her periods"? "tumescent fate"?). In future versions, the passage becomes an ellipsis: "so that once—but what was the good thinking of that?".

30. Ackerley and Clipper also point out this extension of Donnelly's Atlantean theories (324–25). They further note the anomaly of the reference to "the Vedic storm god Vindra"—which persists through the manuscripts—suggesting that Lowry may have confused Indra and Vrinda. The notes from which Lowry worked, however (derived from Rawlinson 126–27), suggest that the confusion may be less learned: "Vishnu," they read, "has been identified with the Vedic storm-god, Rudra," and "Vishnu" appears directly in the line above "Rudra." I would suggest Lowry's eye "slipped" to produce the impossible hybrid "Vindra."

31. Only a few scattered pages of the typescript survive, found in 15:14, 13–15 (versos 16–18) and 16:2, 10 (verso 5). My estimate of length is based on the fact that the last numbered of those survivals, ts. 15, corresponds with material found on page 10A of the holograph base, a complete manuscript that runs twenty-four pages.

32. The Rebecca-like woman is rescued from the discarded 1940 Chapter II; see 25:18, 3. The very same sentence from that old version of II also gave Lowry two small pigs moving along at a "gallop," and "scattered aloft eddies of green and yellow birds . . . into wider circlings like rings on water," both of which appear with slight alterations on the second page of this draft; and, for later in the chapter, an anteater chained to a kennel. Elsewhere, the hills "white with blossoms" already cited and Yvonne's recollections of New York City that appear here before being moved to IX both come from the opening pages of the 1940 Chapter II.

33. Lowry was also keeping in mind linking associations for his planned trilogy; in his notes from Rawlinson, at "firesticks" he has a bracket: "{mem. firesticks in In Ballast: Aarlesrund {?} scene.}" (Templeton 1:10, 1).

34. For historical and geographical information, Lowry had already made use of Younghusband, as Ackerley and Clipper have pointed out. His notes

derived from Younghusband, however, are quite distinct from (and presumably earlier than) those derived from Rawlinson, which he draws on here for myths, beliefs, and rites (see note 30 above). Lowry's notes from Younghusband are in Templeton 1:12, those from Rawlinson in Templeton 1:10.

35. Rawlinson (29–30) has, "Agni (Ignis) is the Sacred Fire, burning upon the family hearth, and summoned from heaven by the priest with his firesticks. . . . Soma was . . . an intoxicating drink, which was consumed sacramentally and offered to the gods. . . . Soma was mystically identified with the moon, who controls vegetation, and whose cup is forever filling and emptying, as he waxes and wanes." Lowry copied out this passage (Templeton 1:10, 1), and although he did not inscribe Rawlinson's note of p. 30, he clearly recalled its substance: "Soma has been identified as a plant of the *Sarcostemma* or *Asclepias* genus. It has been suggested that it was *bhang* or Indian hemp, still widely used as an intoxicant."

36. Younghusband ends his look at Kashmir by commenting on the impression made by the vast and ancient Himalayas on the human imagination. Some, he notes, might feel "depression" in contemplating the great forces and "aeons of time" involved in bringing them into being, but man himself, he exhorts is "young and recent": should he not look confidently to the future rather than despairingly to the past?

For these and the Consul's following speech on mountains, see Younghusband, 272–74, 254, 257–58. No notes on these later passages survive, but the verbal exactness and, particularly, the accuracy about the number of degrees the theodolites are off true level make it unlikely Lowry is simply drawing on memory.

37. As Ackerley and Clipper say (384), Lowry's information here comes from Younghusband 129–130; the basic "facts" appear briefly in his notes (Templeton 1:12, 5). A longer version of Hugh's speech, which uses phrasing from Younghusband *not* in Lowry's notes, is crowded onto the top of the first page of notes from Rawlinson (Templeton 1:10, 1).

38. Geoffrey characteristically recalls only one of the meanings of "Eridanus," which will be described in "The Forest Path to the Spring" as "both the River of Death and the River of Life" (226).

39. Lowry's information came from another article in the same issue of *The Sky* 3, no. 8 (June 1939) that contained "The Astronomy of the Mayas," Hugh. M. Johnson's "Jupiter's Red Spot," pp. 14, 21.

40. See Clipper, and Ackerley and Clipper 125–28, for a different reading of this passage. As the *Volcano* abundantly shows, Lowry was fascinated with the possible malleability of time: his interest in J. W. Dunne's *An Experiment with Time*, for instance, is well known. "Mac's" relevance to Yvonne, it might be

noted, comes not only from its being the month of fertility, but also from her Scottish lineage.

41. The complete, final holograph draft, which shows signs of going through more than one stage, is found in 29:17 (discarded earlier versions of individual passages are in 29:19 and in Texas, Chapter V, versos pp. 15, 16, 16A, 17, 23, 24). The twenty-eight-page typescript prepared from this manuscript, however, now resides in three places: (1) Texas, Chapter V for pages 1–14, 18, 28 (the last refolioed "31"); (2) 29:17 for pages 15–17, 19–26; (3) 29:18 for page 27 (refolioed "7"). Templeton 1:12, 1 contains not only notes from Younghusband that Lowry used for the new dream opening of the chapter, but also early draftings of his transformation of those notes.

42. Lowry here uses his notes from Younghusband and Rawlinson (as well as echoes they seem to have awakened of Eliot's *The Waste Land* and "Gerontian."). Although Rawlinson (33–34) quotes a longer passage from the *Mahabharata*, Lowry's notes contain only the four lines he actually used—used without altering a syllable of the translation (Templeton 1:10, 3). His notes from Younghusband on the seasons in Kashmir, on the other hand, are much more extensive (Templeton 1:12, 1–3). From these he selected and telescoped to produce his rapid fragmentation and shifting of image.

CHAPTER FOUR. 1943–1944

1. California: see p. 92 above. Mexico: see *DAG* 232.
2. What enables us to determine this is the unique use in the new typescript of Chapter V ("E") of a thin yellow paper (27:10, 166–82). The only other appearance of a sheet of this paper is in the working copy of Chapter VI, where Lowry replaces an earlier typescript page, according to his note burned in the June fire, with a holograph on this same paper. As the pagination above suggests, Margerie was now numbering seriatim as she typed and would do so through Chapter VIII, another indication that the *Volcano* is now being thought of as a single entity: this is the first time since the 1940 *Volcano* that consecutive pagination has been employed.

I have stated that "the first five" chapters were ready for this retyping, but VII and VIII may also have been complete, simply waiting their turn behind the refurbishing of VI. What suggests their revision in Ontario rather than at Dollarton is the combination of their existence in the "Texas" manuscript in holograph together with the consecutive pagination on their typed versions in the "E" fair copy. Since Lowry's practise was not to find a chapter draft "done" until it was typed, the fact that we know the typing done in Ontario argues that the handwritten base was probably done there also. A further note from Malcolm to Margerie under the heading "Chapter six–seven–eight" says, "Gerald has the *neater* copies of these, being typed by you at Wynywood" [*sic*] (Templeton 1:9, n.p.). "Wynwind" was the Oakville house shared by the Noxons and the Lowrys in July and August 1944, and the fact that the Noxons have moved on (Margerie's notes on this same sheet direct "Bring from Gerald's" and "Take to Gerald's") dates this note to September 1944, before the Lowrys too moved to Niagara-on-the-Lake. The note makes no mention of chapters after VIII, a piece of negative evidence perhaps also suggesting that VII and VIII were at that time the most recently completed.

My tentativeness on these points confesses that it is not now always possible to be entirely certain what was written before going to Ontario and what afterward, but the manuscripts provide more compelling (and less contradictory) testimony than Lowry's declarations elsewhere. According to the Cape letter, he was at work on Chapter VI when the fire occurred, and his return to it "later in 1944 comprised the first work I had been able to do since the fire" (*Letters* 77), a description that accords with his note on the burned page mentioned above. However, he told Albert Erskine that "I was working partly on the revision of [Chapter VIII] when [our fire] happened" (2:6, July 8, 1946). The fair copy of the Cape letter lists Chapters VII and IX through XI as revised in 1944 (it does not always make clear whether these revisions took place before or after June 7 and is simply silent on the revision of VIII). However, an earlier draft had claimed "there were but three other chapters to rewrite, part of 8, 9, 10, and 11, when one day in late 1943 I picked up a review of The Lost Week End," and again, "six months later while [*sic:* read "after"] my house burnt down ... I rewrote 9, 10, and 11 and the book was finished" (2:3, first typescript of letter of January 1946). While Margerie was in New York in July of 1944, Malcolm wrote her that he was working on "the bull chapter" (IX), and in a letter dated September 2, 1944, Margerie assured Harold Matson that "Malcolm is hard at work on the last three chapters of the Volcano" (51:2).

There is, I think, little question that Chapters IX, X, and XI were completely rewritten in Ontario, that VI received at least refurbishment there, and that XII got some isolated and specific revision. I suspect that most, if not all, of the holograph versions of VII and VIII now part of the "Texas" manuscript were also written there: certainly their typed versions ("E") were done in Oakville. In my text, I treat the chapters of this stage in order and leave to these notes questions of place and date of composition.

3. Letter to Conrad Aiken dated March 2, 1945, in Noxon 28–29; Gerald Noxon, taped interview, n.d. [late 1966–early 1967] for BBC TV show, "Malcolm Lowry" (45:9).

4. A notebook of inserts for Chapter I in 28:22 refers to the (missing) manuscript base for 28:23, which may have been composed in a (missing) "Maytime" notebook referred to therein. However, two different versions of the same material in the notebook suggest that there were at least two holograph phases before the typescript of 28:23, whereas the three refoliations of 26:18, 22 (as 24, 19, 18) raise the possibility that in addition to the 1941 revision and the 28:23 typescript, there was another typescript, of which the only other evidence is a sheet folioed in pencil "21," that contained the ending of the chapter. This sheet now resides in the same folder as the "Chapter I–Chapter II" typescript (28:23), which has its own final page (ts. 20).

Later records are even scantier. The partially burned typescript "3" referred to in my text is the next survival, followed by (?) a holograph leaf that experiments with two openings (inserted in 28:23, but clearly postdating the typescript there). After that, holograph drafts that seem preliminary versions of passages for the manuscript forming the basis of the Texas typescript, part of which survives in 28:24, can be found on various versos in Chapters I, II, and VI of the Texas typescript, and in 30:4 and Templeton 1:8.

5. In developing Bustamente's case for the Consul as political secret agent, Lowry availed himself of John Kenneth Turner's *Barbarous Mexico*, partly importing Turner's descriptions of spies during Porfirio Díaz's regime into Cárdenas's Mexico of several decades later. He apparently worked directly from Turner, not from notes: the first clear use of this source (Templeton 1:8, verso ts. 42) contains the marginal notation, "166.149. Turner." The first of these page references to *Barbarous Mexico* is to the account of the 1902 raid by government-controlled gendarmes and soldiers on the Liberal club "Ponciano Arriaga" of San Luis Potosí which Lowry gives to Señor Bustamente's father (see Ackerley and Clipper 53, and Ackerley, "Barbarous Mexico"). The second, however, Lowry drew on even more directly. Turner quotes an American newspaperman:

"There are twice as many secret police as regular police. . . . leaning against the wall of that alley entrance is a man whom you take to be a loafer; over on the other side lounges a man whom you think is a peon. Just start something and then try to get away. . . . There is no getting away in Mexico; every alley is guarded as well as every street!

"Why," said he, "they know your business as well as you do yourself. . . . When you cross the border they take your name and business and address, and before you've reached the capital they know whether you've told the truth or not. They know what you're here for and have decided what they're going to do about it." (149)

Lowry has:

> [the Consul was pursued by other spies] who without his knowing it guarded every street and alley entrance . . . who should he see leaning against the wall but a man in dark glasses he takes to be a loafer, while over on the other side lounges a man in dark glasses he thinks is a peon. . . . Just start something and try to get away and both those men will be after you. . . . Did he suppose that he, Laruelle, could even cross the border in a cattle truck, for example, say, without their knowing about it in Mexico City before he had arrived and having decided what they were going to do about it? (Templeton 1:8, verso ts. 42)

At virtually the same time, Lowry was also reading John Gunther's *Inside Latin America* (1941) as part of the general research into matters Mexican he took up at this stage. Among his notes were some on the description of Cárdenas's Ejido program (Templeton 1:21, 5–6), including, "Ejido means exit or way out." This became the source of a Lowryan error in Chapters I and VIII: by way of creating a link with other references to the Ejido program, a "motif," he placed the sign "EJIDO" over the theatre exit and later over the exit door of the camion (which persisted until the editorial substitution of the correct "SALIDA").

6. Lowry copied from Rawlinson 113 (Templeton 1:10, 9) a part of the Chinese pilgrim Hiuen Tsang's description of medieval India:

> The towns and villages have inner gates; the walls are wide and high; the streets and lanes are tortuous and the roads winding. The thoroughfares are dirty and the stalls arranged on both sides of the road with appropriate signs. . . . In coming and going these persons are bound to keep to the left side of the road till they arrive at their homes. Their homes are surrounded by low walls and form the suburbs. The earth being soft and muddy, the walls of the towns are mostly built of brick or tiles.

Below this, Lowry wrote, "Similar description of Quahnahuac [*sic*] at the beginning of The Volc." As the holograph shows, that fragment is an imperative, not an indicative.

7. Templeton 1:8, verso ts. 53 reads (in holograph) in its entirety:

I

Two mountain chains traverse the republic, forming between them a number of valleys and plateaus. The plateau of Anahuac, on which the capital is situated, is the largest and most important. The eastern edge of the plateau is formed by the Sierra Madre Oriental. On the western edge of the plateau the Sierra Madre Occidental shows a steep front and narrow ridges broken by canyons; in both Sierras the highest peaks are about 10,000 feet. {At the southern edge of the plateau, confused ranges of mountains fall sharply to the Isthmus of Tehuantepec, where the lowest point on the watershed between the Atlantic and Pacific is a little over 700 feet. The physical division eastward of the Isthmus of Tehuantepec include[s] the highlands of Chiapas, and the narrow low plain of Soconisco on the Pacific side. These highlands range from 6000 to 8000 feet in extreme elevation. Northeast of them is the peninsula of Yucatan.}

Mexico is a federative republic, divided into states, each of which has a right to manage its own local affairs, while the whole are bound together in one body politic by fundamental and constitutional law. The powers of the supreme government are divided into the legislative, executive and judicial. The legislative power is rooted in a congress consisting of a house of representatives and a senate and the executive power in a president. Representatives are elected for two years by universal sufferage. The senate consists of fifty-eight members, two for each state, and are elected in the same manner as the deputies [?]. Mexico is divided into twenty eight states, one federal district, and two territories.

"{ }" are Lowry's brackets, probably added later to mark what he wished to omit. The passage reads as if copied out of a basic source, such as a travel guide or an encyclopedia.

8. Worksheets for this version of Chapter II survive on versos and one recto of a draft of a four-page letter (ostensibly from Margerie, although the hand here is Malcolm's) to Harold Matson (2:2). The draft is undated; it refers to the problems Margerie is having with Scribner's over publication of *The Shapes That Creep* and wonders if Matson has shown them the manuscripts of her other two novels. The draft of a later letter to Matson is, however, dated "October 25" and refers to the earlier letter, sent "about two months ago" (that is, around the end of August). No year is given, but Lowry's letters to Gerald Noxon of September 7 and 28 and November 14, 1943 (*Lowry-Noxon* 56–62) all refer to Margerie's problems with agent and publishers. The connection between the draft of the earlier letter to Matson and the new version of Chapter II is the appearance of a part of the new "Oaxaca" passage in Margerie's hand on the top half of one of the recto sheets and a version of the same passage in Malcolm's hand on one of the versos.

Furthermore, one discarded holograph sheet from this stage of Chapter II (Yvonne rejoined by the Consul outside the abarrotes) contains in its margin a shopping list in Malcolm's hand for supplies (jars, fruits, sugar) for making preserves, in British Columbia a late-summer activity (Texas II, verso 23). Of such are the fruits of scholarship, other evidence lacking!

9. The new portions of the holograph of Chapter II at this stage are found in 29:5, but these were supplemented by refolioed leaves from the typescript in 29:3, and with holograph 10 filed in 29:6 (which, however, belongs with leaves in 29:5). However, not all leaves found in 29:5 are from this stage. This rather confusing situation may be clarified thus: the draft that became the basis for the Texas Chapter II was made up of the following components: (a) 29:3, ts. 3, 6, 7, refolioed 4, 8, 9; (b) 29:5, holograph 1, 2, 3, insert 3, 5, 6, 7, 7A, 10, 10A; A, B; 1–9, 11–12; (c) 29:6, holograph 10. Together these form an almost complete draft, lacking only the brief passage between the encounter with the public scribe and the pause before the print shop.

10. See Brian O'Kill's impressive analysis of this sentence ("Aspects" 75–79). O'Kill argues that it reveals Lowry's typical syntactical construction of "open" (rather than periodic or "closed") sentences. The "centrifugal development" in such sentences "shows a dangerous tendency towards formlessness and lack of definition: this sentence displays some awkwardness and loss of momentum in the final phrases." But it seems noteworthy that the sentence begins with a periodic structure and only midway, after the predicate, shifts to "open" form. What O'Kill finds "loss of momentum" at the end is what I have called the "slower rhythms" that return Yvonne's perception to the present scene. And one might ask what is meant by "lack of definition" in such constructions: surely it depends on what is being defined?

11. Although Lowry's notes from Gunther's *Inside Latin America* (Templeton 1:21, 2) refer to recent Mexican history as well as earlier events derived from Gunther's summary of Henry Bamford Parkes's *History of Mexico*, and thus contain such familiar references as those to Cortez and Cárdenas, Juarez and Díaz, Huerta the "murderous drunk" and *pelados*, the Ejido and *sinarquistas*, virtually all of these (the likely exceptions are Huerta and the term "Ejido") almost certainly were in Lowry's text before he read Gunther.

12. That Lowry was quite conscious of the psychological process he was dramatizing here is shown by the notes on an earlier worksheet (Texas II, verso 19), which has "suppressed" and "repressed" followed by what look like dictionary definitions of these often-confused terms

13. See Sherrill Grace's fine analysis of this passage in terms of a "serial universe" (*Voyage* 57). Grace also notes the suggestion of a "Venus-like Yvonne."

14. Perhaps the association runs "eggs"–chicken–capon–"Capone." Strangely, the Capone reference does not appear in the typescript version of this page (Texas II, 17). Margerie seems to have missed an entire line of holograph text, and since syntax and sense were not awry, neither of the Lowrys noticed the omission. In any case, the reference disappears from II only to turn up later in XII, where the capon/Capone association is captured in the spelling "Capón."

15. An early worksheet for III contains an amusing echo of the draft sheet of Chapter II mentioned in n. 8 above, with its shopping list for fruit preserving: "the Burke's Irish loosened a screw . . . it was still tight, but his consciousness was like a jampot of preserves, the cap of which, after the glass has cooled, needs rescrewing" (Texas III, verso I). Apparently the preserving experience—and the draft of the preceding chapter—were not far behind Lowry at this point.

Although a number of discarded sheets of this stage of Chapter III survive on the versos of Texas typescript (see Appendix B), the final draft itself presents no difficulties: 29:10 contains a complete holograph.

16. The ambiguity with which cabalistic material is handled can perhaps be gauged from the more definite forms it took on early worksheets. A sketched start of the lovemaking, for instance, went this way: "Analogous to the task of the young neophyte bound for Yesod—Firmin years ago—who must control the astral plane and sometimes imagine a gate miles high with a sacred banishing symbol upon them through which he must enter a paradise (although for his present purposes it would have [been] better to have been a Zelator.)" (Texas III, verso 14). While "guiltily" climbing the Calle Nicaragua, one of his voices was to call him "the ex-cabbalist," and he was to be overtly conscious of his lapse. "All very difficult for a chap on the plane of Jupiter," he remarks, "except that I've no right to mention or even think of these things now" (Texas III, verso 12). The assertion on worksheets of extensive knowledge of cabalistic concepts and practices is far stronger, more insistent, than what Lowry permitted to remain.

17. Geoffrey recognizes this as an hallucination, and thinks, "So 'it' or 'they' had come again." On the typescript (Texas III, 33) Lowry worries that the reader will think he means the familiars, and with the laconic "See Chap. 2," alters the wording to "So the 'other' had come again." The passage in Chapter II Lowry is referring to is Geoffrey's assertion that "'It's really the shakes that make this kind of life [of drinking] insupportable. . . . You get to like the other after a while'" (Texas II, 9). Even with this echo, one doubts that many readers make the connection Lowry intended.

18. It is possible that this new draft of Chapter IV was written somewhat earlier, at about the same time as that of Chapter I (28:24), for both drafts (and only these drafts) make use of Turner's *Barbarous Mexico*, and apparently do so directly from the book, not from notes, as both manuscripts contain marginal page references to Turner (see n. 5 above). Aside from unmistakable use of material from Turner, the manuscript of IV (29:14, 11) has "see 127 B.M." for the spelling of "Tomosachics" (which Lowry nonetheless manages to spell "Tomasachics"). The holograph of this stage, 29:14, is complete.

19. The identification of the history of Mexico with that of man himself

is also made marginally in Lowry's notes from Gunther (Templeton 1:21, 2). See also n. 5 above.

20. In this phase of revision Lowry was much concerned with the debilitating effects of remorse. In one draft of the Consul's imagined speech to Hugh in Chapter III, this sometime-reader of Hawthorne had his protagonist identify it as the unpardonable sin: "Remorse, Hugh, that is the all-poisoning sin that God cannot forgive, cannot because he cannot help" (Texas III, verso 27). Nonetheless, it can be wrestled with successfully, as Juan was to show—and as, on another plane, the *Volcano* itself was to demonstrate. One draft here has, "It struggled upward = art, struggles. Even in the cantinas you could see the grotesque malformed imitations of the great murals" (Texas IV, verso 4); and indeed in the ensuing draft of Chapter VII, El Bosque will acquire its "small mural, aping the Great Mural in the Palace." In the end, the redemptive possibilities of aesthetic struggle, both personal and communal, were allowed to remain implicit, although elsewhere Lowry would point to his book as the justification for years that otherwise gave all too many reasons for remorse (cf., e.g., *DAG*, 24).

21. The emphasis on Hugh's remorse, already so strong in the previous (29:13) draft of IV, would have been underlined still further had Lowry pursued other holograph notes on that typescript. For instance, as Hugh sips his beer, Lowry pencils, "A glint of remorse winked in the draught, died" (ts. 21), and against the falling leaf "like a sudden footstep," "It was the footstep of the spectre of indefatigable remorse, disguised this time as guilt. Next time it would be the spectre of atonement" (ts. 22). Instead, Lowry chose to show Hugh struggling against remorse. At the base of his obsession is, of necessity, an inverted egotism: both Firmin brothers, like their creator, are quite familiar with it. See "The Garden of Etla."

22. However, with Lowry, "substantially" when preceding "unaltered" is a relative term: here it signifies only that changes could be carried out without rewriting an entire page. Noteworthy individual additions in the early part of the chapter include "Cathartes atratus" in the series of cat puns, the Consul's histrionic citation of Marston ("Thou mighty gulf, insatiable cormorant," etc.) and new designation of "donga" for the barranca, and the "monstrous" paranoiacally imagined headlines of Vigil's "accusing newspaper."

23. The manuscript survivals here are rather complex, but the stages can be identified as follows:

1. The complete clean holograph of the previous version, 29:17A.
2. The complete typescript made from that holograph, now located in two places:
    (a) pp. 1–14, 18, 28 (refolioed "31") are part of Texas Chapter V;

(b) pp. 15–17, 19–27 (plus holograph inserts) later rejected from this stage, now found in 29:17B.
   3. The complete clean holograph for the new "blackout" section, 29:18. These pages are numbered 1–6, but Lowry also reused ts and holograph inserts from (2b) above as the basis for the new version of the section of the chapter immediately preceding the blackout, and another such typed leaf in its midst: the pages so used were 29:17B, pp. 15–20, with inserts 15–16, 17, 19, and p. 27, refolioed "7."
   4. Typescript pages 15–17, 19–30, based on (3) above, compose the remainder of the Texas Chapter V.

There are also surviving worksheets from these stages on the versos of Texas V, 18–30, and IV, 14, 31.

24. Lowry identified the source on galley proofs (28:14, galley 50). See also Ackerley and Clipper 211–12.

25. It survives, however, in several places:

1. The opening (holograph) page is found on the verso of p. 2 of Lowry's letter dated "August 1951" to David Markson (2:19).
2. (Holograph) pages 2–6 are in the Einar Neilson Collection, 1:2, at UBC.
3. The remaining holograph-typescript pages are in 30:3. These are folioed or refolioed 7–46, of which pages 10, 17, 19, and 34 are missing. The first three are now part of the Texas typescript of the chapter (refolioed 13, 23, 25 respectively); the last was presumably removed at Lowry's behest when he discovered that the corresponding page (43) in the Texas typescript had been burned, but the holograph p. 43 in Texas Chapter VI consists of a sheet of the thin yellow paper employed only in Ontario for part of the "E" typescript of Chapter V. Thus it is not the missing page from 30:3 (although doubtless based on that page).

Since the two phases are not entirely separate, this is probably the best place to note the evidence for the several stages of the Texas Chapter VI:

1. Dark-ribbon typescript, refolioed pages 13, 23, 25, see (3) immediately above. Another dark-ribbon page, refolioed 17, is also included, headed, "Keep for correcting final." This is not a part of the text of Texas VI; it precedes the regular page 17 typed on medium ribbon of (2) below.
2. Medium-ribbon typescript, all other typed leaves.
3. Holograph p. 43 (on thin yellow paper used only in Chapter V of "E" [27:10]).
4. Holograph pp. 51A, 53 (on "Revenue Bond," used only in Chapters VI and VII of "E" [27:11, 12]).

26. Ackerley and Clipper (226) suggest, rightly, that Nordahl Grieg's *The Ship Sails On* and Melville's *Redburn* may have influenced Lowry's description of Hugh's treatment by the crew, but these works do not, presumably, influence *Hugh's* expectations. However, their contention that "Hugh's version of what life should be on board seems to have been derived almost entirely from his reading, in particular of R. H. Dana's *Two Years Before the Mast*," has the support of Hugh Fernhead's enthusiasm for Dana in the 1940 text. By the time of this much later draft, nonetheless, the influences hardly seem so exclusive: much of the sea-lore Hugh "knows" has been diffused beyond even London and O'Neill into the stereotypes of popular culture; it is "literary" in the broad, rather than the narrow, sense. Indeed, in his corrections to the E typescript of VI, Lowry cut the specific reference to London because he himself was "not sure about Jack London," that is, not sure whether "men fought, whored, drank and murdered" warranted the concluding "much as they did in Jack London" (27:11, 196; 30:4, A).

27. Repeating his words to Cape (*Letters* 74), Lowry told Erskine that the chapter was "the heart of the book," and in an early draft of that letter was more specific: "Mention always scene of turn of tide is centre of book." A later draft expanded, "I feel the scene where the two ships, the Oedipus Tyrannus and the Philoctetes drift closer and closer together with the tide as the point where the two halves of the book are knit together: or the tide of the book is changing. Please don't ask me what I mean by that because I don't know. It is just a feeling" (2:5, letter of June 22, 1946). Neither sentence survived into the final draft, which says simply that Chapter VI may be long, but "it has already been cut to the bone. And I think the book can support the chapter's great length" (3).

Lowry's phrasing gives at least a pseudo-structural basis to the significance of this connection between the ships, but his mordantly facetious language to Cape suggests that more is at stake than structure: he would resist an editor's excisions, he joked, because "even though I do live in Mexico, I'm damned if I'm going to help him cut out his heart. (And then, when he's dead, 'just flop it back in again anyhow,' as the nurse said to me having just attended the post mortem)" (*Letters* 77).

28. Names that disappear are William Beckford, Tourneur, Ibsen, John Deth, John Clare, Romains, Peacock, Chatterton, Keats, Freud, the Bible, Hume, all of whom (excepting John Deth, one of Conrad Aiken's poetic personae, an in-joke) give the list a more literary and "mainstream" air than later versions. The library lacks (until a pencilled insert on Texas VI, 32) "Vice Versa, Shakespeare, a complete Taskerson, All Quiet on the Western Front, The Clicking of Cuthbert."

29. The intermediate version (Texas-E) provides Hugh with lines from Dante to fit his current political obsession:

> The Ebro falling under lofty Libra
> And waters in the Ganges burnt with noon.

Here Spain and India are conjoined at an appropriate time of day, but Lowry was unable to work the lines in plausibly. Although Hugh cites the opening of the *Commedia*, that is common cultural currency; this later passage, from (we are informed) "some half-forgotten translation of Longfellow's," appears all too well-remembered, possible for the Consul, unlikely in his brother (Texas VI, 52; 27:11, 234).

30. In these notes, directives remind Lowry, on one sheet, "Mem: the Cambridge Cabbalists," and on the other, "also something from Abremalin the Mage." A separate sheet presents an early draft of the Consul's discourse to Hugh about "the Cambridge Cabbalists" (which he distinguishes, without explanation, from "the Cambridge Platonists"), ending, like the version quoted in my text, with "Whoever shall know the quality which is the secret of darkness shall know why the evil demons are more hurtful in the night than in the day." This is immediately followed by the list of those "evil demons":

> "The servitors of Amaymon
> Yes, I know them all, the mighty strongholds,
> the devouring fire of God,—
> Erekia, the one who tears asunder
> [and so on, as in the draft and the novel, down to "the evil questioners"]
> all these, at one time or another, have visited my bed," said the Consul, smoking and drinking.

All the foregoing is in response to the directive, "Abremalin the Mage" (properly, *Abra-Melin the Mage* by MacGregor-Mathers, as identified by Ackerley and Clipper, 262–63).

On the worksheet, the dialogue with Hugh was to begin "'It is true that at Cambridge, Hugh, you might have learned that we go back to Aristotle for the right questions,'" and a note above this directed "and repeated, in the next chapter: It is true, Jacques, that at the Sorbonne." Most of what follows is what appears in the chapter draft, as quoted above, but the untransformed angel is here a six-winged creature; and among the questions tossed at Hugh is, "'Who said that Malkuth was the invisible, archetypal moon, and if so, why?'"

31. The holograph draft (Texas VII) went through two quite distinct major phases and, refoliations suggest, an indeterminate number of minor ones. For once, paper differences show the way: earlier stage(s) appear on the ubiquitous yellow foolscap, later on white "Revenue Bond." In addition, a smaller, cramped hand and, frequently, "dirty" copy (with cancellations, marginalia,

etc.) characterize the yellow sheets, whereas a larger, more fluent hand and "clean" copy appear on the white leaves. Pages belonging to the earlier (yellow) stage are 4A, 5, 6–8, 21–24, 25A, 29–30A, 34–37; to the later (white) stage, 1–4, 5A, 9–20, 25, 26–28, 31–33.

At least the second of these stages was certainly composed in Ontario: the white paper makes its first appearance in Texas VI as pp. 51A and 53, the latter of which replaces an earlier (yellow) ts. 53 (which survives in Templeton 1:8). This "Revenue Bond" then is used for the typing of "E" VI (27:11) and the first portion of "E" VII (27:12), which makes clear how close Margerie's typing of the fair copy of the manuscript was behind Malcolm's composition. Furthermore, if we consider that Lowry characteristically did not let a chapter go until a typescript was made, we might assume that both holograph phases of Texas VII were made in Ontario, for the only typescript at this stage is that of "E." (Alternatively, it is possible that the Lowrys' fire interrupted composition before the typescript could be made, so that the yellow holograph dates from Dollarton, the white revisions plus typescript from Ontario.)

32. Lowry is here cannibalizing the manuscripts of the work later published as *Lunar Caustic*, where the protagonist suffers a like trauma. See *Psalms and Songs* 303–4.

33. In one draft (30:5, 25) Lowry put quotation marks around "releases the mystical in man." A pencil notation took the next logical step and inserted "William James."

34. "Original" in this context means the 1940 *Volcano*. The other meaning of "see original" in these manuscripts, a typing direction to Margerie, is, "see original document—poster, menu, telegram, travel folder, etc.—on which this passage is based, and check for accurate transcription." Context easily indicates which meaning applies.

In this case, because of incomplete survivals in the 1941 Chapter VII, we cannot now be entirely certain exactly what Lowry went back to: while we can regain the 1940 base from the "C" carbon, we cannot be sure that this was precisely what Lowry worked from in 1943–44.

35. As with the holograph of Chapter VII at this stage (see n. 31 above), there are signs of two major (and an indeterminate number of minor) phases of composition in the Texas holograph of VIII, although here paper proves a less sure guide than in the case of VII. The older phase, entirely on yellow sheets, again bears the stigmata of "dirty" copy, refoliations, and a crowded hand; the newer phase begins on white sheets of "Revenue Bond," but soon reverts to yellow sheets, at which point one must rely on the freer hand, lack of refoliation, and the relatively "clean" copy to distinguish later pages from earlier ones. Inevitably, one does so with less certainty. Nonetheless, the older phase seems made up of pp. 1, 5, 10, 13–19, 21, 25; the newer of pp. 2–4, 6

(white paper to this point, yellow hereafter), 7–9A, 11–12, 20, 22–24. Precisely the same speculations on place(s) and time(s) of composition made above on Texas VII may be applied to Texas VIII.

36. Such comic-sinister pairs as the assistants of *The Castle* and the arresting warders of *The Trial* seem behind the reference, as in more specific ways they seem behind the "chiefs" of Chapter XII.

37. It is conceivable that either VII or VIII (or both) were finally revised *after* IX at this stage. Evidence for this, anything but conclusive, rests on the fact that the consecutive pagination of the "E" typescript breaks down only at Chapter IX, which might suggest that it had been typed earlier and that the Lowrys saw no reason to bother to repaginate.

However, the draft under discussion (ms. 31:2; ts. Templeton 1:4) is not the one destined to become part of the Texas-"E" sets of drafts: Chapter IX went through yet another set of drafts (see following note). All this of course suggests Lowry's difficulties with the chapter and may indicate not that any of these versions of IX was created before the Texas-"E" versions of VII or VIII, but rather that because of these difficulties—at least three versions of the chapter were apparently typed in the summer and fall of 1944—Margerie simply reverted to her practice of pagination by chapter, uncertain, as Lowry himself may have been, which would prove final. After all, "E," still on yellow sheets, would need to be retyped before being sent out to publishers anyway, so consecutive pagination was hardly a necessity. However, it is also clear that in Ontario the Lowrys became less consistent about moving directly and immediately from holograph to typed versions of chapters.

38. The possibility of multiple "drafts" here depends on two peculiar factors in the manuscript record. One is the absence of all holograph remains from this stage. Clearly there was a holograph, certainly for the new passages concerning Yvonne's past, probably for the entire chapter, since adjustments appearing elsewhere are often not indicated on the preceding typescript (Templeton 1:4). The other anomaly is what seems a transposing of the Texas and "E" typescripts of IX. Whereas we should find that the Texas version is the earlier, what signs there are point the other way, suggesting that "E" was actually the first typed and Texas was its fair copy (which may account for sequential pagination ceasing in the "E" typescript at this point: see the preceding note). The differences between the two typescripts are so small that one hesitates to be dogmatic, but that similarity may explain why Lowry confused them, giving to the Noxons as part of the gift manuscript the fair copy of IX he should have kept for himself. In any case, the Texas IX is altogether clean copy, without refoliations or marginalia except for the typing directive "italics" (in Margerie's hand) next to Yvonne's press release. Typescript "E" (27:14), however, shows early refoliation: the current pages 20–28 and 31–33 were originally 14–22 and

25–27 respectively, indicating a considerably shorter earlier typescript. Nothing survives to tell us precisely what was added, but certainly the expansion came in the retrospective material, and here there is some basis for conjecture. Yvonne in Los Angeles and New York, including the Yvonne Griffaton film, is the only part of the flashback altogether unmentioned in the previous draft's sketch, and it consumes almost exactly the requisite number of pages (13–18 in "E") to account for the refoliations. The very few textual differences between the two scripts seem also to suggest (if they suggest anything at all) the priority of "E."

39. The granting of a past to Yvonne in Chapter IX gives rise to a small rash of anticipatory references, most of which are inserted on the typescripts of the Texas chapters. For instance, a "Born in Hawaii . . ." sentence gets dropped into II (13), a truncated reference to "Bill Hod—" into IV (2), Jacques Laruelle's desire to have been her director into I (12), and his recollected comment on the films she did make into III (9).

40. The three stages:

1. A "dirty" holograph, for part or all of the chapter. Only p. 3 survives (Templeton 1:22), heavily overwritten. There is no way of determining whether this stage was represented by a full draft or only by new and revised versions of individual passages. At the bottom of this single surviving sheet, as Lowry returns to familiar material, an "etc." directs him to the previous draft.
2. The clean holograph of Texas X, complete. The survival of an earlier draft of p. 10 of this phase (Templeton 1:9) indicates, again, an indeterminate number of drafts behind the complete holograph. In an apparently unique step, Lowry at this stage wrote out four pages of specific notes and queries (Templeton 1:9, A–D) to be taken up with Margerie (and Gerald Noxon?) before proceeding to typescript. Alterations on the holograph indicate that these were often acted on.
3. A complete typescript made from (2) above, now resident in two files: 27:15 ("E"), 1-3, 6-7, 9-13, 32-35, 40-41, 44; and 31:6, 4-5, 8, 14-31, 36-39, 42-43.

41. In Lowry's existence, of course, there is no difficulty in "accounting for" the passage, especially since its first draft occurs in letters he wrote to Margerie in the summer of 1944 while she was on a brief trip to New York (2:1). However symbolic it may be, the experience is recognizably rooted in Oakville, Ontario. See Nimmo.

42. Lowry was fond of the name "Quattras." In one version of *Lunar Caustic* (at this time known as "The Last Address") the black who in the published

version is called "Battle" bears this name (spelled with a double "s"), and in "Elephant and Colosseum" (*Hear Us O Lord*) it is given to a secondary figure, a Manx sailor.

There are also two literary analogues worth mentioning here:

(1) The second chapter of *Moby-Dick* (a chapter Lowry knew well enough to quote from in a 1931 letter to Aiken; see chapter 3, n. 20 above). Here in the context of the language and imagery of light and dark, black and white, heaven and hell, Ishmael stumbles into a nighttime service in a "negro church," where the black congregation, the biblical text on "the blackness of darkness," and the setting create a play with traditional categories: Ishmael is in a Christian house of worship, but it reminds him of "Tophet."

(2) F. Scott Fitzgerald's *Tender Is the Night*, where a drunken Abe North becomes obscurely involved with blacks and is indirectly the cause of the death of one of them. Fitzgerald writes, "Peterson [the black] was rather in the position of the friendly Indian who helped a white. The Negroes who suffered from the betrayal were not so much after Abe as after Peterson" (106). In Lowry's manuscripts, the source of Mr. Quattras's problems remains obscure until Lowry has him say, "'I was brought up with whites, so the blacks don't like me'" (31:6, insert 4).

The Fitzgerald analogue is particularly intriguing, for it is unclear whether we are dealing with echo or anticipation. Several years later (1949), Lowry and Margerie will launch into a film adaptation of *Tender Is the Night*, but it is not certain when he first read the novel. Binns (57–58) has noted the similarity of Hugh's (late-added) reflection on Yvonne as typical American woman in Chapter VI to Fitzgerald's presentation of Nicole Diver. Specifically, Hugh's reflections seem remarkably reminiscent of the paragraph which precisely sets Nicole into a symbolic American-female role (Fitzgerald, 233).

43. Strictly speaking, in *this* draft (Texas) the Consul does seem actually to have left dining room for toilet. One voice (probably Hugh's) remarks, "Geoff's a long time away" (24), and later he finds himself back at the table with "most" of the Tlaxcala brochure in his possession (26). However, the cutting of both these presumptive links in revision also cuts, whether deliberately or not, confirming evidence for the reality of the move to the *excusado*.

44. *1940 294*. On Lowry's use of Houghton, see York.

45. The single alteration in Geoffrey's attack on Hugh, from "'What have you ever done for humanity, Hugh, with all your orations about the capitalist system'" (31:5, 25) to "'with all your *oratorio obliqua* about the capitalist system'" (27:15, 40), is curious, the technical literary term seeming rather anomalous. A slur beyond "mere talk instead of action" (indoor Marxmanship), adequately conveyed by "orations," appears intended, probably including a pun

on *"obliqua"* to suggest "not straight, devious." The basic sense seems something like, "talk to which you have no real commitment and therefore refuse to take responsibility for by saying 'I'." Indirectly (obliquely), of course, the term is an indication of Lowry's own concern with literary matters, one of the several signs of covert or overt self-consciousness to appear late in the composition of the *Volcano*.

46. The visionary Tlaxcala seems a stylized version of Conrad's "whited sepulchre" of a city in *Heart of Darkness*, immediately behind which lies Matthew 23:27. A general wash from "The Whiteness of the Whale" also seems inevitable.

As echoes of Melville remind us, Lowry worked while in Ontario on a radio script of *Moby-Dick* for the CBC, a script never used (nor, apparently, fully written). While it is impossible to pinpoint just when he did such work, certainly it was contemporary with late revisions of the *Volcano*, for superseded drafts from the novel appear on versos of the *Moby-Dick* script (16:1; 16: 2).

47. Survivals of this stage suggest that Lowry had Margerie make a typescript from a holograph overtly incomplete, apparently a unique event in the composition of the novel: the latter part of a preliminary précis for the passage about the stars (31:10, 8–9) is visible, cancelled, as part of Texas XI, 9A. This is an omen of the complexity of the record at this stage. We begin with the fair (incomplete) holograph of 31:10, some of which is the basis for the typescript in Texas, some of which is the basis for an earlier typed version now lost.

Discernible stages:

1. First fair holograph: most of 31:10, supplemented by the August 25, 1951, letter to David Markson (2:19, versos 4–8, 13, for pages 10, 10A, 10B, 10C, 11, G of the chapter draft). Incomplete: changes in the system of foliation suggest that this is itself the survival of earlier stages.

2. First typescript(s), based on the above. It is not possible to be certain whether originally there was a single typescript, consecutively numbered, from which the latter half was discarded and replaced by a new version whose foliations began again at 1, or whether Lowry for compositional purposes divided the chapter in half (the break coming just after Hugh and Yvonne's arrival at El Popo) and instructed Margerie to number each separately, starting again at 1 for the second group. In any event, a light ribbon distinguishes both, and the leaves in Texas XI involved are the following:

    (a) 1, 3, 4, 9A (refolioed from 9), 10, 11A (12).
    (b) 20–21 (9), 22 (10), 23 (11), 24 (12).

3. New fair holograph leaves: 31:10, insert 2, insert 5–6 [2 leaves], insert 7–8 [2 leaves, also headed B and C].

4. New typescript in Texas XI based on (3) above and (we must assume) on corrected leaves from (2) above: these ts. leaves are distinguished by a notably darker ribbon than those in (2): 2, 2A, 5–9, 11, 12 (1)–19 (8), 25–26.

5. Finally, holograph "insert 25" follows all of the above.

(Discarded holograph drafts from this stage can be found in Templeton 1:22, 3; 15:14, versos 4–15; 27:17, versos 1, 7–11, 15–16; Texas XI, versos 1–9, 11–26. Corrections for the Texas typescript are found in 16:1, verso 8 and 16:2, versos 1–3.)

The fair typescript, "E," is in 27:16. However, a note in Margerie's hand on the opening page of the 31:10 holograph, "perhaps keep for G's [Gerald's] gift version," suggests that at one point the Lowrys had hoped that the typescript of XI now at Texas—the one, in short, that *did* go into the "gift version"—might prove their own fair copy.

Much of the holograph in 31:10–and several of the leaves elsewhere clearly discarded from it—have another distinction: here alone among the *Volcano* drafts do we find Lowry making a neat marginal column, usually on the right, sometimes headed "Notes." These are comments, queries, directives of various kinds, relevant to the text at hand, but usually clearly separated from it. On one leaf, however (31:10, 7), Lowry reveals his awareness of the porous border, writing at the top of the page, "Stuff in margin part of text save one note at bottom." The entire method of "Through the Panama" lies in that note.

48. It does not seem irrelevant that Lowry had in the past associated the actual menu with judgment upon a woman. The *Volcano* "erases" from the face a fragmentary poetic draft quite different from the one on its back, this one entitled "A Curse," beginning, "How shall we apostrophise the vileness of women," and ending, "But think not to escape the wrath of life for all your children will be born dead." (cf. Scherf, #438: my transcription differs somewhat from the text published there.)

49. A still earlier draft (Templeton 1:22, 3) makes it plain that this passage in XI stems from the same nighttime experience Lowry had in Oakville, recounted to Margerie by letter, and made partial use of in the train vision of X (see n. 41). The sheet in question is basically an early draft for the train vision, but near the bottom, a line is drawn, and in a quite separate passage Lowry develops his sense of the effects of light and shadow made by car headlights sweeping along a fence. "[E]aten up in reverse by night," they also contribute to the illusion of "a Grecian temple, dim, with the slender pillars, approached by two broad steps." A note at bottom reads, "This was the El Popo." (At the start of this passage, not obviously connected to anything else, tantalizingly, a line reads, "more like a cup perhaps—Parsifal's cup that this Amfortas held lacking a spear–.")

50. Lowry said he had both in mind, and of course the Pleiades are referred to overtly in the chapter. He told Jonathan Cape that Hugh and Yvonne's search "would have added meaning to anyone who knows anything of the Eleusinian mysteries" (*Letters* 83). It seems a safe enough claim, since no one knows very much of the Eleusinian mysteries except that they were fertility rites connected with the Demeter-Persephone myth. The natural setting and the celebration of the Day of the Dead are general justification for such a reference, but it should be noted that Yvonne's death (like the Consul's) apparently reverses the theme of the dead returning to consort with the living. In her case, Lowry overdetermines the language of transcendence, resurrection, rebirth (without committing himself to any specific meaning of those terms), so that when she evokes the "dark waters of Eridanus," we can imagine her as Persephone returning to the underworld or Persephone restored to earth, just as in the search earlier she has assumed the role of Demeter. Lowry's use of the myth (insofar as it is not merely an afterthought) is loose and reversible, as are the various reflective images Yvonne has of herself.

51. The famous opening of Henry Vaughan's "The World" was referred to in Chapter VI at this stage. See above, p. 238.

52. While avoiding literary echoes in his eagle later in the chapter, Lowry may here have in the back of his mind the end of "The Try-Works," chapter 96 of *Moby-Dick*, a chapter already alluded to in Hugh's recollections of Cambridge (30:3, 27). Melville's bird that reconciles heights and depths, dark and light, is the Catskill eagle; the passage in question goes this way: "there is a Catskill eagle in some souls that can alike dive down into the blackest gorges, and soar out of them again and become invisible in the sunny spaces. And even if he for ever flies within the gorge, that gorge is in the mountains; so that even in his lowest swoop the mountain eagle is still higher than other birds upon the plain, even though they soar." It is a revealing difference that Lowry does not resolve the extremes he presents. Whereas Melville's bird is evoked precisely as a metaphor of reconciliation, Lowry's vulture alternates between extremes, dramatizing "the eternal horror of opposites."

53. An early draft (27:17, verso 8) suggested succinctly, if somewhat ambiguously, what "home" was in question here: in the margin appears "My Blue Heaven" ("When whipoorwills call / And evening is nigh / I hurry to. . . ."). To underscore this new passage and new theme, Lowry will later insert another non-Mexican bird, this time briefly and metaphorically. As they near the "cascada," "The noise of the approaching falls was now like the awakening voices downwind of five thousand bobolinks in an Ohio savannah. Toward it the torrent raced furiously" (27:16, 4).

54. The earliest version (Texas XI, verso 1) has the bird headed "toward the stars, though she had not seen any." Yet within a very few pages Yvonne was to

see a vast panorama of stars, as if Lowry's night has fallen with the absurd suddenness of Beckett's in *Waiting for Godot*. Then again, the note of aspiration is more convincingly struck if there appears a goal, which the single star of subsequent versions provides.

55. The passage begins in the square but moves quickly to the sky ("–they were the cars at the fair that were whirling round her, but no, they were not cars, stars they were and they were not stars, they were planets, while {the great(?) sun(?) stood, burning and twirling and glistening in the middle,} here they came round again {NAME THEM i.e. the planets} . . ." etc.), then dissolves into the butterflies ("{go through some of the chaos of arrival in II}"), then into a generalized recollection of the wood ("and they had lost their way") followed by the horse, which as it rears becomes "a statue," containing successively Yvonne Griffaton, Huerta, and the Consul, then a merry-go-round horse that abruptly strands her in a ravine down which "a million horses were thundering," from which she "escapes" to the house (15:14, versos 8, 7, 5). Individual sections will be trimmed or, more often, filled out, but Lowry's design here essentially holds.

56. The new holograph drafts are placed before the earlier, full holograph of Chapter XII in the Texas manuscript; they are numbered 1, 7A, 8, 9, 9A, 12A, 12B, 12C, 12D, 13. Since these do not quite account for all the new typescript in the "E" Chapter XII (27:17), we must assume that other revisions were executed on some earlier typescript pages of "E." Unfortunately, all the superseded typescript of "E" at this stage was discarded, so that discussion of alterations must be based on the earlier holograph of Texas XII.

That this procedure may not always stand on firm ground is revealed by some survivals of an earlier revision of the "E" typescript (31:13, 4, 9, 10, 15, 32, 32 [sic], 33, plus holograph inserts). A comparison of Texas XII, 14–15A, with discarded 31:13, 15–insert 15, from "E" and the new 20–21 of "E" reveals changes made at the intermediate stage that without the survival of discarded typescript one would assume to have come later. However, since for virtually all of the alterations here the intermediate stage(s) has been lost, we can only proceed on the assumption that these changes were executed at this latest phase.

57. At least the incident of the drunkard husband seems to have an autobiographical base, the clue lying in his having told the barman "at too great length last night how somebody's house burned down" (9). In *DAG* 170, Sigbjørn Wilderness recalls patronizing the Riverside Inn in Niagara-on-the-Lake, whose proprietor, as in the *Volcano*, was named "Sherlock." Having returned, at least at times, to serious drinking after the Dollarton fire, Lowry may well have considered himself "another kind of drunkard, in different circumstances, in another country," than he had been when in Mexico.

58. See Noxon's letter of March 2, 1945 to Aiken: "before he left he gave me the original manuscript of the book which is complete except for a [few] changes which were made in his later working copy. So if there are more fires and disasters, the thing will not be lost" (Noxon 29).

CHAPTER FIVE. 1945–1946

1. Lowry's letter to Matson, dated June 6, reports that he has mailed the manuscript "several days ago" (*Letters* 45), and on June 22 Matson wrote to say that he was reading it. On July 31 he sent Lowry a discouraging report from Duell, Sloan and Pearce that echoed his own response to the novel (*Letters* 420), along with a copy of a covering letter to Henry Holt and Company, to whom he was next submitting it (1:45).

On January 12, 1946, Matson forwarded a letter of rejection from Henry Holt to Lowry in Dollarton. Signed by Helen K. Taylor, Managing Editor, the letter acknowledges that Holt has had the manuscript for "a very long time" and explains the delay this way:

> There were two quite different camps. A few of our editors insisted that the script showed too much brilliancy to reject and were in favor of publishing it provided the author would consent to certain rather extensive revisions. The other camp believed that the brilliant ingenuity of the man's writing, although it showed tremendous talent, was not sustained, that the book showed such a fundamental unbalance and lack of discipline together with overwriting that an extensive job of cutting, supposing the author were willing to submit to it, would not make an acceptable book. There was no one of us who denied the terrific power which the author very often displays. Some of the scenes of alcoholism make The Lost Weekend look like a Sunday school picnic. In fact, there is as good writing in the book in snatches as one could find anywhere in the prose of the last half century.

With these perceived problems and with Holt's crowded schedule, Taylor concluded, they had reached a "negative decision" (1:45).

On February 18, Matson sent on to Dollarton a copy of his letter accompanying the manuscript to Reynal and Hitchcock. On March 27 he wrote to say that the publisher was near a decision and that "there's a very good chance that decision will be favorable." However, he cautioned, the decision might be conditional on Lowry's doing "some" editing of the novel.

By the time of this last letter Lowry had had an outright acceptance from British publisher Jonathan Cape. But all Matson's correspondence went to

Dollarton: after November 1945, the Lowrys were in Mexico, and news of the to-and-fro in New York did not reach them until after the *Volcano* had been accepted.

2. He also now correctly attributed the Bunyan passage to *Grace Abounding* rather than, as he first had it, *Pilgrim's Progress,* an error doubtless stemming from his encountering the passage in William James's *Varieties of Religious Experience* (also suggesting he had not read *Grace Abounding?*).

As with these first changes on the "E" typescript, it is once again not always possible to determine when such alterations were made. Enough sheets of corrections for the "E" chapters survive, almost certainly done immediately after the initial typing, to suggest that this was regular practice for all chapters at this stage (and for at least some typed chapters in the Texas manuscript). When there is evidence that alterations were made at that earlier stage, I have included them in my consideration of those drafts treated in Chapter 4. All other changes on the "E" typescripts I consider as belonging to the later phase taken up in this chapter. Once more, the presence of Margerie Lowry's hand (as in the correction of the Bunyan title) does not seem to warrant special notation; following my general practice, I speak simply of "Lowry's" emendations.

3. This insertion postdated the typing of Chapter VII. In his corrections for that chapter (28:3, 1), Lowry wonders, "Should not Jacques have thought of that post card in 1. That post card Geoff must have put maliciously under his pillow: then quote the postcard in toto—would that confuse, spoil surprise, or tremendously heighten the tragic irony when the postcard arrives in VI. As things stand the irony of it is not very evident I think anyhow at the end of VI. Perhaps the p. c. can be quoted in part in I. It would be a bitter pill to Laruelle, for it shows him she loves Geoff after all."

4. Some of this revision may have been done in Ontario (none of the correction sheets from that stage survive), but the new version of the Tlaxcala-"excusado" episode (31:7) was made in Dollarton, as corrections for portions of "F" appear, cancelled, on some versos. Most of Lowry's revising of Chapter X was done on earlier typed leaves, supplemented by inserts where necessary. The new Tlaxcala-"excusado" episode is a "Margie version," revised by Lowry. When the dust had cleared, instead of the simple "E" typescript the Lowrys brought from Ontario, one could distinguish four separate groups involved in preparation of the "F" fair copy:

1. Original typescript leaves of "E" that are retained: pp. 1–3, 6–7, 9–13, 32–35, 40–41, 44 (27:15) and p. 28 (31:6). (Through an error in cataloguing p. 28, while not rejected, was filed with superseded sheets.)
2. Original typescript leaves of "E" that, revised and supplemented by holograph inserts, are superseded: pp. 4, insert 4, 5, 8, insert 8, 14, 15, insert

15, 16–27, 29, insert 29, 30, insert 30–31, 31, 36, 37, insert 36–37, 38, insert 38A, insert 38B, 39, insert 39, 42, 43 (31:6).

3. Nine-page typescript-holograph (A-I) of the Tlaxcala-"excusado" episode (31:7). A "Margie version," which, annotated and altered by Malcolm, became the basis for this section (pp. 17–"26 and 27") of "E."

4. New typescript leaves of "E": 4–5A, 8–8A, 14–"26 and 27," 29–31, 36–39A, 42 (27:15), based on revisions in (2) and version in (3) above (the latter of which supercedes the comparable pages [17–27] in (2) to complete a forty-five-page typescript.

5. According to Jonathan Cape's letter of November 29, 1945, he had heard from Lowry in August in a letter expressing reluctance to undertake much (anything?) in the way of revision. Lowry's letter (which seems to have been lost: Bowker, *Pursued* 339 refers to a draft) apparently accompanied the manuscript. Why was it sent when and as it was? Insofar as events can be pieced together in the absence of relevant documents, something like this seems to have happened: Matson's discouraging letter of July 31 (*Letters* 420) was the latest in a series of dissatisfactions both the Lowrys felt with him in the early 1940s. Malcolm apparently reacted by sending Cape, publisher of *Ultramarine*, a typescript of the novel and inviting him to act as his agent both for Britain and the U.S. Here is how Lowry recalled events in his May 30, 1946, letter to Cape (2:3):

> Although I had previously told you I would prefer you to act as my American agent, it turned out that my New York agent, who is also my wife's agent, had sold it in America, and all this news I received on the same day [that he received Cape's acceptance]. I had not heard from my agent since he wrote me an extremely disappointing letter saying that he did not believe in the book as it stood.... All this was about the time, as I recall, that I replied to your first letter, when I said I was not altogether satisfied with my American connection ... we hadn't indeed had a word from our agent save this discouraging one for months and months and when we left for Mexico, though your letter had given me hope of another kind, it was with the assumption that the copy of Under the Volcano I'd sent to our agent in America would undoubtedly be returned to our Canadian address.

(Lowry's reference to a "first letter" seems to confuse Cape's letter of October 15 with an imagined earlier letter: there is no other reference to such a letter by either party.) Lowry goes on to say that Margerie had written to Matson "telling him to return it, if that was all he thought about it, and hence my say-so to you on this matter"—a considerable stretch of Margerie's letter of the previous

August (*Letters* 420–23). However, it was surely out of the call in Matson's letter for yet further revisions (echoed by Duell, Sloan and Pearce) that Lowry composed his August letter to Cape, refusing such revisions in advance.

6. There were of course other considerations as well (state of finances, of the shack, etc.). See Day 306ff.; Bowker, *Pursued* 341–42.

7. Apparently, the actual letters of acceptance do not survive, so one must piece together terms and immediate responses from other references: Matson's letters of March 27 and April 16; his telegram of April 13 (all 1:45); Margerie's letter, undated [April], to "Mother and Sis and Bert"; Malcolm's letter to Cape, May 30 (both 2:3).

8. All of Erskine's surviving letters are found in 1:20. I will refer to them simply by date.

9. Lowry's first draft here is often less tactful and ingratiating than the letter sent Erskine. For instance, on the issue of the border, he agrees that an "apparently rather stupid border" around the name would be pointless, but opines that Erskine's suggestion of simply printing the name in capitals was actually "more eccentric" than using the border. In the end, reluctantly, "I suppose I pass the buck to you" (2:5, first ms. 1).

10. Reynal and Hitchcock originally proposed publishing the *Volcano* in the fall of 1946, and Lowry's sense of haste has that earlier deadline in mind. A few days later, he learned of the probable postponement of publication until after Christmas.

Most of the June 30 letter (*Letters* 114–17) is an expression of Lowry's plagiarism anxiety ("a slight neurosis of mine," he discreetly terms it). Should he append explanatory notes "to elucidate such matters in the deeper layers as that the garden can be seen not only as the world, or the Garden of Eden, but legitimately as the Cabbala itself . . . a la Childe Harolde"? Ought he to acknowledge any "borrowings, echoes, design-governing postures, and so on" (à la *The Waste Land*, as he does not say). Almost as if he cannot help himself, examples pour out: "bangs and cries" from a J. C. Squire story; "personal battle" and "with their secret mines of silver" perhaps from D. H. Lawrence's letters; "There's always the abyss" from Julian Green's *Personal Record*; "unbandaging of great giants" not from *To the Lighthouse*, for "I had not read that book when I wrote this passage," but "a not dissimilar image"; "jonquil," a "favorite" word of Faulkner's "in relation to dawn"; "Compañero," vaguely suggested by Ralph Bates's "The Rainbow Fields" [*The Fields of Paradise*].

Before Erskine had a chance to respond to this barrage, Lowry appeared to reverse himself. A draft of a letter with "July 5" scrawled at the top withdraws the suggestion of annotation, declaring, "There are really no echoes etc. that I do not myself really consider to be absolutely justified and assimilated, *absorbed*, and I have mentioned them to you partly for my own psychological benefit and partly in case you might somewhere disagree" (2:7; the fair copy has apparently been lost. The draft is published in Woodcock, *Malcolm Lowry* 110–12). Despite his retraction here, Lowry will continue to "confess" borrowings, certain or possible, to Erskine; it will not be long before he has the hapless editor reading through Faulkner's *Wild Palms* in search of another fugitive echo (see Lowry's letter, n.d. [early November] [2:9] and Erskine's reply, November 7 [1:20]).

11. Surviving letters and notes that Lowry sent Erskine in July 1946 are in 2:6. However, his own notes, drafts, and discards arising out of that correspondence are in 2:7.

12. Referring to Geoffrey's address to the pariah dog in El Bosque, Lowry must tell Erskine, "Consul's declamation . . . is a purposeful echo of Nordahl Grieg's The Ship Sails On, in which protagonist contemplates suicide with ship's dog" (2:6). His draft of this note had gone further, beginning, "I could write you a book on the significance of the dog that would take in everything from the Rig Veda to Eric Von Stroheim's Foolish Wives, and from the Eleusinian mysteries to Djuna Barnes' Nightwood" (2:7).

13. As Erskine said, "your suggested cuts in X were so plaintively and reluctantly suggested I can't bear to make any of them" (August 28/September 20). He had certainly caught his author's tone, but the substance of Lowry's resistance also bears repeating: "this [cutting] does some damage to what I conceive to be my intention, which was to have some fun and games with the word churrigueresque and overloading, as if the chapter were satirizing its own style, while at the same time providing a crazy counterpoint of the very beginnings of Christendom in the Western World."

14. The hand recognizable on the galleys is almost always Margerie's; she had the more legible handwriting.

15. Lowry marked "He left a little for Hugh, however" for a cut, which, unaccountably, did not get made. He may have recognized that the sentence was dubious as coming from Yvonne's point of view; he may have felt the irony excessive. In any case, apparently against his wishes, the sentence remains.

16. By now Lowry could become playful. Two misprints in Chapter X provoked the following: "morrior" (for "mirror," that the Consul wants in the stone toilet)–"He gets it; but what if he had broken this sinister article? 77 years bad luck?" (98); "drunkark" (for "drunkard")–"What about an alternate title? Under the Volcano or the Dunkird of a Drunkark?" [Dunkirk of a Drunkard] (103).

In Chapter XI he admires the graphic hand and notes "it has a nice tweed suit on too" (111), and in a triple-header, draws together an error here ("darknees" for "darkness") with the "drunkark" noted above, and still another in

Chapter III ("to disrepute [rather than "dispute"] with Lucretius") to produce, "A subtle improvement, making the El Popo a more exciting place altogether, where some drunkark, half in darknees, might even disrepute with a Lucretius" (109, 24).

17. Or perhaps not: a letter to Jonathan Cape (n.d. [November? 1946]; *Letters* 130–31) declares, "You will have my proofs soon." In the draft of his November 21 letter to Erskine, Lowry asked permission to send corrected proof from the Reynal and Hitchcock edition directly on to Cape, "that is, *after* I've corrected your page proofs on their basis" (2:9, draft 4), but the request (and much else) was cut from the fair copy of the letter. No other correspondence on the matter survives, but the probable dating of the Cape letter and the assurance that proofs will be sent "soon" strongly suggest that Lowry was not launching into a new set of corrections.

There are several asterisks and the directive "See letter" throughout the corrected galley proofs, but an accompanying letter does not survive. Lowry did correct page proofs for Reynal and Hitchcock in December in New Orleans (see *Letters* 132–34, and 2:9, letter of December 17, 1946). The page proofs do not survive. The official publication date for the *Volcano* in New York was February 19, 1947; in London, September 15, 1947.

CHAPTER SIX. The Complete Consort

1. Lowry's view of the *Volcano* as unfinished was not simply theoretical. When there seemed a possibility that Knopf might reissue the novel, he began to fuss over alterations. A letter to Markson (February 22, 1957) raises some of the questions raised a decade earlier by Albert Erskine: "I think M. Laruelle should see the le gusta esta jardin notice perhaps in I: Chap VI could be tautened, I feel," etc. (3:13).

2. See Wright for an examination of one (but only one) side of this tension.

3. My use of the terms "story" and "discourse" follows that of Chatman (who is himself following French structuralists).

4. Bowker (*Pursued* 117) claims that while at Cambridge, Lowry's talking over his work with Charlotte Haldane "meant discussing musical form as a basis for the novel, especially the fugue, echoing earlier discussions with Aiken." Indeed, Bowker points out that her novel *I Bring Not Peace*, "was structured like a fugue for four voices, each chapter told from the viewpoint of a different character, a technique Lowry used later in *Under the Volcano*" (102). (He would, of course, have found comparable "technique" in Faulkner's *The Sound and the Fury* and Joyce's *Ulysses*.)

5. A minor echo out of the Las Novedades material does, in fact, get developed later. From 1940 onward, discovering that there was no way to telephone for help, the Consul had returned to his companions with some version of "Forward to the arena." Initially, this is a gentle shepherding of his "children," even when Yvonne has become the ex-wife, especially as a response to her tears. The echo toward the other end of the chapter—"Forward to the Salón Ofélia!"—appears only in the draft that first begins the chapter inside Arena Tomalín (31:1, 16), which also seems to produce in the *next* draft an adjustment near the start, "'Forward to the bloody arena then,' the Consul had said savagely, and she had cried" (31:2, 2). Geoffrey has evolved here from the kindly old guide to not quite a travesty of a military leader.

6. Lowry refers to the dog myth in *DAG* 227. As Ackerley and Clipper say (445) he would have encountered it in Spence's *Gods of Mexico*.

7. Jonathan Arac, who is the first to point out the comic importance of this passage, assumes it is a single speech by Wagner, a "misreading" encouraged by Lowry's arrangement. (Does it also ironically echo Laruelle's misreading of the genuine lines from Marlowe?) See Arac 482, and my discussion of these issues ("Revision" 108–9).

8. The most attentive student of Lowry's style has been Brian O'Kill; see also the article by Joan Huddleston.

APPENDIX A

1. My transcription varies slightly from any in *Collected Poetry* because I have retained Lowry's cancelled "Uno mescalito?" Its relevance to Chapter VII of the novel is, I trust, evident.

2. Lowry claimed to Clemens ten Holder that Cervantes's menu had actually existed and been in his possession but was "now" (1951) lost. There are no signs that it was in his possession in 1940, however. In any case, Lowry admits to ten Holder to "certain reservations and improvements" of his own. See Hilton, 51.

WORKS CITED

Ackerley, Chris. "*Barbarous Mexico* and *Under the Volcano*." *Notes and Queries* 229 (n.s. 31) (1984): 81–83.
———. "Malcolm Lowry and Hermann Broch: The Aesthetics of Somnambulism in *Under the Volcano* and *The Sleepwalkers*." *Malcolm Lowry Review* 26 (1990): 10–15.
———, and Lawrence J. Clipper. *A Companion to "Under the Volcano."* Vancouver: UBC Press, 1984.
Aiken, Conrad. *Ushant*. London: W. H. Allen, 1963.
Arac, Jonathan. "The Form of Carnival in *Under the Volcano*." *PMLA* 92 (1977): 481–99.
Asals, Frederick. "Henry Buckley's Spanish Civil War and Lowry's." *Malcolm Lowry Review* 25 (1989): 13–28.
———. "Lowry's Use of Indian Sources in *Under the Volcano*." *Journal of Modern Literature* 16 (1989): 113–40.
———. "Revision and Illusion in *Under the Volcano*." In *Swinging the Maelstrom*, edited by Sherrill Grace, 93–111. Montreal and Kingston: McGill-Queens University Press, 1992.
Binns, Ronald. *Malcolm Lowry*. London and New York: Methuen, 1984.
———. "Materialism and Magic in *Under the Volcano*." *Critical Quarterly* 23 (Spring 1981): 21–32.
Blackmur, R. P., ed. *The Art of the Novel: Critical Prefaces*, by Henry James. New York: Scribner's, 1934.
Bogan, Louise. *Body of This Death*. New York: Robert M. McBride, 1923.
Bowker, Gordon, ed. *Malcolm Lowry Remembered*. London: Ariel Books, 1985.
———. *Pursued by Furies: A Life of Malcolm Lowry*. Toronto: Random House of Canada, 1993.
Breit, Harvey, and Margerie Bonner Lowry. *Selected Letters of Malcolm Lowry*. Philadelphia: J. B. Lippincott, 1965.
Buckley, Henry. *Life and Death of the Spanish Republic*. London: Hamish Hamilton, 1940.

Calder-Marshall, Arthur. "A Visit from the Calder-Marshalls, Cuernavaca, 1937." In Bowker, ed., *Malcolm Lowry Remembered*, 109–13.
Chatman, Seymour. *Story and Discourse*. Ithaca: Cornell University Press, 1978.
Clipper, Lawrence J. "Yvonne's Astronomy Magazine." *Malcolm Lowry Newsletter* 6 (Spring 1980): 3–6.
Costa, Richard Hauer. *Malcolm Lowry*. New York: Twayne, 1972.
Corrigan, Matthew. "The Phenomenology of Failure." *Boundary 2* 3 (1975): 407–40.
Day, Douglas. *Malcolm Lowry*. New York: Oxford University Press, 1973.
Deck, Laura M. Interview with Margerie Bonner Lowry: "His Mind Was Just Like a Fireworks Factory." In Bowker, ed., *Malcolm Lowry Remembered*, 130–43.
Doyen, Victor. "Fighting the Albatross of Self: A Genetic Study of the Literary Work of Malcolm Lowry." Ph.D. diss., Catholic University of Louvain, 1973.
———. "La genèse d' *Au-dessous du Volcan*." *Les lettres nouvelles* 2–3 (May–June 1974): 87–122.
Edmonds, Dale H. "Mescalusions or The Drinking Man's *Under the Volcano*." *Journal of Modern Literature* 6 (1977): 277–88.
———. "*Under the Volcano:* A Reading of the 'Immediate Level.'" *Tulane Studies in English* 16 (1968): 63–105.
Fitzgerald, F. Scott. *The Portable Fitzgerald*. Selected by Dorothy Parker. New York: Viking Press, 1945.
Gabrial, Jan. "Marriage beneath the Volcano." In Bowker, ed., *Malcolm Lowry Remembered*, 113–27.
Grace, Sherrill E. "The 'Asperin Tree' and the Volcano: Carol Phillips and Malcolm Lowry." *Journal of Modern Literature* 17 (1991): 509–20.
———. *The Voyage That Never Ends: Malcolm Lowry's Fiction*. Vancouver: UBC Press, 1982.
Gunther, John. *Inside Latin America*. New York: Harper and Bros., 1941.
Hilton, Terry, ed. "Malcolm Lowry: Three Letters from Mexico." *Malcolm Lowry Review* 21–22 (Fall 1987–Spring 1988): 31–40.
———, ed. "Malcolm Lowry: Letter to Clemens ten Holder." *Malcolm Lowry Review* 21–22 (Fall 1987–Spring 1988): 41–71.
Huddleston, Joan. "Noun Modification as an Index of Style in Lowry's *Under the Volcano*." *Language and Style* 10 (1977): 86–108.
Kermode, Frank. *The Genesis of Secrecy*. Cambridge: Harvard University Press, 1979.
Killorin, Joseph, ed. *Selected Letters of Conrad Aiken*. New Haven: Yale University Press, 1978.

Lowry, Malcolm. "Bulls of the Resurrection." *Prism International* 5, 1 (Summer 1965): 5–11.

———. *Dark As the Grave Wherein My Friend Is Laid*. Edited by Douglas Day and Margerie Lowry. Toronto: General Publishing Co., 1968.

———. "Garden of Etla." *United Nations World* 4 (1950): 45–47.

———. "Hotel Room in Chartres." *Story* 5, no. 26 (1934): 53–58.

———. "In Le Havre." *Life and Letters* 10 (1934): 462–66.

———. "June 30th, 1934." In *Malcolm Lowry: Psalms and Songs*, edited by Margerie Lowry, 36–48. New York: New American Library, 1975.

———. *Lunar Caustic*. London: Jonathan Cape, 1968.

———. "On Board the West Hardaway." *Story*, 3.15 (1933), 12–22.

———. "Under the Volcano." *Prairie Schooner*, 37, no. 4 (Winter 1963–64): 284–300. Reprinted in Margerie Lowry, ed., *Malcolm Lowry: Psalms and Songs*, 187–201.

———. *Under the Volcano*. New York: Reynal and Hitchcock, 1947. Reprinted, with introduction by Stephen Spender, Philadelphia: J. B. Lippincott Co., 1965.

Nimmo, D. C. "Lowry's Hell." *Notes and Queries* 16 (1969): 265.

Noxon, Gerald. *"On Malcolm Lowry" and Other Writings*. Edited by Miguel Mota and Paul Tiessen. Waterloo, Ontario: The Malcolm Lowry Review, 1987.

O'Kill, Brian. "Aspects of Language in *Under the Volcano*." In *The Art of Malcolm Lowry*, edited by Anne Smith, 72–92. London: Vision Press, 1978.

———. "A Stylistic Study of the Fiction of Malcolm Lowry." Ph.D. diss., Cambridge University, 1974.

———. "The Role of Language in Lowry's Fiction." In *Apparently Incongruous Parts*, edited by Paul Tiessen, 174–86. Metuchen, N.J.: Scarecrow Press, 1990.

———. "Why Does Nobody Write Like This Any More?" In *Malcolm Lowry Eighty Years On*, edited by Sue Vice, 9–17. Basingstoke and London: Macmillan, 1989.

Pottinger, Andrew J. "The Consul's 'Murder.'" *Canadian Literature* 67 (Winter 1976): 53–63.

———. "The Revising of *Under the Volcano*: A Study in Literary Creativity." Ph.D. diss., University of British Columbia, 1978.

Rawlinson, H. G. *India: A Short Cultural History*. London: The Cresset Press, 1937.

Saalman, Dieter. "Malcolm Lowry and Hermann Broch: The Metaphysics of Somnambulism in *Under the Volcano* and *The Sleepwalkers*." *Malcolm Lowry Review* 25 (1989): 29–41.

Scherf, Kathleen, ed. *The Collected Poetry of Malcolm Lowry*. Vancouver: UBC Press, 1992.

Sugars, Cynthia, ed. *The Letters of Conrad Aiken and Malcolm Lowry, 1929–1954*. Toronto: ECW Press, 1992.

Tiessen, Paul, ed. *The Letters of Malcolm Lowry and Gerald Noxon, 1940–1952*. Vancouver: UBC Press, 1988.

———, and Miguel Mota, eds. *The 1940 "Under the Volcano."* Waterloo, Ontario: MLR Editions, 1994.

Turner, John Kenneth. *Barbarous Mexico*. Chicago: Charles H. Kerr, 1910.

Vice, Sue. "Narrator Dethroned: The Making of *Under the Volcano*." *Encounter*, 69, no. 3 (Sept.–Oct. 1987): 46–52.

Walker, Ronald G. "'The Weight of the Past': Toward a Chronology of *Under the Volcano*." *Macolm Lowry Newsletter* 9 (Fall 1981): 3–23.

Welty, Eudora. "Some Notes on Time in Fiction." In *The Eye of the Story*, 163–73. New York: Random House, 1978.

Wintringham, Tom. *English Captain*. London: Faber and Faber, 1939.

Woodcock, George. ed. *Malcolm Lowry: The Man and His Work*. Vancouver: UBC Press, 1971.

Wright, Terence. "*Under the Volcano:* The Static Art of Malcolm Lowry." *Ariel* 1, no. 4 (1970): 67–76.

York, Thomas. "The Post-mortem Point of View in *Under the Volcano*." *Canadian Literature* 99 (Winter 1983): 35–46.

Younghusband, Sir Francis. *Kashmir*. With paintings by Major E. Molyneux. 1909. Reprint, New Delhi: Sagar Publications, 1970.

GENERAL INDEX

Ackerley, Chris, 85, 433
Ackerley and Clipper, 8, 170, 179, 250, 407, 425, 429, 430, 433, 440, 441, 456
Aiken, Conrad, 6, 14, 21, 26, 29, 30, 71, 92, 191, 192, 296, 297, 298, 381, 383, 387, 391, 407, 409, 414, 422, 425, 432, 445, 450; and Mary Hoover Aiken, 13, 388
Arac, Jonathan, 456
Asals, Frederick, 157, 344, 421, 456
As the World Turns, 59

Back to the Future, 53
Bakhtin, Mikhail, 384
Barbarous Mexico (Turner), 433–34, 437
Barnes, Djuna, 85, 454
Beckett, Samuel, 449
Binns, Ronald, 3, 11, 200, 421, 445
Blackmur, R. P., 5, 407
Bonner, Mrs. John Stuart, 388
Bowker, Gordon, 2, 73, 137, 297, 452, 453, 455
Bruce, Nigel, 219
Buckley, Henry, 140, 404, 421, 425
Burnett, Whit, 69, 71, 74, 387, 412

Calder-Marshall, Arthur, 19, 28, 407, 412, 417

Cape, Jonathan, 305–6, 404, 450, 452–53, 455; January 1946 letter to, 3, 7–8, 18, 19, 68, 70, 140, 159, 182, 193, 200–201, 229–30, 231, 251, 269, 291, 306, 340, 346, 347–48, 349, 353, 361, 363, 369, 372, 408, 432, 440, 448
Chatman, Seymour, 455
Chaucer, Geoffrey, 283, 379
Chekhov, Anton, 243
Chung, Kathy, 407
Clipper, Lawrence J., 179, 430
Conrad, Joseph, 228
Corrigan, Matthew, 327
Costa, Richard Hauer, 180

Day, Douglas, 1, 11, 73, 76, 192, 286, 407, 425
Díaz, Porfirio, 433
Dickens, Charles, 41
Dostoyevsky, Fyodor, 182
Doyen, Victor, 407–8, 417

Edmonds, Dale, 58, 59
Erskine, Albert, 235, 260, 298, 306–9, 311, 313, 316–17, 425, 428, 432, 440, 453–55

Faulkner, William, 456
Fielding, Henry, 41
Fitzgerald, F. Scott, 445

Foley, Martha, 72
Frost, Robert, 288

Gabrial, Jan, 18, 19
Grace, Sherrill, 436
Grieg, Nordahl, 408, 440
Gunther, John, 207, 405, 434, 436

Haldane, Charlotte, 455–56
Hardy, Thomas, 41
Hawthorne, Nathaniel, 438
Hemingway, Ernest, 160
Hilton, Terry, 153, 344, 417, 456
Huddleston, Joan, 456

Jackson, Charles, 293, 432, 450
James, Henry, 5, 322, 325, 332, 381, 428
Joyce, James, 94, 148, 156, 336, 342, 385, 426, 456

Kermode, Frank, 69, 377

Lawrence, D. H., 41, 78
Levi, Norman, 397, 417
Linscott, Robert, 71, 415, 417
Lowry, Arthur O., 388, 397
Lowry, Malcolm: "Bulls of the Resurrection," 391; *Dark As the Grave Wherein My Friend Is Laid*, 2, 8, 17, 191–92, 306, 408, 409, 431, 438, 449, 456; "Elephant and Colosseum," 445; "Forest Path to the Spring," 430; "For *Under the Volcano*," 392; "Garden of Etla," 438; "Hotel Room in Chartres," 412; *In Ballast to the White Sea*, 1, 79, 191, 296, 408, 409, 416, 429; "In Le Havre," 390, 411; "In the Oaxaca Train," 409; "June the 30th, 1934," 98, 411; "Last Address" (*Lunar Caustic*), 20, 391, 413, 416, 442, 444; "On Board the West Hardaway," 412; plagiarism anxiety of, 72, 296, 384, 426, 453–54; "Preface" [to French translation of *Under the Volcano*], 92; Sigbjørn Wilderness (character), 8, 17, 191, 408, 449; "Thirty-five Mescals in Cuautla," 391; "Through the Panama," 246, 384, 447; *Ultramarine*, 69, 191, 283, 296, 321, 379, 452; "Under the Volcano" [short story], 18–19, 73, 412, 414; *Under the Volcano* (see index to *Under the Volcano*)
Lowry, Margerie Bonner, 6, 12–15, 18, 29, 30, 34, 41, 68, 73–76, 109–10, 192, 200, 219, 231, 245, 251, 259, 286, 289, 296–98 passim, 300, 303–4, 306, 319, 380, 390, 396, 405, 413, 415, 416, 425, 431–32, 435, 436, 442–45 passim, 447, 451–54 passim; *Shapes That Creep*, 74, 435

Markson, David, 298, 319, 352, 401, 402, 403, 426, 446, 455
Márquez, Juan Fernando, 30
Matson, Harold, 18, 68, 69, 71–74, 79, 85, 297, 306, 387, 390, 399, 400, 412–16 passim, 432, 435, 450, 452–53
Melville, Herman, 69, 440
Molyneux, E., 178

Nimmo, D. C., 444
Noxon, Gerald, 152, 191–92, 259, 297, 298, 401, 404, 432, 435, 444, 447, 450; and Betty Noxon, 92, 99, 192, 296, 297, 404
Nuttall: *Ornithology*, 283, 405

O'Kill, Brian, 408, 436, 456
Ontario, 192, 266, 296, 380, 431–32, 442, 443, 446, 451; Niagara-on-the-Lake, 283, 298, 432, 449; Oakville, 192, 259, 269–70, 432, 444, 447

Parkes, Henry Bamford, 436
Parks, Benjamin, 19, 20
Pétain, Henri, 34
Pethick, Derek, 426
Phillips, Carol (Betty Atwater), 20–22, 26, 27, 29, 85
Poe, Edgar Allan, 182
Pottinger, Andrew, 12, 135
Prescott, W. H., 322

Rawlinson, H. G., 171–72, 429–31, 434
Reynal and Hitchcock, 298, 306, 307, 312, 395, 396, 450, 453, 455

Saalmann, Dieter, 85
Scherf, Kathleen, 195, 281, 391, 447, 456
Sky, The, 430

Sommerfield, John, 425
Spence, Lewis, 322
Spender, Stephen, 407, 411
Stansfeld-Jones, Charles, 238
Stern, James, 388, 395
Stevens, Wallace, 32, 210
Story Press, 71–72, 74, 387

Taylor, Helen K., 450
Ten Holder, Clemens, 153, 344, 456
Treacher, Arthur, 219

Walker, Ronald G., 421
Watkins, Ann, 19, 412
Welty, Eudora, 1
West, Nathanael, 425–26
Westcott, Glenway, 283
Wintringham, Tom, 425
Woodcock, George, 454
Woolf, Virginia, 336
Wright, Terence, 455

Yeats, William Butler, 8, 283
York, Thomas, 445
Younghusband, Sir Francis, 170, 172, 405, 429–31

INDEX TO *UNDER THE VOLCANO*

Chapters

Chapter I, 6, 25, 27, 32–35, 37, 44–45, 52, 61, 62, 63–65, 67, 68, 75, 83, 93, 94, 98, 100–103, 136, 141, 154, 184, 193–206, 242, 247, 250, 266, 294, 300–301, 302, 309–10, 320, 322, 328–29, 330, 340, 353–54, 356–65, 368, 374–76 passim, 381–82, 383, 410, 411, 418, 424, 433, 444, 455

Chapter II, 39, 56, 67, 68, 76, 80, 82, 84, 85–86, 90, 94–95, 104–9, 152–55, 163, 165, 166, 206–16, 222, 251, 256, 283, 294, 304, 310, 325, 330, 331–34, 335–36, 341, 343, 344, 349, 353, 356–58, 370, 383, 409–11, 416, 418, 421, 429, 435, 437, 444, 449

Chapter III, 38, 60, 67, 83, 84, 86–89, 94, 95–97, 98, 106, 116–20, 154, 177–81, 183, 188, 194, 196, 213, 214, 216–24, 239, 274, 294, 301, 310, 321–22, 325, 329–30, 341, 343, 344, 346, 347–48, 409–10, 419, 437, 438, 455

Chapter IV, 35, 56, 68, 82, 111–13, 144, 148, 150–52, 224–27, 266, 280, 299, 314, 334–35, 338–39, 343, 346, 347–49, 373, 379–80, 418, 419, 420, 425, 428, 437, 438, 444

Chapter V, 60, 67, 84, 89, 120–24, 136, 141, 145, 177, 181–90, 196, 214, 216, 227–31, 235, 239, 242, 244, 271–73, 304, 307, 308, 310, 323–27, 330, 334, 343, 344, 346–48, 370, 372, 419

Chapter VI, 36, 55, 56, 62, 82, 110–11, 113–16, 144, 145–50, 212, 231–39, 245, 266, 280, 299, 302, 307, 308, 310, 314, 320, 334, 338–39, 340, 344, 351–52, 383, 419, 424, 426, 427, 440–41, 451

Chapter VII, 23, 37, 46–48, 61, 66, 84, 89–90, 114, 124–30, 141, 145, 168, 239–51, 255, 299, 301–2, 305, 310–11, 314, 320, 327, 330, 341, 344, 351, 363–64, 373, 375, 379, 419, 422–23, 425, 438, 441–42, 451

Chapter VIII, 18, 43, 56, 68, 77–79, 84, 90, 114, 140–45, 251–59, 260, 261, 288, 302, 308, 311, 334, 343, 346, 362, 413, 416, 442–43

Chapter IX, 3, 37, 39, 43, 56, 67, 68, 81, 84, 90, 103–4, 155–59, 166, 172, 192, 259–69, 285, 287, 299, 313, 315–16, 320, 340, 345, 346, 349–51, 383, 419, 420, 425, 429, 443–44

Chapter X, 36, 38, 53, 56, 60, 62, 81, 84, 90, 131, 140, 157, 168–77, 226, 269–79, 280, 291, 292, 303, 305, 311–12, 316, 330, 341–44 passim, 346, 352–53, 362, 364, 366, 371, 373–74, 384, 413, 444–46, 447, 451–52, 454

Chapter XI, 10–11, 36, 40, 51, 53–57 passim, 63, 68, 76, 81, 84, 90, 103–4, 111, 159–68, 194, 245, 259, 269, 279–92, 299, 302, 305, 307–8, 312, 316, 320, 338, 341, 356, 366, 368, 373–75, 383, 411, 416, 419, 446–49, 454

Chapter XII, 3, 30, 36, 38, 53, 57, 65–67, 81, 84, 101, 114, 130–40, 146, 148, 152, 164, 166, 167, 168, 180, 192, 242, 250, 251, 272, 291, 292–96, 300, 301, 305, 307–8, 310, 312–13, 316–18, 328–29, 339–40, 342–45 passim, 353–65, 368, 370, 372, 373, 374, 383, 384, 436, 443, 449, 513

Characters

A Few Fleas (XII), 131–32, 138, 300, 356

Barman of the Bella Vista/Fernando (II), 107, 131, 152, 208, 216, 336, 356–57

Bolowski, David (VI), 147, 233, 235

Carruthers (VI), 23, 114, 230, 390

Cartero (postman) (VI), 113, 115, 127

Cerillo, Juan (IV), 5, 152, 224–27, 239, 266, 339, 357–59, 379–80, 418, 438

Cervantes (X), 48, 60, 168, 170, 171, 273, 276, 303–4, 310, 384, 392–93

"Chiefs" (Jefes) (XII), 131–32, 135–36, 138, 301, 317, 339, 342, 354, 357, 361, 363, 443; Chief of Gardens/Sanabria, 135–36, 314, 363; Chief of Rostrums, 135–36, 317–18, 361, 362–64, 373

Cinema manager/Bustamente (I), 31, 100–103, 130, 197–98, 205, 206, 212, 328–29, 355, 361–62, 382, 433–34

Consul/William Ames/Jeffrey Ames/Geoffrey Firmin, 20, 22, 27, 31, 38, 42, 43, 50–52, 53–55 passim, 57, 58–67, 68, 75, 78–84 passim, 86, 87–89, 94–95, 96–97, 98, 100–103, 105, 113–15, 116–40, 141, 144–45, 150–51, 152–54, 156–58, 163–67, 168–77, 178–90, 194–98, 201–6, 208–24, 226, 227–31, 233–51, 252, 258, 263–67, 269–89, 292–96, 299–302 passim, 310, 312–18, 320–32 passim, 335–38, 342, 344–49, 351–79, 381–82, 384–86, 390, 391, 405, 410, 412, 415, 424, 426, 430, 438, 445, 448, 449, 454, 456

Consul's brother/daughter's lover/Ed/Hugh Fernhead/Hugh Ames/Hugh Firmin, 20, 22, 24, 25, 27, 34–36, 38–40, 42, 43, 48–50, 51–53, 54–57, 59, 61–63 passim, 68, 79–83 passim, 87–89, 98, 108–16, 119, 125–27, 131–34, 138, 140–52, 153–55, 159–61, 163–68, 169, 180–81, 186, 195, 205, 212–14, 217–18, 224–27, 228, 231–39, 241–43, 247–48, 252–59, 263–67, 270, 273–77, 279–88, 299, 301, 307, 308, 310, 311, 314–17 passim, 320–23 passim, 329–30, 331, 334–35, 337–40, 341, 342, 346,

348-49, 351, 357, 361, 365-67,
373-75, 379-81, 383, 386, 390,
405, 410-11, 415, 419-20, 424,
438, 445, 446, 448, 454

Consul's daughter/Joey/Yvonne
Ames, 20, 22, 24, 25, 27, 35-36,
39, 42, 43-44, 48-49, 51-53,
55-57, 60, 62, 63, 67, 68, 410-11,
412

Consul's ex-wife/Enid/Priscilla/
Yvonne, 22, 27, 31, 51-52, 55, 57,
58, 60, 65, 79-83 passim, 85-89,
94, 95, 97, 98, 102-9, 112-13,
125-29, 132-34, 136-39, 141-47,
150-69, 174-76, 178-81, 183, 186,
189, 201-4, 206-18, 221-24, 226,
228, 232, 238-43, 245-49, 252,
258-69, 272-75, 277, 278-92, 293,
299, 310, 312, 314-16, 318, 320,
321, 323, 330-38, 340, 342,
344-51, 353, 355-60, 363, 365-67,
370-71, 373-75, 377, 379-83, 388,
390, 405, 412, 415, 419-20, 426,
446, 448, 454

Consul's maid/Josephina/Concepta
(III), 87, 96, 179, 415

Diosdado (XII), 131-32, 293, 328,
355, 356-57, 361-62

Englishman in sportscar (III), 196,
216, 219-20, 273, 301, 322, 367

Firmin, Geoffrey. *See* Consul

Firmin, Hugh. *See* Consul's brother

Firmin, Yvonne. *See* Consul's
ex-wife

German silver miner (XII), 38, 342,
345

Gregorio (VII), 48, 130, 194, 277,
327, 358, 366, 392

Guzman, 246

Indian "grandees," 300-301, 350,
381

Indian rider (VIII), 127-28, 141, 144,
249, 252, 256-58, 270, 276, 311,
334, 341

Hodson, Bill (IX), 267, 444

Japanese restaurateur (XI), 163,
167

Laruelle, Jacques, 20, 24, 30, 31, 34,
37-38, 43, 44, 50-52, 56, 58, 59,
61-63 passim, 67, 68, 80, 86, 89,
94, 98, 100-103, 105, 113-15, 122,
124-30, 141, 153, 154, 194-98,
202, 205, 209, 212, 224, 239-49,
300, 301, 310, 313, 314, 328-29,
331, 334, 337, 340, 341, 353, 354,
361, 363-65, 367-70, 373,
375-77, 381, 388, 390, 404, 444,
451, 455, 456

María (XII), 132-34, 294-95, 307,
357-58, 360, 362, 374-75

Old woman from Tarasco (II, XII),
156, 209, 261, 334, 354, 362

Pelado (VIII), 61, 62, 141, 145,
255-58, 277, 307, 309, 311, 354,
356, 390

Quattras (X), 271, 311, 444-45

Quincey (V), 24, 122-23, 130, 183,
184, 188-89, 227, 323, 346, 412

Taskersons (I), 196, 205, 213, 219-20,
340, 382; Abraham Taskerson (V),
184, 190, 347, 440

Unemployed actor, anecdote of (III),
84, 220-21, 273, 322

Vigil (doctor), 30, 31, 37-38, 48, 94,
100-103, 123-24, 127, 130, 136,
184, 186, 189, 194, 198, 214, 222,
227, 228, 230, 244, 246, 273, 277,
323, 346, 354, 357, 362, 364, 366,
381, 391, 438

Weber, 56, 152-53, 170, 208, 273,
342-45 passim, 354, 356, 390

Wilson (V), 121-22

Yvonne's father (Major/Captain Constable) (IX), 260, 262, 284, 345
Yvonne's first husband and child, 98, 108, 110, 214, 419, 429

Locales

Abyssinia, 256
Anochtitlan, 286–87, 302
Bella Vista, Hotel/Bar, 82, 95, 105–8, 119, 152–54, 201, 209, 212–13, 331–33, 361, 428
Borda Gardens, 170
Bosque, El, 130, 131, 194, 201, 251, 299, 364, 390–92, 438, 454
Cambridge, 110, 114, 167, 219, 230, 235–38, 253, 448
Canada (country), 134, 150, 178, 204, 226, 281, 360, 375, 379–80, 382
Canada (hotel in Mexico City), 177
Cape Horn, 54, 57, 106, 162, 337
Casino de la Selva, 31, 200, 381
Cervecería Quauhnahuac, 334–35, 379
Chapultepec, 140, 417–18, 424, 425
China, 111, 149–50, 173, 338, 422
Cholula, 22, 103, 200
Farm (destination proposed by Yvonne), 104, 150–51, 158, 164, 286, 417–18, 419–21, 426
Farolito, 38, 39, 65, 81, 97, 125–27, 130–38, 169, 176, 190, 201, 242, 264, 279, 314, 343, 354, 357, 359–65, 375, 384, 424
"Genteel Siberia" (destination proposed by Yvonne), 112–13, 150–51, 417–18, 419–21
Granada, 132, 136, 272, 275, 362

Guanajuato, 102, 124, 127, 228, 323
Hawaii, 33, 164, 200, 268, 376, 444
Himavat, 139, 181
India, 33, 98, 113–14, 166, 199, 200, 322, 376, 441. *See also* Kashmir; Indian religions
Infierno, El, 294–95, 357, 375
Ixtaccihuatl, 156
Kashmir, 134, 139, 157, 165, 169–73, 178, 182, 343–44, 430, 431
Maximilian's Palace, 24, 25, 27, 31, 113, 151, 195, 205, 382
Oaxaca, 64, 119, 201–2, 204, 215–16, 276, 294–95, 357–60, 374, 382, 395, 435
Parián, 131, 166, 168, 176, 190, 201, 287–88, 301, 302, 303, 317, 344, 359–60, 405
Petate, El, 81, 161, 279, 283, 286, 316
Popo, El, 5, 81, 104, 134, 163–67, 194, 279, 286, 299, 302, 316, 446, 447, 455. *See also* Menu: El Popo
Popocatapetl, 82, 139, 142, 156, 226, 285, 316, 365
Puebla, 22, 23, 409
Salón Ofélia, 97, 131, 133, 160, 265, 271, 456
Spain, 61–62, 68, 82, 110, 111, 132, 142, 146, 149–50, 163, 173, 174, 205, 224, 225, 232, 252, 337–38, 357, 412, 421, 441. *See also* Spanish Civil War
Tlaxcala, 171–72, 269, 273, 275–78, 303–4, 310, 311, 342, 352–53, 364, 366, 373–75, 395, 445, 451–52
Tomalín, 140, 158, 168, 258, 264, 302, 314, 317, 360, 361, 405, 417–18, 425

Technique, Methodology, Writerly Concerns

Alcoholic consciousness, rendering of, 119–22, 129–30, 168–77, 181–90, 216, 220, 222, 230, 239, 259–60, 271–79, 286, 288, 367, 385, 422; blackout as, 124, 181, 182, 185–88, 216, 222, 227, 230, 235, 239, 244, 269, 271–73, 325–27, 330, 337, 346, 439. *See also* Alcohol; Consciousness, rendering of

Central consciousness technique, 80, 85–91, 93, 103, 105–8, 159, 252, 320, 323, 330–31, 364. *See also* Roving narrator

Chapters: divisions of, 94, 113, 320, 350–52; openings of, 94–97, 124, 130, 145–46, 155, 159, 198, 253; unity of, 349

Cinematic devices, 33, 200, 212, 219

Circles/circularity, 158, 193, 258, 282–83, 289, 350–51, 364, 368, 378, 382, 429. *See also* Wheels

Comedy, 58, 60, 89, 119–22, 141, 144, 149, 150, 154, 177, 181, 188–90, 196, 202, 204, 211, 218, 219–24, 228–29, 233, 243–44, 251, 271–72, 276, 277–78, 347, 365–69. *See also* Irony; Tragedy; Tragicomedy

Consciousness, rendering of, 49, 78, 169, 175, 178, 190, 203, 206–16, 220, 227, 228, 232, 243, 321, 323, 326, 330–33, 337, 385. *See also* Alcoholic consciousness, rendering of

Counterpoint, 56, 125, 137, 141, 152, 156, 181, 235, 237, 260, 276–77, 279, 303, 340–46, 354, 355, 366, 374. *See also* Musical sense of text; Rhythm

Dialogue, 48–50, 98–99, 128–29, 137, 148, 151, 159, 166, 177, 194, 220, 242, 279, 303, 321, 325–26, 341

Doppelgänger, 38, 129, 154, 162–63, 231, 235, 237, 247, 288, 348

Expansion of text, 89, 98–99, 100, 107, 112, 118, 124, 151, 152, 154, 158, 159, 168, 194, 201, 269, 381. *See also* Reduction of text

Female characters, 52, 55, 57, 156, 261

Inception of novel, 17–18

Indeterminacy, textual, 129–30, 187–88, 209–10, 216–17, 222, 230, 240, 247, 269, 295, 299, 323

Irony, 54, 56, 58, 89, 111, 121, 135, 138, 142, 143, 146, 149, 153, 154, 156, 164, 169, 175–77 passim, 190, 197, 207, 209–10, 220, 223–24, 229, 233, 241, 243–44, 253, 257, 268, 272, 274, 278, 280, 294, 299–301 passim, 304, 312, 315, 316, 346, 351, 356, 360, 367, 368, 372, 374, 385, 426, 451

Landscape, 24, 31, 44–45, 67, 98, 106, 142–43, 151, 154, 159–61, 176, 178, 195, 204, 215, 270, 282, 292, 321, 322, 331, 335, 360. *See also* Objective correlative

Method of revision, 2–3, 11–14, 91

Motion/kinesis, 46–48, 91, 164, 207–8, 228, 250–51, 265, 266, 283, 285, 290, 295, 309, 335–36, 337, 339, 341, 347, 349, 365, 377, 378

Musical sense of text, 196, 307, 340–53, 354–65 passim, 455–56. *See also* Counterpoint; Rhythm

Objective correlative, 44–45, 108, 142, 161, 195, 259, 321, 322. *See also* Symbolism

Oratorio oblique, 198, 243, 274, 341, 445

Particularity/specificity, 98–99, 100, 103, 109–10, 117, 118–27, 141–45, 149–50, 152–53, 154, 158, 161, 163, 167, 178, 205, 213

Pluperfect tense, 198, 223, 228, 275, 327–34, 349, 350

Reduction of text, 75–79, 80, 86, 89, 103, 151, 159, 168, 177, 201, 303, 320. *See also* Expansion of text

Relocation of material, 130–32, 180–81, 364

Rhetoric, 33, 44, 174, 204, 217, 221, 243, 256, 259, 288, 290–91, 294–95, 321

Rhythm, 33, 99, 106, 116–18, 131, 133, 139, 160, 171, 181, 190, 207, 208, 239, 241, 246, 251, 253, 261, 268, 270, 278, 285, 287, 290–91, 321–32, 340–45, 358, 385. *See also* Counterpoint; Musical sense of text

Roving narrator, 41–42, 43, 48, 90, 322–23, 326, 331

Symbolism, 40–41, 57, 65, 69, 157, 163, 195, 204, 250, 255, 261, 263, 271, 280, 422. *See also* Objective correlative

Tragedy, 20, 25, 58, 96, 102, 145, 155, 158, 177, 200, 222, 234, 265, 268, 315, 350–51, 365–69, 381. *See also* Comedy; Tragicomedy

Tragicomedy, 365

Typography, 260–61, 265, 277, 279, 292, 302, 311, 349

Understatement, 45–48

Voice, 96–97, 99, 115–18, 120–24, 131, 135, 138, 169, 189, 190, 217, 221, 224, 227, 230, 232, 243–44, 273, 276–77, 321–22, 332–33, 341, 383, 437

Themes, Motifs, References

Abortion, 27, 51, 53, 55, 56. *See also* Children, desire for

Abra-Melin the Mage (MacGregor-Mathers), 441

Abyss/barranca, 22, 25, 31, 45, 116–17, 173, 189, 195, 253, 352, 438. *See also* Hell; Hell Bunker

Aeneas, 248

Ahab, 25, 35. *See also* Melville, Herman

Alastor (film), 84, 241

Alchemy, 60, 221

Alcohol, 6, 20, 23, 26, 53, 55, 59–60, 63–64, 68, 82, 83, 86, 96–98, 109, 110, 112, 114, 116, 119, 123–24, 126–27, 128, 136, 141, 153, 165, 176, 178, 181, 184, 201, 203–4, 213–14, 216–17, 242–46, 252–53, 261–62, 264, 266, 269–79, 280, 285–86, 293, 316, 325–27, 331, 334, 346, 347, 366, 370, 378, 384, 408, 449. *See also* Alcoholic consciousness, rendering of

All Quiet on the Western Front (Remarque), 440

Anarchist card, 132, 138, 339, 361, 384

Aristotle, 441

Arnold, Matthew, 270, 273, 274
Astronomy magazine, 179–80
Atlantis, 60, 139, 157, 172, 230, 316
Atlas, 84
Babel, Tower of, 103, 132, 137–38, 272, 342, 354–55, 384
Baudelaire, Charles, 40
Beckford, William, 440
Beiderbecke, Bix, 28, 427
Betrayal, 51–52, 58, 65, 125–26, 164, 217, 225, 226, 235, 275, 303, 314, 366, 370, 378
Bible, 440; New Testament, 134; Revelations, 310
Birds, 141, 143, 163, 164, 254, 259, 283–85, 309, 311, 316, 318, 332, 381. *See also* Cock; Parrot joke; Trogon *ambiguus ambiguus*
Blackstone, William, 23, 120–22, 138, 354
Blake, William, 202, 374, 422
Bogan, Louise, 112, 422
Book, the Consul's, 60, 93, 203, 274, 287, 382
Boxing advertisements, 212
Broch, Hermann, 56, 84–85
Brooke, Rupert, 39, 253
Browne, Sir Thomas, 274
Bull, 157–58, 263, 268, 315, 345
Bullthrowing, 43, 60, 156, 323, 420. *See also* Chapter IX
Bunyan, John, 375; *Grace Abounding*, 299, 451; *Pilgrim's Progress*, 451
Cabala/the occult, 169, 203, 222, 229–30, 235, 237–38, 247–49, 250, 288, 365, 371–72, 373, 382, 437, 453
Cabinet of Dr. Caligari, The (Wiene), 85

Caesar, Julius (Shakespeare), 84
Caligula, 84, 115
Cambridge Platonists/Cabalists, 237–38, 441
Capone, Al, 214, 436
Cárdenas, Lázaro, 144, 433–34, 436
Case Is Altered, 242, 382
Cat, 40, 115, 158, 189, 194, 217, 438
Chamberlain, Neville, 102, 109, 141
Chatterton, Thomas, 440
Childe Harold's Pilgrimage (Byron), 453
Children, desire for, 51–52, 133, 174–75, 251. *See also* Abortion
Child's funeral, 214
Chubchakum, 84
Clare, John, 440
Clicking of Cuthbert, The (Wodehouse), 440
"Clorinda and Damon" (Marvell), 219, 223
Cocanada, 178
Cock, 134–35, 138, 168, 276, 318, 350, 360. *See also* Birds
Coffee beans, 25, 96–97
"Compañero," 66, 139, 144–45, 206, 231, 303, 362. *See also* Pelado
Conquest of Mexico, 27, 275, 304, 376
Conrad, Joseph, 233, 278, 446; Lord Jim (character), 197
Cornford, John, 236
Cortéz, Hernán, 102, 145, 171, 276, 343, 436
Crime and Punishment (Dostoyevsky), 84
Dante, 64, 202, 206, 231–32, 288, 296, 352, 405, 440–41

Day of the Dead, 20, 31, 37, 39, 56, 85, 102, 109, 143, 198, 200, 249, 301, 320, 355, 363, 365, 373, 376–78, 448
Death, 62, 91, 102, 104, 107, 141, 175, 202, 204, 254, 256, 268, 271, 278, 281–82, 295, 300, 448; and love, 39, 53, 57, 81, 139, 167, 169, 248, 280, 295, 320, 365, 370. *See also* Love
DeQuincey, Thomas, 196
Despedida, La, 109, 142, 209, 211, 354
Destin de Yvonne Griffaton, Le, 268, 289, 345, 444, 449
Diana of the Ephesians, 84
Díaz, Porfirio, 205, 225, 436
Dickens, Charles: Scrooge (character), 23, 130, 251
"Dies Irae," 250
Disguise/performance, 254, 335
Dismas, St., 66, 84, 139
Dog, 66, 112, 136, 155, 178, 182–83, 187, 261, 300, 342–43, 346, 347, 349, 351, 368, 370, 372, 373, 429, 454
Doré, Gustave, 28
Dowlah, Suraj-ud, 424
Dream sequence, 181–82, 186, 431
Dr. Jekyll and Mr. Hyde (Stevenson), 162–63
Dunne, J. W., 52–53, 72, 430
Ebro, battle of, 140–45, 149, 252, 322, 338, 343, 349, 417, 425. *See also* Spanish Civil War
Economic themes, 37–40, 53, 57, 58, 65, 104, 138, 174, 194, 313. *See also* Marxism
Eden, 28, 122–23, 126, 169, 188, 250, 372, 453. *See also* Garden; Paradise

Einstein, Albert, 147, 180, 235
Eisenstein, Sergei, 313
Ejidal/Ejido, 144, 170, 224–25, 305, 418, 434, 436
Eleusinian mysteries, 282, 448, 454
Eliot, T. S., 242, 327; "Gerontian," 431; *The Waste Land*, 134, 287, 431, 453
Elizabethan plays, book of, 31, 100, 103, 245, 329, 361, 373
Emmaus, supper at, 169
Eridanus, 179, 430, 448
Escape/evasion, 67–68, 117, 136, 164, 174, 281, 289, 293, 295, 339, 374–75, 420, 449
Eternal return, 27, 378, 379
Faulkner, William, 382, 453; *The Wild Palms*, 454
Faust/Faustus, 3, 58, 129, 177, 249, 343, 366, 368–69, 373, 376–77, 382
Fields of Paradise, The (Bates), 405, 453
Flying Dutchman, 234
Foolish Wives (von Stroheim), 454
Ford car, 24, 44–45
Franco, Francisco, 62, 102, 141, 343. *See also* Spanish Civil War
Freud/Freudianism, 248, 266–67, 440. *See also* Oedipus complex
Garden, 25, 85, 95–97, 99, 111, 120–23, 178, 183, 188, 190, 227, 311, 346, 348, 372, 410, 422, 454. *See also* Eden; Paradise
Garden sign, 5, 139, 183, 190, 236, 307–9, 310–11, 370, 373, 376–77, 455
Goat, 112, 199, 311, 422
Goethe, 117, 339, 368, 375
Golf, 239, 242

"Grey Champion, The" (Hawthorne), 36, 84
Guilt, 81, 83, 88, 111, 116, 119, 122, 141–45, 148–49, 151, 165, 170, 184, 197, 209, 218, 224–27, 231, 232, 256, 258, 336–37, 343, 367, 379. *See also* Remorse
Hamlet (Shakespeare), 52, 58, 65, 84, 134, 243
Hand, pictograph of, 161, 167, 287, 312, 454
Hastings, Warren, 134, 424
Hell, 64, 65, 101, 176–77, 202, 204, 225, 270, 278, 284, 293, 352, 359–60, 374–75, 380, 382. *See also* Abyss/barranca; Tartarus
Hell Bunker, 196, 382
Heloise and Abelard, 296
Heraclitus, 327
Hitler, Adolf, 102, 233, 237
Hoare, Sir Samuel, 102
Hope, 51, 62, 66, 138, 151, 156, 226–27, 260–65, 315–16, 345
Horse, 104, 112, 114, 115, 132, 135, 138–39, 167, 226, 267, 268, 276, 281, 283, 289, 316–17, 354, 355, 449
Houghton, Claude, 273, 445
"Hound of Heaven, The" (Thompson), 298–99
Huckleberry Finn (Twain), 134
Huerta, Victoriano, 207, 225, 289, 312, 333, 436, 449
Hume, David, 440
"Hymn to God the Father" (Donne), 242
Ibsen, Henrik, 440; Solveig, 25
Indian religions, 157, 164, 170–73, 273–74, 315, 330, 341, 343–44, 366. *See also* India; Kashmir

Infernal machine, 46–48, 119, 239, 250–51, 294, 335, 358, 366
James, Henry, 252
James, William, 248, 442; *Varieties of Religious Experience,* 451
Jazz, 147–48, 427–28
Jesus Christ, 51, 64, 66, 96–97, 139, 143, 157, 172, 218, 223, 229, 232, 275, 288–89, 310, 373
Jews, 135, 147–48, 232, 237; and antisemitism, 138, 233, 373
Johnson, Samuel, 300
Jonson, Ben, 129, 203, 248
Journalism, 98, 110–14, 148, 151, 227, 258, 267, 338, 373, 383, 421
Jude the Obscure (Hardy), 312
Kafka, Franz, 28, 135, 258, 443
Keats, John, 43, 440
King Lear (Shakespeare), 25, 52, 58, 59, 65, 84
Kopic, Colonel, 140–41
Landrock, Maria, 205, 362, 382
Lang, Eddie, 28
Lawrence, D. H., 204, 453
Letter, the Consul's: to his mother, 24, 25, 27; to his ex-wife, 6–7, 31, 52, 61, 63–65, 82, 111, 193, 201–5, 215, 248, 266, 274, 294, 299, 310, 329, 355, 359–60, 365, 375, 382
Letters, the ex-wife's, 39, 51, 57, 82, 119, 132, 137–38, 166, 175, 201–2, 204, 282, 293, 296, 328–29, 342, 345, 355, 359–60, 375, 384; the postcard, 45, 58, 113, 115, 127, 280, 301, 312, 351–52, 364, 374, 375, 381, 451
London, Jack, 233, 440; *Valley of the Moon,* 142
Love, 27, 55, 61, 64, 83, 96, 109, 111, 112, 125–26, 158, 195, 201, 212, 217, 240, 269, 312–13, 314, 315,

Index to Under the Volcano | 473

Love (*cont.*)
  337, 338, 355, 358, 363, 381; and death, 39, 53, 57, 81, 139, 167, 169, 216, 248, 280, 295, 320, 342, 356, 358, 359, 370, 378. *See also* Death
Lucifer, 207, 333
Lucretius, 455
Macbeth (Shakespeare), 85, 122, 123
Mahabharata, 181, 431. *See also* Dream sequence; Indian religions
Manos de Orlac, Las, 28, 145, 328–29, 373, 382
Mar Cantabrico, 137, 273, 343
Marlowe, Christopher, 129, 248, 313, 368, 370, 376–77, 456. *See also* Faust/Faustus
Marston, John, 438
Marxism, 34, 39, 54. *See also* Economic themes
Maugham, Somerset, 312
Maximilian and Carlotta, 21, 151, 225, 376. *See also* Maximilian's Palace
Mayan astronomy, 179–80, 183, 430
Melville, Herman, 36, 169, 233, 278, 299, 424; "Cock-a-Doodle-Doo!," 424; *The Confidence-Man*, 36; "The Encantadas," 424; *Moby-Dick*, 84, 248–49, 425, 446, 448. *See also* Ahab
Menu: El Popo, 166, 279–82, 292, 373–75, 383–84, 392–93, 405; Salón Ofélia, 48, 177, 280, 312, 366, 383–84, 392–93, 456
Mephistopheles, 147, 163
Merry Wives of Windsor (Shakespeare), 245
Mescal, 97, 98, 102, 122, 128–30, 164, 168–77, 230, 259, 269–72, 278, 286, 292–93, 299, 352, 354, 364, 375, 392, 413

Mexican Revolution, 21, 27
Moctezuma, 102, 275–76, 426
Much Ado about Nothing (Shakespeare), 245
Munich agreement, 102, 109, 141
Nationalism, 34–36, 202
Nawanipur, 178
Noemijolea, 141, 226, 299, 338–39, 343, 425
Nuns, dream of, 264, 313, 315
Oedipus complex, 21, 27, 218, 225, 234–35, 266. *See also* Freud/Freudianism
Oedipus Tyrannus, 233–35, 440
O'Neill, Eugene, 233, 262, 440; *The Emperor Jones*, 39
Othello (Shakespeare), 175–76
Ouspensky, P. D., 52–53, 72
Oxen song, 84
Pangloss (Voltaire), 255
Paradise, 65, 66, 85, 176, 202, 204, 262, 278–79, 284, 294, 360, 374, 379, 380, 381, 382. *See also* Eden
Paradise Lost (Milton), 28
Paranoia, 87–88, 122–23, 130, 184, 190, 244, 269, 273, 438
Parrot joke, 84, 138, 141, 254
Past, 241, 265, 268, 275, 287, 292, 294, 320, 327–36, 337, 339, 345, 349, 351, 355, 376–77, 379–80; of Geoffrey, 184, 195, 271; of Geoffrey and Hugh, 110; of Hugh, 147–49, 196, 266; of Laruelle, 205, 266; of Yvonne, 108–10, 166, 196, 260–68, 430–31
Peacock, T. L., 440
Pelado, 66, 139, 257, 302–3, 311, 354, 436. *See also* "Compañero"
Pennsylvania, 106, 208
Personal Record (Green), 453
Peter, St., 275

Peter Rabbit (Potter), 235–36, 310
Philoctetes, 149, 233, 440
Plagiarism, 147–48, 302. *See also in general index*
Plane, 106–7, 207, 333, 382
Pleiades, 179, 282–83, 286, 290, 448
Poe, Edgar Allan, 230; "Arthur Gordon Pym," 84; "The Fall of the House of Usher," 206
Police, 114, 127, 132, 144, 360. *See also* "Chiefs"
Political themes, 34, 39, 54, 56, 82, 84, 98, 132, 138, 141, 144, 146, 163–64, 170, 174, 176, 205, 256, 274–77, 282, 289, 292, 335, 445
Prescott, W. H., 142, 172, 275
Prometheus, 189, 242, 284
Quartermain, Allen (Haggard), 197
Quauhnahuac Nuevo, 205
Quixote, Don, 82, 84, 138, 178–79, 277
Racine, Jean, 132
Raleigh, Sir Walter, 233
Remorse, 45, 103, 148, 151, 218, 223, 225–26, 249, 256, 275, 336–38, 367, 379–80, 438. *See also* Guilt
Revolutionary songs, 147, 279–80, 292
Rig Veda, The, 454. *See also* Indian religions
Rimbaud, Arthur, 202
Rip Van Winkle, 84
Romains, Jules, 440
Samaritan, 60, 146, 197, 205, 249, 310, 335, 343, 361, 382, 424
Scorpion, 290, 295, 300, 310
Scribe, 251, 354
Self-destruction, 45, 61, 64, 83, 355
Sex, 96–97, 107, 175, 180, 188, 196, 214; between Geoffrey and María, 133–34, 294–95, 358, 360, 374, 383; between Geoffrey and Yvonne, 86, 118–19, 125, 178, 188, 294, 415, 437; between Hugh and Yvonne, 164–65, 217–18, 316, 337–38, 366
Shack, 262–64, 269, 282, 284, 286–89, 292, 299, 312, 345, 448, 449
Shakespeare, William, 366, 440
Shaving episode, 113–14, 145–49, 234–35
Shelley, Percy Bysshe, 43, 127, 173, 241, 248
Ship Sails On, The (Grieg), 454
Shoemaker's Holiday, The (Dekker), 196, 206, 368–69, 376–77, 382
Siegebert of East Anglia, 236
Sino-Japanese War, 163–64. *See also* China
Sleepwalking, 85, 160–61
Snake, 122, 183, 225–26, 270
Solipsism, 182, 240, 323, 370
Sonnet 31 (Shakespeare), 124
Sortes Shakespeareanae, 196, 206
Spanish Civil War, 22, 23, 26, 34, 37, 62, 84, 102, 109, 112, 128, 140–45, 163, 275, 322, 338, 343, 422. *See also* Ebro, battle of; Franco, Francisco; Spain
Spengler, Oswald, 3, 174, 274
Spying, 101–2, 197–98, 212, 257, 361–62, 382, 433–34
Stars, 10, 56, 161, 179–80, 267–68, 279, 283, 285, 289–92, 368, 378, 383, 446, 448–49
Station sign, 307–8, 381, 453
Strychnine, 97, 109, 119, 154, 186, 222
Swedenborg, Emanuel, 101, 202
Tartarus, 189, 296. *See also* Hell

Telegram, 111, 114, 138, 144, 280, 301, 339–40, 342, 348–49, 361, 373–75, 383–84, 404
Time, 27, 37, 46, 110, 180, 183, 186–87, 198, 207, 210, 222, 229, 235, 253, 270, 277–78, 312, 320, 327, 336, 365
Timon of Athens (Shakespeare), 39, 65
Titus Andronicus (Shakespeare), 258
Tolstoy, Leo, 127, 173–74, 274; *War and Peace*, 139, 170
To the Lighthouse (Woolf), 453
Tourneur, Cyril, 440
Train, 82, 95, 104, 202, 264, 270–72, 276, 278, 303, 352–53
Trogon *ambiguus ambiguus*, 22, 25
Trotsky, Leon, 361
Turner, W. J., 154
Two Years Before the Mast (Dana), 440
Typhoeus, 296
Union Militar, 146, 424
Universal, El, 114, 366

Valhalla, 129
Venezuelan Embassy card, 219, 301
Venus, 106, 180, 207, 211, 267, 332
Venuti, Joe, 231–32, 427
Verne, Jules, 230
Vice Versa (Anstey), 440
Wagner, Richard: *Parsifal*, 447; *Tristan and Isolde*, 358
Wells, H. G., 84
Wheels, 70, 91, 157, 158, 168, 204, 251, 255, 280–82, 289, 91, 335, 341, 349, 365, 376, 378, 380, 382, 422. *See also* Circles/Circularity
"Wibbly-Wobbly Song, The" 249
Wilde, Oscar, 222
Winter's Tale, The (Shakespeare), 175–76
"World, The" (Vaughan), 238, 283, 448
World War I, 60, 205, 376
World War II, 27, 34, 35, 84, 102, 163–64, 173, 205, 338, 380–81, 416
Yeats, William Butler, 174, 229

www.ingramcontent.com/pod-product-compliance
Lightning Source LLC
Chambersburg PA
CBHW012041290426
44111CB00021BA/2933